2011863

THE POLITICAL ECONOMY OF FINANCIAL REGULATION

This collection of cutting-edge scholarship examines the law and policy of financial regulation, using a combination of conceptual analysis and strong empirical research. The book's authors range from global leaders to rising stars in the field, all of whom shed light on complex questions of financial sector regulation theory and practice in major economies, ranging from the EU to China. Key topics include the role of law in constituting financial markets, the efficiency of markets, the role of interest groups in shaping financial regulation, the interdependence and interactions of international financial regulation with international trade and monetary regimes, and problems of regulation in state capitalism economies. This exciting volume opens the road for further enrichment of the academic and policy-making dialogue on financial regulation and regulatory practice, and reflects new trends in legal and social-science scholarship.

EMILIOS AVGOULEAS holds the International Banking Law and Finance Chair at the University of Edinburgh, where he founded and has directed the LLM in International Banking Law and Finance. An internationally renowned scholar in the field of banking theory and financial regulation, he has also published extensively in the fields of international and European finance law and economics, behavioral finance, and global economic governance. He is a Member of the Stakeholder Group of the European Banking Authority (EBA) elected in the so-called "top-ranking" academics section. He has held visiting posts with leading academic institutions and he is currently a visiting Research Professor at the Faculty of Law, University of Hong Kong (HKU) and a Visiting Professor and Senior Fellow at the School of European Political Economy, LUISS, Rome. He holds an LLM and a PhD in law and finance from the London School of Economics.

DAVID C. DONALD has been a professor in the Faculty of Law at the Chinese University of Hong Kong since 2008. From 2003 until 2008, David taught at the Institute for Law and Finance of Goethe University. During the decade preceding that he worked as a commercial, corporate and securities lawyer in Washington, Milan, Rome and Frankfurt. David's publications focus on market structure, securities clearing and settlement, corporate law and comparative law. He holds a PhD in law and an LLM from Goethe University, a Juris Doctor from Georgetown University and a PhD in comparative literature from SUNY Buffalo.

THE POLITICAL ECONOMY OF FINANCIAL REGULATION

Edited by

EMILIOS AVGOULEAS

University of Edinburgh

DAVID C. DONALD

Chinese University Hong Kong

CAMBRIDGE UNIVERSITY PRESS

CAMBRIDGE
UNIVERSITY PRESS

University Printing House, Cambridge CB2 8BS, United Kingdom

One Liberty Plaza, 20th Floor, New York, NY 10006, USA

477 Williamstown Road, Port Melbourne, VIC 3207, Australia

314–321, 3rd Floor, Plot 3, Splendor Forum, Jasola District Centre,
New Delhi – 110025, India

79 Anson Road, #06–04/06, Singapore 079906

Cambridge University Press is part of the University of Cambridge.

It furthers the University's mission by disseminating knowledge in the pursuit of
education, learning, and research at the highest international levels of excellence.

www.cambridge.org
Information on this title: www.cambridge.org/9781108470360
DOI: 10.1017/9781108612821

© Cambridge University Press 2019

First published 2019

Printed and bound in Great Britain by Clays Ltd, Elcograf S.p.A.

A catalogue record for this publication is available from the British Library.

ISBN 978-1-108-47036-0 Hardback

CONTENTS

v

FIGURES

TABLES

CONTRIBUTORS

EMILIOS AVGOULEAS holds the International Banking Law and Finance Chair at the University of Edinburgh. He has published extensively in the fields of international and European finance law and economics, behavioral finance, and global economic governance. He is a member of the Stakeholder Group of the European Banking Authority (EBA) elected in the so-called "top-ranking" academics section. He holds an LLM and a PhD in law and finance from the London School of Economics.

GIULIANO G. CASTELLANO is an associate professor of law at the University of Hong Kong. He holds a law degree (Bocconi), a PhD in economics and social sciences (Polytechnique), and a PhD in law (Turin). He has published extensively in the fields of financial regulation and international financial law.

SHUONAN CHEN is the Founding Partner of Agile VC and CEO of Shinect, as well as a lecturer at UC Berkeley and faculty at Singularity University. Previously, Shuo was with Goldman Sachs in investment banking. Shuo has a BS and BA from the University of California, Berkeley and a JD from the Chinese University of Hong Kong.

DAVID C. DONALD is a professor of law at the Chinese University of Hong Kong and directs its Center for Financial Regulation and Economic Development. He publishes on market structure, corporate law and comparative law. David previously taught at the Institute for Law and Finance of Goethe University and was a commercial, corporate and securities lawyer in Washington, Milan, Rome and Frankfurt. He holds a PhD in law and an LLM from the Goethe University, a JD from Georgetown University and a PhD from SUNY Buffalo.

JAKOB ENGEL is a PhD student at the University of Oxford's School of Geography and Environment, where his research focuses on the governance and organization of commodity markets since the start of the Global

Financial Crisis. His research focus is on issues related to the economics and politics of regional integration, the emergence and impact of global value chains and production networks, trade and industrial policy, and financial regulation. He also is a staff economist in the Macroeconomics, Trade and Investment Global Practice of the World Bank. The findings, interpretations, and conclusions in his chapter do not necessarily reflect the views of the World Bank, the Executive Directors of the World Bank or the governments they represent.

LI GUO is a professor at Peking University Law School, and the chief editor of *PKU Journal of Legal Studies*. He has taught and researched at Cornell, Duke, Freiburg, Sydney, and Vanderbilt, and is the recipient of a Humboldt Foundation Fellowship. His scholarly interests cover financial laws, social development and comparative studies.

GENEVIEVE HELLERINGER is a law professor at ESSEC Business School, IECL Lecturer at Oxford University and ECGI Research Member. Geneviève is an executive editor of the *Journal of Financial Regulation*.

IVAYLO IAYDJIEV is European Affairs adviser to the Minister of Foreign Affairs of Bulgaria. His research interests are in the area of international political economy and in particular euro area governance, EU financial regulation, and international financial institutions. He holds a PhD in public policy from the University of Oxford.

DENIZ IGAN is the Deputy Chief of the IMF Research Department's Macro-Financial Division. She is also an EUI Young Policy Leaders Fellow. Her research interests include financial crises and the political economy of financial regulation. She holds a PhD in economics from Princeton University.

JIN SHENG is a senior research fellow at NUS Centre for Banking and Finance Law. Jin holds law degrees from NYU, HKU, University of Toronto, and Peking University. She also visited University of Michigan Law School, Max Planck Institute for International and Comparative Law, and Melbourne Law School.

THOMAS LAMBERT is an assistant professor of finance at Rotterdam School of Management, Erasmus University. His research interests are in banking, corporate finance, FinTech, and political economy. Thomas holds a PhD in Finance from the Université Catholique de Louvain.

UGO PAGANO is Professor of Economics at the University of Siena and the Director of the joint PhD program in economics of the Universities of Florence, Pisa and Siena. He received his PhD from the University of Cambridge where he was a university lecturer and a fellow of Pembroke College.

KATHARINA PISTOR is Edwin B. Parker Professor of Comparative Law at Columbia Law School and Director of the Columbia Law School Center on Global Legal Transformation. Her research spans corporate law, corporate governance, money and finance, property rights, and comparative law and legal institutions. She holds numerous international awards for outstanding research and is an elected member of the Berlin-Brandenburg Academy of Sciences. Prior to joining Columbia Law, Pistor held academic positions at Harvard University and the Max Planck Institute. She holds degrees from the University of Munich, Harvard University, the University of London and Freiburg University.

RUTH PLATO-SHINAR is Professor of Banking Law and Financial Regulation, and Director of the Center for Banking Law at the Netanya Academic College, Israel. She is a member of the Advisory Committee of the Israeli Minister of Finance; the Advisory Committee of the Governor of the Bank of Israel; the Advisory Board of the Commissioner of Capital Markets, Insurance and savings; and a former Board Member of the Governmental Fund for Class Actions.

WEI SHEN is Dean and Professor of Law at Shandong University Law School. His research focuses on financial regulation, corporate governance, international investment law and commercial arbitration. He is a Global Professor of Law at NYU and taught at National University of Singapore, Tel Aviv University, Copenhagen Business School, among others.

NIKHILESH SINHA is a Research Fellow and member of faculty at the Hult International Business School, London. He holds an LLM in Law and Economics and is in the final stages of a PhD at University College London. Nikhilesh's research spans the fields of urban economics, development studies, law and institutional economics.

CHANG-HSIEN TSAI is a professor of law and business at the Institute of Law for Science and Technology, College of Technology Management, National Tsing Hua University, Taiwan. His research focuses on corporate law, securities regulation, financial law and financial technology. He holds an LLB from the National Taiwan University College of Law, an LLM from New York University and a JSD from the University of Illinois.

AD VAN RIET studied Economics at Erasmus University Rotterdam and holds a PhD from Tilburg University. His career in central banking encompasses positions at De Nederlandsche Bank, the European Monetary Institute, and the European Central Bank. He has published on European integration, monetary policy, fiscal policy, structural reforms, financial regulation, and the flow-of-funds.

DAILE XIA is an assistant professor at Shanghai University of Finance and Economics School of Law. She was a post-doctoral fellow of Tsinghua University School of Law and an adjunct researcher at the Center for Banking and Financial Law in National University of Singapore Faculty of Law before she joined SHUFE Law. She obtained her LLM degree in Columbia Law School, and her PhD degree from Peking University Law School.

~

Introduction

EMILIOS AVGOULEAS AND DAVID C. DONALD

1. The Case for "Political Economic" Analysis

Financial crises spawn regulatory reform.[1] Before a crisis, "the fickle nature of confidence"[2] enables markets and regulators to ignore the vulnerabilities caused by false policy assumptions, changes in the economic and technological environment and inadequate regulation. Part of the problem lies in the invisible competition between interest groups, where the industry normally holds the upper hand and the constraints of "bounded rationality" restrict the actions of regulatory decision-makers.[3] These subjective constraints on regulators often go unnoticed when the scope and powers of a financial regulator are reviewed from a legal or economic point of view. In fact, the "invisible hand" of industry lobbying may be an even more significant barrier to reform than is bounded rationality.[4] Certain arrangements can help industry money to flow easily in ways some politicians find attractive, and "the power of a political coalition is precisely the power to get a public official to go along with something that he knows is not in the long-run public interest because it

[1] "The pattern is that each crisis leads to a new set of regulations." R. Z. Aliber and C. P. Kindleberger, *Manias, Panics, and Crashes: A History of Financial Crises*, 7th edn (Basingstoke: Palgrave Macmillan, 2015), 239. Also see S. Banner, *Anglo-American Securities Regulation: Cultural and Political Roots, 1690–1860* (Cambridge: Cambridge University Press, 1998).

[2] C. M. Reinhart and K. S. Rogoff, *This Time Is Different: Eight Centuries of Financial Folly* (Princeton NJ: Princeton University Press, 2009), Kindle Locations 594–595.

[3] H. Simon, "A Behavioral Model of Rational Choice," *The Quarterly Journal of Economics*, 69 (1955), 99. Bounded rationality means here: "limited access to information ... and [incomplete] computational capacities." On how bounded rationality played a key role in the decisions/inertia of financial regulators in the period up to October 2008, see E. Avgouleas, *The Governance of Global Financial Markets – The Law, the Economics, the Politics* (Cambridge: Cambridge University Press, 2012), chap. 2.

[4] See, e.g., S. Johnson and J. Kwak, *13 Bankers: The Wall Street Takeover and the Next Financial Meltdown* (New York: Vintage Books, 2010), 92–104.

is in his own short-term interest."[5] As Sinclair once observed, "it is difficult to get a man to understand something, when his salary depends on his not understanding it."[6] Even when problems are recognized and regulators have the will to take action, limitations "hardwired" into the financial system by the conceptual framework of law and the social position of market participants can block improvement.[7] Thus desirable and achievable reform can as a result be neglected, whether from over-confidence, bounded rationality, self-serving neglect of duty or the limitations of the very tools through which reform must act.

With its interdisciplinary and systematic perspective, political economic analysis can uncover such hidden causes within the organization (rules and structures) of financial regulation impeding the success of its expressed goals. Unger defines political theory as "the study of how men organize their societies and how society should be organized."[8] On such organization, Bentham, in his *Manual of Political Economy*, observes that a "desirable effect" cannot be achieved in government without the combination of "power, knowledge or intelligence, and inclination."[9] This is the nexus where modern political economy scholars focus their efforts. Such works investigate the epistemological and environmental limitations facing regulators, the way power is structured and competences are allocated within a regulatory framework, and the forces influencing regulatory action or inertia. These factors are systematically interdependent, so that when an actor lacks any one of them – such as when a knowledgeable and powerful actor is paid to turn away from the public good – this will prevent desired action. Studying these aspects of the modern regulatory framework and activity is of critical importance not

---

[5] See e.g., C. W. Calomiris and S. H. Haber, *Fragile by Design: The Political Origins of Banking Crises and Scarce Credit* (Princeton NJ: Princeton University Press, 2014) 212 ("There were public officials – congressmen, senators, bank supervisors, and regulators – who understood the game but who had good reason not to try to interrupt play or change the rules . . . the power of a political coalition is precisely the power to get a public official to go along with something that he knows is not in the long-run public interest because it is in his own short-term interest.").

[6] U. Sinclair, *I, Candidate for Governor: And How I Got Licked* (Los Angeles CA: University of California Press, 1935), 109. This is cited in A. Lo, *Adaptive Markets: Financial Evolution at the Speed of Thought* (Princeton NJ: Princeton University Press, 2017), Kindle Locations 6377–6395, with reference to Citibank CEO Charles Prince's famous need in 2007 to "dance" as long as the "music played."

[7] K. Pistor, "A Legal Theory of Finance," *Journal of Comparative Economics*, 41 (2013), 315–330, 338.

[8] Roberto M. Unger, *Knowledge and Politics* (New York: The Free Press, 1975), 3–4.

[9] Jeremy Bentham, *A Manual of Political Economy* (1843), 34.

only in order to construct an accurate narrative about a past crisis, but also in order to formulate well-informed and balanced normative propositions.

For Polanyi, the political economic project begins with realizing the significance of something the knowledge of which exercises moral suasion over behavior. He writes that, "[w]hen the significance of poverty was realized, the stage was set for the nineteenth century ... [and] poor relief ... never ceased to occupy men's minds for another century and a half."[10] This closely parallels the definition of "political economy" offered by the *Encyclopaedia Britannica*, which observes that the early political economists "took a secular approach, refusing to explain the distribution of wealth and power in terms of God's will and instead appealing to political, economic, technological, natural, and social factors and the complex interactions between them."[11]

When Bentham observes that a working balance of power, knowledge, and inclination allow desirable government action, he is also suggesting that a failure to act could be the result of a hidden deficit in one or the other of these elements. Such failure could arise from "political, economic, technological, natural, and social factors and the complex interactions between them." The details of such "complex interactions" may be ignored, as they were in the 1990s and early 2000s, when market forces were viewed in awe as essentially "God's will" elevating the "invisible hand" of market forces to an automatically and self-adjusting competitive equilibrium.[12] Where that is the case, a political economic analysis would appear to be distrustful or even resentful of the natural order. Yet, an analysis that uncovers what was previously hidden opens the future to new possibilities. With regard to trust, whether that is trusting regulators, the wisdom of "market forces," or some other phenomenon, Luhmann observes that "the problem of trust is that the future contains many more possibilities than can be actualized in the present and transferred to the past."[13] Unless the present and past are viewed with a certain amount of *dis*trust, those hidden possibilities cannot be freed for actualization.

---

[10] Karl Polanyi, *The Great Transformation: The Political and Economic Origins of Our Time* (Boston MA: Beacon Press, 2001), 116.

[11] *Encyclopedia Britannica*, entry for "Political Economy" (2017).

[12] S. Deakin, "The Evolution of Theory and Method in Law and Finance," in N. Maloney et al. (eds.), *The Oxford Handbook of Financial Regulation* (Oxford: Oxford University Press, 2015), 14–15.

[13] N. Luhmann, *Vertrauen: Ein Mechanismus der Reduktion sozialer Komplexität*, 5th edn. (Stuttgart: UTB, 2014), 14; translation from the German. D. Donald.

2. Political Economy of Financial Regulation

As regulatory change often follows financial crises, it is not surprising that the 2008 global financial crisis and the eurozone debt and banking crisis provoked intense study of financial regulation.[14] The configuration of knowledge, power, and inclination in the 2000s was particularly problematic, both leaving gaps that were unforeseen or unnecessary and creating concentrations of wealth and power at record-setting levels. The systemic collapse in credit that gradually arose in 2007 and burst in late 2008 had been understood by most to be extremely unlikely, given the quality of the regulators and the regulatory framework, the abundance of academic literature and the enormous amount of data available daily from the highly transparent financial markets. Exactly because of this highly sophisticated eco-system of monitoring and control, governments had permitted risk to be created and embraced in unprecedented quantities and allowed regulatory deficits to arise at every level, from the shape of law to the daily operation of regulatory authorities. A global failure of the size that occurred indicates problems going far beyond poorly calibrated risk management or insufficient monitoring. The epistemic grid for markets and risk, the incentive system within government regulation and their regulators, as well as the way knowledge, power and inclination interacted in the face of innovation, invited fundamental reassessment.

The multifaceted nature of political economic analysis, particularly its focus on systemic problems within the relationships between information, understanding and power – the will to use it, and the reasons for using it – can uncover flaws that are otherwise overlooked. This volume contains nine chapters from law and finance experts, and six from economists and political scientists, giving flesh and meaning to the term political economic analysis. They examine from a political economy perspective six national and supranational regulatory systems, as well as the conceptual and epistemological frameworks underlying market structure and regulation. The analyses are empirical in the tradition of social science methodology as well as doctrinal in the tradition of law. They include institutional comparisons among national regulatory systems and between national and international frameworks, as well as epistemological and conceptual

---

[14] Aliber provides a rundown of the most notable thirty books written about the global financial crisis between 2008 and 2015. Aliber and Kindleberger, *Manias and Panics*, 16–18.

analyses of the underpinnings of the financial system and its causal relationship to law on the one hand and the economy on the other.

The combined result disperses the constituent elements of financial regulation within a prism of perspectives, allowing the study of its epistemological, conceptual and policy bases and structural designs both with regard to economic function and constitution/allocation of national and international regulatory power. Requisite analysis even extends to offer explanations of how the human agents charged with the implantation, operation and application of financial regulation have dealt with their power vis-à-vis rich and influential constituencies, including financiers, other industry actors, and consumers.

3. Environmental Determinants and Impact of Financial Regulation

The financial system should fund and facilitate the real economy, smooth out liquidity shortages and facilitate monitoring of agents for the long-term benefit of society. To understand whether a disruption of the balance of power, knowledge or incentive has been overlooked, it is necessary not only to evaluate the financial system for effectiveness, fairness and efficiency within existing mechanisms, but also to explore the sources and conduits of power and knowledge. This exploration includes law in every form, the infrastructure enabling transactions, the way regulation affects differently situated parties, the impact of finance on the real economy and the even-handedness of regulatory personnel. These points of entry allow the play of power in financial regulation to be charted for improvement.

Pistor, whose chapter begins this collection, sees the shape and content of law itself as the constitutive element of finance, and in the chapter published here adds that "we need to understand both public and private law" in order to grasp how law affects finance and how regulation can be improved. The Legal Theory of Finance (LTF), which Pistor has developed over the last decade, exposes the shape of publicly enforceable private law as a source of power determining the shape and operation of finance: "many choices are made in a highly decentralized fashion that are difficult to track; and most are made outside the public eye, with their effects remaining hidden for years, typically coming into the open view only in a crisis, when it is too late."

A conceptual infrastructure previously understood as neutral and natural contains, as anyone who has drafted a contract knows, built-in choices allocating advantages and detriment. She concludes that because the financial system is "the product of many small decisions taken over years and decades by private actors, courts, regulators and legislatures," "small but persistent moves that roll back legal privileges and reassert sovereign rights could go a long way in rebalancing the playing field."

Donald also examines the environment of financial transactions and regulations, arguing that the stance of regulation should fundamentally change as the twin beliefs underpinning the efficient capital markets hypothesis – instant impounding of information into prices and perfect rationality of decisions – no longer present tenable assumptions. He explains how from different starting points, market microstructure studies and both behavioral psychology and neuroscience have shown that neither seamless pricing nor full and neutral judgment exist.

Donald then argues that when pricing is no longer assumed to "just somehow happen," regulators should pay close attention to the infrastructure arrangements of financial markets in which prices are created. Traditionally, the financial industry and their contractors hold all designs and operational details regarding these systems, despite the fact that any arrangement chosen will necessarily create advantages for some and disadvantages for other. Donald also argues that something of a Reformation is necessary regarding public belief in markets, and that this should be done by shifting daily disclosure away from "which stock won today" toward how the market affects economic growth, pension values, jobs, income, and employment conditions.

Chen, on the other hand, focuses on the contrast between the environment in practice and regulatory assumptions, exposing a fundamental problem in the primary market disclosure framework that has been seen but not perceived for decades. Institutional investors receive significantly more and better information in connection with an initial public offering (IPO) than do retail investors. The law she examines is that of Hong Kong, which has an unusually active base of retail investors and perhaps above-average treatment of the same. Nevertheless, by working through the means of disclosure offered institutional investors and retail investors from the moment the underwriter begins informally to test the market, through the roadshows, to the publication of the securities prospectus, she finds that retail investors receive considerably less information and receive it later than do institutional investors.

Selective disclosure is unacceptable pursuant to the best practices of securities regulation, yet rules ensuring fair disclosure do not take into account the specific instances in the actual IPO-building environment. In light of the gap that Chen identifies, she advises adjusting the disclosure ecosystem by introducing "deal-specific resources" for retail investors to access information in ways similar to institutional access and "general education" to "enhance the overall knowledge and skills of the investing public."

Pagano addresses the opposite side of the primary market environment by highlighting a deep legal-economic nexus that has previously gone unexplored: the relationship between the "privatization" of knowledge through expanding intellectual property rights (IPRs) and the growth of equity financing. He argues that "financialization of the economy and privatization of intangibles have reinforced each other." This is the case, as Pagano explains, because IPRs "are highly specific and often even unique assets, which cannot have thick markets like buildings and machines. For this reason they cannot be a good source of collateral for traditional types of banking," such as collateralized lending. As such, the growth in an economy based on IPRs has "been an important cause of a shift towards other forms of finance," primarily equity.

Pagano shows how this trend has tended to choke off innovation through IPR monopoly and squeeze future effective returns. He argues that to overcome the economic distortions created by the monopolization of knowledge through IPRs, financial regulation will not be sufficient. Instead, regulation could "change the nature of the assets held" through an arrangement of "IPRs buy outs" undertaken by public authorities, together with a set of international rules designed to prevent free-riding on technology developed in and bought out by other countries.

4. Political Economy Analysis of Regulatory Choices

Just beyond law lie the regulatory frameworks. The most intractable political economic problem of regulation is influence over the shape and application of regulatory measures. As Stigler observed in his 1971 paper that did much to establish the study of "regulatory capture":

> The ... machinery and power of the state ... is a potential resource or threat to every industry in the society. With its power to prohibit or compel, to take or give money, the state can and does selectively help or hurt a vast number of industries .... The central tasks of the theory of economic regulation are to explain who will receive the benefits or

burdens of regulation, what form regulation will take, and the effects of regulation upon the allocation of resources .... as a rule, regulation is acquired by the industry and is designed and operated primarily for its benefit.[15]

Three chapters in this volume advance the literature on the important problem of channeling the "machinery and power of the state" through financial regulatory authorities for the general good or otherwise. Lambert and Igan bring together a number of points of evidence to analyze the presence and power of lobbying against banking regulators in the years preceding the global financial crisis. They examine average money spent by type of institution and regulatory changes to establish a robust ratio of lobbying to regulatory impact. Castellano and Helleringer move beyond tangible influence to examine the important and less visible aspects of capture through the sociological and psychological perspectives of financial regulators. They use EU regulators in which members have different national backgrounds connected to differing interests and agendas to explore their theory. Plato-Shinar focuses on one case study, recounting the interaction and inaction of banking regulators, the national legislature, and ad-hoc action committees established by the latter in connection with reforming banking fees in Israel.

Lambert and **Igan** acknowledge that lobbyists are an integral part of the regulatory ecosystem, driving rulemaking forward "by providing policy research, sponsoring think tanks, mobilizing grassroots constituencies, building and maintaining relationships with key decision-makers and influencers, drafting and amending bills, and assisting agencies in writing complex rules." They examine various sticks in this bundle of lobbying activity in connection with banking regulators during the decade preceding the global financial crisis. Their analysis finds "clear bank-level evidence suggesting that regulatory capture lessens the support for tighter rules and enforcement," leading to undesirable "economic outcomes."

Castellano and **Helleringer** begin the project of offering a deeper analysis of regulator motivation than either the "public choice" notion that regulators automatically seek to expand administrative power or the classical explanation that they are a simple "emanation of the structure of rules that regulates markets." Their investigation would open analysis to seek bias that arises even without the kind of economic or informational

---

[15] George J. Stigler, "The Theory of Economic Regulation," *The Bell Journal of Economics and Management Science*, 2(1) (1971), 3.

pressure used in traditional lobbying. Leveraging newer work in social and behavioral psychology, they test for the presence of heuristics or forms of sociality in the thinking of regulators staffing regulatory bodies within the European Union and charged with formulating policy on banking regulation.

Examining intra-regulatory action among EU bodies, they map out the "multi-level architectural framework for financial regulation and supervision, offering a typology of EU financial regulators," and "isolate the dominant relational models for selected institutions that, within the EU legal order, are engaged in regulating and supervising financial markets," using the decision of the UK to leave the EU (Brexit) to expose "fault lines that become especially powerful following that decision."

Plato-Shinar provides an interesting case study that also captures the full environment populated by various institutions with distinct characteristics. This includes law-makers, regulators and specially constituted ad hoc committees in a long effort to address problematic banking fees in Israel. Against the background of theories predicting administrative behavior and regulatory capture, Plato-Shinar presents the historical sequence of events and measures, counter-measures and reversals taken and made by various groups. This analysis presents good evidence of how the entire ecosystem, including the press, reacts to opposing stimulus from industry and the public in order to achieve reform.

Sinha deals with the virtually intractable problem of microfinance regulation in India. After scoring some tremendous growth (above 170 percent) in the 2007–2010 period, the microfinance industry was brought to a stuttering halt after the microfinance crisis in Andhra Pradesh in 2010, and the private microfinance sector has yet to recover. Sinha offers a number of explanations for causes of the crisis that are well grounded in political economic theory. He identifies as principal culprit the fact that while microfinance is essentially an innovative financial product, it was instead treated as a device for social and economic development. He thus dismisses the dominant hypothesis of a "mission drift" or the shifting of focus from social inclusion toward profit. The chapter draws on Pistor's Legal Theory of Finance and the regulation of financial markets to analyze the characteristics of the Indian microfinance ecosystem that led to the crisis.

Tsai also applies Pistor's Legal Theory of Finance to a specific case study, which offers excellent comparison to the Israeli problem examined by Plato-Shinar. Tsai explains how the peculiar political balance of constituencies in Taiwan led its government to bail out investors – rather than the institutions that sold them risky instruments – during the global financial crisis.

Tsai examines the interplay of institutional actors in the legal and regulatory frameworks, showing how a legal remedy to provide relief in "changed circumstances" existed in the Taiwanese Civil Code, yet was not applied by courts due to existing judicial precedent. Then a spontaneously organized victims group spurred the Financial Supervisory Commission into action by creating an atmosphere of emergency recognized by the public and the government. That Commission then created a "makeshift Alternative Dispute Resolution system," which itself applied the "changed circumstances" relief denied by the courts. Tsai maps the web of motivations, influences and adjustments of law that led the Taiwanese legal system to provide a kind of relief that appeared on its face contrary to law.

5. The Political Economy of Global Financial Regulation – Discord, Conflict, and Cooperation

Political complexity reaches its highest level when sovereign states enter into bi- or multilateral collaboration without external enforcement by a fully binding, overarching institution. While the frameworks that have been adopted to address individual questions, such as to prevent war (United Nations), manage trade disputes (World Trade Organization) or stabilize international finance (International Monetary Fund) are based on formal treaties under international law, the bodies that govern international finance are largely voluntary. Each of these frameworks maneuvers carefully around the sovereignty of its participants, and are thus left at a workable minimum.

Avgouleas discusses the impact of instability in foreign exchange markets, and currency dumping/manipulation which as he explains can be a cause of systemic risk. For example, foreign currency exposure was a key vulnerability behind the series of emerging market crises in 1997–1998.[16] The Global Financial Crisis also showed that currency mismatches are not just a concern for emerging markets. Greater foreign currency exposure increases country vulnerability to sudden stops and currency depreciations, limiting the ability of the exchange rate to act as a shock absorber as well as

---

[16] See for an overview R. Buckley, E. Avgouleas, D. Arner, "Twenty Years of International Financial Crises: What Have We Learnt and What Still Needs to Be Done?" ADB Background paper, September 2017.

the ability of monetary policy to support the economy. Instability in foreign exchange markets and currency dumping/manipulation can act as a stimulant vis-à-vis sudden reverses of short-term capital flows cultivating further mistrust in international economic relations. He suggests that such mistrust exposes as flawed the notion that an international financial order may exist separately from the global monetary order and the trade and investment order on a self-standing basis through the technocratic standards promulgated by the Basel Committee and the Financial Stability Board (FSB), notwithstanding the importance of such standards. While said separation achieved in the first three decades of the existence of transnational regulatory networks for International Finance, at the same time, it has worked to promote financialization and the global shadow banking sector. This has meant that cross-border financial and especially currency transactions became separated from any links to trade and long-term investment. The paradox of the separation of the three international economic orders, albeit for defensible reasons, has given rise to massive rent-seeking by the global financial services industry and the rentier investor classes and has weakened the case for free trade, since financial flows and global markets, the most potent integrative force in the realm of global finance, are seen as an entirely separate matter. It has also undermined any thoughts of creating coherent international structures for the governance and regulation of global finance, since these would have to move from the current "soft law" status quo and they could be defended only if they were seen as integral in the buttressing of the global trade and investment order.

Engel offers a complex comparison of decision-making dynamics within the regulatory ecosystems of the United States and the EU while each of these jurisdictions worked toward adoption of new regulation for commodity derivatives following the global financial crisis. In particular, he focuses on the "long tail" of the complex implementing rules that had to follow enabling legislation. The differing powers of interested industries in the United States and Europe led to distinct types of influence being applied on a cluster of regulators in each jurisdiction, which themselves were organized differently, opening them to internal disagreement and influence in different ways. The chapter posits a hypothetical framework of organization types and intensity of industry influence to develop a schema of four potential regulatory outcomes.

Engel's conclusions affirm the robustness of his schema of governmental unity and industry opposition. He finds that (in the United States) where the regulator does not disagree with the shape of the enabling legislation and receives limited opposition from industry, the resulting "technical rules were in line with the legislation." On the other hand, where (in the EU) again there was agreement within the primary regulator about the enabling legislation, but they faced "strong opposition from multiple industry groups, extensive efforts were made to develop carve-outs and exemptions for large industries" in the resulting rules.

The European Union and the eurozone provide a rich set of circumstances for the interaction of state power, expert and lay knowledge, and incentives. In a precarious balance on incomplete institutions, a patchwork of bargains and enthusiastic hope for integration, Europe lurched into one of the most dangerous markets in history in the late 2000s.[17] The consequences have been significant, including a contributing factor in the UK's exit from the Union.

Iaydjiev poses an interesting and much discussed question in international financial regulation: "Who governs cross-border banking?," enhancing the literature surrounding the so-called "host's dilemma." His main focus is on situations where "host regulators find themselves with a de facto lack of control over their financial systems while being at the same time largely shut out from key international decision-making forums." His main focus is on the banking markets of emerging European countries, which during the transition period of the late 1990s and early 2000s were largely dominated by Central and Western European banks. The case study is very important in connection with actual distribution of power between different financial regulators in the governance of cross-border banking. In the case Iaydjiev examines such cooperation was rare, with host countries bearing the costs of adjustment to the needs and requirements of the dominant home jurisdiction. Yet, once the external shock of the global financial crisis hit the region, "there was extensive cooperation between all actors in the crisis response, facilitated by the informal Vienna Initiative." According to Iaydjiev, from a political economy perspective this shift in regulatory attitudes "demonstrates international institutions could be an effective solution to the host's dilemma – at the cost of accepting reduced sovereignty."

Van Riet shows that the reform of European finance has not just removed financial market distortions, corrected flawed regulations and strengthened supervisory institutions, it also significantly widened the scope of the existing preferential regulatory treatment for sovereign debt.

---

[17] On the institutional side, see P. Craig, "The Financial Crisis, the European Union Institutional Order, and Constitutional Responsibility," *Indiana Journal of Global Legal Studies*, 22 (2015), 243.

This makes it easier for governments to obtain market funding at favorable interest rates and to manage the crisis legacy of high public debt. In plain terms the financial industry is implicitly encouraged to "disregard the risks from high government exposures and contributes to captive sovereign credit markets." Namely, the principal makers/producers of EU financial regulation gave preferential treatment to their own debt in order to enable themselves to refinance their debt mountains cheaply regardless of whether they were creating, at the same time, a new source of systemic risk and distortions in the global debt markets. European policymakers may have felt compelled to follow relevant parallel regulatory developments in other advanced economies, notably the United States. However, from a political economy perspective preferential regulatory treatment of government debt "may offer EU countries some compensation for the fact that their ability to exercise political dominance over the domestic financial industry and capital markets in general is being constrained by … the centralisation of banking supervision and resolution under the European Banking Union, and … the … harmonisation of capital market law as part of the Capital Markets Union," notwithstanding the fact that "extensive government privileges in public debt financing create moral hazard on the part of sovereigns and undermine incentives for fiscal adjustment and economic reforms." At the same time, "the regulatory bias towards large sovereign exposures in financial institutions may become an economic and prudential concern, given the possible crowding out of private sector funding."

6. Financial Regulation and State Capitalism: A Political Economy Perspective

When a national government owns most large institutions in a financial system, political economy is central to every aspect of their operation, including regulation. This is the case in China, and the final three chapters in this volume apply political economic analysis to the Chinese financial sector and its regulation, examining the formal banking and shadow banking sectors, and the securities markets. These chapters reveal something about the analytical stance found in the political economic approach that might have otherwise not been noticed – it apparently seeks a balance between public and private power. The chapters in this volume examining regulations and regulators in the United States, Europe, Israel, Bangladesh and Taiwan show how private interests work to sway regulators away from the public good in most cases. However, three chapters by scholars who are not affiliated to each other and are based in separate locations addressing the Chinese regulatory system all argue the opposite, that too much government "represses" market forces so that public authority is swaying regulation away from the private good. The combination of views found in this volume on different systems of regulation may well point toward a new goal of "balance" in regulatory analysis.

Guo and **Xia** examine the specific political risks connected to the Chinese financial industry's tacit and explicit support for troubled institutions. They find that as the government seeks to introduce prudential requirements, triggering failures, the cost of the support guarantee is becoming unsustainable. Yet, "without the support of the government, financial institutions are unable to gain trust from the public to run their business." This is a situation that the authors compare to Japan up to the 1990s, a comparison – and a risk for China – often made. They explain that the deposit insurance scheme launched in 2014 may eventually allow the Chinese government to back out of its guarantee, but this is still uncertain.

Guo and Xia also find the government responsible for this problem by adopting policies of "financial repression" that hamstrung commercial banks and forced the growth of a shadow banking industry, an activity that presents even greater risks of failure. They also argue that the Chinese "government has not really understood why all of this happened." As a worst case, they see China introducing another "round of financial repression" that could trigger more failures and make shadow banking even more attractive, creating more exposure for government support, in a vicious cycle.

Shen argues that government ownership in the financial sector has skewed its judgment in banking regulatory matters because of the combination of "continuing state ownership (i.e., majority ownership of large SOEs)" with the need to support "the political foundation and legitimacy of the ruling party or state capitalism," which has led China to adopt untenable policies. Shen argues that these polices and their consequences are, in sum, "that the government has inefficiently overregulated finance, and market forces have efficiently provided liquidity and returns to those neglected by the government through the medium of shadow banking." The solution Shen offers for this problem would therefore be to end "financial repression" and follow a "free-market approach allowing the financial market more effectively and efficiently to allocate financial resources in the lending market."

Jin turns to an examination of the Chinese securities markets, in particular the performance of the Chinese regulatory ecosystem during its equity market crash of 2015. She finds a comparably damaging imbalance of government interference, as do Guo, Xia and Shen in their analysis of the Chinese banking system. Particularly, "that using the planned economy approach to control IPO pricing and pace resulted in an imbalance in the supply and demand of new stocks on the primary market, while inadequate surveillance of trading on the secondary market leaves loopholes for market manipulation, insider dealing and false statements."

Jin argues that because "the China Securities Regulatory Commission is not an independent agency," yet has "expansive powers," it overshadows "courts and self-regulatory organizations" which "only play a passive role" in China. She sees a solution to this ineffective arrangement in a regulatory model similar to that currently found in the United States, with market forces freely at play to determine listings and an independent regulator to enforce rules together with self-regulatory organizations and private plaintiffs against market misconduct in courts endowed with significant power.

7. Progress in Political Economy

The chapters in this volume bring multiple perspectives and novel research approaches to our understanding of the crucial balance among power, knowledge, and incentives in finance and its regulation. From the theoretical underpinnings of law, market order, and the financial regulation ecosystem to the special problems of developing countries and state managed economies, this volume shows that financial regulation is not only in need of political economic analysis, but that such analysis might provide the brightest light for fixing finance.

Chapters examining the state-controlled Chinese economy turn to the concepts of "market efficiency" and "public choice" as somewhat transcendental forces that could be used as fulcrums to free the financial system from government control, while other chapters in this volume offer proof that these same theories are no longer understood as founded in good science. The theories' use in the Chinese context is clearly aspirational, and an understanding of the aspirational function of "market efficiency" in working through the transition from a planned to an unplanned economy could provide insight into why these same conceptual supports were adopted as true at a time when western economies moved from industrial and commercial to financialized economies. In this respect it is interesting, as Lo points out, that Herbert Simon, who is the creator of "bounded rationality" and the theory of limited judgment according to heuristics, and Paul Samuelson, who is the creator of a mathematical economics emulating physics and assuming rational actors in efficient markets, both published their doctoral dissertations in the same year – 1947.[18] If Simon had proved dominant in the immediately subsequent decades, economic and financial development in the West would have likely been very different.

By systematically investigating the financial regulatory framework and its keepers with a political economic approach, the chapters in this volume have brought much to light that had previously gone unnoticed. We are confident that they will form the basis of future regulatory scholarship on financial regulation.

---

[18] Lo, *Adaptive Markets*, Kindle Location 3563.

PART I

The Environmental Determinants and Real
Impact of Financial Regulation

PART I

The Environmental Determinants and Real Impact of Financial Regulation

1

Regulating Financial Markets – An LTF Perspective

KATHARINA PISTOR

This chapter applies the "Legal Theory of Finance" (LTF) I developed in a paper, which was published in the *Journal of Comparative Economics* in 2013.[1] Together with other research projects, conferences, and workshops conducted in the intervening period, this chapter illustrates the explanatory powers of the theory and its ramifications for the regulation of financial systems. I am grateful for the conference and this volume, and to the other authors in it who have tested LTF in application to new circumstances,[2] as they offer a good opportunity to step back and ask more basic questions about LTF:

1. What is the nature of this theory and how can it help us understand financial markets?
2. What are the possible implications of this theory for *regulating* financial markets, both nationally and globally – the topic of the conference that motivated this book's publication?
3. What are the implications of the theory for democratic governance?

To start, I will briefly summarize the building blocks of the original theory. In the second part of this chapter, I will extend these building

---

[*] I should take this opportunity to express my gratitude to the Institute for New Economic Thinking for sponsoring several doctoral fellows as well as the annual workshops of the Global Law in Finance Network. I should also thank the doctoral students, postdocs, and co-investigators who all participated in their own research and at the workshop in pushing the boundaries of GLawFiN. For details about the workshops and their output, please visit the website of my center at http://blogs.law.columbia.edu/global-legal-transformation/law-in-finance/.

[1] K. Pistor, "A Legal Theory of Finance," *Journal of Comparative Economics*, 41, no. 2 (2013). For comments on this paper, see G. M. Hodgson, "Observations on the Legal Theory of Finance," *Journal of Comparative Economics*, 41, no. 2 (2013). Funding for this research project and for follow-up studies by doctoral students and research fellows was funded by the Institute for New Economic Thinking (INET), which is gratefully acknowledged.

[2] For example, Sinha in Chapter 9 and Tsai in Chapter 8, as well as the analogies drawn by Castellano and Helleringer in Chapter 6 and Donald in Chapter 2, between LTF and related analytical perspectives.

blocks to a process analysis of the financial system. I will argue that a better understanding of financial systems, their construction, regulation, and failure, we need to understand both public and private law, and the use of one to undo the other. Private law, I will argue, furnishes the basic elements for financial assets and their issuers, while public law and regulation seeks to mitigate the risk they might pose for stability. It is often feared that excessive public regulation can "kill" the market; less well appreciated is that with the help of private law, the effects of most regulation can be muted.

1.1   The Legal Theory of Finance Revisited

The Legal Theory of Finance (LTF) is an inductive theory that uses insights drawn from the observation of real markets in good and in bad times, during phases of expansion as well as severe crisis, to theorize about financial markets and financial systems. As originally, conceived, LTF has four building blocks:

First, contemporary financial systems are rule-bound systems. This may seem trivial and there are, of course, many accounts already that highlight the centrality of law to finance. Still, LTF treatment of law as endogenous to finance marks a departure from the existing literature on law *and* finance,[3] which views law as a supportive device for financial systems that are conceived of, at least in theory, to operate outside the law. I am not disputing that borrowing and lending precedes the rise of states and state sponsored legal systems; nor that fairly complicated financial arrangements (such as rotating credit associations) operate without the need for formal law;[4] or that new information technologies are on the rise, which may create digital money and perhaps even entire financial and monetary systems in digital rather than legal code.[5] Still, as of now, the shadow of the coercive enforcement powers of states has been critical to scale

---

[3] See the seminal paper by R. La Porta et al., "Law and Finance," *Journal of Political Economy*, 106, no. 6 (1998) and its conceptual predecessor, A. Shleifer and R. W. Vishny, "A Survey of Corporate Governance," *The Journal of Finance* 52, no. 2 (1997).

[4] This would include, for example, rotating credit associations, or long distance trade and finance based on reputation bonds, as in A. Greif, "Reputation and Coalitions in Medieval Trade: Evidence on the Maghribi Traders," *Journal of Economic History*, 59, no. 4 (1989).

[5] See Szabo on bit gold, for example, or the Bitcoin manifesto by its anonymous founder. For a legal analysis of crypto-currencies, compare A. Wright and P. De Filippi, "Decentralized Blockchain Technology and the Rise of Lex Cryptographia," *SSRN*, https://ssrn.com/abstract=2580664 or http://dx.doi.org/10.2139/ssrn.2580664.

financial systems beyond local settings where mutual monitoring is possible.

Law was a critical ingredient already in early long-distance trade finance, which relied extensively on legal devices, such as the bill of exchange. The bill is often hailed as an example of a private system of financial ordering, but, in fact, was supported by case law in England and statutes that major trading cities across Europe adopted over the course of the seventeenth and the early eighteenth centuries.[6] They were adopted in order to increase the probability that such an instrument would in fact be enforceable against anyone who had endorsed it along the chain of payment transactions, and critically, without allowing counter claims arising out of contract or even crime.[7] The digital revolution may offer an alternative to state-sponsored law, but we have yet to find out whether it can match the scale and scope of financial systems that are coded in law, which extend to trillions of assets traded globally. In any event, digital codes are also rule-bound systems, and LTF's analytical tools and predictions should therefore be applicable to them as well.[8]

The second building block of LTF is the Law-Finance Paradox. This holds that the function of binding commitments – upheld by the threat of coercion or an immutable digital code, as the case may be – makes the system scalable. Critically, however, insisting that commitments, which were made in the past will be enforced "no matter what" and irrespective of intervening change, can set the system on course to self-destruction. It can be rescued from this fate only by suspending the very rule of enforceability that enabled the scaling of the system in the first place. This, of course, undermines the foundations on which the system was built, the same foundations that will be needed for rebuilding it.

Because there have been some misunderstandings about the nature of the Law-Finance Paradox, I would like to clarify that the paradox lies neither in the fact that a rule-bound system might crash, nor in the possibility of rescuing it by relaxing or suspending these rules. The key is that these actions undermine the credibility of law as the foundation for relying on the enforceability of claims embedded in assets that are traded globally without spending much time considering who the debtors are on

---

[6] E. Kadens, "The Myth of the Customary Law Merchant," *Texas Law Review*, 90 (2011).

[7] For an excellent analysis of the common law of bills of exchange in England, see J. S. Rogers, *The Early History of the Law of Bills and Notes: A Study of the Origins of Anglo-American Commercial Law* (Cambridge: Cambridge University Press, 1995).

[8] See also K. Pistor and A. Wang, "RE-imagining Finance: The Promise of Decentralized Technologies," (2017), working paper on file with the author.

the other end.[9] This tension is built into a system that puts a premium on credibility of commitments made that cannot be renegotiated; within such a system there is no obvious solution for what to do when the enforcement of these commitments will precipitate a crisis and possibly the system's self-destruction. Indeed, this dynamic affects not only debt, but also the formation of equity, or even property rights in land, if only because they too are affected by fundamental uncertainty. But debt finance makes the mix of uncertainty and legal rigidity toxic. To prevent the system's self-destruction, it is necessary to step outside such a system and relax or suspend the rules that governed them. Critically, the Law-Finance Paradox is an element of a positive or descriptive theory, not a normative call for inaction or for relying on ex-post emergency responses rather than precautionary measures.[10]

The suspension of law can take many forms, including a halt of *all* enforcement actions not only against individual debtors (as in bankruptcy), but against all debtors. It may be possible to craft more targeted interventions, such as debt moratoria that limit creditors' discretion in seizing and selling debtors' assets at fire-sale prices.[11] Importantly, the suspension of law is also present when bailing out select entities or extending liquidity support to them, even if these measures are backed by ad hoc legislation[12] or fall within the scope of the discretionary powers of an agency, such as central banks.[13] The reason is that they undermine the foundational rules of the game for a competitive market economy, namely that individuals or entities that are unable to balance their assets and liabilities must exit.

[9] Gorton uses the concept of "information insensitivity" to refer to a similar phenomenon, but ignores the foundational function law plays for turning claims to pay at a future date in assets that are traded as if they were a valuable object in and of themselves. See G. Gorton et al., "Regulating the Shadow Banking System [with Comments and Discussion]," *Brookings Papers on Economic Activity* (2010).

[10] See, however, J. N. Gordon and C. Muller, "Confronting Financial Crisis: Dodd-Frank's Dangers and the Case for a Systemic Emergency Insurance Fund," *Yale Journal on Regulation* 28, no. 1 (2011).

[11] See P. Bolton and H. Rosenthal, "Political Intervention in Debt Contracts," *Journal of Political Economy* 110, no. 5 (2002); for the historical account on which this theoretical paper has been based, see M. N. Rothbard, *The Panic of 1819* (New York: Columbia University Press, 1962) and L. J. Alston, "Farm Foreclosure Moratorium Legislation: A Lesson from the Past," *The American Economic Review* 74, no. 3 (1984).

[12] The United States and many European countries passed bailout legislation in the midst of the 2008 crisis. See C. Woll, *The Power of Inaction: Bank Bailouts in Comparison* (Ithaca NY: Cornell University Press, 2014).

[13] Many of the Federal Reserve Bank's interventions were justified by emergency powers enshrined in section 13 of the Federal Reserve Act.

The interplay of rules that are designed to bind participants and can be enforced against their will, if necessary with the coercive powers of the state, implies that financial systems in all their dimensions invoke state power; they are never entirely private, but always hybridic, and essentially so. This is *the third building block* of LTF. It is impossible to explain the rise of financial systems on such a scale simply as the sum of private agreements; beyond a certain threshold, financial systems (just as other complex systems of social ordering) require a commitment to binding rules, whether backed by the credible threat of enforceability,[14] or a self-executing "smart" contract, envisioned by the technologists who code blockchains. A careful institutional autopsy of the assets shows that they make ample use of legal devices that can be upheld against the world (*erga omnes*), such as property rights, secured interest law, and the asset shielding functions of trust and corporate law.[15]

The *fourth building block of LTF* seeks to locate power; it suggests that there are two critical points where power creeps into a system that is otherwise bound by rules: First, where "the rules of the game" are made;[16] and, second, where these rules are suspended in the name of rescuing the system from self-destruction. In rule-bound systems there are rule-makers and rule-takers, the former having the power to frame the game. We may be playing "Chess" or "Go," American football or European soccer; somebody sets the rules for the respective game – if only by codifying practices that have become settled over time. Setting the rules of the game entails "framing powers," as sociologists would call it. Rule-making also occurs in subtler forms in the course of the game itself as the players test the limits of existing rules, the umpires interpret and enforce them, and somebody decides whether to alter the rules in response to what players and umpires have done in the field. Viewed in this light, the players themselves partake in the rule-making (alone, or

---

[14] See G. M. Hodgson, "On the Institutional Foundations of Law: The Insufficiency of Custom and Private Ordering," *Journal of Economic Issues* 43, no. 1 (2009).

[15] For an excellent advancement in property rights that builds on the legal notion of rights *in rem* vs. rights *in personam*, see B. Arrunada, "Property as Sequential Exchange: The Forgotten Limits of Private Contract," *Journal of Institutional Economics* 13, no. 4 (2017). On the asset-shielding functions of trust and corporate law, H. Hansmann and R. Kraakman, "The Essential Role of Organizational Law," *Yale Law Journal*, 110, no. 3 (2000), 387–440.

[16] North's dictum is that ultimately, the economic theories on which the rules of the game are being built are just stories. See D. C. North, *Institutions, Institutional Change, and Economic Performance* (Cambridge: Cambridge University Press, 1990).

with a smart lawyer at their side) by exploiting ambiguities and gaps in the rules to advance their own interests.

Economists have discovered that contracts are incomplete and have built entire theories around this insight – some have even won the Nobel Memorial Prize for this.[17] The basic insight is quite intuitive: It is impossible for private parties to anticipate all future contingencies and take precautions for them in their contracts. Even trying to get close to the ideal of a fully state-contingent contract would be too costly – another reason why publicly maintained default rules has proven so useful. Moving from contracts to law, it should be apparent that law, too, is incomplete, and if anything, even more so than contracts.[18] After all, law is meant to offer solutions for many "like" cases in the indefinite future. Legislatures usually create rules with an infinite lifespan subject only to repeal by a future legislature (or the occasional verdict of a court that a law violates the constitution and is therefore struck down) – the practice of including sunset provisions into some laws in some countries notwithstanding.[19] It should be obvious that legislatures can hardly consider every possible case that might arise long after the statute has been passed. They therefore delegate, implicitly or explicitly, the power to apply general laws in specific cases to courts or regulators.[20] Inevitably, delegating the enforcement of incomplete laws to others leaves a substantial amount of discretion in the hands of these agents.

In common law systems, the law-making authority of courts is readily accepted. Civil law countries, in comparison, assert that courts only interpret and do *not* make law, but the line between interpretation and law-making is not always easy to draw.[21] Either way, judges play a critical

---

[17] O. Hart received the Nobel Memorial Prize in 2016 for his work on incomplete contract and the property rights theory of the firm, which is derived from incomplete contract theory. Foundational is S. J. Grossman and O. D. Hart, "The Costs and Benefits of Ownership: A Theory of Vertical and Lateral Integration," *Journal of Political Economy* 94, no. 4 (1986); for a comprehensive treatment see O. Hart, *Firms, Contracts, and Financial Structure* (Oxford: Clarendon Press, 1995).

[18] K. Pistor and C. Xu, "Incomplete Law," *Journal of International Law and Politics*, 35, no. 4 (2003).

[19] Examples in the US include funding provisions for regulators, such as the Commodities Future and Trading Commission (CFTC).

[20] Pistor and Xu, "Incomplete Law."

[21] K. Zweigert and H. Kötz, *Introduction to Comparative Law* (Oxford: Clarendon Press, 1998) offer a comparative overview of these two major legal systems in their introduction. See also S. Deakin and K. Pistor, "Legal Origin Theory: Introduction," in S. Deakin and K. Pistor (eds.), *Legal Origin Theory* (Cheltenham: Edward Elgar, 2012).

role in ensuring that decades- if not centuries-old codes[22] can be used to resolve current issues by way of legal interpretation, including analogy and gap-filling. These differences notwithstanding, both systems have come to rely heavily on administrative agencies and regulators as secondary lawmakers and law enforcers. In fact, under conditions of uncertainty it becomes necessary to rely on agents that can enforce law proactively, especially when the likely damages are substantial, rather than relying on victims litigating for compensation only ex post.[23]

The second juncture where power is made visible in a rule-bound system is when rules are suspended ex post, whether selectively or wholesale.[24] In no sports game can the players simply declare that they will no longer be bound by the rules; they will most likely face expulsion. They may and often will, however, try to push the boundaries of the rules, and the more incomplete the rules ex ante or ex post, the greater the opportunities to do so. This allows them to get away with the claim that "it is legal," even though in this process they have helped alter the rules of the game.

Suspending the law goes substantially further than delegating well-circumscribed lawmaking and law-enforcement powers to regulators. In this scenario, rules that were considered to be binding on all are either overridden or declared to be no longer binding on grounds of exigencies, not normative reconsideration. When binding rules are suspended, all bets are off. Whoever suspends the rules may now rule by fiat, devise ad hoc rules for a limited time, or for however long it takes to establish stability, order, or whatever other objectives were used to justify the state of exception.[25] Once emergency rule is proclaimed, it falls on the "power wielder"[26] who called the emergency to determine whether to return to the original rules, or to create new ones. Even legal systems that incorporate emergency rules designed to set a path back to the old normal are not entirely safe from rule by fiat, because enforcing them is next to impossible. Ultimately these systems also rely on the goodwill of the power wielder to return to the ex-ante state.

---

[22] The French Code Civil was first enacted in 1804, and the German Civil Code in 1900.

[23] This is the core argument that Chenggang Xu and myself developed for explaining the increasing reliance of modern states on regulators. See Pistor and Xu, "Incomplete Law."

[24] Note that this ex-post treatment of legal rules is what I called the "elasticity of law" in the original paper, to be distinguished from the ex-ante incompleteness of law just discussed.

[25] See G. Agamben, *State of Exception* (Chicago IL: University of Chicago Press, 2005).

[26] The term was introduced by R. Grant and R. O. Keohane, "Accountability and Abuses of Power in World Politics," *American Political Science Review*, 99, no. 1 (2005).

In short, power is contained by rules; however, when these rules result, endogenously, in the self-destruction of the system, as predicted by the Law-Finance Paradox, it can be rescued only from the outside. Suspending the rules of the game is where power lies, and implies the power to rule and to pick winners and losers. Emergency rulers may be benevolent or predatory, they may believe that they rule in the interest of society (as most central bankers argue they did during the Global Financial Crisis, for example).[27] This, however, cannot disguise the fact that by suspending the existing rules of the game, they exercise enormous powers. It should therefore come as no surprise that the central banks, which were created as "independent" agencies, have become much more politicized after the crisis. They have brought this onto themselves by rescuing the system from its self-destructive tendencies. To be sure, these tendencies can be mitigated, though not eliminated, with the help of regulation. Any system that relies on debt finance to make bets on an uncertain future is afflicted by this problem at some level.

Taken together, LTF's four building blocks link micro-level legal institutions to the organization and operation of national and global financial systems and calls for a closer examination of its governance structure, both in normal times when the system appears to be functioning well, and in times of crises. Critically, not only the legal rules but also crises are endogenous to the system; they are not fixes or shocks external to it.

1.2 LTF – A Restatement

In the original paper, I argued that I was presenting a "construction site" on which to develop a new theory of finance. To demonstrate the potential power of the theory, I drew from various segments of the financial system, including the case studies my collaborators on the broader research project had developed,[28] and which were published in the same special issue.[29] In this introductory chapter, I will build on these

---

[27] See Bernanke's recent memoir, tellingly called *The Courage to Act*, about the crisis, his role and that of his colleagues during the crisis. B. S. Bernanke, *The Courage to Act: A Memoir of a Crisis and Its Aftermath* (New York: W.W. Norton, 2015).

[28] These projects were funded by the Institute for New Economic Thinking. See also n. 1 supra.

[29] See the May 2013 issue of the *Journal of Comparative Economics*.

Table 1.1 *Legal Structure of Actors and Assets*

	Issuers	Assets	Investors
Entry Rules	Corporate, Trust Law Entry Requirements Capital Rules	State Monopoly	Corporate, Trust Law Entry Requirements Capital Rules
Asset Rules	Asset Types	Contract, Property & Secured Interest Law Corporate & Trust Law	Portfolio Rules

foundations, first by adding flesh to the bones of the legal institutions that are central to financial actors and assets.

Table 1.1 depicts two types of actors: issuers and investors; and two types of rules: entry rules and asset rules. At the most basic level, trust, corporate and other business organization law offers off-the-shelf rules for creating actors, both issuers and investors. There are no formalities whatsoever for a simple partnership, and very few for a trust. In fact, courts will deem an undertaking to be a partnership if two or more persons engage in a joint undertaking for profit, even if they themselves have not contemplated this. For a trust, a deed must be written up, but there are no registration requirements or other formalities that would otherwise be associated with transferring title. In contrast, limited partnerships, limited liability companies, corporations, and business trusts must be registered and comply with additional requirements, such as a name, address, and corporate seal for entities that acquire the status of an independent legal person (as is the case for limited liability companies and corporations).

Some legal systems impose capital rules even on non-financial firms, requiring them to demonstrate that they have raised a minimum amount of capital from shareholders prior to registration. Successful firms quickly outgrow any safeguarding function of these requirements, which therefore are best viewed as (perhaps obsolete) entry barriers. More common at least today are capital *adequacy* rules for financial intermediaries, in particular for banks. Under these rules, banks have to ensure that they maintain a certain ratio of equity to debt funding for their operation throughout their existence. International standards originally set the ratio at 8 percent equity capital; this was subsequently relaxed for the most sophisticated banks, only to be tightened again under the last iteration of the Basel Accords.[30]

Issuers face not only entry rules, but also some rules concerning the assets they can issue. I use the term "asset" broadly, to include, for example, the stakes of partners in a partnership. This particular asset gives a partner a claim to future profits, but also exposes her to the liabilities the firm incurs. It may not be transferable at all, or only with the approval of the other partners. In contrast, the limited partners in a limited partnership and the shareholders of publicly traded corporations can freely sell their shares.

A corporate share has been classified as personal property of the shareholder, but it is, of course, a special kind property, in that they confer right rather than physical control of things. Most importantly, holders of common shares have the right to elect representatives to the board and jointly decide on "life and death" decisions of the corporation, such as mergers and acquisitions, changes in the corporate capital and voluntary liquidation. They have the right to receive dividends, and to trade their shares. However, corporations can also issue preferred or convertible shares with very different bundles of rights attached to them. Shares, in short, are made contractually, even if they are treated by law as personal property. In fact, most shareholders no longer "own" their shares in a technical sense. The shares of publicly traded corporations are owned by central depositories, which hold them on behalf of shareholders who have a claim to share of a certain kind and all the rights it embodies.[31]

Debt instruments display an even greater variation than shares. Corporate debt can be short-term or long-term; secured or unsecured; convertible into shares, or not. Securitization has engendered the creation of an even greater variety of debt instruments – from simple securitized claims, all the way to complex synthetic derivatives. When taken apart, however, the legal components are not as new as the fancy labels such as "repos," "squared" or "cubed" CDOs might suggest. Property and secured interests law, trust and corporate law also play a critical role in their production.

---

[30] The rules have become more complicated and now place greater emphasis on common (not preferred) shares, for which the minimum requirement has been set at 4.5 percent. For an excellent and highly accessible account of capital adequacy rules, see A. Admati and M. Hellwig, *The Bankers' New Clothes* (Princeton NJ: Princeton University Press, 2013). They advocate a capital cushion of up to 30 percent.

[31] J. S. Rogers, "Policy Perspectives on Revised U.C.C. Article 8," *UCLA Law Review*, 43, no. 5 (1996) discusses the legal challenges for custodians and traders of assets held in this fashion.

Consider first a "repo," which has become a crucial tool for obtaining short-term funding, a critical source of liquidity for the shadow banking system. "Repo" of course stands for repurchase agreements, contracts by which one party sells an asset (a claim to future cash-flows) to the other on the condition that the seller will repurchase it (or an asset of a similar kind) on a certain date. The legal title of the asset changes hands, even though functionally speaking, the entire transaction operates like a secured loan. This raises interesting questions if one of the party defaults, because then it really matters whose asset it is to keep.

Securitized assets and their derivatives give investors claims against various "tranches" or slices (stratified by risk, payout, and loss absorption obligations) of assets pools held by a trust or corporate entity. In short, a mortgage-backed security or collateralized debt obligation is a complex asset that combines contract law with property, collateral, trust, and corporate law.

Examined closely, the basic structure of financial assets is more consistent than it may first seem. Moreover, efforts have been made to achieve some level of standardization in order to scale the market for a particular type of asset. Stock exchanges, for example, have imposed listing rules that have standardized the tradable common share. Even assets that are traded "over-the-counter," such as most swaps and other derivatives prior to the regulatory backlash that followed the Global Financial Crisis of 2007/08, have seen some standardization. In this case not exchanges, but trade associations, have developed standardized master agreements that streamline the basic rights and obligations of the parties, while leaving them with ample flexibility to meet their specific needs.[32]

There is, however, an important exception to the free-wheeling private creation of financial assets, and that is state money. Most states retain a monopoly over the money they issue, and exercise the power to designate it as the final means of settlement. Some countries have relinquished their power to issue their own money by adopting the currency a foreign country has issued, or by joining a currency union. But this decision too is a sovereign determination of what counts as money within

---

[32] On standardization as an important prerequisite for liquidity, see Bruce Carruthers and Arthur L. Stinchcombe, "The Social Structure of Liquidity: Flexibility, Markets, and States," *Theory and Society*, 28, no. 3 (1999). On the role of the International Swaps and Derivatives Association in creating and amending a master agreement for these market segments, see G. Morgan, "Market Formation and Governance in International Financial Markets: The Case of OTC Derivatives," *Human Relations*, 61, no. 5 (2008).

a given jurisdiction.[33] Private parties can make their own money, in the form of debt or Bitcoins, but they cannot pay their taxes with them; they have to convert these assets and thereby reconfirm state money as the means of final settlement.

Turning finally to the investors, we find the same entry rules that also govern issuers. Individual investors are largely free to choose what they want to buy, but even they face some regulatory restrictions. Unless they are deemed "sophisticated" investors and can invest a minimum amount over several million dollars, they are precluded from investing in hedge funds,[34] for example. Investors that use other people's money, such as pension funds, money market funds, or insurance companies, are often subject to more extensive portfolio regulations. They may invest only in assets of a certain risk profile or a certain liquidity to meet payout demands.

Taken together, the entry and asset rules that govern issuers, investors and the assets themselves are all it takes to create financial markets. The analysis would, however, be incomplete without mentioning two additional set of rules that have a huge impact on the choice of issuers to make and of investors to buy certain types of assets: tax and bankruptcy law. The importance of tax law is easy to understand. Not all entities or assets are taxed equally. Take only debt and equity: the cost of debt, but not that of equity, can be deducted from gross revenue prior to taxation.[35] Tax authorities have taken pains to minimize the difference between corporations and partnerships by allowing corporations to opt into pass-through tax-treatment, but this does not eliminate all differential treatment. Tax is a huge debt obligation that private parties face, and even a small reduction can greatly boost their profitability. This explains why so much effort goes into tax planning.

The importance of bankruptcy law may be less obvious. I like to think of bankruptcy as the "acid test" for all claims that have been created

---

[33] For an elaboration of monetary sovereignty from an LTF perspective, see K. Pistor, "From Territorial to Monetary Sovereignty," *Theoretical Inquires in Law*, 18, no. 2 (2017).

[34] For a useful overview of the rise of the hedge fund industry in the 1990s, see, for example, F. R. Edwards, "Hedge-Funds and the Collapse of Long Term Capital Management," *The Journal of Economic Perspectives*, 13, no. 2 (1999).

[35] According to the Modigliani-Miller theorem, the cost of debt and equity should be equal for an issuing corporation; but this assumes tax neutrality. See F. Modigliani and M. H. Miller, "The Cost of Capital, Corporation Finance and the Theory of Investment," *The American Economic Review*, 48, no. 3 (1958); for a good summary see R. C. Merton, "Application of Option-Pricing Theory: Twenty-Five Years Later," *The American Economic Review*, 88, no. 3(1998).

beforehand. When a debtor defaults this usually means that his liabilities exceed his assets with the consequence that not all commitments to creditors, which the debtor had made earlier, can possibly be fulfilled. Bankruptcy law therefore ranks creditors' claims and makes payouts to them accordingly. For the most part, bankruptcy law has tried to mimic the private rights parties created outside bankruptcy.[36] Bankruptcy safe harbors deviate from this principle. They give preferential treatment to certain types of claims; they even exempt them from general bankruptcy rules that apply to everybody else, such as the "automatic stay," which bars individual creditors from enforcing their claim during bankruptcy; or the receiver's prerogative in deciding which contracts should still be performed even as the debtor is in bankruptcy.[37]

As this brief summary of only the basic rules that govern issuers, assets and investors suggest, there are quite a few rules in play that can be fashioned by different actors to achieve optimal treatment. The major takeaway is that the relevant rules include both private and public, or regulatory law – a critical insight for understanding the challenges we face in regulating financial markets domestically and globally.

1.3   Regulating Financial Markets

It is well known that financial intermediaries are heavily regulated and that the regulation extends to what assets they may issue or hold. Less attention is typically paid to the legal institutions from which the issuers, investors, and assets are crafted. Most of the work on this front is done by "private" rather than "public" law. This distinction is somewhat artificial, but as a rule of thumb, private law governs the relations among private parties and offers a set of devices and tool kits, including but not limited to contract and property law, that can be used to structure business organizations, transactions, and assets. These tools can be employed for many purposes, including productivity-enhancing transactions, speculation and regulatory arbitrage, or any combination of the above. In effect, private law is used to mitigate or undo the effects of public law. There is a fine line between tax avoidance (legal) and tax evasion (illegal), and similar fine lines can be drawn between regulatory arbitrage and the violation of a rule; between a risky bet and a wager, and so forth. A lot

---

[36] See D. G. Baird, *The Elements of Bankruptcy* (Westbury NJ: Foundation Press, 1993).

[37] F. R. Edwards and E. R. Morrison, "Derivatives and the Bankruptcy Code: Why the Special Treatment?," *Yale Journal on Regulation*, 22, no. 1 (2005).

of efforts go into neutralizing the cost effects of public regulation without crossing the line into illegality. In an area that is as heavily regulated as the financial sector, pushing the line without crossing it is an enormously lucrative business for regulated entities and their legal advisors.

It might sound odd, but law is central to these law and regulatory avoidance strategies. Private parties can, of course, make deals without relying on formal law. The ingredients for financial assets, however, require state law. You cannot simply set aside some of your assets and tell your private creditors or the tax authorities that they are beyond reach; you need to create a legal shield, such as a trust or corporate entity to do so. You would not be able to benefit from a new business organization in a tax or regulatory haven and book all your transactions through it, were it not for the fact that this entity is recognized as an independent legal entity in your own jurisdiction. And you certainly cannot settle all outstanding repo or derivative transactions with a counterparty that finds itself in bankruptcy without legal rules in place that exempt them, with the help of "safe harbors" from the ordinary rules of bankruptcy. The beauty of the law of property, secured transactions, trust and corporate law is that these institutions of private law are readily available and must even be respected by others, including the state that furnished them.

Without understanding how one type of law (private law) is used to undo what another type of law (public law) is trying to accomplish, we cannot understand modern finance. The reason is very simple: finance is not only regulated by law, it is made *in* law.[38] It is often said that regulators are playing catch-up with the private sector, which appears to be always at least one step ahead.[39] The irony is that the private sector relies on law to do so, and that the strategies they employ are often tolerated if not endorsed by regulators, and often facilitated by legislative change.

Lawyers will seek clearance from regulators prior to putting new legal innovations into the world; the risk of not doing so would be too large to ignore. When issuing "no action" or "interpretative" letters, regulators do not bind their hands, but they rarely renege on them, and private parties have come to extensively rely on them, especially under conditions of regulatory uncertainty. Oftentimes, the guidance is given on a specific

[38]   K. Pistor, "Law in Finance."
[39]   See also A. S. Blinder, "Financial Entropy and the Optimality of Financial Regulation," in D. D. Evanoff, A. G. Haldane, and G. G. Kaufman (eds.), *The New International Financial System: Analyzing the Cumulative Impact of Regulatory Reform* (New Jersey: World Scientific, 2017).

case and may not even be publicly available. Resolving legal issues in this gray area between formal rulings and informality has the advantage of reducing the risk of future law enforcement when the rules themselves are ambiguous, or incomplete; but it occupies a space that is beyond the reach of most. Moreover, a case could be made that legal uncertainty may be a good thing. It is true that some transactions would be undertaken without the informal opinion, but it is not clear that their social benefit necessarily outweighs their social costs.[40] reprimanded the Commodities Future Trading Commission (CFTC) for excessive use of no-action letters and similar instruments, citing concern by market participants about regulatory capture.[41] Capture may, however, not be the only concern. By assuring the regulated that their innovative strategies will most likely not be challenged in the future, the regulators set the system up for gaming by the most resourceful actors with access to the regulators. Instead, a new comparative study of financial regulation proposes that regulators should "force regulatory uncertainty" on financial engineers to keep the upper hand.[42]

The potential for regulatory capture has also been raised in cases where regulators seek a settlement decree from a court rather than litigating a case to the end. In a widely noted ruling, Judge Rakoff of the Southern District of New York, refused to sign off on a settlement between the Securities and Exchange Commission (SEC) and Citigroup[43] for want of explanation why a major bank that was asked to pay $280 million in settlement would be allowed to do so without any admission of guilt. The ruling was overturned on appeal, on the grounds that the SEC had wide discretion in crafting a settlement decree, and that the monitoring function of judges was limited to procedural aspects, not substance.[44] While there is good reason in many instances to ask courts to defer to regulators, especially given their greater expertise, this narrow reading of the court's oversight role seems problematic. In the absence of any other form of effective oversight, it exposes regulators to capture, because it removes the excuse that a judge would not accept a given action.

[40] On the divergence of social benefits and social costs in dispute settlement, see S. Shavell, "The Fundamental Divergence of Social and Private Benefits of Litigation," *Journal of Legal Studies*, 26, no. S2 (1997).

[41] See US Treasury, *A Financial System That Creates Economic Opportunities: Capital Markets* (Washington DC: US Department of the Treasury, 2017), 130.

[42] T. Matthias, *The Growth of Shadow Banking: A Comparative Institutional Analysis* (Cambridge: Cambridge University Press, 2018), p. 255 of the draft on file with the author.

[43] *SEC v. Citigroup Global Markets, Inc.*, 11 Civ 7387, November 28, 2011.

[44] *SEC v. Citigroup Global Markets*, 2nd Circuit, 752 F.3d 285.

There is much to be said for informality; it is more malleable than formal rules, and solutions can be more easily tailored to the needs of the parties involved. Its greatest drawback is that it conflicts with one of the foundations for the rule of law: that everyone is equal before the law. Not everyone has access to no action letters of interpretative guidance, and most ordinary mortals will have to plead guilty to cut a deal with a prosecutor. I argued in the original paper that power is differential relation to law.[45] As these examples suggest, this applies not only to the ex-post suspension or relaxation of legal rules in times of crises; differential treatment occurs in the space where regulators and regulated meet and in the interstices of court rulings that use procedural arguments to limit oversight over this space.

In summary, LTF urges a shift in focus when talking about regulating or governing finance, or when blaming regulatory failure for crises when they occur. Financial systems are built with two interdependent bodies of law: public and private. Private law is primarily enabling, while public law is constraining. The ability to use private law to mute the effects of public law is a powerful tool in the hands of private actors and their skilled lawyers. When pushed far enough and paired with regulatory forbearance, this becomes a toxic mix. In contrast, courts have been on the retreat in monitoring finance. Even in a purely private dispute, settling a case is the norm. For the litigating parties, it is frequently in their own interest to avoid a court ruling, as it could wreak havoc for the carefully crafted contracts and master agreement that support many similar transactions. This implies that the boundaries of using private law to undo public law are rarely policed by anybody but the regulators, which are most vulnerable to regulatory capture.

1.4   Democratic Governance

The current state of financial governance also raises fundamental questions of democratic self-governance. The textbook scenario of constitutional democracy is government in which the constitution sets the ground rules, the legislature adopts general laws, delegates more specific tasks to regulators, and judges resolve disputes that in turn reveal critical information to be used for legislative corrections. Assuming for the sake of the argument that legislatures act with the public interest in mind, which may be a heroic assumption, we can easily see that creeping

---

[45] Pistor, "A Legal Theory of Finance," 316.

informality in the relation between the regulators and the regulated, and the lack of any serious oversight of this relationship, can erode democratic governance. Regulated parties can construct complex systems of deals and transactions in law, and rely on the legitimacy of law in doing so, claiming law's legitimacy, without being subjected to scrutiny by courts as the law's most important guardians. In effect, they create a two-tiered legal system, not so different from the two-tiered market Chen describes in her analysis of the role of disclosure in primary markets.[46] Regulators cannot be compared to courts, because they are much more prone to capture. The lack of openly contested legal disputes also compromises legislative action. Disputes often reveal critical information; moreover, they put the public on notice about the stakes of the game and the players involved. In the end, they too succumb to deal-making over lawmaking.[47]

Taking this a step further from a single system to the global context, it becomes clear that democratic governance of finance is deeply challenged. In the global arena, private actors can largely pick and choose the laws by which they wish to be governed – from tax law all the way to financial regulation. They simply need to take advantage of rules that allow them to opt out of one and into another legal system without an intermediary losing its status as a legal entity, or an asset losing its property or collateral coating.

Many countries make their tax laws available for a registration fee that brings in additional revenue, and others offer contract, corporate or trust law off the shelf to willing takers. It is enough for only a few countries to do so, as long as other countries respect the choices they make without denying them the legal privileges they obtained offshore.

What I am describing is the well-known phenomenon of "regulatory competition," which has often been hailed as a harbinger of efficiency. Private parties know better than any government official, even than legislatures, what is good for them.[48] By picking and choosing the best

---

[46] See Chen, Chapter 3, this volume.

[47] See S. M. Davidoff and D. Zaring, "Regulation by Deal: The Government's Response to the Financial Crisis," *Administrative Law Review*, 61, no. 3 (2009) for an analysis of the "deal"-like structure of the bank bailouts in the midst of the Great Financial Crisis.

[48] See, for example, R. Romano, "Empowering Investors: A Market Approach to Securities Regulation," *The Yale Law Journal*, 107, no. 8 (1998) making an argument for the full portability of securities regulation. See, however, M. B. Fox, "Retaining Mandatory Securities Disclosure: Why Issuer Choice Is Not Investor Empowerment," *Virginia Law Review*, 85, no. 7 (1999), who argues that this disregards that securities regulation should serve also constituencies that are not movable.

rules for themselves, they also exert pressure on legislatures elsewhere to offer laws like goods in a market place, according to the laws of supply and demand. Endorsing market principles to the adoption of laws must assume that what is good for some is good for all; or, in the alternative, accept the notion that some are more equal before the law than others. The former relies on the yet to be proven merits of trickle-down economics; the latter departs from the normative foundation of constitutional democracies.

This then puts LTF face-to-face with the "political trilemma of the World Economy," the assertion that it is impossible to reconcile national sovereignty, democratic governance and deep economic integration; one must pick two of the three.[49] But what if deep economic integration, understood here as the integration of financial systems, is the *product* of national sovereignty exercised by democracies? How should we think about this trilemma if "hyper-globalization" is endogenous – at least for the most advanced economies? This last expresses the LTF perspective, and it has important implications for rethinking globalization itself and the challenges of global governance.

First, shifting governance from the local to the global level is not a solution, because it does not take away the toolkit that can be used to undo it.

Second, the harmonization of private law also fails to present a solution. It is a difficult process to begin with and would not eliminate the duality of public and private law that enables the undoing of one by the other.

Third, even if private law were to be fully harmonized, this would not preclude that individual states could expand or alter the toolkit available for private parties. Such attempts could be thwarted only if other states denied them full legal recognition, thereby retreating from the global back to the national stage.

Fourth, there is much to be said for allowing private actors to innovate with the legal tools that are given to them. The problem lies not in the exercise as such, but in drawing boundaries and in ensuring equal access. These are fundamental problems of political economy that are not unique to the global stage, but are equally present at the domestic level.

Fifth, intermediate solutions that do not force us to choose two of the triangle's corners are feasible. States could, for example, include conditions for recognizing foreign law and make opt-outs costlier.

---

[49] D. Rodrik, *The Globalization Paradox* (Place: W.W. Norton & Co, 2011), esp. chap. 9.

1.5   Concluding Comments

The goal of this chapter is to develop LTF into a richer analytical framework that allows us to explain the inner workings of the financial system as well as the institutional choices that make global finance as we know it possible. Different choices could well produce different results. Critically, many choices are made in a highly decentralized fashion that are difficult to track; and most are made outside the public eye, with their effects remaining hidden for years, typically coming into the open view only in a crisis, when it is too late.

On the more positive side, the financial systems that we have are not given, but made. They were not designed in one big stroke, but are the product of many small decisions taken over years and decades by private actors, courts, regulators, and legislatures. It will be difficult to dislodge these entrenched interests, and it may well take another crisis on an even greater scale to do so. Short of financial crises or similar calamities such as wars or revolutions,[50] small but persistent moves that roll back legal privileges and reassert sovereign rights could go a long way in rebalancing the playing field. LTF's offers a diagnostic kit for identifying the critical junctures where such intervention may be most effective.

---

[50] M. Olson, *The Rise and Decline of Nations: Economic Growth, Stagflation, and Social Rigidities* (New Haven CT: Yale University Press, 1982), arguing that wars, revolutions, but also competition are agents of change.

Information, and the Regulation of *Inefficient* Markets

DAVID C. DONALD

2.1 Introduction: Information's Role in Shaping, Operating and Regulating Financial Markets

The point where financial markets and their regulation meet is determined by information. The dominant understanding of how financial markets process information determines what behavior regulators expect from market participants, and how they should respond. What regulators know about the shape and operations of financial markets determines what regulation they think necessary. The information fed to the public about financial markets in turn greatly determines how the public views markets and the level of regulatory intervention they expect.

These three facets of information create three different points of analysis. The first sets the parameters of the intellectual and conceptual framework. How information is understood to circulate and the degree to which prices are thought to reflect it within the market environment will determine how regulators understand the dangers of this environment. That is, a market in which the regulator believes all prices fully and automatically reflect public information due to rational decision-making will attract a different kind of regulation than a market in which it is thought prices are driven by sales narratives pitched to buyers whose decisions are determined by strategically or contextually adopted heuristics. The second facet of information presents a classic information asymmetry: the builder of financial market infrastructure knows more about its structure and operation than do others, including regulators. If the transmission of information and funds within the market microstructure is deemed significant (because it no longer is merely assumed to be efficient), this regulatory deficit of information should be eliminated. The investing mice of the market are running in a maze of others' design. The third facet of information shapes the public environment and perspective in which financial regulation rests. If available information about financial markets encourages every member of the public to assume the perspective of market insiders, financial market impact on the larger economy and general public can go unrecognized. This resembles reporting on a sporting event, in which goals, wins and player statistics are the highlight, rather than whether tickets and refreshments sold to fans are fairly priced. Such perspective-shifting is ill-suited to an economic phenomenon as important as the financial markets.

Markets can no longer be assumed efficient in the classical sense. The previously dominant understanding of how information forms market prices has been shedding layers of mystery, like a shared superstition giving way to science. From the 1970s until the very recent past, the efficient capital market hypothesis (ECMH)[1] was the leading theory of how market prices reflect reality by incorporating all information. It provided a solid pillar of trust in financial markets during the ascent of finance. This quasi-religious belief in spontaneous balance supported a stripping away of regulation. As evidenced in Chapters 14, 15 and 16 in this volume, by Guo and Xia, Shen, and Jin respectively, hope in the beneficence of market efficiency through the "invisible hand" edifies the aspiration to roll back state control. The belief that securities prices perfectly and instantly incorporate available information, pursuant to the rational decisions of investors, allows regulators to ignore the mind-numbing complexity of the strata of actors, channels of information distribution and mechanisms for trading (what is called "market microstructure"),[2] as well as the vagaries of the human mind and how it reaches conclusions.[3] "Efficiency" beyond understanding or observation works out the details for us. But, as Lo has observed, "complexity is actually a polite way of saying 'ignorance'. If something is too complex, it means we don't understand it."[4]

---

[1] See E. Fama, "Efficient Capital Markets: A Review of Theory and Empirical Work," *The Journal of Finance*, 35 (1970), 383–417, 404.

[2] See e.g., P. G. Mahoney, "Market Microstructure and Market Efficiency," 28 *Journal of Corporation Law*, 28 (2003), 541. An excellent primer on the reality of how prices are formed in equity markets is R. A. Schwartz and R. Francioni, *Equity Markets in Action: The Fundamentals of Liquidity, Market Structure & Trading* (Abingdon: John Wiley & Sons, 2004).

[3] See e.g., Amos Tversky and Daniel Kahneman, "Judgment under Uncertainty: Heuristics and Biases," *Science*, 185 (September 27, 1974), 1124–1131. An excellent primer on behavioral psychology is D. Kahneman, *Thinking, Fast and Slow* (New York: Farrar, Straus and Giroux, 2011).

[4] A. Lo, *Adaptive Markets: Financial Evolution at the Speed of Thought* (Princeton NJ: Princeton University Press, 2017), Kindle Locations 7123–7124.

For decades, belief in the ECMH simplified our world by providing a presumption that prices were correct and random, and this was coupled with the dominant assumption that market participants act rationally on the basis of full information to maximize return.[5] This lent markets a sublime perfection: an order no observer was able to verify, but one for which each liked to hope, and its clear benefit for the growing financial industry allowed the ECMH to become an article of faith. Faith can be socially useful, as it permits members of a community to endure hardship without panic or crisis. However, ill-placed faith can also create "suckers," when others have a better view of reality than do the faithful. In both word and deed, George Soros has shown that a skeptic in an environment of faith can prosper. As Soros explains, Keynes' "beauty contest" analogy[6] invites a trading strategy that "looks for the flaws" in existing narratives about price and works on "convincing people" to accept one narrative or another:

> The fact that a thesis is flawed does not mean that we should not invest in it as long as other people believe it in and there is a large group of people left to be convinced. The point was made by John Maynard Keynes when he compared the stock market to a beauty contest ... Where I have something significant to add is in pointing out that it pays to look for the flaws; if we find them we are ahead of the game because we can limit our losses when the market also discovers what we already know.[7]

While Soros was building a fortune on the shifting inefficiency of price narratives, the ECMH provided decades of serenity to most investors in financial markets, advising light regulatory intervention with a focus on disclosure. This community of belief was disturbed by a few market crashes of diverse severity (1987, 2001 and 2008) arising from bubbles or misallocation of risk, by the growth of successful hedge funds capitalizing on market inefficiency, and by the award of three Nobel Prizes to

---

[5] The rational man, or *homo economicus*, is canonised in the work of Muth. See J. F. Muth, "Rational Expectations and the Theory of Price Movements," *Econometrica* 29 (1961), 315–335. This is discussed in Lo, *Adaptive Markets,* Kindle Locations 903–956.

[6] See J. M. Keynes, *The General Theory of Employment, Interest and Money* (Kindle Edition, 1936), Kindle Location 2418 ("each competitor has to pick, not those faces which he himself finds prettiest, but those which he thinks likeliest to catch the fancy of the other competitors ... It is not a case of choosing those which, to the best of one's judgment, are really the prettiest, nor even those which average opinion genuinely thinks the prettiest. We have reached the third degree where we devote our intelligences to anticipating what average opinion expects the average opinion to be").

[7] G. Soros, *The Alchemy of Finance* (Abingdon: John Wiley & Sons, 2003), 25.

behavioral theorists.[8] History and science both gave solid testimony to Soros' position, that far from inherently efficient, "markets are always wrong in the sense that they operate with a prevailing bias."[9]

When markets are assumed to process information with rational perfection, the details of the plumbing are of limited importance. However, both financial market participants and students of market microstructure understand that infrastructure creates information asymmetries that are challenging to overcome.[10] Contemporary financial markets reside within interlocking systems of data transmission networks and processing hubs very similar to those used for telephony, the internet or (at the abstract level of logistics), transportation.[11] This interlocking web of arrangements significantly determines the shape of financial dealings, just as does the system of private law discussed by Pistor in Chapter 1 of this volume.

Securities exchanges and the networks that provide communications both to exchanges and between financial institutions for trading purposes are built by the leading institutions that use such infrastructure. Through private research and numerous planning meetings and consultations between market leaders and their contractors, sometimes over years, these institutions understand exactly how and why a given piece of infrastructure will take the shape it does.[12] Regulators learn about this infrastructure from its owner-builders as they plan and construct it, sometimes pursuant to regulatory guidelines, but often in advance of regulatory understanding.[13] The driving force behind financial architecture is maximum benefit to the

---

[8] Daniel Kahneman (2002), Robert Shiller (2013), Richard H. Thaler (2017), see www.nobelprize.org/nobel_prizes/facts/economic-sciences/index.html.

[9] Soros, *Alchemy*, 5.

[10] See e.g., R. Lee, *What Is an Exchange? The Automation, Management, and Regulation of Financial Markets* (Oxford: Oxford University Press, 1998), 111.

[11] See e.g., the definition of financial infrastructure in R. Lee, *Running the World's Markets: The Governance of Financial Infrastructure* (Princeton NJ: Princeton University Press, 2011), 9–21.

[12] For example, about 70 large financial institutions backed 3r (see 3r.com) to develop blockchain infrastructure for the financial industry. Jemmina Kelly, "Exclusive: Blockchain platform developed by banks to be open-source," *Reuters* (October 20, 2016).

[13] John Kay compares the growth of payment systems to other infrastructural projects: "The physical networks of transport, telecoms and other utilities were planned by engineers. Resilience and robustness were design objectives from the beginning. Payment systems evolved in a more haphazard way and over a longer period of time. To the extent that there was design at all, such design was the work of financiers and administrators." John Kay, *Other People's Money: Masters of the Universe or Servants of the People?* (Profile Books, 2015), Kindle Locations 3146–3148.

users,[14] and that will generally be enough to justify its approval by regulators.[15] Once the system is in place, any imbedded unfairness remains structurally determined.[16] While any industry – such as aviation, shipping or telecommunications – will have specialized information about the airports, ports and networks they construct, the asymmetry of information vis-à-vis regulators, and the degree to which such regulators trust the information provided by the industry, appears to be higher in finance.[17] Nevertheless, no jurisdiction other than a planned economy like China has seriously challenged the model of broker-dealers using self-built markets with light supervision to exit regulated stock exchanges.[18]

The success or failure of financial markets can have a real impact on the general economy and society.[19] A serious problem of perspective and banking for financial regulation is the way information about financial markets is selected, processed and distributed for public consumption. Markets are reported on like a sporting event, while they should be explained and monitored as the crucial arterial system providing financial liquidity to the economy. Every casual observer receives rich data about market prices and trends, the winners and losers in a day's trading,

---

[14] As a leading academic on market microstructure, and the former CEO of the Frankfurt Stock Exchange, put it, broker-dealer members of exchanges find "investors and the listed companies ... important primarily because they are critical for the profitability of the members. Nevertheless ... the interests of the intermediaries come first. R. A. Schwartz and R. Francioni, *Equity Markets in Action: The Fundamentals of Liquidity, Market Structure & Trading* (Abingdon: Wiley & Sons, 2004), 93.

[15] In a separate paper, I call this a "narrow" definition of market quality, as opposed to a "broad" concept that would assess the market infrastructure in the context of the entire economy using the financial system to invest or seek investors. See D.C. Donald, "From Block Lords to Blockchain: How Securities Dealers Make Markets," *Journal of Corporation Law*, 44 (2018) 29, 31–35.

[16] This has been the case with the indirect holding system's blackout of shareholder information for issuers. The problem is discussed in section 2.2, below.

[17] Andrew Lo laments the absence of a body like the National Transportation Safety Board (NTSB) in the financial industry, to investigate problems like the "flash crash" of 2010, with "experts in each relevant field, led by an experienced investigator-in-charge who manages the process." Lo, *Adaptive Markets*, Kindle Locations 7456–7457.

[18] China's two stock exchanges, the Shanghai Stock Exchange and the Shenzhen Stock Exchange, are owned by the China Securities Regulatory Commission. On the diverging systems of achieving securities trading throughout the national territory, see D. C. Donald, "Bridging Finance without Fragmentation: A Comparative Look at Market Connectivity in the US, Europe and Asia," *European Business Organization Law Review*, 16 (2015) 173–201.

[19] See, e.g., J. K. Galbraith, *The Great Crash* (Boston MA: Houghton Mifflin, 1954); P. M. H. Bell, *The Origins of the Second World War in Europe* (Abingdon: Routledge, 1986).

and the standing of one or more opaquely constituted indexes. Regulators receive disclosure to monitor the financial health of market participants, but seldom delve deeper or broader.[20]

Argument that markets should be freed of "red tape," or that public money should be spent rescuing large banks rather than allowing them to fail, are rooted in both regulatory policy and public perception of the markets. The public will know the name of stock indices and perhaps remember whether brokers are currently "riding a bull market" or are being "hammered in a bear market," but they will not know exactly how any of this affects their pension fund, the quality of jobs in the economy, labor's share of corporate profits, or the median pay in a given sector of employment. Information flows do not work to generate similar pictures of social importance and sympathy for bakers, butchers, telephony providers, or airlines. Unlike the generally accepted subsidies provided to the banking industry,[21] there are no discount windows to hand out cheap oil or cut-rate microchips to the non-financial industries during economic downturn.

On the other hand, no good knowledge is gathered and disseminated on how the prices of shares, bonds or derivative instruments in the secondary market actually affect the operations of issuers, which may have sold the listed securities into the market decades earlier.[22] There is a generally held assumption that an issuer's "cost of capital" will suffer, but it is far from certain that an issuer which finances itself through ongoing revenues will suffer in this way.[23] Beyond very specialized and relatively esoteric venues, the public also does not receive detailed information on such important matters as the financial markets' impact on

---

[20] Following the global financial crisis, the UK undertook an extraordinary study of its equity markets in this regard, and the findings were not positive. See "The Kay review of UK equity markets and long-term decision making," (July 2012), www.gov.uk/government/consultations/the-kay-review-of-uk-equity-markets-and-long-term-decision-making.

[21] This point is made by John Kay in his critical analysis of the financial system. See Kay, *Other People's Money*, Kindle Locations 5090–5091.

[22] Foroohar describes how a CEO of IBM came under investor pressure when taking the company from the PC business to an AI-focused service orientation, and essentially had to ignore share price temporarily in order to complete a successful transition. R. Foroohar, *Makers and Takers: The Rise of Finance and the Fall of American Business* (New York: The Crown Publishing Group, 2016), 136–137.

[23] Thin use of equity for actual financing has been known for decades. See e.g., C. Mayer, "Financial Systems, Corporate Finance, and Economic Development," in R. G. Hubbard (ed.), *Asymmetric information, corporate finance and investment* (Chicago IL: University of Chicago Press, 1990), 307–332.

executive pay levels, overall levels and stability of employment, the financing of research and development, or the "contagion" factors connected with an individual job loss or home foreclosure.

Despite recognition that information is vital to financial markets, not enough thought is given to how financial regulation should change in light of a new understanding of market efficiency and real historical evidence of the power of financial markets over the entire economy. This chapter takes on that task in the following way. Section 2.2 will present the growing body of thought on the *inefficiency* of markets, with particular focus on Andrew Lo's application of behavioral psychology and market history to argue that the ECMH should be replaced by his "adaptive market hypothesis." Section 2.3 will examine the problem of generally unrecognized asymmetry of information in the creation of major market infrastructure, using construction of the US consolidated audit trail as an example. Section 2.4 will examine the way in which information about financial markets given to the general public creates a "sporting event" perspective that downplays the impact of finance on the general economy and set regulators within an environment that is largely sympathetic to the financial industry. Section 2.5 offers conclusions.

2.2   Real Financial Markets Consist of Proprietary Labyrinths

In any social context, if the actors are assumed to be rational and fully informed, the dangers to be expected will be minimal. An assumption of efficient pricing in a market populated by rational actors can lend financial markets an aura of natural perfection that regulators would be loath to disrupt. In fact, this was the stance taken by the US Congress in 2000 when it enacted the Commodity Futures Modernization Act to "eliminate unnecessary regulation for the commodity futures exchanges,"[24] and by President Clinton when he encouraged the resignation of a Commodity Futures Trading Commission Chair who recommended that derivatives should be regulated.[25] Magically efficient markets do not attract regulation, but they do attract academic criticism, especially when the rationality assumed to exist cannot be found in

---

[24] The Commodity Futures Modernization Act of 2000, H.R. 5660, 106th Congress (December 14, 2000), sec. 2(2).

[25] S. Johnson and J. Kwak, *13 Bankers: The Wall Street Takeover and the Next Financial Meltdown* (New York: Vintage Books, 2010), 136.

nature and the asserted efficiency of pricing is repeatedly refuted by historical price trends. A religion of market efficiency is gradually giving way to a very complex reality.

In 2005, Eugene Fama received the first Deutsche Bank Prize in Financial Economics.[26] In connection with the award, a panel was set up at Goethe University in which a number of Fama's former students, all prominent economists in their own right, respectfully "roasted" him by gently recounting cases in which markets had famously not been efficient.[27] At the close of these light-hearted but substantive presentations, Professor Fama stood up and with a smile called each of his former students a "dunce." The future Nobel Laureate then forcefully explained that every crash following a supposed "bubble" recovered to full price, showing that only a lack of faith in the efficiency of markets had caused the price instability. Professor Fama's faith in the perfection of market price was edifying, giving the audience something useful they could believe. Indeed, that audience had suffered from the collapse of the dot.com bull market (called by some the "dot.com bubble") that had debilitated the Frankfurt equity market and was pushing toward the subprime crisis (thought by some to be related to a "housing bubble") by investing in asset-backed securities.

As mentioned above, not everyone at the close of the 20th century shared Fama's faith. George Soros' idea of market "reflexivity" accompanied the ECMH for decades, like a hedge fund performing statistical arbitrage in a market dominated by index investors. As Soros expresses it: "the efficient market hypothesis does not fit the facts, and it is also questionable on theoretical grounds: the illusion that markets are always right is created by the reflexive interaction between the participating and cognitive functions."[28] The idea expressed in the term "reflexivity" has received significant academic backing by Lo. In his 2017 *Adaptive Markets*, which pulls together about 30 years of his own work, Lo explains much of the theoretical support for this shift away from the efficiency/rationality "dogma." Looked at carefully, the ECMH demands investment behavior which is simply not human:

> to reach the equilibrium price – as hypothesized by the Efficient Markets
> Hypothesis and rational expectations theory – requires an infinite chain of

---

[26] See the website of the Frankfurt Center for Financial Studies, www.ifk-cfs.de/dbprize/2005.html.

[27] The author was present at this event and the narrative here is from his own recollection.

[28] Soros, *Financial Alchemy*, 5.

reasoning ... It's as though a buyer and seller were trapped in a hall of mirrors: the seller knows that the buyer knows that the seller knows that the buyer knows ... that the asking price is too high. In other words, market equilibrium requires a rather *sophisticated* theory of mind, and presumably a high level of abstract thought ... [But decades of neuroscience has shown] our rationality is *biologically* too limited for the Efficient Markets Hypothesis to hold at all times and in every possible context.[29]

Both the content of price discovery in the actual trading process (where buyers and sellers input orders from a fixed menu of several types of trading systems triggering various kinds of matching engines) and long-term history of markets (where upward and downward momentum continuously is at play) confirm the relative *inefficiency* of markets. Different traders have different views of market information and assign different values (according to different needs, or heuristics) to the information they have, pursuant to needs, policies and personal histories. This behavior is neither rational in an absolute sense nor does it reflect all available information. Just as Kahneman and Tversky,[30] Shiller,[31] and Thaler[32] before him, Lo, when rejecting *homo economicus*, examines recent work done in behavioral psychology and neuroscience to reach a conclusion on human behavior similar to that held in most fields of law, that "our irrationality is far from directionless random," but shows "an all-too-human tendency to explain the world in terms of motives ... we use heuristics."[33]

Examining the history of markets, Lo observes that traders will develop heuristics adapted to a given market environment, and when adaptation is complete, behavior appears rational (for a given ecosystem at a given point of inflection), but when the environment changes and existing traders are no longer well-adapted, decisions using the same heuristics appear irrational, although in fact they are merely "maladaptive." Lo's adaptive markets hypothesis broadly agrees with Soros' theory of reflexivity, by focusing on "species" of financial actors in relation to their "environment," and finding that the heuristics of species adaption

---

[29] Lo, *Adaptive Markets*, Kindle Locations 2327–2390.
[30] See D. Kahneman and A. Tversky, "Prospect Theory: An Analysis of Decision under Risk," *Econometrica*, 47 (1979), 263–292.
[31] See R.J. Shiller, "From Efficient Markets Theory to Behavioral Finance," *Journal of Economic Perspectives*, 17 (2003), 83–104.
[32] R. H. Thaler, "From Homo Economicus to Homo Sapiens," *The Journal of Economic Perspectives*, 14 (2000), 133–141.
[33] Lo, *Adaptive Markets*, Kindle Locations 2392–2393.

move toward increased efficiency but will become maladaptive as the environment evolves, such as through changes in technology or law.[34] Lo also refuses to completely reject the descriptive term "market efficiency" because data shows that "the US market was a remarkably reliable source of investment return from the mid-1930s to the mid-2000s, yielding relatively uninterrupted and steady growth over seven decades."[35] He sees the belief in efficient markets as a heuristic that was adapted to that time. However, he also observes that market data show the time for that heuristic has past. Acknowledging Soros' importance, Lo uses the "species" of the hedge fund to show how they thrived as the period of great moderation was decaying under technological and legal changes from the 1980s to the 2000s, so that active funds could profit from anomalies within markets generally believed to be efficient by most investors and regulators.

As Stiglitz observed in 2002, our understanding of how information behaves in a market has "a profound effect on how we think about economic policy."[36] In a market where it is thought prices perfectly reflect available information that is processed rationally, regulators need not give much thought to the environment. Key information about issuers and their securities would have to be disclosed, non-public information should not be acted upon (insider dealing) and prices must not be distorted in an artificial way (market manipulation). Otherwise, efficiency is left to take its course. However, in a market conceived as an "ecosystem" in which various "species" of participants prey upon others, constantly spinning out heuristic narratives to serve their own comfort and advantage, regulators have to consider the shape of the environment in relation to every actor, and the manner in which the environment changes over time. The market would be a melee in which some participants would have predictable advantages over others, although which group is privileged may change with evolution of the environment.

Unevenness could be found in the design of market infrastructure, and the advantages this design entails, as discussed in section 2.3, below. Changes in technology could disrupt an equilibrium of fairness as did the latency arbitrage used in early high-frequency trading and addressed through the creation of the Investors' Exchange (IEX). If, as Soros argues,

---

[34] Ibid. 6597–6600.
[35] Ibid. 5188–5190.
[36] J. E. Stiglitz, "Information and the Change in the Paradigm in Economics," *The American Economic Review* 92 (2002), 460–501, 460.

in an environment of this type, "predator–prey" relationships arise,[37] regulators must decide whether the market should actually be permitted to contain such predatory relationships or the "prey" should be protected, as market rules have historically done with some types of investors in some types of situations, such as short selling or margin trading.

If the period of extraordinary market stability from the 1930s until the early 2000s that Lo calls the "great modulation"[38] fits the ECMH well as an explanatory narrative, this begs the question, "whether the last fifteen years should be regarded as a temporary blip in an otherwise smooth upward trajectory, or a harbinger of a new world order. There's growing evidence for the latter."[39] If this is correct, regulators need to start thinking about information flows in new and more carefully articulated ways. Like judges in a reality where suffering is seen as divine justice, regulators of a mysteriously efficient market need not be anxious to intervene. However, if losses are revealed to be zero-sum results of some players duping others into maladapted heuristics while an evolving market ecosystem creates surprises due to new technology (understood only by some), political developments or law, the maintaining of fair and orderly markets will require a more active and agile regulator.

2.3   Information Asymmetry in Transactional Labyrinths

Modern finance takes place within interlocking pipelines designed to bring buyers and sellers together and deliver their cash and securities to counterparties, both local and international. Over the 400 years since the Amsterdam Stock Exchange was established,[40] the ownership of information about how such infrastructure is built has changed little.[41] Unlike

---

[37] Soros, *Financial Alchemy*, 28.

[38] Lo, *Adaptive Markets*, Kindle Locations, 5177–5191.

[39] Ibid., 5202–5203.

[40] On the early history of the Amsterdam Stock Exchange, see L. O. Petram, *The World's First Stock Exchange: How the Amsterdam Market for Dutch East India Company Shares Became a Modern Securities Market, 1602–1700* (The Netherlands: Eigen Beheer, 2011), chap. 1.

[41] A very good example of this was the approval process for one of the world's newest and most strongly contested stock exchanges, the Investors' Exchange (IEX), which was licensed in 2016 to create a matching venue in which high-frequency traders would not have an unfair advantage. The current US licensing process requires disclosure of extensive corporate and financial information, as well as the full system rulebook, but requires only targeted specifics on actual processing within the architecture. The IEX application was opposed by some broker-dealers (such as Citadel LLC) because of its 350-microsecond "point-of-presence" "speedbump" that slows down order processing; this

the construction of infrastructure with similar social importance – such as for transportation, water, sanitation or electricity – full knowledge of the system architecture and operation remains closed within the financial industry.[42] While regulatory scrutiny and public comments do precede the approval of major financial infrastructure, in the US and Europe, the weight of commentary depends on authoritative knowledge of system architecture, which is not made available beyond a few items known in advance to have been of interest.[43] The history of such approval processes shows that parties external to the financial industry – unless expressly invited into the data by system architects – will not have access to the information necessary to offer a convincing critical analysis of an infrastructure project.[44]

"speedbump" was brought out in detail by the give-and-take among IEX and its critics. However, even in this heated debate, only the basic scheme, structure and characteristics of the infrastructure were disclosed for comment, so that neither the regulator nor any external party could gain an understanding of the arrangement equal in expertise to that of the system architects. Patent applications provide more public detail than the lengthy regulatory approval process for financial infrastructure. See, "Investors' Exchange LLC – Form 1 Application and Exhibits," www.sec.gov/rules/other/2015/investors-exchange-form-1.htm.

[42] As this area does not receive the attention it deserves, hard evidence on the extent to which private parties themselves control the process of arranging financial infrastructure is rare. For one high-profile example of how complex financial projects develop, see the following statement by Neil Barofsky, overseer of the Troubled Asset Relief Program (TARP), introduced in 2008 by the US federal government in connection with the global financial crisis. Barofsky writes that he complained to a US Treasury official that he was "being kept in the dark" about the multi-trillion dollar Public-Private Investment Program (PPIP) being developed by the US Treasury, and that his "primary source of information about PPIP's development came from the *Wall Street Journal.*" He was told that that there was nothing to tell because "nothing had been decided," and then he learned: "Although it was going to be funded overwhelmingly with taxpayer dollars, PPIP had been designed by Wall Street, for Wall Street. We only later learned . . . that at the same time that Treasury had been keeping us in the dark, it had been working on the design of the program with BlackRock and the Trust Company of the West Group." N. Barofsky, *Bailout* (New York: Simon & Schuster, 2012), 129. We can also see how regulators depend on banks for knowhow in the case of the development of Basel II, where the Bank for International Settlements relied on the "creditmetrics" system developed by JP Morgan. See Bank for International Settlements, "Credit Risk Modelling: Current Practices and Applications," (April 1999), 21–22, www.bis.org/publ/bcbs49.pdf. Generation of private know-how with only generalized disclosure to public regulators also corresponds to my own experience on a major European infrastructural project.

[43] In the US, this would be the "Form 1" filed with the SEC. In the EU, the European Securities and Markets Association authorization process for authorization of trading venues is less formalized and transparent.

[44] See the discussion of the direct registration system, below.

Yet these projects shape, and even determine the content of, many forms of financial activity. They are the hardware corresponding to the software "coding in law" that Pistor discusses in Chapter 1 as determinants of the financial system. This hardware constitutes specific channels that limit the flow of information and funds within finance. The earliest stock exchanges were built as private clubs by leading broker-dealers to focus trading in one place controlled by the club,[45] and the most recent exchanges follow a similar pattern, but with government authorization and oversight. All financial infrastructure generally tracks this model. Banks and their law firms built the cash clearing systems, such as the US Clearing House Interbank Payments System (CHIPS) and the UK Clearing House Automated Payment System (CHAPS), used by every country as pipelines to link one bank to others and allow easy funds transfers in their national currency. The Euroclear securities clearing system, built in 1968 by Morgan Guaranty as an extension of one of its in-house services, has received an above-average amount of historical documentation.[46] Another example is the message network for interbank transfers created in 1973 – the Society for Worldwide Interbank Financial Telecommunication (SWIFT) – which remains the primary channel used to notify such transfers.[47] In 1969, the National Association of Securities Dealers launched an automated quotation system (NASDAQ) linking together market makers to create the first dedicated market for over-the-counter stock trades, and it was soon found that market makers were using the closed system to manipulate prices.[48] In 1971, the US Banking and Securities Industry Committee (BASIC) successfully advocated the

---

[45] See e.g., on Amsterdam, F. Braudel, *Civilization and Capitalism, 15th–18th Century,* *Vol. 2, The Wheels of Commerce* (New York: Harper & Row, 1992), 101–104; on New York, C. R. Geisst, *Wall Street: A History from its Beginnings to the Fall of Enron* (Oxford: Oxford University Press, 1997) 10–15; on London, R. Michie, *The London Stock Exchange: A History* (Oxford: Oxford University Press, 2001), chap. 2.

[46] The creation of the system is outlined in P. Norman, *Plumbers and Visionaries: Securities Settlement and Europe's Financial Market* (Abingdon: John Wiley & Sons, 2007), 31–35; and R. Chernow, *The House of Morgan: An American Banking Dynasty and the Rise of Modern Finance* (New York: Grove/Atlantic, 1990), 550.

[47] "In 1973, 239 banks from 15 countries got together to solve a common problem ... SWIFT is now a global financial infrastructure that spans every continent, 200+ countries and territories ... connection of the first central banks in 1983 reinforced SWIFT's position as the common link between all parties in the financial industry ... During the 80s SWIFT strengthened its coordinating role by organising various forums to address standards, business and operational issues." www.swift.com/about-us/history.

[48] The history of NASDAQ is presented in J. Seligman, *The Transformation of Wall Street: A History of the Securities and Exchange Commission and Modern Corporate Finance,* 3rd edn. (New York: Aspen, 2003), 490–500, 698–703. Market manipulation by NASDAQ

creation of the Depository Trust Company (DTC) to hold all US listed securities in the name of its nominee, Cede & Co., despite knowledge that the model would sever the communication link between issuers and shareholders.[49]

Around 2000, the financial industry sought regulatory support to move trade matching out of exchanges and into private platforms, which resulted in adoption of Regulation National Market System (NMS) in the US and the Market in Financial Instruments Directive (MiFID).[50] This move was supported by an argument that it would reduce trading costs. By 2012 fragmentation of trading was so problematic for price discovery that both jurisdictions called for new infrastructure to patch the fragmented price data back together. In the US, this was the Consolidated Audit Trail (CAT), and in the EU, the Consolidated Tape (CT). As discussed below, these important patches for the fragmented securities markets will be designed, developed and operated by private vendors, and have estimated costs in the tens of billions of dollars.

In each of the instances listed above, financial institutions created the infrastructure on which public markets operate. In each case, the only persons with a full understanding of the project details were financial institutions and their agents. Elsewhere, I have explained how the indirect holding system found in the DTC model of securities settlement contradicted some of the most careful thinking at the time and eliminated transparency of corporate shareholdings.[51] That earlier work also notes that an attempt to correct the system twenty years after its establishment was blocked by the broker-dealers, based on information in their sole possession, and thus on the basis of perspectives that only they could have formed.[52] As a result, an opaque system was cemented in the US and actively spread to other countries as markets internationalized in

---

dealers was presented in W. G. Christie and P. H. Schultz, "Why do NASDAQ Market Makers Avoid Odd-Eighth Quotes?" *Journal of Finance*, 49 (1994), 813–1840.

[49] For a critical history of this process, see D. C. Donald, "Heart of Darkness: The Problem at the Core of the US Proxy System and Its Solution," *Virginia Law & Business Review*, 6 (2011), 41–100.

[50] For a critical analysis of this process, see Donald, "Bridging Finance," 182–188.

[51] Donald, "Heart of Darkness," 54–59.

[52] As the internet began to mature in the1990s, transfer agents and listed companies proposed creating a direct registration system to return shareholder data to the listed companies that had been deprived of such data when DTC was created in 1972. Brokers objected to this on unspecified grounds of operational stability, and the SEC agreed, sealing the broker-dealers' usurped ownership of shareholder data until this day. See Donald, "Heart of Darkness," 89–91.

the 1990s. The following paragraphs will present the development of the market's most recent infrastructural project, the Consolidated Audit Trail, or CAT, which as of writing is being built to tie together the numerous exchanges and proprietary matching venues that have propagated since the impact of Regulation NMS began to fragment the US equities market.

As has been explained elsewhere,[53] the fragmentation of markets, which between 2000 and 2012 dispersed trade matching from concentration in a few major stock exchanges to over 100 alternative trading systems (ATSs), new exchanges, and bank internalizers, created serious problems for market price discovery and liquidity. The US Securities and Exchange Commission (SEC) also found "that the regulatory data infrastructure on which" it had to rely was "outdated and inadequate to effectively oversee a complex, dispersed, and highly automated national market system."[54] The solution selected was to create the CAT, a data network that would gather and consolidate all post-trade (i.e., orders, cancellations and execution prices) data from all venues.[55]

This was accomplished by requiring all self-regulatory organizations (SROs), such as stock exchanges and clearing houses, to devise a common plan to build a CAT and solicit bids from potential contractors. A development advisory group consisting of "broker-dealers of varying sizes, the Options Clearing Corporation, a service bureau and three industry trade associations" was created so that the SROs could interact with the broader securities industry to select an operator for the CAT.[56] In January 2017 the SRO group selected as operator Thesys Technologies,[57] a high-frequency trading company active in many areas of financial technology, as its contractor. The plan to build the CAT lines up with the general guidelines originally published by the SEC in 2012, but tells the reader little about operational technology and nothing about alternatives considered and rejected, or the operational features of such alternatives.

---

[53] Donald, "Bridging Finance," 182–185.
[54] SEC Release No. 34-67457, "Consolidated Audit Trail," 77 *Federal Register* (1 August 2012), 45722, 45722.
[55] *See* 17 CFR §242.613(c)(7)(i)–(vii).
[56] SEC Release No. 34-77724, "Joint Industry Plan; Notice of Filing of the National Market System Plan Governing the Consolidated Audit Trail," 81 *Federal Register* (April 27, 2016), 30614, 30617.
[57] Letter from the parties to the National Market System Plan Governing the Consolidated Audit Trail, 18 Jan. 2017, www.sec.gov/divisions/marketreg/rule613-info-notice-of-plan-processor-selection.pdf.

Disclosure focuses on how much market participants will have to contribute to the cost of the CAT's construction and maintenance,[58] and what technology participants will have to implement to hook up with the CAT.[59] Like most other instances of financial infrastructure, outsiders know enough about the CAT to grasp its main purposes and functions and how to become a user and pay for its services, but not nearly enough to understand whether an alternative model could have been developed that would generate greater benefit for persons outside of the immediate circle of its architects. As in the days of the clubs, those outside the inner circle are expected to trust the leaders. Once the estimated $9 billion sunk costs are paid to set the CAT into operation for its first year,[60] arguments for a change in overall structure will face an extremely high burden to be heard. Although the transparency of financial infrastructure unquestionably improved during the twentieth century, the information necessary to ensure adoption of designs that serve broader market quality is still absent.

If regulators envision a magically efficient market – where prices impound all information without actual bid and ask orders being placed and investment decisions are made with a kind of rationality foreign to human actors – the details of market infrastructure are generally irrelevant. However, if the market itself is built by leading broker-dealers following adaptive heuristics that have utility exactly to yield advantage over other market participants, the structure of the trading environment becomes crucial. It can become an aggressively militant labyrinth. The creation of IEX shows exactly how much of an uphill struggle is necessary to create a fair market, when some market participants notice that other market participants have designed infrastructure to extract unfair advantages.[61] In that case, the main proponents of adjusting the

---

[58] SEC Release No. 34-82451, "Joint Industry Plan; Notice of Filing and Immediate Effectiveness of Amendment No. 4 to the National Market System Plan Governing the Consolidated Audit Trail," 83 *Federal Register* (11 Jan. 2018), 1399.

[59] See the website of the CAT organizing SROs: www.catnmsplan.com/technical-specifications/.

[60] The SROs that devised the CAT plan project "initial aggregate cost to the industry related to building and implementing the CAT would range from $3.2 billion to $3.6 billion. Estimated annual aggregate costs for the maintenance and enhancement of the CAT would range from $2.8 billion to $3.4 billion. Additionally, costs to retire existing systems would be approximately $2.6 billion." SEC Release No. 34-77724, "Joint Industry Plan," 31034.

[61] From formal application to approval, the process took ten months, including the filing by IEX of five amended applications forced by nearly 500 comment letters filed with the SEC. See SEC Release No. 34-78101, "In the Matter of the Application of: Investors' Exchange,

market structure were buy-side institutions, which although not as central to the market as broker-dealers (who were once the exclusive set of exchange members and owners who built the "clubs"), are still wealthy and powerful in the financial industry. When market structure damages non-financial issuers, as in the case of the indirect holding system's destruction of corporate ownership transparency, it is unlikely an adjustment can ever be achieved.

2.4 Financial Markets Are Not Football, and More Information for Impact Assessment Is Needed

The "financial market exceptionalism" discussed indirectly by many chapters in this volume presents a real problem that most scholars here represented are working to solve. The financial industry was cloaked for decades in a belief (unsupported by evidence) of rational efficiency that encouraged regulators to back off restrictions and ignore the fine points of market structure. The financial industry collapsed in 2008, but received financial support from governments enabling the largest institutions to gain an *even stronger* position than they had in the run-up boom to their failure.[62] Ten years after the global financial crisis, the industry is not characterized by efforts to present itself as safer or more oriented to the real economy, as one might expect. While lenders foreclosed on real estate, private equity funds and other financial institutions became one of the largest owners of the same, so the share of Americans that could own a home was driven down.[63] Moreover, banks and broker-dealers have thrown themselves into FinTech-labeled innovation that will allow them to shed large numbers of employees through automation.[64] This dysfunctional connection between the needs of society and the development of the financial industry is in part due to how the public views that industry, which largely depends on what people know from the information made available.

LLC for Registration as a National Securities Exchange; Findings, Opinion, and Order of the Commission," 81 *Federal Register* 41142 (June 23, 2016).

[62] R. J. Barth and A. P. Prabha, "Resolving Too-Big-to-Fail Banks in the United States" (24 March 2013), https://ssrn.com/abstract=2238702.

[63] R. Foroohar, *Makers and Takers: The Rise of Finance and the Fall of American Business* (New York: The Crown Publishing Group, 2016), 212–214.

[64] Laura Noonan, "Growth of Fintech Forecast to Spur Almost 2m Banking Job Cuts," *Financial Times* (31 March 2016).

Here is an illustration: When securitizing a portfolio of loans, the actual loans included in the transfer to the special purpose vehicle are fully recorded as part of the transaction documentation. These records are kept electronically on spreadsheets. In the US, the Internal Revenue Service has means of communicating with every taxpayer by regular mail and may also have taxpayers' wire transfer details. Because of this data, in 2008, either before or after the failure of Lehman Brothers, when the Federal Reserve was evaluating possible courses of action, one powerful solution available was to allow the maladaptive banking industry to learn proper adaption from "pain"[65] while returning the economy quickly to stability. The banking regulators could have ordered the relevant banks to provide complete lists of all mortgages and mortgagors in default, and the US Treasury could have arranged debt relief with the mortgagees, or transferred funds to each of the mortgagors for their defaulted mortgage amount plus a reasonable number of future payments.[66] This "FinTech" version of Franklin Roosevelt's Home Owner's Loan Corporation (HOLC)[67] would have injected funds into the real economy,[68] addressing the problem raised by both Stiglitz[69] and Krugman[70] that bailout money was kept within banks to prop up their balance sheets for new stress tests, while the spending activity of ordinary consumers failed to receive necessary stimulus. In the competitive environment, it was the banks that had shown themselves lacking, maladapted, and needing change. Nevertheless, instructive messages of "pain" were instead sent to ordinary citizens who may well have been using credit from rising housing value to compensate for an income that had become insufficiently stagnant.[71]

---

[65] Following the biological adaptation paradigm, Lo suggests that the financial industry be given a central nervous system, to feel pain from its maladaptive behavior.

[66] In fact, various forms of mortgage relief were actively discussed and a mortgage modification program was eventually introduced (see Barofsky, *Bailout*, 198) but not as immediate and alternative measures.

[67] D. Dayen, *Chain of Title: How Three Ordinary Americans Uncovered Wall Street's Great Foreclosure Fraud* (The New Press, 2016), Kindle Locations 418–430.

[68] If begun early enough, it could also have worked against the generalized fraud conducted in connection with the foreclosure practices of many mortgage lenders and documented in Dayen, *Chain of Title*, Kindle Location 5174.

[69] J. E. Stiglitz, *The Price of Inequality: How Today's Divided Society Endangers Our Future* (New York: Norton, 2012), 167.

[70] See P. Krugman, *End This Depression Now!* (New York: Norton, 2012), 125–129.

[71] T. Piketty, *Capital in the Twenty-First Century* (Cambridge MA: Harvard University Press, 2014), 297 ("one consequence of increasing inequality was virtual stagnation of the purchasing power of the lower and middle classes in the United States, which inevitably made it more likely that modest households would take on debt").

Such a FinTech solution employing big data to inject funds into the
roots of the credit crisis probably strikes most readers as ridiculous. Why?
For one, we know exactly how connected (systemically important) a big
bank is.[72] We know nothing about the borrowers. Our ignorance prevents them from having much importance at all. They remain faceless to
banking regulators while banks themselves cultivate the kind of relationship that Igan and Lambert explain in Chapter 5. The result is that
regulators would place more trust in the reliability and rationality of
a banking executive who just drove his firm to ruin, than in an ordinary –
and perhaps honestly diligent – defaulting mortgagor.

Banking executives are known quantities to regulators, but ordinary borrowers are not. Systemically important financial institutions
have often been rescued from suffering accountability to the market
because of their connections and due to the hope that they will pass
funds down into the capillaries of the economy.[73] Ordinary borrowers are not known, and are held accountable for their misjudg-
ments. The financial, economic and social contagion that comes
from thrusting an ordinary person into insolvency is not specifically
known and thus does not have much of an existence. There can be
no contagion for the common man because no data is gathered, or if
it is, such data is not seen as generalizable.

Markets and regulatory systems collect data about things that are
considered important. The connectedness of systemically important
financial institutions is very important. The connectedness of millions
of ordinary citizens is not. Such knowledge makes a difference. Dayen, in
Chain of Title, attempts to reverse this by approaching the sub-prime
crisis from the point of view of one borrower, Lisa Epstein, a nurse from
Maryland who moved to Florida, got married and had a child:

> She had blue eyes, soft features, and a laugh you could hear across
> a crowded room. When she got excited she got very loud. But at the
> moment she focused on her daughter in the tub. Blond-haired, big-eyed
> Jenna had been born with a mild form of spina bifida. Her spinal cord was
> tethered at the base, something that could generate motor control pro-
> blems as she grew. The child would turn two in March; surgery had been
> scheduled for April. And Lisa could think of practically nothing else,

---

[72] For the assessment factors, see Bank for International Settlements, "Global systemically
important banks: Assessment methodology and the additional loss absorbency requirement" (Updated November 21, 2017), www.bis.org/bcbs/gsib/.

[73] See, e.g., E. Avgouleas, *Governance of Global Financial Markets: The Law, the Economics,
the Politics* (Cambridge: Cambridge University Press, 2012), 134–136.

ministering to Jenna at nearly every waking moment. As a cancer nurse, she worked with families coping with the stress of a sick child. Now she was experiencing the same emotions ... Lisa was forty-three, a nurse, a wife, and a new mother. She had only lived in the house two years. And her life was about to change forever. KNOCK KNOCK KNOCK! She did not hesitate for a second. "That's about the house, Alan!" she yelled out to her husband. "They're from the bank, and it's not good news!"[74]

Information of this type makes a great deal of difference. When Lisa Epstein suffers from her foreclosure, we can see the contagion affect her daughter, husband, and patients. But we do not normally receive the information to allow us to understand the connectedness of an ordinary borrower or investor. This position is reserved for financial institutions. On a daily basis, many people will know whether the national stock index is up or down, and thus may develop a need to know on the basis of this habit. That information tells the recipient who is winning or losing on the securities market, essentially whether narratives convincing investors to buy shares (a rising index) or narratives convincing investors to sell shares (a falling index) are currently more successful. Many of these narratives are insubstantial and will be forgotten with the passing of one week, but they are reported with an urgency that shapes our view of what is important.

As a society, we do not receive regular updates on information that directly affects the broader economy, such as the number of important patents approved, or firms entering insolvency, or the number of new firms that were granted or refused start-up funding. Each of these data may tell us more about economic health than the stock index. A pay package to a CEO might well be news, as it should be for corporate governance purposes, but changes in the median pay of all employees is something that only specialized organizations like labor unions make known. Corporate profits are announced regularly, but labor's share of such profits is not. An overall unemployment rate is announced, but statistics on the status of jobs (portion that are full- or part-time, with or without benefits) are not.

It is not entirely accidental that the ordinary person's view of the financial industry takes on that industry's own perspective. This narrative has been well sold. In a multi-year anthropological study of the investment banking industry from the late 1990s to the global financial crisis, Ho finds that the industry worked to generate narratives to sell a finance-

---

[74] D. Dayen, *Chain of Title: How Three Ordinary Americans Uncovered Wall Street's Great Foreclosure Fraud* (New York: The New Press, 2016), Kindle Locations 146–156.

centered world and financial transactions (their product) to their non-financial clients. The financial institutions project their "'own' experiences of downsizing as empowerment," "to project a local model of employee liquidity and financial instability onto corporate America . . . Wall Street imagines and uses globalization further [to link] Wall Street's corporate culture (especially employee liquidity and corporate liquidation) and wildly gyrating financial markets, prone to stratospheric booms and far-reaching, devastating busts."[75]

This argument is complementary with the conclusions of the Kay Study of the UK equity markets, which found that at least two failing non-financial "companies [had] reacted to weaknesses in their operating activities by trading in businesses rather than by trading in chemicals or electrical goods. Both were influenced in these decisions by external financial advice and by market perceptions of their activities," and that this culture was "significantly affected by the pre-eminent role established by US investment banks, which favoured transactions and trading over relationships."[76]

If investment banks are able to sell such narratives despite historical evidence of negative effects on earlier clients, information about potential or ongoing negative impact could serve to correct the situation, similarly to the warnings on tobacco that can help to counteract even its addictive hold on consumers. Rather than simply feeding the public a daily dose of abridged information about and tailored for broker-dealers (the winners and losers of the day's trading and the final score), information about the financial industry's impact on the economy and society should also be distributed. In a market where narratives are packaged and polished to move prices high or low, public authorities have a duty to nudge the public into a more circumspect frame of mind.

We receive information about a takeover offer or a merger, which is important for the relevant company's shareholders, but should also learn the size of the fees paid for the advisors or receive follow-up reports on whether the companies involved in the transaction prospered or collapsed three years down the line. We should receive information on any change of share price in connection with such transactions, but should also receive information on changes in

---

[75] K. Ho, *Liquidated: An Ethnography of Wall Street* (Durham NC: Duke University Press, 2009), Kindle Locations 5906–5911.
[76] "The Kay review," 18.

employment or changes in research budgeting as a result of the transaction. We receive information about an improvement, year-to-year, in a company's performance and the executive pay awarded, but we should also receive the results of an audit that estimates the actual cause of the improved performance, which would rarely be work solely of the executive. Abstracting an entire corporation into its CEO is similar to abstracting a team into its captain or the entire financial market into a game among financial institutions, and while such narratives may sell, they are very significant distortions of important activity. Without a public informed of the role and impact of the financial industry in the economy, regulators cannot be expected to receive the support necessary to become effective in a complex – and often treacherous – market.

2.5 Conclusion

We are at the close of an era that has treated market efficiency with something bordering on religious awe. The ramifications of understanding the securities markets as sublimely efficient, with prices reflecting all information in consummate perfection, is obvious for regulation. In the face of a perfection that exceeds their understanding, regulators should hesitate to interfere. They should make sure information is available, but otherwise keep their hands off. This efficiency could arise because of a second accepted fiction that market participants and investors alike make decisions with a rationality that transcends human capability.

The twin beliefs of price efficiency and choice rationality arise from ignoring actual environment and the characteristics of actual decision-makers. Securities prices arise from the interactions of multiple market participants who receive and process information in different ways and contexts, and the price at which a security is sold is determined by bid and ask orders triggering each other in systems that are limited through choices about matching criteria and the latency of their order routing technology. Decisions are made for reasons determined by the history and environment of each decision-maker and with information that is available to that decision-maker.

Thus, in addition to the very important problems arising in the recognized channels of information flow and the imbalances they bring, as examined by Lambert and Igan and Chen in this volume, this chapter has focused on how the unraveling of the ECMH has changed the foundation of financial regulation. Freed of their mystical mantle of efficiency, the financial markets become trading environments in which real people (and their machines) trade financial assets for real purposes (making a profit) *against* each other in what are usually zero-sum transactions.

In a market where, as Voltaire expresses it, every eruption "works out for the best," regulators may depend on regulated entities in any case to act rationally to protect their reputation, ensure repeat business, avoid punishment in cost of capital and a whole host of rational reactions to the potential indirect costs of bad behavior. In short, regulators can depend on the regulated to behave *as if* under perfectly designed regulation. If, on the other hand, market prices are understood to be the result of competing narratives vying for supremacy in a predator-prey context (all within many levels of highly complex information processing systems), the tenor of regulation takes on a completely different level of earnest importance. In an atmosphere where fundamental value is difficult to ascertain and market value is the result of narrative-building and a gaming of market structure and momentum, enumeration of acceptable behavior and active regulation become essential for investor safety.

The environment is no longer a neutral given. When one group of market competitors design the infrastructure for everyone, this is not a public service, but a red flag. The problem of expert control is present in all public infrastructure but exaggerated in finance, thanks to the aura of exceptionality the financial industry has cultivated and the disproportionate funds available to industry actors when compared to regulators. Financial institutions designing market infrastructure control all detailed information regarding architecture, operations, alternatives that might have been considered in planning sessions, and the reasons for choosing a given arrangement. Most of this information will never come to light provided that the system built also meets generally imposed regulatory criteria, which themselves will be "realistic" – i.e., determined within the range of what the industry represents to the regulators as possible and practical. This means that the construction of more socially useful alternatives will not even be considered. Such alternatives might be a transparent system of securities holding that allows shareholder communication rather than a central depository that disrupts it, or a model of connected markets that stimulates broker-dealer competition rather than a fragmented archipelago of trading platforms that benefits the largest broker-dealers, and the multibillion-dollar CAT this approach necessitates. While the infrastructure eventually implemented will in most cases dutifully match the regulatory parameters, the entire model may well generate large externalities that damage the economy. These problems never come on the regulatory radar because proprietary industry information is necessary to set the parameters correctly.

Narratives also have broad power, both for price and for policy-making. Perhaps no narrative has had more impact on contemporary economies and societies than that which presents finance as an economy's heart. When the information about financial markets that a factory worker receives daily is a simplified form of the same information that broker-dealers find most relevant, the factory worker will come to see her own interests aligned with those of the broker-dealer. Whether Adidas AG is up, or Nike Inc. is down, will have little connection to whether she can afford a new pair of shoes, but she will in any case be told. When the Dow or FTSE goes up or down, she will be expected to take this as a sign of the national health, but no specifics will be given to her about the effect on her pension scheme.

On the other hand, something as directly relevant to most people as employees' share of corporate profits or disproportionate effects of GDP growth on various income groups remains unknown and is socially understood as an esoteric and perhaps therefore unreliable metric. Imagine a tape at the bottom of Bloomberg Television with scrolling information on changes in median pay in relation to changes in corporate profits, or percentage of workers receiving full health care benefits, or jobs replaced by automation in a given month. While this information would be highly relevant to most people, we do not expect to receive it and may not even be able to find a reliable source to obtain it. This is perhaps why the public is concerned with financial regulation only for the brief period following a market crash. As public support is essential for regulatory action, the broader narrative used to condition public opinion largely determines the shape of financial market regulation.

Unless we return to the belief that "all is for the best in the best of all possible financial markets," it is crucial that financial regulators accurately understand the way information is gathered, conceptualized, sold and processed in set channels prior to affecting the human and mechanical decisions that create market price. It is also crucial that we change the public understanding of financial markets by providing information that shows their real impact on ordinary people rather than as a series of exotic football scores. The technology going into financial market infrastructure can now harvest and display nearly any imaginable data relationships showing impact on the real economy. A close look at the grit of real financial markets is necessary for both regulators and the public they serve.

The Information Gap between Institutional and Retail Investors during the IPO Process

SHUONAN CHEN

3.1 Introduction

Since the financial crisis, policy-makers have focused on regulating financial intermediaries to ensure a balance between providing the best valuation for issuers and fair pricing for investors. However, what has often gone unnoticed is the different treatment given to institutional as opposed to retail investors. This is particularly evident in the initial public offering (IPO) process,[1] where institutional investors tend to be favored, given their greater financial prowess and ability to take on large portions of the deal. Issuers and underwriters alike tend to view institutional investors to be of higher quality when compared to retail investors, as institutions are often more knowledgeable and longer-term stockholders.

On the other hand, retail participation in IPOs has become increasingly valued by issuers and underwriters alike. Given the increasing importance of retail investors, it is crucial to consider how they are treated in the IPO process, compared to institutional investors. This chapter conducts such analysis in three key stages. First, the chapter will examine the information gap between institutional and retail investors, and analyze the extent of this gap in each stage of the IPO process. Second, referencing principles drawn from relevant legislation, the chapter demonstrates that this information gap is unfair regardless of its extent. Lastly, in stages of the IPO process where the gap is in principle too unfair, the chapter makes initial recommendations – including deal-specific resources and general education provided by issuers and policy-makers, respectively – to bridge this gap.

---

[1] This chapter considers the most generic cases of IPOs, which are primary offers for subscription and listed only in Hong Kong.

As a leading global financial center, Hong Kong has played a vital role in setting regulatory standards for the capital markets.[2] Furthermore, Hong Kong also has been one of the most multicultural markets, with influences from China, the United Kingdom as well as the United States. Thus, this chapter will use Hong Kong as one of the primary examples to analyze the information gap between institutional and retail investors.

3.2   Literature Review

Academics and regulators alike have often focused on the issue of information asymmetry between issuers and investors in relation to pricing for IPOs.[3] A smaller body of literature has considered the role of institutional investors in comparison to retail investors in IPOs,[4] which incidentally recognizes an information gap between the two groups of investors.[5] In other words, existing papers use the notion of an information gap to make their arguments. For instance, Kevin Rock contends that, consistent with information production and acquisition theories,[6] IPOs tend to be underpriced, since institutional investors possess an informational advantage over retail investors, and only underpricing incentivizes retail participation.[7] Similarly, other literature on IPO pricing such as those by Lawrence Benveniste and Paul Spindt[8] and Thomas Chemmanur[9] assume that institutional investors are better informed in order to argue that the IPO book-building process is a mechanism for extracting information to price IPOs.

In addition to recognizing the information gap, other works present evidence for its negative consequences – such as excess profit to institutions and lowering of market quality. For example, Thomas Chemmanur

---

[2] Hong Kong Information Services Department, "Hong Kong Fact Sheets: Financial Services," unpublished Hong Kong fact sheets, Hong Kong Information Services Department (2018), 1.

[3] V. Fleischer, "Insight: IPO Intelligence," unpublished thesis, The Ohio State University Moritz College of Law (2008), 762.

[4] T. Jenkinson and H. Jones, "IPO Pricing and Allocation: a Survey of the Views of Institutional Investors," unpublished research, University of Oxford, Saïd Business School (2007), 2.

[5] J. MacIntosh, "The Role of Institutional and Retail Investors in Canadian Capital Markets," unpublished research, University of Toronto Faculty of Law (1993), 371.

[6] L. M. Benveniste and P. A. Spindt, "How Investment Bankers Determine the Offer Price and Allocation of New Issues," unpublished research, Boston College (1989), 344.

[7] K. Rock, "Why New Issues Are Underpriced," *Journal of Financial Economics*, 188 (1986).

[8] Benveniste and Spindt, "How Investment Bankers," 24.

[9] T. J. Chemmanur, "The Pricing of Initial Public Offerings: A Dynamic Model with Information Production," *Journal of Finance*, 48 (1993), 285–304.

and Gang Hu use transactional-level trading data to conduct quantitative analysis and find that institutional trading is predicative of long-run IPO performance even after controlling for publicly available information.[10] They contend that institutional investors have significant private information about IPOs, receive considerable profit from participating in these IPOs, and retain a residual information advantage in post-IPO trading.[11] Similarly, Reena Aggarwal et al.,[12] as well as Kathleen Hanley and William Whilhelm[13] argue that institutional investors disproportionately profit more from IPOs. In fact, Phillip Zweig et al.[14] and Matti Keloharju and Sami Torstila[15] recognize that institutional investors generally have easier access to relevant information and resources, which can be used to generate excess profit.

Several papers also back the idea that equal access to information is an important measure of market quality, which would be lowered by an information gap. David Donald, in discussing the importance of good infrastructure to the operation of the financial system, highlights how major market participants can shape financial infrastructure in their own favor. He thus argues that, "[i]ssues of unequal treatment, bias and incentives should be included as measures of market quality."[16] Research from the HKEx similarly argues that improving information and education for public investors can help enhance market quality,[17] indicating that vice versa, an information gap lowers market quality.

Existing research recognizes an information gap and highlights the undesirable consequences of this gap. This chapter takes specific aim at how this gap emerges, why it may be unfair from a legal perspective, and how to mitigate this discrepancy. The answers provided in this chapter solidify the foundation of existing work and provide insight into how the negative consequences of such a gap can be averted. In fact, this chapter

---

[10] T. J. Chemmanur and G. Hu, "The Role of Institutional Investors in Initial Public Offerings," unpublished research, Boston College (2009), 23.

[11] Chemmanur, "The Role of Institutional Investors," 23.

[12] R. Aggarwal, "Institutional Allocation in Initial Public Offerings: Empirical Evidence," *Journal of Finance*, 57 (2002), 1421–1442.

[13] K. W. Hanley and W. J. Wilhelm Jr., "Evidence on the Strategic Allocation of Initial Public Offerings," *Journal of Financial Economics*, 37 (1995), 239–257.

[14] P. Zweig, "Beware the IPO Market," *Business Week*, 42–46 (1994).

[15] M. Keloharju and S. Torstila, "The Distribution of Information among Institutional and Retail Investors in IPOs," *European Financial Management*, 358 (2002).

[16] D. C. Donald, "'Market Quality' and Moral Hazard in Financial Market Design," in R. P. Buckley et al. (eds.), *Reconceptualising Global Finance and Its Regulation* (Cambridge: Cambridge University Press, 2016), 217–235, 235.

[17] E. Tsoi, "Understanding Investors in the Hong Kong Listed Securities and Derivatives Markets," unpublished research, SFC (2004), 18.

clearly demonstrates the existence and extent of this information gap in each stage of the IPO process by identifying the point from which it emerges. The perspective offered here is a legal and principle-driven one, rather than an analysis driven by quantitative differences, and argues why this gap is fundamentally unfair, regardless of the severity of outcomes. Preliminary recommendations discussed herein could do much to bridge this gap.

3.3   The Existence and Extent of an Information Gap

While existing regulations in Hong Kong appear to be quite comprehensive, retail investors and even small institutional investors are relatively disadvantaged during IPOs. Overall, in terms of information, while retail investors typically only receive the prospectus, institutional investors have access to tailor-made materials analyzing investment highlights, professional assistance from financial intermediaries – underwriters in particular[18] – and insights offered directly by the management of the issuer. While the prospectus contains all material information and is ultimately available to all investors, retail investors tend to receive this information at a later point in time. This section analyzes the existence and extent of an information gap in each stage of the IPO process.

3.3.1   IPO Process

The typical Hong Kong IPO can span from a few months to a few years from initial discussions to listing.[19] Investors are involved in four main stages: pre-marketing, marketing, book-building and pricing, as well as allocation, spanning eight to ten weeks. Throughout this process, there exists an information gap between institutional and retail investors, which is particularly evident from marketing to allocation.

3.3.1.1   Pre-Marketing: Early-Look, Cornerstone and Anchor Meetings

Overview   Pre-marketing is the process during which research analysts from underwriters meets investors to collect feedback on the prospective

---

[18] Financial intermediaries include but are not limited to investment banks, accountants and auditors. Given the focus on information received by institutional and retail investors, out of all the financial intermediaries, this paper will focus on the role of investment banks who act as underwriters.

[19] LexisNexis, "Hong Kong IPO Guide 2014," unpublished research, Lexis Nexis (2014), 24–26.

transaction, lasting from weeks to months. The purpose is to have a reasonably firm idea of the likely demand, to determine an initial pricing range, and to prepare the schedule for marketing. Another key purpose of this process is to encourage key investors to express their interest early in the book-building process.

To ensure information equality, the number of investors approached at an early stage is restricted to only a few who are foundational to the transaction. In other words, with just a few necessary exceptions, all investors should have the same access to information. As a result, smaller institutional and retail investors are excluded. On balance, while retail investors are disadvantaged because they have later access to information, the extent of this gap may not be too great, given the importance of key institutional investors to a successful deal.

Early-Look Meetings   Early-look meetings allow underwriters to introduce a company and its management to key investors without a detailed discussion of the offering before any public announcements, generally within six months of the IPO, prior to the analyst presentation (AP).[20] These meetings are typically permissible given that a very limited number of leading IPO investors are targeted in order to generate pre-deal demand and add certainty to the deal.

Measures that Mitigate the Gap

In order to restrict the flow of information to only select investors, each potential investor met during early-look meetings is carefully selected, subject to approvals internal to the underwriters, and is expected to sign a confidentiality agreement with the issuer. Also, presentation materials used are typically limited to historical financial information and a brief description of the issuer's business. By market practice, these materials are usually reviewed by outside counsel, who also brief management on appropriate responses to questions regarding the potential transaction and information not included in the presentation.[21]

---

[20] This applies to non-SEC registered offerings.

[21] Insights drawn from a series of conversations with industry professionals at various financial intermediaries between June and November 2014. In particular, discussions with senior personnel in investment banking legal and compliance at Deutsche Bank, Bank of America, Goldman Sachs, JP Morgan and Morgan Stanley, as well as counsels in corporate law at Clifford Chance, Freshfields, Latham & Watkins and Linklaters formed the foundation of assumptions about market practices. The same basis was used in other discussions of market practices in the rest of this chapter.

All materials are collected after the meetings and no information is left with the investors. An online system called NetRoadshow is often used to provide compliant online communication tools during early-look meetings, by allowing materials to be viewed online for only the duration of the meeting and disabling printing options.[22] Under no circumstances can research analysts participate in investor meetings with management, so their opinions remain unbiased.

While information leaks can occur, these cases are not common and news leaks tend to become available to all investors simultaneously. In such cases, underwriters are typically held responsible by the regulator, the Securities and Futures Commission (SFC), which derives its power from the Securities and Futures Ordinance (SFO).[23] In the worst-case scenario that underwriters abuse their ability to approach investors in the pre-marketing stage, the SFC provides a platform for supervision, investigation and enforcement.[24] As of the second quarter of 2017,[25] the SFC has conducted 539 investigations in total, of which 186 were regarding intermediary misconduct.[26] The SFC has conducted 202 investigations in terms of persons subject to proceedings just in the second quarter of 2017.[27] Thus, it is clear that the SFC has been actively monitoring the market for potential abuses of the pre-marketing process.

Persistence of Information Gap

Retail investors are excluded altogether from early-look meetings. Furthermore, since there is no numerical cap on the number of investors allowed to be approached during pre-marketing, it is possible that underwriters may speak with too many institutions. While this provides underwriters the flexibility to approach the number of investors they judge sufficient, it can also result in information being provided to more investors than necessary.

[22] NetRoadshow (2018).

[23] Cap. 571 (2018).

[24] D. C. Donald, *A Financial Centre for Two Empires: Hong Kong's Corporate, Securities and Tax laws in Its Transition from Britain to China* (Cambridge: Cambridge University Press, 2014), 188.

[25] Quarter ended June 30, 2017. This was the latest data available publicly as of the end of March 31, 2018.

[26] SFC, "Investigations by Nature," unpublished research, SFC (2018), 1. This was the latest data available publicly as of the end of March 31, 2018.

[27] SFC, "Persons Subject to Ongoing or Concluded Enforcement Proceedings," unpublished research, SFC (2018), 1. This was the latest data available publicly as of the end of March 31, 2018.

Is the Gap Too Great?

Since Hong Kong IPOs are typically split into a Hong Kong public offering (HKPO) and an international offering – to institutional investors in markets including New York, London and Singapore – international practices must be considered. The laws in the United States are particularly relevant. The US Jumpstart Our Business Startups Act (JOBS Act) of 2012 permits "emerging growth companies" to "test the waters" by engaging in communications with investors to determine their interest in a potential SEC-registered offering, either before or after the filing of the registration statement.[28] Thus, it is accepted market practice for underwriters to participate in testing the waters if authorized by the issuer, thereby providing support for practices in Hong Kong.

Overall, it appears that in allowing for exceptions such that institutional investors receive additional information, Hong Kong can maintain a good balance between market equality and deal facilitation. While an information gap still exists during pre-marketing, the extent of this gap may not be too great, given the strict guidelines in place that limits the information shared and that allows exceptions only for purpose of market facilitation.

Cornerstone Investor Meetings　These meetings seek to confirm cornerstone investors (cornerstones), who would make a firm commitment to subscribe for a specified number of shares or monetary value at a to-be -determined final offer price within the marketed price range prior to the formal marketing period and agreed upon lock-up. In return, cornerstones are usually guaranteed their agreed amount. Since cornerstones would be disclosed in the prospectus, the presence of high-profile cornerstones helps generate further demand and encourages earlier orders. Cornerstones are common in Hong Kong IPOs, participating in approximately one-third of all transactions since 2011.[29] For IPOs with cornerstones, the cornerstone tranche ranges from 5 to 70 percent of the deal, averaging 30 percent.[30]

In terms of aftermarket performance, it is possible to evaluate the benefit of cornerstones by categorizing them into two groups: long-

---

[28] H.R. 3606 (2012).

[29] Collating data from all Hong Kong IPO prospectuses since 2010.

[30] HKUSpace, "Accounting & Finance Professional Seminar – Hong Kong Initial Public Offering: Overview and Recent Trends," unpublished research, Hong Kong University (2014), 1.

term investors – sovereign wealth funds (SWFs), strategic and long-only – as well as non-institutional investors – corporates, private individual and China state-owned enterprises (SOEs).[31] Diverging aftermarket performance can be observed between the groups. IPOs with participation by long-term investors have outperformed IPOs with participation by "non-institutional investors" – by more than 3 percent on average, one month after listing.[32] This provides some justification for the additional information given to institutional investors during the pre-marketing stage.

Measures that Mitigate the Gap

While confirmed cornerstones receive guaranteed allocation and additional information, such as a general sense of valuation and potential access to pre-deal research, they agree to be price-takers and to be subject to a lock-up period of six to twelve months, which prevents them from disposing of their shares.[33] Key terms of the cornerstone agreement – size of investment and lock-up terms – as well as background information on the cornerstones will be disclosed in the draft prospectus to provide transparency and build deal momentum.

There are other market practices in place to help restrict the flow of information to cornerstone targets.[34] First, for cornerstone meetings, issuer and underwriter legal counsels are consulted before any written information can be provided to potential investors. A teaser consistent with the draft prospectus is provided only upon clearance by issuer and underwriter counsels. Oral communications are typically scripted based on specific talking points prepared by the deal team, with input from legal counsel as well. These measures together help ensure adequate restrictions on information during pre-marketing.

Persistence of Information Gap

Given that it takes time to convince cornerstones to commit, investors are often engaged months ahead of launch. In addition, cornerstone targets are sent one or more drafts of the prospectus on a confidential basis and also offered opportunities to meet with management and

---

[31] J. Song, "HKEx Gets Tough on Cornerstones," unpublished research, IFRAsia (2013), 2.
[32] Song, "HKEx Gets Tough," 2.
[33] Song, "HKEx Gets Tough," 2.
[34] Non-SEC registered, since this chapter focuses on Hong Kong listings.

undertake site visits. Furthermore, given the additional requirements for cornerstones, it is extremely difficult to find investors who are interested. As a result, a large number of investors are often provided additional information without any being interested to undertake as a cornerstone, placing these investors at an informational advantage.

While investors solicited as potential cornerstones may have to sign non-disclosure agreements (NDAs), they still benefit from receiving information at a much earlier stage. While underwriters have internal guidelines on the number of investors that should be approached, this is difficult to follow and regulate, likely resulting in information distribution to too many institutional investors. This clearly indicates that the information gap persists strongly.

Is the Gap Too Great?

Despite the persistence of the information gap, the benefits of deal stabilization, momentum building and strong aftermarket trading that cornerstones can bring, as well as restrictions on information dissemination in place during the cornerstone process makes the gap more reasonable.

Anchor Investor Meetings   Anchor investor (anchor) meetings, also known as pilot-fishing meetings, are held before or during pre-deal investor education (PDIE) to acquire early orders in return for earlier access to the issuer and a better – although not guaranteed – allocation of shares. These meetings typically take place no more than one month prior to the publication of research and commencement of PDIE.[35]

Measures that Mitigate the Gap

General guidelines for anchor meetings are similar to early-look meetings, particularly in terms of requirements on due diligence, prospectus drafting, confidentiality agreement, as well as limitations on presentation materials and exclusion of research analysts. However, in anchor meetings there are different restrictions on what information can be shared. First of all, given that the draft prospectus is typically fully prepared by the time these meetings take place, materials must be sourced directly from the prospectus. Key deal metrics may be discussed with potential

---

[35] P. Espinasse, "IPO Research: Theory and Practice," *South China Morning Post*, 1 (2012).

investors, close to the time of or during PDIE, for purposes of soliciting valuation input or encouraging early orders. Similarly, bankers or sales representatives who are briefed on the materials and potentially wall-crossed should attend meetings alongside management by market practice.

Persistence of Information Gap

During anchor meetings, even with all the guidelines in place to restrict the flow of information, targeted investors are still offered various types of information that the general public otherwise do not have. This is similar to information received by target cornerstones, such as management meetings and site visits. Furthermore, anchors are not disclosed in the prospectus nor are they subject to a lock-up as are cornerstones. Thus, anchors are another source of an information gap between institutional and retail investors.

Is the Gap Too Great?

Balancing the information gap against the amount of support that anchors can provide, it appears that exceptions allowing for information advantages to institutional investors may be necessary to facilitate deals. Also, given the various informational restrictions regulating the anchor process, the extent of this gap is not too great.

Information Gap in the Pre-Marketing Process

Overall, the pre-marketing process provides various informational advantages to investors identified by underwriters as having potential to invest in large tickets over the rest of institutional and retail investors, as the involvement of cornerstones and anchors has become essential for large deals, particularly in difficult market conditions.[36] Recently, market conditions for IPOs have become increasingly difficult globally, particularly in Hong Kong. In such markets, getting a core group of large, well-known institutional investors to anchor the deal at an early stage has also become a pre-requisite in most cases.[37]

As already mentioned, there are various measures in place to mitigate the information gap in the pre-marketing process, by restricting the

---

[36] B. Andrews, "Hong Kong IPO Guide 2013," unpublished professional guide, Hong Kong (2013), 58.

[37] Andrews, "Hong Kong," 60.

institutional investors approached as well as requiring approvals and records. Given the benefits that such investors provide and the additional restrictions placed on target investors, the extent of the information gap in the pre-marketing process seem limited and reasonable.

3.3.1.2   Marketing: PDIE and Roadshow

Overview   The marketing process is designed to ensure that the issuer formally communicates to prospective investors and briefs equity analysts to gauge market acceptance and determine pricing. This takes place approximately two to four weeks before pricing in order to allow one week for PDIE and approximately two weeks for roadshow, although the roadshow can overlap with PDIE.

PDIE   Issuers and their underwriters ordinarily commence the marketing stage of offering after receiving the Post-Hearing Letter from the Stock Exchange of Hong Kong (SEHK). Key milestones for the PDIE include kick-off, period before AP, the AP and report drafting. The AP assists research analysts in drafting pre-deal research reports, which are sent selectively to institutional investors. These reports are for marketing purposes and only vetted for factual data, thus playing an important role by guiding investors' views.[38]

Key market participants have adopted standard measures and documentation that assess the objectivity of the pre-deal research reports – to prevent these reports from being used by issuers to disseminate information without formal prospectus liability – and track the dissemination of pre-deal research reports. Once these reports have been published, research analysts will travel globally to meet with institutional investors, again excluding retail investors from the process.

Investors' feedback is then collected to set a book-building price range and tailor the roadshow presentation, which builds up investor momentum before formal deal launch and helps analysts estimate investors' demand. However, this outreach covers only institutional investors.

Measures that Mitigate the Gap

To better understand the nature of pre-deal research reports and the information they include, it is helpful to refer to the SFC Code of

---

[38] SFC, "Code of Conduct for Persons Licensed by or Registered with the Securities and Futures Commission," (2018), 1–2.

Conduct.[39] First of all, to ensure that these reports do not mislead any investors, the SFC Code of Conduct highlights independence and transparency as crucial elements of pre-deal reports. In other words, pre-deal research reports are merely publicity materials and should not be characterized to resemble an offering document.

The general publicity restrictions discussed earlier will apply to pre-deal research reports as well. Otherwise, such reports would be constituted as a prospectus and liability rules would apply as such.[40] To avoid the appearance of being an offering document, an institution would consider the timing of the report's publication. The SFC Code of Conduct does not establish any quiet period restricting the publication of a pre-deal research report before the making of an IPO offer.[41] However, there is a risk that the report could be seen as part of the offering and trigger liability if the period in between its publication and the offering is too short. In the SFC's "Consultation Conclusions on the Regulatory Framework for Pre-Deal Research,"[42] the SFC stated that it did not yet consider it appropriate to establish a pre-IPO quiet period. Nonetheless, the consultation noted that many underwriters impose a quiet period of at least two weeks after they issue a pre-deal research report. Ultimately, the length of a pre-IPO quiet period is a matter for underwriters to consider in light of the nature, complexity and scale of the issuer's business.

As publicity material, pre-deal research reports must also comply with all applicable statutory requirements for such. Specifically, forecasts, projections and valuations may be included in research reports if they are prepared independently. Thus, it is clear that there are many restrictions and prudent market practices in each key stage for PDIE to restrict the flow of information.

In addition, although retail investors do not receive the pre-deal research reports, they do have access to the A1 or Application Proof prospectus and Post-Hearing Information Pack ("PHIP") – essentially draft prospectuses[43] – on the HKEx website, which issuers are required to

[39] SFC, "Code of Conduct," 2.
[40] SFC, "Consultation Conclusions on the Consultation Paper on Possible Reforms to the Prospectus Regime in the Companies Ordinance," Hong Kong (2006), 1–2.
[41] SFC, "Code of Conduct," 2.
[42] Kirkland and Ellis, "Due Diligence Guidelines – Provision of Information to Analysts," unpublished professional guide, Kirkland and Ellis (2018), 3.
[43] S. Birkett and J. Moore, "Consultation on the Regulation of Hong Kong IPO Sponsors – The Top Five Things You Need to Know," unpublished professional guide, Morrison Foerster (2012), 2.

post essentially around the same time as when draft prospectuses are provided to institutional investors before the start of the roadshow.[44] This provides more basic information on the business of the issuer. These draft prospectuses are substantially in its final form, and any subsequent changes are specifically highlighted, therefore making this information accessible to the public.

Persistence of Information Gap

While pre-deal research reports provide information and analysis, they are only provided to institutional and not retail investors. The investors who receive the reports are usually those who have accounts open with the relevant underwriters and who have indicated in their account preferences that they would like to receive pre-deal research reports. Retail investors are also not offered meetings with research analysts, and thus must solely rely on the offering circular for their investment decision. In fact, contrary to the pre-marketing process where the additional information is restricted to the individuals who play foundational roles in the deal, pre-deal research reports can be sent to thousands of institutional investors without considering retail investors at all in the process.[45]

Although pre-deal research reports do not contain material information otherwise not found in the prospectus, this information is typically available to institutional investors much earlier than to retail investors. In fact, pre-deal reports are available at the beginning of PDIE, which takes place approximately two weeks before HKPO and the release of the prospectus to the general public. This is the case despite retail investors having access to the A1 and PHIP, as crucial information – such as expected timetable, use of proceeds, and offering-related details including size – is redacted and therefore not available to retail investors until the full prospectus. In contrast, this redacted information is often indicated during meetings to institutional investors. Moreover, these reports contain much more sophisticated analysis of the overall industry and specific business. While more analysis does not necessarily guarantee a better decision, the availability of more information provides the potential for more informed decision-making.

In addition, whereas issuers actively engage institutional investors to provide information and guidance on pre-deal research reports and draft

---

[44] Birkett and Moore, "Consultation," 2
[45] C. Tam, "Hong Kong IPO Guide 2014," unpublished professional guide, Claris Tam (2014), 75.

prospectuses, retail investors must actively check the HKEx website for new information themselves. Also, given that no timetable is published with the A1 and PHIP, retail investors may not even be aware of the pending deal, unless it is highlighted by news and media, by the time that institutional investors have learned all about the upcoming transaction from the PDIE stage. Hence, it is clear that the information gap persists, as institutional investors have a time advantage in terms of basic information and an absolute advantage of access to in-depth analysis, as retail investors are overlooked altogether.

Is the Gap Too Great?

The key question in the PDIE process is whether or not a selective offering of publicity materials to institutional investors creates a gap that is too great. Given that all institutional investors rather than only a select few have the opportunity to be approached and offered information in this process, it would appear that the extent of this information gap is too great.

Roadshow   The roadshow is the final stage of the marketing process and typically lasts for approximately two weeks, concurrent with bookbuilding. The roadshow is intended to present the investment story of the issuer to confirm the understanding and interest of potential investors to place their orders.

This process has three key components, including group presentations, small group meetings and one-on-one meetings. Roadshow materials typically include a presentation slide book and the preliminary prospectus that in essence is a near-final draft, conventionally only omitting pricing and related financial and offer size information. Up to hundreds of institutional investors can be contacted directly.

Given that the roadshow takes place simultaneously with bookbuilding, this is a crucial step in the price discovery process, as underwriters gather feedback and information to make an informed decision in terms of pricing. However, retail investors are not involved in these presentations.

Measures that Mitigate the Gap

Despite other materials being used during the roadshow, the prospectus is nonetheless intended as the principal offering document. Thus, it must contain all information necessary for investors to make an informed assessment of the company's assets and liabilities, financial position, profits and losses, business prospects and rights attached to the shares.[46] Underwriters also conduct extensive due diligence and verification and the HKEx vets and approves the prospectus to ensure compliance with all disclosure requirements. In cases of any inaccurate, misleading or hidden information, the issuer and its underwriters can be held to civil and criminal liabilities. As a result, given that retail investors will ultimately gain access to the full prospectus, these procedures ensure that retail investors have all the necessary information to make an informed investment decision.

Persistence of Information Gap

Retail investors are excluded altogether from the roadshow process. While they eventually have access to the prospectus, they still have much later access to offering-specific information, such as the amount of offering, which are redacted from the A1 and PHIP.

Moreover, it has been market practice that institutional investors often base their investment decision on roadshow presentations,[47] indicating that this is a crucial source of information beyond those outlined in the prospectus to which retail investors do not have access. At these meetings, institutional investors can make decisions based on personal interactions – such as via Q&A[48] – with management. Through speaking with the management, institutional investors can get a better sense of the management's expertise and dedication to their business. Institutional investors also receive tailor-made roadshow materials. While these materials may contain similar information, it is presented in much more user-friendly formats that better highlight points most relevant to the investment case. Institutional investors at group events can also gather information from other investors and have a better sense of deal momentum throughout the marketing process.

Furthermore, the roadshow process is crucial for gathering feedback. Underwriters consider comments on valuation and overall investment case from investors, and use this to determine the price range. However, retail investors are again excluded from this process. Therefore, it is clear that the information gap persists in the roadshow stage.

---

[46] Tam, "Hong Kong," 75.

[47] This applies to non-SEC registered offerings.

[48] Roadshow meetings typically conclude with a question and answer segment where investors can ask management on any topic of interest.

Is the Gap Too Great?

Given that issuers widely approach all institutional investors during the roadshow stage, and these investors tend to make decisions during this stage, it appears that the extent of this gap is too great for fair treatment of retail investors, who are excluded altogether.

Information Gap in the Marketing Process   Hence, the PDIE and roadshow processes are crucial steps to which retail investors do not have access – they do not receive certain information, and their feedback is not considered.

3.3.1.3   Book-Building and Pricing

Toward the middle of the roadshow, underwriters meet with the issuer to determine a price range based on feedback from pre-marketing. Upon setting the price range, the book-building process for institutional investors commences, during which non-binding orders can be placed into the demand book, typically indicating desired sizes at different price levels within the range. Toward the end of the roadshow, the offer to retail investors – also known as subscription for the Hong Kong public offering (HKPO) – kicks off with the release of the listing prospectus on the HKEx's website,[49] typically spanning three-and-a-half business days.[50] One day prior to the start of the HKPO, the HKPO press conference takes place to communicate the offer and relevant information via media sources to the public.[51]

Once the demand book closes, issuers and underwriters meet to determine the final offer price. This discussion is crucial in ensuring that the stock trades well in the aftermarket. Based on investor demand and feedback – particularly the size, quality and price sensitivity of orders – the underwriters will recommend an offering price to the issuer.

---

[49] §§ 44A(1) and 342B(1) of the Companies Ordinance.

[50] HKEx & SFC, "Joint Consultation Conclusions on the Proposal to allow a Companies Ordinance (CO) Offeror to issue a CO Paper Application Form for Shares in or Debentures of a Company to be listed on the SEHK, and a Collective Investment Scheme (CIS) Offeror to supply a CIS Paper Application Form for Interests in an SFC-authorized CIS to be listed on the SEHK, with a Listing Document Displayed on Certain Websites," unpublished legislative guideline, HKEx and SFC (2010), 22.

[51] Baker and McKenzie, "Due Diligence Guidelines – Overall Management of a Public Offer," unpublished professional guide, Baker and McKenzie (2013), 1.

Measures that Mitigate the Gap   By the book-building stage, given extensive marketing conducted by the issuer, the key objective is no longer to restrict the flow of information to select investors as in the pre-marketing process. On the other hand, this process contains requirements by the SEHK to ensure that retail investors receive all the necessary information to make informed investment decisions. First of all, there is typically a press conference before HKPOs kick-off, to provide the public with more information. Although retail investors do not attend the press conference directly, reporters who do attend will be able to assist in passing on key information to the general public. At the press conference, reporters are typically given the opportunity to listen to the same management presentation as was given for the roadshow, ask questions as well as receive copies of the draft prospectus, which constitutes similar access to information as institutional investors. Thus, it is up to the reporter to select the most relevant information to pass on to retail investors. The day after the press conference, the HKPO officially kicks off, and retail investors have access to the full prospectus. The HKEx requires that the prospectus be published electronically on its website to ensure that all investors have equal access to information.

Persistence of Information Gap   HKPOs thus typically begin days after the roadshow and book-building for institutional investors have already started. A large majority of IPOs allow an offer period of three-and-a-half days between the issue of the final prospectus and the close of offer. It is only during this period that the general public investors have access to the full prospectus to make an investment decision. This gap in timing most likely disadvantages retail investors, as they only obtain the offering-specific information long after institutional investors do. Furthermore, retail investors also have less time – three-and-a-half business days – to consider their investment decision in the context of full information disclosure, whereas institutional investors can have as long as months to consider and place orders.

Furthermore, the process during which underwriters determine the price with the issuer is typically dependent solely on feedback collected from institutional investors. However, there is usually no representation of retail investors and their feedback is often only heard through market rumors. Given the importance of achieving a balance between maximizing price and ensuring support in the aftermarket, information on the level of subscription can often provide better guidance in terms of where the deal is likely to price. Thus, retail investors are often excluded from access to such information.

Is the Gap Too Great?   Issuers and underwriters provide information and guidance throughout the book-building and pricing process, whereas retail investors do not receive any information. Hence, it appears that the extent of the information gap between institutional and retail investors is too great.

3.3.1.4   Allocation

Upon setting the offer price, underwriters go through line-by-line institutional allocations to ensure not only that investors receive an amount of stock that encourages them to purchase more in the aftermarket, but also that a core group of significant holders can anchor the transaction and remain as long-term investors. Underwriters consider a number of factors, including the quality of investor, consistency throughout the pre-marketing and market process, coherence of order size relative to funds under management and peer holdings, track record in comparable offerings, price sensitivity and time of order. The aim is to reward early, strong commitment while ensuring a quality, supportive shareholding base. Finally, upon the issuer's approval, the final price and allocations are released.

The stock commences trading typically three business days after pricing and allocation. It is established practice that the immediate aftermarket is stabilized via the over-allotment or green-shoe option.[52] This typically takes place within the first month of trading, helps smooth imbalances between short-term sellers and buyers, and provides support for the stock price.

Measures that Mitigate the Gap   There are mainly two measures in Hong Kong that help mitigate the gap in information for retail investors at the allocation stage: SFC guidelines and the clawback mechanism – a re-allocation of offer shares between HKPO and the international offering in the event of oversubscription under the HKPO. There are explicit SFC guidelines against certain malpractices to prevent underwriters from putting retail investors at an informational disadvantage by providing additional information to institutional investors. The SFC guidelines prohibit quid pro quo and reports of indications of interest

---

[52] Securities and Futures (Price Stabilisation) Rules.

and final allocations.[53] Quid pro quo describes a situation of exchange,[54] such as where institutional investors offer commitment to place orders in return for additional information, or institutional investors offer future orders in return for information on or promised allocation. Regulators step in to prohibit the aforementioned situations where underwriters may be incentivized to act in ways contrary to equal information access by all investors.

Additionally, Practice Note 18 (PN18) requires that the initial minimum allocation to retail must be at least 10 percent of the total offering for all Hong Kong IPOs.[55] Where the HKPO is oversubscribed, clawback kicks in, whereby given proportions of the shares will be transferred from the institutional tranche to the HKPO tranche. The standard clawback requirements range from 10 percent to 50 percent, depending on the level of oversubscription. The policy consideration is to protect the interests of local investors, particularly where it is anticipated that there will be significant public demand. This requires a balance between ensuring a sufficient supply of shares to satisfy the demand of retail investors while also allowing issuers and underwriters a sufficient degree of flexibility to determine their offer structures. While there is a PN 18 waiver, such cases are rare and are considered on a case-by-case basis, and such waivers typically do not allow worse allocations to retail investors.[56] This mechanism helps to mitigate the information gap, as retail investors are guaranteed more allocation given appropriate levels of oversubscription, despite not having information on the existing level of subscription.

Persistence of Information Gap   SFC guidelines against quid pro quo and indications of interest and final allocations may not be sufficient, as it is inevitable that market rumors travel among institutional investors and news leak through the media.[57] Also, the clawback mechanism may not necessarily be useful, as many retail investors do not understand how to use the clawback provision. In fact, even with the clawback mechanism, while the effect of the information gap on retail investors may be more limited, the fundamental issue of lack of access to information still exists.

Furthermore, in allocation, investors that are considered to be top quality are ones that consistently participate in the primary and

---

[53] SFC, "Guidelines," unpublished professional guidelines, SFC (2018), 1.
[54] Oxford dictionary definition of quid pro quo.
[55] PN 18 (1998).
[56] HKEx-LD60-1(2008).
[57] IFR, FinanceAsia and DealReporter articles.

secondary markets, provide in-depth analysis of the issuance, and hold a long-term investment horizon. These are typically large institutional investors – large long-only funds, sector specialist funds, one-on-one meetings attendees and some selected large hedge funds, for which the underwriters seeks to maximize allocations.[58] This creates a situation where those are perceived to be more likely investors are offered more information at an earlier stage, on the basis of which they are more likely to demonstrate interest and ultimately receive larger allocations, thereby fundamentally disfavoring retail and even smaller institutional investors without providing them the opportunity to engage.

Moreover, allocations for retail investors are much more mechanical, as they are done through a balloting process.[59] Practically, this makes sense, as there are a large number of investors, making line-by-line allocation impossible. However, the extensive allocation principles for institutional investors illustrate a lack of regard for retail investors and lack of incentive for underwriters to consider retail investors. Retail investors are also not provided opportunities for interaction with representatives from underwriters and therefore prevented from gaining further insight on the deal.

In addition, after the issuer is listed, the company is likely to have an active investor relations department that schedules regular meetings and earnings calls with key investors. Retail investors typically would not be offered the opportunity to attend such meetings. While the company has obligations to disclose price sensitive information, disclosure is still often not sufficient. In fact, research has found that institutional investors retain a residual informational advantage in post-IPO trading.[60]

Is the Gap Too Great? Overall, throughout the allocation process, issuers and underwriters communicate continually with institutional investors. In fact, institutions can also reach out actively to issuers and the underwriters for more information. In contrast, retail investors are excluded altogether from this process, which makes the extent of the information gap too great. While there are important reasons why allocations favor institutional investors – such as their ability to provide necessary support for the deal – it does not change the fact that retail

---

[58] Tam, "Hong Kong," 84.
[59] SFC, "Consultation Paper on Offering Mechanisms," unpublished professional guidelines, SFC (2012), 1.
[60] T. J. Chemmanur and G. Hu, "Institutional Trading, Allocation Sales, and Private Information in IPOs," unpublished research, Boston College (2007), 2.

investors are subordinated and not provided crucial information in this process.

Given increasing participation by local retail investors in the markets,[61] it would appear that such a gap is too great and that it would make sense to provide proper information and guidance so that retail investors can be a positive influence in the markets.

3.3.1.5   Conclusion: The Gap Is Too Great

Overall, throughout the IPO process, retail investors are disadvantaged greatly in terms of access to information – which includes providing institutions tailored analysis, insights on the issuer's management and general sense of market sentiments. Retail investors are also provided information at a much later point in time compared to institutional investors.

It may be argued that providing merely the prospectus to retail investors is enough to protect them, as the law makes clear that only the full prospectus – which includes the relevant risk factors, disclaimers and disclosures – should be used in making an investment decision, rather than building on selective information from other sources. However, having only the full prospectus can also make it more difficult for retail investors to digest the information about the issuer, ultimately making information less accessible. Thus, it is clear that there exists a significant gap in information between institutional and retail investors, despite the extensive regulation and market practices currently in place. In fact, as illustrated above, the extent of this information gap is too great in the marketing, book-building and pricing as well as allocation stages.

3.3.2   General Knowledge/Analytical Skills

In general, retail investors are not well-versed in finance and may not know where to look for information and be unable to conduct thoughtful analysis. While there are strong regulations limiting material non-public information (MNPI) to investors during the IPO process,[62] institutional investors still tend to have access to more relevant information and can thus make more informed judgments than retail investors. Although a fair system may still result in information inequality, policy-makers

---

[61] Research and Corporate Development Department, "Local Retail Investors in the HKEx Stock Market Reach All-time High," unpublished professional research, HKEx (2012), 33.

[62] C. W. Betts, "Legal and Regulatory Issues in Hong Kong PIPE Transactions," unpublished professional research, Skadden (2012), 3.

should aim to establish a good structure so that investors have at least an equal start.

3.4   The Unfairness of the Gap

Given there is an information gap between institutional and retail investors – a gap that is too great at various stages of the IPO process – it is important to evaluate whether or not this gap is fair. While issuers and underwriters tend to see retail investors as higher in quantity but lower in quality, and therefore focus on institutional investors for efficiency, this does not mean that such practice is fair. By examining the relevant regulatory structure and legislation in Hong Kong, there is evidence that this gap is unfair. In fact, principles expounded explicitly or implicitly in relevant legislation in Hong Kong – which includes the former Companies Ordinance (CO), now the Companies (Winding Up and Miscellaneous Provisions) Ordinance (CWUMPO),[63] the SFO, the non-statutory Listing Rules of the SEHK (the Listing Rules) and the Securities and Futures (Stock Market Listing) Rules (the SFC Listing Rules), the Joint Policy Statements of the Stock Exchange of Hong Kong (SEHK) and SFC (the JPSs), as well as SEHK Guidance Letters covering topics relating to publicity restrictions – demonstrate the importance of equal access to information.

These principles have been confirmed in practice, as evidenced in decisions made by regulators.[64] However, it is important to note that these principles of equality have not been applied consistently to all areas of the finance, as is evident in the information gap between institutional and retail investors during the IPO process. Hence, the principles underlying relevant legislation should be applied to rectify the information gap for stages in the IPO process, where such gap is both too great and unfair, whereas practices that only result in a limited gap – albeit still unfair – can be addressed at a future date.

3.4.1   Overview of Regulatory Structure

Issuers in Hong Kong are typically governed by a three-tier regulatory structure, which consists of the government, the SFC and the HKEx.[65]

---

[63] Cap. 32 (2018).
[64] SFC, "Investigations by Nature," 1.
[65] HKICS, "'Corporate Governance at the Crossroads' Conference Opening Remarks," unpublished speaking transcript, Paul Chow Chief Executive of the HKEx (2008), 1.

The government sets the overall policy direction and initiates legislation. The SFC, an independent statutory body, is the principal regulator and market supervisor that regulates the HKEx, and licenses and disciplines underwriters. The HKEx, a public organization and business entity, is the frontline regulator and administrator of the Listing Rules and regulates stock exchange participants with respect to trading matters and listed companies through its wholly owned subsidiary, the SEHK.[66] The SFC and SEHK overlap in some matters; for example, both the SFC and SEHK vet prospectuses for companies seeking to be listed.

3.4.2   Companies Law

The CWUMPO sets out the prospectus regime, which follows a "document-based" approach, focusing on the existence of a document containing an offer to the public. The law provides safe harbor exceptions, such as offers made only to "professional investors," under which offers of shares can be made without authorization of a prospectus under the CO. Thus, it would be evident that the provisions are intended to protect those who do not qualify as professionals – retail investors. In addition, the Companies Law prescribes other disclosure requirements, such as material contracts, valuation reports and accountant's reports,[67] to ensure that the prospectus contains sufficient information to enable a reasonable person to form a justifiable opinion of the issuer.[68] Therefore, the law's disclosure requirements illustrate the importance of transparency for all investors, particularly retail investors, which indicates that unequal information provided – as in the information gap between institutional and retail investors – is unfair.

3.4.3   SFO

As a statutory body, the SFC's work is defined and governed by the SFO. Outlined in the SFO, the regulatory objectives of the SFC are "to develop and maintain . . . fair . . . and transparent securities and futures markets; to help the public understand the workings of the securities and futures

---

[66] P. Bowie, "Strategies for Going IPO," unpublished professional research, Deloitte (2007), 21.

[67] Pt. II for companies incorporated in Hong Kong, Pt. XII for companies incorporated outside Hong Kong, and in the Third Schedule.

[68] S. Birkett, "The MoFo Guide to Hong Kong IPOs," unpublished professional guide, Morrison Foerster (2012), 7

industry; to provide protection for the investing public."[69] These suggest that the SFC aims to ensure equal access to information and assist the public or retail investors where necessary to safeguard fairness.

In fact, the SFC is the only Hong Kong financial regulator with an express mandate to educate the investing public.[70] The SFC published the Consultation Paper on Proposals to Enhance Protection for the Investing Public in 2009,[71] which established a number of measures for improvement[72] and following the enactment of the Securities and Futures (Amendment) Ordinance 2012 (Amending Ordinance),[73] the Investor Education Centre (IEC) was formed as a SFC subsidiary to educate the public on a broad range of retail financial products and services.[74] This indicates that the SFC acknowledges the gap in access to information and general knowledge of the public compared to institutional investors to be unfair, and is providing resources to rectify these gaps. However, these efforts are clearly insufficient, given the earlier analysis of the persistence of an unfair information gap in the IPO process.

3.4.3.1   Overlap with CO

Similar to the principles set out in the Companies Law, one of the regulatory objectives of the SFO is to provide protection for the investing public. Per the SFO, it is an offense for a person to issue IPO offering documents to the public.[75] Exceptions can be granted for prospectuses that comply with or are exempt from the CO to avoid duplication. Similar to the CO, advertisements of securities to professional investors or those outside of Hong Kong are exempt as well.[76] The placing of similar responsibilities in multiple organizations further reveals the emphasis that Hong Kong regulatory entities place on providing accurate information to the public. Principles that encourage accurate provision of information indicate that the same should apply to crucial sources of information outside of the prospectus, to which retail investors often

---

[69]   § 4 of the SFO.
[70]   SFC, "Regulatory Objectives," unpublished professional guidelines, SFC (2012), 1.
[71]   SFC, "Consultation Conclusions on Proposals to Enhance Protection for the Investing Public," unpublished professional guidelines, SFC (2010), 1.
[72]   SFC, "Consultation Conclusions on Proposals," 2.
[73]   Ord. 9 (2012).
[74]   SFC, "Regulatory Objectives," 2.
[75]   § 103 of the SFO.
[76]   § 105 of the SFO.

do not have access, demonstrating that the information gap between institutional and retail investors is clearly unfair.

3.4.3.2   Information Disclosure

While legislation requiring information disclosure in connection with the sale of securities only applies to listed companies, they provide insight into the types of information to which regulators consider all investors should have equal access. The Amending Ordinance introduced a statutory regime for the disclosure of inside information,[77] supplementing prior disclosure requirements under the SEHK Listing Rules,[78] which the SFC may seek to enforce.[79] This regime substantially expanded the previous framework by imposing personal liability on company management, indicating the importance that regulators place on information disclosure.

The Amending Ordinance was accompanied by Guidelines on Disclosure of Inside Information issued by the SFC. While SFC guidelines do not have the force of law, a breach will be taken into account in determining whether or not the statutory disclosure requirements have been complied with. These guidelines explained that this regime was implemented to ensure "the maintenance of a fair and informed market."[80] The legislation states explicitly that "[d]isclosure should be made in a manner that provides for equal, timely and effective access by the public."[81] This indicates in principle that there should be equal and fair information dissemination for all investors, both institutional and retail, and perhaps suggests that similar measures should be followed in an IPO context.

The guidelines also discuss "[striking] an appropriate balance between encouraging timely disclosure of inside information and preventing premature disclosures which might prejudice a corporation's legitimate interests."[82] In an IPO context, while it is important for the public to gain fair access to information as soon as possible, it is also crucial that the potential transaction is not announced until the issuer is sufficiently

---

[77] SFC, "Guidelines on Disclosure of Inside Information," unpublished professional guidelines, SFC (2012), 1

[78] Rule 13.09.

[79] M. Brown, "A Quick Look at the New SFC Guidelines on Disclosure of Inside Information," unpublished professional guide, Mayer Brown (2012), 1.

[80] SFC, "Guidelines on Disclosure," 2.

[81] Ibid., 3.

[82] Ibid., 2.

ready. This supports the idea of approaching select investors to form the foundation of the IPO before a public announcement, thereby indicating that a gap during the pre-marketing may be acceptable.

The guidelines summarize the principle underlying information disclosure by stating that "all disclosure of information must be made [so] that it does not place any person in a privileged dealing position and allows time for the market . . . to reflect the latest available information."[83] For IPOs, given that retail investors tend to have less general knowledge and access to resources than institutional investors, it is difficult to justify providing the former with less information and less time to fully digest the information that is available to the general public.

The guidelines added that "[t]he disclosure required . . . is only the minimum mandatory standard."[84] In other words, companies must consider their own circumstances when deciding whether any information should be disclosed to the public. It is evident that these measures to enhance disclosure are in the spirit of valuing market transparency for all investors and leveling the playing field by taking the advantage away from those who may more easily possess inside information. Given that information transparency and equal disclosure are fundamental market values, as articulated in the Amending Ordinance and supporting guidelines, it is clear that such values should apply to the IPO process as well, thus making clear that the information gap between institutional and retail investors is unfair and should be mitigated.

3.4.4 Listing Rules

Listing rules include both non-statutory elements adopted by the SEHK and statutory elements required by the SFC, although the former are more often referenced. The sections that cover strategic investors and pre-IPO placings in particular provide further insight into principles underlying the Listing Rules.

3.4.4.1 Non-Statutory: Listing Rules of the SEHK

While the Listing Rules do not have the force of statute and do not provide the SEHK with statutory regulatory powers, they are contractual obligations that listed companies undertake to fulfill with the SEHK – including

---

[83] HKEx, "Guide on Disclosure of Price-Sensitive Information," unpublished legislative guidelines, Hong Kong (2002), 1.

[84] HKEx, "Guide on Disclosure," 1.

both pre-conditions for listing and continuing obligations after approval of listing. These rules are extremely helpful in analyzing principles fundamental to the listing environment in Hong Kong.

In fact, it is illuminating that the first sentence in the Listing Rules' introduction states that "[t]he principal function of the [SEHK] is to provide a fair, orderly and efficient market for the trading of securities."[85] Moreover, the general principles section clearly states the SEHK should ensure that "the issue and marketing of securities is conducted in a fair and orderly manner and potential investors are given sufficient information [for] a properly informed assessment of an issuer."[86] The fact that "fair" is used as the first adjective – in describing the type of market that the SEHK seeks to provide and the manner in which a listing should be conducted – is revealing. This emphasizes the importance of fair and equal treatment for all investors, evidencing that the existing information gap needs to be rectified.

Strategic Investors and Pre-IPO Placings

In the context of fair and equal treatment for all investors, the Listing Rules place restrictions that limit the information advantages that may be held by strategic investors and pre-IPO investors, such as timing of investment and restrictions on rights upon listing – controlling shareholders are subject to lock-up.[87] Also, any pre-IPO investment that will result in the pre-IPO investors obtaining shares of a listing applicant at a price other than the IPO price must be disclosed in detail in the prospectus. Connected persons of the issuer need to comply with additional connected transaction rules.[88] These all indicate principles strongly in favor of achieving market and information equality through protecting minority and retail investors.

Moreover, while pre-IPO investors may be entitled to additional information rights before listing, they can only receive information simultaneously as it is made publicly available upon listing per the Listing Rules.[89] This again demonstrates principles that promote equality. Thus,

---

[85] Paragraph 2 of Appendix 7 of the Main Board Rules (the "Listing Agreement") and Rule 17.10 of the GEM Rules.

[86] Listing Rule 2.03.

[87] Listing Rule 10.07.

[88] Chap. 14A of the Listing Rules.

[89] HKEx, "Rules and Guidance on Listing Matters," unpublished legislative guidelines, HKEx (2010), 1.

such principles should apply to prohibit unequal distribution of information in the IPO process.

3.4.4.2   Statutory: The Securities and Futures (Stock Market Listing) Rules

Under the dual-filing regime, the SEHK passes to the SFC copies of materials submitted by listing applicants and listed issuers, treated as if materials have been submitted to the SFC by the prospective issuer.

3.4.5   JPS: PHIP

A listing applicant is required to post a PHIP[90] to ensure earlier disclosure of information[91] and therefore provide equal access to information for the general public.[92] Given this intent, it is clear that unequal access to information in the IPO process has been determined to be unfair. In order to better understand the principles and intentions underlying the PHIP, it is important to see how it evolved from a JPS establishing the web proof information pack (WPIP) to the current day PHIP regime.

In 2007, after consultation with industry experts and experimentation, the SEHK and the SFC published a JPS on a pilot scheme requiring all new listing applicants to post a WPIP – a near-final draft prospectus – on the HKEx website prior to publishing the official prospectus. The SEHK required the WPIP to be submitted for posting before the information is provided to institutional investors. In other words, the WPIP must be published online before the start of the roadshow. The logic is to ensure equal dissemination of information to all investors who may be unable to attend the roadshow. Practically, this requires issuers to publish information to the general public at an earlier stage of the listing process which mirrors the existing practice of distributing draft prospectuses to institutional investors. The JPS also requires that any supplemental materials and revisions involving material changes to the WPIP be published via HKEx's website as well, which again mirrors the existing market practice

---

[90] HKEx and SFC, "Pilot Scheme Regarding the Posting of a Web Proof Information Pack on the HKEx Website Prior to the Issue of a Prospectus in IPO Cases," unpublished legislative guidelines, HKEx and SFC (2007), 1.

[91] HKEx and SFC, "Earlier Disclosure of Information by IPO Applicants," unpublished legislative guidelines, HKEx and SFC (2007), 1.

[92] Stock Exchange of Hong Kong Ltd, "Publication of Application Proofs and Post Hearing Information Packs (PHIPs)," unpublished professional guidelines, Stock Exchange of Hong Kong (2013) 1.

for institutional investors. With these requirements in place, the SEHK and SFC raised the bar for distribution of information to retail investors closer to that available to institutional investors.

The scheme began in 2008 as a pilot and was codified in the Listing Rules later in the same year. The JPS described the WPIP scheme as "represent[ing] one of the various initiatives the [SEHK] has been considering to further refine the [IPO] vetting process with a view to enhancing investor protection and supporting HK's continuing role as an international financial center."[93]

The JPS clearly states, "the rationale for requiring the WPIP at an earlier stage in the listing process is to address the apparent inequality of information available to institutional and retail investors in the lead up to IPOs."[94] This acknowledges forthright that there exists a gap in information and that this gap is unfair. In support of this, then HKEx's Head of Listing, Richard Williams, stated, "[t]he pilot scheme is intended to help level the playing field for institutional and retail investors in the receipt of information about an applicant prior to the commencement of the public offering."[95] In fact, the public is provided the opportunity to raise any issues in the quality of disclosure to the SEHK after the WPIP posting. The SEHK can then determine whether or not the allegation warrants further investigation and can require the issuer involved to address or clarify any issues before distributing its prospectus, ensuring more fair information dissemination to all investors.[96]

In view of the rationale behind WPIP-posting, the SEHK and SFC do not consider a WPIP to constitute a prospectus or an advertisement under the CO or the SFO. As a result, other than information that is required, select transaction-specific information – particularly any disclosure relating to the offering, such as size of offer, pricing and timetable – must be redacted to avoid any implication that it is a prospectus.[97]

In 2012, the SFC published its Consultation Conclusions concerning the regulation of IPO sponsors,[98] which replaced the WPIP with the PHIP and required for the A1 or Application Proof prospectus filed with

---

[93] HKEx, "Pilot Pre-IPO Information Scheme Supports Hong Kong's Position as an International Financial Centre," unpublished legislative guidelines, HKEx (2008), 1.

[94] HKEx, "Pilot," 2.

[95] HKEx and SFC, "Pilot Scheme," 2.

[96] SFC, "Consultation Conclusions on the Regulatory Framework for Pre-Deal Research," unpublished legislative guidelines, SFC (2011), 9.

[97] Fried, Frank, Harris, Shriver and Jacobson LLP, "SFC Proposals to Enhance Regulation of IPO Sponsors in Hong Kong," unpublished professional guidelines, Jacobson (2012), 1.

[98] SFC, "Consultation Conclusions," 2.

the listing application to be published on the HKEx website, which gave the public earlier access to information.[99] This came into effect in 2013,[100] with the PHIP replacing the WPIP to fit the new regime, although the PHIP is similar in essence to the WPIP. The PHIP is required to be published after the listing hearing when material comments from the regulators have been reflected, and should not be published later than the distribution of draft prospectuses, commencement of book-building and any overseas publication of similar information. The PHIP also does not constitute a prospectus, so the information that is required to be included and redacted from the PHIP remains in-line with the WPIP regime. The principles drawn from the regulations in place demonstrate the emphasis placed on equal access to information for all investors, which indicates that the information gap between institutional and retail investors is unfair and needs to be rectified.

3.4.6   Decisions Demonstrating Hong Kong's Commitment to Market Equality

In fact, protecting retail investors' interests through a fair market has been fundamental to Hong Kong's status as a global market leader, as evident through Hong Kong's principles about transparent pricing, certainty of corporate structure and fair representation through one share, one vote.[101] For example, Hong Kong's loss of e-commerce giant Alibaba's IPO, for which the HKSE and SFC refused to adapt rules to allow the company to nominate the majority of the board after being listed, illustrates Hong Kong's dedication to fairness for all shareholders, no matter how small.[102]

Recent cases involving public investors' investment losses indicate a genuine prospect of shareholders' action.[103] If retail investors are denied proper access to information and equal treatment, then it is essentially only large institutional investors with privileged access to more information who profit at the detriment of those without access

---

[99] Birkett and Moore, "Consultation," 1.

[100] S. Waite, "New Filing Regime Weighs on HK Issuance," *Finance Asia*, 1 (2014).

[101] C. Chan, "Fairer Deal Needed for Retail Investors in IPOs," *South China Morning Post*, 1 (2014).

[102] D. Thomas and E. Barreto, "Alibaba's choice of U.S. IPO spurred by rivals, Hong Kong impasse," *Reuters*, 1 (2014).

[103] Hong Kong Financial Services Development Council, "Positioning Hong Kong as an International IPO Centre of Choice," unpublished professional research, Hong Kong Financial Services Development Council (2014), 2.

to the same information. Therefore, the current inequality in information between institutional and retail investors is unfair and violates principles underlying various pieces of legislation in Hong Kong.

3.4.7 Conclusion: The Gap Is Unfair

Overall, compared to efforts undertaken by the US Securities and Exchange Commission ("SEC"), Hong Kong regulators offer less specific guidance around the defined terms and permissible exceptions to standard disclosure and enforcement by HKEx and SFC appears less active as relates to dealings with institutional investors. In other words, the rules in Hong Kong are less delineated than those in the United States. Nonetheless, the principles enshrined in Hong Kong's regulatory framework clearly demonstrate the city's commitment to protecting retail investors and providing equal access to information for all investors. As Hong Kong regulators at least subconsciously recognize an information gap, and consider this gap between institutional and retail investors unfair, it is crucial for Hong Kong to take steps toward bridging it.

3.5 Recommendations for Bridging the Gap

In stages of the IPO process where the extent of this unfair information gap is too great, market participants and policy-makers alike should act to rectify the problem.[104] While there is regulation as covered by legislation including the CO, the SFO and the Listing Rules, "the rules on the books are not enough to guarantee fair and balanced regulation," as Donald has observed.[105] Other than increased regulation, which may create negative externalities,[106] issuers and regulators can reference initiatives taken in other jurisdictions and consider implementing a two-pronged approach to overcome this gap. First, issuers can make deal-specific improvements to each stage in the IPO process. Second, policy-makers can better educate retail investors to bridge the information gap. While these recommendations require further research and refinement prior to implementation, they provide the basis for positive change.

---

[104] G. C. Bible, "NYSE/NASD IPO Advisory Committee," unpublished professional guidelines, FINRA (2003), 1.

[105] Donald, *A Financial Centre for Two Empires*, 188.

[106] Ibid., 226.

3.5.1   IPO Process

Issuers and their underwriters can take deal-specific measures in each stage
of the IPO where an unfair information gap exists. As aforementioned,
while the gap in the pre-marketing process can be acceptable in the spirit of
market facilitation, the gap in the marketing, book-building and allocation
processes need to be mitigated. Issuers can be incentivized to implement
these measures by considering that retail investors form a solid foundation
of companies' shareholding base, particularly given the clawback mechanism. Better engaging retail investors can further build demand momentum
in IPOs and support higher share price in the aftermarket by encouraging
investor confidence and long-term investments.

3.5.1.1   Marketing

Retail investors receive the prospectus only immediately before HKPO.
Thus, issuers can provide better access to information for retail investors
via two key tools: online publications and media – earned, paid and
social. While these additional materials cannot substitute the additional
information received by institutional investors, they are crucial to lessen-
ing the gap. This is due to the fact that although financial factors disclosed
in the prospectus are extremely important, institutional investors often
rely on various non-financial factors such as management credibility and
experience to make investment decisions.[107] These non-financial factors
are often best conveyed through personal interaction, and when not
available, through multi-media contact. It is true that any misrepresenta-
tions in such a medium can trigger greater liability for issuers and
underwriters if investors rely upon information received to make investment decisions. However, this risk can be managed with assistance from
legal counsel.

To elaborate, issuers can first publish selective content from existing
roadshow materials for institutional investors on their investor relations
sites. These materials can include slides from roadshow presentations
and marketing videos. In fact, the use of advertisements and publicity
materials in roadshows are already regulated to ensure that all information is accurate.[108] Minimal work and costs are required as the issuer can
publish existing content on readily available websites without significant
regulatory hurdles. Users should register and agree to online disclaimers

---

[107] M. Pinelli, "Institutional investors Support IPOs That Come to Market Well Prepared,"
unpublished professional guidelines, Ernst and Young (2013), 2.
[108] Listing Rule 9.08.

before they are provided access to these materials to minimize issuers' liability and track retail engagement.

Second, media can be extremely effective. In fact, per a recent SFC Retail Investor Survey (RIS), media is the best channel for retail marketing.[109] Issuers can use a variety of paid and earned media including advertisements, interviews via TV and newspapers, as well as presentations at relevant forums to communicate with retail investors. For example, Alibaba created effective marketing videos featuring its management and clients during its IPO, to engage more broadly with public investors.

3.5.1.2   Book-Building and Pricing

The US can provide useful reference, as SEC Commissioner Luis Aguilar recommended engaging retail shareholders through electronic forums.[110] In fact, online forums on corporate websites allow for monitored discussion among retail investors, interaction between investors and issuers, as well as compliant guidance on the status of book-building and on pricing from issuers to retail investors, all of which had been previously available to only institutional investors. This gives retail investors better access to information and allows them to better gauge market sentiment.

Currently, retail investors in mainland China utilize a popular social platform called Snowball,[111] which is a social platform where investors, many of which are retail, discuss various IPOs and stocks. It also provides investors with cross-market and cross-product data search as well as news subscription, covering not only A-share stocks, but also Hong Kong and US stocks. While it is possible for underwriters and issuers to monitor information via these platforms, it would be beneficial for such platforms to be centralized and provided by the issuers or regulators, so that quality information can be exchanged in a more efficient and moderated manner.

3.5.1.3   Allocation

Per market practice, the allocation process focuses on allocating to high quality institutional investors to achieve an optimal mix of short-term

---

[109] SFC, "Retail Investor Survey 2011," unpublished professional research, SFC (2011), 2.

[110] L. A. Aguilar, "Looking at Corporate Governance from the Investor's Perspective," unpublished professional research, Harvard University (2014), 2.

[111] Snowball xueqiu.com (2014).

investors creating liquidity and long-term investors supporting long-term growth.[112] While it is difficult to meaningfully change the allocation mechanism given the sheer number of retail investors, it is possible to help retail investors better understand the process and incentivize them to have a more optimal mix of short-term and long-term holders.

First, guidance from issuers on allocation can encourage retail investors to be less prone to disposing shares right after the IPO, which also mitigates downward pressure on the share price and volatility in the aftermarket.[113] While tailored guidance may be prohibitively expensive, online announcements incur minimal costs. A brief announcement of the allocation rationale and how it strengthens aftermarket trading can foster trust and encourage more long-term investments. It is true that misleading guidance can incur additional liability such as lawsuits from unfair losses.[114] However, general guidance on book-building information that is accurate and not misleading, as has been practiced in the market for institutional investors, can be effective for retail investors as well.[115]

Second, as retail investors tend to hold more short-term, companies have offered incentives to encourage more long-term retail participation. For example, Hong Kong's subway operator, MTR Corp, implemented a Retail Investor Incentive Plan during its IPO, and on its one-year and two-year IPO anniversary, it distributed stock dividends to shareholders who held their stake since the IPO.[116] In 2014, Hong Kong Airlines discussed implementing a Retail Investors Lottery Reward Plan – which would have rewarded mileage and airport VIP memberships – to retail investors holding above a certain amount of the stock for the long-term from the IPO.[117] While companies in these previous examples may have contemplated doing so given its retail-driven business, their strategies are nonetheless helpful for all issuers to consider, as these can simultaneously promote their underlying business – such as by offering deals for their products and services – and incentivize retail investors to hold more long-term.

---

[112] Birkett, "The MoFo Guide," 75.

[113] T. Sifert, "Think Tank Takes Up HK IPO Woes," *IFR Asia*, 2 (2014).

[114] J. Stempel, "Facebook, Zuckerberg, Banks Must Face IPO Lawsuit: Judge," Reuters, 2 (2013)

[115] I. H. Davison, "The Operation and Regulation of the Hong Kong Securities Industry," unpublished legislative research, FSTB HK (1988), 291.

[116] MTR, "Investor Relations," unpublished corporate releases, MTR (2003), 1.

[117] S. Wong, "Long-Term Shareholders May Receive Flying Rewards," *Apple Daily*, 2 (2014).

Third, after the IPO, since retail investors continue to be excluded from regular communications, such as earnings calls,[118] companies can use social media to publicize important corporate announcements and encourage retail participation, thereby mitigating this gap.[119]

3.5.2   General Knowledge/Analytical Skills

Other than deal-specific measures, policy-makers can also enhance the overall knowledge and skills of the investing public to mitigate the unfair information gap, since educated investors can better protect themselves. Moreover, education would help retail investors better analyze the information to which they do have access, so as to avoid being overwhelmed with information.[120] As Victor Fleischer put it, "[t]he Internet makes it easier to acquire information and access markets, but it does not necessarily improve the quality of information."[121]

Per the SFC RIS, close to half of retail investors do not know the latest data on attributes they consider most important in investment decisions.[122] Moreover, the attributes they consider most important may not provide them with the best analysis, as retail investors look at different metrics from institutional investors, whose investments tend to perform better.[123] For example, retail investors are more likely to sell their shares in the short-term, before fully monetizing on capital gains, which is evidence of less informed decision-making.[124] In other words, retail investors often disregard or misinterpret readily available public information.[125] In an environment where available information is already limited, retail investors need better knowledge to be able to fully use what is available. This will enhance the quality of their investment decisions and improve overall

---

[118] Chemmanur and Hu, "The Role of Institutional Investors," 23.

[119] Pinelli, "Institutional Investors," 3.

[120] T. A. Paredes, "Blinded by the Light: Information Overload and Its Consequences for Securities Regulation," unpublished academic research, Washington University in St. Louis School of Law (2003), 1.

[121] Fleischer, "Insight," 761.

[122] SFC, "Key Findings of Retail Investor Survey," unpublished professional research, SFC (2008), 2.

[123] Chemmanur and Hu, "The Role of Institutional Investors," 23.

[124] BlackRock, ""Bad News Is Good" – A Hard Habit for Investors to Kick," unpublished professional research, BlackRock (2014), 2.

[125] L. C. Field and M. Lowry, "Institutional versus Individual Investment in IPOs: The Importance of Firm Fundamentals," unpublished academic research, Penn State University (2009), 490.

market quality.[126] In fact, investor education allows the SFC to better achieve all of its regulatory objectives outlined in the SFO, limits the need for further information disclosures, and makes existing disclosures more meaningful to retail investors.[127]

3.5.2.1   Supplementary Materials

Given that the prospectus is the only offering document and most important source of information for retail investors in making investment decisions for Hong Kong IPOs, it is essential that it is read by retail investors in the intended manner. However, retail investors often do not have the necessary knowledge to fully digest the content of a prospectus within the limited time of HKPO.[128] Regulators can mitigate this by providing supplementary materials to better educate investors on the general structure of prospectuses so that retail investors are aware of what information is included and where to look for particular attributes they want to focus on.[129] This will encourage more retail investors to read the prospectus and feel comfortable navigating through the long and dense document. This manner of providing general guidance on prospectuses can be possible without incurring significant additional liability, provided that there are clear disclaimers – disclaimers should explicitly state that the materials provide general guidance for educational purposes and only the full prospectus should be relied upon for making investment decisions.

3.5.2.2   Access to Data

The SFC can publish existing data in more user-friendly formats and consider publishing additional types of data otherwise available to institutional investors for retail investors. First, data currently published by the SFC, such as open short, is only available in PDF and CSV formats for isolated dates.[130] Allowing the data to be easily exportable to Excel for selected stocks over a specified period of time would be much more useful for retail investors. Second, the SFC can publish other data points, such as

---

[126] Field, "Institutional versus Individual," 514.

[127] § 4 of the SFO.

[128] S. Finch, J. Grant, J. Hamer, J. Hudson and J. Muraca, "Improving Prospectus Disclosure For Retail Investors," unpublished academic research, Australian Securities and Investments Commission (2011), 2.

[129] R. Bashford, "Global Investor Survey International Competition for Capital Intensifies," unpublished professional research, FTI Consulting (2014), 4.

[130] SFC, "Aggregated Reportable Short Positions of Specified Shares," unpublished professional research, SFC (2014), 2.

trading volumes, to give investors a better sense of liquidity.[131] While this information may be already available via brokers, it may be valuable for the SFC to provide it as an authoritative source.

3.5.2.3   Internet and Social Media

The Investor Education Center ("IEC") is a subsidiary of the SFC established by the SFO to enhance financial literacy in Hong Kong. It offers helpful resources for retail investors both in-person and online.[132] For instance, it provides a wide range of informative pamphlets and educational videos on its website. However, retail investors nonetheless use resources from well-known online personalities, such as David Webb,[133] as well as third-party websites such as aastocks,[134] ET net,[135] Sina Finance and Yahoo Finance as major sources of information. It would be beneficial for the IEC to analyze these websites for crucial sources of information relevant to retail investors to provide better materials covering IPOs by using the Internet via social media, regular activity and interactive communication.

First, the IEC can use the HKEx website and social media to bring more traffic to its own website, as many retail investors may not be aware of these helpful resources. Second, the IEC can reference efforts by the SEHK for institutional investors. Currently, the SEHK sends bi-monthly newsletters via email to various institutional investors and underwriters that highlight the latest listing activities, IPO statistics, Hong Kong stock market performance reviews as well as major business initiatives and events.[136] These newsletters are also published on the SEHK website, but can be easily buried and difficult to find. In fact, as of November 19, 2014, the same newsletters can be found in two different locations, one of which is not updated for the latest newsletter.[137] The HKEx also has published newsletters containing more comprehensive information, but it has only been published twice – in January and July of 2012.[138] The IEC can learn from the HKEx's experiences and consider sending regular newsletters to those who subscribe and publish periodically via social

---

[131] SFC, "Market & Industry Statistics," unpublished professional research, SFC (2014), 2.

[132] Investor Education Centre, www.hkiec.hk/web/en/index.html (2018).

[133] Webb-Site Reports, webb-site.com/ (2014).

[134] AAStocks, www.aastocks.com/en/default.aspx (2012).

[135] ETNet, www.etnet.com.hk/www/tc/home/index.php (2014).

[136] Currently sent by the issuer marketing team, client business development, global markets, Hong Kong Exchanges and Clearing Ltd.

[137] HKEx Listing in Hong Kong Bi-Monthly Newsletter 2014.

[138] HKEx Exchange Newsletters 2014.

media to attract subscribers. Third, the IEC can engage retail investors through online forums as well, particularly those that allow for Q&As.[139] While transaction-specific Q&A sessions may be costly, general Q&A sessions through online resources similar to Reddit[140] may be effective and cost-efficient in resolving common inquiries among retail investors. Discussion via similar tools should be monitored by the IEC to ensure quality discussion.

3.5.2.4   Workshops and Events

The HKEx has held events for retail investors, such as the latest, Third Annual Retail ETF Event series,[141] which includes an ETF and stock investment simulation game offering awards, an ETFs and Options Investment Expo, which invited various institutions to give workshops on their products and offered free giveaways, as well as an Options Education TV Program. While such announcements can be found on the SEHK website via the Circulars section,[142] they are not easily accessible nor well publicized to the public. In fact, the Circulars section had no mention of any retail related publications before 2013, where even the First Annual Retail ETF Event series announcement was not available on the website.

3.5.2.5   Survey

While the SFC RIS can be extremely helpful, none has been done since 2009.[143] This would be an extremely helpful starting point to learn more about the retail population in the present in order to better tailor recommendations for improvement.

3.6   Conclusion

Given the growing importance of retail investors in the IPO process and aftermarket trading,[144] it is crucial for capital markets to better engage retail investors in the IPO process. While retail investors have historically

---

[139] Aguilar, "Looking at Corporate Governance," 3.

[140] S. Macale, "A Rundown of Reddit's History and Community," *The Next Web*, 1 (2011).

[141] HKEx, "Third Annual Retail ETF Event Information," unpublished professional guideline, HKEx (2014), 1.

[142] HKEx, "The Stock Exchange of Hong Kong Limited (SEHK) Circular," unpublished legislative circular, HKEx (2018), 1.

[143] HKEx, "Retail Investor Survey – Past Issues," unpublished professional research, HKEx (2010), 1.

[144] HKEx, "Shareholding Analysis," unpublished professional research, HKEx (2013), 116.

been unfairly provided with less information, this will need to be resolved to uphold the market principles of fairness and equality that are enshrined in each major piece of financial legislation, as is the case in Hong Kong. In fact, limiting the information gap is crucial to each capital market's success and standard-setting as an international financial center, as it forms the foundation of what roles different investors can play and how well they can engage in the market. Hence, policy-makers and market participants must take action to bridge this unfair information gap between institutional and retail investors.

Finance, Intangibles and the Privatization of Knowledge

UGO PAGANO[*]

4.1 Introduction

Financialization of the economy and privatization of intangibles have reinforced each other. In many ways, they make two sides of the same coin. Consider, for instance, knowledge. Knowledge is an intangible, and as with many intangibles it can be used without consuming or even touching it. As most intangibles, knowledge is a non-rival good: using more of it in one application does not reduce its availability for another application. If knowledge is publically available, it cannot be the object of financial claims: everyone can use it and no one can claim an income from the fact that others use it, or a monopoly rent from the fact (s)he is the only agent who is allowed to use it. Similarly, if knowledge is in the mind of an individual, in non-slave societies financial claims on knowledge are impossible, because they would imply the ownership of person. Also, a trade secret cannot be the object of financial claims because, to understand its worth, the knowledge should be disclosed, which would destroy its value as a trade secret. Also, for this reason, the value of a trade secret is so uncertain that it is impossible to hold any financial claim on it.

Unsurprisingly, until recently, intangibles like knowledge could not be a relevant part of the capital of a firm. They lacked the attributes of priority, universality and durability. Only these attributes can allow financial claims on a machine or a building and give them the qualification of capital.[1] For instance, the holder of a trade secret cannot claim any priority against the holder of identical trade secrets. Moreover, her claims would not be universal but would be limited to the persons who had had

---

[*] I am very grateful to David Donald for all his useful comments and suggestions. David is not responsible for my mistakes but he has greatly helped me to avoid some mistakes and to improve many parts of this chapter.
[1] This important point has been made by K. Pistor, *The Code of Capital* (Princeton NJ: Princeton University Press, 2019, forthcoming).

some working relations with her. And finally, the durability of the privilege could end at any moment when other independent discoverers of the substance of the secret disclose it. Knowledge in the form of a trade secret – and even more if held by humans or in the public domain – could not be part of the capital of a firm.

The situation has substantially changed with the introduction and the massive diffusion of intellectual property rights (IPRs). IPRs give a priority to their holders also against individual who make an independent discovery, have a duration longer than most machines and, thanks to recent international treaties, have almost universal application.

Intangibles, such as privatized knowledge, have therefore become part of firms' capital and have greatly increased the assets on which it is possible to have financial claims. However, the increasing share of intangible assets has not only meant a dramatic expansion of finance but also an impressive change of its characteristics. Most intangible assets, including IPR, are highly specific and often even unique assets, which cannot have thick markets like buildings and machines. For this reason they cannot be a good source of collateral for traditional types of banking, so that their expansion has been an important cause of a shift toward other forms of finance.

Section 4.2 of this chapter compares different types of financing in a framework of incomplete law, which does not require that the rights and the duties of the individuals are completely specified. The focus is on two very stylized typologies of finance: loans secured by collateral (banking) and equity funding of firms run by professional managers (equity), which turn out to have a different distribution of ex-ante and ex-post rights.

Section 4.3 considers the relationship between finance and specificity. It is shown to be a complex one, where financial structure influences the degree of specificity of the assets, and the degree of specificity of the assets influences the financial structure of firms. We may have multiple equilibria, and the selection of a particular equilibrium can depend on a different mix or a new regulation of financial activities, or it may be due to the fact that the degree of specificity of the underlying assets has changed.

Section 4.4 argues that, while the changes of financial claims have received much attention, some relevant structural changes may be rather due to the nature of the underlying assets. In particular, the spectacular increase of intangibles is likely to have increased the role of equity and other firm-basis forms of finance relative to traditional forms of banking, guaranteed by assets with thick markets and intelligible market values.

The concluding section argues that excessive financialization mirrors the abnormal growth of intangibles and, in particular, of the assets related to the privatization of knowledge. For this reason, international regulations should also tackle the negative effects of over-enclosing the knowledge commons.

4.2   Incomplete Law and the Nature of Financial Transactions

According to Fuller, law is the activity of subjecting human behavior to rules. Since humans are also engaged in other activities (such as producing food), there are trade-offs between law and other activities.[2] These trade-offs make law incomplete. Completing the law is sometimes not feasible, and is often a costly enterprise. Only within certain limits is it worthwhile to complete the law. Moreover, some other trade-offs are internal to law. For instance, if rules have to guide human behavior, they cannot change too often. At the same time they have to adapt to a changing reality. There is a trade-off between flexibility and rigidity of rules.

Another important trade-off considered by Fuller is that between the comprehensibility and the technical precision of a rule. Even more important are the trade-offs between the specificity (deepness) and generality (wideness) of rules considered by Pistor and Xu,[3] which we represent in Table 4.1 and Figure 4.1. Ex-ante specific rules prescribing in detail what to do in particular situations favor effective enforcement in particular cases, but they fail to cover a large number of cases. Here, incompleteness may be due to an insufficient generality of the rule involving *wideness incompleteness*. Ex-ante general rules that cover a large range of possible situations suffer from the opposite problem. Incompleteness may stem from their lack of precision and their superficial nature may involve a form of *deepness incompleteness*.

---

[2] This trade-off emerges in what Fuller defines as the morality of aspiration that is the human effort to make the best of their lives. However, Fuller's view is much broader and also includes what he calls the morality of duties, which has important consequences, including singling out the characteristics that a legal system should satisfy. L. Fuller, *The Morality of Law* (New Haven CT: Yale University Press, 1969).

[3] K. Pistor and C. Xu, "Incomplete Law," *International Law and Politics*, 35 (2003), 931–1013.

Table 4.1 *Forms of Legal Incompleteness*

	Detailed ex-post Enforcement	Wide ex-post Enforcement	Form of Incompleteness
Ex-ante specific rule	Yes	No	Wideness Incompleteness
Ex-ante general rule	No	Yes	Deepness Incompleteness

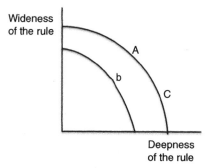

Figure 4.1 The Legal Incompleteness Trade-off

Hence we must face a legal trade-off between *wideness incompleteness* and *deepness incompleteness*. In some cases, rules can be revised without sacrificing one objective for the other. If we can move from b to point A of Figure 4.1 we can improve both the wideness and the deepness of legal rules. By contrast, moving from A to C involves improved deepness at the expenses of reduced wideness of the rules. When wideness and deepness of rules can both be improved with no reduction of the other, no choice between them is required but, when we reach a point where a trade-off exists, we must balance the costs of one form of legal incompleteness against the other and face the problem finding the less damaging forms of legal incompleteness.

Observe that in Kelsen's mainstream legal approach, law is treated as a consistent set of rules and no incompleteness is admitted in the rule of law. In terms of the Hohfeldian tradition,[4] this involves a consistency among the legal positions of all the persons acting in the same legal

---

[4] W. N. Hohfeld, "Fundamental Legal Conceptions as Applied in Judicial Reasoning," *Yale Law Journal*, 26 (1917), 710.

system. In the framework of complete law, rules would specify both the extension of the rights of a certain individual (i.e., their boundary with the exposures of this individual) and the corresponding extension of the duties of other individuals (i.e., their boundaries with their liberties).

By contrast, in a situation of incomplete law only the rights, or only the duties (or none of them!), would be completely defined ex-ante. Some ex-post adjustment is necessary. When some legal positions can be better defined than the others, an obvious strategy, and sometimes even a necessity, of law-making is to define the positions that can be defined ex-ante, leaving to ex-post decisions the definition of the other positions on the basis of additional future information. In this respect, we can define different legal arrangements arising from some stylized forms of legal uncertainty.

Complete law with fully defined rights and duties is feasible when it is possible to define both with certainty the rights and the corresponding duties (case 1 of Table 4.2). We have two intermediate situations. In one situation, it is possible to spell out precisely some rights but not the corresponding duties (case 2). In the other situation, it is possible to spell out the duties but not the corresponding rights (case 3). Because of the first type of legal uncertainty we may therefore have situations when ex-ante rights or duties are defined and some ex-post governance of duties or rights is necessary. In this case, while the governance cannot be entirely ruled by the initial agreements, it is however guided by the legal positions that it was possible to define ex-ante. Some legal interpretation and disagreement on the ex-post nature of the rights (duties) matching the ex-ante duties (rights) is likely to arise and the initial constraints may in some cases include a certain number of possible outcomes. Such guidance is obviously absent in case for case 4 where legal uncertainty involves both rights and duties and ex-post definition of rights and duties cannot be guided by some initial definitions of some legal positions.

Table 4.2 *Legal Positions and Uncertainty*

	Certain Duties	Uncertain Duties
Certain Rights	(1) Ex-ante defined rights; Ex-ante defined duties	(2) Ex-ante defined rights; Ex-post defined duties
Uncertain Rights	(3) Ex-ante defined duties; Ex-post defined rights	(4) Ex-post defined rights; Ex-post defined duties

The possibility of defining ex-ante rights and/or duties characterizes different systems of legal orderings considered in Table 4.3. The ex-ante definition of rights and duties allows a complete legislation under which it is possible to write complete contracts. In case (1) contract law can here be a pervasive system of legal ordering and the theoretical construction of an economy with complete contracts can even sound as a reasonable description of an economic system.

When the rights can be clearly defined ex-ante but the corresponding duties are uncertain, the initial contracts fail to offer a satisfactory legal ordering and contract law needs to be integrated with liability law and bankruptcy law. This is case (2). Much constitutional law and international law also offer a clear definition of rights leaving to policy-makers the task of making the necessary ex-post adjustments of duties. Judicial proceedings are required to define the ex-post duties that are consistent with the ex-ante rights. This is the case of accidents, analyzed by Guido Calabresi, and it is also the case of individuals unable to fulfill the duties that were agreed under the initial contract.

By contrast, negligence law, criminal law, duties of care and regulations fall under case (3), where duties are precisely defined ex-ante and rights adjusted to the existing duties only ex-post. Since the goal of the system is still the satisfaction of the rights, regulatory activity has to verify continuously how in practice the ex-ante duties satisfy the targeted ex-post rights. For this reason, regulatory activity bundles together rule-making and enforcement powers.

Case (4) is a case in which both ex-ante duties and ex-ante rights cannot be defined. In this case pervasive ex-ante legal uncertainty means

Table 4.3 *Legal Outcomes in a World of Uncertainty*

	Ex-ante Defined Duties (Liberties)	Ex-post Defined Duties (Liberties)
Ex-ante Defined Rights	(1) Complete legislation; complete contracts	(2) Liability law and judicial decision; social and welfare policy; bankruptcy law
Ex-post Defined Rights	(3) Regulation, rules of negligence, rules on duties of care	(4) New law-making power; corporate and public executive powers

that there is wide discretionary power in the ex-post rules. In this case the only thing that can be done ex-ante is to agree on a legitimate authority (private or public), which has the power to establish and balance the ex-post rights and duties.

It is very difficult to find real-life governance systems that fall under one of these pure four cases. However, we can see how traditional banking activity and equity finance are both characterized by legal uncertainty and differ in the type of legal positions that can be defined ex-ante.

Traditional banking falls mainly under (2). Creditors have well-defined ex-ante rights to which the ex-post duties of the borrowers are adjusted. In some particular cases, such as default, some ex-post governance of the relation is necessary. Bankruptcy rules differ in different countries and involve some redefinitions of the duties of the borrowers to which the ex-ante rights of the creditors have to be readjusted.[5]

Shareholding finance falls mainly under (3). Corporate managers have well defined ex-ante duties, which involve ex-post rights (dividends and values of the shares) of shareholders. Their duty of care involves a certain vagueness of the ex-post actions that best fits the rights. Because of the discretionary power of managers, shareholders have to monitor that managers are fulfilling their ex-post duties.

In a regime of incomplete law, equity and debt finance turn out to be also different for different types of the underlying investments that we will consider in the following section.

4.3   Finance and Specificity

The Modigliani-Miller equivalence of equity and debt financing relies on the idea that it is the same to contract a loan and buy a firm or to buy directly a firm that has contracted a loan at the same conditions.[6] Their argument ignores the fact that agents with different reputations and assets available as collateral face different costs when they borrow. Moreover, it ignores bankruptcy costs.

However, this chapter will argue that the main problem with the Modigliani-Miller theorem is that it ignores the relationship between

---

[5] For instance, in the United States an insolvent debtor can file under Chapter 11 of the Bankruptcy Code to obtain some rearrangement of the ex-ante rights of the creditors. Other legislations do not allow a similar rearrangement.

[6] See F. Modigliani and M. Miller, "The Cost of Capital and Theory of Investment," *The American Economic Review*, 48 (1958), 261–297 and in particular pp. 268–269 where they formulate their famous theorem.

technological choice and governance structure. The technical assets that are best under one governance system are not necessarily the best assets under a different system. If we are in a world without bankruptcy, where managers' duties can be completely specified, then the two systems turn out to be equivalent. However, in a world with legal uncertainty the two systems operate best with different technical assets and tend, in turn, to bias the choice of technical assets. In particular the two systems tend to favor the use of assets characterized by different degrees of specificity.[7]

The degree of specificity of an asset is the share of its value that is lost when it is moved from one use to another best employments. Thus, the specificity of an asset is not an intrinsic characteristic of the asset. Its degree of specificity may increase because some alternative employments have vanished or may increase because new opportunities have opened. We will see in section 4.4 how institutional changes have increased the specificity of assets in the modern economy. In this section we focus on the relation between different forms of finance and different degrees of asset-specificity.

Under traditional banking, creditors have well defined ex-ante rights to which the ex-post duties of the borrowers are adjusted. Their rights have priority over shareholders in case of bankruptcy. Their interests are best protected if the borrower engages in projects that involve the development of low specificity assets that can be easily redeployed in case of bankruptcy. By contrast they are not interested in high returns of risky projects involving high asset specificity.

Under equity financing, shareholders have ex-post rights (e.g., to receive dividends) corresponding to managers' ex-ante duties to the corporation. Shareholders are the last ones to be compensated in the case of bankruptcy, and gain little from low-specificity assets in the event of liquidation. By contrast they share the gains of risky projects characterized by high asset specificity.[8]

---

[7] The degree of specificity is the share of its value or productivity of the resource, lost when the resource is moved to its next best use. Williamson attracted the attention of economists on the importance of specificity to understand the nature of the different governance systems. O. E. Williamson, *The Economic Institutions of Capitalism* (New York: The Free Press, 1985).

[8] This chapter treats here debt and equity as two forms of financing and assumes that each group of financiers when prevalent can exercise some pressure on the management of the organization. The important issue concerning the shareholders as "owners" of the corporation is not considered. The view that the shareholders are the owners of the corporation is increasingly challenged by the recent legislation. In this chapter, equity appears only as a form of finance, and not as a form of ownership of the corporation.

Higher degrees of asset specificity increase the value of the company for shareholders and decrease its value for creditors. One may argue that for each degree of asset specificity there is an optimal debt-equity mix maximizing the value of the company.

Debt is a cheap system of governance where the financier needs only to monitor the liquidity (non-specificity) of its assets. However when the sacrifice of valuable high-specificity projects exceeds a certain threshold, some equity finance increases the value of the company.

An optimal debt-equity ratio should correspond to each degree of asset-specificity. Low levels of specificity favor low equity/debt ratios, and high levels of specificity favor high equity/debt ratios.[9]

However, specificity characteristics cannot be assumed to be independent of the existing governance mechanism.

If creditors have control over the governance of the firm, they will favor low-specificity investment projects. Their ex-ante rights of recovering their capital are particularly valuable if managers have (over-)strong duties to adopt low-specificity projects. Low-specificity investments are easily recoverable in case of liquidation of the assets of the firm.

By contrast, if shareholders control the governance of the firm they will favor high-specificity investments. Their ex-post rights to earn profits will be translated in over-strong duties of high-specificity projects that increase the value of the shares.

In other words, the rights of creditors and shareholders protect and truncate their earnings in different ways. Creditors have an ex-post priority right to receive back the funds lent, with agreed interest, in case of the debtor's insolvency, but their rights are truncated in receiving the profits of the enterprise. Shareholders have no protection for their capital contributions and no priority (over creditors) in the case of insolvency, but they are not truncated in their right to receive ex-post earnings from projects. Because of their different interests, shareholders and creditors tend to favor different asset structures.[10]

Thus, causation can run in opposite directions. It can run from the financial form of governance to the degree of asset-specificity, or vice versa. Figure 4.2 joins these two directions of causation and suggests how

---

[9] The account of this direction of causation (from degree of specificity to governance structure) is based on Williamson, *Institutions of Capitalism*.

[10] The account of this direction of causation (from financial structure to degree of specificity) is based on A. Nicita and U. Pagano, "Finance-Technology Complementarities: an Organizational Equilibria Approach," *Structural Change and Economic Dynamics*, 37 (2016), 43–51.

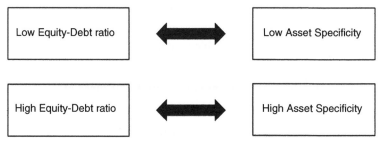

Figure 4.2 Financial Equilibria

they can generate multiple financial equilibria characterized by different finance-technology complementarities.[11] Financial equilibria define self-reinforcing processes. A certain type of assets may reinforce its nature by favoring the corresponding form of financial governance and, vice versa, a certain form of financial governance may reinforce its characteristics by favoring the related types of assets.

Because of the self-reinforcing nature of each system of governance, one may expect a certain polarization of the different organizations.

One may argue that appropriate regulations, such as limits on permissible leverage, may try to avoid extreme polarizations. However, they may also produce useless standardized hybrids, unable to cover the different nature of the assets characterizing the firms to be financed.

Moreover some regulations may have unintended effects. For instance, by making managers duties more responsive to shareholder ex-post rights, regulations may push firms toward an excessively high level of asset-specificity, and damage creditors' interests. Or, in other cases, by making managers more responsive to ex-ante creditors rights to collateral, regulations may push toward excessively low levels of asset-specificity and damage shareholders interests.

Other problems of regulation have to do with the complex nature of asset-specificity. In comparison to traditional societies, modern societies have decreased the degree of specificity of many assets but in many cases, the employment of specific assets is still necessary to increase productivity and for many innovative activities.

However, an increase of the productivity of specific assets does, not seem to be the main cause of the recent increase in their intensity. As we will see

---

[11] For a formal analysis of financial equilibria and the precise conditions necessary for their multiplicity, see Nicita A., Pagano U. (2016) Finance-Technology Complementarities: an Organizational Equilibria Approach. *Structural Change and Economic Dynamics.* V. 37 pp. 43–51.

in section 4.4, this increase has more to do with the increasing monopolization of modern capitalism and the related privatization of the knowledge commons, than with an inevitable tendency of modern technology.

4.4   Intellectual Monopoly and the Enclosures of Knowledge Commons

According to Schumpeter, capitalism is characterized by a process of "industrial mutation." This process "incessantly revolutionizes the economic structure *from within*, incessantly destroying the old one, incessantly creating a new one. This process of Creative Destruction is the essential fact about capitalism. It is what capitalism consists of and what every capitalist concern has got to live in."[12]

In spite of Schumpeter's influence on the discipline of economics, his analysis of capitalism may be rather outdated. Schumpeter almost ignored the role of intellectual property (the term "intellectual property" was not even generally used at the time he was writing). He did not perceive the protection that legal intellectual monopoly could offer against his process of creative destruction. His analysis belongs to a period in which the dramatic reinforcement of what came to be known as intellectual property had not yet taken place. Moreover, his emphasis on entrepreneurial innovation ignores the fact that the distribution of the fruits of innovation and of working knowledge has always been a source of fierce conflict also within the capitalist firm.

In a world of complete law and contracts, the problem of the ex-post distribution of the fruits of working knowledge and of other productive factors would not arise. However, in a situation of incomplete law and contracts the division of the production surplus is highly uncertain. Some institutional solutions, which are available for avoiding opportunistic behavior for non-human capital, are not feasible to reward working knowledge and, in general, human effort.

If machines are specific to each other, different owners can decide to own them jointly and have shares in the same entity. In this way, owners may sell their shares, but not the single machine, whose withdrawal from production might have a dreadful effect on the productivity of the other machines. Moreover, if additional machines are required for production, one can borrow money to buy them, using machines as collateral.

---

[12] J. A. Schumpeter, *Capitalism Socialism and Democracy* (London: Unwin University Books, 1952), 83.

Analogous solutions for the skills and the working knowledge held by workers are much more difficult. One worker cannot own parts of other workers and, in general, individuals cannot own shares of other individuals. Moreover, absent slavery for debt, individuals make an unreliable collateral.

The problem is made even more complex by the non-rival nature of knowledge. The same working knowledge can be used in many other firms even if they contribute very little to its development. Specificity is not an intrinsic characteristic of resources. If new opportunities arise, what is now specific working knowledge may become general-purpose knowledge. Vice-versa, what is general working knowledge may become specific, if existing opportunities close.

Indeed, referring again to the scheme considered in Table 4.3, a new analogous scheme (Table 4.4) may be obtained, showing the different legal systems by which the production of knowledge can be organized.

In a regime of complete law we may define ex-ante the rights on future knowledge and the consequent related (case 1) restrictions on the liberties to use this knowledge. In the case of new knowledge, this solution is particularly difficult. If we have not yet produced the knowledge we are unlikely to be able to specify the future restriction of liberties applicable to given rights of knowledge.

The second approach (case 2) states ex-ante well-defined liberties on the use and the production of knowledge. Some rights on the new knowledge can be attributed ex-post, but only insofar as they do not

Table 4.4 *Knowledge Economy Arrangements*

	Ex-ante defined liberties	Ex-post defined liberties
Ex-ante defined rights	1) Complete contracts on very well defined research projects	3) Intellectual property; closed science; trade secret restrictions
Ex-post defined rights	2) Academic research; rewards and prizes for publications and discoveries; open science; *artisanal independence*	4) Free and creative intellectual exchanges; governance of collective learning

contradict the ex-ante stated liberties to engage in the production of knowledge. Academic research with rewards and prizes for publications and discoveries, open science and the principles of artisanal independence share a clear ex-ante priority of research liberties over the future rights to be rewarded for its outcomes.

The third approach (case 3) specifies ex-ante the rights on knowledge and limits in unpredictable ways the future liberties of the individuals. Intellectual property and closed science developed for profits under a regime of secrecy have these characteristics. Trade secret restrictions and intellectual property rights give employers ex-ante rights on the many fruits of the knowledge acquired by their employees and limits in unpredictable ways the future ex-post liberties of the individuals.

Finally, case 4 is one in which both ex-ante rights and liberties cannot be specified and requires complex forms governance of collective learning under which free and creative intellectual exchanges can take place.

The conflicts related to the appropriation of the working knowledge were treated in different ways by the legal system in different periods. Fisk shows how the capitalist system evolved from regimes of strong workers liberties and weak corporate intellectual property rights to regimes of strong corporate intellectual property rights and of weak workers liberties (or, in terms of Table 4.4, it moved from case 2 to case 3). According to Fisk,[13] three periods marked the transition of American and British common law from the emphasis on workers' liberty to use their knowledge in all employments, to the emphasis on the corporate ownership of intellectual property rights, implying also the enforcement of trade secrets and of restrictive covenants.

As Fisk points out, from 1800 to 1860, courts stated repeatedly that skilled workers had no fiduciary responsibilities.[14] They could not be restricted in their liberties to change employment and use somewhere else the working knowledge acquired in previous employments. Trade secrets were considered to be a limitation of competition and of the fundamental liberties of the workers. Post-employment covenants were usually considered to be illegal, or at least unenforceable.

---

[13] See L. C. Fisk, "Working Knowledge: Trade Secrets, Restrictive Covenants in Employment, and the Rise of Corporate Intellectual Property 1800–1920," *Hastings Law Journal*, 52 (2001), 441, 449, where she explains how the "article is organized chronologically."

[14] See ibid., Pt. I.

From 1860 to 1890, courts started to regard trade secrets as a possible obligation of employment, which should however be explicitly included in the initial contract.[15]

The period 1860–1920 witnessed the diffusion of a more radical view regarding trade secrets as an implicit condition of employment. The breach of trade secrets started to be seen as a misappropriation of property, automatically forbidden by the employment contract.[16]

> In enforcing contracts first, only if they were express, and later by recognizing such contracts as implied-to maintain secrecy of the employer's methods, courts created a new species of "intellectual" property at the expense of older notions of artisanal independence. This was undoubtedly a case of "creative destruction" of one form of economic privilege to create another – the corporate intellectual property.[17]

Artisanal independence was also limited and often destroyed for the majority of workers by the scientific management movement of Frederick Taylor. According to Taylor, artisanal skills had another major drawback for the employers: the traditional system of management was ill-suited to increasing workers' effort.[18] Traditional management relied on the knowledge of the workers, in the sense that the managers believed that the workers knew better than they did how to perform their jobs. Under traditional management, the workers could work less than "fairly" by claiming that a certain amount of time was required to perform a certain job. The situation of "asymmetric information" existing under traditional management implied that the managers had no means of challenging this claim. Taylor's solution to this problem was straightforward: the managers, and not the workers, should know how the jobs could be best performed, plan how they should be executed, and give the workers detailed instructions about their execution.

It was only by gaining control over the labor process that the managers could reverse the situation of asymmetric information and control the workers. Braverman summarizes the content of Taylorism in three different

---

[15] See ibid., Pt. II.
[16] See ibid., Pt. III.
[17] See ibid., p. 445.
[18] In his *Principles of Scientific Management*, Taylor considered how production should "scientifically" be organized by management independently of the knowledge of the workers. A critical and interesting account of Taylor's is contained in H. Braverman, *Labour and Monopoly Capital* (New York: Monthly Review Press, 1974).

principles:[19] (1) dissociation of the labor process from the skills of the workers, (2) separation of conception from execution and (3) use of this monopoly over knowledge to control each step of the labor process and its mode of execution. These principles had not only the effect of controlling workers' effort. It monopolized working knowledge in few individuals and together with trade secrets law contributed to the protection of the private property of the knowledge of the firm.

Even if trade secrets could be seen as a form of corporate intellectual property, they lacked a key-factor distinguishing property from implicit or explicit contracts among the involved parties: the possibility of enforcing the rights *"erga omnes"* and not only *"in personam"* against the contracting parties. Property requires the involvement of a third agent, such as a State, which guarantees the owner's rights against all other parties. This universality of intellectual property makes it tradable and allows its inclusion in the capital of the enterprise. The full-blown institution of intellectual property changes the role and the rights of all parties.[20] With trade secrets obligations or restrictive covenants, anyone who discovers independently a technology used by others has the right to use it. By contrast, if a person has acquired intellectual property in a technology, even persons who have re-discovered independently that technology are forbidden to use it without the owner's permission.

As Radder points out, a product patent is a patent on the product as such:

> That is to say, it is valid for *any* known or unknown process through which the product has been or might be produced. Thus, with the help of the questionable distinction between the invention itself and the patent claims allegedly based on it, the protection acquired through a product patent goes far beyond what has been made available through the actual invention.[21]

Thus, a product patent effectively amounts to appropriating a concept because the patent claims made through a product patent are, effectively, conceptual or theoretical claims. According to Radder, this kind of privatization appropriates full, non-exhaustible potential of knowledge

---

[19] According to Braverman, ibid., p. 86, the analysis of Taylorim is essential to an understanding of the real-life capitalist economy because in Taylor's work "lies a theory which is nothing else than an explicit verbalization of the capitalist mode of production."

[20] This point is a particular application of the general framework developed by K. Pistor, *The Code.*

[21] H. Radder, "Which Scientific Knowledge Is a Common Good?," *Social Epistemology,* 31 (2017), 431, 446–467.

on the basis of a limited scientific achievement and it prevents the (wider and possibly improved) realization of this potential by other researchers (including the present research workers if they leave the firm where they have contributed to the development of the product).

If firms are entitled to take ownership of the intellectual property developed by their workers, and can sell or license it to third parties, this entitlement tilts definitively the balance against employee's independence and in favor of corporate intellectual property.

Once trademarks, industrial designs, patents and all sort other intangibles have become property of the corporation, much working knowledge becomes specific to the corporation for legal reasons. The ex-ante rights on intellectual property of the corporation impose a tight constraint on its employees' liberties to use their working knowledge in other firms. With the ownership of these intangibles the firm may acquire a monopoly of some productive activities and their future improvements. Thus, it is not too surprising that intangibles have become the lion's share of the assets of big corporations and that, in the case of the top 500 corporations, their share grew from 17 percent in 1975 to 87 percent in 2015.[22]

A dramatic mutation of capitalism has occurred. Big corporations have moved from being rich in machines and other physical assets to being rich in intellectual monopoly and other intangible assets, which is a distinctive characteristic of a new form of intellectual monopoly capitalism.

The 1980 Bayth Doyle Act and the 1994 TRIPs agreement[23] (an annex to the institution of the WTO) marked two crucial steps of this dramatic mutation of capitalism. The first allowed the acquisition of private intellectual property rights for innovations developed with the support of public funding. The second introduced a much stronger legislation and enforcement for intellectual property at global level.

In this way, corporations have been able to exploit the huge economies of scale and of scope that arise when knowledge becomes a private input.[24] They have also been able to decentralize production to firms in

---

[22] See U. Pagano, "The Crisis of Intellectual Monopoly Capitalism," *Cambridge Journal of Economics*, 38 (2014), 1409–1429.

[23] The Bayth-Dole Act is US legislation dealing with intellectual property arising from government funded research. The TRIPs agreement is an annex to the institution of the WTO. For a more detailed analysis, refer to U. Pagano, "The Crisis of Intellectual Monopoly Capitalism," *Cambridge Journal of Economics*, 38 (2014), 1409–1429.

[24] In some other cases, this privatization is not even necessary. The infrastructures, used to exchange knowledge are characterized by such network externalities to be a natural monopoly needing very little legal protection.

low labor cost countries without the fear that their competitors could use their know-how.

According to Boyle a second enclosure movement has taken place.[25] The first industrial revolution capitalism was preceded by the enclosure of lands. Modern intellectual monopoly capitalism has been made possible by a second great enclosure, fencing ideas in privately owned fields. Even if there is some evidence against this thesis, as Ostrom suggests,[26] some theories claimed that land enclosures may have even prevented its over-exploitation by the commons crowding the land with an excessive number of animals. No similar claim can be made for the case of intellectual enclosures. Knowledge is a non-rival good, and its fields are not subject to overcrowding. By contrast, the privatization of the field of knowledge sets limits to its access, which decrease productivity and welfare. The agents are forced to specialize in activities based on narrow fields and suffer a dramatic squeeze of investment opportunities which Heller and Eisenberg have appropriately called the anti-commons tragedy.[27]

The so-called knowledge society emerges from the following paradox. The non-rival nature of knowledge, which could in principle favor small, and even self-managed, firms, is used to create artificial economies of scale which make cheap acquisition and defense of property rights possible only for big business. Absent knowledge privatization, the need to provide incentives to invest in human capital would be an argument favoring the labor-hiring-capital solution.

Because of the monopolization of intellectual capital the knowledge economy can become the least friendly environment for small labor-managed firms and an ideal setting for big corporations. Only the latter centralizing the ownership of much intellectual property can give a partial solution to the anti-commons problem.

---

[25] Boyle claims that we "are in the middle of a second enclosure movement." J. Boyle "The Second Enclosure Movement and the Construction of the Public Domain," *Law and Contemporary Problems*, 66 (2003), 33, 37.

[26] Ostrom provides a large number of cases in which commons for rival goods subject to overcrowding are successful. E. Ostrom, *Governing the Commons: The Evolution of Institutions for Collective Action* (Cambridge: Cambridge University Press, 1990).

[27] Heller and Eisenberg used this term to point out that, because of the non-rival nature of knowledge, the tragedy of the second enclosure movement had an origin opposite to the one that was supposed to justify the enclosure of land in the first enclosure movement. M. A. Heller and R. S. Eisenberg, "Can Patents Deter Innovation? The Anticommons in Biomedical Research," *Science* (May 1, 1998), 698.

The increased intensity of intangible assets has increased the degree of specificity of the assets of the firms. Trademarks, patents, reputation, copyrights, design and projects ownership and industrial secrets are often unique assets. Mainly for legal reasons, they cannot be replicated and have an unclear, and often lower, value outside the firm. Unlike, buildings, land, plants, industrial machines, trucks or airplanes, they do not have thick markets and cannot be used efficiently as collateral. Thus, the weightless economy makes traditional banking increasingly difficult and the equity–debt ratio increases. Because of the self-reinforcing process considered in section 4.3, the increase of the debt–equity ratio in turn favors the increase of asset-specificity.

The fact that intangibles have no thick markets is one of the factors that contributes to increase the volatility of the values of the companies. At the same time, the enormous growth of intangibles has greatly increased financial wealth and companies with a great percentage of intangibles are greatly valued on stock markets.

Financialization of the economy and privatization of intangibles have reinforced each other. In many ways they make two sides of the same coin.

When embodied in human beings or available as public goods, knowledge as intangibles cannot offer a significant basis for securing financial rights. By contrast, commodified and privatized pieces of knowledge become assets on which financial claims can be defined and traded.

In turn, the financialization of the economy induces companies to commodify their intellectual capital. The higher the intensity of private commodified knowledge relative to other types of knowledge, the easier it is to attract cheap finance. Thus, financialization of the economy and commodification of knowledge reinforce each other. The behavior of modern corporations is characterized by an increasing influence of the financial sector and by a high share of intangible assets.

The massive increase of financial wealth and intangible assets has not gone together with an increase of productive capital and of social wealth. Indeed the opposite has been true. The increase in financial wealth has often caused a decrease of total productive capital or, in other words, we have often had a form of capital-destructive financial wealth. As Stiglitz has observed:

> If monopoly power of firms increases, it will show up as an increase in the income of capital, and the present discounted value of that will show up as

an increase in wealth (since claims on the rents associated with that market power can be bought and sold).[28]

By contrast, knowledge that is freely available increases output, but does not show up in balance sheets. Therefore, it would not normally be reflected in the national accounts as wealth. While increasing financial wealth, a process of privatization of knowledge could destroy productive intellectual capital, which becomes available only for a much-decreased number of uses. However, sooner or later, also the financial wealth of society will be threatened by the monopolization of the economy.

When IPRs are reinforced (as happened with the 1994 TRIPs agreements), the surpluses of the different firms are likely to diverge. Some firms enjoy a virtuous circle, where intellectual property induces them to develop new capabilities and, in turn, these capabilities induce them to acquire more intellectual property. Other firms become trapped in a vicious circle. They do not develop skills, because they lack the complementary intellectual property. At the same time, they do not acquire intellectual property, because they have not developed the complementary skills.

Because of IPR protection, many "tangible" production activities can be safely decentralized to low-cost countries, increasing even more the inequality among firms. The firms intensive in the types of jobs advocated by Taylor can be separated from those where more skilled activities take place. These jobs are done in firms which compete for the tasks outsourced by the firm holding the intellectual monopoly, and they become very precarious and poorly paid.

Unsurprisingly, there is a very high level of inequality among firms. As Schwartz points out:

> Using a standard measure for inequality, the Gini index (where 1 equals perfect inequality and 0 equals perfect equality), to assess the distribution of profit just within the [Forbes Global 2000] shows levels of inequality for profits that are significantly higher than any given national economy. The Gini index for the distribution of profits among the [Forbes Global 2000] over the ten year period 2005 to 2015 is .809. By comparison, some of the most unequal societies in the world, South Africa and Brazil, typically have Gini indices of roughly .600, and the highly egalitarian Nordic countries have Ginis typically around .250.[29]

---

[28] J. Stiglitz, "New Theoretical Perspectives on the Distribution of Income and Wealth among Individuals," NBER Working Paper 21189 (2015), 24.

[29] H. M. Schwartz, "Club Goods, Intellectual Property Rights, and Profitability in the Information Economy," *Business and Politics*, 19 (2017), 191, 205.

Workers tend to share part of the benefits of the profits of their firm. Thus, the inequality in the profitability of the different firms causes inequality in the earnings of their employees. Virtually the entire rise in earnings dispersion in the United States from 1978 to 2012 between workers is accounted for by increasing dispersion in average wages paid by the employers of these individuals.[30]

In spite of all striking outcomes, these studies are based only on non-financial firms. We should add to this bleak outlook for (in)equality the fact the new intellectual monopoly capitalism had implied a shift from traditional banking to equity with additional adverse effects on wage dispersion. This has in turn changed the nature of the work in finance from routine business to hedging and other sophisticated activities. According to Philippon, the new setting of financial industry has con- tributed to increase the earnings of the individuals in this sector relative to other sectors. Philippon observes how workers in finance "earn the same education-adjusted wages as other workers until 1990, but by 2006 the premium is 50 per cent on average," with executives in finance earning "250% more than executives elsewhere."[31] Thus, the change in the nature of finance, associated to new intellectual capitalism based on intangibles, has contributed to increase even more the overall level of inequality.

High inequality not only involves an unjust distribution of income, which has devastating social consequences. It also has bad consequences at the level of the general economy. It gives more money to individuals who have a low need to consume and may be simply engaged in competi- tion to overcome others in the wealth rankings. It is true, as Keynes observed: it is far better that an individual tyrannize over his bank balance than over his fellow citizens. However, savings are no guide for future consumption and investment. If no investment in productive capacity is made, the higher the saving the lower will be the future production that is available, and as a consequence the future savings that will be possible. Keynes' paradox of thrift is counterintuitive only because many individuals confuse an act of saving with a future demand for goods or an immediate demand for capital goods.[32]

---

[30] On this point, see J. Song, et al., "Firming up Inequality,' National Bureau of Economic Research Working Paper w21199 (2015).

[31] T. Philippon and R. Ariell, "Wages and Human Capital in the U.S. Finance Industry,"*The Quarterly Journal of Economics*, 127 (2012), 1551, 1605.

[32] "The absurd, though almost universal, idea that an act of individual saving is just as good for effective demand as an act of individual consumption, has been fostered by the fallacy,

The inequity in the distribution of tangible and intangible assets entails that money is given to the individuals who are less likely to specify an effective demand and more likely to increase their savings. However, it is difficult to maintain that excess liquidity in the advanced countries, arising due to a "saving glut" in the low-income countries, was the main cause of the recent financial crisis. In the advanced countries, the recycling of the savings of the low-income countries has, at most, compensated for the decrease in the savings of the high-income countries. In the high-income countries many people needed to borrow because globalization (and stronger intellectual property rights) allowed a decentralization of productive activities in the low-income countries, increasing income inequality in the core countries. At the same time, because of strong intellectual property rights, the low-income countries could not digest their own savings, which had to be recycled through high-income country firms, rich in intellectual property rights. Until the American corporations began investing in China, America (and in general the global economy) boomed.

However, *intellectual monopoly capitalism*[33] was doomed to have an investment crisis also in the intellectual property-rich countries. A reinforcement of intellectual property rights such as occurred with the TRIPS agreements has two effects on investments. The first is an incentive effect. Firms invest to get the benefits of future monopoly rents. The second is a blocking effect. The monopoly rights of other firms may make each investment risky because it may require technologies infringing the intellectual property rights of other firms.

The time profiles of the incentive and of the blocking effects of IPR reinforcement are different. The incentive effect is immediate. As soon as the reinforcement of intellectual property is introduced (and even before, when it is expected to happen) firms are pushed to invest in innovations

---

much more specious than the conclusion derived from it, that an increased desire to hold wealth, being much the same thing as an increased desire to hold investments, must, by increasing the demand for investments, provide a stimulus to their production; so that current investment is promoted by individual saving to the same extent as present consumption is diminished.

It is of this fallacy that it is most difficult to disabuse men's mind. It comes from believing the owner of wealth desires a capital-asset as such, whereas what he desires is its *prospective yield*. Now prospective yield wholly depends on the expectation of future effective demand in relation to conditions of supply." J. M. Keynes, *The General Theory of Employment, Interest, and Money* (London: Macmillan, 1936), 210–212.

[33] On the nature and the crisis of intellectual monopoly capitalism see U. Pagano, "The Crisis of Intellectual Monopoly Capitalism," *Cambridge Journal of Economics*, 38 (2014), 1409–1429.

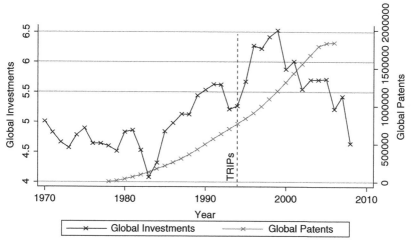

Figure 4.3 Trips and Investment Crisis

that can be patented. The blocking effect comes later, when a substantial number of innovations has been patented and many technological paths are forbidden, or too costly, for non-owners.

Even if complex historical processes always have multiple causes, it is interesting that the reinforcement of IPR could explain both the investment boom of the roaring nineties and the investment famine of the 2000s, leading to the great recession. Figure 4.3 shows how the introduction of the TRIPs agreement was unsurprisingly followed first by a boom of global investment crisis.[34]

4.5 Property and Global Protectionism

While it is commonly accepted wisdom that the financial crisis was due to a savings glut, the crisis was more due to a famine of good investment opportunities than to an increase in the propensity to save.

The monopolization of the global economy has contributed to this famine of investment opportunities. In the crisis of the 1930s, protectionism was considered one of the worst consequences of the financial crisis. However, unlike IPR, even the highest tariff can at most protect the

---

[34] Figure taken from F. Belloc and U. Pagano, "Knowledge Enclosures, Forced Specializations and Investment Crisis," *The European Journal of Comparative Economics*, 9 (2012), 445–483.

national industry against foreign competitors. In the recent downturn, protectionism (in the new form of global IPR rights and costs) has been a cause instead of a consequence of the financial crisis. Because of the lack of good investment opportunities, a flood of savings rushed into the American housing market and other similar speculative business.

Tougher financial regulations have been seen as the main remedy to the financial crisis. The Dodd-Frank Act in the US contains a diluted requirement reminiscent of the 1933 Glass-Steagall Act. With some exceptions, commercial banks should not engage in proprietary trading. Enhancements to Basel II (before the crisis) and the adoption of Basel III (after the crisis) have increased the capital and liquidity requirement of the banks.[35]

These regulations are useful to restore some space for finance in a "banking equilibrium" that had been overtaken by the speculative mood of the pre-crisis economy.

However, the regulations cannot do too much to correct an investment crisis. In some cases they may have made banks too cautious during a period in which quantitative easing was being advocated to re-launch the economy. Low effective demand and the monopolistic nature of many intangible assets were as important in causing the crisis as the nature of the financial claims on assets.

4.6   Conclusion

Contemporary capitalism has seen an exceptional growth of finance, and is often defined as financial capitalism. Securitization and equity finance have gained an unprecedented role with respect to traditional banking. We have seen that this kind of financial capitalism could also be understood as the other face of intellectual monopoly capitalism. While financial regulations can improve the stability of contemporary capitalism, some of the characteristics of the financial arrangements are related to the assets on which the financial claims are made. Many underlying assets have become discounted rents of intellectual monopoly, which are poorly suited to secure loans granted in traditional banking. In this respect overregulating the traditional banking sector may simply have the effect of pushing the economy even further toward an equity-based (or possibly shadow banking-based) financial equilibrium, which would in turn

---

[35] On the flaws of the Basel regulations, see E. Avgouleas, *Governance of Global Financial Markets: The Law, the Economics, the Politics* (Cambridge: Cambridge University Press, 2012).

reinforce a security-based equilibrium. In this respect, it may be more attractive to regulate the intangible assets on which the financial claims are exercised, thereby taming the negative effects of intellectual monopoly.

Consider that IPRs may generate huge incomes for a monopolist but they depress the average returns of the economy and squeeze future effective demand by making the monopolist a lazy investor and by depriving competitors of valuable investment opportunities. Moreover, intellectual monopoly creates huge inequalities depressing the average propensity to consume.

To overcome these problems we need regulations that change the nature of the assets held. This could be done by the means of IPRs buy out and by introducing new international regulations.

In some cases, public buy-outs of IPRs could be useful. They could leave the former monopolies with more money and more competition and stimulate their investments. At the same time, competitors would be empowered to enter new markets and increase their investments.

The standard multiplicative properties of public investments would be reinforced by the intrinsic multiplicative properties of a public good such as knowledge. Keynes' multipliers can become super-multipliers in a knowledge economy!

More generally, National States must produce international regulations, concerning the levels of public spending on knowledge in the different countries. Public knowledge is a global common and each nation-state has the incentive to free ride on the public knowledge produced by other states. Free-riding on the production of public knowledge of other nations should be seen as a damaging form of unfair competition, as one country reaps the benefits of another country's costly investments. The WTO should be reformed in such a way that this unfair competition is tamed. The charter of the WTO should include rules stating that fair participation in international trade requires a GNP fraction of each member state to be invested in open science and to be made available to all countries as a global common.

Closed science and closed markets can be perverse institutional complements, organizing and shaping the nature of excessive amounts of assets. New institutional complementarities, based on open science and open markets should shape and organize an increasing numbers of assets, fitting a more equal and dynamic society. Regulations cannot only be about the financial claims on assets. They should also be about the assets themselves.

Law will always be incomplete. However, in some fields, its enterprise (subjecting human behavior to rules) has barely started and its incompleteness is particularly painful!

PART II

The Political Economic Analysis of Regulatory Choices

Bank Lobbying: Regulatory Capture and Beyond

DENIZ IGAN AND THOMAS LAMBERT[*]

> Even if social welfare could be defined, and methods of maximizing it could be agreed upon, what reason is there to believe that the men who run the government would be motivated to maximize it? To state that they "should" do so does not mean that they will.

Anthony Downs[1]

5.1 Introduction

Lobbyists play a pervasive role in the US political system. They attempt to sway the opinion of legislators and regulators on specific issues, using their expertise, network connections, persuasion, public relations skills, or some combination thereof. While in principle any private interest group could find a use for services of lobbyists, the majority of lobbyists in Washington represents business interests.[2] Lobbyists literally move business interests forward. They do so by providing policy research, sponsoring think tanks, mobilizing grassroots constituencies, building and maintaining relationships with key decision-makers and influencers, drafting and amending bills, and assisting agencies in writing complex rules.

The more complicated the policies (and policy-making processes) are, the more valuable the activities performed by lobbyists become. Lobbyists gain greatly from policy complexity because it offers them room to insert narrow provisions into legislation under discussion with

---

[*] The views expressed here are those of the authors and do not necessarily represent those of the IMF, its management and Executive Board, or IMF policy.

[1] A. Downs, "An Economic Theory of Political Action in a Democracy," *Journal of Political Economy*, 65 (1957), 135–150, 136.

[2] J. de Figueiredo and B. K. Richter, "Advancing the Empirical Research on Lobbying," *Annual Review of Political Science*, 17 (2014), 163–185; L. Drutman, *The Business of America is Lobbying. How Corporations Became Politicized and Politics Became More Corporate* (Oxford: Oxford University Press, 2015).

limited public scrutiny, and because it gives them an advantage when it comes to providing legislators and regulators with information and expert opinion.

It is therefore not surprising to see many lobbyists actively working for the banking industry, as it is one of the most heavily regulated and supervised industries. Copious and complex regulations define acceptable behavior and shape the environment in which banks operate. A supervisory system encompassing both on-site and off-site elements aims to ensure compliance with these rules. At the same time, banks perform important functions for the economy – producing ex-ante information on investment opportunities and allocating capital, monitoring investments and exerting corporate governance, facilitating risk management, mobilizing savings, and easing transactions – and, as a result, any dysfunction in the banking system may pose significant risks for the entire economy (in the form of financial crises and through macro-financial linkages), with large socio-economic, and possibly political, costs.

It is thus imperative to understand not only how regulation and supervision affect bank decisions and performance, but also how regulation can be influenced by the banking industry itself. An expansive literature has examined the first part of this question, namely, the effects of regulatory and supervisory actions on bank activity, including efficiency and risk-taking.[3] Research on the second part, by comparison, has been scarce but has gained momentum in the wake of the global financial crisis. In these studies, the concept of *regulatory capture*, introduced in

---

[3] See, for example, C. M. Buch and G. DeLong, "Do Weak Supervision Systems Encourage Bank Risk-Taking?" *Journal of Financial Stability*, 4 (2008), 23–39; L. Laeven and R. Levine, "Bank Governance, Regulation, and Risk Taking," *Journal of Financial Economics*, 93 (2009), 259–275; J. R. Barth, et al., "Do Bank Regulation, Supervision, and Monitoring Enhance or Impede Bank Efficiency?" *Journal of Banking and Finance*, 37 (2013), 2879–2892; A. N. Berger and C. H. S. Bouwman, "How Does Bank Capital Affect Bank Performance during Financial Crises?," *Journal of Financial Economics*, 109 (2013), 146–176; S. Ongena, A. Popov, and G. F. Udell, "When the Cat's Away the Mice Will Play: Does Regulation at Home Affect Bank Risk-Taking Abroad?," *Journal of Financial Economics*, 108 (2013), 727–750. For theoretical and empirical aspects of bank regulation and supervision, see also J. R. Barth, G. Caprio Jr., and R. Levine, *Rethinking Bank Regulation: Till Angels Govern* (Cambridge: Cambridge University Press, 2006); J. R. Barth, G. Caprio Jr., and R. Levine, *Guardians of Finance: Making Regulators Work for Us* (Cambridge MA: MIT Press, 2012); A. Admati and M. Hellwig, *The Bankers' New Clothes: What's Wrong with Banking and What to Do about It* (Princeton NJ: Princeton University Press, 2013); R. B. Myerson, "Rethinking the Principles of Bank Regulation: A Review of Admati and Hellwig's 'The Bankers' New Clothes'," *Journal of Economic Literature*, 52 (2014), 197–210.

modern economic analysis by Stigler,[4] received particular attention. Regulatory capture arises when banks exert excessive influence on the regulators such that regulators act primarily in the interest of the industry they regulate rather than in the public interest.[5] In this context, regulators are not only the agencies establishing and enforcing the final rules by which banks need to abide, but also the legislature whose actions form the basis for these rules. Hence, we use the term "regulatory capture"[6] to encompass "legislative capture," whereby elected representatives are also motivated by pursuing private interests of the regulated industry instead of the public interest.[7]

In this chapter, our goal is to discuss whether and how bank lobbying in the United States leads to regulatory capture. In section 5.2, we provide an overview of the importance of bank lobbying in the United States and further highlight some empirical characteristics. In section 5.3, we discuss the motivations behind bank lobbying by outlining a conceptual framework of regulatory capture. In section 5.4, we examine the impact of lobbying on financial regulation and supervision by reviewing recent empirical evidence. We close section 5.4 by presenting evidence on the effect of the rising political influence of the banking industry on the global financial crisis. Finally, we conclude in section 5.5 with policy implications.

---

[4] G. Stigler, "The Theory of Economic Regulation," *Bell Journal of Economics and Management Science*, 2 (1971), 3–21.

[5] E. Dal Bó, "Regulatory Capture: A Review," *Oxford Review of Economic Policy*, 22 (2006), 203–225.

[6] A related concept is "intellectual capture," loosely defined as the inability or difficulty to question the tenets of the dominant viewpoint in a field and adoption of someone else's views as one's own. To put it more concretely, those working in regulated firms make regular contact with regulatory agencies while few members of the general public do. As a consequence of such regular interaction, regulators' mindset would more closely resemble that of the industry representatives and groupthink would take hold, making it difficult to come up with or voice unconventional ideas. Hence, identification with the regulated ends up in rationalization and institutionalization of industry views as the regulator's view. Ultimately, the society as a whole may start believing that what is good for the regulated industry is good for all (see, e.g., M. W. Brandl, *Money, Banking, Financial Markets and Institutions* (Boston MA: Cengage Learning, 2016), chap. 14. While captivating, intellectual capture is hard if not impossible to appraise. That said, lobbying is an obvious channel through which intellectual capture may materialize. For discussions on the conceptions of capture, their mechanisms and outcomes, see D. Carpenter and D. A. Moss, *Preventing Regulatory Capture: Special Interest Influence and How to Limit It* (Cambridge: Cambridge University Press, 2013).

[7] It is important to emphasize upfront that regulatory/legislative capture, in the way we interpret it here, does not imply corruption. The latter has been defined in many ways but almost always involves the abuse of public office for private gain, often through illegal means such as bribery and theft.

5.2   Bank Lobbying in the United States

In the United States, special interest groups, including the banking industry, can legally influence the policy formation process by carrying out
lobbying activities in the executive and legislative branches of the federal
government. Some hire lobbying firms; others have lobbyists working in-
house. These lobbying activities dwarf campaign contributions:[8] the whole
financial sector (encompassing finance, insurance, and real estate companies) spent $7.4 billion on lobbying in the period that ran from 1998 to
2016.[9] Considering the scale of this politically targeted expenditure, it has
received insufficient attention in the literature, as compared to campaign
contributions, in part owing to the scarcity of data on who lobbies and by
how much.[10] Public scrutiny and academic interest in lobbying has

[8] In the US campaign finance system, electoral campaigns can gather funding from various
sources including public funds, political party and candidates' own funds, and private
contributions from individuals and businesses. Political action committees (PACs) solicit
money from employees or members and make contributions in the name of the PAC to
candidates and political parties. Individuals contributing to a PAC may also contribute
directly to candidates and political parties. PAC and individual contributions are "hard
money" and are subject to limits: a PAC can give $5,000 to a candidate per election and up
to $15,000 annually to a national political party. PACs may receive up to $5,000 each from
individuals, other PACs and party committees per year while individuals may contribute
$2,700 per election to candidates, $5,000 per year to a PAC, and $33,400 per year to
a political party (as of 2016). Contributions made outside these limits are labeled "soft
money" and, while unlimited in amount, are subject to rules under the Bipartisan
Campaign Reform Act of 2002 (BCRA) on how they can be used. Note however that, in
the years that followed, federal court decisions, including *Citizens United* v. *Federal
Election Commission*, have eroded parts of the BCRA, giving rise to super PACs and
"dark money" organizations – politically active nonprofits that do not have to disclose
their donors. We refer the interested reader to the Center for Responsive Politics (CRP,
www.opensecrets.org) for more on campaign finance basics and definitions.
[9] Based on data compiled by the CRP. Between 1998 and 2016, the whole financial sector
contributed $675 million to PAC contributions, making the financial sector a top con-
tributor along with other regulated sectors (e.g., utilities) and sectors that tend to be
government-dependent (e.g., healthcare). By comparison, the utilities sector (encompassing communications, energy, and natural resources) contributed $521 million while the
healthcare sector contributed $465 million. The financial sector has also been the biggest
spender in individual contributions and soft money. In total (counting individual contributions and soft money), the financial sector outspent all others, pouring $4.6 billion to
elections. Utilities and healthcare have been distant runners-up at $2.3 billion and
$1.5 billion, respectively.
[10] A partial list of campaign finance studies includes: D. M. Hart, "Why Do Some Firms
Give? Why Do Some Give a Lot? High-Tech PACs, 1977–1996," *Journal of Politics*, 63
(2001), 1230–1249; G. Wawro, "A Panel Prohibit Analysis of Campaign Contributions
and Roll-Call Votes," *American Journal of Political Science*, 45 (2001), 563–579;
R. S. Kroszner and T. Stratmann, "Corporate Campaign Contributions, Repeat Giving,
and the Rewards to Legislator Reputation," *Journal of Law and Economics*, 48 (2005),

increased since the public disclosure of data on lobbying became regular, thanks to the passage of the Lobbying Disclosure Act of 1995 (LDA), which requires lobbyists to provide a substantial amount of information on their activities. In particular, lobbyists have to disclose the dollar amounts they receive from their client, and the issue areas as well as agencies they target. This information makes clear the economic motives of lobbying expenditures, which are unlike campaign contributions in that the latter may also reflect partisan or ideological motives. We provide in the appendix a description of the reporting and recording of lobbying data and some indications for their use in empirical research.

The disclosure of lobbying expenditures gives us a good measure of the size of the bank lobbying market during the past twenty years. The question is thus: how much do banks lobby? At first sight, a short answer would be quite a lot. Within the financial sector, the leading industries in lobby spending are insurance, securities and investment, and real estate (see Figure 5.1).[11] Banks – encompassing commercial banks, credit unions, savings and loans, and mortgage bankers and brokers – come fourth, having spent a total of $1.2 billion over the period between 1998 and 2016. This is likely a lower bound for lobbying spending on issues that affect banks because part of the activity is reported under the parent organization – which may be recorded as a securities and investment company – and some seemingly unrelated industries may also lobby on issues directly related to banks.[12]

Lobbying by banks increased in absolute terms over most of this period, rising from a trough of $36.3 million in 1999 to a peak of $88.2 million in 2014. When scaled by the industry value-added (i.e., gross domestic product-by-industry), this pattern remains largely

41–71; R. J. P. de Figueiredo and G. Edwards, "Does Private Money Buy Public Policy? Campaign Contributions and Regulatory Outcomes in Telecommunications," *Journal of Economics and Management Strategy*, 16 (2007), 547–576; M. Cooper, H. Gulen, and A. Ovtchinnikov, "Corporate Political Contributions and Stock Returns," *Journal of Finance*, 65 (2010), 687–724; P. Akey, "Valuing Changes in Political Networks: Evidence from Campaign Contributions to Close Congressional Elections," *Review of Financial Studies*, 28 (2015), 3188–3223; J. L. Kalla and D. E. Broockman, "Campaign Contributions Facilitate Access to Congressional Officials: A Randomized Field Experiment," *American Journal of Political Science*, 60 (2016), 545–558.

[11] It is worth noting that the biggest clients in the insurance industry are often attached to the healthcare sector (e.g., Blue Cross/Blue Shield and America's Health Insurance Plans).

[12] For instance, in 2016, the National Retail Federation lobbied on seven specific issues that fell under the general issue category of banking. These issues included implementation of mobile payment systems, data security and breach notification, and competition in debit routing and other payment innovation.

Lobbying Spending by Financial Industries
(percent of total spending by the financial industry in 1998–2016)

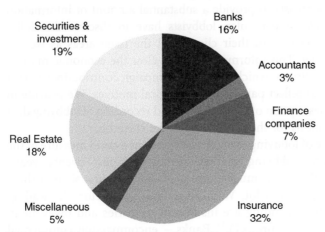

Figure 5.1 Lobbying Spending by Financial Industries
Note: Miscellaneous mainly include companies providing financial data, consulting
and support service (e.g., Bloomberg LP, Experian).
Source: Center for Responsive Politics; authors' calculations.

unchanged (see Figure 5.2). Interestingly, the growth in bank lobbying
expenditures during the period was faster than that of other financial
industries. This difference can perhaps be explained by two major factors.
First, the real estate industry – a major contributor to overall financial
sector lobbying – considerably cut down on lobbying during the Great
Recession. Second, legislative and administrative activity picked up significantly for banks during the global financial crisis and remained
intense following the passage of the Dodd-Frank Act in 2010.

Banks' lobbying expenditures declined somewhat during the period
2015–2016, to an annual average of $86.3 million. The decline looks more
pronounced in relative terms since the industry value added continued to
grow in these years. That said, this decline in lobbying activities of the
banking industry has coincided with a decline in total lobbying spending.[13]

---

[13] One possible reason for this generalized decline may be the political gridlock that
characterized Congress in these years. Yet, the gridlock started earlier and Congress
actually enacted more laws in 2015–2016 than it did in 2013–2014 or 2011–2012 (www
.govtrack.us/congress/bills/statistics). Other factors likely played a role: the energy and
natural resources sector recorded the largest drop in lobbying spending, coinciding with
the oil price slump.

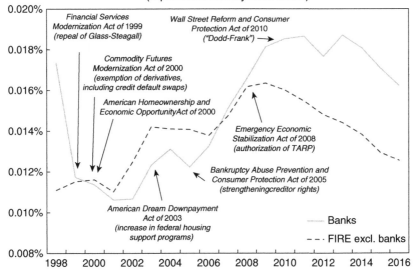

Figure 5.2 Lobbying by Banks and Other Financial Industries
Source: Center for Responsive Politics, Bureau of Economic Analysis; authors'
calculations.

Although the size of the bank lobbying market looks big according to
these nominal figures and by comparison to other industries, when we
contrast them with the size of the banking industry, it is rather the
opposite that prevails.[14] For example, in 2016 Citigroup Inc. spent
\$5.47 million in lobbying, while it reported \$17 billion in revenues for
the fourth quarter 2016 only. In a same vein, if we compare the total

---

[14] However, it is quite likely that our numbers significantly underestimate the real size of the
bank lobbying market. The definition of a lobbyists by the LDA is narrow enough to allow
many people who are actually engaged in lobbying to not register as such – the major
loophole being "20 percent of the time" an individual should at least spend on lobbying.
Indeed, recent reports suggest that the underworld of hidden lobbying is bigger than what
formal disclosures and registries reveal. LaPira and Thomas estimate that the actual total
amount spent on hidden lobbying is probably as big as the amount spent on "registered"
lobbying. T. M. LaPira and H. F. Thomas III, "Just How Many Newt Gingrich's Are There
on K Street? Estimating the True Size and Shape of Washington's Revolving Door,"
unpublished manuscript, 2013. See also G. Rolnik, "Uber, the Mayor's Private Email, and
the Underground Lobbying Complex," https://promarket.org, February 28, 2017, and
G. Rolnik, "How Many Newt Gingrich's Are There in Washington? Much More Than
You Might Think," https://promarket.org, April 3, 2017.

lobbying expenditures made by banks with the value of policies and benefits at stake, again these numbers are rather small.

These comparisons raise a puzzle: why do special interest groups spend so little in politics? This puzzle has been debated at length in the literature, and most prominently by Tullock.[15] We underscore here three important considerations accounting for this puzzle in bank lobbying.[16] One is that the interests of the banking industry are aligned and well-organized, while it faces a diffuse, unorganized opposition (i.e., the general public). Therefore, special interest groups need not spend much money to further push for their particular interests. Another consideration relates to the informational content of lobbying. Special interests do not need to spend much because once they reach out the legislator or regulator and provide them with the key, relevant piece of information, the value of all additional information is basically zero. For example, for a congressman, the key piece of information could be the impact of his vote for or against a particular bill on his reelection prospects, while for a regulator it could be about the chances of getting her appointment renewed or about the odds that a strict stance could prompt banks to go "charter shopping" and potentially engender a race-to-the-bottom among regulators.[17] Our third consideration is about the idea that lobbying expenditures are supplemented by other mechanisms of influence, such as quid pro quo agreements, career concerns, relationships, and persuasion. Although lobbying may encompass some of these mechanisms, lobbying *money* only facilitates the purchase of access to legislators and regulators. In a recent study, Brown and Huang analyze the Obama Administration's White House visitor logs from 2009–2015.[18] Identifying 2,286 meetings between federal government officials and corporate executives from S&P 1500 firms, they show that firms having access to high-level federal government officials

---

[15] G. Tullock, "The Purchase of Politicians," *Western Economic Journal,* 10 (1972), 354–355.

[16] See also S. Ansolabehere, J. M. de Figueiredo and J. M. Snyder Jr., "Why Is There So Little Money in Politics?" *Journal of Economic Perspectives,* 17 (2003), 105–130; and L. Zingales, "Towards a Political Theory of the Firm," *Journal of Economic Perspectives,* 31 (2017), 113–130.

[17] Charter shopping refers to the argument that a complex, multi-regulator system may generate regulatory arbitrage by incentivizing banks to change their charter to pick regulators that are laxer. See, for instance, S. Agarwal, et al., "Inconsistent Regulators: Evidence from Banking," *Quarterly Journal of Economics,* 129 (2014), 889–938. See also J. Silver-Greenberg, "Small Banks Shift Charters to Avoid U.S. as Regulator," *New York Times,* April 2, 2012.

[18] J. Brown and J. Huang, "All the President's Friends: Political Access and Firm Value," NBER Working Paper No. 23356, 2017.

experience higher stock price performance. Consistent with this notion that money buys access, the authors also find that firms that spent more heavily on lobbying and contributed more to Barack Obama's presidential election campaigns had an increased probability of gaining access to influential federal officials at the White House.

The relatively small size of the bank lobbying market is also explained by its breadth. Only a small number of (big) banks actually lobby.[19] The existence of barriers to entry for the lobbying process accounts for this empirical regularity. In particular, the high fixed costs and returns to experience both act as barriers to entry.[20] The fixed costs include the costs of creating a government affairs department, hiring the right lobbyists and educating them about the bank's interests. These are also the resources necessary to develop a lobbying agenda and a strategy for influencing the complex political process. Lobbying experience can also be viewed as a barrier to entry, because experience is necessary to establish a continuing relationship with legislators and regulators and to become more effective at lobbying them. These barriers to entry induce persistence in lobbying. Firms tend to stay in the lobbying process once they get into it, because they do not want to incur these fixed costs to set up a lobbying operation again in the future. Lee Drutman writes in this respect: "Once companies encamp on the Potomac, they rarely depart."[21]

5.3 Bank Lobbying and Regulatory Capture: A Conceptual Framework

After having explained the importance of bank lobbying, we now turn to the reasons why banks lobby. For this purpose, we use a conceptual framework to clarify how lobbying can lead to regulatory capture. This conceptual framework, shown in Figure 5.3, is adapted from Mitnick's seminal work and also partly draws from Dockner.[22]

---

[19] Bombardini shows that industries, such as the banking industry, with a higher share of firms above a certain size exhibit higher intensity of lobbying activity. M. Bombardini, "Firm Heterogeneity and Lobby Participation," *Journal of International Economics*, 75 (2008), 329–348.

[20] W. Kerr, W. Lincoln, and P. Mishra, "The Dynamics of Firm Lobbying," *American Economic Journal: Economic Policy*, 6 (2014), 343–379.

[21] Drutman, *The Business of America Is Lobbying*, 2.

[22] B. Mitnick, *The Political Economy of Regulation: Creating, Designing, and Removing Regulatory Forms* (New York: Columbia University Press, 1980); E. J. Dockner, "Regulatory Capture: Why? How Much? What to Do About It?," 42nd Economics Conference of the Oesterreichische Nationalbank, 2014.

Panel A: Regulation/Supervision Serving the Public Interest

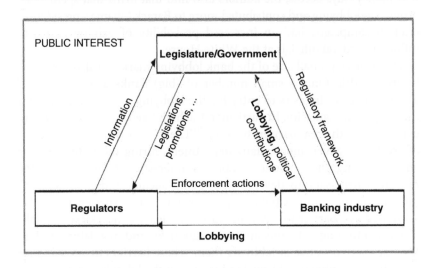

Panel B: Captured Regulation/Supervision

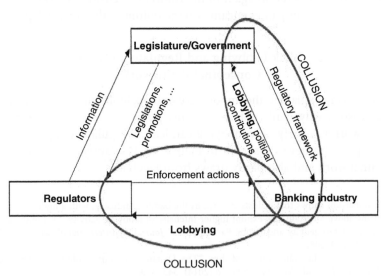

Figure 5.3 Conceptual Framework

Figure 5.3 presents the players involved – the legislature, the regulator put in place by the government, and banks, that is, the regulated industry. The role of all these players are intertwined in a complex way, so the arrows of the figure indicate the two-way interactions between each of them, with the first best solution of the system serving the public interest (i.e., Panel A). It is not trivial to identify what the public interest is, and it is beyond our scope to do so, but we refer to it as the economic welfare of agents referenced in the system. Our purpose here is not to provide a complete description of this system and its first best solution, but is rather to show how regulatory capture through lobbying comes up from it.

The role of the legislator is to design rules in such a way that economic agents (here, banks) behave and take actions best serving the public interest. Because in the real world, information asymmetries and externalities are present, the regulator comes into play in order to implement and enforce these rules again with the objective of supporting the public interest. The arrows in Panel A going from banks to either the legislator or the regulator primarily indicate the flow of information transmitted between these players. In this regard, bank lobbying plays a crucial role from a public interest standpoint as it enables the transmission of information. This information is seen as expert (or private to banks) by the regulator/legislator, who can act accordingly.[23]

However, capture can also arise in this framework: when the interests of the regulator (or the legislator) are in conflict with the public interest and serve instead that of banks.[24] In other words, regulatory capture is characterized by a situation in which the regulator/legislator and the regulated industry collude and maximize the sum of their own returns at the expense of the public interest. In terms of Figure 5.3 this is exhibited in Panel B, which stresses the collusion between the regulator or legislator alike, and the banking industry.

The economic drivers of regulatory capture have their roots in the same concepts that drive the need for regulation: information asymmetries and externalities. In practice, these economic drivers operate

---

[23] See Grossman and Helpman for detailed discussions on the informational role of firm lobbying. G. Grossman and E. Helpman, *Special Interest Politics* (Cambridge MA: MIT Press, 2001).

[24] The definition of the OECD Guidelines for "managing conflict of interest in the public service" reads as follows: "A 'conflict of interest' involves a conflict between the public duty and private interests of a public official, in which the public official has private-capacity interests which could improperly influence the performance of their official duties and responsibilities." OECD, *Managing Conflict of Interest in the Public Services: OECD Guidelines and Country Experiences* (Paris: OECD, 2003), 13.

through two main channels: career concerns of the regulators and the regulators' need for information that can only be provided by the industry.[25]

To illustrate the first channel, suppose regulators aim to maximize their lifetime earnings.[26] If public-sector salaries are on average lower than those paid in the private sector, regulators would have an incentive to establish their expertise as well as their networks within the industries they regulate. When the right opportunity presents itself, a regulator would leverage the network connections she has built to increase her chances of getting a job offer.[27] In this context, having a track record of being "industry friendly" may be a useful asset. Another way regulators may increase their value to the private, regulated firms is to generate complex, industry-specific rules and regulations that would require a great deal of institutional knowledge and experience to navigate. The regulated firms might then find it attractive to hire ex-regulators to help them comply and avoid penalties.[28]

Turning to the second channel, for the regulator to do a good job and maximize her utility, she would require access to the same information set as the industry she is tasked to regulate/supervise. Given information asymmetries and in the absence of perfect disclosure, she may find herself

---

[25] L. Zingales, "Preventing Economists' Capture," in D. Carpenter and D. A. Moss (eds.), *Preventing Regulatory Capture: Special Interest Influence and How to Limit It* (Cambridge: Cambridge University Press, 2013). Laffont and Tirole were the first to theoretically study regulatory capture in an analysis based on asymmetric information and the principal–agent model. J. Laffont and J. Tirole, "The Politics of Government Decision-Making: A Theory of Regulatory Capture," *Quarterly Journal of Economics*, 106 (1991), 1089–1127.

[26] While this may seem obvious, there may be cases where the regulator's utility function puts non-negligible weight on, e.g., civic pride in serving the public.

[27] The term "revolving doors" has been coined to refer to public office holders or public servants taking positions in the private industry and vice versa. For theoretical developments on revolving doors, see Y.K. Che, "Revolving Doors and the Optimal Tolerance for Agency Collusion," *RAND Journal of Economics*, 26 (1995), 378–397; P. Bond and V. Glode, "The Labor Market for Bankers and Regulators," *Review of Financial Studies* 27 (2014), 2539–2579. For recent empirical evidence on revolving doors, see D. Lucca, A. Seru, and F. Trebbi, "The Revolving Door and Worker Flows in Banking Regulation," *Journal of Monetary Economics*, 65 (2014), 17–32; S. Shive and M. Forster, "The Revolving Door for Financial Regulators," *Review of Finance*, 4 (2017), 1445–1484.

[28] Note that having complex rules and regulations does not necessarily mean having strict rules and regulations. Adding complexity may hurt firms by increasing compliance costs but helps the regulator in increasing the value of her expertise. As an additional consideration, complexity may actually be welcome by the regulated industry and the lobbyists it hires if it generates room for loopholes.

trading preferential treatment for information.[29] A preferential treatment for banks can be a change in existing rules or policies, or the provision of private benefits in the form of bailout guarantees, privileged access to licenses (allowing market power and boosting charter values), or more lax treatment in supervision.[30]

Bank lobbying mostly operates through this second channel, as suggested by the arrows in Panel B of Figure 5.3 going from the banking industry to the legislator and the regulator, respectively. These arrows indicate that banks collude to obtain preferential treatment and suggest another definition of lobbying as a legal activity aiming at changing existing rules and procuring private benefits. This definition of lobbying is consistent with and in part builds upon the interest-group theories of regulation as developed by Stigler, Peltzman and Becker, which are also the basis for regulatory capture.[31] In this context, lobbying is indeed arguably more conducive to being interpreted in a regulatory capture view than other forms of politically targeted activities. This is because lobbying involves one-to-one interaction between industry and both legislative and executive branches of the government, including numerous agencies that exercise certain degrees of discretion in implementing and enforcing regulations. Campaign contributions, by contrast, would influence a smaller circle.

---

[29] This pertains particularly to financial infrastructure where information asymmetries can be extremely severe and, crucially, the builder/owners of the infrastructure have exclusive information about how and why these systems are designed the way they are. Differently from most other forms of infrastructure, financial infrastructure – stock exchanges, the Consolidated Audit Trail, SWIFT, and payment systems like TARGET, CHIPS or CHAPS – are built and owned by financial institutions. For more on this, see Chapter 2 and D. C. Donald, "Heart of Darkness: The Problem at the Core of U.S. Proxy System and Its Solution," *Virginia Law & Business Review*, 6 (2011), 41–100.

[30] Less often in the financial sector but quite prominently in the non-financial sector, firms may also benefit from preferential access to credit and procurement contracts. See, e.g., S. Claessens, E. Feijen and L. Laeven, "Political Connections and Preferential Access to Finance: The Role of Campaign Contributions," *Journal of Financial Economics*, 88 (2008), 554–580; M. Faccio and D. C. Prasley, "Sudden Deaths: Taking Stock of Geographic Ties," *Journal of Financial and Quantitative Analysis*, 44 (2009), 683–718; E. Goldman, J. Rocholl and J. So, "Politically Connected Boards of Directors and the Allocation of Procurement Contracts," *Review of Finance*, 15 (2013), 1617–1648; S. Agca and D. Igan, "The Lion's Share: Evidence from Federal Contracts on the Value of Political Connections," unpublished manuscript, 2015; Brown and Huang, "All the President's Friends."

[31] Stigler, "The Theory of Economic Regulation"; S. Peltzman, "Towards a More General Theory of Regulation," *Journal of Law and Economics*, 19 (1976), 211–240; G. Becker, "A Theory of Competition among Pressure Groups for Political Influence," *Quarterly Journal of Economics*, 98 (1983), 371–400.

Furthermore, this second channel of regulatory capture works because all interest groups including the public do not have the same access to information and to influence as the regulated industry. Put in simpler terms, consider the case in which the regulator makes a mistake and puts in place regulation that fails to maximize total welfare (in a Pareto-efficient way) by favoring one interest group over the other. Given its superior access to information, the industry is more likely to know of and expose the mistake, while the public is unlikely to notice the mistake or react to it. In addition to the information gap, the public also faces a bigger free-rider problem, making it difficult to coordinate a reaction. This gives the regulator the incentive to err on the side of being more lenient to the industry. Banking regulators are particularly prone to such incentives because it is difficult for them to convince the public that there would have been a crisis but for their successful efforts to avoid it. Rather, it is easier for them to persuade the public that crises are the outcome of complex interplay among various factors – many of which the regulator cannot control.[32] Similarly, not all interest groups have the same level of access to influence. If lobbying by one interest group is perfectly matched by the lobbying of the opposing interest group, the regulator would not be swayed in favor of one or the other. However, access to influence is asymmetric across interest groups, especially in our context, because of the extent of the free-rider problem or the resources available for politically targeted activities. The latter can be particularly important if there are fixed costs involved (as seen in section 5.2). These differences in access to both information and influence reinforce the effect of bank lobbying.

Empirical research is broadly in line with the regulatory capture view of (bank) lobbying. Bertrand, Bombardini and Trebbi study the role of lobbyists in the United States and show that a pure informational (or expertise) view of lobbying is rather inconsistent with the data, whereas maintaining contacts to regulators and legislators to influence (capture) them is central to what lobbyists do.[33] Section 5.4 summarizes some

---

[32] By comparison, in the aviation industry for example, it is more straightforward to pin point the reason for a crash, allocate the blame, and punish the responsible party. For more on this contrast between aviation safety and banking regulation, see A. Admati, "It Takes a Village to Maintain a Dangerous Financial System," in L. Herzog (ed.), *Just Financial Market: Finance in a Just Society* (Oxford: Oxford University Press, 2016).

[33] M. Bertrand, M. Bombardini and F. Trebbi, "Is It Whom You Know or What You Know? An Empirical Assessment of the Lobbying Process," *American Economic Review*, 104 (2014), 3885–3920.

recent empirical findings of the literature specifically on bank lobbying and financial regulation, supervision, and outcomes in the United States. This summary is primarily based on four of our own studies.[34] It is noteworthy that the empirical literature on political connections (broadly defined) also confirms that politically connected firms have an influence on the regulatory and supervisory framework that affects their industry but also have consequences on firm-specific economic outcomes.[35]

5.4 Bank Lobbying and Regulatory Capture: Recent Evidence

5.4.1 Banking Regulation

As laid out conceptually in Section 5.3, a primary reason for banks to engage in lobbying is to exert influence on the process through which regulations are put in place. The legislative branch of the government is often the first stop in getting regulations in place. The disclosure of information on lobbying allows study of whether and how a regulated industry influences the creation of regulations. This is because one can identify which legislative and regulatory proposals are targeted by lobbyists working for the industry. Igan and Mishra study this issue in the context of financial regulation between 1999 and 2006, that is, the run-up to the global financial crisis.[36] The empirical analysis of that paper is set in the context of the federal law-making process in the Unites States, which is arranged as follows.

From the initial idea for a legislative proposal through its publication as a statute, the process is not a simple or short one. It is initiated by the introduction of a proposal in the form of a bill by (a) member(s) of the House of Representatives or the Senate ("the sponsor" or the "co-sponsors"). Each bill must have a sponsor and may have a number of co-sponsors.

---

[34] That is, D. Igan and P. Mishra, "Wall Street, Capitol Hill, and K Street: Political Influence and Financial Regulation," *Journal of Law and Economics*, 57 (2014), 1063–1084; D. Igan, P. Mishra and T. Tressel, "A Fistful of Dollars: Lobbying and the Financial Crisis," *NBER Macroeconomics Annual*, 26 (2012), 195–230; D. Igan, T. Lambert, et al., "Winning Connections? Special Interests and the Sale of Failed Banks," CEPR Discussion Paper No. DP12440 (2017); T. Lambert, "Lobbying on Regulatory Enforcement Actions: Evidence from U.S. Commercial and Savings Banks," *Management Science* (2018).

[35] For a survey of the literature, see T. Lambert and P. F. Volpin, "Endogenous Political Institutions and Financial Development," in T. Beck and R. Levine (eds.), *Handbook of Finance and Development* (Cheltenham: Edward Elgar, 2018).

[36] Igan and Mishra, "Wall Street, Capitol Hill, and K Street."

If a bill ultimately reaches the floor,[37] the vote on it in either house of Congress may be done in one of three ways: voice vote (where the chair asks first for all those in favor of the motion to speak out, and then asks all those opposed to the motion also to say so), the division (where the members supporting and opposing the motion stand successively and are counted) and the written, recorded vote.

There are various points in the legislative process at which a legislator makes her stance on the proposed bill known to others. Obviously, recorded votes on passage constitute one such point, but not all bills get to this final stage. For those that do, roll-call records for all senators and representatives are publicly available. For bills that never make it to the final voting stage (or do, but do not have recorded votes), one can analyze the information from the earlier stages of the legislative process, namely, data on the sponsorships and co-sponsorships. The (co-)sponsorship of a bill usually translates into voting in favor of that bill.

Throughout the law-making process, lobbyists approach members of Congress – especially those in key committees, who tend to receive larger amounts in campaign contributions – and administrative offices to make a case for the support or opposition of a bill. Anecdotally, the sought outcome is the defeat (passage) of unfavorable (favorable) legislation. This is supported by lobbying reports, which occasionally spell out the client's objective or position on an issue: for example, Bear Stearns

---

[37] After introduction by (co-)sponsor(s), the bills are referred to committees that deliberate, investigate, and, if necessary, revise them before they are accepted for general debate. Arguably, this is the most important phase of the process because, for the majority of bills, this marks the end of the road. The original bill, if not dead in a committee, often leaves the committee with several amendments. Once a bill is recommended by the committee-(s) to which it was referred, it comes to the house of Congress that originated the bill for consideration and debate. At the end of the reading and discussion of the bill in its entirety, the originating house first votes on whatever amendments have been reported by the committee(s) and then immediately votes on the passage of the bill with the amendments it has adopted. If the bill passes, a copy, with all the amendments and in the exact same format that it was passed by the originating chamber, is sent to the other chamber of Congress. At this point, the measure technically ceases being a bill and becomes an act. It then goes through similar steps in the other house of Congress: referral to committee(s), debate, and vote. The original, together with the engrossed amendments, if any, from the second house, is then returned to the originating house with a message stating the action taken by the second. If there are any differences between the two versions, a conference may be called to resolve any disagreements or competing versions bounce between the two houses until the disputes on legislative text are resolved. Once an agreement on an identical form of the act is reached, a copy is presented to the President. A bill becomes law on the date of approval or passage over the President's veto, unless it expressly provides a different effective date.

reported that it "advocated the concepts in the proposal but not the proposal" in its filing regarding lobbying activities on the Mortgage Reform and Anti-Predatory Lending Act of 2007 (a bill that would have established stricter requirements and standards on mortgage loans) while Citigroup Inc. reported that it sought passage of the Bankruptcy Reform Act of 2001 (a bill making it more difficult to file for individual bankruptcy). Albeit incomplete, this information can be used to make an educated guess on whether the banking industry would support or oppose a particular financial regulation proposal.

If efforts to influence the law-making process on behalf of the banking industry are successful, one would expect to see bills deemed favorable and supported through lobbying by the banking industry to have a higher likelihood of passage. By contrast, bills that are unfavorable would be defeated if the industry spent enough on lobbying to do so.

In an empirical set-up, the complication is that there are many other factors that may influence the ultimate fate of a financial regulation proposal. A possible solution is to focus instead on the voting and/or (co-)sponsorship patterns. To be more specific, one can use the actions of an individual legislator on a given bill to examine whether a legislator's likelihood of taking a particular position or changing her previous position on a proposal relates to how much lobbying is done on the proposal. This would also allow one to control for a range of fixed effects to capture legislator characteristics (e.g., ideology) and the general political environment (e.g., anti- or pro-regulation sentiment). Of course, it would also be imperative to control for lobbying by the "other side," that is, groups that are likely to advocate against the position of the financial industry.[38]

Igan and Mishra explore the effect of lobbying by asking two main questions.[39] First, did lobbying by the financial sector have a link to the

---

[38] Note that the discussion focused on the politically targeted activities of the industry as a whole. An interesting question is how the incentives at the industry level are reflected at the individual bank level, given the free-rider problem. Why do individual banks lobby rather than free ride the industry-wide effort to influence regulation? The short answer is that not all banks are created equal, and some have stronger incentives (and hence a lower threshold for fixed costs) to engage in these activities. Banks differ in their screening technology, underwriting and securitization techniques, specialization, or capacity to acquire private information regarding future states of the world. Given these characteristics, some banks would have the incentive (and perhaps the capacity) to take more risk. These banks would also gain comparatively more from a relaxation of the regulatory rules that limit risk-taking and, thereby, lobby on them, even if other banks may free ride and also benefit (but to a lesser extent) from lax regulations – a point we come back to in section 5.4.3.

[39] Igan and Mishra, "Wall Street, Capitol Hill, and K Street."

legislative outcomes of bills on financial regulation? Second, were legislators' network connections with the lobbyists and the financial sector related to their decision to support certain proposals?

The authors construct a comprehensive dataset that combines firm-level data on lobbying expenditures targeting specific bills and on campaign contributions to particular legislators with information on employment histories of legislators and lobbyists hired to work on these specific bills to pin down the network connections among the legislators, lobbyists, and the financial sector. Then they gather detailed information on the forty-seven financial regulation bills that were considered in Congress between 1999 and 2006, including their provisions, so that they can be grouped into broad categories on the basis of their similarities ("tight" or "lax" bills that have common provisions). This categorization is important because their empirical strategy exploits the cases in which legislators switched positions on a given legislative proposal. In other words, they use the variation in bank lobbying at the bill level and the variation in the position taken by the same legislator on the same issue through its various incarnations. Hence, their econometric specifications, similar to Stratmann,[40] allow to identify whether an individual legislator's switching her support for a particular bill is linked to the lobbying expenditures made by financial institutions affected by the bill.

Igan and Mishra first document that no tight bill passed both chambers of Congress and ultimately got signed into law, while 16 percent of the lax bills did.[41] This difference is even more striking when individual bills are grouped into common concept categories. The majority of lax-regulation proposals were ultimately signed into law, whereas none of the tight-regulation proposals succeeded.

Next their empirical analysis reveals that both lobbying expenditures by affected financial institutions and network connections between lobbyists and legislators who worked on a particular bill are positively associated with the probability of a legislator changing positions in favor of deregulation.[42] In economic terms, a one-standard-deviation

[40] T. Stratmann, "Can Special Interests Buy Congressional Votes? Evidence from Financial Services Legislation," *Journal of Law and Economics*, 45 (2002), 345–373.

[41] Igan and Mishra, "Wall Street, Capitol Hill, and K Street," 1073.

[42] Other evidence on the link between the political influence of the banking industry and financial regulation comes from an analysis of campaign contributions prior to the global financial crisis: Mian, Sufi, and Trebbi examine how different interest groups may have influenced US housing policy during the subprime mortgage credit expansion that took place between 2002 and 2007. The authors measure "special interests" by campaign contributions from the mortgage industry and "constituent interests" by the share of subprime borrowers in a congressional district. They also use co-sponsorship

increase in lobbying expenditures is associated with an increase of 3.7 percentage points in the probability of switching, while lobbying by individuals who previously worked for a legislator is associated with an increase in the probability of switching of 2.5 percentage points. Further analyses show that network connections of legislators with the financial sector and certain legislator characteristics affect the strength of the relationship between lobbying and the probability of switching in favor of deregulation prior to the crisis. Specifically, they find that lobbying has a stronger link to moving support toward deregulation if the legislator has previously worked in the financial sector and if she has more conservative tendencies.

The documented correlation among lobbying, network connections and voting patterns is robust to a battery of robustness tests, yet it does not translate directly to any particular causation story. The estimates lend themselves to several interpretations. First, lobbying firms may have better information than the legislators, and they partly reveal their information by endogenously choosing their lobbying effort, consistent with information-based view as discussed above in connection with Figure 5.3 (Panel A). Second, lobbying may simply be a reflection of the political negotiation process and good-faith compromise, also consistent with an information-based view. Legislation evolves as various interest groups lobby to garner support. The negotiations start with an extreme position and then slowly move toward compromise. Lobbying efforts on the earlier, more extreme versions of a bill may be small, focusing on the marginal legislator. As the bill evolves, more compromises are made, and lobbyists may elect to reach out to a broader set of legislators as the bill gravitates toward the center and becomes more appealing to them, which increases the odds of a position switch. Hence,

information in addition to actual votes in their analysis. They first document that, beginning in 2002, mortgage industry campaign contributions increasingly targeted US representatives from districts with a large fraction of subprime borrowers. During the expansion years, mortgage industry campaign contributions and the share of subprime borrowers in a congressional district increasingly predicted congressional voting behavior on housing-related legislation. This suggests that both lenders and borrowers influenced government policy toward housing finance during the subprime mortgage credit expansion. As mentioned earlier, while using campaign contributions has the attractiveness that they can be linked to particular legislators, they are mute on what the objective of the contributor is on a specific issue or proposal. Moreover, this analysis focuses on six bills selected on an ad hoc basis, rather than the more systematic analysis provided in the Igan and Mishra study. A. Mian, A. Sufi and F. Trebbi, "The Political Economy of the Subprime Mortgage Credit Expansion," *Quarterly Journal of Political Science*, 8 (2013), 373–408.

more lobbying in a given round may coincide with more compromises being made and more votes being switched from the preceding round as a result of the negotiation process. Finally, a less benign story is that financial institutions lobby to buy off legislators, and in this case their motive for lobbying is to extract rents from them. In other words, lobbyists compete for influence over a policy by contributing to politicians strategically, consistent with the regulatory capture view as depicted in Panel B of Figure 5.3.

While it is difficult to firmly distinguish among these explanations, two additional pieces of evidence from the study deserve attention. First, the probability of switching does not increase systematically over successive incarnations,[43] which raises doubts about the compromise explanation. Second, the result that legislators' employment experience in the financial sector and use of connected lobbyists enhance the link between lobbying expenditures and voting patterns is consistent with the regulatory capture view and, hence, seems to support rent-seeking motives.[44]

5.4.2 Banking Supervision

Looking back at Figure 5.3, the evidence discussed so far shows that bank lobbying affects the ability of the legislator to design proper rules: i.e., we have followed the arrows between banks and the legislature. Banks may also succeed in avoiding regulation by lobbying the regulator directly, so as to affect her ability to enforce the rules in place, as highlighted by the arrows of the figure going from banks to regulators and vice versa.

---

[43] Igan and Mishra, "Wall Street, Capitol Hill, and K Street," Table 6.

[44] The influence of banks on regulation has not disappeared in the aftermath of the global financial crisis. In another study, Mian, Sufi, and Trebbi show that constituent and special interests theories also explain voting on key bills in 2008. They examine the effects of constituents, special interests, and ideology on congressional voting on two of the most significant pieces of legislation: the Foreclosure Prevention Act and the Emergency Economic Stabilization Act. Representatives whose constituents experienced a sharp increase in mortgage defaults were more likely to support the Foreclosure Prevention Act, especially in competitive districts. Interestingly, representatives were more sensitive to defaults of their own-party constituents. Special interests in the form of higher campaign contributions from the financial industry was associated with an increase in the likelihood of supporting the Emergency Economic Stabilization Act. However, ideologically conservative representatives were less responsive to both constituent and special interests, potentially reflecting their opposition to bailouts and concern about moral hazard. A. Mian, A. Sufi, and F. Trebbi, "The Political Economy of the U.S. Mortgage Default Crisis," *American Economic Review*, 100 (2010), 1967–1998.

In a recent study, Lambert analyzes the relationship between bank lobbying and supervisory decisions of regulators by focusing on enforcement actions imposed by regulators on banks.[45] More precisely, an enforcement action is initiated when regulators identify during their examination financial or managerial problems, or even violation of banking laws and regulations. Enforcement actions constitute key components of micro-prudential supervision, as they require a troubled institution to take corrective measures. Such actions are meant to restore safety and soundness by stabilizing the institution, modifying its practices and risk-taking behaviors, and averting potential losses to the deposit insurer. Enforcement actions translate more or less directly into costs for the punished bank and its management (monetary penalties, partial loss of managerial control, loss of reputation or potentially negative market reaction). Regulators can impose several types of enforcement actions that differ in terms of severity.

The supervisory process gives broad discretionary power to regulators in assessing the seriousness of a bank's problems and in determining whether (and which types of) enforcement actions should be taken. In his study, Lambert examines whether banks may interfere in the process by lobbying the regulator (i.e., the Office of the Comptroller of the Currency (OCC), the Federal Deposit Insurance Corporation (FDIC), or the Federal Reserve System (Fed)) to avoid costly enforcement. He concentrates his analysis on the most severe types of enforcement actions (i.e., formal written agreement, cease and desist order, prompt corrective action, or deposit insurance threat), which have a direct impact on a bank's activity and risk-taking. Examining a sample comprising virtually all commercial and savings banks during the period of intense enforcement around the global financial crisis, he shows evidence that both lobbying status and experience of banks reduced the probability of being targeted by a severe enforcement action. According to his estimates, lobbying status reduces the probability of being subject to a severe enforcement action by 44.7 percent, while one additional year of lobbying experience decreases this probability by 11.4 percent. These results are robust to controlling for the CAMELS rating and endogeneity. Consistent with our discussion in section 5.2 on the existence of barriers to entry, he also finds weaker results at the intensive margin of how much banks spend on lobbying once the decision has been undertaken to participate in the lobbying process.

---

[45] Lambert, "Lobbying on Regulatory Enforcement Actions."

Lambert also seeks to disentangle two explanations of the result that banks lobby to circumvent costly enforcement actions: regulatory capture versus informational lobbying.[46] To do so, he explores the risk-taking behavior of lobbying banks and their performance, and finds evidence that aggregate risk (as measured by the Z-score) increases at lobbying banks. Further analyses of liquidity and credit risk reveal similar insights: lobbying banks expand more aggressively (on and off the balance sheet) in the years leading to the global financial crisis, and experience an increase in nonperforming loans afterwards. He also finds that lobbying banks have lower performance than other banks, and this underperformance persists in the longer run as well as when regulators face greater uncertainty (normally favoring informational lobbying).

Taken together, these findings appear consistent with the theory of regulatory capture. As discussed above, preferential treatment in supervision is viewed as regulators' response to the rent-seeking pressures and political influence of banks (see Panel B of Figure 5.3). Under this view, captured regulators provide an implicit guarantee to the risk-taking activities of lobbying banks, which is consistent with the results on risk taking documented by Lambert and discussed above. These risk-taking activities are in turn likely to generate distortions in the allocation of resources, translating into poor subsequent performance – and a build-up of risk that may ultimately unwind in a financial crisis. We explore this important consequence in the section 5.4.3. Lambert's findings on bank performance are in line with this view, but not with an information-based view of lobbying.

5.4.3   Financial Outcomes: The Case of the Global Financial Crisis

So far, we summarized the evidence on how bank lobbying influences regulatory and supervisory frameworks. Now we turn our attention to the outcomes banks faced during the global financial crisis to close the circle on the potential consequences of regulatory capture.

As demonstrated above, financial regulation became less strict in the run-up to the global financial crisis in part due to the lobbying efforts of the banking industry while banks that lobbied were more likely to avoid enforcement actions. The argument then goes: this lax environment allowed certain banks to engage in riskier lending during the period 2000–2007 and end up with worse outcomes during the crisis.

---

[46] Lambert, "Lobbying on Regulatory Enforcement Actions," 20–22.

To illustrate with an example, the *Wall Street Journal* on December 31, 2007 reported:[47]

> Data from federal and state campaign-finance records, Internal Revenue Service filings, and the National Institute on Money in State Politics show that from 2002 through 2006, Ameriquest, its executives and their spouses and business associates donated at least $20.5 million to state and federal political groups . . . Ameriquest became a player in the business of lending to low-income homeowners. The company persuaded many homeowners to take cash out of their houses by refinancing them for larger amounts than their existing mortgages . . . Home loans made by Ameriquest and other subprime lenders are defaulting now in large numbers.

Once the financial crisis hit and the government was forced to intervene, the factors that determined who would be bailed out included, for example, how badly the financial institution was hurt, how systemically important it was, how healthy the balance sheets were, and perhaps how well connected the institution was to the politicians. For instance, on January 22, 2009 the *Wall Street Journal* reported:[48]

> Troubled OneUnited Bank in Boston didn't look much like a candidate for aid from the Treasury Department's bank bailout fund last fall . . . Nonetheless, in December OneUnited got a $12 million injection from the Treasury's Troubled Asset Relief Program, or TARP. One apparent factor: the intercession of Rep. Barney Frank, the powerful head of the House Financial Services Committee . . . Some powerful politicians have used their leverage to try to direct federal millions toward banks in their home states. "It's totally arbitrary," says South Carolina Gov. Mark Sanford. "If you've got the right lobbyist and the right representative connected to Washington or the right ties to Washington, you get the golden tap on the shoulder.

The channels highlighted in such anecdotes suggest that one is likely to observe an empirical association (i) between lobbying and ex-ante riskier lending, and (ii) between lobbying and ex-post performance as well as the likelihood of bailout in 2008.

These expectations motivate the empirical analysis of outcomes during the crisis conducted in Igan, Mishra and Tressel.[49] They construct a dataset combining information on banks' lobbying and mortgage

---

[47] Glenn Simpson, "Lender Lobbying Blitz Abetted Mortgage Mess," *Wall Street Journal*, December 31, 2008.

[48] D. Paletta and D. Enrich, "Political Interference Seen in Bank Bailout Decisions," *Wall Street Journal*, January 22, 2009.

[49] Igan, Mishra and Tressel, "A Fistful of Dollars."

lending activities and ask whether lobbying lenders behaved differently from non-lobbying lenders in the 2000–2007 period and how they performed in 2008.

First, the authors look at three measures that capture the ex-ante riskiness of mortgage lending: loan-to-income ratio, proportion of loans sold, and loan growth rates. They find that banks that lobbied more intensively originated mortgages with higher loan-to-income ratios, securitized a faster-growing proportion of loans they originated, and had faster-growing mortgage loan portfolios.[50]

Then they turn to ex-post performance and find that faster relative growth of mortgage loans by lobbying lenders in the decade prior to the crisis was associated with higher delinquency rates in 2008.[51] The authors also carry out an event study during key episodes of the global financial crisis to assess whether the stocks of lobbying lenders performed differently from those of other financial institutions. They show that lobbying lenders experienced negative abnormal stock returns at the time of the failures of Bear Stearns and Lehman Brothers, but positive abnormal returns around the announcement of the bailout program (i.e., TARP).[52] In addition, they analyze the determinants of how bailout funds were distributed, finding that being a lobbying lender was associated with a higher probability of being a recipient of these funds.[53]

Taken together, these findings indicate that lobbying is associated ex ante with more risk taking and ex-post with worse performance. In other words, some lenders lobbied more aggressively; the ensuing lax regulatory environment let them to engage in riskier lending; and such lending exposed them (directly or indirectly) to worse outcomes during the crisis. In the aftermath, the market anticipated lobbying lenders to benefit more from the bailout, and they indeed did, partly because they had closer connections to policymakers.

Again, there are several possible explanations for these results. Lobbying lenders, for example, may be specialized in catering to riskier

[50] Ibid., 206–215.

[51] Ibid., 216–218.

[52] Ibid., 218–220.

[53] Ibid., 220–221. Duchin and Sosyura also investigate the relation between political connections, including lobbying activities, and bailouts under TARP. They find that politically connected firms are more likely to be funded, controlling for other characteristics. Yet investments in politically connected firms underperform those in unconnected firms. They interpret these findings as suggestion that connections between firms and regulators can distort investment efficiency. R. Duchin and D. Sosyura, "The Politics of Government Investment," *Journal of Financial Economics*, 106 (2012), 24–48.

borrowers, or they may be overly optimistic and may have honestly underestimated the likelihood of an adverse shock. Then, these lenders may have lobbied to signal their private information to the policymaker and prevent tighter regulation that would otherwise have restricted profitable lending opportunities. If lobbying lenders are specialized or overly optimistic, their motive for lobbying is consistent with an informational view (Panel A of Figure 5.3). Alternatively, certain lenders may have engaged in rent seeking and lobbied to increase their chances of preferential treatment, for example, a lower probability of scrutiny by regulators or a higher probability of being bailed out (Panel B of Figure 5.3). Igan, Mishra and Tressel do not disentangle these explanations but further document that large lenders were the ones lobbying more aggressively and ultimately getting bailed out with a higher probability.[54] These suggest that lobbying might be conducted with too-big-to-fail issues in mind – consistent with moral hazard elements and rent-seeking explanation.

Igan et al. look into another aspect of the crisis aftermath: the resolution of failed banks.[55] They explore, using the perspective of lobbying, whether discretion by the FDIC may compromise, or improve, the efficiency of the resolution process. Lobbying can reflect both sides of discretion. On the one hand, the FDIC can receive from lobbying useful private information for its decisions (e.g., on the potential synergies between the target and the acquirer). On the other hand, lobbying may lead to the capture of the FDIC, hindering the resolution actions.

Their analysis utilizes detailed information on failed-bank auctions conducted by the FDIC during the period between 2007 and 2014. They show evidence that bidders lobbying banking regulators are in a better position to win an auction: for them, the probability of winning is 26.4 percentage points higher, while a one-standard-deviation increase in lobbying expenditures targeted on banking regulators leads to an increase of 6.6 percentage points in the probability that a bidder wins an auction.[56] These results hold after controlling for bidder characteristics and target fixed effects, and accounts for endogeneity concerns by using an instrumental variable strategy. Compellingly, the analysis also shows that the usage of revolving-door lobbyists and of lobbying contact with the FDIC have the largest effects on auction outcomes.

---

[54] Igan, Mishra and Tressel, "A Fistful of Dollars," 222–224.
[55] Igan et al., "Winning Connections?"
[56] Ibid., 16.

Further empirical evidence suggests that rent seeking for preferential treatment accounts for this finding. The authors assess the economic magnitude of the cost associated with the lobbying on failed-bank auctions. To do so, they compare the actual resolution cost to the cost that the FDIC would have incurred if another bid had been chosen and report that lobbying is associated with a smaller cost differential. This indicates that lobbying acquirers pay relatively less than other bidders, resulting in an even more severe drain for the Deposit Insurance Fund (DIF). In particular, they estimate the cost due to lobbying at 16.4 percent of the total resolution losses, amounting to a transfer of $7.4 billion from the DIF to lobbying bidders.[57] More generally, these findings suggest that the FDIC makes more use of its discretion when bidders lobby. Finally, Igan et al. show that eventual acquirers with lobbying activities deliver inferior outcomes in terms of post-acquisition efficiency.[58]

This evidence sheds light on the channel through which lobbying affects regulatory outcomes. Under the rent-seeking view, the finding that lobbying banks acquire other banks at lower prices suggests an economic misallocation, as the bank offering the highest price is not necessarily the winner. This comes on top of the DIF's burden of paying larger resolution costs. Of course, consistent with the information channel, regulators may allocate banks at lower prices to bidders who have conveyed private information that convince the regulators that they are in a more favorable position to acquire the failed bank. However, the finding that lobbying banks underperform other acquirers ex post appears inconsistent with the efficiency-improving role of bank lobbying. Instead, it is consistent with agency-type inefficiencies in the allocation of failed banks predicted by rent-seeking theories à la Shleifer and Vishny as in Panel B of Figure 5.3.[59]

5.5   Lessons and Policy Implications

The idea that powerful organizations with private interests may capture the government in order to pursue their private benefits is certainly not new. Similar ideas go back at least to Montesquieu and, later, to Marx. But the concept of *regulatory capture*, introduced in modern economic

---

[57] Ibid., 23.

[58] Ibid., 24–26.

[59] A. Shleifer and R. Vishny, "Politicians and Firms," *Quarterly Journal of Economics*, 109 (1994), 995–1025.

analysis by Stigler,[60] received particular attention in the aftermath of the global financial crisis. In particular, regulatory capture has been blamed by many commentators for the failures and gaps in banking regulation and supervision that led to a buildup of risk ahead of the crisis.[61] Because of the difficulty in quantifying captured interests, this narrative is mainly anecdotal.

This chapter summarizes recent, systematic evidence on the banking industry capturing the government through its lobbying activities. Specifically, it focuses on financial regulation, supervision, and outcomes during the global financial crisis. Employing detailed data on lobbying available thanks to the LDA of 1995, this line of research shows clear bank-level evidence suggesting that regulatory capture lessens the support for tighter rules and enforcement. A lax regulatory environment is generally understood to allow riskier practices and worse economic outcomes. More generally, from this line of research we gain insights into how the rising and concentrated political power of the banking industry in the first decade of the 2000s propelled the financial system and the "real" economy into crisis.

The appropriate policy response depends on the true motivation for lobbying, which is extremely difficult to pin down empirically, as shown in the studies surveyed. Regulatory capture would suggest that curtailing lobbying is a socially optimal outcome. However, if the banking industry, along with other stakeholders such consumer protection groups, lobbies to better inform the legislator/regulator, lobbying would remain a socially beneficial channel to facilitate decision-making. Overall, the findings summarized here are consistent with a regulatory capture view of bank lobbying. While these findings should not be interpreted as evidence in support of an outright ban of lobbying, they clearly point in the direction of a need for rethinking the framework governing interactions between regulators and the industry, including their lobbyists.

Without pretending to provide a complete set of solutions,[62] we want to stress two avenues that we think are crucial to contain regulatory

---

[60] Stigler, "The Theory of Economic Regulation."

[61] See, e.g., Simpson, "Lender Lobbying Blitz Abetted Mortgage Mess"; S. Labaton, "Back to Business; Ailing, Banks Still Field Strong Lobby at Capitol," *New York Times*, June 4, 2009; B. Hallman, "FDIC Slow to Pursue Failed Bank Directors, Recover Tax Dollars," *Center for Public Integrity*, March 15, 2011 (updated May 19, 2014).

[62] See, e.g., L. G. Baxter, "'Capture' in Financial Regulation: Can We Channel It Toward the Common Good?" *Cornell Journal of Law and Public Policy*, 21 (2011), 175–200; L. G. Baxter, "Understanding Regulatory Capture: An Academic Perspective from the United States," in S. Pagliari (ed.), *Making Good Financial Regulation: Towards a Policy*

capture at more "acceptable" levels, that is, at a level where the benefit of regulation exceeds the cost of regulatory capture. The first avenue is to enhance the transparency of regulatory decisions by mandating the ex-post disclosure of how they are made. The information disclosed (possibly with a delay and perhaps using the regulator's own web portals) should include the deliberations, minutes of meeting, names of regulatory staff involved, data and models used, number and nature of contacts with registered lobbyists (including their names and the position they advocate on the issue), and an assessment of how the inputs of lobbyists were factored into the final decision. In various circumstances (enforcement action, capital support, resolution), regulators enjoy broad discretion, which is valuable in order to undertake better-informed actions. But, at the same time, regulatory discretion further buttresses the risk of capture. We think that the systematic, ex-post disclosure of information on regulatory decisions would increase regulators' accountability both toward the general public and toward other (potentially competing) parties. Indeed, this would prevent the reputational cost of defending positions the general public would consider as improper collusion with banks. In this regard, the role of the media is of primary importance as it acts as a watchdog by effectively overcoming the private cost that individuals face in gathering, digesting and analyzing information.[63]

The second avenue is about placing checks and balances within the decision-making process for regulators. Of course, this starts with setting up properly structured and resourced agencies as well as internal change (of culture and liability rules) within the industry itself,[64] but we mean here implementing structures tackling the enduring disproportionate influence of banks and their lobbyists as interest group. As access to influence is asymmetric across interest groups, and regulatory power has become more diffuse, the interactions between the regulator and the regulated should be subjected to procedures that ensure the inclusion of dissenting views, that is, views of legitimate groups with different interests, such as customers, smaller financial institutions, and trade

---

Response to Regulatory Capture (Guildford: Grosvenor House Publishing, 2012); Carpenter and Moss, "Preventing Regulatory Capture."

[63] For example, in the global financial crisis, when information did leak, it pointed to mistakes made both by large banks and the regulators, helping in turn to produce more informed views on financial regulatory policy (see https://seekingalpha.com/article/158046; accessed: August 16, 2017). Although new regulation (Dodd-Frank, Basel III) explicitly stresses increased transparency, this requirement of more information being publicly disclosed is not put forward in the way we propose.

[64] See Baxter, "Understanding Regulatory Capture," for recommendations along these lines.

unions. Implementing structures of checks and balances involving these less politically powerful interest groups would induce a rebalance of the dominant position currently held by the banking industry. In the spirit of the model of "tripartism" proposed by Ayres and Braithwaite, these interest groups should have lobbying powers and a voice during the deal-making process – namely, having a seat at the negotiation table, having full access to the same information, and standing to take legal action when warranted.[65]

We believe these two avenues should constitute the basis of policy interventions aimed at preventing (or reducing the effects of) regulatory capture in the banking industry. In any case, more research is needed to better apprehend the drivers of capture in its many forms, and also its incidence for both the industry and the society at large. The post-crisis era can provide new insights. For example, the consolidation in the financial sector during that period and the ongoing implementation of new regulations – under the Dodd-Frank Act in particular – see rigorous lobbying activity, with incumbent survivors adopting different strategies by bypassing the Congress.[66]

5.6   Appendix: Reporting and Recording of Lobbying Data

In general, the LDA requires registration by any individual lobbyist (or the individual's employer if it employs one or more lobbyists) within 45 days after the individual first makes, or is employed or retained to make, a lobbying contact with either the President, the Vice President, a Member of Congress, or any other specified Federal officer or employee, including certain high-ranking members of the uniformed services.[67] Since 1996, all lobbyists (intermediaries who lobby on behalf of companies and organizations) have filed semi-annual reports with the Secretary of the Senate's Office of Public Records (SOPR), listing the

---

[65] I. Ayres and J. Braithwaite, "Tripartism: Regulatory Capture and Empowerment," *Law & Social Inquiry*, 16(1991), 435–496.

[66] B. Bain, "Here Are Ways Regulators Can Revise Dodd-Frank without Congress," *Bloomberg*, June 14, 2017.

[67] Under section 3(10) of the LDA, an individual is defined as a "lobbyist" with respect to a particular client if he or she makes more than one lobbying contact (i.e., more than one communication to a covered official) and his or her "lobbying activities" constitute at least 20 percent of the individual's time in services for that client over any six-month period. "Lobbying activity" is defined in section 3(7) of the LDA as "lobbying contacts or efforts in support of such contacts, including background work that is intended, at the time it was performed, for use in contacts, and coordination with the lobbying activities of others."

name of each client (firm) and the total income they have received from each of them. In parallel, all firms with in-house lobbying departments are required to file similar reports stating the total dollar amount they have spent (either in-house or in payments to external lobbyists).

The LDA requires the disclosure of not only the dollar amounts actually received/spent, but also the issues lobbying activity has targeted. To be more specific, the LDA requires the filer to state the general issue areas on which the registrant engaged in lobbying during the reporting period. There are seventy-six general issue areas, of which at least one has to be entered by the registrant/filer. The filer can list more than one issue. In that case, she has to use a separate page of the form for each area selected and provide the relevant information on each activity. Specifically, for each general issue, the filer is required to list the specific issues which were lobbied for during the semi-annual period. For example, specific bills before Congress or specific executive branch actions are required to be listed in the form. Thus, unlike PAC contributions, lobbying expenditures of companies can be associated with very specific, targeted policy areas.

The datasets compiled in the studies summarized in this chapter are based on the semi-annual lobbying disclosure reports filed with the SOPR and can be compiled from two sources: (i) the SOPR website and (ii) the website of the CRP. The latter provides information on the lobbying expenditures as well as the general issue area (e.g., bankruptcy) with which lobbying is associated. For detailed information including specific issues targeted (e.g., the name and number of the bill introduced in Congress) and executive/legislative offices contacted, one needs to go over the individual PDF reports posted on the former website to extract the desired information.

Lobbying firms (or lobbyists) are required to provide a good-faith estimate rounded to the nearest $20,000 of all lobbying-related income in each six-month period. Likewise, organizations that hire lobbyists must provide a good-faith estimate rounded to the nearest $20,000 of all lobbying-related expenditures in a six-month period. An organization or a lobbying firm that spends less than $10,000 in any six-month period does not have to state its expenditures. In those cases, the CRP treats the figure as zero.

Occasionally, income that an outside lobbying firm reports receiving from a client is greater than the client's reported lobbying expenditures. Many such discrepancies can be explained due to filer error. In cases not already resolved in previous reports and where the discrepancy exceeds the $20,000 that can be attributed to rounding, the client's expenditures rather than the lobbying firm's reported income are used. The only exception is when a client reports no lobbying expenditures, while the outside lobbying firm lists an actual payment. In such cases, the figure reported by the lobbying firm is used.

Annual lobbying expenditures and income (of lobbying firms) are calculated by adding mid-year totals and year-end totals. Whenever a lobbying report is amended, income/expense figures from the amendment are generally used instead of those from the original filing. Often, however, CRP staff determine that the income/expenditures on the amendment or termination report are inaccurate. In those instances, figures from the original filing are used.

In cases where the data appear to contain errors, official Senate records are consulted and, when necessary, the CRP contacts SOPR or the lobbying organizations for clarification. The CRP standardizes variations in names of individuals and organizations to clearly identify them and more accurately represent their total lobbying expenditures.

In cases where both a parent and its subsidiary organizations lobby or hire lobbyists, the CRP attributes lobbying spending to the parent organization. Therefore, the lobbying totals reported by the CRP for a parent organization may not reflect its original filing with the Senate, but rather the combined expenditures of all related entities. However, to calculate lobbying expenditures by sector and industry, each subsidiary is counted within its own sector and industry, not those of its parent. The CRP makes this distinction when it has the information necessary to distinguish some or all of the subsidiary's lobbying expenditures from either the subsidiary's own filing or from the receipts reported by outside lobbying firms.[68] In addition to firms' own lobbying expenditures, lobbying expenditures by associations (such as the American Bankers Association, the Securities Industry and Financial Markets Association, American Council of Life Insurers, National Association of Realtors, etc.) are also filed on the CRP website and included in the sector and industry totals.

---

[68] For example, tobacco giant Altria Group owns Kraft Foods. Although Altria Group's original filing includes lobbying for Kraft in its expenditures, in the dataset the CRP isolates Kraft's payments to outside lobbyists and includes them in "Food Processing and Sales."

6

The Social Psychology of Financial Regulatory Governance

GIULIANO G. CASTELLANO AND GENEVIÈVE
HELLERINGER

6.1 Introduction

This chapter builds on the enriched understanding of financial regulation put forward in this volume by offering a social and psychological understanding of financial regulation. The aim is to address a fundamental question: how do financial regulators "think?" To answer this question the chapter isolates and examines the group dynamics that – within regulators – influence decisions concerning the achievement of key policy objectives, such as maintaining financial stability or promoting market integrity. Our contribution builds on a novel strand of research that we have been developing and that applies the analytical tools of social psychology to financial regulatory theories.[1] Through these lenses it is possible to identify and explain how conflicts are managed and decisions concerning regulated markets and firms are taken.

Financial regulators, in discharging their supervisory and regulatory functions, are key players in the financial ecosystem. Yet, in classical political economic thinking, their role tends to be explored by relying on simplified assumptions largely influenced by economic theories. Under the public choice theory, regulators are considered as rational operators routinely engaged in a process of maximization of different interests, such as acquiring more power or better reputation.[2] Neo-institutional

---

[1] This chapter is in part based on our article "Shedding Light on EU Financial Regulators: A Sociological and Psychological Perspective," *Hastings International and Comparative Law Review*, 40 (2017), 69.

[2] See G. Tullock, "Public Choice" in S. N. Durlauf and L. E. Blume (eds.), *The New Palgrave Dictionary of Economics*, 2nd edn. (Basingstoke: Palgrave Macmillan, 2008).

economics, by distinguishing between "rules of the game" and "players" as key components of markets,[3] depicts regulators either as players or as an emanation of the structure of rules that regulate markets. In any respect, regulatory agencies are considered as units, in the form of social actors or organizations. Albeit offering a useful simplification, such understandings neglect that organizations are composed of individuals with objectives that may conflict.[4] Steering away from this unitary conception, there is a flourishing literature in anthropological and sociological studies that considers organizations, such as companies or administrative agencies, as collective entities.[5] In this chapter, such an approach is applied to financial regulators to isolate the relationship between the legal rules defining the architectural framework for financial regulatory governance and behavioral dynamics driving regulatory choices and modus operandi.

A deeper understanding of the relationship between interpersonal dynamics and the legal framework guiding, or even shaping, the decision-making process of financial regulators leads to acquiring a more complete understanding of the role of regulators in financial markets. This is all the more important in the aftermath of the 2007–2009 Global Financial Crisis and against the backdrop of inquiries into the role of law in the financial sector that has followed. The interaction between financial entities and legal rules has been re-examined. Novel theories have focused on the idea that legal norms are constitutive elements of finance,[6] rather than exogenous phenomena that intrude upon markets. In a similar vein, financial markets have been approached through socio-legal lenses, highlighting, inter alia, the recursive interaction between markets, firms, and legal rules.[7] In addition, the behavioral dynamics influencing the choices of financial consumers, professional investors, and other actors of the financial markets has been scrutinized: the postulate of rationality developed in financial economics and influencing the

---

[3] D. C. North, *Institutions, Institutional Change and Economic Performance* (Cambridge: Cambridge University Press, 1990), 3–5.

[4] See generally G. M. Hodgson, "What Are Institutions?," *Journal of Econ. Issues*, 40 (2006), 1.

[5] See, e.g., M. Douglas, *How Institutions Think* (Syracuse NY: Syracuse University Press, 1986).

[6] K. Pistor, "A Legal Theory of Finance," *Journal of Comp. Econ.*, 41 (2013), 315.

[7] J. Black, "Reconceiving Financial Markets – From the Economic to the Social," *Journal of Corporate Law Studies*, 13 (2013), 401.

regulators' understanding of finance has been questioned.[8] It is now largely understood that individual cognitive processing has limited capacity and that the brain economizes upon such processing by relying on heuristics and other shortcuts, which will save time but also generate biases and predictable errors.[9] Regulatory actions are thus refined in order to take into account these insights that depart from the traditional rationality paradigm.[10]

With the intent of applying these novel and multi-disciplinary approaches to the institutional framework of financial regulation, this chapter considers regulators as organizations composed of individuals whose conduct is impacted by legal design as well as by the conduct of investors, depositors, and the various financial firms populating the heterogeneous financial ecosystem. They are also impacted by legal provisions which define membership criteria, as well as organizational structures with collegial governing bodies, and the powers, responsibilities, goals or objectives of each institution. This is to say that our focus is on how the legal dimension influences the relational dynamics *within* regulators, rather than focusing on the external relationship of regulators.

Drawing on insights from social psychology, regulators appear to reach decisions shaped by social roles, cultural norms as well as legal design.[11] Social psychology provides a language that enables us to capture and analyze these aspects,[12] as it focuses on the result of individual interactions within or among groups.[13] Hence, with specific reference

---

[8] In the UK, see Financial Services Authority [FSA], "The Turner Review: A Regulatory Response to the Global Banking Crisis" (March 2009) Ref. No. 003289.

[9] K. Erta et al., "Applying Behavioral Economics at the Financial Conduct Authority," (Financial Conduct Authority, Occasional Paper No. 1, April 2013), www.fca.org.uk /publication/occasional-papers/occasional-paper-1.pdf.

[10] E. Avgouleas, "The Global Financial Crisis, Behavioural Finance Regulation: In Search of a New Orthodoxy," *Journal of Corporate Law Studies*, 9 (2009) 23.

[11] See F. H. Allport, "A Structural Conception of Behavior: Individual and Collective – Structural Theory and the Master Problem of Social Psychology," *Journal of Abnormal Psychology and Social Psychology*, 64 (1962) 3.

[12] A classical definition of social psychology was given by Gordon Allport: "Social psychology is the attempt to understand and explain how the thoughts, feeling, and behaviours of individuals are influenced by the actual, imagined, or implied presence of other human being"; G. W. Allport, "The Historical Background of Modern Social Psychology" in G. Lindzey (ed.), *Handbook of Social Psychology*, vol. 1 (Cambridge, MA: Addison-Wesley, 1954) 5.

[13] Although there is some overlap between sociology and social psychology, there are also differences. Sociologists tend to relate social behaviors to norms, roles, social class and other structural variables. Differently, social psychologists focus on the goals, motives and cognitions of individuals operating in a social context.

to the primary decision-making bodies of financial regulatory agencies, social psychology provides an analytical grid to observe group dynamics and isolate what Alan Fiske, in his seminal work, defined the "fundamental forms of sociality."[14] Fiske, bridging different studies and building upon his own ethnographic research, isolates four relational models into a unified theory of social relations. These relational models, illustrated in detail in section 6.3, are archetypes describing elementary forms of sociality that feature in every culture and characterize all social interactions.[15] They operate in all domains of social action and cognition, such as transfer of property, standards of social justice, group decisions, social influence, organization of labor, moral judgments, response to suffering, and interpretation of human behavior. Combinations between the four models result in various forms of social interaction pursuant to general cultural rules.[16] At a more fundamental level, "the relational models theory explains social life as a process of seeking, making, sustaining, repairing, adjusting, judging, construing, and sanctioning relationships."[17]

Fiske's perspective finds a natural application in the context of the European Union, as its multi-layered governance structure leads to diversified interests which converge toward different decision-making centers. Typically, the College of Commissioners and the Board of Supervisors are the primary decision-making bodies of the European Commission (the Commission) and the European Supervisory Authorities (ESAs), respectively. While they operate through very different legal structures and mandates, these organizations are composed of civil servants and representatives of each Member State and are therefore considered, for our purposes, as groups of individuals whose behaviors reflect archetypical relational models.

Isolating one or more forms of sociality which characterize the decision-making bodies of different regulators has profound theoretical and practical consequences. First, it sheds new light over the relationship between the architectural framework and group dynamics, indicating

---

[14] A. P. Fiske, "The Four Elementary Forms of Sociality: Framework for a Unified Theory of Social Relations," *Psychology Review*, 99 (1992), 689 (Fiske, "Four Forms of Sociality").

[15] Identified by Fiske through field study in West Africa and also uncovered at the same period in other branches of social sciences. See A. P. Fiske, *Structures of Social Life: The Four Elementary Forms of Human Relations* (New York: Free Press, 1991) (Fiske, *Structures of Social Life*).

[16] Fiske, "Four Forms of Sociality," 690.

[17] Ibid. at 689.

whether given institutional structures and apparatuses favor specific behavioral patterns and modus operandi. Second, the forms of sociality allow us to understand how conflicting dynamics emerge. It similarly shows how they are resolved between individuals partaking in a collective (regulatory) enterprise when the interest of the group as a whole no longer matches the interest pursued by some of its members and the equality relationship among individuals is compromised. The infra-institutional dynamics that followed the decision of the United Kingdom to leave the EU are an example of where this can be applied. The Brexit process is now formally commenced. Nonetheless, the disentanglement of the UK from the decision-making processes and the administrative apparatuses of the EU has not occurred immediately. Meanwhile, since the vote to leave was casted, the UK, being still part of the EU, has been participating – thorough its representatives – in the decision-making bodies of EU financial regulators. Hence, a socio-psychological analysis offers a fresh perspective over the unfolding dynamics. Marginalization, or even the genesis of different subgroups, may emerge in the College of Commissioners, affecting the agenda of the Commission. In examining this transition period from a social and psychological perspective, it will emerge that the role of the ESAs is likely to change. Any future reorganization of the EU regulatory and supervisory framework that Brexit will entail stems from within the current institutions. Members of core decision-making bodies, such as the Supervisory Boards of the ESAs, are required to adjust to a novel relational setting. In observing this process of adjustment, the isolated forms of sociality help predict whether, following Brexit, the EU regulatory governance for financial services and markets could be characterized by a divide between eurozone and non-eurozone Member States.

The chapter develops in four sections. Section 6.2 introduces the EU multi-level architectural framework for financial regulation and supervision, offering a typology of EU financial regulators. Section 6.3 illustrates the theory of relational models. It then applies this theory to isolate the dominant relational models for selected institutions that, within the EU legal order, are engaged in regulating and supervising financial markets. Part IV offers an application of the socio-psychological framework in the context of Brexit with particular attention to its implication for the tension between eurozone and non-eurozone countries.

6.2   EU Multi-Level Financial Regulation

EU institutions perform their activities and roles within the perimeters of EU law, as defined by the constitutional provisions enshrined in the Treaty of the European Union (TEU) and the Treaty of the Functioning of the European Union (TFEU).

In light of EU primary and secondary law, a typology of financial regulators is constructed around two core dimensions.[18] The first dimension is represented by the institutional status of a given entity within the EU legal order. In particular, financial regulators are regrouped into two main categories: institutions that are established through EU primary law, such as the Commission and the European Central Bank (ECB), and agencies established through secondary law, such as the ESAs and the European Systemic Risk Board (ESRB). The former category represents the pantheon of EU institutions, for which mandates, competencies, and composition are enshrined in the Treaties.[19] The latter category is wider and has been witnessing a constant expansion.[20]

In the context of financial regulation, the three ESAs – i.e., the European Banking Authority (EBA), the European Securities and Markets Authority (ESMA) and the European Insurance and Occupational Pensions Authority (EIOPA) – deserve particular attention. They are new administrative agencies (established in 2011) and epitomize the process of progressive "agencification" of EU law which has emerged to meet the growing demand for regulatory interventions in the European single market.[21] The rule-making powers of the ESAs emanate from (and are

---

[18] For further detail on this typology see Castellano and Helleringer, "Shedding Light on EU Financial Regulators," 80 et seq.

[19] TEU Art. 13 enlist the seven EU institutions: The European Parliament, the European Council, the Council of the European Union, the European Commission, the Court of Justice of the European Union (including the General Court and the Court of Justice), the European Central Bank, and the European Court of Auditors.

[20] For an analysis and a critique over the establishment of regulatory agencies in the EU see E. Chiti, "An Important Part of the EU's Institutional Machinery: Features, Problems and Perspectives of European Agencies," *Common Market Law Review*, 46 (2009), 1395–1442.

[21] On the genesis of the ESAs in comparison to other, alternative models for regulatory governance see G. G. Castellano, A. Jeunemaître and B. Lange, "Reforming European Union Financial Regulation: Thinking through Governance Models," *European Business Law Review*, 23 (2012) 437. For an accurate critique of the legal ground sustaining the ESAs and, in particular the EBA, see E. Fahey, "Does the Emperor have Financial Crisis Clothes? On the Legal Basis of the European Banking Authority," *The Modern Law Review*, 74 (2011), 581–595.

conducted under the aegis) of the Commission.[22] The EU constitutional structure significantly curtails their discretion in exercising decision-making powers. Hence, supervisory tasks are discharged only in limited circumstances and occur within the limits set by the European Court of Justice in the *Meroni* doctrine.[23] Notwithstanding these narrow constitutional premises, the ESAs have swiftly become a critical component of the EU architectural framework and are located at the forefront of EU regulatory governance of the financial sector. The EBA is the custodian of the Single Rulebook and has been engaged in the definition of its key elements, i.e., the rules concerning capital requirements for credit institutions and investment firms, as well as in the new special resolution regime.[24] The ESMA has been involved, inter alia, in the drafting of the Markets in Financial Instruments Directive and Regulation,[25] whereas EIOPA has been primarily preoccupied with the implementation of the directive concerning capital and liquidity requirements for insurance companies (Solvency II).[26]

Despite this, their current functions – following the impressive rule-making efforts recently completed – are shifting toward supervisory convergence. The ESAs are striving to accrue their institutional weights within the EU and at the international level.[27] Given that the ESAs are not (and cannot be) empowered with sufficient discretion to perform (outside exceptional circumstances) supervisory functions toward firms and markets, the oversight of cross-border operations and entities occurs through a network-based structure. Memoranda of understanding and secondary law provisions are established for national authorities to coordinate through Colleges of Supervisors and, within the Banking Union, Joint Supervisory Teams. In this respect, the EU multilayered

---

[22] On the rule-making powers attributed to ESAs, see N. Moloney, *EU Securities and Financial Markets Regulation*, 3rd edn. (Oxford: Oxford University Press, 2014), 854 et seq.

[23] Case 9/56 *Meroni* v. *High Authority* [1957–1958] ECR 133. On the supervisory powers see ibid. 942 et seq.

[24] Directive 2013/36/EU [2013] OJ L176/338 and Regulation EU No. 575/2013 [2013] OJ L176/1; and Directive 2014/59/EU [2014] OJ L173/90.

[25] Directive 2014/65/EU [2014] OJ L173/349 and Regulation (EU) No. 600/2014 [2014] OJ L173/84.

[26] Directive 2009/138/EU [2009] OJ L335/1.

[27] On the role of the ESAs in the international regulatory arena, prior to and after Brexit, see N. Moloney, "International Financial Governance, The EU, and Brexit: The 'Agencification' of EU Financial Governance and The Implications," *European Business Organization Law Review*, 17 (2016) 451.

Table 6.1 *The Legal Status of EU Financial Regulators*

Status	Institution	Scope
Treaty-based	European Commission	EU
	European Central Bank (ECB)	Eurozone/Banking Union
Secondary law-based	European Supervisory Authorities (ESAs)	EU
	European Systemic Risk Board (ESRB)	EU
Networks of national authorities	Colleges of Supervisors (CoS)	EU
	Joint Supervisory Teams (JST)	Eurozone/Banking Union

approach to financial regulation and supervision is composed of entities with different legal statuses and structures, as summarized in Table 6.1.

The second dimension in our typology represents the relation that selected EU institutions have, according to the Treaties, toward the *common interest* of the Union. EU regulators perform three key functions vis-à-vis this general interest, which are: advancing and protecting its existence, defining its content and ensuring its operation throughout the Union. The existence of a common interest represents a prerequisite to establishing a legal community that binds together different social actors – e.g., sovereign States, public administrations, citizens, and businesses.[28] This means that the EU is an entity that is autonomous and transcends the interests of its members when individually considered. Thus, EU institutions are established to pursue the interest of the community.[29] Although the common interest of the Union stemmed from the establishment of a single market, the concept – given its blurred contours – appears to be, in essence, the preservation and the prosperity of the Union.[30]

---

[28] The idea of the EU as a legal community operating under a common interest – that transcends the interests of individual members – emerges decisively from early case law; see, in particular, Case 26/62, *Van Gend en Loos* v. *Nederlandse Administratie der Belastingen*, 1963 ECR, 2–15.

[29] TEU Art. 13(1) states: "The Union shall have an institutional framework which shall aim to promote its values, advance its objectives, serve its interests, those of its citizens and those of the Member States, and ensure the consistency, effectiveness and continuity of its policies and actions."

[30] See Castellano and Helleringer, "Shedding Light on EU Financial Regulators."

A closer examination reveals that, in promoting the advancement of these overarching objectives, EU institutions have different prerogatives. In this regard, as illustrated in Table 6.2, within the EU financial regulatory framework, institutions and agencies perform different functions vis-à-vis the realization of the common interest. To the Commission, the Treaty expressly attributes the role of promoting the general interest of the Union.[31] The ECB, within the European System of Central Banks (ESCB), advances the primary interest of the monetary union of maintaining price stability.[32] The discretionary powers attributed to both institutions, e.g., in setting the policy agenda, initiating the legislative process, or in determining the appropriate monetary policy tools to safeguard the single currency, equip them with the ability to determine the contents of the general interest. This process benefits from the expertise of specialized agencies, such as the ESAs or the ESRB, which in turn contributes to defining – under the Commission's aegis – the general objectives of the Union. Leaving aside specific considerations concerning monetary policy activities, the interest of the Union is pursued through the EU legal order and by the voluminous corpus of rules and administrative provisions enacted to regulate financial firms and markets. Specific institutional arrangements to ensure supervisory convergence and coordination are thus required to ensure the correct and harmonized application of these rules. Without a change in the Treaty, this function is mandated to network-based mechanisms involving the authorities of EU Member States.

The complexity of the resulting framework, with different constitutional statuses, structures, and prerogatives, generate critical legal and political issues. First, the ECB discharges its newly acquired – yet enshrined in the Treaty – supervisory duties in line with its function of protecting the general interest of the monetary union. In giving operational value to such a common interest, the ECB will apply technical standards that have been de facto drafted by an institution that is not established by the Treaty, i.e., the EBA. Second, the risk of the three ESAs to be politicized – as noted also by the International Monetary Fund – may ultimately undermine the effectiveness of the regulatory governance apparatus established, within and outside the Banking Union.[33] The overlaps of different national and supranational interests within an

---

[31] TEU, Art. 17(1).

[32] TFEU, Art. 127(1)

[33] International Monetary Fund Country Report, *European Union: Publication of Financial Sector Assessment Program Documentation—Technical Note on European Banking Authority*, 7–87 Report No. 13/74 (2013).

Table 6.2 *The "Common Interest" of the Union and Financial Regulators*

Relation with the "common interest"	Example	Institution	Scope
Advancement and protection	*TEU Art. 17(1)* "The Commission shall promote the general interest of the Union and take appropriate initiatives to that end."	Commission	EU
	TFEU Art. 127(1) and Art. 129(1) Price stability and general support to the Union's economic policy.	ECB (European System of Central Banks)	Eurozone
Definition of contents	*TEU Art. 17(2)* Right of legislative initiative, power to set policy agenda (in pursuit of the general interests of the Union).	Commission	EU
	TFEU Art. 127(2) and Art. 129(1) Monetary policy tools (to achieve price stability).	ECB (European System of Central Banks)	Eurozone
	TFEU Art. 114 Legal harmonization	Commission + ESAs	EU
Operation and application	*TEU Art. 17(1)* Application of the Treaties and of EU law.	Commission	EU
	TFEU Art. 127(4) and Art. 128 Possibility to issue opinion and recommendations. Printing banknotes and minting coins.	ECB	Eurozone
	TFEU Art. 127(6) Prudential supervision (Banking Union).	ESAs	
	TFEU 114 Supervisory convergence Cross-border coordination and supervision	CoS JST	EU Eurozone/Banking Union

institutional framework that cannot sufficiently curb the risk of politicization and which is grounded on unstable constitutional premises, is likely to harbor conflicts between those Member States that have adopted the euro as a single currency and those that have not. The first group of Member States considers the ESAs and, in particular the EBA, as a forum where undue pressures may be directed toward Treaty-based institutions. The second group of states perceives the new supervisory role of the ECB as an expansion of the institutional perimeters of the eurozone, which thus reduces the weight of the ESAs.[34] Ultimately, this indicates that Member States within and outside the Banking Union (and the eurozone) have different priorities.[35] In this respect, it appears that, as part of being engaged in a supervisory convergence across the EU, non-Treaty based agencies will be naturally called to offer a bridge between the two groups of Member States within the single market. This chapter approaches these issues as phenomena related to the relational dynamics among the individuals participating in the decision-making process of the relevant EU institutions.

6.3 Elementary Forms of Sociality in Financial Regulatory Governance: The Case of the European Union

6.3.1 The Four Elementary Forms of Sociality

The theory of social relations identifies four relational models that characterize any social interaction in every culture[36]: Market Pricing (MP), Equality Matching (EM), Communal Sharing (CS), and Authority Ranking (AR). Combinations of these four models build various social forms in accordance with the contingent cultural framework. Through these lenses the social dimension of interactions among individuals is understood as a process that involves "seeking, making, sustaining, repairing, adjusting, judging, construing, and sanctioning relationships."[37] The four relational models operate in all domains of social action and cognition. For example, transfer of property, definition of standards of conduct, group decisions, or organization of labor.

---

[34] House of Lords, *European Banking Union: Key Issues and Challenges*, 2012, HL Paper 88, at 28.

[35] The point was also noted by A. Enria, "Challenges for the Future of EU Banking" (Speech, 3rd Financial Meeting, Madrid, January 2015).

[36] Fiske, "Four Forms of Sociality," 689.

[37] Ibid. at 690.

The core characteristics for each of these relational models are briefly presented here, drawing primarily from Fiske's unified view of the theory of social relations.

MP is the epitomic form of sociality in Western cultures.[38] Within this model, relationships among individuals are based on cost-and-benefit considerations to sustain self-interested exchanges. Market prices, exchange rates, or other forms of measurements are devices to facilitate such relational structure. Individuals interact and enter into consensual agreements with the intent of maximizing their return according to utilitarian and individualistic logics. From a socio-psychological perspective, rationality is not a necessary element for MP to occur, as irrational choices may still underpin self-interested exchanges. In general terms, MP arises whenever a coordinated action among individuals is necessary to attain an agreed general goal, provided the goal is pursued through voluntary interaction sustained by a calculative attitude. Relational dynamics based on MP require defined parameters and established criteria which individuals can consider to measure demands and assess whether their objectives are met. Explicit rules, often formally stated, are prerequisites for groups operating (primarily) under this form of sociality. Although MP is widely diffused, it is not the only mode of relating to others in Western cultures.

In EM, a form of sociality exchange is also a core feature.[39] However, in comparison to MP, EM presents a distinctive focus on ensuring an even balance within the group, rather than an individual maximization of value or resources. The principles of equality and reciprocity are cardinal features and individuals are willing to reduce personal gains in order to avoid imbalances or unfairness in the group.[40] A balanced distribution of resources is incentivized, echoing the economic concept of Pareto efficiency, whereby a given allocation of resources among individuals is considered optimal when it is impossible to make any one individual better off without making someone worse off.[41] In this form of sociality, individuals relate among themselves as equals and differences are taken

---

[38] Ibid., 706.

[39] Ibid., 702. As also noted by M. S. Clark and J. Mills, "Interpersonal Attraction in Exchange and Communal Relationships," *J. Personality & Soc. Psychol.*, 37 (1979), 12; and J. Mills and M. S. Clark, "Exchange and Communal Relationships," in *Rev. of Personality & Soc. Psychol.*, 3 (1982).

[40] Rawls' "veil of ignorance" is epitomic of the ethical dynamics underlying EM; *see,* John Rawls, *A Theory of Justice* (Cambridge MA: Harvard University Press, 2009).

[41] *See* V. Pareto, "The New Theories of Economics," *Journal of Political Economy*, 5 (1897) 485.

into account to reach an optimal point. This is represented by an even balance.

In relationships governed by CS, the equality principle is taken further and members of a group consider each other as part of the same family, sharing a common identity and, possibly, a common history.[42] A sense of responsibility for the well-being and preservation of the group as a whole is a core feature in the communal relationship. Unlike MP and EM, where resources are distributed according to merit or as part of exchanges, in CS resources are distributed (primarily) in response to the needs of individuals.[43] In modern societies, CS mostly characterizes familial and friendship relationships, but it is also common when the cooperative attitude toward a common objective is fueled by an *organizational identity*.[44] In such a circumstance, members of an organization, e.g., a company or an administrative authority, share an understanding of what characterizes their organization as unique. Within this framework, members of a group identify themselves under a common denominator – be it an ideology, a shared identity, a cultural element, a mission, or a common interest – and tend to change their behaviors to conform to the behaviors of the others in order to maintain their membership.[45] An idealized social norm, often accompanied by rituals and traditions, provides the core social bond. The ordering principles of consensus, unity, and conformity lead individuals to act in order to preserve the group and its existence. In its extreme manifestation, CS leads to *groupthink*, which is a psychological phenomenon that occurs when members of a group or a community impede critical thinking in order to avoid conflicts.[46] When conflicts among individuals are openly managed and not discouraged, CS still operates.

Finally, AR relationships reflect a hierarchical ordering among members of a group.[47] By adopting a linear structure, each individual is either above or below another member. Higher ranked individuals enjoy various benefits and are in command. Military ranks are epitomic of this

---

[42] Fiske, "Four Forms of Sociality," 693.

[43] The idea is advanced by Clark and Mills, "Interpersonal Attraction," and "Exchange and Communal Relationships."

[44] The concept is well established in the organizational literature, see S. A. and D. A. Whetten, "Organizational Identity," *Res. Org. Behav.* 7 (1985), 263.

[45] See M. D. and H. B. Gerard, "A Study of Normative and Informational Social Influences upon Individual Judgement," *J. Abnor. & Soc. Psychol.*, 51 (1955) 629.

[46] See I. L. Janis, "Groupthink," in *Psychological Studies of Policy Decisions and Fiascoes* (Boston MA: Houghton Mifflin, 1982).

[47] Fiske, "Four Forms of Sociality," 700.

relational model. In contrast to CS and EM, AR demands that resources are allocated depending on the ranking of individuals instead of being traded, equally distributed, or pooled. A hierarchical structure may be imposed or may develop spontaneously, for instance when individuals emulate or defer their decisions to someone considered superior.[48]

The four models often coexist, and a group that operates according only to one model is a rare phenomenon. Within the same group, different forms of sociality may be adopted depending on the activity the group has to perform.[49] Empirical investigation has shown that individuals recognize which form of interaction should be used in any given circumstance and (more or less consciously) opt for one of the forms of sociality.[50] This indicates that, depending on circumstances, there are cultural and contextual rules that drive individuals to adopt one of the four relational models of interaction. Drawing from these observations, the fundamental forms of sociality are applied to identify the relational dynamics that characterize selected EU institutions tasked with financial regulatory and supervisory functions.

6.3.2   The Forms of Sociality in the EU Regulatory Framework

To apply the theory of relational models to the EU regulatory framework, three points of methodology should be clarified. First, the decision-making bodies of EU institutions and agencies are approached as *groups of individuals* that organize themselves in *collective structures*. Here the achievement of one's activity may only occur if other individuals perform their assigned task or activity.[51] This implies that our findings and considerations concern primarily the body observed and do not necessarily reflect the general culture of the entity in which such a decision-making body operates. Second, basic contextual rules against which the scrutinized decision-making bodies organize themselves should be identified. To this end, the organizational structure and the powers of a given institution or agency define the context in which its decision-making

---

[48] *See* Charles Horton Cooley, *Human Nature and the Social Order* (New York: Transaction Publishers, 1992); and Benjamin R. Barber, *Strong Democracy: Participatory Politics for a New Age* (Berkeley CA: University of California Press, 2003).

[49] Fiske, "Four Forms of Sociality," 701.

[50] *See* R. A. LeVine, "Properties of Culture: An Ethnographic View," in R. A. Shweder and R. A. LeVine (eds.), Culture Theory: Essays on Mind, Emotion, and the Self (Cambridge: Cambridge University Press, 1984) *and* Fiske, "Four Forms of Sociality."

[51] This idea draws from F. H. Allport, "A Structural Conception," 3. The idea that institutions are groups of individuals has been also advanced by Douglas, *Institutions Think*.

body has been established. Third and related, a fundamental group norm bonding together individuals should be identified. The composition of the various decision-making bodies of Treaty-based institutions and non-Treaty-based agencies, as well as their functions vis-à-vis the pursuit of a common interest, are powerful proxies indicating whether there is an organizational identity. For instance, bodies which are composed of national representatives operate under a given group norm. This is different from the group norm which drives the decisions of a body composed of civil servants and where individuals are mandated to advance the interests of the body itself or the institution it governs. Ultimately, whether EU institutions and agencies organize themselves in a collective enterprise which is governed (primarily) by communal, bargain, equalitarian, or hierarchal relational models depends on a number of factors, largely engendered in the legal framework.

Through this prism, the application of the forms of sociality in relation to EU regulators is directly linked to the fundamental grammar of the EU legal order. Hence, the typology presented in section 6.2 offers a map that allows for comparison of different institutions and agencies in relation to both their proximity to the general group norm, i.e. the pursuit of the common interest of the Union, and their constitutional status. This means that where a given decision-making body within an institution performs more than one function, more than one model of sociality is observed. In advancing this approach, we hope to stimulate a new strand of empirical studies that connects with greater accuracy the legal (and constitutional) dimension of administrative agencies and political institutions with forms of sociality. Publicly available official documents, scholarly inquiry, and legal documents provide for an abundance of data on the modus operandi that characterizes the EU bodies under scrutiny.[52] Consequently, for each body examined it is possible to isolate a dominant relational model, as summarized by Table 6.3 and as further illustrated in the remainder of this chapter.

A pattern emerges from this data. CS is the dominant mode for institutions engaged in the advancement and protection of the common interest. EM and MP are the dominant modes for institutions involved in defining the content of the common interest (under the principles of mutual recognition). They are also the dominant modes for institutions operating the common interest, where regulatory and supervisory convergence occur through a balancing of the interests of the community, with

---

[52] For a more complete treatise over the methodological approach and the source of data, see Castellano and Helleringer, "Shedding Light on EU Financial Regulators."

Table 6.3 *The Form of Sociality in Respect to the Legal Status of Selected EU Bodies and their Relation with the Common Interest of the Union*

Institution	Legal status	Relation with the "common interest"	Form of sociality
Commission	Treaty-based	Advancement and protection	CS
		Definition of the content	EM
ECB	Treaty-based	Advancement and protection	CS
		Definition of the content	EM
ESAs	Secondary law-based	Definition of the content	EM
		Operation and application	MP
CoS/JTS	Network	Operation and application	MP

national and industry's interests. By contrast, due to the very nature of the EU legal framework, AR does not appear to be a dominant mode in any of the three categories elicited. This is not to say that hierarchical arrangements are alien to EU institutions and agencies; rather it signals that linear ordering, albeit present to an extent and in specific instances, is not a dominant form of sociality induced by the legal framework governing the decision-making bodies under scrutiny. Moreover, as expected for any group of individuals, more than one form of sociality is observed. More precisely, the coexistence of multiple forms of sociality appears to reflect the various functions that the observed entities, and their decision-making bodies, are mandated to perform vis-à-vis the common interest. EU Treaty-based institutions appear to be engaging with the logics of two primary forms of sociality: CS and EM. With regards to the ESAs, their ambivalent – and recently acquired – roles lead to EM and MP appearing as their primary forms of sociality.

6.3.2.1   The Treaty-based Institutions and Communal Sharing and Equality Matching Forms of Sociality

In general terms, CS relational dynamics permeate the EU constitutional framework. CS is a direct emanation of the idealized notion of "common interest." Hence, the advancement of such an interest is the raison d'être of Treaty-based institutions that are called on to represent such a community as a whole. In particular, the ECB and the Commission pursue the common interest, however intended, precisely through the realization of specified objectives that shape their regulatory and supervisory action. The Commission acts as a guardian of and represents the community's interest, to the point that it defines itself as the institutional embodiment of the community.[53] The ECB preserves the stability of the eurozone, in the general interest of its members. These institutions' supranational status, with extensive autonomy and independence, separates them from individual members and entitles them to manage resources that are pooled in the pursuit of a collective interest. Within these institutions, the pursuit of a common interest – no matter how vaguely defined – bonds together individuals who, in turn, operate knowing that their actions are directed toward a collective enterprise.[54] The principles characterizing a decision-making structure based on CS, i.e. consensus, unity and conformity,[55] emerge from the status of their civil servants whose activities and roles are above national politics under the principles of *fonction publique européenne* (European civil service). This determines a sense of the group and an organizational identity which is established to manage the (pooled) resources of the community in view of its general interest.

A closer look at the organizational structures and decision-making processes of the Commission and the ECB reveals that EM also characterizes the relational dynamics within their respective decision-making organs. These organs are governed under the principle that distinct but equal individuals acknowledge their differences to reach an even balance.[56] Other than being the guardian of the common interest, the Commission is also the engine of the Union, with its executive, policy-setting, and quasi-legislative powers. The College of Commissioner is the primary decision-making body of the Commission and it is composed of one Commissioner for each Member State[57] (now twenty-eight Commissioners[58]), with one President proposed by the European Council and elected by the Parliament.[59] The debate over the politicization of the College of Commissioners has led commentators to note that,

---

[53] European Commission, *The European Commission: 1995–2000*, 7.
[54] Allport, "A Structural Conception," 13–15.
[55] Fiske, "Four Forms of Sociality," 697.
[56] Ibid., 705.
[57] TEU art. 17(4).
[58] As illustrated below, until the UK formally leaves the EU, i.e., two years after the notification to the European Council of the decision to withdraw from the Union, the EU is still composed of twenty-eight Member States.
[59] TEU art. 17(5) and TFEU art. 244, which stipulates that "Member States shall be treated on a strictly equal footing as regards determination of the sequence of, and the time spent by, their nationals as members of the Commission" TFEU art. 244(a).

in practice, there is little collegial discussion.[60] A socio-psychological perspective indicates that the lack of collegiality could be explained also as a manifestation of a specific form of sociality.

The College of Commissioners observes the "one-person-one-vote" principle. This indicates that the EM is likely to govern interpersonal relationships. A mechanism for social influence is thus created. Individuals receiving a favor feel obliged to reciprocate in order to ensure balance and equality among group members.[61] For example, debating the decisions proposed by one or more Commissioners is likely to delay the decision-making process and compromise the Commissioners' ability to attain their objectives. In order to maintain an overall balance of interpersonal relationships – and avoid the institutional paralysis of such a large decision-making body – the principles of reciprocity and equality encourage a bargaining process.

The EM relational mode can also be found in the ECB governing organs. Within the ECB there are three decision-making organs, namely:

i) The Governing Council, which formulates monetary policy for the eurozone, defines guidelines for national central banks operating under the ECBS, and under the Single Supervisory Mechanism (SSM) of the Banking Union, sets the general supervisory framework with the possibility to object the decisions proposed by the Supervisory Board.

ii) The Executive Board, which implements the guidelines established by the Governing Council and coordinates national central banks.

iii) The newly established Supervisory Board which coordinates the supervisory activities under the SSM.

The Governing Council is the primary decision-making body and is composed of the governors of the national central banks that are a part of the eurozone, plus the members of the Executive Board (President, Vice-President and four other independent individuals).[62] Governors shall not represent the interests of their country and are members in

---

[60] See, e.g., F. Franchino, "Delegating Powers in the European Community," *B. J. Pol. S.*, 34 (2004) 269; and S. K. Schmidt, "The European Commission's Powers in Shaping Policies," in D. G. Dimitrakopoulos (ed.), *The Changing European Commission* (Manchester: Manchester University Press, 2004), 105.

[61] *See* K. S. Cook, C. Cheshire, E R. Rice and S. Nakagawa, "Social Exchange Theory," in J. DeLamater and A. Ward (eds.), *Handbook of Social Psychology* (Dordrecht: Springer, 2013), 61.

[62] TFEU art. 283(1).

their capacity as independent experts. In order to avoid coalitions among Member States, the Executive Board sets the agenda and, since Lithuania's accession to the eurozone as of 2015, the voting follows a rotating system capped at twenty-one voters. Governors are allocated to different groups based on the size of their country's economy and financial sector. As long as the eurozone has between eighteen and twenty-one participating countries, there are two groups. The five largest countries constitute the first group, sharing a total of four voting rights that rotate monthly.[63] Thus, every month one of the governors of the five largest countries cannot vote, but may participate in the discussion. The remaining governors share a total of eleven voting rights, which also rotate on a monthly basis. The six members of the Executive Board are permanent voters. This creates a system based on a collective decision-making process where one person is equal to one vote. The mechanism creates a "veil of ignorance" proper of the EM form of sociality.[64] In fact, members of the Governing Council are in the position to predict when they will not vote, but cannot predict the decisions on which they will be asked to vote.

6.3.2.2 Secondary Law-based Agencies and Market Pricing Form of Sociality

The ESAs and the ESRB have been established under Article 114 TFEU which allows Treaty-based institutions to delegate specific task to ad hoc created authorities, as long as they are devices to serve the community's interest of protecting the single market through the harmonization of EU law. It follows that the ESAs and the ESRB are, from a constitutional perspective, means to achieve the general interest and, following the categorization offered in section 6.2, they operate the common interest by ensuring regulatory and supervisory convergence.

With primary reference to ESMA, we argue that the decision-making bodies of the ESAs are primarily characterized by MP form of sociality. ESMA drafts technical standards, advances proposals, and issues "comply or explain" notices, which harden its non-binding guidelines and recommendations.[65] ESMA's primary decision-making body is the

---

[63] The countries in this group are France, Germany, Italy, the Netherlands and Spain.

[64] Fiske, "Four Forms of Sociality," 705.

[65] Council Regulation 1095/2010, Nov. 24, 2010, art. 16 O.J. (L 331) (EU), establishing a European Supervisory Authority (European Securities and Markets Authority), amending Decision No 716/2009/EC and repealing Commission Decision 2009/77/EC (ESMA Regulation).

Board of Supervisors, which is composed of the heads of Member States' supervisors, themselves defined as National Competent Authorities (NCAs). The Chairperson of ESMA sits on the Board and chairs the meeting, but has no voting right. The Board also includes representatives (also with no voting rights) of the Commission (as for any EU agency), the ESRB, EBA, and EIOPA. With such a configuration, the Board combines scientific expertise functions with political oversight, two functions that are usually separated. The Board gives guidance to the work of ESMA, and adopts opinions, recommendations, decisions and advice. The Board operates under a simple majority vote; each Board member has one voting right and Board members have a duty *not* to advance the interest of their own Member State[66] (but see below). Alongside the Board of Supervisors, there is the Management Board, which is composed of the Chairperson and six members of the Board of Supervisors. The members of the Management Board are elected by the voting members of the Board of Supervisors.[67] Also in this case, the Commission and the Executive Director participate in meetings, but have no voting rights.[68] The Management Board operates on a simple majority rule basis. The Management Board has to propose, for adoption by the Board of Supervisors, an annual and multi-annual work program. In addition, to facilitate consultation with stakeholders, ESMA has established a consultative Securities and Markets Stakeholder Group (SMSG).[69] This Group is consulted by ESMA on various matters, including technical aspects of market practices. Decisions within ESMA – especially those driving supervisory convergence across the EU – are technical in nature and abide to established criteria set by its remit and internal procedures.[70]

Notwithstanding the Board of Supervisors' supranational character,[71] representatives of NCAs within the Board are naturally incentivized to promote national interests. For instance, in deciding how to allocate the limited resources of ESMA – and, in general, of the three ESAs – NCAs

---

[66] ESMA Regulation art. 44(1).

[67] ESMA Regulation art. 45(1).

[68] ESMA Regulation art. 45(2); according to art. 45(3) of the same regulation, the representative of the Commission, however, has voting rights on matters related to the ESMA's budget.

[69] ESMA Regulation art. 37.

[70] See, e.g., European Securities and Markets Authority Annual Report 9 (2011).

[71] According ESMA Regulation art. 42 para 1, ESAs should act independently and autonomously "in the sole interest of the Union as a whole" without seeking instructions from other European institutions or from Member States.

are not bound to a common (European) organizational identity. The 2013 Mazars ESA Review also highlighted that decisions are mostly taken through a process of negotiation that engages the members of the Board, and emphasized the preponderance of national interests over those of the EU.[72] Through the prism of the fundamental forms of sociality, these elements indicate that the group operates primarily through a MP form of sociality, where the individual interests are more prominent.

6.4   Regulators in Disarray

The relational models provide a useful analytical tool to examine the actual or potential conflicts within and among EU institutions. Divergences among individuals partaking in a collective enterprise are also managed following the behavioral patterns ascribed to each dominant form of sociality. Social sanctioning when individuals do not follow the appropriate group norm are commonly adopted to maintain group cohesion. In this respect, the Brexit debate – preceding and following the result of the referendum of June 23, 2016, when the UK voted to leave the EU – offers a perfect case study to examine how different, and often antithetic, positions advanced by EU Member States influence the group dynamics operating within different EU institutions and bodies.[73] The UK has signaled that it no longer shares the common interest upon which the Union has been constructed. As further elaborated below, this emerges from the result of the June referendum and is evidenced in the official talks preceding the public vote. Even after the formal notification of withdrawal, as per Article 50 TEU, the UK would remain a member of the Union. Pursuant to Article 50 TEU, there is a window of two years – set to terminate in March 2019 – to define the UK–EU relationships, after which the UK will be effectively out of the Union. This exit will occur with or without a deal between the UK and the EU.[74] Hence, at least until the moment of exit, the UK has

---

[72] Mazars, *The European Supervisory Agency, Review of the New European System of Financial Supervision* (October 2013); see in particular Pt. 1.

[73] For a first assessment of the possible implications of Brexit see N. Moloney, "Financial Services, The EU, and Brexit: An Uncertain Future for the City?" *German Law Journal*, 17 (2016) 75. For a complete analysis of the legal implications of Brexit for financial services see K. Alexander, et al., *Brexit and Financial Services: Law and Policy* (London: Bloomsbury Publishing, 2018).

[74] In particular, TEU art. 50 para 3 states: "The Treaties shall cease to apply to the State in question from the date of entry into force of the withdrawal agreement or, failing that, two

participated in most of the official meetings of the European Council, and its representatives have still held positions in EU institutions, such as the Commission and the ESAs. In this context, while the Union still performs its tasks and functions relying on an institutional setting designed for twenty-eight countries, the position of the representatives of the UK in the various decision-making bodies of EU institutions is peculiar. A social and psychological perspective over the group dynamics within institutions provides a much deeper understanding of an unfolding debate that will have ripple effects in the years to come.

6.4.1 The Emergence of a Divide

A significant source of tension in EU institutions derives from the emergence and the consolidation of two separate groups of countries, notably eurozone countries and non-eurozone countries. The inclusion of financial stability within the perimeters of the common interests is particularly pronounced for Member States that are taking part in the SSM. The link between the banking regulation and supervision, sovereign debts restructuring, and monetary policy in the eurozone, imposes crisis response solutions tailored to the needs of the monetary union and demanding further integration. Breaking the vicious circle between the banking sector and sovereign debt, whereby the use of public funds to rescue troubled banks increases national debts and weakens the single currency, has been a priority animating the establishment of the Banking Union. However, the greater involvement of the ECB preoccupied many Member States, chiefly the UK, which feared a reduced role of the EBA.[75] In general terms, it is possible to note that, within the EU, there is material misalignment in the understanding of what constitutes the common interest. Drawing from the literature on the forms of sociality, it is possible to examine how this divide within the Union affects the decision-making process and, more generally, the relational dynamics within institutions.

When Communal Sharing (CS) operates, members are not ranked or organized under a hierarchical structure. Decisions made for the group,

---

years after the notification [...], unless the European Council, in agreement with the Member State concerned, unanimously decides to extend this period." For an analysis over the mechanism put forward by TEU art. 50, *see* European Parliament, *Brief: Article 50 TEU: Withdrawal of a Member State from the EU*, European Parliamentary Research Service (Feb. 2016, PE 577.971).

[75] See supra House of Lords (n. 34).

and conflicting interests, are resolved under the overarching objective of preserving the collective enterprise. A powerful illustration of this behavioral structure is offered by the position of the UK in the debate concerning the establishment of the Banking Union, which happened only a few years before the Brexit decision. Here, the UK, while opting out from the project and advancing some concerns, formally supported the creation of a Banking Union among eurozone countries, having in view the common objective of preserving the integrity of the single market.[76]

More generally, prolonged dissent may engender a disagreement around the group norm upon which the collective structure is established. This makes participation in the group less rewarding and ultimately may lead to one or more individuals withdrawing from the group.[77] Hence, lacking a sense of belonging to a collective project, the relational equivalence among members is undermined.[78] It follows that prolonged divergences damage not only groups characterized by CS, but also groups operating under the equality paradigm of an EM relational model. In the EU institutional framework, this implies that if the existence of the common interest is compromised, decision-making bodies entrusted with the powers to define the contents of such a common interest are also compromised.

The problem emerges clearly from the impact that the UK vote to leave the EU had immediately on the College of Commissioners. The Commissioner for the UK, Lord Hill, held the crucial role of advancing the financial regulatory agenda of the Union, being Commissioner for Financial Stability, Financial Services and Capital Markets Union. After the results of the referendum, Lord Hill, a key promoter of the Capital Markets Union, resigned and Mr. Dombrovskis (Latvia), Vice-President of the Commission and Commissioner for the Euro and Social Dialogue, took over his position.[79] Given that the UK is still part of the EU, a new UK Commissioner for the Security Union has since been appointed,

---

[76] On the different positions see D. Howarth and L. Quaglia, "The Steep Road to European Banking Union: Constructing the Single Resolution Mechanism," *J. Common Mkt. L. Rev.*, 52 (2014) 125 and A. Spendzharova, "Is More 'Brussels' the Solution? New European Union Member States' Preferences About the European Financial Architecture," *J. Common Mkt. L. Rev.*, 50 (2012) 315.

[77] Allport, "A Structural Conception of Behavior,"11.

[78] Fiske, "Four Forms of Sociality," 697.

[79] Jim Brunsden, "UK's EU Commissioner Lord Hill Quits as British Departures Begin," *Financial Times*, June 25, 2016; and Jim Brunsden, "Brexit Gives Valdis Dombrovskis Big Sway Over Banks," *Financial Times*, June 30, 2016.

Sir Julian King.[80] However, from the "Mission Letter" issued by the President of the Commission, it emerges that the new Commissioner will be mostly in charge of implementing "concrete operational measures,"[81] rather than focusing on policymaking. Moreover, Sir Julian will not represent the Commission in the European Parliament and at meetings of national ministers; a crucial role maintained by the previous Commissioner.[82] Hence, one member of a key decision-making body within a Treaty-based institution is not mandated to advance and protect the common interest of the Union; instead, differently from other members, he has been allocated operational functions that are proper of non-Treaty-based institutions (see Table 6.3). As a consequence, the representative for the UK in the College of Commissioners is no longer treated as formally equal to the other Commissioners. Ultimately, his role has been curtailed, thus weakening the equality paradigm that characterizes a group dominated by a form of sociality that responds to the Equality Matching relational dynamics.

6.4.2   Insiders v. Outsiders

The existence of Member States that partake in only some features of the Union is not new in the history of the EU, and is often referred to as a phenomenon of *differentiated integration*. Accordingly, Member States may opt for different levels of integration that entail different levels of abdication of state prerogatives, on specific matters, toward the supranational institutional apparatus.[83] Differentiation characterizes the genesis of the EU that from a small group of founding members progressively enlarged and conflated various communities into a supranational union. During this process, opt-out clauses, notably to the Schengen Agreement and to the monetary union, have been conceded to some Member States and, more generally, new members are not expected to adopt the single

---

[80] M. Khan, "Juncker to Appoint New UK Commissioner as 'Security' Chief," *Financial Times*, Aug. 2, 2016.

[81] Mission Letter from Jean-Claude Juncker, President, European Commission, to Julian King, Member of the European Commission, 4 (Brussels, Aug. 2, 2016).

[82] Ibid. at 5.

[83] See B. Leruth and C. Lord, "Differentiated Integration in the European Union: A Concept a Process or a Theory?," *J. Eur. Pub. Pol.*, 22 (2015) 754; F. Schimmelfennig, et al., "The European Union as a System of Differentiated Integration, Politicization and Differentiation," *J. Eur. Pub. Pol.*, 22 (2015) 764; J. Jamet, "The Optimal Assignment of Prerogatives to Different Levels of Government in the EU," *J. Common Mrkt. Stud.*, 49 (2011) 563.

currency at the same pace. Nonetheless, the division between countries that have adopted the euro and countries that have not, either because they opted out or because they are waiting to meet the conditions for joining the monetary union, is becoming more pronounced. Following the recent crises and the establishment of the Banking Union, the risk of a two-speed Europe has been particularly strong. There is even a risk that differentiation could evolve into fragmentation, as already witnessed in the discontent that animated the movement causing the UK to leave the Union. With the Brexit vote, fragmentation is now becoming a tangible risk that the EU has to tackle.

Aside from any speculation over the possible future of the UK and the EU, the unified theory of social relations applied to EU financial regulators helps to identify an increasingly sharp division within groups of individuals entrusted with decision-making powers. Such a division implies that outsiders, i.e. countries not participating in a given project, harden their positions, while insiders, i.e. countries partaking in the new project, expect the former to join.[84] Beyond this, a socio-psychological standpoint indicates that the differentiation between outsiders and insiders may induce insiders to concentrate around a new shared interest that defines a new bond, or even a new common identity. In turn, this is further legitimized by the existence of outsiders who do not share in such a bond and whose common interest may harden as well toward a new shared objective.[85] The unfolding events concerning Brexit offer a powerful illustration of such a group dynamic.

A progressive crystallization of different positions around new or reinforced shared objectives has emerged from the declarations of European politicians during the talks that preceded the formal commencement of EU–UK negotiations. In particular, reports over the alleged stance of EU negotiators to use French, rather than English, as the official language of the negotiation process regarding the EU–UK relationships signals, beyond a possible pre-negotiation tactic, the search for a new group identity for EU Member States.[86] Likewise, the polarization of a group around a hardened common interest, toward which individual interests converge and are superseded, is apparent if one

---

[84] T. Chopin and C. Lequesne, "Differentiation as a Double-Edged Sword: Member States' Practices and Brexit," *Int'l Aff.*, 92 (2016) 531.

[85] Fiske notes that CS, in its extreme form, may imply "a contrast between the subjective 'we' and the objectified 'they.'" Fiske, "Four Forms of Sociality," 699.

[86] F. Guarascio, "Parlez-vous Brexit? EU Negotiator Wants Brits to Talk French," *Reuters*, Oct 21, 2016.

considers that negotiations will be conducted between the EU – a block of twenty-seven countries that is expected to act, by virtue of the legal obligations established in the Treaties, as a unitary entity protecting its existence – and the UK, a single sovereign state. This polarization is exemplified by the fact that the first meetings of the European Council after Brexit – on June 29, 2016 (Brussels) and on September 16, 2016 (Bratislava) – were held informally, without the participation of the UK. They led to what has been labeled the Bratislava Declaration and Roadmap, that deals with the new institutional setting of the Union.[87] In particular, the Bratislava Declaration opened with a reaffirmation of the common interest, enshrined in the following statement:

> Although *one country* has decided to leave, the EU remains indispensable for *the rest of us*. In the aftermath of the *wars and deep divisions* on our continent, the EU secured peace, democracy and enabled our countries to prosper. ... We are determined to make a success of the EU with 27 Member States, building on this *joint history*.[88]

This statement appears to be more than a mere rhetorical device. First, the locution "one country" contraposed to "the rest of us" (as well as "our continent') constructs a hiatus between a generically denominated outsider – i.e., the runaway country – and the subjective insiders.[89] Second, reference to "wars and deep divisions" (as well as to the "joint history") echoes the Schuman declaration of 1950, which represents the first time the idea of a common interest was presented as a necessary premise for an enduring peace.[90] The separation between those members of the club partaking a common interests is manifested also in the subsequent Brexit talks, which have been separated from the agenda concerning "the future of the EU with twenty-seven member countries."[91]

While the result of referendum held in the UK enlarged a fracture in the common interest, the phenomenon has deeper roots. Already during the run-up to the referendum, and as a condition for the UK to remain in the EU, the then-UK Prime Minister negotiated concessions and exceptions that were gathered in an agreement reached during the European

---

[87] European Council, Bratislava Declaration, 1 (informal meeting, Sept. 16, 2016).

[88] Emphasis added. Ibid. at 1.

[89] On this aspect see supra n. 85.

[90] See R. Schuman, "A United States of Europe," speech recorded in *Selection of Texts Concerning Institutional Matters of The Community from 1950 to 1982*, 47, European Parliament Committee on Institutional Affairs (1982).

[91] See, e.g., President Donald Tusk, *Remarks of the President of the European Parliament Following the European Council Meeting* (Oct. 20–21, 2016).

Council (February, 18 and 19, 2016): this already signaled a misalignment of interests between the EU, the monetary union and ultimately the UK.[92] Such an agreement reflects a separation that goes beyond the process of differential integration that allowed the UK to opt out from the single currency; it entailed a general and more profound opt-out for the UK on an ever-closer Union.[93] In this respect, it was expressly stated that reference to an ever-closer Union contained in the Treaties does not constitute a legal basis for expanding the scope, the competencies, or the powers of the EU and of its institutions.[94]

Among the various items of the agreement, of particular interest (for the purposes of this analysis) are those defining the perimeters of the Banking Union and the relationships between eurozone and non-eurozone countries. The agreement advocated for a stronger protection for eurozone Member States and, hence, a sharper separation between the eurozone and non-eurozone countries. From a legal perspective, the agreement, albeit recognizing the necessity to deepen the monetary union in support of a robust Banking Union, reaffirmed two already established principles of EU law. First, it reinstated the principle of non-discrimination toward non-eurozone Member States, thus indicating that regulation and supervision of banking institutions in the EU should have followed two separate paths. Second, the agreement reaffirmed a principle already encountered in the *OLAF* decision and according to which the EU institutions involved in the governance of the eurozone should be subjected to EU law at large, and their decisions should be taken with the participation of non-eurozone Member States when affected.[95] Given that the agreement would have had a limited impact on the existing EU legal framework, the requests therein advanced may signal a departure from the idea of common interest, that is, a fracture in the group norm.

Against this backdrop, different scenarios may develop. Members may be separated under the pressure of a centrifugal force that dissolves the group norm and, thus, the group. The widening gap between eurozone

---

[92] European Council, *Conclusions*, Brussels (Feb. 19, 2016).

[93] The agreement commences the section titled "Sovereignty" with the following statement: "It is recognised that the United Kingdom ... is not committed to further political integration into the European Union. The substance of this will be incorporated into the Treaties at the time of their next revision ... so as to make it clear that the references to ever closer union do not apply to the United Kingdom." Ibid. at Annex 1, p. 16.

[94] Ibid.

[95] C-11/00 *Commission* v. *European Central Bank*, 1999/726, [1991] ECR (EC).

and non-eurozone countries may result in a weakened equivalence relationship in the EU architectural framework for financial regulation. Alternatively, a centripetal force could lead to a convergence around a new or a reinforced group norm. Even if damage to the Union is one of the most probable consequences of Brexit, a socio-psychological perspective indicates that the self-preservation of the group may tighten the group of the "remaining." This dynamic can be observed in the decision, following a large bid, to relocate the EBA from London to Paris. It can also be seen in the Commission stance (backed by several Member States and by the ECB) to deploy a new system to regulate non-EU clearing houses that currently handle a large portion of euro-denominated transactions.[96] In fact, the completion of the Brexit process calls into question the applicability of the protections against discrimination based on location and currency for the UK financial services industry.

In general terms, the theory of social relations helps explaining why, after Brexit, the polarization around two group norms – one for eurozone and one for non-eurozone Member States – may ultimately fade. Under the Maastricht Treaty, any country joining the EU is obliged to adopt the single currency, provided that they fulfill the convergence criteria, which include price stability, soundness and sustainability of public finances, durability of convergence, and exchange rate stability.[97] Denmark and the UK negotiated an opt-out from this obligation. Hence, after Brexit becomes effective, only Denmark is formally exempted from joining the eurozone. Nonetheless, rather than clustering around the choice of the UK, and thus widening the gap between eurozone and non-eurozone countries, Denmark is currently debating joining the Banking Union, with the intent of becoming a stronger financial center. The future is obviously uncertain and any forecast tends toward speculation; however, the dominant form of sociality characterizing the behavioral patterns of

---

[96] See European Commission, "Proposal for a Regulation of the European Parliament and of the Council amending Regulation (EU) No 648/2012 as regards the clearing obligation, the suspension of the clearing obligation, the reporting requirements, the risk-mitigation techniques for OTC derivatives contracts not cleared by a central counterparty, the registration and supervision of trade repositories and the requirements for trade repositories" (Brussels, 4 May 2017 COM(2017)208).

[97] Albeit the Global Financial Crisis slowed the expansion of the eurozone, Bulgaria, Croatia, Czech Republic, Hungary, Poland, Romania and Sweden will join the eurozone eventually. For a review of the different levels economic integration and the legal framework of these countries, see European Central Bank, *Convergence Report 2014* (Frankfurt, Jun. 4, 2014).

the decision-making bodies will directly affect the ultimate outcome. In this respect, the expanding process of financial integration presupposes that members are partaking in an "enhanced group norm." According to this norm the common interest is achieved by pairing regulatory and supervisory convergence with monetary integration. In other words, the shock sent by Brexit tilted the equilibrium between the two coexisting sub-groups that had different understandings of what constituted the common interest. This triggered a centripetal force within institutions governed by Communal Sharing or Equality Matching forms of sociality.

6.5   Conclusion

Studies in the field of social psychology and anthropology highlight four fundamental relational models, or forms of sociality. Such relational structures characterize relationships within every group and call for specific decision-making processes within such groups: the way they think is influenced by the prominence given to shared objectives that can be more or less distinct from individual members' interests.

In the general context of financial regulation, and with respect to EU institutions specifically, this is evidenced by the fact that institutions perform different functions (including advancing and defining the contents of the common interests) and display specific relational – and decision-making – models. Capturing this mosaic opens up the complexity of the multi-layer governance model of the EU. It also clarifies the dynamics at play and therefore provides a deeper understanding of behavior within the multi-layer governance model. This new map helps elucidate why, after Brexit, the eurozone Member State vs. non-eurozone Member State dichotomy may become less pronounced. When institutions must respond and adapt to different political and economic contingencies, the dominant form of sociality characterizing the behavioral patterns of their decision-making bodies has direct consequences on the ultimate outcome. Brexit has revealed how much the understanding of what constitutes the common interest may differ – and triggered centripetal tensions within financial regulators governed by Communal Sharing or Equality Matching forms of sociality.

The Role of Political Economy in Designing Banking Regulation

The Israeli Bank Fees Reform as a Test Case

RUTH PLATO-SHINAR

7.1 Introduction

According to the Public Interest Theory, the aim of regulation is to maintain and promote the public interest. Regulation is supplied in response to the demand of the public for the correction of inefficient or inequitable market practices, and it is designed to improve the public's welfare by correcting market imperfections. The underlying assumption of the concept of regulation is that no other body (private, group, or the market as a whole) can satisfy the public's interest in a more effective manner, and therefore regulation was established as the mission of the regulatory agency. Regulation is assumed to benefit society as a whole, rather than any particular vested interests. The regulatory agency represents the interest of the society in general, within which it operates, rather than the private benefit of certain interest groups or those of the regulator himself. The regulators are perceived as professionals, specialists in their field, honest in their pursuit of public goals, and unbiased, thus capable of fulfilling their goals.[1]

---

[1] M. E. Levine and J. L. Forrence, "Regulatory Capture, Public Interest and the Public Agenda: Towards Synthesis," *Journal of Law, Economics and Organization*, 167 (1990); M. Hankte-Domas, "The Public Interest Theory of Regulation; Non-Existence or Misinterpretation?," *European Journal of Law and Economics*, 15 (2003), 165–194; R. Baldwin, M. Cave and M. Lodge, *Understanding Regulation: Theory, Strategy and Practice*, 2nd edn. (Oxford: Oxford University Press, 2012), 40–43; R. A. Posner, "Theories of Economic Regulation," *The Bell Journal of Economics and Management Science*, 5 (1974), 335, 335–341; J. den Hertog, "Review of Economic Theories of Regulation," Discussion Paper No. 10–18, Tjalling C. Koopmans Research Institute 5–21 (2010), www.uu.nl/sites/default/files/rebo_use_dp_2010_10–18.pdf.

However, this normative theory does not always match reality. The regulator does not always understand his task. He may use poor judgment in the prioritization of his goals. He may not act industriously enough in the fulfillment of his powers. He may prefer the interest of a specific interest group over that of the general public, and may act egocentrically by promoting his own self-interest.[2] As a result of these and other issues, regulators do not necessarily maintain and promote the public interest.

These regulatory failures may also apply in the banking sector and characterize the regulator of banks. Banking is a complex activity, obliging the regulator to use enhanced knowledge and a very high level of specialization. Banking is a dynamic field that requires the regulator to keep pace and adopt an active attitude in order to meet the market's needs. Often, the banking regulator is in charge of both prudential regulation (maintaining the stability of the banking system) and the conduct of business regulation, goals that may contradict each other and may require a sensitive balance between them, which is not an easy task. The banks, as a special interest group with a huge financial and political clout, may attempt to convince the regulator to adopt a policy that suits their needs, to the detriment of the general public. As a result of all these issues, the banking regulation, in many situations, fails to achieve its objective and does not work in favor of the general public.

However, the Israeli experience shows that under certain circumstances, public pressure can overcome such a regulatory failure and result in regulation fashioned to suit the interests of the public. A case that well illustrates this issue is the bank fees reform that took place in Israel in 2007, and which will serve as the test case in this chapter.

The structure of this chapter is as follows: section 7.2 describes the Israeli banking system with its special characteristics – a high level of concentration and a low level of competition. These idiosyncrasies created preliminary conditions for the creation of systemic failures in respect of the bank fees. Section 7.3 provides the background of the banking fees reform analyzed herein. It illustrates the problems that characterized the bank fees arrangements prior to the reform. The following three sections contain a chronological survey of the developments that took place in respect of bank fees throughout the years.

---

[2] This theory has been known as the "Public Choice Theory." See, in general: J. M. Buchman and R. D. Tollison (eds.), *The Theory of Public Choice*, 4th edn. (Ann Arbor MI: University of Michigan Press, 1994).

Section 7.4 analyses the efforts for regulating the bank fees prior to the 2007 Reform, efforts that were unsuccessful in solving the failures of the system. Section 7.5 describes the Bank Fees Reform which, for the first time, established supervision over bank fees. The section also analyzes the Reform's immediate results. Section 7.6 deals with another turning point: The social protest that erupted in the summer of 2011 and which resulted in enhanced supervision over the bank fees. The measures that the Bank of Israel took at that point, together with a slow but consistent reduction of fees as an on-going implementation of the 2007 Reform by the banks, finally resulted in a true change in the bank fees arena.

The impression from the last three chapters is of a passive attitude of the Supervisors of Banks over the years, and of a clear agenda of non-intervention in respect of bank fees. Section 7.7 suggests two explanations for this approach. It argues that Supervisors of Banks tended to focus their attention on prudential regulation, rather than consumer protection, and therefore neglected consumerist issues, such as bank fees. Moreover, in their desire to strengthen the banks' stability, the Supervisors preferred not to take measures that could have cut the banks' profitability, and therefore avoided curtailing bank fees. The section also refers to regulatory capture, as an additional possible explanation for the passivity of the Supervisors. Section 7.8 concludes with a few thoughts regarding the relationship between the passivity of regulators, public pressure, and the role of the political echelon.

7.2   The Israeli Banking System

The banking system in Israel consists of five major banking groups that control about 94 percent of the bank assets in the country. In addition, there are three small independent banks and isolated branches of four foreign banks. The banking corporations provide a wide range of financial services, including corporate, commercial and retail banking, housing loans and credit card transactions. In addition, they provide investment counseling, brokerage services, and pension advice. The three credit card companies that operate in Israel are owned by the large banks.[3]

---

[3] For elaboration on the Israeli banking system, see: R. Plato-Shinar, *Banking Regulation in Israel: Prudential Regulation versus Consumer Protection* (Alphen aan den Rijn: Wolters Kluwer, 2016), 31–37. A recent law obliges the two largest banks to sell their credit card companies. See the Law to Enhance Competition and Reduce Concentration in Israel's Banking Sector (Legislative Amendments), 5777–2017.

In the field of insurance, the activities of the Israeli banks are limited due to statutory restrictions. They market, through special subsidiaries, property insurance and life insurance as incidental services to the provision of housing loans.[4] Other activities, which – due to the restrictions of the law – are performed by subsidiaries, are underwriting and portfolio management.[5] Although the banks are allowed to provide trust services pursuant to section 10 of the Banking (Licensing) Law, in practice these services are provided by subsidiaries of the banks as well. As a result of a 2005 reform in the Israeli capital market, the banks are prohibited from managing provident funds or mutual funds, and from holding companies that manage such funds.[6]

The banks are subject to the Banking Supervision Department at the Bank of Israel. The Department is headed by the Supervisor of Banks, who is appointed by the Governor of the Bank of Israel.[7]

As mentioned above, the Israeli banking system consists of five banking groups, whose joint assets amount to about 94 percent of the total assets of the system. Approximately 58 percent of these assets are held by the two largest groups (Bank Leumi and Bank Hapoalim). This centralized structure constitutes a duopoly, where two players control the vast majority of the activities of the sector.[8]

Concentration in the Israeli banking system is rather high. In 2015, the Herfindahl-Hirschman Index (HHI), which measures the concentration in the system as a whole and is calculated according to the total assets of the banks, was 0.22. The concentration ratio (CR2), which measures the market share of the two largest banks within the system's total assets, amounted to 0.58. An international comparison shows that the concentration in the Israeli banking system is significantly higher than the EU average.[9]

Another conspicuous characteristic of the Israeli banking system is the low level of competition between the banks. This observation is mainly based on the Structure Conduct Performance (SCP) Paradigm, according to which the greater the level of concentration in the system, the greater is the market power of its players, and the lower is the level

---

[4] Banking (Licensing) Law, s. 11(b).

[5] Banking (Licensing) Law, ss. 11(a)(3a) and 11(a)(3b).

[6] For elaboration on the Capital Market Reform, see: Plato-Shinar, *Banking Regulation*, 23–24.

[7] For elaboration on these supervisory powers, see ibid., 14–16, 66–73.

[8] Supervisor of Banks, *Israel Banking System – Annual Survey 2015* (August 2016), 8–9.

[9] Ibid., 9. Supervisor of Banks, *Israel Banking System – Annual Survey 2014* (June 2015), 12.

of competition.[10] A low level of competition was also found using the Contestable Market Theory, according to which competition can exist, even in a concentrated market, on condition that a real threat of competition exists, pressurizing the existing players to behave competitively. Apparently, such a threat does not exist in the Israeli banking system.[11] The Paznar-Rosse H-Statistic value for the Israeli banking system in various years was found to be lower in comparison to other Western countries, thus indicating a lower level of competition.[12]

These characteristics of a high level of concentration and a low level of competition were used by the banks adversely against their customers, as will be explained in section 7.3.

7.3 Failures in the Bank Fees System

In Israel, until the bank fees reform of 2007, there was no supervision of bank fees.[13]

It transpired that, for many years, the banks in Israel had used the mechanism of bank fees in an inappropriate manner, in order to increase

---

[10] See, e.g., Report of the Team to Examine Increasing Competitiveness in the Banking System (March 2013), 51, www.boi.org.il/he/NewsAndPublications/PressReleases/Pages/19032012e.aspx and summary in English at www.boi.org.il/en/BankingSupervision/Survey/Pages/competition.aspx; Committee to Enhance Competitiveness in Common Banking and Financial Services, "Background Survey for the Interim Report: The situation of Competition in the Target Sectors and the Required Measures" (2016), http://mof.gov.il/Committees/competitivenessCommittee2015/MidReport2.pdf; Bank of Israel, *Examination of the Prices of the Banking Services – Recommendations of the Work Teams* (January 2007), 4, www.boi.org.il/he/Research/Pages/neumim_neum226h.aspx.

[11] D. Rotenberg, "The Competitiveness in the Banking Sector: Theoretical Aspects and Empirical Evidence from Israel and Abroad," Banking Supervision Department Research Unit, Working Paper (2002), www.boi.org.il/he/Research/Pages/papers_dp0502h.aspx; Report of the Committee to Enhance Competitiveness in Common Banking and Financial Services, supra n. 10, at pp. 8–13 (in respect of retail credit); *Examination of the Prices of the Banking Services – Recommendations of the Work Teams*, supra n. 10, at pp. 6–12.

[12] Committee to Enhance Competitiveness in Common Banking and Financial Services, "Background Survey for the Interim Report," pp. 8–9. Bank of Israel, *Examination of the Prices of the Banking Services*, 8–9; Parliamentary Inquiry Committee on Bank Fees, Final Report (June 2007), 16–17, in Hebrew at www.knesset.gov.il/committees/heb/docs/bank_inq.pdf.

[13] For an opinion that the bank is subject to a fiduciary duty when determining its fees, see L. Haim, "Bank Fees: Banking Liability in their Determination and Collection (following CA 4619/08 Mercantile Discount Bank v. Ezrat Israel Housing)," *Mishpatim Online*, 5 (2013), 51. For the opposite opinion, see R. Plato-Shinar, *The Bank's Fiduciary Duty: The Duty of Loyalty* (Israel: Bar Publishing, 2010), 103–105.

their profits at the expense of the retail sector (individuals, households and small businesses), that were perceived as weak customers.[14] A few problems could be noted in this regard.

Firstly, due to an absence of competition between the banks, the banks permitted themselves to charge very high fees. The level of fees increased sharply from year to year, even surpassing the rise of the consumer price index. For example, from June 1999 to January 2005, the level of fees increased by an average of 12.2 percent, in comparison to an increase of 7.9 percent in the consumer price index, meaning that the fees actually increased by 4 percent above the index.[15] In addition, in the years 2001–2003 there was a serious economic recession in the Israeli economy, which was accompanied by a sharp decline in real wages. Nevertheless, bank fees continued to rise.[16] In 2007, the average expenditure of an account holder for basic bank services was 73 percent higher than its counterpart in Western countries.[17]

Another problem was the multiplicity of fees charged by each bank for financial and operational services. In 2007, on the eve of the bank fees reform, there were banks that charged more than 300 different types of fees to retail customers. Between 1993 and 2007, the number of fees for actions in current accounts increased by 137 percent; the number of fees for computerized and technological services increased by 147 percent; and the number of fees in respect of credit cards increased by 189 percent.[18] While in other developed countries such as the United Kingdom and the United States, a current account with a positive balance bore no fees, and fees were charged only in cases of no cover or exceeding a credit facility, in Israel customers had to pay fees for each and every action which was executed in their account, no matter its balance, plus expensive fees in cases of a lack of cover or of a credit facility excess.[19] In 2005, the Israeli banks' income from fees charged to households constituted 49.5 percent of their total income from fees.[20]

In addition, the banks used to collect double fees for the same transaction. A good example for such a double fee was the "line-entry fee": For

---

[14] Parliamentary Inquiry Committee on Bank Fees, Final Report, 32.
[15] Ibid., 34. Knesset Research and Information Center, "The Prices of Banking Services," (May 2006), 3.
[16] Parliamentary Inquiry Committee on Bank Fees, Final Report, 41.
[17] Ibid., 36.
[18] Ibid., 32.
[19] Ibid., 35.
[20] Ibid., 37.

every line that was recorded on the bank statement of the customer, the bank charged a fixed fee, even if the customer was charged with an additional, specific fee for the transaction itself. The banks explained that this fee was intended to cover their computer expenses in the handling of the customer's account. However, they used to charge an "account management fee" as well, another variety of a double fee. Other examples for double fees were: A "documents processing fee," a "collection fee" that was charged for every monthly installment of a loan repayment, "credit card membership fee," and more.[21]

A fourth problem was information barriers. The bank fees system was extremely complicated. It not only contained hundreds of types of fees, as explained above, but, in addition, some of the fees comprised a few levels (such as the fees in respect of securities trading). Rules promulgated over the years with the aim of making the fees simpler and clearer did not solve the problem.[22] As a result, customers were unable to understand the cost of banking services. In addition, each bank identified and calculated the fees differently, which made it impossible for customers to compare them from bank to bank.[23]

Last, but not least, one should mention the phenomenon of the great similarity in the level of fees that were charged by the different banks. For years, there was almost complete uniformity in the fees that the banks charged their retail customers. Moreover, when one bank raised a fee, the other banks were quick to update their parallel fee by a similar rate. Although this phenomenon lasted for years, the Supervisor of Banks did not intervene.

This phenomenon of great similarity among fee levels served as the basis for a lengthy investigation by the Director General of the Antitrust Authority. The investigation revealed that from the 1990s until 2004, the five major banks had exchanged among themselves information concerning the fees that they charged, which constituted a criminal offence.[24]

---

[21] Ibid., 38, 42.

[22] See in section 7.4, below.

[23] Parliamentary Inquiry Committee on Bank Fees, Final Report, 38.

[24] Israel Antitrust Authority, "A Ruling regarding Restrictive Arrangements between Israeli Banks regarding the Transfer of Information about the Bank Fees" (April 26, 2009), www .antitrust.gov.il/subject/120/item/25879.aspx. However, in 2014, following an appeal that was filed by the banks with the Antitrust Tribunal against the Director General's ruling, the case was settled and the ruling against the banks was cancelled. In return, the banks undertook to pay the Antitrust Authority ILS 70 million. Not only was this sum much lower in comparison to the amounts involved, the banks were allowed to set off an

7.4   Attempts to Regulate the Bank Fees Prior to the 2007 Reform

Until the bank fees reform of 2007, there was no systemic supervision of bank fees.

The competent authority to set prices on essential goods and services, by virtue of the Supervision of Goods and Services Law, 5756–1996, was the Ministry of Trade, Industry and Tourism. In isolated cases, where the Banking Supervision Department found it fitting to set a ceiling for the price of a specific banking service, it had to rely on the Ministry's authority, recommending it to act in this regard. The Bank of Israel did not see fit to change this situation, nor to assume the authority to set prices for banking services.

In 1993, the Bank of Israel appointed an internal committee to examine the bank fees. The committee reduced the number of fees charged to households and small businesses to 125 and prepared a standard list of fees to be adopted by all banks.[25] These steps were anchored by the Supervisor of Banks in Proper Conduct of Banking Business Directive No. 414. However, over the years, the banks gradually deviated from the Directive, while the Supervisor of Banks refrained to take any measures against them.

In 1998, the Knesset (the Israeli Parliament) amended the Banking (Service to Customer) Law, 5741–1981. It added section 5A, which obliged the banks to provide their customers with written information about the amount or rate of fees they charge. Information that did not refer to a specific customer, such as the bank's tariff of fees, had to be presented in a prominent location in all the bank's branches. In addition, every quarter the banks had to provide each customer with a notice detailing all fees charged that customer during the preceding three months. Section 5A did not deal with the amount of the fees or their structure. The obligations it imposed on the banks were only meant to increase transparency.

At the beginning of the millennium, public criticism of the banks for mistreatment of customers in general, and in regard to bank fees in particular, started gaining momentum. Serious allegations were made regarding the fees that were being charged to households and small

---

amount of ILS 35 million that they paid in settlement proceedings relating to class actions that were filed against them in this regard.

[25] Parliamentary Inquiry Committee on Bank Fees, Final Report, 41; Knesset Research and Information Center, "The Prices of Banking Services," 8–9.

businesses. Expectation arose amongst the public of active intervention on the part of the Supervisor of Banks,[26] but the latter was slow to act.

In 2003, the Israeli Consumer Council launched a campaign concerning bank fees, which attracted intense media coverage and the attention of the Knesset Economic Affairs Committee, which decided to actively intervene in the matter. Between 2003 and 2008 this Committee held 21 hearings that focused or touched upon the banks' excessive fees. In addition, to signal their responsiveness to the public, various members of the Knesset initiated several bills that empowered the Banking Supervision Department in the Bank of Israel, to control bank fees.[27]

In 2003, the Supervisor of Banks appointed an internal team – the Team to Examine the Policy of the Banking Supervision Department in respect of the Prices of Banking Services (the "Fein Team"). In 2004, the Team submitted its report, which determined that the level of fees in Israel was high in comparison to other countries. The Team recommended, inter alia, abolishing many fees, reducing the level of others, and controlling the prices of banking services according to certain criteria.[28] However, it turned out that not everybody in the Bank of Israel agreed with these recommendations. While the Supervisor of Banks was willing to adopt the recommendations, the Governor of the Bank of Israel and other senior officials in the Banking Supervision Departments rejected them.[29] In addition, the Association of Banks in Israel rejected the Team's recommendations, and submitted a counter-report according to which the level of fees in Israel was shown to be similar to the level in other countries.[30]

In 2004, the Knesset Economic Affairs Committee appointed the Team to Examine Issues in the Banking System. It was headed by the Director of the Knesset Research and Information Center, and included representatives from the Economic Affairs Committee, the Israel Consumer Council, the Antitrust Authority, the Association of Banks, the

---

[26] Compare: P. Cartwright, *Banks, Consumers and Regulation* (London: Bloomsbury Press, 2004), 2, noting that "consumer expectations may not only apply to the relation between bank and consumer, but also to that between bank, consumer and the State, particularly the regulator."

[27] S. Gilad, "Political Pressures, Organizational Identity, and Attention to Tasks: Illustrations from Pre-Crisis Financial Regulation," *Public Administration*, 93 (2015) 593, 601.

[28] Knesset Research and Information Center, "The Prices of Banking Services," 23–24.

[29] Gilad, "Political Pressures," 602.

[30] Parliamentary Inquiry Committee on Bank Fees, Final Report, 42; Knesset Research and Information Center, "The Prices of Banking Services," 25–26.

Ministry of Finance, and the Deputy Supervisor of Banks. In July 2004, the Team published its recommendations in respect of competition in the household sector. As to bank fees, the Team adopted nearly all the recommendations of the Fein Team (which had called for intervention in the prices of the fees). In addition, it focused on increasing transparency regarding fees. For example, by sending a monthly fee statement to the customers, by creating a standard and simple tariff of fees that the banks would be obliged to adopt, by notifying the customer in advance of the fees involved in the requested transaction, and by receiving the customer's specific consent before charging expensive fees. The Team also recommended a duty of semiannual reporting by the Supervisor of Banks to the Knesset Economic Affairs Committee, about the measures taken by him in the preceding six months, in respect of the bank fees.[31]

Some of the above-mentioned recommendations regarding the transparency of the fees were adopted by the Governor of the Bank of Israel. In 2004 the Governor amended the Banking (Service to Customer) (Proper Disclosure and Delivery of Documents) Rules, 5772–1992, by adding new rules regarding due disclosure of bank fees. The rules obliged the banks to exhibit their tariff of fees in their branches, in a prominent manner. In addition, the banks were obliged to obtain informed, advance consent of fees changes from each customer before performing any banking transaction. This duty also applied to transactions performed on the phone or by electronic means.[32]

Immediately after these Rules entered into force, Bank Hapoalim (one of the two largest banks in the country) announced an increase of its line-entry fee by a few cents. This announcement created a new wave of public and media criticism. The Knesset Economic Affairs Committee threatened to promote a legislative bill to strictly limit the bank fees. At the end, the Committee, the Supervisor of Banks and the banks reached a "package deal," which came into force in December 2005. The "package deal" allowed the banks to collect a fixed fee (ILS 1.21) for every bank transaction performed in a current account, with a minimum monthly charge. In consideration, the banks agreed to abolish double fees such as the "account managing fee" and the "line entry fee"; to create baskets of fees that included a certain amount of

---

[31] Knesset Research and Information Center, "The Prices of Banking Services."

[32] Banking (Service to Customer) (Proper Disclosure and Delivery of Documents) Rules, 5752–1992, ss. 26 and 26A.

services for a fixed – and lower – price; and to facilitate the possibility for customers to switch between banks.[33]

The package deal was honored by the banks for almost one year. But then, in October 2006, the three largest banks decided one after the other to raise their fixed fees, without raising the prices of the baskets of fees. This move escalated public criticism to a new apex and led the Knesset Economic Affairs Committee to a new initiative – a Parliamentary Inquiry Committee in respect of the bank fees.[34]

Concurrent with preparations for establishing the Parliamentary Inquiry Committee, internal working teams at the Bank of Israel examined the issue of the bank fees. In January 2007, almost simultaneously with the formal establishment of the Inquiry Committee, the Bank of Israel published a report about bank fees. The report recommended a series of regulatory steps, as follows: Empowering the Supervisor of Banks to supervise the prices of banking services, especially in sectors where the level of competition is low; creating standard lists of fees while reducing the number of fees; determining a fixed price for the management of a current account; obliging the banks to provide reports about their fees to the Supervisor of Banks on a regular basis; and obliging the Supervisor of Banks to regularly publish comparative tables of the fees charged by the different banks.[35]

In June 2007, the Parliamentary Inquiry Committee published its report. The report pointed to a long list of failures that characterized the bank fees system in Israel, as was detailed in section 7.3. Moreover, the Committee determined that for years, the banks had taken advantage of their influence as pillars of the Israeli economy in order to increase their earnings, mainly at the expense of the retail sector, which was perceived as the weaker party in terms of its bargaining power in dealings with the bank. The Committee determined that "households in Israel pay a 'lack of competition fee' when purchasing bank services."[36] The Committee further noted that, while Western countries had been implementing reforms since the 1980s, in order to encourage competition in the banking industry as well as the non-bank sector, not enough had been done in this field in Israel, because the policy of the Supervisor of Banks had not been sufficiently active in this regard. Throughout the

---

[33] Supervisor of Banks, *Israel Banking System – Annual Survey 2005* (May 2007), 116, www .boi.org.il/en/NewsAndPublications/RegularPublications/Pages/skira05_skira05e.aspx.
[34] Parliamentary Inquiry Committee on Bank Fees, Final Report.
[35] Bank of Israel, "Examination of the Prices of the Banking Services."
[36] Parliamentary Inquiry Committee on Bank Fees, Final Report, 8.

past decades, the Israeli Supervisors of Banks had not implemented an active regulation policy in the field of retail banking.[37]

Based on these findings, the Committee's main recommendations that directly referred to bank fees, were as follows: (1) to transfer the authority of price control in respect of bank fees from the Industry and Trade Ministry to the Bank of Israel; (2) to cap the price of certain fees for a limited period of time (for this, it was recommended that banks and the Supervisor of Banks reach a voluntary agreement, in order to avoid conferring a new power on the Bank of Israel); (3) to determine a standard list of fees for the retail sector which would be identical for all banks, while reducing the number of fees and canceling double fees; (4) to create a few models of current accounts for which a fixed monthly fee could be charged; (5) to oblige the Supervisor of Banks to publish a comparative index of fees paid by household in each bank, which would thereby enable the public to compare fees between banks.[38]

The recommendations of the Inquiry Committee were immediately adopted by the Government and by the Knesset. In July 2007, based on a bill that was formulated by the Bank of Israel, the Banking (Service to Customer) Law was amended,[39] and the Bank of Israel was statutorily authorized to supervise bank fees.

7.5   The Bank Fees Reform of 2007

According to the above-mentioned amendment of the Banking (Service to Customer) Law, powers are conferred on the Governor of the Bank of Israel to oversee the fees.

The law grants the Governor two main powers: The first relates to retail customer accounts of individuals, households and small businesses, and empowers the Governor to determine and update – from time to time – a closed list of permissible fees.[40] The aim of the closed list was to reduce the number of fees, to prevent the charging of double fees for the same service, and to present the fees to the public in a way that is fair and understandable, giving the same names to the fees that are charged by the different banks, and ensuring that the customer can compare the prices of different banks. However, the aforementioned power does not include intervention in the prices or the level of the fees.

[37] Ibid., 9.
[38] Ibid., 9–13.
[39] Banking (Service to Customer) Law, Chapter B2.
[40] Banking (Service to Customer) Law, ss. 9I, 9J.

The second power conferred on the Governor is to declare certain bank services to be "a service subject to supervision." Such a declaration allows the Governor to limit the amount of the fee charged for that service.[41] A service will be declared "a service subject to supervision" if one of the following circumstances exists: The fee charged for the service may reduce competition between the banks or between banks and other institutions that provide similar services; a customer can only receive the service from the bank where his account is managed; in the Governor's opinion, the service is an essential service for which public welfare recommends supervision.[42]

By virtue of his power, the Governor published in 2008 a list of allowed fees while giving banks discretion to determine actual fees.[43] The result of this move was the abolition of many fees, and uniformity in the names and structure of the rest of the fees that remained in force.

In addition, very few services were declared "a service subject to supervision," and for such services a limited price was specified.[44] However, regarding most of the fees, the Bank of Israel allowed the banks discretion to determine the level of the fees, while expecting competition to trigger a reduction in prices. Unfortunately, these expectations were not realized: It turned out that some banks took advantage of this reform to the detriment of the customers, and actually increased their fees.[45]

Opinions were divided as to the immediate consequences of the bank fees reform. The Bank of Israel determined that the reform led to a reduction in the "average basket of fees."[46] However, the Israel Consumer Council found that the average fee charged to households actually increased.[47] In addition, the hope that the Fees Reform would immediately lead to price competition between the banks proved

---

[41] Ibid., ss. 9K and 9N.

[42] Ibid., s. 9K.

[43] Banking (Service to Customer) (Fees) Rules, 5768–2008.

[44] Services Subject to Supervision according to the Banking (Service to Customer) (Amendment 12) Law, 5767–2007, 5799 The Official Gazette (Yalkut Hapirsumim) 2927 (2008).

[45] Bank of Israel, "Data for the First Quarter after the Implementation of the Bank Fees Reform" (Dec. 30, 2008), www.boi.org.il/he/NewsAndPublications/PressReleases/Pages/081230h.aspx.

[46] Ibid.

[47] Israel Consumer Council, "The Council's Opinion in Respect of the Bank Fees after the Reform" (August 20, 2008), in Hebrew at www.consumers.org.il/files/files/odaot/amlot bemda2.doc.

unfounded. Few real differences have arisen between the prices charged by different banks for same fees. Since no meaningful improvement was seen, consumer organizations argued that the Governor was not active enough in his role, and was succumbing to the industry's power. However, the Governor did not change his policy. Save for a few specific updates, such as giving discounts to senior citizens, the disabled or the underprivileged on fees for basic clerk-assisted services,[48] the Governor did not broaden his supervision over bank fees.

7.6 Strengthening the Supervision over Bank Fees – The Social Protest of 2011

In summer 2011 something changed: A huge social protest erupted against the high cost of living in Israel. The protest did not focus on the high cost of banking services per se, but centered on the high cost of housing, food and transportation. Nevertheless, it also had an impact on bank fees, as will be explained below. The protest was supported by major portions of the public, in particular the middle class. It was encouraged by aggressive media coverage, prominent social leaders and social organizations, and it caused the political echelon to understand that actual change in the Israeli economy should take place.[49]

As a result of the protest, the government established the Committee for a Social-Economic Change (the "Trachtenberg Committee"). The Committee examined the different factors that influenced the cost of living in Israel. To this end, the Committee made an analysis of several key sectors of the Israeli economy where there were apparent failures and significant barriers to competition, including the banking sector. The Committee found that the high degree of concentration in the banking system created a concern as to a lack of competitiveness, as well as over-charging. In this light, the Committee recommended

---

[48] Banking (Service to Customer) (Fees) (Amendment No. 2) Rules, 5768–2008, 6705 Regulations File (Kovetz HaTakanot) 1290.

[49] For a wider description of the social protest and its impact on the regulatory agencies, see: Y. Chernin and Y. Lahav, "'The People Demand Social Justice': A Case Study on the Impact of Protests on Financial Markets," *Accounting Economics and Law – A Convivium*, 4 (2014), 99, 103–105. See also: S. Alon-Barkat and S. Gilad, "Political Control or Legitimacy Deficit? Bureaucracies' Symbolic Response to Bottom-Up Public Pressures," *Policy and Politics*, 44 (2016), 41. S. Gilad, S. Alon-Barkat and A. Braverman, "Large-Scale Social Protest: A Business Risk and a Bureaucratic," *Governance*, 29 (2016), 371.

establishing a team that would work toward increasing competitiveness in the Israeli banking industry.[50]

In 2012, the Minister of Finance and the Governor of the Bank of Israel appointed the Team to Examine Increasing Competitiveness in the Banking System, headed by the Supervisor of Banks. The mandate given to the Team was to focus on the retail banking sector – households and small businesses – and to recommend measures for developing competition in the sector.

The report published by the team in 2013 included recommendations aimed at enhancing competition in the banking sector to reduce the cost of banking services and improve the situation of bank customers.[51] In addition, the Committee expressly recommended more involvement by the Bank of Israel in respect of the bank fees charged to the retail sector. In particular it recommended to cancel a number of fees (in addition to those that were already abolished in the 2007 Reform); to declare additional services to be "a service subject to supervision" and to limit their fees; to alter the structure of fees charged in respect of securities trading and to reprice these fees; and to oblige the banks to provide the customer with comparative information about fees that were actually paid by other customers for similar trading activities, in order to increase the bargaining power of the customer in dealings with his bank.

---

[50] Report of the Committee for a Social-Economic Change (September 2011), 188, http://hidavrut.gov.il/sites/default/files/%20%D7%A1%D7%95%D7%A4%D7%99.pdf?bcsi_scan_99FE300B8A2E1F36=1. Translation at www.bjpa.org/Publications/details.cfm?PublicationID=13862.

[51] Report of the Team to Examine Increasing Competitiveness in the Banking System. It was believed that implementation of the Team's recommendations would result in a loss of revenue for the bank of NIS 500-800 million. See: I. Avisar, "Stability is above everything," *Globes* (July 16, 2012), www.globes.co.il/news/article.aspx?did=1000766233; S. Aizescu, "The Competition Committee Is a Display to the Public as If the Banking System Is Handled," *The Marker* (June 13, 2012), www.themarker.com/markets/1.1730298. On the other hand, various agencies, including the Israel Consumer Council, argued that the Team's recommendations were insufficient to create real competition and significantly strengthen the position of bank customers, and that the real reason for this was the preference given to the prudential over consumer interest. See the speech of E. Peleg, CEO of the Israel Consumer Council, in the Knesset Economic Affairs Committee, following on publication of the Team's Interim Report: Knesset Economic Affairs Committee, Protocol No. 921 (July 17, 2012), http://main.knesset.gov.il/Activity/Committees/Economics/Pages/CommitteeAgenda.aspx?tab=3&AgendaDate=17%2f07%2f2012+12%3a00%3a00. See also criticism of the General Director of the Israel Antitrust Authority, even though a representative of the Antitrust Authority was among the members of the Team: I. Avisar, "With All Due Respect to Gilo, the Ball Is in the Hands of Fisher," *Globes* (July 18, 2012), www.globes.co.il/news/article.aspx?did=1000766963.

In addition, attention was given to the small business sector. It was recommended to expand the small business group that enjoys discounted retail rates, and to require the banks to inform these businesses of their entitlement and how they could exercise it.[52]

The Bank of Israel promptly adopted these recommendations. It was even so quick to act that it implemented some of the recommendations immediately after publication of the Committee's interim report, without waiting for the final report.[53]

Moreover, the Bank of Israel did not stop at adopting the Committee's recommendations, but this time took even further measures. Over the years, it has gradually deepened and strengthened its involvement in respect of fees by initiating and implementing additional measures aimed at enhancing competition and reducing fee levels.

In this context, of particular interest was the initiative of the Bank of Israel in 2014, whereby it compelled banks to introduce uniform "baskets of fees" on current accounts.[54] A "basket of fees" includes a certain number of services at a fixed price, to be determined by each bank separately. Because of the Bank of Israel's concern that the banks might abuse the basket system in order to increase prices, as occurred when the Fees Reform came into effect in 2008, the Governor of the Bank of Israel declared the basic basket of fees a "service subject to supervision," which allowed him to determine the price of this basket.[55] However, as the transition to the basket system was not worthwhile for the banks, they did not bother to inform their customers about this. Another directive of the Bank of Israel required the banks to take proactive measures to bring the matter to the attention of their customers, and to report to the Supervisor of Banks the rate at which the customers subscribe to the basket of fees

---

[52] Report of the Team to Examine Increasing Competitiveness in the Banking System, 111–120, 125–127.

[53] See, for example: Banking (Service to Customer) (Cancelling Supervision of a Certain Banking Service and Its Amendment in Another Case), 5773-2012, 7196 Regulations File (Kovetz HaTakanot) 368; Banking (Service to Customer) (Fees) Rules, 5773-2012, 7196 Regulations File (Kovetz HaTakanot) 369; Banking (Service to Customer) (Fees) (Amendment No. 2) Rules, 5773-2013, 7261 Regulations File (Kovetz HaTakanot) 1385.

[54] Banking (Service to Customer) (Fees) (Amendment) Rules, 5774–2013.

[55] Banking (Service to Customer) (Supervision on Basic Track Service) Order, 5774-2014, 7360 Regulations File (Kovets HaTakanot) 1001; Bank of Israel, "The Price of the Basic and Uniform Basket of Current Account Management Services will be under Supervision and will not Exceed NIS 10 a Month" (March 5, 2014), www.boi.org.il/en/NewsAndPublications/PressReleases/Pages/05-03-2014-BankSupervi.aspx.

system.[56] The Bank of Israel even launched a radio campaign to increase public awareness.[57]

In accordance with the obligation imposed on him by this law, the Supervisor of Banks reports to the Knesset Economic Affairs Committee every six months about actions taken regarding fees, and about the banks' implementation of the provisions of the law. These reports constitute a tool for supervising his actions.[58]

In addition, the Banking Supervision Department endeavors to promote banking services transparency by publishing detailed information about the fees that different banks charge, by issuing comparative tables, and by providing calculators on the Bank of Israel's website that are available for public use.[59]

To summarize, the social protest in the summer of 2011 resulted in enhanced supervision of bank fees. The measures taken by the Governor of the Bank of Israel and the Supervisor of Banks in response to the social protest, together with a slow but consistent reduction of fees through implementation of the 2007 Reform did, finally, result in a true change in bank fees.

7.7 The Passive Approach of the Supervisor of Banks

In section 7.3 we saw the failures that characterized the bank fees system, particularly in respect of the retail sector. Notwithstanding these problems, the Bank of Israel was not enthusiastic to actively intervene in this regard, and surely not to establish a systematic response.

---

[56] Supervisor of Banks, "Letter to the Banking Corporations: 'The Tracks Service'" (July 5, 2014), www.boi.org.il/en/BankingSupervision/LettersAndCircularsSupervisorOfBanks/LettersOfTheBankingSupervisionDepartment/201405.pdf; Supervisor of Banks, "Letter to the Banking Corporations: 'The Tracks Service'" (June 21, 2015), www.boi.org.il/he/BankingSupervision/LettersAndCircularsSupervisorOfBanks/LettersOfTheBankingSupervisionDepartment/201512.pdf; Supervisor of Banks, "Proper Conduct of Banking Business Directives: Directive no. 423 on 'The Tracks Service'," www.boi.org.il/en/BankingSupervision/SupervisorsDirectives/ProperConductOfBankingBusinessRegulations/423_et.pdf.

[57] Supervisor of Banks, Annual Survey 2014, 104.

[58] By virtue of s. 9R of the Banking (Service to Customer) Law. For an example of such a report, see: Bank of Israel, "The Semiannual Report on Common Banking Service Fees was presented today to the Knesset Economic Affairs Committee," (January 26, 2016), www.boi.org.il/en/NewsAndPublications/PressReleases/Pages/26-01-2016-BankingSupervisor.aspx.

[59] By virtue of the authority conferred on him in s. 16K of the Banking (Service to Customer) Law. The information is published on the Bank of Israel website: www.boi.org.il/en/ConsumerInformation/ConsumerIssues/Pages/Amalot.aspx.

From the survey in section 7.4, it seems that until the Bank Fees Reform of 2007, the involvement of the Supervisor of Banks and the Bank of Israel in bank fees was rather limited. They focused mainly on efforts to increase the transparency of the fees, assuming market forces would cure customer mistreatment. Only in sporadic cases did they set a ceiling on the price of a banking service, relying on the general powers of the Ministry of Trade, Industry and Tourism to set the prices of essential services. Yet these interventions were too weak to provide a real solution.[60]

Even when professional teams, such as the Fein Team or the Team to Examine Issues in the Banking System, recommended regulating the prices of banking services, the Bank of Israel still did not take any active measure to implement these recommendations. And in those issues where the Bank of Israel did take an active part, such as the "package deal," it only followed acts that were initiated and promoted by other political players, mainly the Knesset Economic Affairs Committee.

Most of the moves of the Bank of Israel were made only as a response to escalating public pressure, and simply as a gesture with no full commitment. Moreover, due to the general reluctance of the Bank of Israel to intervene in this field, its response was belated and attenuated.[61] The general impression of the Bank of Israel's behavior is that of a firm agenda of non-intervention, an agenda which was even expressly admitted by the Deputy Supervisor of Banks during the Knesset debates.[62]

It was only toward the end of 2006 and the beginning of 2007 that the Bank of Israel could no longer adhere to this agenda. Two main political actors compelled it to intervene: The public, whose escalating pressure now reached a new peak, encouraged by aggressive media coverage; and the Parliament – headed by social activist members who were influenced by the public pressure, which led to the establishment of the Parliamentary Inquiry Committee. Presented with the possibility of serious social and parliamentary censure, the Banking Supervision Department could no longer ignore the issue of bank fees. Therefore, at that point, it changed its attitude and took an active part in the legislative

---

[60] Gilad, "Political Pressures," 601.

[61] Ibid., at p. 604.

[62] See the speech of Mr. Motti Fein, the Deputy Supervisor of Banks, at the Knesset State Control Committee, Protocol 7029 of 30 July 2003: "We do not think that there should be control over the banks' fees, because control is a bad thing."

process promoted by the Knesset, which resulted in the statutory Bank Fees Reform.

However, even after the law was amended, authorizing the Governor of the Bank of Israel to intervene in the prices of the banking services, the Governor used this power in a limited manner, leaving the level of most of the fees to the discretion of the banks themselves. The result was quick to come – there were banks that took advantage of the reform in order to increase their fees, with the Supervisor of Banks taking no measure against them.

Another milestone took place a few years later, once again as a response to a huge public protest. This time it was the social protest of 2011, that swept hundreds of thousands of people who went out on the streets and called upon the government to reduce the cost of living. The strength of this protest caused the Supervisor of Banks not only to head the Team to Examine Increasing Competitiveness in the Banking Sector, but also to immediately adopt the Team's recommendations, and to even take additional measures to reduce the fees.

The interesting question is what was the reason for the passive approach of the Supervisor of Banks and the Bank of Israel? Why, for so many years, did the Israeli regulators adopt such an attitude, despite the existence of public criticism? I believe that the main explanation for this situation is related to prioritization of regulatory goals, namely the preference of prudential regulation over consumer protection. In addition, I will refer to regulatory capture as another possible explanation for regulatory passivity.

7.7.1   Prioritization of Regulatory Goals

The Israeli Supervisor of Banks is in charge of both fields of banking regulation: prudential regulation (maintaining the stability of the banks), as well as consumer protection. However, the prudential role has always occupied the predominant place in the activities of the Supervisors of Banks, while consumer protection has received less attention.[63] This is not surprising. There are several reasons why bank regulators prefer to focus on prudential supervision rather than on consumer protection.

Firstly, banking instability will always attract a more vigorous response from regulators by virtue of its potential severity.[64] A bank that collapses

---

[63] Plato-Shinar, *Banking Regulation*, 84–86, 172–175.
[64] A. D. Schmulow, "Twin Peaks: A Theoretical Analysis," Center for International Finance and Regulation, Research Working Paper Series Project No. E018, at p. 9 (2015).

causes considerable damage, not only to customers and investors, but it may – through the contagion effect –harm the entire banking system and the economy as a whole.[65] Whereas improper conduct regarding a consumer, even if it involves a systemic failure rather than an isolated event, does not usually have such severe consequences.

In addition, the collapse of a bank could be perceived as a professional failure, both by the Banking Supervision Department as an organization, and by the Supervisor of Banks personally. No Supervisor would like a bank to collapse during his term in office. On the other hand, inadequate attention to consumer matters is not seen as a supervisory failure, and will at most attract public criticism. Considerations of protecting personal interests will therefore motivate the Supervisor to devote more attention to the supervision of stability.

A similar explanation is supported by the theory of Risk Based Regulation.[66] According to this theory, regulatory agencies are responsible for reducing risk to the public ("social risk"). However, in the event that a social risk materializes (such as the collapse of a bank), the relevant regulatory agency will be exposed to "institutional risk" as having failed to fulfill its duties, and it could lose its status and its power. Hence, in determining priorities between regulatory goals, the regulatory agency will also take this institutional risk into consideration, and will establish its priorities so as to prevent the institutional risk from materializing.[67]

In addition, it was found that regulatory agencies prefer to handle social risks with high salience (even if the probability of them materializing is low), rather than social risks with low salience (even if the probability of them materializing is high). This is due to the dramatic significance of social risk with high salience on the reputation of the

---

[65] J. R. Macey and G. P. Miller, "Bank Failures, Risk Monitoring, and the Market for Bank Control," 88 *Columbia Law Rev.* 1153, 1156 (1988); L. Dragomir, *European Prudential Banking Regulation and Supervision* 30 (Abingdon: Routledge, 2010); X. Freixas, C. Giannini, G. Hoggarth and F. Soussa, "Lender of Last Resort: a Review of the Literature," *Financial Stability Review* 151, 154 (1999); R. J. Herring and R. E. Litan, *Financial Regulation in the Global Economy* (Washington DC: Brookings Institution Press, 1995), 50.

[66] J. Black, "The Emergence of Risk-Based Regulation and the New Public Risk Management in the United Kingdom," *Public Law*, 512 (2005); J. Black, "Managing Regulatory Risks and Defining the Parameters of Blame: A Focus on the Australian Prudential Regulation Authority," 28 *Law and Policy* 1, 4 (2006); J. Black and R. Baldwin, "Really Responsive Risk-Based Regulation," 32 *Law and Policy*, 181 (2010).

[67] H. Rothstein, M. Huber and G. Gaskell, "A Theory of Risk Colonization: The Spiralling Regulatory Logics of Societal and Institutional Risk," 35 *Economy and Society*, 91 (2006).

organization and on its ability to survive the resulting institutional risk.[68] Because a bank collapse has much higher salience than mistreatment of a customer, we can understand why the Supervisor of Banks prefers to focus on prudential regulation.

Similarly, a recent political economic study examining why multiple-goal agencies succeed in achieving some goals and fail in others, claims that agencies will systematically over-perform on tasks that are easier to measure, and underperform on tasks that are harder to measure and that conflict with the achievement of the more measurable goals.[69] The prudential field is easy to measure because it quotes clear number parameters such as capital adequacy, liquidity and leverage ratios. Likewise, a prudential failure – the collapse of a bank or its inability to meet its obligations – is also visibly obvious. By contrast, the consumer field is difficult to measure because it has a social value orientation rather than a quantitative orientation and it is not based on measurable parameters.

To conclude this point, reputational considerations may well lead to the preference of prudential regulation over consumer protection.

It is worth noting that consumer protection supervision requires more inputs, manpower and resources than those required for prudential supervision.[70] Therefore, even if the Supervisor devotes identical resources to both these fields, the actual results will be more noticeable in the field of prudential regulation.

In addition to all these explanations, we must remember that past history and agency culture may also "lock-in" certain goals as primary over other goals.[71] A few studies that analyzed public agencies' prioritization among multiple tasks and goals, suggested that agencies' allocation of attention is guided by their idiosyncratic sense of mission. Tasks that were not defined as central to the agency's mission, were underperformed.[72] For years, the Banking Supervision Department in Israel saw it as its mission to

---

[68] S. Gilad, "Attention and Reputation: Linking Regulator's Internal and External Worlds," in M. Lodge and K. Wegrich (eds.), *Executive Government in Crisis* (Palgrave Macmillan, 2012), 157, 158-159 (2012).

[69] E. Biber, "Too Many Things to Do: How to Deal with the Dysfunctions of Multiple-Goal Agencies," *Harvard Environmental Law Review*, 33 (2009) 1.

[70] R. K. Abrams and M. W. Taylor, "Issues in the Unification of Financial Sector Supervision," IMF Working Paper 00/213 (2000), 24.

[71] Biber, "Too Many Things to Do," 61.

[72] J. R. DeShazo and J. Freeman, "Public Agencies as Lobbyists," *Columbia Law Review*, 105 (2005), 2217; Gilad, "Political Pressures," 593–594 (using the term "organizational identity").

maintain the stability of the banking system, and it developed its organizational culture around this objective.[73] Hence, it is only natural that the Supervisor continues to promote this mission over the other objective for which he is responsible – regulating the banks' conduct vis-à-vis customers. This is particularly true when the latter objective conflicts with the agency's mission.

The focus of the Supervisors of Banks on prudential regulation, whatever the reasons for this may be, and their desire to strengthen the stability of the banks, led them to encourage high profitability for the banks, and they did so even when it resulted in sacrificing consumer protection.[74] As bank fees are a major source of profit for Israeli banks,[75] the Supervisors have, over the years, preferred not to limit the earnings that derive from fees and not to intervene in this area.

7.7.2   Regulatory Capture

As was explained in section 7.1, regulation is intended to benefit the general public. However, in certain cases, the regulated industry acquires a persistent and excessive influence over the regulator, which causes the latter to prefer the interests of the regulated firms over those of the public. In such cases, the question arises as to the existence of "regulatory capture": i.e. "the result or process by which regulation, in law or application, is consistently or repeatedly directed away from the public interest and towards the interest of the regulated industry, by the intent and action of the industry itself."[76]

---

[73] Plato-Shinar, *Banking Regulation*.

[74] On the conflicts that may occur between prudential regulation and consumer protection, see: Plato-Shinar, *Banking Regulation*, 170–172; M. Taylor, "'Twin Peaks': A Regulatory Structure for the New Century," Center for the Study of Financial Innovation (1995), 1, 15 (noting that the two goals "often conflict"); E. J. Pan, "Four Challenges to Financial Regulatory Reform," *Villanova Law Review*, 55 (2010), 743, 745, 759 ("fundamental differences"); J. J. Norton, "Global Financial Sector Reform: The Single Financial Regulator Model based on the United Kingdom FSA Experience – A Critical Reevaluation," *International Lawyer*, 39 (2005), 15, 42 ("inherent conflict").

[75] In 2016, the total amount of fees collected by the five largest banks was NIS 14.5 billion, whereas the net earnings from interest were NIS 26.2 billion. See: E. Rosenberg, "The Banks' Profit in 2016: More than 8 billion," *YNET* (March 30, 2017), in Hebrew at www.ynet.co.il/articles/0,7340,L-4942689,00.html.

[76] D. Carpenter and D. A. Moss, "Introduction," in D. Carpenter and D. A. Moss (eds.), *Preventing Regulatory Capture* (Cambridge: Cambridge University Press, 2014), 1, 13. For criticism of this definition see: L. Tai, "Regulatory Capture and Quality," New York University Law and Economics Working Papers, Paper No. 397 (2015), 6; D. F. Engstrom, "Corralling Capture," *Harvard Journal of Law & Public Policy*, 36

The classical works on regulatory capture focus on the materialistic capture, which consists of materialistic benefits offered to the regulator by the regulated industry. These benefits may include bribes, gifts and various entrustments given to the regulator by the regulated firms.[77] They may also include career opportunities by way of express or implied promises for recruitment into a higher-paying job in the regulated firms (the "revolving doors" phenomenon).[78]

The more recent literature on regulatory capture deals with non-materialistic capture. One type of non-materialistic capture is "cognitive" or "cultural capture," which is the creeping process of "colonization of ideas"[79] through which the regulator shares the views of the regulated industry. It mostly refers to the regulator's education, background, experience, networks and social interaction with the industry, that may influence his worldview and mold it in a pro-industry manner. The result is that the regulator may identify – albeit even unconsciously – with the industry, its views and its needs.[80] A close interface or a permanent and continuing relationship between an institution and a regulator may increase the chance for a cultural capture. Such a close interface may, for example, be found in highly regulated fields such as the banking field, due to the need for the regulator to constantly design and enforce regulation on the regulated firms.[81]

Another type of non-materialistic capture is the "information capture." For an agency to regulate an industry effectively, it needs to know

---

(2013), 31. See also the definition in: L. G. Baxter, "'Capture' in Financial Regulation: Can We Channel It Toward the Common Good?" *Cornell J. L. & Pub. Pol'y*, 21 (2011–2012) 175, 176. The subject of regulatory capture was recently discussed by the Israeli Committee to Reduce Concentration, in its Draft Methodology for the Examination of Economy-Wide Concentration 5–6 (Jan. 17, 2017), in Hebrew at www.antitrust.gov.il /subject/203/item/34435.aspx.

[77] G. J. Stigler, "The Theory of Economic Regulation," *Bell Journal of Economics and Management Science*, 2 (1971), 3; Posner, "Theories of Economic Regulation"; S. Peltzman, "Toward a more general Theory of Regulation," *Journal of Law and Economics*, 19 (1976) 211. See also: J. Laffont and J. Tirole, "The Politics of Government Decision-Making: A Theory of Regulatory Capture," *The Quarterly Journal of Economics*, 106 (1991) 1089.

[78] Stigler, "The Theory of Economic Regulation"; R. D. Eckert, "The Life Cycle of Regulatory Commissioners," *Journal of Law and Economics*, 24 (1981) 113; E. Dal Bo, "Regulatory Capture: A Review," *Oxford Review of Economic Policy*, 22 (2006) 203.

[79] Engstrom, "Corralling Capture," 32.

[80] J. Kwak, "Cultural Capture and the Financial Crisis," in Carpenter and Moss, *Preventing Regulatory Capture*, 71; ibid., 18–20. Baxter, "'Capture' in Financial Regulation," 183; N. Bagley, "Agency Hygiene," *Texas Law Review*, 89 (2010) 1, 5.

[81] Committee to Reduce Concentration, "Draft Methodology for the Examination of Economy-Wide Concentration," 12–13.

how the industry works and what it is capable of doing. But this information is often in the exclusive control of the regulated firms, resulting in a dependency of the regulator upon these firms. Such a dependency may also create a capture.[82] Information capture is more likely to occur when the regulation is highly complex, and when information asymmetry between the regulated industry and the regulator is greater.[83] These are features that characterize financial regulation and therefore suggest that information capture is more likely to happen in the financial sector.[84]

Banking regulators are not immune to regulatory capture. They, too, may be captured by the industry they are supposed to supervise – the banks. In fact, regulatory capture in the banking field should not surprise us. The banks, as special interest groups with huge financial clout, have a high-stake interest in the outcome of policy and regulatory decisions of the Supervisor. Therefore, the banks focus massive resources and energies on attempting to gain the policy outcome they prefer.[85] In contrast, members of the public, each with only a tiny individual stake in the outcome, ignore it. While the banks are better equipped and incentivized to concentrate their lobbying efforts,[86] the public suffers from "rational apathy," whereby each individual prefers to avoid, rather than contribute, to public oversight of the matter at hand.[87] This situation is a fertile ground for the development of captive regulation.

[82] R. E. Barkow, "Insulating Agencies: Avoiding Capture through Institutional Design," *Texas Law Review*, 89 (2010), 15, 23; Bagley, "Agency Hygiene," 5; W. E. Wagner, "Administrative Law, Filter Failure, and Information Capture," *Duke Law Journal*, 59 (2009–2010), 1321.

[83] C. Knil and A. Lenschow, "Modes of Regulation in the Governance of the European Union: Towards a Comprehensive Evaluation," in J. Jordana and D. Lavi-Faur (eds.), *The Politics of Regulation: Institutions and Regulatory Reforms for an Age of Governance* (Cheltenham: Edward Elgar, 2004), 218, 231.

[84] M. Hellwig, "Capital Regulation after the Crisis: Business as Usual?" CESifo DICE Report 2/2010 (2010), 40; H. Hakenes and I. Schnabel, "Regulatory Capture by Sophistication," Working Paper (2015), https://papers.ssrn.com/sol3/papers.cfm?abstract_id=2531688. For the phenomenon of the "captured regulator" in the Israeli insurance market, see: HCJ 7721/96 *Association of Insurance Appraisers in Israel* v. *The Commissioner of Insurance*, 55(3) PD 625, 653.

[85] See, for example: D. Igan, T. Lambert, et al., "Winning Connections? Special Interests and the Sale of Failed Banks," CEPR Discussion Paper No. DP12440 (2017).

[86] D. Igan and T. Lambert, Chapter 5; T. Lambert, "Lobbying on Regulatory Enforcement Actions: Evidence from U.S. Commercial and Savings Banks," *Management Science* (2018).

[87] M. Olson, *The Logic of Collective Action: Public Goods and the Theory of Groups* (Cambridge MA: Harvard University Press, 1965); Laffont and Tirole, "The Politics of Government Decision-Making," 1089–1090; Barkow, "Insulating Agencies," 22.

Moreover, as was well described:

> The particular processes involved in financial regulation suggest that the opportunity for capture might be greater than ever in financial services, particularly in relation to large-scale financial institutions, which have very deep engagements with the regulators. Banks are not only subject to rules that govern their structure, operations, and activities in advance but they are also subject to ongoing monitoring in a manner that involves broad regulatory discretion. One need not be totally cynical to recognize that the highly discretionary and continuous nature of bank regulation is dependent on and nurtures an environment in which the regulators and the regulated are engaged in such close, daily relationships as to nurture intense mutual empathy – perhaps even a kind of "transference" – between the two sides.[88]

Indeed, various studies determined – some of them based on empirical research – that bank regulators were actually captured by the banks.[89] Some even claimed that captive regulation was one of the causes for the Global Financial Crisis.[90]

Going back to the bank fees in Israel, we saw above the passivity of the Supervisor of Banks throughout the years and the policy of non-intervention in this field; a policy that served the interests of the banks and drifted away from that of the public. However, tempting as it may be, this fact by itself does not automatically lead to a conclusion of regulatory capture. Whereas classical scholars were quick to diagnose capture whenever any interest group appeared to benefit from regulation, or

---

[88] Baxter, "'Capture' in Financial Regulation," 187.

[89] S. Johnson and J. Kwak, *13 Bankers: The Wall Street Takeover and the Next Financial Meltdown* (New York: Pantheon Books, 2010); W. H. Buiter, "Central Banks and Financial Crises," Federal Reserve Bank of Kansas City's symposium, Discussion Paper No. 619 (September 2008), 104–107 (noting that "there has been regulatory capture of the Fed by Wall Street during the Greenspan years, and that this is continuing into the present"); Baxter, "'Capture' in Financial Regulation," 181–187. Hakenes and Schnabel, "Regulatory Capture by Sophistication"; D. Veltrop and J. de Haan, "I Just Cannot Get You Out of My Head: Regulatory Capture of Financial Sector Supervisors," De Nedelandsche Bank, Working Paper No. 410 (January 2014), www.dnb.nl/binaries/Working%20Paper%20410_tcm46-302769.pdf; Kwak, "Cultural Capture"; A. E. Wilmarth, "Turning a Blind Eye: Why Washington Keeps Giving in to Wall Street?," *University of Cincinnati Law Review*, 81 (2012, 2013), 1283.

[90] Johnson and Kwak, *13 Bankers*; S. Claessens, G. R. D. Underhill and X. Zhang, "The Political Economy of Basle II: The Costs for Poor Countries," *The World Economy*, 31 (2008) 313; Kwak, "Cultural Capture," 93; Hakenes and Schnabel, "Regulatory Capture by Sophistication." See also the references in Carpenter and Moss, *Preventing Regulatory Capture*, 1; and in L. G. Baxter, "Capture Nuances in Financial Regulation," *Wake Forest L. Review*, 47 (2012) 537.

when there was merely motive for capture, recent literature emphasizes the need to establish such a conclusion on the basis of empirical findings and their careful analysis.[91]

The Israeli banking system contains some features that may contribute to the creation of captive regulation or, at least, explain the tendency of the Supervisor of Banks to succumb to pressure exerted by the banks.

Firstly, as was explained in section 7.2, the Israeli banking sector is very concentrated. It is dominated by five strong banking groups, and in particular by the duopoly of the two largest groups. In addition, competition between the banks is low. A market of this type allows the banks to join forces and consort in their battle on the Supervisor's opinion, using their cumulative power for the benefit of their mutual interest.

In this regard it should also be emphasized that the interest group that is subject to the Supervisor of Banks is rather homogenous, being comprised of both banks and credit card companies which are subsidiaries of the banks. In contrast, when a regulator is in charge of various and different interest groups, the diversity of their interests reduces their ability to capture the regulator, especially in cases where the interests of these groups contradict each other.[92]

Another factor that may strengthen the power of negotiation of the banks in Israel (or at least of the two largest banks that constitute a duopoly) against the Supervisor, is based on the concept of being "too big to fail." The wide scope of activities of the large banks and their interconnectedness with other key players in the economy may lead the Supervisor to take into account considerations that stem from the systemic risk that such institutions create. The problem, in the current context, is not potential business failures and resulting bailouts, but the influence that such institutions exert when business is going well, thus creating a distortion in the decision-making process of the Supervisor.[93]

---

[91] Carpenter and Moss, *Preventing Regulatory Capture*; D. Carpenter, "Detecting and Measuring Capture," in *Preventing Regulatory Capture*, 57; D. A. Moss and D. Carpenter, "Conclusion: A Focus on Evidence and Prevention," in *Preventing Regulatory Capture* 451. See also: Baxter, "Capture Nuances."

[92] J. R. Macey, "Organizational Design and Political Control of Administrative Agencies," *Journal of Law, Economy and Organization*, 8 (1992), 93, 99; A. Eckstein, "Regulatory Inertia and Interest Groups: Empirical Evidence from the Field of Regulation of Capital Markets," *Bar-Ilan Law Studies*, 30 (2016), 635, 672.

[93] A. Ayal, "The Market for Bigness: Economic Power and Competition Agencies' Duty to Curtail It," *Journal of Antitrust Enforcement*, 1 (2013), 221, 233–238; Committee to Reduce Concentration, "Draft Methodology for the Examination of Economy-Wide Concentration," 6–7.

Secondly, the Israeli banks have very strong lobbying power. Their high profitability and large financial resources allow them to hire the country's most prominent and experienced lobbying firms to attend the Knesset debates on their behalf.[94] Similarly, the banks can afford to hire the best professionals in the market to provide policy makers with opinions and reports that are biased toward banking interests. In addition, the Association of Banks plays an important role as an informal lobbyist of the banks. Whereas, in other countries, banking associations engage in various tasks such as self-regulating their members,[95] the Association of Banks in Israel serves mainly as an intermediary between the banks and the policy-makers in various matters, focusing its efforts on convincing the regulators to shift their policy toward the interests of the banks.

Thirdly, the Advisory Board of the Supervisor of Banks, with which the Supervisor consults in the promulgation of new directives, contains nineteen members, of whom eight are representatives of the banks and only one is a public representative.[96] Needless to say, such a structure of the Board not only allows the banks to express their views, but also affords them the opportunity to convince the Supervisor to adopt a policy that suits their needs. In comparison, the Advisory Board of the Israeli Commissioner of Capital Markets, Insurance and Savings contains no industry representatives. Industry can express views on new directives by providing comments on drafts published by the Commissioner during the rule-setting process.[97]

---

[94] See, for example, the lobbying companies that represent the banks in the current debates about the separation of the credit cards companies from the banks: Z. Zrachya, "The Banks operate Lobbyists to Pressure Members of Knesset to change the Strum Committee's Recommendations," *The Marker* (September 6, 2016), in Hebrew at www.themarker.com/news/1.3059725.

[95] See, e.g., the activity of the Swiss Bankers Association that published guidelines, recommendations and agreements: www.swissbanking.org/en/home/standp unkte-link/regu lierung-richtlinien.htm. In Australia, the Australians Bankers' Association Inc. has developed industry codes and standards: www.bankers.asn.au/Consumers/Industry-Standards.

[96] The Hebrew website of the Bank of Israel: https://www.boi.org.il/he/Banking Supervision/Pages/about.aspx.

[97] On the ability of interest groups to informally influence the regulatory agency, already in the very preliminary stage of the rule-making process, see: N. A. Mendelson, "Regulatory Beneficiaries and Informal Agency Policymaking," *Cornell Law Review*, 92 (2007) 397, 429–431. S. W. Yackee, "The Politics of Ex Parte Lobbying: Pre-Proposal Agenda Building and Blocking during Agency Rulemaking," *Journal of Public Administration Research and Theory*, 22 (2012), 373.

Fourthly, the revolving door phenomenon has become common practice in Israel. Many Supervisors of Banks have found themselves, at the close of their term in office, as chairpersons or holders of other senior positions in banks.[98] Incumbent Supervisors may prefer to keep good relations with the regulated firms to secure future appointment and, in so doing, inadvertently collaborate with the needs and interests of these firms.

These idiosyncrasies may serve as fertile ground for the creation of regulatory capture. For the purposes of this chapter, these indicators may explain the sensitivity of the Supervisors of Banks, throughout the years, to the pressures exerted against them by the banks, and the Supervisors' responsiveness to the banks' desires and needs. This situation, in its turn, may also explain the regulatory tendency to support the banks on the question of fees and serves as an additional explanation for the passivity of the Supervisors in this regard.

7.8 Conclusion

Today, more than ten years after the Bank Fees Reform took place, it seems that Israeli supervision over bank fees resulted in an improved situation in the retail sector. Reports by the Bank of Israel in recent years show a consistent trend of reduced fees and the existence of a "wide variance" in prices between the different banks,[99] which is an improvement in the protection afforded to consumers.

The Supervisor of Banks and the Bank of Israel understood that they could not stay passive and indifferent any longer. Continuous public scrutiny compelled them to stay alert and keep pace, by constantly examining the bank fees system and by imposing additional limitations in response to the changing circumstances. The duty of reporting to the

---

[98] For example: Dr. Meit Heth (1969–1975) became the Chairperson of Bank Leumi; Galia Maor (1982–1987) became the CEO of Bank Leumi; Dr. Amnon Goldschmidt (1987–1992) became a deputy CEO at Discount Bank, and later a director at First International Bank; Zeev Aveles (1992–1998) became the Chairperson of Union Bank; Dr. Yitzhak Tal (1998–2003) became a director at Tefachot Mortgage Bank; Ronny Hizkiyahu (2006–2010) became the chairperson of the First International Bank. Before being nominated as the Supervisor, he served as a senior banker in various banks. In 2016 he was appointed as the State Accountant General. Hedva Ber, the current Supervisor, served as the Chief Risk Operator at Bank Leumi, before being appointed as a Supervisor.

[99] See, e.g., "The Semiannual Report on Common Banking Service Fees." I. Avisar, "A Decrease of 17% in Four Years in Household Bank Fees," Globes (July 16, 2015), in Hebrew at www.globes.co.il/news/article.aspx?did=1001053777.

Knesset, which enhances the accountability of the supervisory process, constitutes an important mechanism for controlling the regulatory echelon.

Before the reform took place, the banks had threatened that supervision of fees would have a negative influence on the market, compelling them to raise interest rates, and that it would ultimately harm customers instead of protecting them. However, although the Reform did decrease banks' earnings, they still exist and thrive. They passed the global financial crisis relatively unscathed, and continue to make enormous profit.[100]

Having said this, two reservations should be made. Firstly, the fact that improvement has been achieved up to now does not mean that the Supervisor can rest on his laurels and let market power continue from here. As was mentioned above, the Supervisor must constantly examine the bank fees system and impose additional limitations in response to changing circumstances. For example, the current trend that the Israeli banking system is undergoing, namely the closing of branches and the move to digital banking, reduces banks' costs and should – respectively – also reduce the fees charged for banking services.[101]

Secondly, the positive results of the Israeli Bank Fees Reform do not necessarily lead to the conclusion that bank fees should be subject to supervision in all countries. However, where banks abuse their market power to the detriment of weaker customers, such as households and small businesses, in a systematic manner and as prevailing practice, as was the case in the Israeli banking market, then supervision should take place, in order to protect the underdog.[102]

---

[100] In comparison, in the United States at the time of intensive banking legislation at the end of the 1960s and the beginning of the 1970s, the banks claimed that the legislation that protected the customers would destroy the credit market and would harm the American economy as a whole. It is interesting that among the opponents were not only the banks but also the Federal Reserve Bank. The claims were rejected, laws and regulations were enacted, and nothing untoward happened in the credit market, which continued to prosper and succeed. See J. A. Spanogle, "'Regulation of the Bank-Customer Relationship in the United States," *Journal of Banking and Finance Law and Practice*, 4 (1993), 18, 22–23.

[101] See, e.g., draft amendment, Banking (Service to Customer) (Fees) Rules, 5768-2008, of Jan. 25, 2017, www.boi.org.il/he/BankingSupervision/DraftsFromTheSupervisor OfBanks/Pages/Default.aspx.

[102] It is interesting to note that even Adam Smith, who supported market freedom and who invented the metaphor of the "invisible hand," justified supervision of the banks for fear that the collapse of a bank would cause damage to the public at large. See: A. Smith, *An Inquiry into the Nature and Causes of the Wealth of Nations* (1776), Book II chap. II, 308. See also E. G. West, "Adam Smith's Support for Money and Banking Regulation:

The lesson that can be learned from the Israeli bank fees reform is that there is sometimes a need for other political actors to intervene when the regulator has adopted a passive approach and neglected the public interest. It was the Knesset that adopted the uncompromising socio-economic approach on banking fees, establishing the Inquiry Committee on Bank Fees, and finally enacting the Bank Fees Reform. The Government also played a role, by establishing the Trachtenberg Committee which, in its turn, led to the establishment of the Team to Examine Increasing Competitiveness in the Banking Sector. Without these initiatives, it is doubtful whether the bank fees reform would have taken place and would have been further developed as it actually was.

Nevertheless, the legislator and the government should be cautious about excessive intervention into the expert discretion of the regulator. They should interfere only in those cases where the public interest is unjustifiably harmed, and to the minimum extent that is required. Indeed, in the Israeli bank fees affair, the legislator did not directly intervene in the level of fees. It sufficed in granting authority to the Bank of Israel as the professional body to determine the list of permissible fees, and to set prices only in exceptional cases. Similarly, the Trachtenberg Committee avoided dealing by itself with the lack of competition in the banking system. Instead, it recommended the establishment of a professional committee to examine this subject. Experience shows that these initiatives constituted an adequate framework for leading the regulator to change its attitude and take active measures to protect the public interest.

Last, but not least, the Israeli experience demonstrates the value of public pressure. It shows that in certain situations, a strong public protest can overcome the passivity of the regulator, and result in improved supervision.

A case of Inconsistency," *Journal of Money, Credit and Banking*, 29 (1997) 127; M. Carlson, "Adam Smith's Support for Money and Banking Regulation: A case of Inconsistency?," *History of Economics Review*, 29 (1999), 1, www.hetsa.org.au/pdf-back /29-A-1.pdf.

Choosing among Authorities for Consumer Financial Protection in Taiwan

A Legal Theory of Finance Perspective

CHANG-HSIEN TSAI

8.1 Introduction

In 2008, an economic crisis struck most of the world's financial markets.[1] During the Global Financial Crisis (GFC), the global markets were devastated by bank over-lending, and several international financial institutions were unable to continue business, precipitating a serious controversy regarding international financial markets. Taiwan's financial market was one of those seriously affected by the GFC. Retail investors in Taiwan who invested in structured notes issued or arranged by Lehman Brothers Holdings Inc. might have been unaware of the real risk these financial products posed ("the structured notes debacle").[2]

According to Professor Pistor's seminal paper, "A Legal Theory of Finance" (LTF), at times of distress or crisis, it may be socially optimal for the state to intervene in private contracting; on top of that, under conditions of extreme uncertainty, future adjustment in contracts can be required not merely at the apex of the financial system, where law tends

---

[1] G. Kirkpatrick, "Corporate Governance Lessons from the Financial Crisis," *OECD Journal: Financial Market Trends*, 1 (2009), 61, 64.

[2] Structured notes are hybrid financial products that combine derivatives and debt securities and link to other investment products in the market. See C. H. Chen, "Structured Notes Fiasco in the Courts: A Study of Relevant Judgments between 2009 and 2010," 中研院法學期刊 *[Academia Sinica Law Journal]*, 10 (2012), 161, 211. See also P. Chen, "Behind the News – Structured Notes: Who's at Fault?," www.amcham.com.tw/content/view/2785/. Chen briefly defined structured notes as "a type of debt instrument whose value is based on an underlying derivative product rather than on fixed rates for periodic payout." To give a snapshot of the scope of the structured notes debacle, "more than 50,000 Taiwanese invested more than NT$42 billion (US$1.25 billion) in structured notes issued by Lehman Brothers alone." Ibid.

to be relatively more elastic, but also at the periphery if ex-ante legal commitments are relaxed or suspended as a sort of "safety valves" so as to take changes in circumstances into consideration.[3] The structured notes debacle in Taiwan during the GFC can shed some light on questions about whether courts, regulators, or other agents would be best placed to create safety valves, especially on the periphery of the financial system.

When it comes to whether courts would be best placed to fashion safety valves, Art. 227–2 of the Taiwanese Civil Code (CC), the legal foundation for applying the rule of changed circumstances in Taiwan, has empowered courts to initiate interventions on behalf of retail investors or financial services consumers in times of distress. As the structured notes debacle showed, some retail investors left holding worthless financial products in the wake of the 2008 crash were quick to seek legal redress for their losses, but these disputes were difficult to address using the civil remedies then available in Taiwan.[4] Few of the possible causes of actions listed in the Taiwanese Civil Code or in other special laws were available to address disputes over structured notes. In theory, the most applicable remedy available in the legislation available at the time was Art. 227–2 of the CC, which governs the rule of changed circumstances, but in practice it was referred to extraordinarily rarely in such disputes. In other words, the substantive aspect of the rule of changed circumstances, which requires courts' intervention, was little applied in Taiwan during the GFC.

However, interventions by the Financial Supervisory Commission (FSC), the sole financial market watchdog in Taiwan, showed that the procedural aspect of the rule of changed circumstances emerged instead to address the structured note controversies at the time.[5] Specifically, the change of circumstances caused by the bankruptcy of Lehman Bros. contributed to a wave of controversies in Taiwan in which retail investors argued that bank salespersons had not fully disclosed the risk of these structured notes. Meanwhile, there was no professional authority to handle this kind of financial product controversy at that time. The FSC, appearing to create a safety valve for retail investors, intervened by establishing the makeshift Alternative Dispute Resolution (ADR) system, which was created in a hurry, partially due to the courts' inability simultaneously to handle such a great number of cases and lack of

---

[3] K. Pistor, "A Legal Theory of Finance," *Journal of Comparative Economics*, 41 (2013), 315, 323, 326, 329.

[4] See section 8.3.1.4 below.

[5] See section 8.3.1.3 below.

professional knowledge and related resources. In addition to setting up the makeshift ADR system, the FSC intervened and used discretionary power to force financial intermediaries selling structured notes to settle complaints from retail investors and share the credit risk of Lehman Bros. and the concomitant systemic risk. This demonstrated a procedural aspect of the rule of changed circumstances.

From the LTF perspective, the FSC seemed to redistribute losses to the banks, thus granting the relaxing of binding commitments to retail investors in such a way as flexibility relief is created for apex players in a theoretical sense. From a political economy perspective, however, it is important to ask why the FSC intervened. Mounting public sentiment agitated by the media and aroused by various Structured Notes Self-Salvation Organizations (SNSSOs), which were formed via social networks on the Internet, insisted that "something must be done." Shaping a national "we must act now" type of environment,[6] SNSSOs exerted pressure on the government by resorting to street protests and various informal channels. The structured notes debacle in Taiwan demonstrates that financial services consumers generally may not be as dispersed, apathetic, and weak as many think, when it comes to pressuring the government by resorting to such methods of political mobilization in times of crisis. This meanwhile indicated that retail investor action groups sought to bring the financial consumer position to the attention of the government, therefore obtaining special, flexible treatment. Therefore, the tentative ADR scheme was created in a hurry during the GFC; in order to prevent similar problems in the future, the Financial Consumer Protection Act (FCPA) was adopted in 2011, formalizing the tentative ADR scheme into the Financial Ombudsman Institution (FOI) in 2012. In doing so, the FSC in theory appears to have treated retail investors' concerns similarly to those of private banks that are closer to the financial system's apex.

Despite these efforts, flaws remain in Taiwan's consumer financial protection infrastructure. The government could manipulate society's perceptions of how the structured notes debacle was addressed through the tentative ADR scheme, leading people to believe that the FOI could use ADR to prevent future problems similar to the structured notes

---

[6] Likewise, in terms of US corporate financial regulations such as the Sarbanes-Oxley Act and the Foreign Corrupt Practices Act, it was easy for interest groups to lobby Congress to impose new requirements and liabilities, "especially during times of a national 'we must act now' type of environment." See M. P. Wilt, "The Political Economy of Corporate Financial Regulatory Legislation" (Feb. 19, 2016), 31, http://ssrn.com/abstract=2734991.

controversy. From a political-economy perspective, executive-branch rule-makers, enforcers and legislators receive the benefit of a public perception that the tentative ADR scheme is pro-investor and the newly enacted FCPA is a tough formalization of an ex post facto ADR channel, avoiding blame for failing to prevent wrongdoing through ex-ante regulation that should have been implemented prior to the GFC.

Ex post action replaces ex ante regulation. This is not just beneficial to legislators and executive branch officials appearing to be tough in establishing an alternative ADR body and forcing banks to share the systemic risk on a small scale. It benefits banks too, because the focus on ex post facto ADR channels directs discussion about responses and remedies away from ex ante regulation and supervision by the FSC. However, the FSC, which under the current financial regulatory architecture is a unified regulator and tends to focus more on prudential regulation concerns than consumer financial protection, might not be best placed to produce a safety valve for financial services consumers.

This chapter argues that in order not to leave Taiwanese retail investors with only one option to influence their position in the financial system via non-legal informal channels such as street protests whenever a financial crisis arises, Taiwan could consider reforming the structure of its financial regulatory system by adopting a stronger consumer financial protection watchdog such as the US Consumer Financial Protection Bureau (CFPB), where prudential regulation concerns do not predominate over consumer financial protection. A professional consumer complaint body that is separate from and independent of the FSC, including having exclusive control over its own rulemaking, supervision, and enforcement of consumer financial protection measures in Taiwan, would be able to create safety valve flexibility when necessary. This would bring the position of financial services consumers to the attention of the government, so that accommodation would flexibly be provided even at the periphery of Taiwan's domestic financial system.

This chapter unfolds as follows: section 8.2 deals with the question of whether the substantive aspect of the rule of changed circumstances is applicable in such circumstances as financial crises, bearing in mind the issue of whether courts are suitable bodies to create safety valves for consumer financial protection. Section 8.3 discusses the emergence of the procedural aspect of the rule of changed circumstances, a variation of its substantive form and the legislation introduced following the GFC. It then offers a political economy analysis of whether the FSC would be a better choice than courts to create safety valve waivers of law on the periphery of the financial system. Section 8.4, from the LTF and political economy perspective, assesses why the FSC intervened in the structured notes debacle and its regulatory aftermath in Taiwan. To conclude, this paper advocates creating an independent agency such as a Taiwanese version of the CFPB to act independently of the FSC and exclusively control its own rulemaking, supervision and enforcement of consumer financial protection measures in Taiwan. This body would be better placed to offer the legal flexibility of safety valves within the financial system. In short, the structured notes saga illuminates the power relationships within the Taiwanese financial system, illustrating how law is applied under pressure.

8.2   Courts as Bodies Creating Safety Valves for Consumer Financial Protection

8.2.1   Basic Theories

If the effects of GFC on contracts in Taiwan are taken into account, the theoretical basis appears to rest on the rule of fundamental change of circumstances (*clausula rebus sic standibus*), or the concept of frustration of contracts.

The first issue to be explored under the GFC herein is the "rule of changed circumstances," which is related to sudden events that impact the foundation of transactions. In the GFC context, the question may involve whether those structured note contracts can be terminated or rescinded, just as some retail investors assert, because in some instances the GFC has totally changed the circumstances at the moment a contract is signed.

As a matter of legal theory, the rule of changed circumstances is an exception to the principle of *pacta sunt servenda* – that is, the promise must be kept. The rule of changed circumstances has been developed under both the common law and the civil law,[7] and is often applied to dramatic changes resulting from wars.[8] The idea of changed circumstances was also created and applied in German civil law cases.[9] Pistor

---

[7] C. T. Lo, "An Introduction to Contract Defenses in U.S. Contract Law and the Rule of Changed Circumstances in Taiwanese Law," 萬國法律 [*FT Law Review*], 186 (2013), 68, 70.

[8] C. C. Hou, "A Study on Rules of Changed Circumstances in Civil Law," 法學叢刊 [*China Law Journal*], 191 (2003) 107.

[9] F. Z. Peng, "Theories and Legislations on the Rule of Changed Circumstances in the Modern German Civil Code," 政大法學評論 [*Chengchi Law Review*], 30 (1984), 159, 161, 175, 179, 190.

explains that court-made principles designed to adapt contracts to new circumstances have been incorporated into the German Civil Code:

> If circumstances which became the basis of a contract have significantly changed since the contract was entered into and if the parties would not have entered into the contract or would have entered into it with different contents if they had foreseen this change, adaptation of the contract may be demanded to the extent that, taking account of all the circumstances of the specific case, in particular the contractual or statutory distribution of risk, one of the parties cannot reasonably be expected to uphold the contract without alteration.[10]

The rule of changed circumstances also exists in the Taiwanese Civil Code, albeit with somehow different wording, as discussed below.

8.2.2   The Substantive Aspect of the Rule of Changed Circumstances in the Taiwanese Civil Code

Some provisions of the CC share certain characteristics of the rule of changed circumstances. Even prior to the codification of the Taiwanese version of this rule, similar concepts were present in other Taiwanese laws and court decisions.

8.2.2.1   Historical Review

Article 227–2[11] of the CC is equivalent to the rule of changed circumstances in Taiwan. The CC follows the approach of civil law and is mainly fashioned after the German Civil Code. Before the codification of Art. 227–2, when it came to the issue of changed circumstances, Taiwan's and Germany's laws even shared similar developmental backgrounds with regard to changed circumstances. The problems with enforcing contracts during and after a time of war shed light on the demands to address this issue,[12] in that local market conditions then tended to be extremely unstable.[13]

---

[10] Pistor, "A Legal Theory of Finance," 329.

[11] The full text and elements necessary to apply this Article will be discussed in section 8.2.2.2.

[12] The current ROC government moved to Taiwan after the end of the Second World War due to the defeat of Kuomintang forces by the Chinese Communist Party during a civil war. Therefore, cases relating to contract enforcement during a time of social change were often brought to the court during and after the war. See Hou, "A Study on Rules of Changed Circumstances," 108.

[13] Ibid.

Although the rule of changed circumstances was not directly imported from Western legal systems, Taiwanese courts have long relied on the principle of good faith to address contact disputes under changed circumstances, thus sharing the same basis as its development in other civil law countries such as Germany.[14] In Taiwan, the idea of changed circumstances was usually cited by courts to deal with dramatic changes of price levels and the change of currencies after the Second World War.[15] The first attempt to codify the rule of changed circumstances was Art. 397 of the Code of Civil Procedure (CCP),[16] which is worded similarly to the current Art. 227-2 of the CC. The former also emphasizes that the circumstances in question must not result from the actions of either party.[17] In 1968, this Article was initially placed in the CCP rather than the CC, for the sake of expediency.[18] Prior to the codification of the rule under the CC, courts repeatedly tried to apply similar concepts to this rule based on previous court decisions, such as the interpretation of the principle of good faith and Art. 397 of the CCP.[19]

Article 227-2, an official legal basis of the rule of changed circumstances, was finally added in 1999 when the CC was amended.[20] This is

[14] Chen Erh Lin, *Rethinking the Rule of Changed Circumstances*, 台灣本土法學雜誌 [*Taiwan Law Journal*] 12 (2000), 57, 61. For example, the German Supreme Court (*Reichsgericht*) used to invoke the principle of good faith under Germany's civil code to adjust contracts to changed circumstances. Pistor, "A Legal Theory of Finance," 329 (noting that the German Supreme Court "used the principle of good faith embodied in the civil code to adapt contracts to new circumstances").

[15] Hou, "A Study on Rules of Changed Circumstances," 108–109. Taiwan's currency changed once after the end of the Second World War in an effort to control inflation. Most of the court cases related to this event dealt with the value difference between the New Taiwan Dollar and the original Taiwan Dollar.

[16] Art. 397 formerly stipulated: "(1) The court shall, *ex officio*, make just determination and give judgment to increase, decrease, or make payment, or change other effect of any juristic act which has its effect become unjust after it is done due to change of circumstances upon cause not attributable to the parties concerned and beyond their expectation. (2) The above provision shall apply *mutatis mutandis* to legal relationship originated from non-juristic act." Please note that this Article was later modified in February 2003, and now no longer covers changed circumstances in terms of substantive law (as opposed to procedural law).

[17] Lin, "Rethinking the Rule of Changed Circumstances," 66–67.

[18] The amendment was made in February 1968, when there was no official plan to amend the CC, so that the rule of changed circumstances was placed under the CCP as a temporary solution. See ibid., 66.

[19] C. T. Lo, "An Introduction to Contract Defenses in U.S. Contract Law and the Rule of Changed Circumstances in Taiwanese Law: An Introduction to Contract Defenses in U.S. Contract Law and the Rule of Changed Circumstance in Taiwanese Civil Law (Part II)," 萬國法律 [*FT Law Review*] 187 (2013) 68, 69.

[20] Ibid.

now the legal or statutory foundation for applying the rule of changed circumstance under the CC, as will be discussed in detail as follows.

8.2.2.2   The Elements

Article 227–2 of Taiwan's Civil Code states:

(1) If there is change of circumstances which is not predictable then after the constitution of the contract, and if the performance of the original obligation arising therefrom will become obviously unfair, the party may apply to the court for increasing or reducing his payment, or altering the original obligation.
(2) The provision in the preceding paragraph shall apply mutatis mutandis to the obligation not arising from the contract.

Nevertheless, even after the enactment of this Article, the requirements for applying the rule of changed circumstances did not become fully clear, and continued to be supplemented by legal theories and court decisions. With those elements in the CC, the question is therefore whether the events of the GFC qualify as exceptional circumstances. If so, we must then discuss whether this rule has legal applications that retail investors can take advantage of.

Concepts similar to the rule of changed circumstances had already been invoked by courts before enactment of Art. 227–2,[21] and these decisions are important references for interpreting the Article.[22] In the context of financial crises, the core issues requiring interpretation seem to be the standards of "obviously unfair" and "foreseeability."

Firstly, the wording of Art. 227–2 itself provides no clue as to how to decide what constitutes "obviously unfair." There are two cases that may serve as particularly clear demonstrations of the problem: both share a similar factual background, but came to different conclusions.

In 2009 the Taiwan Supreme Court ruled[23] that if a contractor is not economically disadvantaged, and if there is a price-index adjustment term included in the contract, a rise in price is insufficient justification for invoking the rule of changed circumstances.[24] Nonetheless, the Supreme Court also

---

[21] See section 8.2.2.1 above.
[22] Lo, "An Introduction to Contract Defenses (Part II)," 74.
[23] Zuigao Fayuan [Supreme Court], Civil Division, Tai-Shang No. 2470 (2009) (Taiwan).
[24] Cases addressing price level changes also exemplify the standard to determine foreseeability. In these typical cases, the courts determined that if the price level term had been included in a contract, the rule of changed circumstances would generally not apply, unless the result of a change was unconscionable. See M. C. Cheng, *The Rule of Changed Circumstances Applied*

held[25] that when a significant rise in price would lead to unfair results if the contract remained in force, then the rule of changed circumstances could be invoked and the contract terms adjusted. In this case the Supreme Court applied the rule without additional requirements such as weighing the economic strength of contracting parties.

Secondly, an unforeseeable event is another element that might necessitate invoking the rule of changed circumstances. In another 2009 case, the court determined the following precedent that the worsening of marine conditions was not unforeseeable because the contractor knew that the construction site was in an area where the weather was unstable, and therefore the change was foreseeable.[26]

Regardless of whether the rule of changed circumstances can be applied in controversies resulting from the GFC, it is another question whether the legal effects of this rule meet the needs of retail investors. That will be explored closely below.

8.2.2.3   The Legal Effects

In accordance with Art. 227–2, the legal effects of applying the rule of changed circumstances appear to be clear, including "increasing or reducing payment" or "altering the original obligation."

Nonetheless, in theory there are two tiers of possible judicial action when applying the rule of changed circumstances. The first is to adjust the contract terms while maintaining its validity. However, if adjustment cannot produce a fair result, the second tier would theoretically come into play: i.e., termination or rescission of a contract.[27]

Civil courts in Taiwan have been found to have jurisdiction to decide contract adjustment in cases involving a change of a currency value.[28] The Supreme Court stated that the advantages and disadvantages faced

---

to *Price Level Changes*, 174萬國法律 [*FT Law Review*], 9, 11–12 (2010). See also the following similar court decisions: Zuigao Fayuan [Supreme Court], Civil Division, Tai-Shang No. 760 (1995) (Taiwan); Gaodeng Fayuan [High Court], Civil Division, Jian-Shang No. 126 (2007) (Taiwan); Gaodeng Fayuan [High Court], Civil Division, Jian-Shang No. 99 (2007) (Taiwan); Gaodeng Fayuan [High Court], Civil Division, Jian-Shang-Geng (Yi) No. 32 (2009); Gaodeng Fayuan [High Court], Civil Division, Jian-Shang No. 59 (2009) (Taiwan); Gaodeng Fayuan [High Court], Civil Division, Jian-Shang No. 53 (2008) (Taiwan). Based on these court decisions, the interpretation of terms in a contract involving financial products such as structured notes might be an important key to the issue of whether the investment or credit risk thereof is unforeseen.

[25] Zuigao Fayuan [Supreme Court], Civil Division, Tai-Shang No. 2299 (2009) (Taiwan).

[26] Hou, "A Study on Rules of Changed Circumstances," 114.

[27] Ibid., 114.

[28] Ibid., 115.

by both parties due to the change of circumstances should be taken into consideration in order to reach a fair adjustment.[29] Only if an adjustment would fail to achieve a fair result, as one commentator has argued, would the court rescind the contract and award damages if necessary, based on the principle of good faith.[30] The idea behind this two-tier approach is that the validity of a contract should be maintained to the extent possible, as, in accordance with the principles of the CC, the court should not interfere in private transactions unless absolutely necessary.[31]

The second tier of rescission has yet to be applied by a Taiwanese court, so opinion has it that only "adjustment" – the primary consequence – is allowed by the CC.[32] As one commentator pointed out, the only choice provided in Art. 227–2 and the former text of Art. 397 in the CCP is "adjustment," and it is possible that Taiwanese courts have never tried to broaden this interpretation to cover the secondary consequences of the rule.[33]

8.2.3   Application of Changed Circumstances to Investor Contracts?

It is thus possible to make a temporary argument concerning the application of the rule of changed circumstances to a dispute over structured notes. According to the current text of Art. 227–2, the interpretation of investment or credit risk will determine whether the rule of changed circumstances can be applied. Even if the rule does apply, the Article and previous court decisions imply that the court may only adjust, not rescind, the contract. More importantly, it is necessary for retail investors who took part in transactions involving structured notes to apply to the court in order to benefit from this remedy.[34]

However, as shown in section 8.3, the makeshift ADR system was created in a hurry due to the courts' failure to handle the volume of cases filed and the courts' lack of professional knowledge and related

---

[29] Ibid. See also the following court decisions supporting this ruling: Zuigao Fayuan [Supreme Court], Civil Division, Tai-Shang No. 1771 (1958) (Taiwan); Zuigao Fayuan [Supreme Court], Civil Division, Tai-Shang No. 2630 (1997) (Taiwan).
[30] J. Y. Lin, "The Theory and Practice of the Rule of Changed Circumstances (II)," 法律評論 [Chas Yang Law Review], 29 (1963) 19, 20.
[31] Lo, "An Introduction to Contract Defenses (Part II)," 75.
[32] Hou, "A Study on Rules of Changed Circumstances," 114.
[33] Ibid., 115.
[34] K. C. Huang, "Should a Claim on the Rule of Changed Circumstances Necessarily Be Made Via an Action?," 月旦法學教室 [Taiwan Jurist], 29 (2005), 22–23.

resources.[35] Moreover, it was extremely rare to apply Art. 227–2 in cases of structured notes. This may be due to the strict conditions required by law, which deter retail investors from applying the rule of changed circumstances in actual cases.[36] In other words, even though courts, independently of the FSC, have been empowered to act to create safety valves for consumer financial protection in times of distress, the rule of changed circumstances as potentially applied through court intervention was impeded from working in Taiwan during the GFC.

8.3   The Financial Supervisory Commission as a Maker of Safety Valves for Consumer Financial Protection

8.3.1   The Procedural Aspect of the Rule of Changed Circumstances: A Case Study on the Structured Notes Debacle

8.3.1.1   The Background

Financial institutions in Taiwan began promoting structured notes around 2001, and at that time investors had to purchase them through foreign banks.[37] In 2003, the Ministry of Finance (MOF) announced retail investor protection regulations on disclosing information related to investment-linked insurance policies. In September 2008, Lehman Bros. went bankrupt, and all transactions involving structured notes issued or arranged by Lehman Bros. were suspended during the period of bankruptcy protection in Taiwan.[38] This event set off a wave of lawsuits against banks, in which retail investors argued that the banks' sales representatives had not fully disclosed the risks inherent in the structured notes.[39]

8.3.1.2   Common Disputes

At the core of the disputes outlined above are "Designated Money Trusts" (DMTs), a type of contract used by banks to sell structured notes to retail investors.[40] Under DMT contracts, investor clients retain the right to

---

[35] See section 8.3.1.3 below; see also section 8.3.2.2 below.

[36] See section 8.3.1.4 below.

[37] C. H. Lin, 金融消費者保護法之理論與實務 [*Financial Consumer Protection Act: Theory and Practice*] (Taipei: Taiwan Law Journal Publishing, 2012), 82.

[38] Y. T. Lin, "Reviewing Current Mechanisms of Financial Consumer Dispute Resolution after The Lehman Brothers Bankruptcy," 全國律師 [*Taiwan Bar Journal*], 13 (2009), 45.

[39] Ibid. at 46.

[40] L. C. Li, "An Analysis of Disputes in Sales of Financial Products and Relevant Cases: Centered on Structured notes," 全國律師 [*Taiwan Bar Journal*] 13 (2009), 29.

decide how to use their money, while banks are required to offer financial products that entail a risk level appropriate for the respective client, as well as to disclose investment risks.[41]

In cases where a dispute over structured notes entered into renegotiation procedures or the parties to a DMT contract went to court, the most common sort of dispute was that the client lacked information for one reason or another. For example, a retail investor lacked the necessary knowledge to understand the financial product(s) he or she was offered, a bank did not fully disclose necessary information, or information was not given at a proper time.[42] Another common dispute was whether banks (or their salespersons) had adequately discharged their fiduciary duties.[43]

8.3.1.3   Makeshift Resolution

Before the FCPA was passed, there was no professional authority to handle these kinds of disputes over financial products. The provisional authority in charge was the Bank Bureau under the FSC, dealing with cases in which the disputed value was larger than 1 million New Taiwan Dollars (NTD). Other cases for less than 1 million NTD were handled by either the Securities and Futures Investors Protection Center (SFIPC) if a Lehman product was involved, or by the Bankers Associations of ROC (BAROC) if non-Lehman structured notes were involved. All such cases, if they passed procedural review, were finally assigned to the Appraisal Committee of Financial Consumer Disputes under the BAROC (Appraisal Committee) for substantive review.[44] Regardless of whether they were nominally public or private in their capacity, these are the organizations that the FSC controlled.

Nonetheless, some cases involving structured notes did not fit the legal definition of "consumer disputes" in the Consumer Protection Act (CPA), and therefore did not fall under the BAROC's jurisdiction. In response to public pressure, the BAROC addressed this issue by

---

[41] Ibid.

[42] H. I. (Grace) Ku, "A Study on the Most Updated Court Decisions on Structured Note Disputes – A Survey of Banks' Fiduciary Duties," in LCS & Partners (ed.), 後ECFA實戰財金法律 [Post–ECFA Financial Laws] (Taipei: Shu-Chuan Publishing, 2010), 119.

[43] Ibid., 120.

[44] W. Y. Wang, "Developments in the Law: A Review of Financial Regulation: Global Perspective and Local Reexamination," 國立臺灣大學法學論叢 [National Taiwan University Law Journal] 40 (2011), 1980.

amending its own internal administrative rules to include any cases referred to it via the appropriate authorities mentioned above.[45]

As at April 1, 2011, 25,214 cases had been reviewed under this provisional system; nevertheless, only the first 100 decisions made by the Appraisal Committee were open to the public for reference at that time.[46] Members of the general public were thus not in a position to acquire information about the provisional ADR procedures introduced above. Moreover, adjudications made by the Appraisal Committee had no binding force on individual complaints when neither party had agreed to settlement terms; decisions were only binding on banks under certain conditions.[47] Meanwhile, with a view to maintaining its neutral position, the Bank Bureau under the FSC could not itself make any decision on an individual case unless the bank in question had been proved to have violated the law. In this regard, the BAROC was therefore the actual authority operating the makeshift ADR mechanism.[48]

8.3.1.4 Hindrance to the Application of Available Remedies

Even though a makeshift mechanism cobbled together in a hurry appeared to be available, the uncertainty over what constituted a valid cause of action was still problematic. Applicable remedies were so scattered among various statutory provisions that it was difficult for retail investors to identify sufficient and effective remedies.[49] Among the other causes of action for retail investors to seek legal redress or to modify a contract term involving structured notes, Art. 227-2 might, in theory, be taken into account to adjust the terms of DMT contracts in structured note cases.[50] In practice, this type of claim was extremely rarely made, which could be attributed to the strict conditions required by law, hence

---

[45] Ibid. For further discussion on how political pressure exerted by SNSSOs pushed the FSC to intervene, together with these controlled organizations, see section 8.4.2 below; see also section 8.4.1 below.

[46] Chen, "Structured Notes Fiasco in the Courts," 211.

[47] Ibid. at 212; Li, "An Analysis of Disputes in Sales," 37.

[48] T. W. Kuo, "The Dispute Resolution Mechanism of Financial Services: A Comparative Study between Taiwan and the United Kingdom," 中正財經法學 [*Chung Cheng Financial and Economic Law Review*] 4 (2012), 52–61.

[49] *See* C. H. Tsai, "Meditations on Liability Rules in the Financial Consumer Protection Act: An Empirical Perspective on Structured-Note Cases," unpublished manuscript, Institute of Law for Science and Technology, National Tsing Hua University, Taiwan (2013), 6–7, 14–17; K. H. Chen, P. H. Li, C. L. Cho and H. M. Hsu, 金融消費者保護法解析 [*Analysis of the Financial Consumer Protection Act*] (Taipei: New Sharing Publishing, 2012), 52–55, 85–132.

[50] See section 8.2.2 above.

deterring retail investors from applying the rule of changed circumstances in actual cases.

Apparently, there were no sufficient and effective rules or regulations targeting so unusual a financial product as the structured note. In order for Taiwan's government to prevent similar problems in the future, the FCPA finally came into effect in 2011.

8.3.2   The Legislation of the Financial Consumer Protection Act: A Thorough Solution?

8.3.2.1   A Profile of the Financial Consumer Protection Act

When the FCPA was enacted in June 2011,[51] the Taiwanese legislature required that the FSC, as the competent authority of this Act, establish an additional professional ADR authority to handle financial consumer controversies for procedural and substantive review.[52]

However, commentators indicated that this legislation merely provided another new ADR channel for seeking relief, not an ultimate solution for every future dispute arising in connection with products similar to structured notes.[53]

In addition, the FCPA imposes new obligations on financial service enterprises, particularly regarding new causes of action to be applied in financial consumer disputes. To summarize, the FPCA supplies two new

---

[51] When it comes to financial services enterprise, the statutory definition includes the following entities: banking enterprises, securities enterprises, futures enterprises, insurance enterprises, electronic stored value card enterprises, and enterprises in other financial services as may be publicly announced by the competent authority. Jinrong Xiaofeizhebaohu Fa (金融消費者保護法) [Financial Consumer Protection Act] Art. 3 (promulgated Jun. 29, 2011, effective Dec. 30, 2011, as amended Dec. 28, 2016) (Taiwan). As for financial consumers, the FCPA defines them as "parties that receive financial products or services provided by a financial services enterprise," but excludes consumers with a certain level of income or with professional knowledge of investment. Ibid. at Art. 4. Therefore, investment companies apparently cannot be consumers under the FCPA. C. T. Chiu, S. I. Hu and K. H. Lin, 金融消費者保護法與案例解析 [Cases & Analysis on Financial Consumer Protection Act] (Taipei: Angle Publishing, 2012), 25. In addition, the FCPA (Art. 5) only copes with CC disputes of financial products or services. Ibid. at 26. However, these financial consumer disputes also include disagreements that arise during contracting or advertising, and other similar disputes between parties that relate to financial products or services. Ibid.

[52] Lin, Financial Consumer Protection Act, 34.

[53] See, e.g., Y. T. Lin, "Effectively Resolving New Financial Disputes – The Past, Present and Future of Alternative Dispute Resolution of Financial Disputes," 月旦法學雜誌 [The Taiwan Law Review] 199 (2011), 27.

causes of action available for financial consumers: (1) Liabilities for false advertising (Art. 8); and (2) Breach of duties for implementing KYC and the suitability test (Art. 9), as well as the duties of explanation and disclosure (paragraphs 1 and 3 of Art. 10).[54] The new causes of action may prove to be more direct and powerful weapons for retail investors to use against financial institutions than the remedies that existed before the FCPA came into effect. More importantly, the FCPA provides other procedural rules to resolve disputes over this kind of financial transaction, as are discussed below.

8.3.2.2   The Creation of the Financial Ombudsman Institution

One major regulatory effort under the FCPA in response to the structured notes saga that followed the collapse of Lehman Bros. is the creation of an independent ADR body that exclusively handles financial controversies: the Financial Ombudsman Institution (FOI).[55] The FOI is an official answer to a previous situation in which financial consumer disputes were widely dispersed in various courts with slow proceedings and not decided under a common guideline.[56]

The FOI is a semi-official foundation funded by both regulated private enterprises and government agencies.[57] The decision-making organ of dispute resolution is the Ombudsman Committee (Arts. 17 and 18), which is composed of between nine and twenty-five members, including scholars, experts, and other professionals with sufficient practical knowledge. Because the FOI is merely a semi-official foundation, the FCPA vests the committee with the power to ask financial services enterprises to provide necessary documents (Art. 20).

However, retail investors still have to make a complaint to those financial services enterprises before they are allowed to apply to the Ombudsman Committee (Art. 24).[58] The process of dispute resolution generally goes as follows: after a retail investor brings a complaint to the financial services enterprises concerned, the investor may then file a case

---

[54] C. C. Wang, "The Control of Financial Marketing and Legal Reform: Application and Interpretation of Financial Consumer Protection Act," 萬國法律 [FT Law Review] 179 (2011), 2–10.

[55] C. C. H. Chen, "Judicial Inactivism in Protecting Financial Consumers against Predatory Sale of Retail Structured Products: A Reflection from Retail Structured Notes Lawsuits in Taiwan," 26 Columbia Journal of Asian Law, 26 (2014), 180.

[56] Tsai, "Meditations on Liability Rules," 16.

[57] Lin, "Effectively Resolving New Financial Disputes," 32.

[58] Ibid.

with the FOI. The FOI will first review the case to determine whether there is any possibility of reaching a settlement; if not, the Ombudsman Committee will start the committee hearing procedure. From the moment the case is referred to the FOI, the decision must be made within three months.[59] The system was designed to address disputes in a reasonable and timely manner.

Nevertheless, some problems remain with the design of the current system. The first issue is the protection of a retail investor's right to choose from various dispute-resolution procedural frameworks. The FCPA leaves room for the two parties to agree freely on whether to be bound by the Ombudsman Committee's decision. The FCPA also devised an "agreement in advance" mechanism: if a financial institution agrees to enter into dispute resolution procedures under the FCPA, either through a written statement before entering into the procedures or in a contract involving the disputed financial products or services, the financial institution will automatically be bound by the Ombudsman Committee's decision in cases where the value of the disputed products or services is less than a certain amount.[60] Nevertheless, in cases where there is no agreement in advance or the value of the disputed products or services exceeds "a certain amount," the financial institution retains the final say on whether it will be bound by the FOI's decision. This is unfair to retail investors with inferior bargaining power.[61]

In addition, the authority of the committee is also important. As it stands, the FCPA does not impose a real duty on financial services enterprises to cooperate with the committee, such as to provide necessary documents. Art. 20, for example, allows the committee to ask financial institutions to provide necessary documents, but it does not grant the committee the power to impose punishment for a failure to cooperate, thus further weakening the committee's authority. Therefore, penalties for non-compliance need to be clearly codified in the FCPA in the future.[62]

---

[59] Chiu, Hu and Lin, *Cases & Analysis on Financial Consumer Protection Act*, 45–46.

[60] C. C. Lian, 金融消費者保護法與評議案例解析 [*The Financial Consumer Protection Act and Case Studies*] (Taipei: Taiwan Academy of Banking and Finance, 2013), 108. Please note that "a certain amount" is to be determined according to product types. Take investment-linked products or services for example, the threshold amount is 1 million NTD, while the amount for non-investment-linked ones is 100,000 NTD. Notice of Financial Supervisory Commission, Executive Yuan, No. 10000423911, 18 *Executive Yuan Gazette* 324, 324 (Jan. 4, 2012) (Taiwan).

[61] Lin, "Effectively Resolving New Financial Disputes," 36; Kuo, "The Dispute Resolution Mechanism," 77.

[62] Lin, "Effectively Resolving New Financial Disputes," 39.

Furthermore, based on the limited range of subjects covered in the FCPA, it appears that different authorities continue to regulate other relevant financial products or services. For example, in one court decision involving investment-linked insurance policies, the financial product in question was in fact linked to structured notes; nonetheless, whether this case could have been reviewed by the FOI under the current provisions of the FCPA is unclear.[63] One commentator indicated that this conundrum substantiates the necessity of integrating the regulation of all financial-consumer-related cases under one law, thus providing full protection to financial consumers just as the United States' Consumer Financial Protection Bureau (CFPB) does.[64]

8.3.3   Merely Adding an Additional Channel Did Not Provide Sufficient Relief

The procedural aspect of the rule of changed circumstance, exemplified by the FSC interventions via the Appraisal Committee of the BAROC during the GFC and the FOI controlled by the FSC after the GFC, remained insufficient. Even though additional ADR channels with more professional resources were set up to handle a huge number of complaints within a short period of time,[65] they remained in the shadow of the FSC with a predominantly prudential focus.[66] Under the current financial regulatory architecture, the FSC cannot help but focus more on prudential regulation concerns than on consumer financial protection. Accordingly, the FSC is not well placed to create safety valves in contract law on the periphery of the Taiwanese financial system.

8.4   Reflections from the Legal-Theory-of-Finance Perspective on the Structured Notes Debacle in Taiwan

8.4.1   The Influence of the Structured Notes Self-Salvation Organizations

The structured notes debacle demonstrates from a political economy viewpoint that whereas substantive application of the rule of changed

---

[63] Wang, "Developments in the Law," 1989.
[64] Ibid. at 1990.
[65] C. Chen, "The Resolution of the Structured Notes Fiasco in Hong Kong, Singapore and Taiwan," *Company Lawyer* 34 (2013), 123.
[66] See section 8.4.3 below.

circumstances in Taiwanese courts could not be achieved, a procedural channel, illustrated by the FSC interventions, did emerge to address the problem. From the LTF perspective, even if retail investors are located on the periphery of the domestic financial system,[67] they formed various Structured Notes Self-Salvation Organizations (SNSSOs) during the GFC to draw attention[68] to the plight of investors and exert pressure on the FSC to intervene.[69] Specifically, in a national atmosphere where "something must be done,"[70] SNSSOs became influential interest groups and pressured the government. They used informal channels like street protests,[71] picketing the FSC building to demand action against the banks,[72] complained that the government was siding with the banks, and called for the resignation of then-FSC Chairman Sean Chen.[73] In the face of the FSC's failure to be firm with banks from the start,[74] SNSSOs

---

[67] Without government bailouts during the GFC, homeowners might still have been at the periphery of the US financial system. Pistor, "A Legal Theory of Finance," 320. Likewise, Taiwanese retail investors in the very beginning of the structured notes debacle needed to assume all the credit risk of Lehman Bros. and the concomitant systemic risk alone, whereas Taiwanese banks selling notes arranged by Lehman Bros. were literally waiting for the final liquidation of its holdings, thereby passing losses on to domestic investors but keeping the fees they had received. See Chen, "The Resolution," 123; Chen, "Judicial Inactivism," 186; Chen, Li, Cho and Hsu, *Analysis of the Financial Consumer Protection Act*, 81–82. In this regard, Taiwanese investors might be deemed to be on the periphery of the domestic financial system as well.

[68] See Lin, "Reviewing Current Mechanisms," 45–46; C. C. H. Chen, "Legal Risk and Investor Protection for Retail Investment Products: An Empirical Study of Lawsuits Regarding Mutual Funds and Structured Notes in Taiwan," 政大法學評論 [*Chengchi Law Review*] 141 (2015), 132. See also Chen, "Behind the News – Structured Notes" (describing that "with the structured notes issue receiving a high degree of media and political attention, the banks wish to resolve the investor complaints quickly and quietly").

[69] See Li, "An Analysis of Disputes in Sales," 26; C. S. Teng, "Profession or Fraud? The Myth of the Financial Derivatives of Structure Notes," unpublished master thesis, Fu Jen Catholic University (2009), 60, 62–64.

[70] Chen, "The Resolution," 119 (noting that "[o]bviously, it is a daunting challenge to settle such a massive number of disputes of such magnitude. Mounting political pressure and public opinions in such situations mean that regulators cannot afford to do nothing . . . . ").

[71] Chen, "Judicial Inactivism," 175 (vividly illustrating that "[f]or example, in Taiwan, some victims of the Lehman-related structured notes protested against a bank by carrying a coffin to the door of the bank").

[72] Teng, "Profession or Fraud?," 1, 8, 10, 66. The SNSSOs also held a press conference on May 30, 2008 before the headquarters of the China Trust, one of the banks involved in the dispute, which happened to be the most successful private commercial bank in Taiwan at the time.

[73] Chen, "Behind the News – Structured Notes."

[74] Chen, "The Resolution," 121.

held press conferences, announcing they were preparing to file lawsuits against banks and even the FSC to recover losses.[75] SNSSOs also complained to legislator Wei-cher Huang, who helped them hold a public hearing in the legislature on July 11, 2008.[76] On September 12, 2009, SNSSOs initiated a large-scale demonstration, marching to the Presidential Palace, the Control Yuan,[77] the Legislature, and the Cabinet.[78] The Control Yuan further issued an investigation report, concluding that the FSC failed to adequately supervise banks in selling structured notes.[79]

From the LTF perspective, mounting political pressure and public sentiment meant that SNSSOs representing Taiwanese retail investors, who could traditionally be regarded as less concentrated interest groups, raised their message to the apex of the domestic financial system, where they could benefit from informal flexibility via various non-legal means.[80]

8.4.2   The FSC Interventions

The tide of the political opinion stirred up by SNSSOs forced the FSC to react in order to create the perception of toughness and avoid blame for failing to prevent or take regulatory action against banks for their wrongdoing.[81] Even if the FSC could not simply require banks to absorb all of the losses, the second-best option for the FSC was to help retail investors recover as much as possible via "elastic" means.[82] For example, the FSC started to lay a heavier hand on banks by requiring the BAROC

---

[75] See Lin, "Reviewing Current Mechanisms," 45; Teng, "Profession or Fraud?," 60, 62.

[76] Teng, "Profession or Fraud?," 62–63; Chen, "Judicial Inactivism," 183.

[77] The founding father of the Republic of China (Taiwan), Dr. Sun Yat Sen, drew from the Western system of checks and balances among the legislative, executive, and judicial powers and added two traditional Chinese government powers of examination and supervision (control) to complete the five-power system. The Constitution of the Republic of China (Taiwan) was enacted on December 25, 1947; on June 5, 1948, the Control Yuan was officially established, following the enactment of the Constitution. See Control Yuan's website, www.cy.gov.tw/ct.asp?xItem=6036&CtNode=989&mp=21 (visited Dec. 10, 2017) (Taiwan).

[78] Teng, "Profession or Fraud?," 64.

[79] Ibid. at 69.

[80] See Pistor, "A Legal Theory of Finance," 325.

[81] Li, "An Analysis of Disputes in Sales," 26 (a commentator then wrote an op-ed in a major Taiwanese newspaper, arguing that officials of the FSC should be legally liable for its inaction or slackness in dealing with the structured notes controversies).

[82] Lin, *Financial Consumer Protection Act*, 84–85.

to amend its own internal administrative rules to include any cases involving structured notes referred to it, thereby expanding the jurisdiction of the tentative ADR channel with a view to alleviating public sentiment aroused by SNSSOs.[83] In response to initial recalcitrance on the part of banks, the FSC in mid-2009 intervened to increase the settlement rate by auditing the business operations of those targeted banks with a low settlement rate. The FSC also held up applications for new businesses made by non-cooperating financial institutions and threatened to forfeit licenses of trust enterprises that had sold structured notes to unsophisticated investors but declined to fully compensate those investors.[84] Therefore, during the GFC, the FSC intervened through structuring the makeshift ADR system[85] while forcing financial intermediaries selling structured notes to settle complaints from retail investors and hence to share both the credit risk of Lehman Bros. and the concomitant systemic risk. From the LTF perspective, the FSC in theory redistributed loss to the banks, thus bailing out retail investors, or rather giving them treatment normally reserved for the financial system's apex.[86]

According to the LTF, "law tends to be relatively elastic at the system's apex, but inelastic on its periphery."[87] Owing to the dramatic political mobilization of SNSSOs, however, retail investors managed to influence the government, eliciting treatment at the apex of the domestic financial system, where law tends to be relatively more "elastic," not least as

---

[83] See Li, "An Analysis of Disputes in Sales," 26; see also section 8.3.1.3 above.

[84] See Lin, "Effectively Resolving New Financial Disputes," 31; Lin, *Financial Consumer Protection Act*, 85, 87; Teng, "Profession or Fraud?," 56, 66. Interestingly, similar intervention measures to bail out those at the periphery of the financial system could also be observed in the United States to an extent: "In the wake of financial crises, public authorities often respond by using law to modify private contracts, transferring value from those who fare better in the crisis to those who fare worse. From the perspective of the crisis victim, this is a bailout. ... Recent examples include staying foreclosures, authorizing bankruptcy courts to modify mortgage terms, or threatening criminal prosecution to induce banks to undo transactions made with their clients." A. Aviram, "Bailins: Cyclical Effects of a Common Response to Financial Crises," *University of Illinois Law Review 2011* (2011), 1633.

[85] Chen, "Judicial Inactivism," 175 (noting that "[a]s required by the Financial Supervisory Commission (FSC), the sole financial regulator in Taiwan, the Bankers Association of the Republic of China (Bankers Association) was tasked to form a dispute resolution panel to handle structured note disputes").

[86] Pistor, "A Legal Theory of Finance," 320 (describing that "the Hungarian government intervened and forced creditors to adjust loans and share their currency risk. In doing so they have brought homeowners a step closer to the system's apex").

[87] Pistor, "A Legal Theory of Finance," 320.

illustrated by the FSC interventions to force banks to share the systemic risk via "elastic" means. Alternatively, from the other perspective (from the periphery of the system), during the GFC, when the FSC was pressured to exercise its discretionary power via "elastic" means to rescue retail investors ex post facto to some extent, it played a tentative and unexpected role as a provider of safety valves even for financial services consumers on the periphery of the system.[88]

8.4.3   Did the Interventions by the FSC and the Enactment of the FCPA Have a Placebo Effect?

While in hindsight the FSC providing elastic safety valves for retail investors or financial consumers at the periphery in the system may be a fait accompli beyond anyone's control, the next question would be whether the FSC is best placed to perform such a role and to initiate an intervention in times of future distress.[89] In reality, there are still flaws in Taiwan's consumer financial protection infrastructure, as the government might arguably have just manipulated society's perceptions of regulatory quality rather than actually achieving it. We formulate this manipulation as a "placebo effect" below.

The FSC did not come down hard on banks from the start of the structured note controversies, possibly because "the overall exposure was simply too massive for banks to swallow."[90] In the LTF view, "the survival of the system is determined at its apex,"[91] and this systemic risk explanation could account for the FSC's light-handed approach from the start, because the rhetoric (public-spirited justifications) of banks' systemic importance reinforces their location at the apex in the system by influencing regulators through social or political ties.[92] However, the political

---

[88] See ibid., 329.

[89] See ibid.

[90] Chen, "The Resolution," 121. The FSC and the BAROC in the FSC's shadow might worry that requiring banks to highly compensate retail investors for their losses would severely damage the business safety and soundness of banks. See Teng, "Profession or Fraud?," 57, 69; Chen, "Legal Risk and Investor Protection," 130–131.

[91] Pistor, "A Legal Theory of Finance," 329.

[92] From a political economy perspective, banks as concentrated, motivated industries have a strong incentive to band together and affect policy. From the "public choice" perspective, the political process is a competition among interest groups to secure rents with "public-spirited justifications used to disguise interest group rent-seeking." See M. Kahan and E. Rock, "Symbolic Corporate Governance Politics," *Boston University Law Review* 94 (2014), 2027; see also B. Orbach, *Regulation: Why and How the State Regulates* (New York: Foundation Press, 2013), 199 ("The term 'rent-seeking' is often used to

sentiment later aroused by SNSSOs insisted that the FSC do something. This chapter thus argues from a political-economic perspective that the procedural aspect of the rule of changed circumstances (i.e., the FSC interventions) emerged to address the structured note controversies because public pressure was brought to bear on the apex of the system. Under pressure from SNSSOs, the FSC set up the tentative ADR body (i.e., the Appraisal Committee under the BAROC) and used its discretionary power to increase the settlement rate. Finally, the FOI was created under the FCPA as a formalized and strengthened version of the tentative ADR channel.[93]

Being seen to do something had tangible benefit for both legislators and the FSC as executive-branch rule-makers and enforcers. It allowed each group to avoid blame for failing to prevent wrongdoing through regulation and scrutiny that should have been implemented prior to the GFC.[94] This political action is well described by Aviram's bias arbitrage theory:

> Bias arbitrage is the extraction of private benefits through actions that identify and mitigate discrepancies between actual risks and the public's

describe the pursuit of private interest through regulation. Rent-seeking activities are all actions that interest groups may take to promote their goals, and their costs are added to the burden interest groups impose on society" (footnote omitted)). That is, interest groups will become involved in the political process to advocate for the common interests of their members. D. C. Mueller, *Public Choice III* (Cambridge: Cambridge University Press, 2003), 475. Banks, as strong interest group lobbyists, might, in the name of avoiding systemic risk, indirectly interfere in the process of the FSC's decision-making with respect to how to deal with retail investors' complaints in the very beginning of Taiwan's structured notes debacle, in effect "captur[ing]" regulatory agencies. See B. Orbach, "Invisible Lawmaking," *University of Chicago Law Review* 79 (2012), 15. See also B. Orbach, "What Is Regulation?," *Yale Journal on Regulation Online* 30 (2012) 5–6; Orbach, *Regulation*, 199 ("Capture" theories or regulatory capture indicate that "regulators are captured by the regulatees; that is, they serve those they intend to regulate rather than the public"); George Stigler, "The Theory of Economic Regulation," *Bell Journal of Economics and Management Science*, 2 (1971), 3, 5 ("[A]s a rule, regulation is acquired by the industry and is designed and operated primarily for its benefit").

[93] See section 8.3.2.2 above. The structured notes debacle was one of the reasons for the enactment of the FCPA; the FOI was established as another ADR body for financial disputes. See Lin, *Financial Consumer Protection Act*, 92–93, 95; Wang, "Developments in the Law," 1974–1975, 1989; Lin, "Effectively Resolving New Financial Disputes," 27.

[94] From a public choice perspective, government agencies such as the FSC tend to be averse to risk, "defensive, threat-avoiding, scandal-minimizing," and "reluctant to take on activities that embrace seemingly intractable problems and that are fraught with the danger of unintended consequences including regulatory failure and criticism." M. L. Stearns and T. J. Zywicki, *Public Choice Concepts and Applications in Law* (St. Paul MN: West Academic Publishing, 2009), 348 (footnotes omitted).

perception of the same risks. Politicians arbitrage these discrepancies by enacting laws that address the misperceived risk and contain a "placebo effect" – a counter-bias that attempts to offset the pre-existing misperception. If successful, politicians are able to take credit for the change in perceived risk, while social welfare is enhanced by the elimination of deadweight loss caused by risk misperception.[95]

Accordingly, it can be inferred that Taiwan's government might have complex incentives to ensure consumer financial protection. Specifically, why is bias arbitrage beneficial for legislators and the FSC to look tough through setting alternative ADR bodies during the GFC and in its aftermath? It might be because the Taiwanese government, by setting additional ADR bodies that appear to be very strict actually allowed most banks to avoid generously compensating retail investors and financial consumers or writing off their losses. Taiwanese politicians could try to maximize their positions by manipulating the public's perception of the effectiveness of the seemingly pro-investor regulations and enforcement while reaping a private profit from the placebo effects of the FSC interventions and the enactment of the FCPA, which mitigated the discrepancy between the actual and the perceived risk of future disputes such as the structured notes saga.[96] This argument is to an extent supported by retail investors' low expected recovery rate offered by either courts or the Appraisal Committee under the BAROC both during and after the GFC.[97] Therefore Taiwanese banks in the very beginning of the GFC had few incentives to share the credit risk of Lehman Bros. and the concomitant systemic risk – or rather, to offer much in settling investors' complaints voluntarily and then to proactively negotiate with liquidators of Lehman Bros. or a foreign issuer to recover remaining value.[98] Even though the FSC, as the sole financial market watchdog, has taken action, including its interventions during the GFC and later pushing through the enactment of the FCPA, it might not strive to put consumer financial protection into practice thoroughly enough.

Why may the FSC be less incentivized to effectively create safety valves for financial consumers at the periphery of the system, especially in times of future distress? When it comes to the institutional design of the FSC, it was created in 2004, patterned after the design of the former Financial

---

[95] A. Aviram, "Bias Arbitrage," *Washington & Lee Law Review*, 64 (2007), 789.

[96] *See* A. Aviram, "The Placebo Effect of Law: Law's Role in Manipulating Perceptions," *George Washington Law Review*, 75 (2006) 101.

[97] Chen, "Legal Risk and Investor Protection," 134.

[98] Chen, "Judicial Inactivism," 183, 185–186.

Services Authority in the United Kingdom (FSA).[99] Nonetheless, the former UK model of a unified regulator places too many responsibilities under one universal regulator, "thereby masking the conflicts that can arise between consumer protection and maintenance of bank solvency and soundness."[100] Under the old UK model, the FSA's supervision and regulation theoretically focused more on the "safety and soundness" of financial institutions than on consumer financial protection.[101] This institutional incentive factor is partially evidenced by the general settlement result of low compensation to retail investors under the Appraisal Committee indirectly controlled by the FSC in Taiwan.[102] Even if the FSC required the Appraisal Committee under the BAROC to handle structured note disputes, a possible reason for the Appraisal Committee not forcing banks to return large amounts of cash to investors might be to protect banks from encountering serious solvency failures and to guard financial soundness of the banking system.[103] In the LTF view, during the GFC, retail investors at the periphery were in practice more likely to face greater economic stress than banks at the apex, even after the FSC interventions; banks in Taiwan could by and large pass on the credit risk of Lehman Bros. and the concomitant systemic risk to domestic investors.[104] With its current institutional design, the FSC is not best placed to create safety valves for financial consumers on the periphery of the financial system.

Furthermore, establishing additional ADR channels such as the Appraisal Committee under the BAROC during the GFC, as well as the FOI in its aftermath, has not solved all the problems,[105] although these measures benefit banks because the focus on ex post facto ADR channels directs discussion about responses and remedies away from the regulatory design of a stronger and independent consumer protection watchdog. Specifically, this chapter argues that in order not to leave financial consumers with street protests or other informal channels as their only option to bring themselves a step closer to the flexibility of the

---

[99] W. Y. Wang (ed.), 金融法 [*Financial Law*] (Taipei: Angle Publishing, 2012), 18, 526–527.
[100] J. C. Coffee, Jr. and H. A. Sale, "Redesigning the SEC: Does the Treasury Have a Better Idea?," 95 *Virginia Law Review*, 95 (2009), 774.
[101] See ibid., 722; Lin, *Financial Consumer Protection Act*, 93–94.
[102] Chen, "Judicial Inactivism," 180–181.
[103] Ibid., 182–183.
[104] See Pistor, "A Legal Theory of Finance," 325.
[105] See Chen, "Judicial Inactivism," 186, 219; Chen, "Structured Notes Fiasco in the Courts," 218; Chen, "The Resolution," 122–123, 125.

financial system's apex whenever a financial crisis occurs, we could consider moving consumer financial protection into a separate and single agency; that way prudential regulation concerns would not predominate over consumer financial protection.[106] This regulatory proposal is to concentrate the mission of consumer financial protection, including rulemaking, supervision, and enforcement, in the hands of a single professional agency such as the United States' CPFB, who would be at the same hierarchical level as the FSC while simultaneously independent of it.[107] Accordingly, a stronger and independent consumer financial protection body could be best placed to create safety valves on the periphery of the system, not least in times of future distress.[108]

8.5   Conclusion

Are courts, regulators, or other agents best placed to offer the flexibility of safety valves and to initiate interventions for retail investors or financial services consumers in times of economic distress?[109] The structured notes debacle in Taiwan during the GFC shed some light on the afore-mentioned issues.

When it comes to whether courts are best placed to fashion safety valves, the structured notes debacle demonstrated that Art. 227-2 of the CC, the statutory foundation of the rule of changed circumstances in Taiwan, was extremely rarely invoked and decided by courts. Even though courts, independently of the FSC, were empowered to intervene per se, they did not in Taiwan during the GFC, possibly due to their inability to handle a great number of cases at the same time with insufficient professional knowledge and related resources, and possibly due to the law's standing, pleading and proof requirements, hence deterring retail investors from applying the rule of changed circumstances in actual cases.

The procedural aspect of the rule of changed circumstances (i.e., interventions by the FSC) emerged instead. Specifically, the FSC interventions via the Appraisal Committee of the BAROC during the GFC and the FOI in its aftermath illustrated the procedural aspect of the rule

---

[106] See A. J. Levitin, "Hydraulic Regulation: Regulating Credit Markets Upstream," *Yale Journal on Regulation*, 26 (2009), 161–162.

[107] See Wang, "Developments in the Law," 1989–1990; Wang (ed.), *Financial Law*, 528.

[108] Of course, fleshing out the detailed regulatory design of a Taiwanese version of the CFPB would remain a difficult issue requiring more research in the future.

[109] Pistor, "A Legal Theory of Finance," 329.

of changed circumstance. The FSC, appearing to produce safety valves for retail investors, intervened by structuring the makeshift ADR system while forcing financial intermediaries selling structured notes to settle complaints and to share both the credit risk of Lehman Bros. and the concomitant systemic risk. From the LTF perspective, the FSC in theory seemed to redistribute loss to the banks, thus bringing retail investors a step closer to the flexibility of the financial system's apex.

But why did the FSC intervene? From a political economy angle, even if retail investors are usually located on the periphery of the domestic financial system, the actions of SNSSOs made the losses of retail investors nationally relevant. In the time of a national "we must act now" mood, SNSSOs exerted pressure on the Taiwanese government through street protests, picketing, publicly complaining that the government was siding with the banks and even calling for the resignation of the FSC Chairman. This moved the traditionally peripheral concerns of retail investors toward the apex of the domestic financial system, where they were most likely to benefit from sympathetic flexibility. Although the FCPA was finally legislated in 2011, hence formalizing the tentative ADR scheme into the FSC-controlled FOI, flaws remained in Taiwan's consumer financial protection infrastructure. The FCPA's lacking bite indicates that the government may arguably just have sought to manipulate the society's perceptions of whether the structured notes debacle was addressed through the tentative ADR scheme, without really preventing potential problems similar to the structured notes controversies from arising or being addressed via the FOI. Even though additional ADR channels with more professional resources were set up to handle a huge number of complaints quickly, they are still in the shadow of the FSC and have a predominantly prudential focus. In short, the FSC might not be best placed to provide safety valves for financial services consumers.

In order not to leave Taiwanese retail investors with informal channels such as street protests as their only option to influence financial regulators whenever a financial crisis occurs, we could preliminarily consider a holistic reform agenda, i.e., adopting a fully independent consumer financial protection watchdog such as the United States' CFPB. With a newly created single professional agency playing the role in creating safety valves for retail investors independently from the FSC, the concerns of financial services consumers might therefore be brought a real step closer from the periphery of Taiwan's domestic financial system to the power found at its apex.

9

The Political Economy of Indian Microfinance

An Application of LTF to the Andhra Pradesh Microfinance Crisis of 2010

NIKHILESH SINHA

Microfinance is widely associated with the Bangladeshi Nobel Laureate Mohammad Yunus, and the Grameen Bank. While there are precedents, the most popular model, involving small loans to groups (most often women) can be traced back to Dr. Yunus's pioneering works in 1976, which laid the basis for the establishment of the Grameen Bank in 1983. There are numerous microfinance institutions operating in many parts of the developing world, including Latin America and Africa, but these markets are dwarfed by the sheer proliferation and density of operation in South Asia, where there are currently almost 80 million clients, representing a gross loan portfolio of $27.4 billion.[1] The Indian microfinance story may be summed up as it was in the title of an article in the *Economic and Political Weekly*: "Microfinance: A Fairy Tale Turn(ed) into a Nightmare." The tremendous growth (above 170 percent) of the 2007–2010 period was brought to a stuttering halt after the microfinance crisis in Andhra Pradesh in 2010, and the private microfinance sector has yet to recover.

Explanations of what led to the crisis range from "mission drift"[2] or the shifting of focus from social inclusion toward profit, to a delayed impact

---

[1] Data retrieved from www.themix.org/mixmarket/countries-regions/south-asia (last visited November 1, 2017).

[2] C. Fouillet and B. Augsburg, "Profit Empowerment: The Microfinance Institution's Mission Drift," *Perspectives on Global Development and Technology*, 9/3 (2010), 327–355; P. Yerramilli, "The politics of the Microfinance Crisis in Andhra Pradesh, India," *Journal of Politics & Society*, 24/1 (2013), 190–225; P. Ghate, "Consumer Protection in Indian Microfinance: Lessons from Andhra Pradesh and the Microfinance Bill," *Economic and Political Weekly*, 42/13 (2007), 1176–1184; M. Kumar, "Crisis at the Bottom of the Pyramid: A Case Study of Micro Finance in India," (November 2012), https://ssrn.com/abstract=2177290.

of the Global Financial Crisis[3] and a failure of regulation.[4] With due respect to the multiple rich and informative narratives presented by other observers, this chapter argues that the Indian microfinance crisis was primarily a subprime credit crisis. In other words, while there are several confounding factors, the key dynamics are most usefully identified by focusing on microfinance as an innovative financial product, as opposed to a device for social and economic development. This does not imply that the perception of microfinance as a development tool is irrelevant to our analysis of the crisis, as this played an important role in shaping the narratives around the crisis.

The chapter draws on Katharina Pistor's pioneering work on the Legal Theory of Finance (LTF) and the regulation of financial markets to analyze the characteristics of the Indian microfinance ecosystem and the factors that led to the crisis and its aftermath. LTF provides a general yet highly adaptable analytical framework for examining financial systems, highlighting the hybrid nature of such systems, and laying bare the intrinsic paradox for regulators. Pistor argues that "it may be time to move beyond the simple state vs market dichotomy in the debate about financial regulation."[5] None of the current theories, Efficient Market Hypothesis (EMH), Imperfect Knowledge Economics, Minsky's Financial Instability Hypothesis (FIH), nor "shiftability" or the Money View of Finance (MVF) completely explain the causes of the microfinance crisis or indeed suggest a useful regulatory response.[6] The chapter therefore proceeds upon the stylized facts presented in Pistor as underpinning the Legal Theory of Finance (LTF):[7]

---

[3] H. Tadele and P. M. S. Rao, "Corporate governance and ethical issues in microfinance institutions (MFIs) – A study of microfinance crises in Andhra Pradesh, India," *Journal of Business Management & Social Sciences Research*, 3/1 (2014), 21–26; R. Sane and S. Thomas, "A Policy Response to the Indian Micro-Finance Crisis," Working Paper 2011-007 (Mumbai: Indira Gandhi Institute of Development Research, 2011); J. de Quidt, T. Fetzer and M. Ghatak, "Microfinance, Market Structure, and Borrower Welfare: Regulatory Lessons from the Indian Crisis," LSE Working Paper (London, 2012).

[4] R. Galema, R. Lensink, and R. Mersland, "Do Powerful CEOs Determine Microfinance Performance?," *Journal of Management Studies*, 49/4 (2012), 718–742; S. Nasir, "Microfinance in India: Contemporary Issues and Challenges," *Middle-East Journal of Scientific Research*, 15/2 (2013), 191–199.

[5] K. Pistor, "On the Theoretical Foundations for Regulating Financial Markets," Columbia Public Law Research Paper No. 12–304 (2012), 0–65.

[6] Section 9.2 of the chapter provides a more nuanced argument for the suitability of the LTF framework for the analysis of the case.

[7] For a complete discussion of LTF please, see K. Pistor, "A Legal Theory of Finance," *Journal of Comparative Economics*, 41/2 (2013), 315–330.

1. Financial assets are legally constructed.
2. The law contributes to financial instability.
3. Finance is inherently hierarchical.
4. The strength of enforcement is inversely related to this hierarchy.

For the sake of brevity and clarity, I present a highly simplified version of the arguments put forward by Pistor. Financial markets do not exist outside of rules but are instead constituted by them, though it is possible to distinguish different rules and rule-makers, both public and private.[8] Hodgson[9] and Pistor contest the possibility of an unregulated market, suggesting instead that "deregulation" implies the implicit delegation of rule-making authority to different, typically non-state actors, affording them the full protection of the law in other respects. Financial markets are neither state nor market, nor indeed private or public, but are essentially hybrid entities.[10] This follows from the requirement that financial instruments be enforceable, that finance is hierarchical and that the sovereign must stand guarantor as the last resort, in order to protect the system from self-destruction. The law-finance paradox in its simplest form can be characterized in this way: The legal scaffolding that lends financial transactions their legitimacy, could also bring the system down, if all obligations are enforced to their fullest extent, ignoring changes in circumstances. On the other hand, if the full force of the law is relaxed or suspended, it undermines the legitimacy of the entire system. Finally, differential relations to the law extend from the elasticity of the structure, and the power of different actors, which can be exercised by those who have resources to extend support to others without being legally obligated to do so.[11] Power becomes salient when the law is elastic.[12]

There is a need for certain caveats when applying LTF to the case of the Indian microfinance crisis. For one, this is a market that is geographically limited not just to the Indian subcontinent, but further the analysis concerns the microfinance market in one subnational region, the erstwhile state of Andhra Pradesh (which has subsequently been subdivided).[13] LTF

[8] Pistor, "A Legal Theory of Finance."
[9] G. M. Hodgson, "Observations on the Legal Theory of Finance," *Journal of Comparative Economics*, 41/2 (2013), 331–337.
[10] Pistor, "A Legal Theory of Finance."
[11] Ibid.
[12] Ibid.
[13] See Internet Desk, "The Story of India's 29th State – Telangana," (2016), and Press Trust of India, "From 1948 to 2013: A Brief History of the Telengana Movement," (2013), for a detailed timeline.

was developed in reference to macroeconomic phenomena, more specifically the case of the US financial system, with the Federal Reserve serving as the apex financial authority. Given the position of the US dollar in the global financial market, it can be extended to an analysis of the entire global financial system without great difficulty. I argue that LTF can also be applied to exploring the dynamics of a subnational financial market, which exhibits similar characteristics including being rule-bound, hybrid and with different actors having differential relations to the law. The third of Pistor's stylized facts has more limited applicability here, as a crisis in a subnational market may not have as dire implications for the entire financial system. However, even within this limited scope, the incentives for state authorities are conflicted, given the economic implications for the region, but also the growth of the microfinance sector across the country. This will be elaborated on in the analysis section.

The chapter begins with a brief look at the history of microfinance in India and more specifically Andhra Pradesh, and the lead-up to the crisis. This section also discusses the probable causes as identified in the economic and development studies literature. In the second section LTF is applied to the analysis of the crisis identifying where the theory fits, and where the specifics depart from the theories predictions. The last section presents some observations related to the applicability of LTF in the context of emerging markets and concluding remarks on regulating microfinance in India.

9.1   A Fairy Tale that Turned into Nightmare

The Grameen model, pioneered and promoted by Muhammad Yunus in Bangladesh is the most widely known form of microfinance; particularly after the Nobel Peace Prize was awarded jointly to the Grameen Bank and Yunus in 2006. [14] Yunus launched the Grameen Bank Action Research Project in 1976, in the Jobra village of Chittagong, and by 1980 the project covered 363 villages. [15] The project transformed into a full-fledged bank in October 1983 with the financial assistance of the Bangladesh Bank, the International Fund for Agricultural Development, the Ford Foundation and others. [16] The Grameen model has been described as being

---

[14] The title of this section is inspired by the title of M. S. Sriram's (2010) article the EPW.

[15] M. A. Auwal and A. Singhal, "The Diffusion of Grameen in Bangladesh: Lessons Learnt about Alleviating Rural Poverty," *Knowledge: Creation, Diffusion, Utilization*, 14/1 (1992), 7–28.

[16] Ibid.

underpinned by the philosophy of "Microcapitalism,"[17] whereby poor clients who do not meet the formal collateral requirements of conventional banking gain access to credit, while also being trained in the skills and expertise required to start and run a business. Grameen borrowers or "members" gain certain privileges which can be likened to those accorded to shareholders in a regular business, such as the ability to participate in decision-making at the board level.[18]

The remarkable success of the Grameen model has been attributed to its pro-people focus, but the financial sustainability of the enterprise rested on the remarkable reported loan recovery rates of 99 percent and over. This high recovery rate, or conversely low default rate, is a consequence of the joint liability group structure, which creates a risk-sharing framework. Loans are advanced to individuals through a group structure, with five members forming a group and six groups forming a village *center*.[19] Center chiefs are charged with conducting weekly meetings, and observing the various rules prescribed by the bank.[20] The group is an essential mechanism, helping to spread risk, to keep members in line through peer pressure, and with inter-group and intra-group competition serving as an impetus for members.[21] For the bank, it is easier to keep track of groups than to monitor individual members.[22] The requirement that every member make a "one taka" deposit every week serves as a hedge, but equally importantly inculcates financial discipline.[23] While interest rates charged were typically higher than those charged on conventional bank loans, they were considerably lower than those charged by informal lenders, and justified on the basis of covering operational costs.[24] By 1991, the Grameen Bank had over a hundred thousand members and a portfolio of close to $400 million.[25] The latest report states that the Bank has disbursed over $22,500 million

[17] M. A. Auwal, "Promoting Microcapitalism in the Service of the Poor: The Grameen Model and Its Cross-Cultural Adaptation," *The Journal of Business Communication*, 33/1 (1996), 27–49.

[18] Auwal, "Promoting Microcapitalism in the Service of the Poor."

[19] Auwal and Singhal, "The Diffusion of Grameen in Bangladesh."

[20] M. Yunus, "Group-based savings and credit for the rural poor," in Panel on People's Participation of the ACC Task Force on Rural Development (ed.), *Group-Based Savings and Credit for the Rural Poor: Papers and proceedings of a Workshop, Bogra (Bangladesh), 6–10 November 1983* (Geneva: International Labour Office, 1984), 9–20.

[21] Ibid.

[22] Ibid.

[23] Ibid.

[24] Auwal, "Promoting Microcapitalism in the Service of the Poor."

[25] Auwal and Singhal, "The Diffusion of Grameen in Bangladesh."

since its inception, with loans outstanding amounting to just under $1,700 million, a membership of close to 900,000, and a reported repayment rate of just over 99 percent.[26]

Three aspects of the Grameen model made it particularly attractive to the international development community. Firstly, the seductive idea that the key roadblock to economic development is the supply of financial services, and that it is possible to unlock the entrepreneurial instincts of millions, allowing them to bootstrap their way out of poverty. The second is the focus on women and the potential for empowerment through financial agency. Finally, the remarkable loan recovery rates meant cost-recovery and replicability in a very short period of time. The last characteristic also meant that the model represented an alluring business opportunity.

While it is beyond the scope of the present discussion to evaluate the merits of the Grameen model, it is important to note that the first two of these aspects continue to be the subject of widespread debate. The link between microfinance and micro-entrepreneurship is tenuous at best, and it is now acknowledged that much of the credit is used for consumption or refinancing of existing debt. Further, the self-selecting mechanism at the heart of the joint liability group structure means that in practice, the poorest are often excluded.[27] The idea of empowerment is both powerful and hard to measure, but there is evidence that many of the beneficiaries of Grameen were in positions of relative privilege within social hierarchies[28] and in addition, the monitoring mechanisms of the group structure may have eroded social cohesion. Nevertheless, the Grameen model served as an inspiration and a template for the proliferation of microfinance programs across the world, including Africa, Latin America, and other countries of South Asia, particularly India.

The existence of multiple aims or multiple bottom lines – poverty alleviation, empowerment and profit – poses a challenge for regulators regardless of geographical context. The founder of the Grameen Bank provides a theory of capitalism in developing countries that includes "social-consciousness driven enterprises"[29] which step in to correct for

---

[26] Grameen Bank, *Monthly Report : 2017–08 Issue 452 in USD* (2017).

[27] A. Rahman, *Women and Microcredit in Rural Bangladesh. An Anthropological Study of Grameen Bank Lending* (Boulder CO: Westview Press, 1999).

[28] H. Todd, *Women at the Center: Grameen Bank Borrowers after One Decade* (Boulder CO: Westview Press, 1996).

[29] M. Yunus, "Poverty alleviation: Is economics any help? Lessons from the Grameen Bank experience," *Journal of International Affairs*, 52/1 (1998), 47–65.

the failure of the state and the conventional private sector to cater for the needs of the poor. This creates in effect three groups of entrepreneurs: traditional profit maximizers, philanthropic organizations that maximize social returns, and entrepreneurs who consider both financial and social returns on investments.[30]

What is interesting is that all three of these categories of entrepreneurs could be found to be operating in the Indian microfinance market. In addition the state was also an active player in the microfinance market, not just as a regulator, but also an enabler and supplier of financial services. In order to simplify the analysis we distinguish primarily between state-aided and private microfinance, while acknowledging that the category of private microfinance includes entrepreneurs with differing and competing aims. These competing aims between state and private on the one hand and between different categories of private microfinance on the other led to what is best described as a crisis of image within the microfinance industry as a whole.

With the launch and proliferation of private microfinance initiatives, some started by non-government organizations (NGOs) operating on a not-for-profit basis, as well as a few that operated on a for-profit basis, there was a shift in emphasis from "financial inclusion" toward "financial sustainability," though many would argue that the two are intimately related.[31] This shift in emphasis attracted its share of criticism, which ranged from the accusation of "mission drift"[32] to outright profiteering.[33] A discussion of the purpose and intended impact of microfinance, while interesting, is beyond the scope of this chapter. We are primarily concerned with private microfinance and its regulation, though some theoretical discussion of its essential nature will feature in the last section.

---

[30] K. Q. Elahe and C. P. Danopoulos, "Microcredit and the Third World: Perspectives from moral and political philosophy," *International Journal of Social Economics*, 31/7 (2004), 643–654.

[31] D. Drake and E. Rhyne (eds.), *The Commercialization of Microfinance: Balancing Business and Development* (Boulder CO: Kumarian Press, 2002); A. Hannig and S. Jansen, "Financial Inclusion and Financial Stability," *Current Policy Issues* (2010); Sane and Thomas, *A Policy Response to the Indian Micro-finance Crisis*.

[32] Fouillet and Augsburg, "Profit Empowerment: The Microfinance Institution's Mission Drift."

[33] D. Mallick, "Microfinance and Moneylender Interest Rate: Evidence from Bangladesh," *World Development*, 40/6 (2012), 1181–1189; P. W. Roberts, "The Profit Orientation of Microfinance Institutions and Effective Interest Rates," *World Development*, 41/1 (2013), 120–131.

9.1.1 The Two Models of Indian Microfinance

The first pilot microfinance program to be launched in India was started by MYRADA[34] in 1983,[35] the same year that the Grameen Bank was founded in Bangladesh. However it was in the post-liberalization period (1991 onwards) that microfinance really began to take off, with the introduction of the state-led bank inter-linkage program.[36]

There are two competing models of microfinance in India (please refer to figure 9.1). The first is the bank-led self-help groupmodel promoted by the State through commercial banks, where banks lend to federations of self-help groups, each composed of between ten and twenty women. The second is the private microfinance model, where the microfinance institution (MFI) acts as an intermediary, borrowing from banks and then lending to groups. One key difference between the two models is that the SHG model emphasizes group savings, which private MFIs are constrained from offering due to regulatory hurdles.

The existence of the two models and the competition between the state and the private sectors plays a crucial role in determining the crisis. As a consequence of the peculiarities of the regulatory environment in

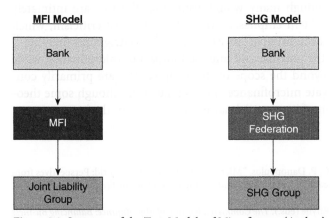

Figure 9.1 Structure of the Two Models of Microfinance (Author's schematic)

---

[34] The erstwhile Mysore Resettlement and Development Agency, which is now simply known by the acronym MYRADA.

[35] A. P. Fernandez, "The Myrada Experience Putting Institutions First," (2003), http://myrada.org/myrada/.

[36] de Quidt, Fetzer, and Ghatak, *Microfinance, Market Structure, and Borrower Welfare.*

India and the challenges of providing allied financial services such as savings, insurance and money transfers, private "microfinance" practice in India was essentially restricted to the provision of credit.

The success and rapid growth of private microfinance in India, and in the southern state of Andhra Pradesh (AP) more specifically, can be directly attributed to positive externalities created by the state's investment in the SHG Bank-linkage program. The SHG program in AP received a further boost in the year 2000 with funds from the World Bank's Velugu program,[37] and this in turn boosted the growth and proliferation of MFIs in the state. Typically private microfinance followed the publicly funded program into districts where the latter had invested in educating potential clients about microfinance. In many cases NGOs played a role in facilitating group formation and training,[38] creating fertile ground for MFIs to launch operations. This may have sown the seeds for the resentment that was to erupt at a later stage.[39]

9.1.2   The Macro Context

In order to understand the peculiarities of the case it is useful to understand some of the macro policy context of the banking sector in India. In the period following independence in 1947, the Indian government has made frequent use of the banking sector to pursue broader development objectives.[40] This has often meant taking direct control. Fourteen of the largest commercial banks operating in India (representing 85 percent of all deposits in the country) were nationalized in 1967, and a further six were nationalized in 1980.[41] One of the key aspects of the state's oversight of the banking sector has been a focus on financial inclusion, most directly through the Priority Sector Lending (PSL) program. This requires all commercial banks operating in India to allocate 40 percent

---

[37] Ibid.

[38] Ibid.

[39] I interviewed and came in contact with several operatives involved in the publicly funded SHG programme in Andhra Pradesh in 2007, and found that many actively discouraged their clients from borrowing money from private MFIs. There was a general consensus amongst them that MFIs were up to no good and complaints that they were poaching their best client groups. The research was part of a project funded by Mahila Abbhivruddhi Society, Andhra Pradesh (APMAS), an NGO involved with supporting and monitoring microfinance in the state.

[40] Yerramilli, "The Politics of the Microfinance Crisis in Andhra Pradesh, India."

[41] J. G. Copestake, "The Transition to Social Banking in India: Promises and Pitfalls," *Development Policy Review*, 6 (1986), 139–164.

of their credit portfolio to specific sectors dictated by the Reserve Bank of India (RBI) at a preferential rate of interest. The interest rate for these loans was capped at the respective bank's prime lending rate, applying to loans of under INR 200,000 ($3,000) rates of interest ranging from 10 to 16 percent at the time.[42] The federal government used the network of nationalized commercial banks to extend credit to rural areas through a range of programs, most notably the Integrated Rural Development Program (IRDP), which was launched as a pilot program in 1978 and extended to the whole country in 1980.[43] The framework for operation left little in the hands of participating banks, with decisions on the eligibility of households being determined by local government staff, and bank branch managers offering little more than a rubber stamp on disbursement.[44] Towards the end of the decade rising default rates led to widespread criticism, and the government implemented a loan waiver in light of the upcoming elections.[45]

With liberalization and the large-scale reform of the financial sector in line with IMF guidelines of the 1990s, the program was cut back, and subsidies to rural borrowers reduced.[46] However the extension of credit to the rural sector remained a key area of priority, though the focus began to shift from agricultural loans toward other sectors of the rural economy. It was around this time that the bank-led SHG model began to take off, and provided an ideal conduit for PSL funds. Banks were willing to lend at preferential rates because NGOs and government subsidies absorbed most of the operating costs involved with setting up and managing groups.[47] The Union Budget of 1998–1999 set a target of promoting 200,000 SHGs, with the government receiving support and guidance from the World Bank and its Consultative Group to Assist the Poorest (CGAP), an effort that was to continue and expand in the following years.[48] This resulted in significant pressure on public banks and institutions like the Small Industries Development Bank of India (SIDBI) to lend to NGOs engaged in microfinance and later to MFIs.[49]

---

[42] de Quidt, Fetzer, and Ghatak, *Microfinance, Market Structure, and Borrower Welfare.*
[43] Copestake, "The Transition to Social Banking in India: Promises and Pitfalls."
[44] Ibid.
[45] S. Young, "The 'moral hazards' of Microfinance: Restructuring Rural Credit in India," *Antipode*, 42/1 (2010), 201–223.
[46] Young, "The 'moral hazards' of microfinance."
[47] de Quidt, Fetzer, and Ghatak, *Microfinance, Market Structure, and Borrower Welfare.*
[48] Fernandez, *The Myrada Experience Putting Institutions First.*
[49] Ibid.

The bank-led SHG program expanded particularly rapidly in the former state of Andhra Pradesh, and as mentioned above, received a boost in the year 2000 with funds from the World Bank's Velugu program. The SHG program was piloted in six districts through an NGO called the Society for Elimination of Rural Poverty (SERP), and was the first push toward a commercial microfinance industry, allowing SHGs to hire skilled professionals instead of relying on free services from NGOs.[50] By 2004, the SHG-Bank Linkage Program in Andhra Pradesh accounted for two-fifths of all SHGs financed by India's National Bank for Agriculture and Rural Development.[51]

9.1.3   The Importance of the Andhra Pradesh Case

While there were initiatives in other parts of the country – the growth and reach of the industry in Andhra Pradesh (AP) was unrivalled. This was not happenstance. The government of AP systematically nurtured and promoted the growth of microfinance, diverting state resources to this end.[52] The investment was aimed at promoting the SHG-Bank Linkage model, but this lowered costs for private microfinance, as they could build on awareness campaigns as well as financial and basic skills training programs for women funded by the state and NGOs. A report on the state of the microfinance sector published in 2010, just prior to the crisis, states that the numbers of SHG members and MFI clients in AP were more than double that of those in the states with the second-highest number in each case.[53]

9.1.3.1   The Political Context

There were political reasons for the state government's promotion of the SHG-Bank Linkage Program, and arguably for allowing private micro-finance to flourish, despite the direct competition between the two. Chandrababu Naidu took over as Chief Minister of AP in 1994, serving for ten years, during which time he undertook an ambitious restructuring of the state economy, with particular focus on the capital city of

---

[50] de Quidt, Fetzer, and Ghatak, *Microfinance, Market Structure, and Borrower Welfare.*
[51] Ibid.
[52] A. Priyadarshee and A. K. Ghalib, "The Andhra Pradesh Microfinance Crisis in India: Manifestation, Causal Analysis, and Regulatory Response," *BWPI Working Paper* 157 (2011), 1–14.
[53] N. Srinivasan, *Microfinance India: The State of the Sector Report 2010* (2010).

Table 9.1 *Comparison of States with Highest Penetration of Microfinance (Data Source: Srinivasan,* Microfinance India: The State of the Sector Report 2010 *(2010))*

Aspects	Karnataka	Andhra Pradesh	Tamil Nadu	West Bengal	Orissa
Number of households (04–05)(million)	11.16	16.02	12.96	16.92	7.72
Number of poor households (million)	2.77	2.52	2.91	4.16	3.56
Number of credit SHG members (million)	3.35	17.31	7.3	6.58	4.64
Number of MFI clients 2010 (million)	3.74	6.24	4.57	3.51	1.59
Total microfinance clients	7.09	23.55	11.88	10.09	6.23
Microfinance clients as proportion of poor households	2.6	9.3	4.1	2.4	1.8
Microfinance clients as proportion of total households	0.6	1.5	0.9	0.6	0.8
Total mf loans SHG+MFI ₹ (millions)	34,844	157,692	62,861	34,324	26,801
Average loans outstanding per poor household ₹	12,579	62,576	21,602	8,251	7,528

Hyderabad.[54] AP was one of the first Indian states to receive a subnational loan from the World Bank, and Naidu developed a strong relationship with that institution. It has been argued that Naidu's vision for the state was deeply influenced by prevailing World Bank ideology,[55] making him something of a poster-boy for what many

[54] L. Kennedy, *Decentralisation and Urban Governance in Hyderabad. Assessing the Role of Different Actors in the City* (Hyderabad: Centre for Economic and Social Studies, 2006); L. Kennedy, "Regional Industrial Policies Driving Peri-urban Dynamics in Hyderabad, India," *Cities*, 24/2 (2007), 95–109.

[55] Young, "The 'moral hazards' of Microfinance: Restructuring Rural Credit in India"; M. Taylor, "'Freedom from poverty is not for free': Rural development and the MicroFinance Crisis in Andhra Pradesh, India," *Journal of Agrarian Change*, 11/4 (2011), 484–504.

describe as "neoliberal" reform.[56] The reduction of subsidies and the introduction of user-fees for public services, along with a largely urban-focused development strategy, had the potential of alienating poor rural voters. Naidu had taken over as leader of the Telegu Desam Party (TDP) from his deceased father-in-law, N. T. Rama Rao, a populist leader whose base was predominantly the rural poor. This meant that Naidu needed to repackage the image of the party as an "enabler" to the poor in order to counter the risk of losing relevance with the traditional voter base.[57] The aggressive rollout of state-led microfinance initiatives served to mitigate this risk, and further endeared Naidu to the World Bank, projecting him as pro-business, but with a wider more inclusive agenda.

By the end of Naidu's first term as Chief Minister, the AP government and the World Bank had forged a strong working relationship, tying together access to other development programs with membership of an SHG through the Velugu project.[58] With CGAP having invested in SHARE,[59] one of the largest private MFIs and their support of private microfinance in general, it would have caused friction if the state government had opposed or obstructed the private sector. This does not how-ever mean that incentives were aligned. In the lead-up to the 1999 State Assembly elections, the TDP began to offer subsidized cooking gas connections to SHG members.[60] The use of the SHG program to build political capital was to prove to be an important contributing factor to the crisis and the nature of the response of the state.

9.1.4   The SKS IPO and the Seeds of the Crisis

The extensive social infrastructure created by the Velugu program and NGO-supported SHG initiatives lowered the costs of entry for private

---

[56] I have written elsewhere about the impact of this reform on the urban economy and housing market in Hyderabad, but few would disagree that AP's "entrepreneurial" Chief Minister had a profound impact on the state, by attracting foreign investment, creating the conditions for the growth of the knowledge economy and putting Hyderabad on the international map.

[57] J. Mooij, "Hype, Skill and Class: A Comparative Analysis of the Politics of Reforms in Andhra Pradesh, India," ISS Working Paper Series No. 413 (2005).

[58] Young, "The 'moral hazards' of Microfinance."

[59] CGAP, Focus On Poverty: CGAP 2000 (2000).

[60] K. Suri, "The Dilemma of Democracy: Economic Reforms and Electoral Politics in Andhra Pradesh," in J. Mooij (ed.), The Politics of Economic Reforms in India (New Delhi, Thousand Oaks: Sage Publication, 2005), 130–170.

microfinance operators, allowing the latter to expand activities at an extraordinary pace. One of the largest and most successful private operators, SKS was to later find itself deeply embroiled in the crisis, and became a symbol of all that was wrong with private microfinance. SKS was founded as an NGO in 1997 by Vikram Akula, and transitioned from a non-profit to a for-profit company in 2005.[61] SKS reported an annual compound growth rate of 165 percent from 2004 up until the crisis, with revenues and profits growing annually at about 100 percent and a loan portfolio of around $665 million.[62] It was also the first microfinance institution (MFI) to go public,[63] with a hugely successful IPO that was thirteen times oversubscribed, allowing it to raise $348 million in fresh capital.

The success of the SKS IPO led several MFIs to try to follow suit. By now a number of international investment funds had begun to eye microfinance as a promising avenue, with the industry being established as its own asset class coupled with the virtuous glow of social responsibility thrown in. Micro investment funds for refinancing MFIs were advertised as one of the "fastest growing segments in the finance industry," with attractively low risks due to their high repayment rate and widespread outreach.[64] The first international fund to be guided by a double bottom-line approach not funded by private donors or development agencies was Dexia Micro-Credit Fund in 1998, but by 2007 increasing commercialization of the microfinance industry had attracted an impressive array of investors from across the world.[65] The years 2008 and 2009 saw a total of venture capital deals of at least $200 million, which corresponded to roughly 10 percent of the market in 2008.[66] The biggest deal by far, was a $75 million investment by Sandstone Capital into SKS.[67] In addition private banks operating in India like ICICI which were not subject to the Priority Lending requirements began building their own retail businesses or partnering with MFIs.[68]

---

[61]   de Quidt, Fetzer, and Ghatak, *Microfinance, Market Structure, and Borrower Welfare.*
[62]   Ibid.
[63]   SKS was the first MFI to go public in India, the second in the world following BancoSol in Bolivia – H. Ming-yee, "The International Funding of Microfinance Institutions: An Overview," *October*, November (2007).
[64]   C. Wichterich, "The Other Financial Crisis: Growth and Crash of the Microfinance Sector in India," *Development*, 55/3 (2012), 406–412.
[65]   Ming-yee, "The International Funding of Microfinance Institutions: An Overview."
[66]   de Quidt, Fetzer, and Ghatak, *Microfinance, Market Structure, and Borrower Welfare.*
[67]   Ibid.
[68]   Ming-yee, "The International Funding of Microfinance Institutions : An Overview."

In short, there was a large amount of capital available, both in terms of potential equity partners and working capital for loans. Interestingly, the financial crisis of 2008–2009 served to increase investor interest in microfinance investments, as they were seen as basically sound, though slightly saturated in some markets,[69] and classed as anti-cyclical assets, de-linked from capital market trends.[70]

9.1.4.1   Capital Adequacy Ratio and Perverse Incentives

The wisdom of the rush to go public is open to debate, but there was a particular difficulty that Indian MFIs faced which has been alluded to earlier in the chapter but deserves further discussion. Private *microfinance* in the Indian context is a bit of a misnomer. The majority of the activity was restricted to credit and excluded other financial services such as savings, insurance and money transfers. One of the major reasons for the absence of savings schemes was that private microfinance companies were not allowed by law to accept deposits from their clients, as they were required to register as a Non-Banking Financial Company (NBFCs). NBFCs are allowed to disburse credit, but may not accept demand deposits or issue checks,[71] and in addition are required to maintain a certain percentage of their loan portfolio with the Reserve Bank, known as the Capital Adequacy Ratio (CAR).

Unlike in the case of the Grameen Bank in Bangladesh where deposit ratios are 1.5 or higher, in the Indian context the only sources available were loans, donations or other overseas funds.[72] As a result, MFIs sourced funds from commercial banks, many preferring to move away from with what some saw as an overly politicized relationship with the government. CRISIL, a credit-rating agency, reported that borrowing from banks by the fourteen largest MFIs doubled between 2002 and 2004.[73] MFIs thus served as intermediaries, but also needed to keep 15 percent of their loan portfolio with the Reserve Bank. This, in the eyes of many in the sector, acted as a severe growth constraint. As Vijay Mahajan, former head of Basix – another prominent MFI in the pre-crisis period – pointed out in an interview conducted in December 2010, equity capital was the cheapest and most sustainable way of filling the CAR gap. Thus while the rationale for restricting demand deposits may lie in

[69] CGAP, *How Have Market Challenges Affected Microfinance Investment Funds?* (2012).
[70] Wichterich, "The Other Financial Crisis."
[71] Government of India, Reserve Bank of India Act, 1934 (2009).
[72] de Quidt, Fetzer, and Ghatak, *Microfinance, Market Structure, and Borrower Welfare.*
[73] CRISIL, "Banking Sector Thrust on MFI Lending Beneficial," *Rating Release* (2005).

consumer protection, it led to perverse incentives. MFIs pursued aggressive growth strategies to court investor interest, in many cases with the sole objective of getting as many clients on their books as possible.

Nevertheless, aggressive growth translated into an overexpansion of credit, a relaxation of the standard client screening procedures, multiple loans given to clients beyond their capacity to repay, and intense competition for clients between rival MFIs as well as SHG promoters. There was a huge demand for MFI "agents," offering employment opportunities to mostly young college-educated males, who were offered various incentives to go out and recruit new clients.[74] As agents of different MFIs went out in search of new clients, often in the same villages, they started poaching from each other, and encouraging women who had no regular source of income to take loans that they had no realistic chance of repaying.[75]

9.1.4.2   The Microcredit Bubble

All of the classic signs of a credit bubble were in place: An overheated market, indiscriminate lending and a lack of adequate regulatory oversight. There were also some regulatory issues relate to the structure of NBFCs and the process of transformation of NGOs to for-profit companies. NGOs looking to commercialize, used mutual benefit trusts (MBTS) to transfer funds from the existing non-profit to the new for-profit NBFC, which represented stakeholder interests but the trust deed made provisions for an employee of NBFC to chair the MBTS and participate in the general body of the NBFC, ensuring complete control of community assets.[76] While this mechanism was ratified by institutions like SIDBI and ICICI in good faith, it turns out that it allowed public purpose funds to be used to enhance the personal wealth of promoters, particularly in the case

---

[74] Wichterich, "The Other Financial Crisis."

[75] Ibid. Note: This story fits with anecdotal evidence collected in the field. In 2007 I led a study on household indebtedness for an organization called Mahila Abhivruddhi Society, Andhra Pradesh (APMAS), which offered capacity-building training to SHG-members, as well as engaging in research and advocacy. The research conducted in three districts of Andhra Pradesh revealed that the average household had three active loans with different creditors. Conversations with field operatives from SHG-support organizations revealed a deep distrust and animosity toward MFIs, with clients often being castigated if they borrowed from the private sector. At the same time the MFI agents revealed that they were asked to find up to six new clients every day, while continuing to service their existing clients, a tall order. Not surprisingly, many opted to lend to clients of competitors, or to offer new loans to existing clients in order to fulfill their quota.

[76] M. S. Sriram, "Commercialisation of Microfinance in India: A Discussion of the Emperor's Apparel," *Economic and Political Weekly*, xlv/24 (2010), 65–74.

of SKS.[77] The founder of SKS was allotted shares worth INR 16 million ($250,000) for the purchase of which he was advanced an interest-free loan. These shares were later sold for INR 150 million ($2.3 million).[78] Akula allegedly bought the shares at a highly discounted rate (1 percent of the IPO rate), benefitting both from an interest-free loan as well as a subsidized price.[79] Aside from raising ethical questions, the more critical issues relate to the governance of the MBTS as well as of NBFCs.

Perhaps most significant was the growing resentment within the community of development practitioners, and government officials involved in the sector and a plausible narrative about "mission-drift," and outright "profiteering" at the expense of poor women. It should be pointed out that promoters of SKS were not alone in reaping the rewards of a maturing microfinance sector, but the SKS IPO and the massive payout to the promoter were the most visible of these transactions. It is also worth noting that the political climate had changed, with a new government in AP as well as at the Center. The stage was set for the crisis, but also for the public outrage and backlash against private microfinance operators that followed.

9.1.5   The Crisis and Its Aftermath

Towards the end of 2010 there were reports in local, national and international media outlets of several suicides in Andhra Pradesh linked to mounting debts and coercive practices of private microfinance operators. The *Economist* reported fifty-seven suicides, seventeen of which were women who had been clients of SKS.[80] Vikram Akula, founder of SKS swiftly responded to allegations, stating that although the women had been clients, they had not defaulted on their loans, and so there was no scope for agents of SKS to apply any form of coercive pressure.[81] However these tragic deaths set in motion a series of events that were to all but destroy the private microfinance sector in Andhra Pradesh. The discourse emerging from the state government and local media

---

[77] Ibid.
[78] Ibid.
[79] P. Mader, "Rise and Fall of Microfinance in India: The Andhra Pradesh Crisis in Perspective," *Strategic Change*, 22 (2013), 47–66.
[80] "Microfinance in India: Discredited," *The Economist* (November 4, 2010).
[81] Ibid.

outlets painted a picture of private microfinance as modern day *sahukars*, unscrupulous moneylenders driven by avarice, uncaring and exploitative.[82] The AP government placed a moratorium on collection of repayments and sought to directly regulate interest rates,[83] which led ultimately to the collapse of the industry. However the more unexpected and ultimately decisive factor was the decision by the banking sector to stop lending to MFIs across the country, regardless of the default probability ratios of their portfolios, or indeed if they operated in AP or not.[84] This transformed the AP crisis into a nationwide microfinance crisis, causing investors and donors to pull out as well.

While the suicides took the headlines, reportage around the SKS IPO earlier that year had begun to unearth disquieting trends in Indian microfinance. A Bloomberg report in June had suggested that actual default rates were much higher than reported ones, and that something on the lines of the subprime crisis might be on the way.[85] Ghate, while analyzing the 2006 AP crisis[86] had identified systemic issues including the tendency of MFIs to place growth above all other considerations, the charging of effective annual interest rates of close to or above 30 percent, and the coercive nature of the group liability system and its fairly draconian implementation.[87] While there was an attempt to curb interest rates, none of the other issues had really been addressed. Another issue

---

[82] Taylor, "Freedom from poverty Is Not for Free."

[83] Ibid.

[84] Sane and Thomas, *A Policy Response to the Indian Micro-finance Crisis.*

[85] R. David, "Threat of Microfinance Defaults Rises in India as SKS Plans IPO," *Bloomberg* (March 14, 2010).

[86] There was a precursor to the state-wide crisis in 2006, when fifty branches of two major MFIs in Krishna district were shut down by the government following protests by their clients, who alleged unethical practices (H. S. Shylendra, "Microfinance Institutions in Andhra Pradesh: Crisis and Diagnosis," *Economic and Political Weekly*, 41/20 (2006), 1959–1963). It was alleged that agents of the two MFIs had, amongst other misdeeds, seized title deeds as collateral (Mader, "Rise and Fall of Microfinance in India"). The protest and actions of the state were reported by local and state media in ways that were highly critical of private MFIs, and the matter was brought up at a State Level Banker's Committee meeting. The Chief Minister of the time Y.S. Rajasekhara Reddy reportedly accused private MFIs of being worse than moneylenders and of charging usurious rates of interest. This is significant because one of the arguments for microfinance was that it would replace informal lenders, associated with high interest rates and the use of violence and intimidation to ensure repayment. The move to shut down the branch offices was seen as "inappropriate and irresponsible use of state power" by some (Ghate, "Consumer Protection in Indian Microfinance"), though many agreed that there was a need for introspection within the MFI community.

[87] Ghate, "Consumer Protection in Indian Microfinance."

that seemed to escape everyone's attention was the missing data on loan utilization. Websites and publicity material aimed at donors and funders always featured smiling women engaged in running a micro-enterprise, and yet it was an open secret amongst field operatives that loans were often used for consumption or to refinance other debts. I attended an annual forum organized by Intellecap, an organization that provided consultancy services to MFIs in August 2006, where a senior manager at SKS informed me that that they did in fact have the data, but were too busy to process it. It is unclear whether the data was deliberately suppressed, or if the low reported default rates were assumed to indicate all was well, but loan utilization data only became public knowledge after crisis prompted scrutiny.

9.1.6   The Policy Response

The government of Andhra Pradesh passed an Ordinance (Ordinance 9 of 2010) on October 15, 2010 temporarily prohibiting the collection of repayments and the issue of new loans by MFIs. This passed into law on January 1, 2011, and was referred to as the Andhra Pradesh Micro Finance Institutions (Regulation of Money Lending) Act, 2011, though the actual title reads "An Act to Protect the Women Self Help Groups from Exploitation by the Micro Finance Institutions in the State of Andhra Pradesh and for the Matters Connected Therewith or Incidental Thereto."[88] The Act makes it mandatory for all MFIs to register with the local authority in the area where they operate,[89] and to obtain permission before lending to members of SHG groups who have an existing loan through the Bank-Linkage scheme.[90] There are also provisions related to interest rates, and the form and manner of MFI repayments and collection.[91] Much of the Act refers to the regulation of MFI activities, except where it is specified that no SHG-member can retain membership of more than one group.[92] This was one of the main criticisms of the Act, which was seen by MFIs as a transparent attempt by the state government to constrain them, so as to maximize the political

---

[88] Government of Andhra Pradesh, Andhra Pradesh Micro Finance Institutions (Regulation of Money Lending) Act, 2011 (2011).

[89] Cl. 3(2) of the above Act.

[90] Cl. 10(1) of the above Act.

[91] Cll. 8, 9 & 11 of the above Act.

[92] Cl. 6 of the above Act.

capital gains from the SHG program.[93] On the other hand, MFIs had shown reluctance to admit wrongdoing, and to address many of the legitimate concerns expressed by clients and state authorities.

In December 2010 the Reserve Bank of India appointed the Malegam Committee to look into the microfinance crisis, identify the key regulatory issues and to propose a way forward. The main recommendations of the committee included the following:[94]

1. The creation of a new category of NBFC, specifically designed for MFIs.
2. Stipulations related to Priority Sector Lending to MFIs.
3. Transparency regarding rates of interest being charged.
4. Stronger supervision of MFIs.
5. The need for more suitable corporate governance structures as well as consumer protection.

The government of India accepted many of the recommendations of the Malegam Committee, creating a new category of NBFC-MFIs for instance, and put forward a draft Bill titled the "Micro Finance Institutions (Development and Regulation) Bill."[95] Interestingly, associations of MFIs like Sa-Dhan and MFIN approved of the need for a national-level policy, but states like AP objected, suggesting that local contexts required specific regulations.[96] The Bill was introduced in the lower house of parliament in 2012, but was never passed. There have been attempt to revive the Bill in recent years, but it remains in draft form.

9.2   Applying LTF to the AP Microfinance Crisis

Section 9.1 laid out the contours of the crisis, and some of the structural factors that led to it. In this section the Legal Theory of Finance is applied to analyze the fallout. As set out in the introduction, one of the key premises of this chapter is that while the dynamics of microfinance crisis

---

[93] A. Feasley, "SKS Microfinance and For-Profit MFIs, Unscrupulous Predators or Political Prey? Examining the Microfinance Credit Crunch in Andhra Pradesh and Assessing the Applicability of the UN Global Compact 'Protect Respect Remedy' Framework," Cornell Law School Inter-University Student Graduate Conference Papers. Paper 49 (Ithaca NY, 2011).

[94] Reserve Bank of India, *Report of the Sub-Committee of the Central Board of Directors of Reserve Bank of India to Study Issues and Concerns in the MFI Sector* (2011).

[95] S. Saxena, "The 2010 Microfinance Crisis in Andhra Pradesh, India and Its Implications for Microfinance in India," *Reconsidering Development*, 3/1 (2014).

[96] Ibid.

and the policy response can be examined through multiple lenses, viewing microfinance as an innovate financial product, as opposed to a development tool has several advantages. Firstly, it allows us to sidestep the contentious issue of the motivations of the various suppliers and the question of mission drift. Secondly, microfinance clients are not then beneficiaries but consumers with agency. Finally, it clarifies the role of the regulator, in requiring the adequate level of consumer protection, while ensuring a well-functioning market. While political theories such as interest group theory[97] can give us a compelling picture of the policy-making process, they are not concerned with the specific issues of financial markets. LTF on the other hand is an institutional theory of financial markets that highlights not just the conflict between state and market actors, but also the paradoxes inherent in the multiple roles of the state as enabler, beneficiary and regulator of a financial system. Further, it emphasizes that the legal structure of finance is of first order importance for explaining and predicting the behavior of market participants as well as outcomes.[98]

There are of course several other theories that can be applied to an analysis of financial markets. It is therefore necessary to discuss why competing theories of financial markets do not provide satisfactory explanations or suggest adequate regulatory responses. We can leave aside the Efficient Markets Hypothesis (EMH), as at the time of the crisis SKS was the only MFI to be publicly traded, and even in the case of SKS, the market value did not reflect the rising default rates and inadequate screening of clients. It could be argued that the weak version of EMH could be applied, since much of this information was not publicly available, but the policy response would be to leave it to the markets, and there is clearly a need for regulation of unscrupulous practices.

The Financial Instability Hypothesis (FIH) builds on Keynesian precepts, but theorizes the financial sector to compose of hedge financing units that can fulfill all of their contractual payment obligations through their cash flows, speculative units that can meet their obligation on

---

[97] The theory that different interest groups vie to influence policy and political action, where the state acts as a kind of referee, and where public policy is merely a temporary equilibrium. James Madison and Alexis de Toqueville are considered early proponents, though more formal treatment can be found in D. B. Truman, *The Governmental Process* (New York: Alfred A. Knopf, 1971) and in R. A. Dahl, *Who Governs?: Democracy and Power in an American City* (Cambridge MA: Yale University Press, 2005 – first published 1961).

[98] Pistor, "A Legal Theory of Finance."

"income account" on their liabilities, and Ponzi units where the cash flows are insufficient to repay either the principal or the interest.[99] FIH predicts that capitalist economies that are dominated by the first of these units are stable, and those dominated by the latter two are unstable, and further that over a protracted period of prosperity, economies tend to shift toward instability, with attempts to regulate through monetary constraints pushing speculative units to become Ponzi units and hastening collapse.[100] The Minsky Hypothesis, while elegant and plausible is unequivocally monetarist, and ignores the effects of other forms of regulation, which are central to understanding the microfinance crisis and its aftermath.

Imperfect Knowledge Economics represents a radical new approach to modeling macroeconomic phenomena, based on the idea that humans are neither "rational" nor "predictably irrational," but that we may revise our preferences from one point in time to the other, and that we have imperfect knowledge of the state of the world, but also of how this as well as our own preferences might change.[101] The theory is one of the first to incorporate "creativity" as a feature of decision-making, and has been applied to the analysis of foreign exchange markets with some success. Despite the theory being innovative and potentially yielding useful insights, it treats political actions as exogenous, and like much of mainstream economic theory, does not meaningfully theorize power.

Pistor's Legal Theory of Finance in contrast encourages a much deeper engagement with the notion of power and how it shapes outcomes, recognizing the hybridity of financial systems as neither purely market, nor state constructions, and with an inherent hierarchy, where the state legitimizes market transactions and has the power to delegitimize these in times of crisis. LTF however draws from and expands on each of the above theories, particularly Minsky's Instability Hypothesis, and additionally Mehrling's "Money View."[102]

There is without a doubt much that can be drawn from the wider field of political economy, particularly the work of Polyani[103] and others, which may be applied to analyzing the impact of market-based credit

[99] H. P. Minsky, *The Financial Instability Hypothesis* (Annandale-on-Hudson NY: Levy Economics Institute, 1992).

[100] Ibid.

[101] Frydman and Goldberg, *"Recognizing the Limits of Economists' Knowledge,"* in *Imperfect Knowledge Economics* (Princeton, NJ: Princeton University Press, 2007), 3–25.

[102] Pistor, "A Legal Theory of Finance."

[103] K. Polanyi, *The Great Transformation* (Boston MA: Beacon Press, 1944).

on customary savings and credit practices and social structures. However the focus of the chapter is on the interface between credit-suppliers and regulators, where MFI clients are only part of the calculus as far as consumer protection considerations are relevant. Within this limited scope LTF provides the best fit, where the assumptions bear a resonance to the characteristics of the market being analyzed. More saliently the predictions of the theory are congruent with the observed fallout.

Certain caveats have been laid out earlier in the chapter. It will suffice here to say despite these caveats, applying LTF is particularly appropriate as it allows for a simultaneous analysis of actions of state and non-state actors in contributing to and dealing with the fall-out of the crisis. In other words, instead of separating state and market actors and resorting to a simplistic narrative of a benign state attempting to regulate market opportunism, or indeed a draconian state interfering and distorting a functioning market – the framework allows for a nuanced analysis of a crisis co-created by state and market actors.

The one limitation is in theorizing the role of actors who are neither state nor market actors, such as international agencies such as the World Bank, or local NGOs. There is no doubt that these actors had a role in the creation of the SHG eco-system and the microfinance industry as well as in the aftermath. The local, national and international media also had a role to play in shifting public opinion against MFIs, and affecting investor confidence. However in as much as the World Bank Velugu Program was legitimized and implemented through state channels, we can see these actions as falling within the purview of state authority. The role of NGOs is more complex, as many of the largest MFIs began as non-profits, and those that continued to operate as such formed a parallel system to both the MFI and SHG operations, while interacting with both. St the same time several NGOs acted as support organizations in the creation of the SHG groups and federations. The three different types of stakeholders involved in the SHG-Bank Linkage structure; NGOs, banks and local government, often had conflicting interests and adversarial relationship.[104] Here it is possible to simplify the narrative by clubbing SHG support organizations as quasi-state, and those that operated in similar ways to MFIs, while retaining non-profit status as quasi-market. Finally, while the media had a visible role to play, which in the case of

---

[104] Feasley, "SKS Microfinance and For-Profit MFIs, Unscrupulous Predators or Political Prey?"

local media may have been influenced by vested interests of the state, it was not a decisive one, though it may have hastened the collapse of private microfinance.

Pistor's "theoretical map" is presented below:[105]

1. Financial markets are rule-bound systems.
2. Financial markets are essentially hybrid: Not public or private but both.
3. They are imbued with the law-finance paradox.
4. Power is defined as the differential relation to the law.

It should be clarified that in Pistor's conception the rules are not necessarily formal rules, in fact as alluded to in the introduction to the chapter, rules may be set by non-state actors, though this is with the tacit permission of the state. The hybridity of financial markets exhibits itself precisely because the scaffolding of state regulations allows private entities to regulate the interstices. The law-finance paradox, as explained in the introduction, consists of the need to enforce legal contracts fully in order to ensure credibility, while full enforcement may also bring down the system. The final point refers to the pattern of enforcement, whereby the state in order to protect the system applies the law differentially, privileging those who are located relationally closer to the apex, while penalizing those who are located on the periphery. Thus power is reflected in the differential pattern of enforcement, though of course power may also manifest itself in the ability to set or flout rules.

In order to make the analysis of the crisis more tractable, certain stylized facts have been drawn from de Quidt et al. (2012):[106]

1. Fast growth led to declines in portfolio quality due to multiple lending, spatial concentration of lending activities and weak incentives for capacity building.
2. Lack of regulation implied that borrowers had no means to protect themselves against coercive actions by some microfinance actors.
3. Financial regulation implied that MFIs could not diversify their product portfolio or their funding sources (e.g., offering savings products), making them highly dependent on bank lending and equity finance which both demand short-term returns on their investments.

---

[105] Pistor, "A legal Theory of Finance," 317
[106] de Quidt, Fetzer, and Ghatak, *Microfinance, Market Structure, and Borrower Welfare*, 5.

4. High staff-turnover and improper incentive schemes may have caused a substitution of portfolio quality for portfolio volume and a neglect of capacity building (e.g., financial literacy training).
5. The conflict of interests between the state's role as regulator and as a market participant through its own lending program (SHG) led to erratic regulation.
6. Supporting infrastructures such as credit bureaus and institutionalized redressal systems did not keep up with the growth of the sector.
7. The existing regulatory framework inhibits the development of MFIs into full financial service providers, over-emphasizing the role of microcredit.

The stylized facts presented above make it clear that while the nature of the microfinance model in AP display the classic characteristics of subprime credit market, with high growth the objectives of MFIs encouraging riskier portfolios, the position of the state as regulator as well as participant created perverse incentives. In order to aid clarity, this section is divided into four sections: One examining the applicability of each of Pistor's four axioms.

9.2.1   The Microfinance Eco-System as a Rule-Based System

As per LTF, financial markets are constituted by rules, and the rule-makers may be private or public.[107] As a financial system moves from relational finance toward entities and markets, it comes to depend on the formal legal system to authoritatively vindicate contractual obligations, or enforce such claims.[108]

Here there is a need to clarify the roles of state and central authorities. While the apex financial institution is the Reserve Bank of India, and its subsidiary the National Bank for Agricultural and Rural Development (NABARD) provided oversight of the microfinance sector as well refinancing of loans to SHGs and MFIs, the state government of AP held the power to regulate the sector. It was the actions of the state government through the passing of Ordinance 9 in October 2010 that enforced a moratorium on loan collections and fresh loans. This Ordinance, along with the actions of local political actors, in some cases preventing MFI agents from entering village, encouraged MFI clients to default.[109]

---

[107] Pistor, "A Legal Theory of Finance."
[108] Ibid.
[109] To complicate matters further, Naidu who played enabler at the time of the setting up of the SHG-Bank Linkage Program through Velugu, and tacitly supported the growth of

It was also the state government that was an active player as a promoter of the SHG-Bank Linkage Program. We will however for the purposes of simplifying the analysis assume that national and state authorities acted in coordination, despite the political differences and existing areas of conflict between state and national actors.

We find that in the case of AP, the state was instrumental in creating the financial system for microfinance lending, in putting in place the SHG-Bank Linkage Program and introducing the concept of the joint liability group, thereby setting in place the culture of group borrowing and internal monitoring. However, the internal structure of groups drew upon existing social structures and hierarchies, and enforcement of payments was determined to a large extent through peer pressure, which made it highly effective. There are competing theories about why repayment rates are as high as they are despite the lack of formal enforcement mechanisms, though the most persuasive recognize the embeddedness of actors in social relations, with norms of reciprocity and mutual enforcement playing prominent roles.[110] Thus while the groups themselves are informal associations with no *locus standi*, as Hodgson[111] suggests, these are not deregulated spaces. The loans themselves were not formal transactions, but rules regarding regular meetings and keeping of accounts were strictly enforced in the case of SHGs as well as MFI client groups.

Further up the chain, MFIs were constrained in having to adopt NBFC status, which placed limits on liquidity through the prohibition of demand deposit collection and the need to meet the CAR requirement for lending. The advantage of NBFC status was access to loans from commercial banks as well as capital investments from Indian and foreign investors.[112] It also opened the door to a possible future IPO. However the shift from non-profit to for-profit changed their legal status without affording them greater protection from defaulting clients under the law.

---

the private MFI sector, was now leader of the opposition and reversed his position, calling for MFI agents to be rounded up and for the cancellation of the SHG-Bank-Linkage Program. S. Ravi, *A Reality Check on Suicides in India* (New Delhi: Brookings Institution India Center, 2015).

[110] A. Haldar and J. E. Stiglitz, "The Indian Microfinance Crisis: The Role of Social Capital, the Shift to for-profit Lending and Implications for Microfinance Theory and Practice," *Global Conversations on Social Innovations and Development Conference* (New York: Columbia University, 2012), 1–75.

[111] Hodgson, "Observations on the Legal Theory of Finance."

[112] Refer to section 9.1.4.1 above.

In fact one can argue that it delegitimized their activity in the eyes of the state, which no longer regarded them as part of an overall development program for the region, and began to regard them as direct competition. The only concession was that the central government continued to include them within the ambit of Priority Sector Lending.

9.2.2   The Hybridity of Microfinance

Pistor[113] asserts that financial instruments must be enforceable, and that since finance is hierarchical, the sovereign must stand between the system and self-destruction. Essentially, financial systems are based on money as a legal tender, reliant on the enforceability of private/private commitments, and ultimately depend on a sovereign backstop.[114]

This is arguably the least applicable aspect of LTF to the case of microfinance. While the AP crisis had major implications for several of the financial actors, at no point was it a threat to the stability of the financial system as a whole. The RBI through NABARD provided refinancing, and as it is the sovereign monetary authority could have rescued banks had the need arisen, but this was not necessary at any point. If the market had been more mature, and innovations like collateralized debt obligations been in play, the contagion could have spread and posed a greater threat. However there is another sense in which microfinance manifests hybridity. It is a system that transforms informal debt obligations into financial instruments, allowing formal financial players to invest and trade in assets that are built upon thousands of individual loans to poor women in villages. This is the issue at the very heart of the crisis. The need for rapid growth, which was a response to the incentives in the formal financial system, when transmitted to the informal structures at the base of the pyramid, was unchallenged by formal regulatory mechanisms like consumer protection. While comparisons between village loan sharks and MFIs may seem harsh, in practice MFI clients were held to have unlimited liability. The formal/informal nature of microfinance is its greatest strength in unlocking the possibility of channeling institutional finance to clients who would otherwise have no access, and at the same time makes the system vulnerable to abuse.

---

[113] Pistor, "A Legal Theory of Finance."
[114] Ibid.

9.2.3 The Law-Finance Paradox in Microfinance

The Law-Finance Paradox relates to the idea that financial systems operate because it is assumed that contracts are enforceable, yet actual enforcement of all commitments would bring down the system and at the same time a failure to enforce would dilute credibility.[115]

Unlike hybridity, the Law-Finance Paradox can apply to a relatively self-contained system like microfinance. Inasmuch as the state sees the value of ensuring clients have access to credit and that exposed sections of the banking system are protected there is an incentive to enforce contractual obligations to the extent possible within the machinery of the state. While waiving of loans may have short-term political benefits for local state interests, the long-term fallout of encouraging default is the potential destruction of the system, as was arguably the case. This is where local and national interests diverged to some extent, with the AP government resisting central efforts to pass legislation that would rationalize regulation of MFIs.

It is significant that the regional government sought to protect the SHG-Bank-Linkage Program, placing the blame squarely on MFIs, though some of the unfortunate clients who chose to end their lives were also members of SHGs. While reports focused on malpractice by MFI agents, and the opportunistic capitalism of MFI promoters, the availability of credit from both sources encouraged clients to take on more debt than they were able to repay. With SHGs representing vote banks, the state was keen to retain members, competing with MFIs by offering subsidized rates of interest. While SHG loans were typically smaller than MFI loans, there was greater flexibility in repayment,[116] this however does not mean that there was no pressure to repay. Indebtedness of rural households was not a new phenomenon in Andhra Pradesh, and tragically these were neither the first nor the last cases of suicides related to debt. During the 2006 microfinance crisis in Krishna district,[117] there were reports of 200 suicides linked to extortion by MFI agents.[118] The state did not however initiate punitive action at the time. Debt-related suicide in India is a complex issue and there are

---

[115] Ibid.

[116] M. A. Guiyazuddin and S. Gupta, *Andhra Pradesh MFI Crisis and Its Impact on Clients* (Chennai; IFMR Centre for Microfinance, 2012).

[117] Refer to supra n. 87

[118] Mader, "Rise and Fall of Microfinance in India."

several contributing factors,[119] however indebtedness of rural households in Andhra Pradesh has been linked to the agrarian crisis, which
the state had a hand in exacerbating.[120] Statistical analysis of suicide rates
in the state suggest the suicide rates amongst MFI borrowers are significantly lower than average.[121] It may have been that in 2006 it served
the state better to allow the MFIs to continue operating. In 2010 however
the state chose to selectively enforce payment obligations, encouraging
MFI clients to default.

9.2.4   Power as the Differential Relation to the Law

This brings us to the final axiom, which proposes that the law is enforced
imperfectly, and that the pattern of enforcement will depend on the proximity of the actors to the apex, with the periphery bearing the full force of the
law.[122] The simplest and most obvious testament to this in the case of the AP
crisis is the actions of the state with respect to MFIs as opposed to SHGs.
The AP Ordinance in its statement of objects and reasons states:

> Of late, many individuals and entities have come up styling themselves as
> Micro Finance Institutions and are giving loans to SHGs at very high or
> usurious rates of interest and are using inhuman coercive methods for
> recovery of the loans. This has even resulted in suicides by many rural
> poor who have obtained loans from such individuals or entities.
>   In the larger public interest and to protect the poor from exploitation,
> and to regulate the lending of monies to the SHGs by the MFIs, the
> Government intends to bring into force a law containing the various
> provisions stated in this Bill in order to check the illegal acts of these
> MFIs.[123]

The drafting of the Ordinance and subsequent Bill makes it appear as if
the regulation was designed to stop for-profit MFIs from competing with
state-sponsored SHGs.[124] It is also significant that SHGs may, under the
provisions of the Bill report misconduct to the local registering authority,

---

[119]   *A Reality Check on Suicides in India.*
[120]   Taylor, "Freedom from Poverty Is Not for Free"; M. Taylor, "The Microfinance Crisis in
        Andhra Pradesh, India: A Window on Rural Distress?," *Institute for Food and
        Development Policy: Food First Backgrounder,* 18/3 (2012), 1–4.
[121]   de Quidt, Fetzer, and Ghatak, *Microfinance, Market Structure, and Borrower Welfare.*
[122]   Pistor, "A Legal Theory of Finance."
[123]   Government of Andhra Pradesh, Andhra Pradesh Micro Finance Institutions
        (Regulation of Money Lending) Act, 2011.
[124]   Feasley, "SKS Microfinance and For-Profit MFIs, Unscrupulous Predators or Political
        Prey?"

and in the presence of "sufficient proof"[125] thereby cause the cancellation of the MFIs registration, and in effect their license to operate.

In essence as stated before, the state tried to protect the SHG-Bank Linkage Program, shielding organizations and entities involved, and disrupting the activities of MFIs. While the spirited defense of MFIs as blameless victims and the allegation that the state fabricated evidence in order to destroy private microfinance[126] should be taken with a large pinch of salt, there is no doubt that the state threw MFIs under the bus, as it were. This led to capital flight, with some investors pulling out and banks refusing to advance loans, leaving those at the periphery to absorb the financial fallout. This resonates with the predictions of LTF.

> When events necessitate the readjustment of investment strategies, inves-
> tors flee to assets they regard as relatively more safe. These actions render
> those left holding assets others have dumped on the periphery of the
> system, where their fate will be decided by the full force of the law – unless
> they find a backstop willing and able to step in and accept these assets
> against more credible ones or cash.[127]

The argument that the state-backed SHG-Bank Linkage Program was shielded, while private MFIs were made to bear the brunt of the crisis with central and state governments acting in accord, is supported by the reluctance of the RBI to relax provisioning rules. The liquidity crunch for MFIs was heightened by the need to meet provisioning requirements mandated by the RBI.[128] The three-month provisioning rule stipulates a disclosure of loans where interest has not been paid for three months, and a payment of 10 percent of the loan amount. MFIs who were unable to collect on their loans could not pay their creditors, and also faced large liabilities related to provisioning requirements. Trident Microfin, for instance which had 70 percent of its loan portfolio in AP, owed an equivalent of 90 percent of its total loan portfolio, worth $22.1 million in 2010.[129] The total amount owed by MFIs was estimated to be $108 million, if they were to meet the provisioning requirement on all

---

[125] Government of Andhra Pradesh, Andhra Pradesh Micro Finance Institutions (Regulation of Money Lending) Act, 2011.

[126] Legatum Ventures, "Microfinance in India: A Crisis at the Bottom of the Pyramid: How the Government of Andhra Pradesh Has Severely Damaged Private Sector and Put 450 Million of India's Rural Poor at Risk" (2011), www.legatum.org.

[127] Pistor, "A Legal Theory of Finance," 324

[128] Reserve Bank of India, "Report of the Working Group to Review the existing prudential guidelines on restructuring of advances by banks/financial institutions" (2012).

[129] J. S. Raja and M. Rajshekhar, "Microfinance Crisis: MFIs with Sizeable Presence in Andhra Pradesh on the Brink of Closure," *Economic Times* (January 13, 2011).

of their bad microfinance debt in AP.[130] In the aftermath of the 2006 crisis in the Krishna district, private equity funds stepped in to solve the liquidity crisis for MFIs, pumping $679 million over the next four years, in contrast with the mere $6 million invested till that point.[131] However PE funds were less keen to go on pumping money after the 2010 crisis for a number of reasons, including the perception that the sector was reaching saturation point.[132]

Several MFIs tried to negotiate with banks to restructure their loans, but banks were skeptical and imposed various restriction. This was understandable, given that they are required to meet the same provisioning requirements that apply to MFIs. Banks faced a difficult decision, not restructuring loans would mean MFIs might collapse, saddling them with large debts, and extending MFIs more time to repay meant big provisions.[133] The RBI stepped in, relaxing the rules related to corporate debt restructuring (CDR) for banks loans to the five largest MFIs, and while SKS was also offered similar terms they opted out.[134] Part of the rationale for the relaxation of the rules may have been to protect the banks from suffering heavy losses, particularly the Small Industries Development Bank of India (SIDBI), which had a large exposure to MFI loans.[135] As a result, small MFIs ended up having to close shop, while some of the larger MFIs including SKS survived the crisis and expanded their portfolios in other states.[136] MFIs also proceeded to diversify into safer more lucrative areas, advancing consumer credit to wealthier urban clients using gold and other fungible assets as collateral.[137]

If we compare the fallout with the predictions of LTF, there is an undeniable resonance. While the narrative of a political plot to kill private microfinance proved invaluable in restoring investor confidence

---

[130] Ibid.

[131] R. S. Arunachalam, *The Journey of Indian Micro-finance: Lessons for the Future* (Chennai: Aapti Publications, 2011).

[132] ET Bureau, "Andhra Crisis Is Now Hurting MFIs' National Interest," (2010).

[133] Raja and Rajshekhar, "Microfinance Crisis."

[134] A. Lele and S. Chakraborty, "A Third of Banks' MFI loans Go into Restructuring," *Business Standard* (April 15, 2011).

[135] D. Unnikrishnan, "MFIs Seek RBI Nod for Another Debt Recast Round," *Live Mint* (July 17, 2013).

[136] Press Trust of India, "From 1948 to 2013: A Brief History of the Telangana Movement," *First Post* (July 30, 2013).

[137] M. Rajshekhar and J. S. Raja, "ET Special: New Journeys, New Challenges as India's Microfinance Promoters Sail into New Lending Areas," *Economic Times* (January 17, 2013).

particularly amongst foreign investors,[138] the evidence suggests otherwise. The AP Ordinance did temporarily plunge the sector into turmoil,
but the subsequent actions of the RBI and the recommendations of the
Malegam Committee were designed to help revive the sector, and the
former provided a quasi-bail-out for the larger operators. The fact is that
while microfinance represented a small proportion of the financial system in terms of value, it was one that was highly visible. For a country that
had liberalized only a couple of decades before, it was vital to continue to
project an image that was investor-friendly. Nothing scares away foreign
capital faster than government overreach and lack of transparency in
governance, and the actions of the RBI convey an acute awareness of this.
The following quote establishes the predictive power of the LTF framework and its applicability to the case of the Indian microfinance crisis.

> However, in times of crisis the periphery is more likely to face the full
> force of the law generating higher default risks and greater economic
> stress. Third, the survival of the system is determined at its apex. Those
> entities (states or intermediaries) in greater proximity to the apex are
> therefore more likely to benefit from a relaxation of the rules or
> a suspension of the full force of the law. Fourth, actors will seek to position
> themselves strategically towards the apex of the domestic or global system
> where they are most likely to benefit from another lifeline. On their own
> they may not have full control over their location in the system, but they
> can influence it by various means ranging from social or political ties,
> influencing the rulemaking process, to making themselves systemically
> important.[139]

While alternative theories may account for many of the actions of state
and non-state actors, LTF frames the essential dilemma of regulator, and
provides a rationale for selective enforcement with specific reference to
the hybridity of financial markets. What becomes salient when applying
LTF to the Indian microfinance crisis, is that the nature of the market,
which required strict financial discipline on the part of clients as well as
credit-providers, held in place by formal rules for the latter, and informal
rules for the former, can be likened to a delicately balanced house of
cards. At the very heart was the effectiveness of the group liability
structure and conditioned regularity of repayment, which translated
into the widely celebrated low rate of default. When the AP government
placed a moratorium on collection of repayments, and essentially

---

[138] P. Mader, " *Mechanisms of a Microfinance Crisis,* " *The Political Economy of Microfinance*
(Basingstoke: Palgrave Macmillan, 2015), 160–194.
[139] Pistor, "A Legal Theory of Finance," 325.

encouraged clients to default, this undermined the carefully established norms that underpinned the viability of the entire system. As can be seen from the response to the 2006 crisis, both central and state governments were in the first instance willing to relax rules to ensure recovery of private sector actors; however, in 2010 it was more difficult to contain the crisis, arguably because of the much wider media coverage.

9.3   Some Concluding Remarks

The Legal Theory of Finance asserts that law and finance are locked in a dynamic process in which the rules that establish the game are continuously challenged by new contractual devices, which in turn seek legal vindication.[140] It was developed in order to analyze the configuration of global financial capitalism and provide insights into the nature of financial crises as well as the politics of the regulatory responses. The challenge of applying LTF to the microfinance crisis is twofold. Firstly there is the question of whether such a theory can be meaningfully applied to a market where capital account convertibility is not yet a reality. The absence of capital account convertibility merely means that the RBI has greater control and can limit the effect of external shocks, but it does not in any way make LTF inapplicable. The second challenge relates to the strength of the rule of law in the context of India, which received a score of 40 on the 2016 Corruption Perception Index compiled by Transparency International, and stands joint 79th along with China, Brazil and Belarus. The second challenge is an interesting one, because on the one hand it implies that the credibility of contracts and the certainty of enforcement are weaker, and that other mechanisms of enforcement may need to fill regulatory gaps for the system to operate, and on the other that the elasticity of the law is greater, which implies that the predictive power of the theory in terms of outcomes for those in greater proximity to the apex of the system should be stronger. This can be seen to hold true in the case of the Indian microfinance crisis, with the SHG program being insulated from the shock, and banks and the larger MFIs benefitting from a relaxation of RBI rules. This demonstrates the power of the theory and its applicability in diverse contexts. The one area for development in the theory is that while there is a recognition of delegated rule-making authority, there is no explicit treatment of the interaction

---

[140] Pistor, "A Legal Theory of Finance."

between formal and informal rule systems, and how these may influence outcomes.

The case of Indian microfinance raises several questions and issues, which are beyond the scope of this chapter. With the proposed MFI Bill continuing to languish in legislative limbo, it is not clear if and when these will be resolved. The central question remains a definitional one. Is microfinance to be regarded as a developmental tool, or should it be treated as a financial innovation that expands the financial system into areas that exposes it to greater volatility? While the clear-sighted might conclude that it is both, the two imply different roles for regulators. In a country where access to financial services remains a major constraint for a large section of the population, the state may want to design incentives to encourage providers. On the other hand, as the 2006 and 2010 crises indicate, there are serious consequences associated with allowing purely profit-driven expansion in the absence of adequate regulation protecting customers and penalizing errant providers.

PART III

The Political Economy of Global Financial
Regulation: Cooperation, Discord and Conflict

PART III

The Political Economy of Global Financial Regulation: Cooperation, Discord and Conflict

The Incomplete Global Financial Order and Spillovers from Instability in Trade and Currency Market Regimes

EMILIOS AVGOULEAS

10.1 Introduction

10.1.1 The Problem

Instability in foreign exchange markets, and currency dumping/manipulation by means of devaluations, or via excessively loose monetary policies (so-called "beggar thy neighbor" policies) seem to be at the heart of today's looming trade wars and accusations and counter-accusations between the world's four main trade blocs: the USA, EU, China and emerging markets such as Brazil. In the financial sector, on the other hand, exposure to foreign currency borrowing and currency mismatch can be a cause of systemic risk. For example, foreign currency exposure was a key vulnerability behind the series of emerging market crises in 1997–1998.[1] The Global Financial Crisis also showed that currency turmoil is not just a concern for emerging markets. Greater foreign currency exposure increases country vulnerability to sudden shocks and currency depreciations, limiting the ability of the exchange rate to act as a shock absorber as well as the ability of monetary policy to support the economy (as interest rates may need to be adjusted at a higher level to support the currency, rather than be cut to boost domestic demand). In fact, instability in foreign exchange markets and currency dumping can act as a stimulus vis-à-vis sudden reverses of

---

[1] See for an overview, R. Buckley, E. Avgouleas, D. Arner, "Three Major Financial Crises: What Have We Learned," AIIFL Working Paper No. 31, UNSW Law Research Paper No. 18-61, Sept. 14, 2018.

short-term capital flows cultivating further mistrust in international economic relations.

Such mistrust exposes as flawed the notion that an international financial order can exist independently of the global monetary order and trade and investment, on a self-standing basis, through the techno-cratic standards promulgated by the wise heads of the Basel Committee and the Financial Stability Board (FSB) (notwithstanding the importance of such standards). Separation of the three international economic orders has achieved a great deal in terms of integration of regulation and governance of international finance. Not only has discussion between regulators in the fora of the G-20, the FSB, and the Basel Committee progressed vis-à-vis setting globally accepted financial standards, because they avoided last decade's vexed discussions on international trade,[2] but also much needed international cooperation in the aftermath of the Global Financial Crisis (GFC) did not have to stumble over unresolved (but not unrelated) trade issues.

At the same time, this separation has, arguably, worked to promote financialization and the global shadow banking sector, since cross-border financial and especially currency transactions were separated from any links to trade and long-term investment.[3] Arguably, the paradox of the separation of the three international economic orders, albeit for defen-sible reasons, has given rise to massive rent-seeking by the global finan-cial services industry and the rentier investor classes. It has also weakened the case for free trade, since trade and investment are subject to different legal orders separate from those underpinning cross-border financial flows and global markets, although it is the latter that have emerged as the most potent integrative force for the global economy. The same fragmentation has also undermined any efforts of creating coherent international structures for the governance and regulation of global

---

[2] E.g., the so-called Doha Round for trade liberalization has made little progress from its inception at the 2001 Doha WTO Ministerial summit (Doha WTO Ministerial 2001: Ministerial Declaration WT/Min(01)/Dec/1, November 20, 2001) up to the middle of 2018, and if anything the predictions on its progress is increasingly pessimistic. For more analysis on the subject matter and scope of this round of trade negotiations, see WTO, "The Doha Round," www.wto.org/english/tratop_e/dda_e/update_e.htm.

[3] One example is the exponential rise of global money market broker-dealers, another the direct recycling of the huge cash reserves of multinational corporations. See Z. Pozsar, "Shadow Banking: The Money View," Office of Financial Research, Working Paper 14–4, July 2, 2014, http://wisburg.com/wp-content/uploads/2018/02/OFR-Shadow-Banking-The-Money-View.pdf.

finance.[4] For these to progress to the next stage, concrete governance structures would have to replace the current "soft law" status quo, but such a move would only be defended or upheld if such structures were seen as integral in buttressing the global trade and investment order.

10.1.2 Setting the Scene

Today, however, with mistrust of the post-1994 global trade status quo[5] at record levels and with efforts for greater integration of the international financial order having come to a halt, some radical rethinking is overdue. Arguably, the agreement of the FSB loss-absorption standards for Globally Systemic Banks (G-SIBs),[6] which has included an extended transition of emerging market G-SIBs, is an indication of widespread consensus within the global regulatory community. But still that was in 2014–2015, and meaningful cooperation on other looming issues, such as reining in the riskiest forms of shadow banking, or cooperation in derivatives clearing and settlement, has moved way beneath the radar. And it will be very hard for these discussions to be resuscitated in today's trade environment. It's unrealistic to believe that finance ministries and central banks, accusing each other of currency manipulation, triggering currency wars, and ferociously undermining or unraveling key parts of the present trade order, would be enlightened enough[7] to sit down in the

---

[4] In this context, far-reaching yet comprehensive international financial governance designs for a world financial council like those contained in the *Report of the Commission of Experts of the President of the United Nations General Assembly on Reforms of the International Monetary and Financial System* (New York: United Nations, September 21, 2009), www.un.org/ga/econcrisissummit/docs/FinalReport_CoE.pdf, also known as the "Stiglitz Report," simply came to pass. The same should be said of the opposition to the proposal for a World Financial Authority in K. Alexander, R. Dhumale, and J. Eatwell, *Global Governance of Financial Systems: The International Regulation of Systemic Risk* (Oxford: Oxford University Press, 2006). For another equally far-reaching but more complex and pluralistic global financial governance design, see E. Avgouleas, *Governance of Global Financial Markets: The Law, the Economics, the Politics* (Cambridge: Cambridge University Press, 2012), chap. 9.

[5] Arguably, this was heralded by the inception of the World Trade Organization (WTO) after the conclusion of the Uruguay Round of trade negotiations with the signing of the Marrakesh Agreement in April 1994 and of the North American Trade Agreement (NAFTA) which came into force on January 1, 1994.

[6] See FSB, "Total Loss-Absorbing Capacity (TLAC) Principles and Term Sheet," November 9, 2015, www.fsb.org/2015/11/total-loss-absorbing-capacity-tlac-principles-and-term-sheet/.

[7] On the interests that national regulators defend in the international regulatory fora, see Avgouleas, *Governance of Global Financial Markets*, chaps. 4–5 and Federico Lupo-Pasini,

refined environment of the FSB, the G-20, the IMF/World Bank synods and the Basel Committee to thrash out new and closer forms of cooperation and integration in the field of international financial regulation. Any sound political economy approach to the workings of these fora would argue that such lofty ideals are in the past, and have probably not been evident at least since the GFC aftermath in 2008. As a matter of fact, it is now an accepted convention that the first wave of Basel capital regulations (so-called Basel I) were not just an attempt to shore up the resilience of international banks, but also a concerted attempt by Western regulators to contain the competitive threat of Japanese banks.[8]

On the basis of the above analysis, this chapter moves away from standard scholarly analysis that has mostly focused on cooperation in the field of international financial regulation, which makes up the bulk of the international financial order, with the balance filled by anti-money laundering and accounting (financial reporting) standards issued by soft law international standard-setting bodies. It will, thus, explore the risks that instability in currency markets, and the absence of an anchor since the collapse of the Bretton Woods system, pose an insurmountable obstacle to all further integration efforts, since it would be very hard for different regulators to open up their financial systems, or cooperate more closely, when at the same time their governments accuse each other of currency wars and trade manipulation.[9]

Accordingly, the objective of this chapter is two-fold. First, to highlight the importance of the much neglected – since the collapse of the Bretton Woods arrangement in 1972 – aspect of the international economic order

---

The Logic of Financial Nationalism: The Challenges of Cooperation and the Role of International Law (Cambridge: Cambridge University Press, 2017), chap. 2.

[8] Avgouleas, ibid. On how the interests of their domestic industry have weighed on the motivation and actions of US regulators in the international financial standard setting fora see S. Gadinis, "The Politics of Competition in International Financial Regulation," John M. Olin Centre, Discussion Paper No. 15, June 2008, www.law.harvard.edu/programs/olin_center/fellows_papers/pdf/Gadinis_15.pdf.

[9] E.g., China took some major steps toward the liberalization of foreign ownership in its financial sector, which it de facto overturned with new measures that require a very high asset threshold for foreign firms that wish to operate within its financial system – a U-turn that mainly affects US firms and probably has much to do with fears of destabilization if there is a capital flight from its markets, as happened in the summer of 2016, as much as with the blistering rhetoric and US sanctions over PRC exports. See G. Wildau, H. Lockett, "China pledges to open finance sector to more foreign ownership" *FT.com*, November 10, 2017. Cf, D. Weinland, E. Dunkley, "China regulators slow to open up say global banks – Beijing's new rules threaten plans to take controlling stakes in securities ventures," *FT* Companies and Markets, April 25, 2018, p. 16.

for global financial stability from a political economy perspective. Secondly, to argue that a system of more objective benchmarks of currency values could act as a partial stabilizer in the case of short-term capital flows augmenting trust between cross-border financial stability regulators and policy-makers. Even if the panic is about the stability of the country's financial sector and the quality of assets held in that financial sector, still the much feared panic outflows can be slower, absent capital controls, when the indication of currency values is less unstable or uncertain.

The second objective of this chapter is to sketch the possible building blocks that may be used to construct a system or more objective benchmarks/measures of value when it comes to currency parities. Given of course the global experience with the gold standard and the Bretton Woods system of currency parities, any new mechanism must steer away from measures that would restrict circulation and capital flows and/or act in a deflationary manner. Similarly, a system of fixed parities that would break up in the face of trade imbalances, as happened with Bretton Woods parities in 1971–1972, should be avoided.

Any attempt to highlight the role of currency markets/parities as a means to further the integrative and cooperative goals of the global financial architecture inevitably encounters nearly insurmountable obstacles. First, even if there is such a thing as regulatory standard neutrality in global financial architecture, any shift of the debate to the field of currency exchange governance takes the discussion away from the (ostensibly) technocratic zone that global financial governance structures/standards occupy, to the realm of geopolitics. Secondly, in the current climate, where economic nationalism and protectionism are unmistakably on the rise, such a discussion could look futile. And this even before one begins to deal with the core economic aspects of global FX markets and their impact on competitive and comparative advantage in the global trade context, a discussion that is firmly outside the scope of this chapter. Third, any attempt to discuss a comprehensive currency exchange mechanism that incorporates, prima facie, objective benchmarks, is from the outset hamstrung by the burden of history.

Finally and more critically, some currencies that are so-called reserve currencies, e.g., the US dollar, the euro, the Japanese yen, the Chinese RMB, may represent value that goes beyond economic fundamentals. Namely, regardless of whether reserve currencies have been designated as such due to the economic might of the issuing state and the regular use of the currency in international payments, parities for such currencies do not merely reflect economic fundamentals, but also the geopolitical importance of the issuing state. But if no objective benchmark of value were to apply to the most common reserve currencies, what would be its utility after all? As a consequence one needs to think long and hard before endeavoring to draft an intervention in this area. To this effect I offer three reasons for doing so here.

First, while no system of measurement of currency values is perfect, still the use of a system that compares a number of different parities with the IMF's Special Drawing Rights basket of currencies[10] and fundamentals can undoubtedly be a measure of value that is well adjusted to market and geopolitical forces. Secondly, the emergence of cryptocurrencies and other tradable electronic units/tokens offers a unique opportunity to structure more objective reference points of currency values. Thus, the indexes incorporated in the here-suggested global unit of account (GUOA), which are simple and tradable and can be calculated by reference to the value of IMF's SDRs,[11] can provide clear guidance without discarding the known methods of measurement of currency values in economics, such as purchasing power parity and so on. Third, unlike the gold standard and other physical commodity anchors used in the past to measure the value of currencies, modern-day benchmarks need not be deflationary, as tokenized benchmarks can instead reflect fundamental properties of fiat money.

---

[10] The IMF's SDRs are an international reserve asset, serving as the unit of account of the IMF and some other international organizations. The SDR is neither a currency nor a claim on the IMF. Rather, it is a potential claim on the freely usable currencies of IMF members. SDRs can be exchanged for these currencies. Currently the value of the SDR is based on a basket of five currencies – the US dollar, the euro, the Chinese RMB and the British pound. SDR allocations can play a role in providing liquidity and supplementing member countries' official reserves, as was the case with the 2009 allocations totalling SDR 182.6 billion to IMF members amid the global financial crisis. See IMF Factsheet, "Special Drawing Rights," April 18, 2018.

[11] The value of the SDR is determined daily based on market exchange rates. It is determined by tallying the value of the composite currencies in US dollars. IMF Data sheet, "SDR Valuation," April 27, 2018. The SDR basket is reviewed every five years, or sooner if warranted, to ensure that the SDR reflects the relative importance of currencies in the world's trading and financial systems. The reviews cover the key elements of the SDR method of valuation, including criteria and indicators used in selecting SDR basket currencies and the initial currency weights used in determining the amounts (number of units) of each currency in the SDR basket. These currency amounts remain fixed over the five-year SDR valuation period, but the actual weights of currencies in the basket fluctuate as cross-exchange rates among the basket currencies move. The reviews are also used to assess the appropriateness of the financial instruments comprising the SDR interest rate (SDRi) basket. This is also important as the SDRi provides the basis for calculating the interest rate charged to members on their non-concessional borrowing from the IMF. See IMF Factsheet, "Special Drawing Rights," April 18, 2018.

This chapter is in five sections with the present introduction. Section 10.2 discusses the valuation intricacies of international currencies and the thorny questions of currency wars and their impact on trade. Section 10.3 discusses the financial stability risks of currency market instability. Section 10.4 discusses remedies under the existing IMF and WTO legal orders, and the possibility of inserting clauses and remedies against currency manipulation in future bilateral and multilateral agreements, or even amending existing ones to this effect. It also offers a concise discussion of an alternative valuation method. Section 10.5 draws the different strands of the present analysis to a comprehensive conclusion.

10.2   Reserve Currencies, Currency Wars and Currency Manipulation

10.2.1   Mars or Mercury?

The identification of reserve currency values/parities is wide open to the so-called Mars and Mercury debate.[12] The Mercury approach/hypothesis emphasizes pecuniary motives and also highlights the importance of currency safety, liquidity, network effects, trade links, and financial connections. This method may explain why some currencies are used disproportionally as a medium of exchange, store of value and unit of account by governments and private entities engaged in international trade and cross-border financial transactions.[13]

There is also another approach that is put forward by political economists, and applied mainly to the choice of reserve currency or currencies. This emphasizes strategic, diplomatic, and military power (together defined here as geopolitical power). If a country has such geopolitical power, foreign governments will see it to be in their national interest to

---

[12] See B. Eichengreen, A. Mehl and L. Chiṭu, "Mars or Mercury? The Geopolitics of International Currency Choice," NBER Working Paper 24145, December 2017, www .nber.org/papers/w24145.pdf and their Vox blog: "Mars or Mercury? The Geopolitics of International Currency Choice," January 2, 2018, https://voxeu.org/article/geopolitics-international-currency-choice. See also the impressive analysis of the mechanics of international currencies in B. Eichengreen, A. Mehl and L. Chiṭu, *How Global Currencies Work: Past, Present, and Future* (Princeton NJ: Princeton University Press, 2017).

[13] See M. Chinn and J. Frankel, "Why the Euro Will Rival the Dollar," *International Finance* 11 (2008), 49–73.

conduct their cross-border transactions using its currency.[14] The leading power for its part will possess political leverage with which to encourage the practice. In other words, international currency choice is from Mars rather than Mercury. As Barry Eichengreen and his co-authors accurately observe, this hypothesis helps to explain some otherwise perplexing aspects of the currency composition of international reserves.[15] Naturally the Mars view casts a question mark on measurements of currency value that focus exclusively on trade surpluses/deficits, and gives credence to the quest for a more encompassing measure of value that wouldn't discount the geopolitical importance of reserve accumulation and parities.

10.2.2   Currency Manipulation and Currency wars

According to a Peterson Institute publication in 2012,[16] until that point at least twenty countries had appreciably increased their aggregate foreign exchange reserves and other foreign assets mainly through intervention in the foreign exchange markets. The purpose was to keep the currencies of the interveners substantially undervalued, thus boosting their international competitiveness and trade surpluses. A former director of the Peterson Institute and former member of the US government's trade team added that:[17]

> As the world's largest trading country, the United States is the largest loser
> from the manipulation of recent years. Because most of the intervention
> takes place in dollars, the dollar has been pushed to systemically

---

[14] See, inter alia, B. Cohen, *The Geography of Money* (Ithaca NY: Cornell University Press, 1998); B. Cohen, *Currency Power: Understanding Monetary* (Princeton NJ: Princeton University Press, 2015); S. Liao and D. McDowell, "No Reservations: International Order and Demand for the Renminbi as a Reserve Currency," *International Studies Quarterly*, 60 (2016), 272–293.

[15] "[The Mars hypothesis] helps to explain why Japan holds a larger share of its foreign reserves in dollars than China. It helps to explain why Saudi Arabia holds the bulk of its reserves in dollars, unlike another oil exporter, Russia. It helps to explain why Germany holds virtually all of its official reserves in dollars, unlike France. Germany, Japan and Saudi Arabia all depend on the US for security. China, Russia, and France, on the other hand, possess their own nuclear weapons as deterrents." See Eichengreen et al., Vox blog n. 12 supra.

[16] C. Fred Bergsten, J. Gannon, "Currency Manipulation, the US Economy, and the Global Economic order," Peterson Institute Policy Brief 12–25, December 2012, https://piie.com /sites/default/files/publications/pb/pb12-25.pdf.

[17] C. Fred Bergsten, "Currency Wars, the Economy of the United States, and Reform of the International Monetary System," *Stavros Niarchos Foundation Lecture*, May 16, 2013, https://piie.com/sites/default/files/publications/papers/bergsten201305.pdf.

overvalued levels. Bergsten and Gagnon (2012) estimate that the US current account deficit has averaged $200 billion to $500 billion per year higher as a result of the manipulation ... [it] translates into a loss of between one and five million US jobs within the environment of continuing high unemployment and shortage of alternative policy instruments to remedy the problem.

What US sources belatedly acknowledged, however, was that so-called currency manipulation also adversely affected large emerging economies such as Brazil, India and Mexico, but the source of their discontent was not intervention in foreign exchange markets on behalf of the biggest world economies, but rather expansive monetary policies, such as very low interest rates and quantitative easing (QE). These, while initiated in the period after the GFC, in fact continued for the best part of a decade afterwards. Arguably, QE and very low interest rates push down returns on domestic debt, rather than shaking confidence in the value of the currency per se. But as returns in local debt instruments diminish, investors can chase yield in debt assets denominated in other currencies, leading to a shift in the supply of excess funds to anther country's economy. The exodus, however, triggers the readjusting of currency values, having a beneficial impact on the exports of the country that applies very lax monetary policies (the "devaluing" country) and harming the competitiveness of the country that does not follow the same kind of policy, possibly because it experiences a relatively high rate of inflation or good growth. Now this development not only hurts the second state's exports but it also raises the possibility of financial stability risks, since asset bubbles may form following the excess influx of foreign money.

It was thus under these conditions that the term *currency wars* resurfaced for the first time since the era of the Great Depression devaluations, gaining particular prominence when the Brazilian Finance Minister Guido Mantega used it to characterize the impact of US monetary policies on the trading parity of the US dollar.[18] The same accusations were voiced against Japan by its Asian neighbors during 2012–2013, namely at the height of so-called Abenomics when the Bank of Japan raised its inflation target and implemented a massive program of asset purchases to increase liquidity and push up asset prices. Essentially, the representatives of developing economies extended the charge of currency dumping

---

[18] See BBC, "Currency 'war' warning from Brazil's finance minister," October 28, 2010, www.bbc.com/news/business-11424864. See also T. Murphy and L. Magalhaes, "Brazil Minister Says Global Currency War Is Intensifying," *Wall Street Journal*, 23 February 2012, www.wsj.com/articles/SB10001424052970203960804577241460407096338.

on developed countries' unconventional monetary policies. Namely the term currency manipulation has acquired a meaning that goes much beyond state/central bank intervention in foreign exchange markets or purchase in bulk of foreign assets by domestic operators.

Accordingly, currency wars are the consequence of action taken by countries facing macroeconomic shocks (a recession/sustained period of weak growth), an imbalanced balance of payments (more imports than exports), and fiscal troubles (budget deficit) – sometimes all three – seeking to devalue their currency to gain a competitive advantage in terms of trade, or in the case of monetary expansion in order to stimulate domestic demand. However, in all of these cases trading partners or competing exporting countries become less competitive and may respond by weakening their own currencies too.

Some of these modern-day "beggar thy neighbor" policies, whether used by the US Federal Reserve to control deflation and stimulate a distressed economy, or by the Bank of Japan to revive an economy that had by then been stagnant for the best part of two decades, have as their principal objective the revival of domestic demand, rather than manipulation of trade surpluses/deficits. Regardless of the motive, currency instability discourages investment and trade in all scenarios, even if policies that aim to boost money supply in countries facing a recession and/or deflation could increase the level of imports. The latter are of course made more expensive by the implementation of expansive monetary policies and attendant falls in the value of the importing country's currency.

10.3   Global Financial Stability Risks

10.3.1   Financialization and Shadow Banking

In general, shadow banking is a collection of unregulated institutions using a variety of debt instruments, credit enhancement and securities borrowing and lending techniques to extend credit and boost the liquidity of, in principle, illiquid assets and perform maturity transformation. Shadow banking is also a great booster of financialization, given the spaghetti of transactions and counter-transactions and the commission income that each of these generates for the financial sector, even if the funding is not sourced from the financial sector or not even from the capital markets. It may instead come from the real sector, both corporates and individuals, looking for a way to gain a return on cash reserves or to enhance the return on their savings. Namely, the various shadow banking channels are also a good way to recycle cash reserves, including FX reserves and direct savings away from productive investment. In fact, it seems that the bulk of this recycling and redistribution of liquidity does not escape Lord Turner's old adage that most modern financial activity is wasteful. The accumulated and recycled cash reserves seem to be, while secular[19] rather than cyclical, the result of forgone real economy investment.

It is thus not surprising that a large part of international FX transactions amount these days to the recycling of liquidity reserves through the use of global shadow banking channels.[20] One example is the exponential rise of global money market broker-dealers, another the direct recycling of the huge cash reserves of multinational corporations,[21] which increases interconnectedness in a number of invisible ways.[22] Given the

---

[19] See Z. Pozsar, "Shadow Banking – The Money View," Office of Financial Research WP 14–04, July 2, 2014, www.financialresearch.gov/working-papers/files/OFRwp2014-04_Pozsar_ShadowBankingTheMoneyView.pdf.

[20] Ibid., p. 60.

[21] The numbers, as reported by Pozsar, are simply staggering: "First, on the global level, the secular rise of managed FX regimes in relation to the U.S. dollar is one explanation for the rise of cash pools held by FX reserve managers in the form of FX reserves' liquidity tranches, which are estimated at $1.5 trillion. Second, on both the global and local levels, the largest global corporations are holding more cash than ever before, estimated at more than $1.5 trillion. Unlike in previous decades, corporations today are net funding providers. There are many possible explanations for the increase in corporate cash pools. A likely contributing factor is the long-term secular increase in corporate profits as a share of national income, relative to wages. Corporations hold cash as a liquidity buffer for future investments; multinational firms may hold cash in foreign subsidiaries to defer or avoid taxes . . ." Pozsar, ibid., pp. 60–61.

[22] E.g., Pozsar argues that the secular rise of shadow banking due to structural imbalances in the real economy has also turned broker-dealers to "matched-book money dealers that stand between cash pools in search for safety, and various kinds of leveraged bond portfolios across the asset management complex in search for yield" which of course brings unleveraged fund managers well into the net of the leveraged shadow banking system developing "deep linkages" between shadow banking and asset management, including not only hedge funds but also what are assumed to be unleveraged, "long-only" mutual funds. Whereas cash pools' problem is the structural shortage of safe, short-term, public assets (a shortage of public money), real money investors' problem is structural asset-liability mismatches driven by the secular decline of yields on safe, long-term, public assets relative to "sticky" return targets/expectations. The secular rise of leveraged betas (that is, the secular increase in the use of both cash and synthetic forms of leverage in bond portfolios) has been asset managers' way of helping real money investors bridge structural asset-liability mismatches through the provision of "equity-like returns with bond-like volatility." See Z. Pozsar, "A Macro View of Shadow Banking: Levered Betas and Wholesale Funding in the Context of Secular Stagnation" Draft of January 31, 2015, pp. 2–3, https://ftalphaville-cdn.ft.com/wp-content/uploads/2015/07/Pozsar-

increasing commingling of short-term debt with cash exposures, this recycling also increases short-term (but also long-term) borrowing and lending in a foreign currency. A panic in global FX markets may start from nothing more than falling bond prices and a market sell-off, and not just the widely discussed problem of debt refinancing in a foreign currency. In fact, Pozsar's study offers, in a different context, examples of the consequences of a bond market sell-off which, in the view of this author, could also trigger a panic in FX markets.[23]

Even though Pozsar stresses the fact that most of the transactions are hedged/"insured" by means of repo transactions, still the absence of a liquidity backstop means that global FX markets hide global financial stability risks that are often underappreciated, covered in secrecy, or merely ignored. Given that these exposures are not just dollar denominated, and thus not merely dependent on the magnanimity of the Federal Reserve's market operations, but involve multiple underlying monetary regimes.[24] In the event of a liquidity shock a number of these exposures may not be able to be rolled over. And the more frosty trade relations become, the less central bank or other state actor coordination will ensue in global FX markets. Nor are restrictive/controlled FX regimes the answer to this conundrum, as it is the bypassing of those regimes that has created many of those global money pools and facilitated the activities of global money brokers in the first place.[25]

A-Macro-View-of-Shadow-Banking-Levered-Betas-and-Wholesale-Funding-in-the-Context-of-Secular-Stagnation.pdf.

[23] "If all goes well with the risk PM's [Portfolio Manager's] plan, falling bond values would be offset by speedy cash collateral transfers on the swaps, keeping the TRB [Total Return Bonds] fund's net asset value stable amidst a temporary market sell-off, enabling the risk PM to outperform the benchmark. But what if the plan backfires? If, instead of a sell-off, unexpectedly positive data and hawkish policy comments spark a rally in EM and corporate spreads and a selloff in rates, the swaps intended as a hedge become a drain on the TRB fund's performance. Instead of harvesting cash collateral as a result of mark-to-market gains, the fund has to post cash collateral (as specified by its dealer) on mark-to-market losses before closing out the swaps. As a bond investor, the TRB fund would carry only minimal cash balances, which it needs to hold for redemption purposes. Thus, to pay its counterparty (Dealer A), the fund has to repo some of its bonds to raise liquidity to settle derivatives payables." Pozsar, "Shadow Banking – The Money View," 39–40.

[24] E.g., carry trades in the non-dollar markets have been found to be riskier than carry trades only exposed to the US dollar. See K. Daniel, R. J. Hodrick, and Z. Lu, "The Carry Trade: Risks and Drawdowns," Columbia Business School, mimeo, August 27, 2014, www0.gsb.columbia.edu/mygsb/faculty/research/pubfiles/6378/DanielHodrickLu2014.pdf.

[25] Pozsar, "Shadow Banking – The Money View, p. 60.

10.3.2   The Risks of "Carry" Trades

Similar concerns have been voiced about the risks of carry trades, a form of interest rate arbitrage between currencies.[26] While carry trades may earn a seemingly low-risk profit, since they receive higher interest rates on the money invested and pay lower interest rates on the money borrowed, a global unwinding of carry trades, as happened with Japanese yen trades,[27] can spell a string of defaults/bankruptcies for these highly leveraged traders. The most inherent risk of carry trades is of course FX market uncertainty, namely, the fact that the exchange rate between the two currencies is changeable. The carry trade is profitable only if the high interest rate currency depreciates relative to the low interest rate currency by less than the interest differential. It seems that even hedging with currency options cannot eliminate this risk.[28] Another reason that accentuates risks in this case is that traditional finance science tools for risk measurement were conceived to measure capital markets and currency markets risk.[29] Either way, the risk for contagious instability in global markets arising from these trades is far from theoretical. Empirical research has identified that short-term multicurrency investment strategies such as carry trade, momentum and term spread strategies present significant downside risk properties over historical episodes

[26] "Carry trading is one of the most simple strategies for currency trading that exists. A carry trade is when you buy a high-interest currency against a low-interest currency. For each day that you hold that trade, your broker will pay you the interest difference between the two currencies, as long as you are trading in the interest-positive direction... Trading in the direction of carry interest is an advantage because, in addition to your trading gains, there are also interest earnings. Carry trading also allows you to use leverage to your advantage." J. Russell, "Introduction to Carry Trading," Balance.com, January 24, 2018, www.thebalance.com/introduction-to-carry-trading-1344843.

[27] The yen carry trade dominated FX markets in the 2000s, but a little after the collapse of Lehman Brothers in September 2008 and the triggering of what is now called the Global Financial Crisis, the unwinding of the yen carry trade commenced in earnest as speculators began to be hit with margin calls, since the prices of practically every asset began sliding. To meet the margin calls, assets had to be sold, putting even more downward pressure on prices. As credit conditions tightened dramatically, banks began calling in the loans, many of which were yen-denominated. Speculators not only had to sell their investments at fire-sale prices, but also had to repay their yen loans even as the yen was surging. In addition, the higher-yielding countries slashed interest rates to stimulate their economies, eliminating earlier gains. For a preliminary analysis see M. Hattori and, H. S. Shin, "Yen Carry Trade and the Subprime Crisis" 56(2) IMF Staff Papers 384–409, June 2009.

[28] See Daniel, Hodrick, and Lu, "The Carry Trade: Risks and Drawdowns."

[29] C. Burnside, "Carry Trades and Risk," NBER Working Paper No. 17278 issued in August 2011, revised in December 2011, www.nber.org/papers/w17278.pdf.

of financial market turmoil.[30] In fact, they exhibit substantial tail risks against which it is nearly impossible to hedge, especially because most of these strategies may be seen as complementary but, in fact, perform far from uniformly during distress periods in global markets. Worse, as equity market investments feature an even greater downside risk,[31] a global equity portfolio would not be an adequate protection either.

Accordingly, foreign debt and not just FX market exposures can trigger instability in currency markets and beyond. In fact, they can be the source of currency value spirals in the absence of any fundamental reasons for currency movements.[32] The fact that most of these investors will be highly leveraged can even give rise to a self-feeding spiral of defaults and further currency misalignment due to abrupt unwinding of currency swaps or carry trades to generate cash.[33] Combined, the aforementioned investment techniques can be the source of much-ignored global systemic risk that a more objective benchmark of currency values could contain, given the anchoring properties of such a benchmark, in the event of a generalized liquidity crisis. They can also disturb the natural/expected flows of investment capital to countries whose economic fundamentals are improving, or alternatively raise interest rates to make themselves a more attractive investment destination.[34]

---

[30] See J. Gyntelberg and A. Schrimpf, "FX Strategies in Periods of Distress," *BIS Quarterly Review*, December 2011, 29 et seq., www.bis.org/publ/qtrpdf/r_qt1112e.pdf.

[31] Ibid.

[32] "We conjecture that sudden exchange rate moves unrelated to news can be due to the unwinding of carry trades when speculators near funding constraints. This idea is consistent with our findings that (i) investment currencies are subject to crash risk ... (ii) the carry, that is, interest rate differential, is associated with positive speculator net positions in investment currencies; (iii) speculators' positions increase crash risk; (iv) carry trade losses increase the price of crash risk but lower speculator positions and the probability of a crash; (v) an increase in global risk or risk aversion as measured by the VIX equity-option implied volatility index coincides with reductions in speculator carry positions (unwind) and carry trade losses." M. K. Brunnermeier, S. Nagel and L. H. Pedersen, "Carry Trades and Currency Crashes"; K. Rogoff, M. Woodford and D. Acemoglu (eds.), *NBER Macroeconomics Annual* 23 (2008) 313–347, at 314.

[33] The author's assumption here tallies well with Brunnermeier et al.'s observation that: "[FX market shocks] share several features of the 'liquidity spirals' that arise in the model of Brunnermeier and Pedersen (2009) ... shocks that lead to speculator losses are amplified when speculators hit funding constraints and un-wind their positions, further depressing prices, increasing the funding problems, volatility, and margins, and so on. Conversely, shocks that lead to speculator gains are not amplified." Ibid.

[34] A conclusion extrapolated from Brunnermeier et al. who note: "In the currency setting, we can envision a country suddenly increasing its interest rate and thereby attracting foreign capital ... In a frictionless and risk-neutral economy, this should lead to an immediate appreciation of the currency – associated with an inflow of capital – and

10.3.3   Cross-Border Financial Crises

Credit exposures in foreign currencies have historically proved a substantial source of financial stability and appreciable recession risk for two reasons. First, when another country's banks dominate the host's financial sector, home FX risk is transferred to the host's economy. For the devastating effects of this in the Baltic countries and elsewhere in the EU, a good analysis is offered by Ivaylo Jaydijev in Chapter 12 of this book. The second and more common scenario is when lots of loose or speculative foreign investment enters an emerging market and then at the first sign of macroeconomic difficulty or political and economic instability reverses course, wreaking devastation on the recipient country's economy and financial system. This was the typical form of international financial crisis in the 1980s and the 1990s. As observed by Buckley, Avgouleas and Arner:[35]

> Short-term debt contributed significantly to East Asia's economic problems, particularly that not denominated in local currency. Short-term indebtedness increased significantly in 1995 and 1996 across the region ... The primary problem with foreign investment in the short-term debt of emerging markets is the fluidity of the investment. Adverse economic news is likely to halt the rolling over of outstanding debt upon maturity and thus resulting in net capital outflows. This risk is analogous to capital flights. The secondary problem is that these outflows may foment a collapse in investor confidence. When the short-term debt is not denominated in local currency, volatility is heightened because a substantial devaluation will decimate a local currency portfolio. Accordingly, the first signs of a pending devaluation will prompt a severe sell-off.

The problem is compounded in countries with weak financial sectors where the domestic financial system cannot serve as an effective intermediary to allocate funds to productive uses. So capital inflows often end up as speculative gambles in the stock and property markets, boosting in the process asset bubbles.[36] Such speculative investments often cannot generate the foreign currency reserves needed to repay foreign currency

---

a future depreciation of the exchange rate such that UIP holds. In the presence of liquidity constraints, however, capital only arrives slowly such that the exchange rate only appreciates gradually, occasionally disrupted by sudden depreciations as speculative capital is withdrawn." Ibid., p. 315.

[35] Buckley, Avgouleas, Arner, supra n. 1, p. 6.

[36] Shigemitsu Sugisaki, "Economic Crises in Asia" (Address at the 1998 Harvard Asia Business Conference, Harvard Business School, January 30, 1998).

debt. As a result, faced with a steep yield curve, local banks succumbed to the dangerous temptation to borrow short and lend long, and largely did so without hedging their foreign exchange exposures. Especially in the context of the Asian financial crisis, indiscriminate international borrowing and domestic lending was common throughout the region, and when the bubble burst, domestic banks virtually collapsed in most countries in the region, particularly Indonesia, Korea and Thailand.[37] Moreover, premature liberalization of the banking sector in Thailand and elsewhere just made matters worse.

Over the last few years, concerns about foreign-currency exposure have shifted from banks, in spite of an explosion of bank FX borrowing and lending from the 1990s to 2014,[38] to FX exposure in the non-banking and corporate sector, including in major emerging markets such as China. In the aftermath of the Global Financial Crisis macroprudential measures were adopted to reduce bank lending and borrowing in foreign currencies, and thus the corresponding exposure of banks to currency movements. This goal is important since banks are key to the stability of financial system and regulators seek to insulate them from sharp currency movements. Empirical research shows that such measures have been effective in curbing FX risks in the banking sector.[39]

On the other hand, the macroprudential FX regulations seem to have shifted a portion of currency exposure risks to sectors of the economy that lie outside the regulatory perimeter signalling a trend for FX risk migration from the regulated to unregulated sector. Anhert, Forbes and Reinhart note that while these investors and other financial institutions may not be viewed as systemically important financial institutions, as they wouldn't enter bankruptcy even if they did suffer losses after currency movements,[40] still these operators, "may be less well informed than banks, less able to screen for the risks inherent in corporate borrowing in FX, and potentially less able to handle any subsequent losses after a depreciation."[41] Therefore, shifting currency risk to the non-bank

---

[37] R. Dornbusch, "A Bail-out Won't Do the Trick in Korea," *Business Week*, December 8, 1997, 26; R. Garran, "Korea Crisis," *The Australian*, November 19, 1997, 36, col. 1.

[38] In fact, from the mid-1990s through to end-2014, total FX borrowing in international debt securities and bank loans more than tripled, to about $12 trillion. See T. Anhert, K. Forbes and D. Reinhard, "Macroprudential FX Regulations: Shifting the Snowbanks of FX Vulnerability?" MIT mimeo, December 28, 2017, p. 3, http://web.mit.edu/kjforbes/www/ShiftingSnowbanks_2017_12_28.pdf.

[39] Ibid., p. 7.

[40] Ibid.

[41] Ibid.

sector could increase systemic risk in ways that could be harder to monitor and assess, especially as these institutions (e.g., hedge funds, cross-border money brokers etc.) and large corporates are outside the regulatory perimeter. While a first approach to account for the impact of such leakages is to incorporate this scenario into macroprudential analysis, the macroprudential framework has thus far not proved effective for non-financial sector firms, making thus the case of an anchoring benchmark even more compelling.

10.4 If Full International Coordination or the Revival of Bretton Woods Arrangements Is Not Expected, What Are the Alternatives?

10.4.1 Overview

International co-ordination of monetary policies of the type achieved, in a sense, by the Bretton Woods arrangements is not universally advocated. For example, the eminent US economist Barry Eichengreen indicates that international coordination of lax national monetary policies might not have led to financial markets losing confidence in national currencies during the height of Depression-era "beggar thy neighbor" action,[42] but the overall macroeconomic gains from international policy coordination would be relatively small. However, Eichengreen hastens to add that the situation is much different today, since the so-called extraordinary monetary policy programs undertaken by the developed countries, especially in the period between 2008 and 2011, were entirely uncoordinated and inflicted considerable losses on the growth rate of emerging economies.[43] This section will examine the effectiveness of already available and possible future remedies against currency wars, acknowledging that stronger international cooperation may not be feasible in the current climate.

10.4.2 Remedies Embedded in the International Monetary (IMF) and Trade (WTO) Legal Orders: Why Are They Ineffective?

10.4.2.1 Article IV of the IMF Articles

Following the breakdown of the Bretton Woods arrangement in 1971, a new version of Article IV was added to the IMF Articles of Agreement

---

[42] B. Eichengreen, "Currency War or International Policy Coordination?" mimeo, University of California, Berkeley, January 2013, https://eml.berkeley.edu//~eichengr/curr_war_JPM_2013.pdf.

[43] Ibid.

that became effective in 1978 and which prohibits currency manipulation for the purpose of gaining unfair trade advantage. This was the least that could be done in view of the collapse of the previous regime, but it doesn't necessarily mean that the IMF can force a country to change its exchange rate policies. In specific, the amended Article IV, which went into effect in 1978 said that countries should seek, in their foreign exchange and monetary policies, to promote orderly economic growth and financial stability, and they should avoid manipulation of exchange rates or the international monetary system *to prevent effective balance of payments adjustment or to gain unfair competitive advantage over other members.*[44] Policies are not in violation of Article IV when they are not seeking to gain competitive advantage (though this may be the result of their actions) but rather *to stabilize the value of their currency in order to prevent disruption to their domestic economic system.*

The amended Article IV also required the IMF to "exercise firm surveillance over the exchange rate policies of all members and [to] adopt specific principles for the guidance of all members with respect to those policies." The IMF adopted the requisite guidance in 1977 (before the amendment went into effect) and updated it in 2007. The 1977 agreement said that, among other things, "protracted large-scale intervention in one direction in exchange markets" might be evidence that a country was inappropriately manipulating the value of its currency.[45] The 2007 agreement added a key requirement to the effect that "[a Fund] member should avoid exchange rate policies that result in external instability."[46] When a country's current account (balance of payments) is not in equilibrium, the IMF said in its explanation of the new provision, the exchange rate is "fundamentally misaligned" and "should be corrected."[47]

---

[44] Section 3 (iii) of the amended Art. IV which became effective in 1978 allows countries to maintain fixed rates or to adopt floating or market-based rates of exchange for their national currencies. The IMF must approve the exchange system countries adopt but it no longer has a role in determining relative currency values. See IMF, "Article IV of the Fund's Articles of Agreement: An Overview of the Legal Framework" briefing prepared by the Legal Department, June 28, 2006, www.imf.org/external/np/pp/eng/2006/062806.pdf.

[45] Ibid.

[46] IMF, "IMF Surveillance – the 2007 Decision on Bilateral Surveillance," Factsheet, June 2007.

[47] Ibid.

In a June 2007 Executive Board Decision on Bilateral Surveillance[48] (retained in a later decision of July 2012 that included multilateral surveillance),[49] the IMF added "a concept of external stability as an organizing principle for bilateral surveillance," whereby "[e]xternal stability encompasses both the current account of the balance of payments – and thereby also issues of exchange rate misalignment – and the capital account of the balance of payments." In the IMF's words: "the [2007] Decision add[ed] a principle recommending that members avoid exchange rate policies that *result* in external instability, regardless of their purpose, thereby capturing exchange rate policies that have proven to be a major source of instability over the past decades."[50] This broadened the scope of surveillance rather than the Article IV requirement that members manipulating their currency act inconsistently with Article IV principles if they do it for the *purpose* of gaining unfair competitive advantage. The latter required the Fund to establish that the objective of the policies in question was to undervalue the currency to increase net exports. So in practice, the effect of this broader language is unclear.

The Annex to both the 2007 and 2012 IMF surveillance decisions clarifies that "[a] member would only be acting inconsistently with Article IV, Section 1(iii) if the Fund determined both that: (a) the member was manipulating its exchange rate or the international monetary system and (b) such manipulation was being carried out for one of the two purposes specifically identified in Article IV, Section 1(iii)." The two purposes are: "(a) 'Manipulation' of the exchange rate is only carried out through policies that are targeted at – and actually affect – the level of an exchange rate. Moreover, manipulation may cause the exchange rate to move or may prevent such movement … (b) … [and] such manipulation [is] being undertaken in order to prevent effective balance of payments adjustment or to gain an unfair competitive advantage over other members."[51] In that regard, a member will only be considered to be manipulating exchange rates in order to gain an unfair competitive advantage over other members if the Fund determines both

[48] IMF, "Public Information Notice: IMF Executive Board Adopts New Decision on Bilateral Surveillance Over Members' Policies," PIN 07/69, June 21, 2007, www.imf.org /en/News/Articles/2015/09/28/04/53/pn0769#decision.

[49] IMF, "Public Information Notice: IMF Executive Board Adopts New Decision on Bilateral and Multilateral Surveillance," PIN 12/89, July 30, 2012, www.imf.org/en/ News/Articles/2015/09/28/04/53/pn1289.

[50] IMF 2007 Decision on Bilateral Surveillance.

[51] Annex s. 2.

that: "(A) the member is engaged in these policies for the purpose of securing fundamental exchange rate misalignment in the form of an undervalued exchange rate and (B) the purpose of securing such misalignment is to increase net exports."[52] This dual-purpose requirement is very restrictive, since as explained in a briefing of the IMF's legal department, "determination of intent [is] required" to be in breach of Article IV.[53]

Moreover, the 2007 Decision offered a number of plausible caveats. First, as is stated in the IMF decision itself, estimates of misalignment require the exercise of careful judgment. In practice, an exchange rate would only be judged to be fundamentally misaligned if the misalignment is found to be *significant*. The benefit of any reasonable doubt would be given to the authorities in establishing whether fundamental misalignment is present, and the potential market-sensitivity of estimates of misalignment was emphasized.[54]

In specific, the IMF defines a number of criteria that will use to in its surveillance of member state compliance with the rules against fundamental misalignment:[55]

- large-scale intervention in one direction in the exchange market;
- excessive and prolonged official or quasi-official accumulation of foreign assets; and
- large and prolonged current account deficits or surpluses.

These criteria have proved ineffective for a number of reasons. First, assuming that QE and extraordinary low interest rates are captured by this framework, states engaging in extraordinary monetary policies can plead that their purpose is to revive the domestic economy or counter the threat of deflation and recession, rather than manipulation of their currency. Secondly, they can argue that the pursuit of independent monetary policy is outside the remit of the IMF Agreements. In addition, a policy that leads to a revival of demand, especially in a major economy like the USA or a trade bloc like the eurozone,

---

[52] Ibid.

[53] "[A] specific obligation under Article IV, Section 1 is the requirement that members "avoid manipulating exchange rates or the international monetary system in order to prevent effective balance of payments adjustment or to gain an unfair competitive advantage ... the potential applicability of the obligation to avoid manipulation is constrained by the need to determine intent." IMF Briefing, "An Overview of the Legal Framework," 2; see also ibid., 15–16.

[54] IMF 2007 Decision on Bilateral Surveillance.

[55] Ibid.

ultimately benefits imports as well and not just exports. Either way, in the case of the USA a reduction of trade deficits means a beneficial rebalancing of the global economy. These arguments are very hard to refute in the absence of a mechanism that offers an objective indication of currency value. Third, there is the problem of what is large and prolonged, especially if the "manipulation" doesn't happen through formal devaluations or other patently unsubtle ways such as exchange market intervention or foreign asset accumulation for a long time. Clearly there are other more subtle ways at a state's disposal to achieve a similar outcome, such an expansionary monetary policy.

Fourth, there is always the defense that is frequently used by the German governments about their high and persistent trade surpluses. Namely, that these are due to structural discrepancies in economic competitiveness and productivity and not currency misalignment, rendering the third criterion of the IMF Guidance redundant. Finally, the IMF can exercise "firm surveillance," and it has made a genuine effort to revamp its financial surveillance in recent years to include a more macroprudential/systemic strategy,[56] but it cannot compel a country to change its exchange rate. Nor can it order commercial foreign exchange dealers to change the prices at which they trade currencies. All it can do is offer economic advice and discuss how changes in countries' exchange rates might be in their own interest.[57] However, in the end, the authority to make the change resides with the country alone.

10.4.3   Currency Manipulation and the WTO

The WTO seeks to expand international trade through the reduction or elimination of tariffs or other barriers to trade while the IMF pursues this goal mainly through efforts to promote international monetary and exchange rate stability. Trade policy issues may feature prominently in the IMF's surveillance, but as we have already explained there is probably no effective enforcement mechanism in the case of currency manipulation given the discussed above very high burden of proof. Unlike most

---

[56] See IMF, "The IMF's Financial Surveillance Strategy," August 28, 2012, www.imf.org /external/np/pp/eng/2012/082812.pdf and IMF, "Triennial Surveillance Review – Managing Director's Action Plan for Strengthening Surveillance," December 2014, www .imf.org/external/np/pp/eng/2014/112114.pdf.

[57] The IMF can also "provide a forum, such as its new multilateral consultation mechanism or discussion on the IMF executive board, where other countries can urge a country to change its exchange rate procedures."

other major international trade and finance bodies, the WTO has a mechanism for enforcing its rules. If a member country feels aggrieved by the conduct of another which it deems to be in violation of WTO rules, it may request the appointment of a dispute settlement panel to hear its complaint. The country complained of cannot block the establishment of a panel which reviews the arguments of both parties and renders judgment on whether a breach of the WTO rules has taken place. If the losing party does not comply with the decision of the panel within a reasonable timeframe, then the WTO may authorize the endorsement of countervailing measures by the complaining party.

The WTO rule that can be invoked in this case is the prohibition of export subsidies.[58] WTO members are entitled to levy countervailing duties on imported products that receive subsidies from national government. Arguably, an undervalued currency lowers a firm's cost of production "relative to world prices and therefore helps to encourage exports." But, whether undervaluation of a country's currency, even if it proves to be itnetional, amounts to an export subsidy under the WTO's current definition of the term[59] is highly debatable. The term has a precise definition in the WTO Agreements which require that there must be a financial contribution by a government to the exporter or some other form of income or price support. In addition, an export subsidy is a subsidy that is "contingent on export performance." They must also be "specific to an industry," and not provided generally to all producers.[60] Therefore, the WTO prohibition of export subsidies is very narrow and specific and does not seem to encompass currency manipulation.

The IMF and WTO could use their interagency agreement[61] to promote better coordination in the treatment of this concern.[62] The IMF and GATT signed an agreement aimed at facilitating inter-agency cooperation soon after the trade organization was formed in 1947. The IMF and WTO adopted a revised and updated version of that agreement in 1996.

---

[58] WTO Agreement on Subsidies and Countervailing Measures, Arts. 2–3.

[59] See J. E. Sanford, "Currency Manipulation: The IMF and WTO," Congressional Research Services, January 28, 2011, p. 2, https://fas.org/sgp/crs/misc/RS22658.pdf.

[60] For more discussion see Sanford ibid., p. 3.

[61] Agreement between the International Monetary Fund and the World Trade Organization, para. 2, republished in IMF, *Selected Decisions and Selected Documents of the International Monetary Fund*, 31st Issue, Washington DC, December 31, 2006. NB: the preamble to the agreement acknowledges that there are increasing links between the issues addressed by the two institutions and it notes that the Marrakesh Agreement, establishing the WTO, called for greater coherence internationally in economic policies.

[62] Sanford, supra n. 59, pp. 8–9.

The two organizations agreed (in paragraphs 1 and 2 of the agreement) that they "shall consult with each other in the discharge of their respective mandates," with a view toward "achieving greater coherence in global economic policymaking." Article XV of the GATT agreement says that the WTO shall cooperate with the IMF in order to "pursue a coordinated policy with regards to exchange questions that are within the jurisdiction of the Fund." The WTO and IMF also agreed in 1996 (in paragraph 8) that they would communicate with each other about "matters of mutual interest."[63] WTO dispute settlement panels are specifically excluded from this agreement to communicate, but the agreement says that the IMF shall inform the WTO (specifically including its dispute settlement panels) when the WTO is "considering exchange measures within the Fund's jurisdiction [in order to determine] whether such measures are consistent with the Articles of Agreement of the Fund."[64] The IMF also agreed, in 1996, that it would participate in any WTO discussion of any such measures countries may have taken to safeguard their balance of payments. But in the absence of an amendment of the WTO Treaties and IMF Articles which would allow a relevant complaint to be adjudicated by the WTO panels, it is very hard to see what "teeth" this cooperation has, and indeed so far, it has not produced any binding legal action in this context.

Of course, the WTO Agreements (or even the Articles of Agreement of the IMF) could be amended to make their treatment of currency manipulation more consistent. Equally, negotiations may be pursued, on a multilateral as well as a bilateral basis, to resolve currency manipulation disputes on a country-by-country basis without changing the IMF or WTO treatment of this concern. But in the current climate such amendment looks far-fetched even though more than necessary.

Given perceived difficulties to achieve the said change in the WTO/ IMF agreements another solution would be to insert relevant clauses and enforcement mechanisms into bilateral or regional trade agreements. Naturally, as it has been accurately noted linking exchange rate to trade

---

[63] For a very comprehensive discussion of the IMF/WTO agreement and quotes see Sanford, ibid., pp. 4, 8.

[64] Earlier (in paras. 3 and 4), the IMF agreed that it would inform the WTO about any decisions it had made approving any restrictions a country might impose on international payments, discriminatory currency practices, or other measures aimed at preventing a large or sustained outflow of capital.

agreements would be historically unprecedented.[65] At the same time, currency manipulation can in the end prove to be unsubstantiated, or reversible, as has been the case with China, whose currency has appreciated by 40 percent against the US dollar in the past few years.[66] Either scenario makes it impossible to take measures under the IMF Articles or the WTO provisions, and probably under those of a future regional or bilateral Treaties. But linking trade and investment and financial flows to some notion/binding understanding of relative exchange rate stability is, in principle, a good idea. Relevant understanding might have to move away from the IMF definitions and framework to make enforcement a realistic prospect giving it a deterrent value, but it is nevertheless an idea worth exploring. In fact, adding a clause on currency manipulation to bilateral and multilateral trade agreements, such as the currently negotiated Transatlantic and Transpacific Trade Agreements, has been widely promoted by US think tanks.[67]

Naturally, such an initiative would still face several key obstacles. First, any workable clause would inevitably not mirror the IMF guidelines,[68] meaning more fragmentation instead of the required integration of the international trade and monetary orders. Secondly, determining the existence and extent of currency misalignment, especially as a possible trigger for remedial action, has historically proven enormously difficult both intellectually and politically. So why the problem of objective evidence would be different in this case? It has thus been suggested that the determination of "misalignment" be ignored in favor of more straightforward and objective indicators.[69] The goal of the exercise would

---

[65] F. Bergsten, "Addressing Currency manipulation through Trade agreements," *Policy Brief* 14–2, Peterson Institute for International Economics, January 2014, 1, https://piie.com /publications/pb/pb14-2.pdf. As Bergsten hastens to add: "Currency issues and trade agreements, indeed virtually all trade policy issues, have traditionally been handled under separate negotiations and legal constructs and by different institutions at both the national and international levels. Integrating them would require fundamental changes in the conduct of international economic policy in the United States and around the world." Ibid.

[66] T. Worstall, "Bad News for Allegations of Currency Manipulation: IMF Says China's Yuan Correctly Valued," *Forbes, Economics & Finance*, May 26, 2015, www.forbes.com /sites/timworstall/2015/05/26/bad-news-for-allegations-of-currency-manipulation-imf-says-chinas-yuan-correctly-valued/#2c70c5065d94.

[67] Bergsten, supra n. 65, pp. 4–5.

[68] See M. Solis, "The Answer Is Still NO on a Currency Manipulation Clause in the TPP," Brooking op-ed, January 15, 2014, www.brookings.edu/blog/up-front/2014/01/15/the-answer-is-still-no-on-a-currency-manipulation-clause-in-the-tpp/.

[69] J. Gagnon, "The Elephant Hiding in the Room: Currency Intervention and Trade Imbalances" Peterson Institute for International Economics Working Paper 13–2, March 27, 2013, https://papers.ssrn.com/sol3/papers.cfm?abstract_id=2238170.

be simply to prevent a country from running large and persistent external surpluses that result from efforts to depress the value of its exchange rate in the currency markets.[70]

However, these ideas still revolve around the concept of "intervention," seen as "substantial amounts of direct purchases of foreign exchange with local currency." As in some cases this will involve secretive sovereign wealth funds, the picture would still be less than crystal-clear. Worse, the concept of "intervention" is far less convincing in the case of "indirect intervention" through capital controls, uncoordinated macro-prudential and monetary policies such as quantitative easing (QE),[71] or even loose fiscal policies, all of which have an impact on private capital outflows and, as is likely, exchange rates.

For all of the above reasons, and in order to resolve the present conundrum which spreads mistrust in all parts of the rules-based global economic order, this chapter suggests instead in section 10.5 a more objective mechanism/benchmark to measure currency values. The creation of such a benchmark may play a pivotal role at some point in the future when the present cycle of mistrust in international trade has fizzled out. In specific, it will make it possible to implement a currency monitoring regime that will look firmly into excessively loose monetary policies that destabilize global trade. In reality what the world faces today, apart from the diminishing goodwill in international trade, is the absence of any benchmark that could objectively approximate fundamental currency values.

Still, even if the issue of a relatively objective measurement of currency values is addressed, other problems will remain from the point of view of political economy analysis. First, why would the US government wish to do such a thing in the end, beyond talking about it, when it has itself been guilty of weakening the dollar on many occasions? It was in fact the US that brought down the Bretton Woods fixed to floating rates with two unauthorized devaluations of the dollar in 1971. Secondly, why would US trade counterparts accept such a commitment when, at the same time,

---

[70] See Bergsten, supra n.65, pp. 4–5.

[71] Even empirical studies conducted by doubters have found that extraordinary monetary policies have an appreciable impact on current account imbalances, albeit in their view only when capital mobility is low, with the implication being that in the case of financially integrated countries this impact dissipates over time. See J. E. Gagnon, T. Bayoumi, J. M. Londono, C. Saborowski and H. Sapriza, "Direct and Spillover Effects of Unconventional Monetary and Exchange Rate Policies" IMF WP/17/56, March 13, 2017, www.imf.org/en/Publications/WP/Issues/2017/03/13/Direct-and-Spillover-Effects-of-Unconventional-Monetary-and-Exchange-Rate-Policies-44743.

the US will be demanding safeguards on wage levels and environmental standards from its negotiating partners. While these concessions could correct some of the deficiencies of existing NAFTA and WTO, they also fundamentally alter the post-1994 trade status quo which brought immense wealth and prosperity to countries like China, but seems to have weakened the US economy overall. What would US trade partners demand then to also abolish the weapon of exchange rate realignment?

10.4.4   A Composite Benchmark of Value?

There is currently an accentuated trend in the international sphere to use composite indices to further public interest/social good goals. For example, respected Franco-German economists have suggested a composite index of GDP values to be built as a form of a tradable synthetic euro-asset that would replace member states' bonds in eurozone bank balance sheets, thus resolving the infamous "doom loop" under which bank over-indebtedness or a financial crisis can soon morph into a sovereign debt crisis, and vice versa.[72] Similarly, the EU Commission is toying with the idea of client indices to foster sustainable finance investments.[73] While both of these proposals may be open to the charge of inducing excessive financialization, the index suggested here is intended to have the opposite effect: namely to stabilize FX markers. It could curb excessive speculation/volatility in FX markets and also unmask predatory countries.

It is thus suggested that a global unit of account (GUOA) could be created that would be freely tradable in the same way that virtual currencies are, which will have an exchange rate with SDRs but its composite value will be made of easily observed and uncorrelated indices of value. The GUOA may serve as an alternative and objective measure of value if it is not directly dependent on trade flows and other highly volatile

---

[72] "Exploring a euro area-level 'safe asset' that could be scaled up in conjunction with the regulatory incentives to reduce the home bias of banks." See A. Bénassy-Quéré, M. K. Brunnermeier, H. Enderlein, E. Farhi, M. Fratzscher, C. Fuest, P.-O. Gourinchas, P. Martin, F. Pisani, H. Rey, I. Schnabel, N. Véron, B. Weder di Mauro and J. Zettelmeyer, "Reconciling Risk Sharing with Market Discipline: A Constructive Approach to Euro Area Reform," *CEPR Policy Insight* No. 91, January 2018, p. 4, https://cepr.org/sites/default/files/policy_insights/PolicyInsight91.pdf.

[73] See EU Commission Communication, "Action Plan: Financing Sustainable Growth," Brussels, 8.3.2018, COM(2018) 97 final, esp. para. 2.5 (Sustainability Benchmarks), http://eur-lex.europa.eu/legal-content/EN/TXT/?uri=CELEX:52018DC0097.

measures. The idea is to create a system that would measure national fiscal and macroeconomic health against global trends rather than just focusing on the balance of payments of trade partners. To this effect and on the basis of extensive empirical research into the most representative indications of global macroeconomic trends, it is suggested here that the GUOA first of all should measure: (a) the rate of (global) GDP growth, (b) volatility (change in value) of global commodity and energy prices, and (c) the volatility (change in value) of the key global stock market indices. Each of the three indicators (GGDP+GCVC-E+GSI) could be allotted one-third of the overall value of the GUOA, since we have no reliable data as to which of the three is the more representative. Then the GUOA's appreciation/ decline will be compared with the growth in the value of the country's imports or exports for a given year, represented in SDRs. E.g., if the GUOA has appreciated by 5 percent and the country's imports by 7 percent, whereas its exports have appreciated by 3 percent, this is an objective though imperfect (since country productivity rates and structural or cyclical competitive advantage are not measured) indication that this country's currency is overvalued, whereas those of its trade partners are undervalued, and so on. The onus is then on its trade partners to explain themselves to the WTO or the adjudicating body of a future multilateral or bilateral trade treaty that would incorporate an anti-manipulation clause.

The GUOA index suggested here has several prima facie advantages which could help rebuild trust in the international economic sphere. First, it is not bound to any particular reserve currency. Secondly, it is built on such a broad base that it cannot be manipulated. Third, it is rather representative of the economic reality and prospects of both developed and developing countries. Thus, while the stock exchange index, which is an internally uncorrelated composite index, as developed world economies do not have symmetrical growth and stock market cycles, will be over-weighted in developed world economies, the global energy and commodity index will be representing the high price volatility that commodity exporters (mostly developing nations) and energy producers experience.

10.5 Conclusion

Relative stability in currency values or avoidance of excessive instability is essential for the development of global trade and investment and for cross-border financial stability. One would call it a global public good, which like all such goods is often subject to "tragedy of the commons" situations presenting a short-sighted trade advantage to predatory countries, or market speculators. The international financial order generically lacks any credible enforcement mechanism against currency manipulation practices and is thus impotent to buttress cross-border financial stability in the event of a widespread cross-border currency run. At present the only workable measures seem to be capital controls, which, however, are a very blunt instrument and in many cases they might go on for a very long time, in spite their evident short-term benefits. They should be used as the last and not the first resort measure. In addition, the international trade and monetary orders have proved very weak enforcers of the IMF's currency tampering prohibitions. Arguably, this is not so much due to lack of will as to the fact that a mechanism approximating an objective benchmark of currency values is largely missing.

The fact that at present the international framework doesn't have effective tools to control "currency wars" creates conditions of heightened mistrust in the global economic sphere. To this effect this chapter has suggested an objective, transparent and impossible-to-manipulate reference unit of account which can be used to test present currency value and given an objective indication of under- or overvaluation. Arguably, a collateral (yet virtuous) effect of the use of the suggested objective benchmark (or of any equivalent measure) is the deceleration of currency wars and of their impact on the propagation of geopolitical risks. In addition, given widely observed stagnation in the evolution of the global financial architecture, especially in the areas where cooperation is required the most, namely, the field of cross-border macroprudential policies, any idea that can offer a new impetus to the process ought to be welcome, unless terribly flawed. Clearly a transparent benchmark of value is the first step in a long process aiming at the containment of speculative currency trades such as the carry trades. It also builds stores of trust for the rethink of the global financial architecture with a view of aligning it closer to trade and investment rather than mostly buttressing the loose money flows discussed in this chapter.

Much of the social utility of the gigantic cross-currency flows discussed here is questionable, given their "recycling" nature away from the needs of the real economy. On the other hand, the possible social cost of those trades coming unstuck, in the event of a global liquidity shock, could prove incalculable. Therefore, any steps toward realignment of the global financial order with those for trade and investment would inevitably prove a great boon to global financial stability and can provide a solid basis to restart transnational cooperation efforts in the sphere of international financial governance and beyond.

11

The Politics of Commodity Derivatives Reform in the EU and the USA

JAKOB ENGEL[*]

11.1 Introduction

Both physical and financial commodity markets remained in upheaval following the end of the 2003–2012 commodity price super-cycle and financial regulatory reforms in the European Union and the United States. These reforms had their origin in the "triple crisis" of 2007–2009, when a spike in the price of grains coincided with a boom in other commodity prices, and a financial crisis that led to the most severe recession in decades. Food prices for some crops reached almost three times their 2002 levels, and annualized price indices for metals, energy and agricultural goods increased by at least 30 percent year-on-year between 2006 and 2008 (see Figure 11.1). This contributed to widespread riots and a rise in protectionist measures in numerous developing countries, in many cases further exacerbating price volatility. Energy and metals prices also increased significantly during this time, with surging oil prices dominating the 2008 US presidential election until the failure of Lehman Brothers and the start of the global financial crisis overtook events. These concurrent dynamics galvanized public outrage, and the search for appropriate political and legislative responses centered in part on bringing greater transparency and stability to markets for commodity derivatives.[1]

[*] Jakob Engel is a D.Phil. student at the School of Geography and Environment at the University of Oxford. The author wishes to thank David C. Donald, Emilio Avgouleas, Stefano Pagliari and Darisuz Wójcik for comments on an earlier version of this chapter, along with the audience at the 2016 Conference on "The Political Economy of Financial Regulation, "held at the CUHK Faculty of Law for discussions.
[1] See G-20 Leaders, "Cannes Summit Final Declaration: Building Our Common Future: Renewed Collective Action for the Benefit of All," November 4, 2011, 6–7; J. Clapp and S. Murphy, "The G20 and Food Security: A Mismatch in Global Governance?" *Global Policy*, 4 (2013), 129–138.

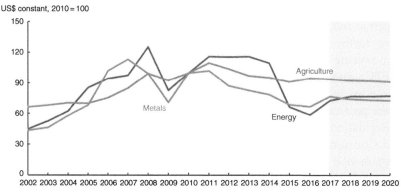

US$ constant, 2010 = 100

Figure 11.1 Commodity Price Indices (annualized)
Source: World Bank Commodity Markets Group
Note : Shaded area (2017–2020) denotes forecast

During this extended rise in the price of commodities, the rapidly growing commodity derivatives market was viewed by many as a source of instability.[2] While the precise role of "financialization"[3] in driving the price spikes of 2006–2008 and subsequent volatility remains a far from settled matter, the scale of financialization and the perceived lack of transparency in many of these markets motivated the leaders of the Group of 20 (G-20), and particularly some policy-makers and regulators in the EU and United States, to favor stronger constraints on market activity related to short-term speculation[4] rather than longer-term risk-hedging. This included limits to the size of trader positions and greater

[2] See M. W. Masters and Adam K. White, "How Institutional Investors are Driving Up Food and Energy Prices: Special Report" *The Accidental Hunt Brothers*, July 31, 2008; J. Mayer, "The Growing Interdependence between Financial and Commodity Markets" *UNCTAD Discussion Papers* (2009) 195.

[3] The definition and implications of the term "financialization" are highly contested. In the context of this chapter I broadly endorse Epstein's definition of financialization as referring to "the increasing importance of financial markets, financial motives, financial institutions, and financial elites in the operation of the economy and its governing institutions, both at the national and international levels." G. Epstein, "Financialization, rentier interests, and central bank policy," Manuscript, University of Massachusetts, Amherst (2003), p. 3.

[4] Likewise a contested term, for the purposes of this chapter I define speculation as "[t]he taking of above-average risks to achieve above-average returns, generally during a relatively short period of time. Speculation involves buying something on the basis of its potential selling price rather than on the basis of its actual value." D. Logan Scott, *Wall Street Words: An A to Z Guide to Investment Terms for Today's Investor* (Boston MA: Houghton Mifflin Harcourt, 2003), 351.

market transparency.[5] Measures had the purported aim of reducing systemic risk and reining in "excessive" speculative activity. Legislators have further brought about significant regulatory changes, greatly empowering the US Commodity Futures Trading Commission (CFTC), and in the case of the EU, creating an entirely new agency, the European Securities and Markets Authority (ESMA) within the context of the post-crisis financial regulatory overhaul.

Regulations embodied in the 2010 Dodd-Frank Wall Street Reform and Consumer Protection Act (Dodd-Frank) appeared to represent a fundamental change in the governance of the commodity derivatives market. It required "strong measures to limit speculation in agricultural commodities," and called upon the CFTC to introduce position limits and bring the over-the-counter (OTC) derivatives market under regulatory control for the first time.[6] New EU commodity derivatives regulations passed as part the European Markets Infrastructure Regulation (EMIR), the Market Abuse Regulations (MAR) and the revised Market in Financial Instruments Directive (MiFID II) have been largely viewed as a defeat for the light-touch approach to the financial sector and as an indicator of the effectiveness of a mobilized civil society.[7] In both the EU and the United States, stronger transparency requirements, regulations limiting the number of open positions that traders can hold, and restrictions on proprietary trading were passed. In both cases, the CFTC and ESMA were authorized to draft technical specifications and implement regulations. These regulations, according to a report by the UK Financial Conduct Authority (FCA), are "of unprecedented scope and complexity both for commodities and [for] more generic measures."[8]

The significance of these measures has been broad and relevant to actors outside financial markets as well. Primary commodities (and in turn the functioning of financial commodity markets) are essential to

---

[5] See E. Helleiner, "Towards Cooperative Decentralisation: The Post-crisis Governance of Global OTC Derivatives," in T. Porter (ed.), *Transnational Financial Regulation after the Crisis* (Abingdon: Routledge, 2014), 132–154.

[6] Dodd–Frank Wall Street Reform and Consumer Protection Act, Pub.L. 111–203, H.R. 4173 (2010).

[7] See J. Clapp and E. Helleiner, "Troubled Futures? The Global Food Crisis and the Politics of Agricultural Derivatives Regulation," *Review of International Political Economy*, 19(2) (2012) 181–207; J. Petry, "Regulatory Capture, Civil Society & Global Finance in Derivative Regulation: An Analysis of Commodity Derivative Regulation in Europe," (June 14, 2014). ECPR Standing Group on Regulatory Governance, 5th Biennial Conference, 25–27 June 2014, Barcelona, Spain.

[8] FCA, "Commodity Markets Update," February 2014, p. 6.

economic development throughout the world – whether in producing or consuming nations. The emerging regulatory changes are likely to affect how risks from commodity trading are assessed and managed, impact liquidity in markets, and could limit or broaden the scope for certain forms of financial activity, ownership, and vertical and horizontal integration in the commodities sector. In short, the new regulatory frameworks have the potential to affect how the commodity price formation process functions for actors at all stages of the supply chain. This in turn influences whether, where and how value can be captured, and by whom. Normative questions assessing the benefits and risks of "financialization" and "speculation" in commodity markets are also receiving significant attention.[9]

This chapter addresses the related and equally important question of how the new regulatory frameworks arose, and particularly their implementation by the ESMA and the CFTC. Seven years after the passage of Dodd-Frank and over three years after the completion of the Level 1 process of MiFID II, few issues in these very broad legislative acts of financial market re-regulation remain as controversial as those governing commodity derivatives. And with the election of Donald Trump, who campaigned on a broad agenda of deregulation and of revisiting Dodd-Frank, many of the new rules relevant to commodity derivative markets under Dodd-Frank are being reviewed and, in many cases, repealed. As these regulatory frameworks are – at the time of writing – approaching their completion, with both the CFTC and ESMA hoping to finalize their work in late 2017, this chapter is interested in the "long tail" of regulatory implementation and technical rule-making, arguing that this phase is essential for understanding the future functioning of commodity derivative markets. The chapter also postulates that this process has operated in a different political and economic context and with different interest group dynamics in Europe than the legislative and executive process that resulted in Dodd-Frank and its subsequent implementation. Moreover, the almost finalized rules differ in nuanced but significant respects in the

---

[9] These debates, while important, are not central to this chapter and are covered extensively elsewhere. See for example S. H. Irwin and D. R. Sanders, "Index Funds, Financialization, and Commodity Futures Markets," *Applied Economic Perspectives and Policy*, 33(1) (2011), 1–31; Secretariat of the United Nations Conference on Trade and Development (UNCTAD), *Price Formation in Financialized Commodity Markets: The Role of Information* (New York and Geneva: United Nations, 2011); S. McGill, "The Financialization Thesis Revisited: Commodities as an Asset Class," in G. L. Clark, M. P. Feldman, M. Gertler and D. Wojcik (eds.), *The New Oxford Handbook of Economic Geography* (Oxford: Oxford University Press, 2018), 645–664.

EU and United States. In this regard, two variables are presented as being of particular salience in determining outcomes during the rule-making process: the breadth and intensity of opposition from interest groups, and the internal level of agreement within the agency itself.

In this context, the regulatory implementation of commodity derivatives reforms presents two interesting puzzles, one of which is related to process and the other to outcome. Firstly, it is striking that this area of financial market regulation, which is relatively small within the scope of the OTC derivatives market, has been one of the most contested during its implementation, and remains unfinished to this day. Thus, despite the comparatively minor role of commodity derivatives trading, reaching an agreement on regulating these products has played an outsized role for legislators, industry actors and civil society groups. There has been no issue on which the CFTC has held more consultative meetings since 2008 than on position limits for commodity derivatives. Within the EU consultative process, the issue that received the most written responses was the reform of commodity markets. This begs the question as to why commodity derivatives regulation has been so contested, and why it remains unfinished?

Secondly, drawing on two distinct aspects of the new regulatory frameworks for commodity derivatives – the setting of position limits and decisions on where to set exemption thresholds for hedging purposes – this chapter examines why seemingly divergent regulatory outcomes in key areas of regulation have emerged in the EU and the United States. More specifically, what role have the differences between the two regulatory agencies, CFTC and ESMA, their different institutional structure, and the differing incentives they face, played in this context? A central premise of this chapter is that focusing on the processes themselves may yield a more fruitful analysis than just looking at outcomes, and therefore the chapter will examine the politics of implementation, and more specifically, the internal dynamics and capacity of the key regulatory agencies and their interactions with legislators and interest groups as primary sources of variation.

This chapter thus joins the work in this volume by Giuliano G. Castellano and Geneviève Helleringer on the social psychology of financial regulatory governance, and by Thomas Lambert and Deniz Igan on bank lobbying, in contributing to what is still a rather limited literature focusing on the regulatory agency itself as an internally complex and often divided actor making decisions about priorities and allocation of resources. These decisions are based on internal debates and processes that change throughout economic and political cycles. Moreover, although an extensive literature focusing on central banks has emerged post-crisis, the historical evolution and internal dynamics of the two main financial regulatory agencies remains poorly understood.

As such, a central contribution of this chapter is its analysis of the potentially substantial impacts at the level of implementation of nuanced changes to thresholds, exemptions and carve-outs within the decade-long regulatory processes. In its focus on the post-legislative process of rule-making by the relevant regulatory agencies, and on how interest group dynamics and the potential returns to lobbying may differ at this stage, this chapter aims to open the "black box" of the regulatory agency. In this context it focuses primarily on the "long tail" of the rule-making processes and aims to address Moschella and Tsingou's call for a better academic understanding of the *processes* of regulatory change in finance, rather than just the regulatory (and legislative) outcomes.[10]

In this regard, the chapter allows for an empirical analysis of what John C. Coffee, Jr. has called the "regulatory sine curve," namely that there is a cyclical progression from "intense to lax enforcement" that is "driven by a basic asymmetry between the power, resources and organization of the latent group (i.e., investors) and the interest groups affected by the specific legislation."[11] It aims to provide an analysis of how the governance, institutional structure and incentives operating within these agencies may determine outcomes. Moreover, even though there is an extensive literature on the development of post-crisis financial regulatory frameworks, particularly in the United States and increasingly also in the EU, far less scholarly work exists on the implementation of this legislation and the politics of rule-making by these agencies, as well as on the determinants of outcomes at the technical level. This gap is likely due to the less public nature of these processes, their highly technical nature, and the fact that they have yet to be finalized.

This chapter is structured as follows. Section 11.2 provides an overview of the two regulatory agencies central to implementing new regulations: the CFTC and ESMA, in the context of commodity derivatives reform. Section 11.3 develops a conceptual framework for the chapter, drawing on the literature on post-crisis regulation for OTC derivatives broadly, and commodity derivatives specifically. Section 11.4 focuses on two

---

[10] M. Moschella and E. Tsingou, "Regulating Finance after the Crisis: Unveiling the Different Dynamics of the Regulatory Process," *Regulation & Governance*, 7(4) (2013), 407–416.

[11] J. C. Coffee, Jr., "Political Economy of Dodd-Frank: Why Financial Reform Tends to Be Frustrated and Systemic Risk Perpetuated," *Cornell L. Rev.*, 97 (2011), 1019–1082 at 1030.

distinct aspects of the new regulatory frameworks for commodity derivatives: the setting of position limits and decisions on where to set
exemption thresholds for hedging purposes. Section 11.5 concludes
with a discussion of the key findings and implications arising from this
comparative analysis of two core aspects of commodity derivatives regulation across the two primary jurisdictions.

11.2   Historical Context

11.2.1   The Re-regulation of Commodity Derivatives: Overview of Key Events

Starting with the establishment of the Chicago Mercantile Exchange,
commodity derivative markets have existed for over 150 years in order
to provide producers and commercial traders with means to hedge
against price risks. These markets sell various financial instruments,
including forward contracts, options, futures and swaps, and have served
as a mechanism for price discovery and to provide producers and commercial traders with a means to hedge against various forms of risk.[12] To
do this effectively, prices need to largely reflect supply and demand
fundamentals for the physical commodity itself. Prior to the 1990s
there was very limited engagement by non-commercial traders in commodity markets. However, restrictions limiting the size of positions were
lifted and the participation by other shorter-term investors was facilitated
during the late 1990s and early 2000s.[13]

The growth of commodity derivatives markets over this time was
caused in large part by the rising popularity of commodity index funds
and the assumption that they would be effective hedges against equity
risk. This was deemed by many to be a major driver of volatility – a
hypothesis popularized by the investor Michael Masters – and in the
subsequent years has led to dozens of econometric papers aiming to
isolate precisely the role of the financialization of commodity markets,
as opposed to supply and demand fundamentals, in price developments.[14] But in reviewing data for this time period, it is clear that there

---

[12] See J. Markham, *The History of Commodity Futures Trading and Its Regulation* (Wesport,
CT: Praeger, 1987).

[13] For an overview see Clapp and Helleiner, "Troubled futures?" and A. Chadwick,
"Regulating Excessive Speculation: Commodity Derivatives and the Global Food
Crisis," *International & Comparative Law Quarterly*, 66 (2017), 1–31.

[14] Despite being one of the most extensively researched areas of financial economics in
recent years, determining the impact of short-term speculative activity (i.e., the buying

was a dramatic shift particularly by institutional investors and increasingly also retail investors betting consistently long on commodity markets during the super-cycle. From about 2005 until late 2008, trading in commodity derivatives exceeded trading in equities on derivatives markets. That said, in the scheme of the overall derivatives markets – both exchange-traded and especially OTC – these were still relatively minor compared to foreign exchange and interest rate forwards, options and swaps, hovering at around 10 percent of exchange-traded derivative contracts, and never exceeding 2 percent of all OTC derivative market activity. However, the scale of trading increased rapidly in both markets until the crisis and then collapsed much more quickly in the OTC market than was the case for other OTC non-commodity contracts, while continuing to increase steadily in exchange trading.

These developments resulted in widespread calls by international organizations, civil society groups, and governments to incorporate commodity derivatives reforms in post-crisis financial reforms. Large-scale speculation and the perceived lack of transparency in many of these markets led leaders of the G-20, and particularly policy-makers and regulators in the EU and United States, to favor stronger constraints on market activity related to short-term speculation rather than longer-term risk hedging. This was in part motivated by substantial pressure from civil society organizations who ran highly effective campaigns against what was termed "the financialization of food." These groups were echoed by officials in several international agencies as well as numerous parliamentarians and heads of state – most notably French president Nicolas Sarkozy. Exemplifying this view, Olivier de Schutter, the UN Special Rapporteur on the Right to Food, argued "[t]he global food price crisis that occurred between 2007 and 2008, and which affects many

and selling of contracts for short-term profits rather than for genuine hedging purposes), and "financialization" more broadly on commodity prices and their volatility has not been conclusively answered, with numerous studies arguing that there has been a causal effect of financial markets on spot markets and others claiming that behavior of commodity prices was largely linked to demand and supply fundamentals; see Irwin and Sanders, "Index Funds," 1. Results depend largely on the choice of the "financialization" variable, the type of the model and estimation technique, and the type of data, among numerous other parameters. However increasingly – as more data has become available – a consensus is emerging that financial investors have had a role in contributing to both the high prices of commodities, and to their volatility over the past decade. For an overview, see R. Arezki, L. Prakash, R. van der Ploeg, and A. J. Venables, "Understanding International Commodity Price Fluctuations," *Journal of International Money and Finance*, 42 (2014), 1–8; Ke Tang and Haoxiang Zhu, "Commodities as collateral," *The Review of Financial Studies*, 29(8) (2016), 2110–2160.

developing countries to this day, had a number of causes. The initial causes related to market fundamentals ... However, a significant portion of the increases in price and volatility of essential food commodities can only be explained by the emergence of a speculative bubble."[15]

Following the very light-touch regulatory approaches taken both at national levels and through trans-national bodies (such as the Basel Committee of Banking Standards as well as through IOSCO), it soon became clear that commodity derivatives trading would be subject to much heavier transnational regulation, though it was unclear what forum would take the leading role in this regard. Despite the impetus and momentum coming from other organizations – most notably the UN's Food and Agriculture Organization (FAO) – the G-20 became the primary forum for the development of new rules for the commodity derivatives market, providing overarching guidance on the development of central clearing of standardized OTC derivatives, exchange and electronic platform trading of standardized OTC derivatives, trade reporting to trade repositories, initial and variation margin requirements for non-centrally cleared OTC derivatives and bank capital requirements for derivatives exposures.[16]

With the G-20 driving the process for the development of new rules of the commodity derivatives market, discussions on commodity derivatives were included within reforms of the broader OTC derivatives market. This further allowed the United States and EU to set the agenda. Discussions on commodity derivatives regulation became part of the broader debate on financial stability, and were thus divorced from debates about the role of derivatives in causing volatility in commodity spot markets. This made a certain degree of intuitive of sense: with over 80 percent of commodity derivatives traded globally sold in the United States and the European Union, where the main exchanges (including the Chicago and New York Mercantile Exchanges, the London Commodity Exchange, the London Metal Exchange and the Frankfurt Eurex are located), regulation in these two primary jurisdictions was likely to be of central importance to the nature of derivative market governance globally. Therefore, international discussions on commodity derivatives regulation – at least until the French G-20 presidency – became part of the broader debate on financial stability, becoming divorced from

---

[15] Olivier de Schutter, "Food Commodities Speculation and Food Price Crises," OHCHR Briefing Note No. 2, p. 1.

[16] C. Amariei and D. Valiante, "The OTC derivatives markets after financial reforms," (May 2014) 36 *CEPS ECMI Commentaries*.

discussions about the role of commodity derivatives in causing volatility in commodity spot markets. It also resulted in regulatory outcomes that were subject to interest group politics in Brussels and Washington DC.

The first G-20 summit in Washington DC in November 2008 at least implicitly placed the commodity derivatives market on the agenda, with extensive discussion on improving transparency, mitigating risk related to the OTC market and preventing market abuse. With the French G-20 presidency, there was a greater focus specifically on the implications of commodity derivatives trading as part of its broader prioritization of food security. The French presidency called for a series of studies on the effect of speculation and commissioned a report by IOSCO that recommended a set of principles for market regulators to be granted effective intervention power to address disorderly markets and prevent market abuse, including through position limits. However, for those hoping for stronger measures to curtail speculation on agricultural markets, the French presidency was seen to have missed an important opportunity, focusing instead on "smoothing and coping" issues with the primary recommendations related to an improved information mechanism to address price volatility as well as market-based risk management strategies for primary commodity markets.[17] IOSCO, together with the Bank for International Settlements (BIS), has been a central authority in implementing G-20 commitments. It published "Principles for the Regulation and Supervision of Commodity Derivatives Markets" that provide guidance on expected regulatory standards in the form of twenty-one separate principles that cover contract design, market surveillance, enforcement and information-sharing, and price discovery.[18]

Among leading economies, the United States acted first after the crisis to reform its financial system. Trends in this direction started even before the bankruptcy of Lehman Brothers, with the CFTC withdrawing a proposal to increase position limits, marking the first time in decades that it had chosen not to loosen regulations in this area. In August 2009, position limit exemptions given to Deutsche Bank for soybeans, corn and wheat were revoked.[19] Despite these dynamics, new regulations embodied in Dodd-Frank appeared to represent fundamental change in the governance of the commodity derivative market. It required "strong measures" to limit speculation in agricultural commodities and called

---

[17] See Clapp and Murphy, "G-20 and Food Security."

[18] See IOSCO, "Principles for the Regulation and Supervision of Commodity Derivatives Markets," (Madrid: IOSCO, 2011).

[19] P. Gibbon, "Commodity Derivatives: Financialization and Regulatory Reform" (2013) No. 2013–12 DIIS Working Paper.

upon the CFTC to introduce position limits and bring the OTC market under regulatory control for the first time.[20] Among other measures, it included the following rules specifically applicable to the commodity derivatives sector:

i) Standardization of OTC swaps and clearing requirement for all financial entities with notional value of greater than $8bn as well as a margin requirement equivalent to 15 percent of position. Non-financial entities were exempt from central clearing requirement but required to notify positions.

ii) Requirements that all parties entering swaps obtain five quotes in advance for the swap in question (later reduced to two and eventually three by the CFTC).

iii) The "Volcker Rule" – i.e., a requirement for banks to spin off commodity swap activities and not engage in proprietary derivatives trading directly related to trading with customers.

iv) An extension of federal position limits to all exchange-traded commodity contracts and aggregation of individual positions on a commodity for position limit purposes (also including non-US exchanges).

v) A hedgers' exemption from position limits narrowed to entities with positions exclusively in cash-settled contracts.

vi) Setting of spot month position limits at 25 percent of estimated deliverable supply.

These changes entailed a significant strengthening of the CFTC in the United States, which has become the main implementing agency of new rules in this area. However, it also came under heavy attack from the financial sector.[21] Particularly on position limits and margin controls, this has had some success, with a US Court of Appeal for the Federal Circuit overturning these provisions for re-consideration by the CFTC due to a lack of evidence that market manipulation was behind price developments from 2004–2009 and the lack of cost-benefit analysis by the CFTC on position limits (and thus, inadequate concern for the impact of limits on market liquidity).[22] The CFTC voted to drop its appeal and would develop new rules.

---

[20] See Pub.L. 111–203, H.R. 4173 (2010).

[21] S. Pagliari and K. L. Young, "Leveraged Interests: Financial Industry Power and the Role of Private Sector Coalitions," *Review of International Political Economy*, 21(3) (2014), 575–610.

[22] *International Swaps and Derivatives Association, et al., Plaintiffs, v. United States Commodity Futures Trading Commission, Defendant* (D. Col., 11-cv-2146 (RLW), September 28, 2012.

The process of weakening legislation continued in several other areas over the past two years. In June 2013, the Federal Reserve allowed for wide-ranging exemptions to the "Lincoln Rule" (which prohibited federal assistance to swap entities), allowing for insured depository institutions to engage in swaps used to hedge or mitigate risk and allowed for a three-year transition period for non-exempted swap activities. In the immediate fallout of the crisis, large investment banks, including Goldman Sachs, JP Morgan Chase and Morgan Stanley, were turned into bank holding companies. Such banks were initially granted the right to continue owning physical trading infrastructure, with a review scheduled for 2013. This review was in part driven by concerns about market manipulation by Goldman Sachs and JP Morgan Chase and other major commodity trading houses. This also coincided with the adoption of the Volcker Rule in late 2013. At the start of 2014, the Chairman of the CFTC, Gary Gensler, was replaced temporarily by Mark Wetjen, and in turn by Timothy Massad, who was confirmed as Chairman in June 2014. This resulted in a more conciliatory approach toward the financial industry.[23]

The EU regulatory process has, on the whole, lagged behind that in the United States. The European Commission announced its intention to examine new initiatives in the area of financial market regulation in December 2008, working in close contact with other non-EU regulatory authorities.[24] In October 2009, the Commission broadly signaled that it would seek to follow the US regulatory approach, including by giving regulators "the possibility to set position limits to counter disproportionate price movements or concentrations of speculative positions."[25] The first proposal for the European Market Infrastructure Regulation (EMIR), following G-20 commitments, was submitted by the Commission in 2010. It included regulations on information reported on all OTC derivative transactions; standardized clearing through central counterparties; improved risk assessments (including margin rules) for non-standardized and non-cleared OTC derivatives exceeding the clearing threshold; common rules for CCPs and trade repositories; and an exemption for hedgers (also if only one side is a non-financial

---

[23] For a more detailed overview of these shifts, see E. Helleiner, "Positioning for Stronger Limits?" in E. Helleiner, S. Pagliari and I. Spagna (eds.), *Governing the World's Biggest Market* (Oxford: Oxford University Press, 2018), 199–225.

[24] Clapp and Helleiner, "Troubled Futures?"

[25] Commission of the European Communities, "Ensuring efficient, safe and sound derivatives markets: Future policy actions" COM(2009) 563.

counterparty). A compromise on EMIR between the Council of Ministers and the European Parliament, which had put forward 125 amendments, was not agreed until over one year later (October 2011) and it took almost a further year, until August 2012, for EMIR to be adopted, for entry into force in March 2013.

The Commission released its first proposals to revise the Markets in Financial Instruments Directive (MiFID) and the Markets in Financial Instruments Regulation (MiFIR) in October 2011, calling for the following key measures as part of the joint legislation MiFID II: i) the creation of new trading platforms (organized trading facilities, OTFs); ii) shifting standardized OTC derivative trading to regulated trading places; iii) real-time reporting by traders to trading platforms of all derivatives eligible for clearing and weekly public reports by trading platforms on positions of classes of traders; and iv) position limits or alternative equivalent measures. These were intended to consider developments in trading environments since the 2007 implementation of MiFID (such as advances in technology and gaps in transparency) as well as to respond to the events of the financial crisis. In March 2012, the European Parliament recommended changes to MiFID II, including by providing ESMA the ability to impose European position limits, a deletion of "alternative measures" for position limits, stronger regulation of high-frequency trading and reducing the hedging exemption for MiFID rules for commercial traders pursuing hedging activities. The vote in the EU's Economic and Monetary Affairs Committee (ECON) clarified that position limits should only apply to net positions and determined a minimum holding period for high-frequency trading.

In June 2013, the Council of Ministers agreed a position on MiFIR/MiFID II that provides member country discretion on the implementation of position limits and argued for competent authorities in each country themselves establishing and applying limits. The trialogue negotiations in September 2013 focused on whether real-time reporting would be required, the strength of trading obligations, whether OTC trade would be subject to position limits, and whether national or EU authorities would set position limits. These were concluded in January 2014, with the European Parliament approving MiFID II "Level 1" in April 2014 and for its implementation to begin in 2016.[26]

---

[26] MiFID II comprises two levels of European legislation. "Level 1" is the framework legislation comprised of two linked pieces of legislation: MiFID II and the Markets in Financial Instruments Regulation (MiFIR). There is provision in a wide range of areas for the framework legislation to be supplemented by implementing measures, so-called

In May 2014, ESMA published its first detailed consultation document, comprising 860 pages of rules for trading commodities and OTC derivatives, as well as addressing high-frequency trading and dark pools.[27] ESMA's Chairman, Steven Maijoor, called this "the biggest overhaul of financial markets regulation in the EU for a decade."[28] Central to EU regulations had been the development of the European Market Infrastructure Regulation (2011) as well as MiFID II, which was agreed by the Commission and heads of member state governments in January 2014. It also included provisions for position limits on commodity derivatives, and measures to increase transparency, particularly in the OTC market. In both the EU and the United States, stronger transparency requirements, regulations limiting the number of open positions that traders could hold, and restrictions on proprietary trading were passed. In both cases, regulatory agencies, CFTC and ESMA were authorized to draft technical specifications and implement regulations.

11.2.2 The Role of the Primary Regulatory Agencies: ESMA and CFTC

As discussed earlier, the analysis presented in this chapter examines the structure and governance of the two key regulatory agencies: the CFTC and ESMA.

Table 11.1 outlines some of the major differences. At the level of agency governance, CFTC commissioners are appointed by the president, while the Commission appoints the Chair and Executive Director of ESMA. These in turn must report biannually and seek approval from their Board of Supervisors. Their mandate is not entirely different from that of their CFTC counterparts, though ESMA has broader direct oversight responsibilities and must also concern itself with issues of supervisory convergence among member states. ESMA also is required to report to the European Parliament, the European Council and European Commission; for historic reasons the main oversight body for the CFTC is the Senate Agricultural Committee.

"Level 2 legislation," which takes two forms: 1. "delegated acts," which are drafted by the European Commission (EC) on the basis of advice by the European Securities and Markets Authority (ESMA), and 2. "technical standards," which are drafted by ESMA and approved by the EC.

[27] "Dark pools" are private exchanges for trading securities, derivatives and other financial products that are not accessible by the investing public.

[28] Philip Stafford, "European Exchanges Warn on Market Data Cost," *Financial Times*, July 4, 2014.

Table 11.1 *Understanding the Regulatory Agencies: the CFTC and ESMA*

	CFTC (founded in 1974)	ESMA (founded in 2011)
Governance structure	5 commissioners – all political appointees but not more than 3 from same party.	Chair and Executive Director appointed by Commission but 28-member Board of supervisors (heads of NCAs).
Mandate	Foster open, transparent, competitive, and financially sound markets, to avoid systemic risk, and to protect from fraud, manipulation, and abusive practices related to derivatives and other products (from 1974 Commodities Exchange Act).	Enhance investor protection, promote stable and orderly financial markets by assessing risks to investors, markets and financial stability, completing a single rulebook for EU financial markets, promoting supervisory convergence.
	Oversee exchanges, SEFs, CCPs, etc. and swap dealers (since Dodd-Frank).	Directly supervising credit rating agencies and trade repositories.
Legislative oversight body	Senate Agricultural Committee and House Committee on Agriculture	European Parliament Economic and Monetary Affairs Committee as well as to Council and Commission
Nature of legislative oversight	Periodic reauthorization and approval of budget requests.	Regular appearances in front of ECON; budget proposed by Commission and accepted by other institutions.
Overall budget and staff	$250 m. (FY 2015); $322 m. requested for FY16 – not self-funding	€39.4 m. (split through NCA and EU contributions as well as fees)
	690 FTE staff members (2015)	186 staff members (16 working on MiFID II)

Finally, in terms of budget and human resources available, the CFTC is far better equipped. Even the Finnish financial supervisory authority (*Finanssivalvonta*), which supervises an economy with a market capitalization that has fluctuated between $100 and $200 billion over the past decade (as opposed to over $5 trillion market capitalization for the entire EU), has more staff than ESMA; the UK's FCA has more than thirteen times more staff than ESMA. Budgetary cuts over the past years by the Commission have meant that ESMA has had to downscale investments in areas such as IT infrastructure.

However, it is important to point out that there are some substantial differences – both structural and strategic – that impact how these agencies have gone about regulating commodity derivatives (see Table 11.2). Firstly, during the legislative process, the CFTC could more actively articulate preferences and concerns early on, with former Chairman Gary Gensler being particularly vocal, while ESMA officials have largely been confined to a more passive role. ESMA officials could mention concerns informally to national authorities and these in turn would be passed on to the respective finance ministries to voice in Brussels, but they lacked the direct access to legislators that CFTC officials often had (in part purely due to the fact that ESMA is headquartered in Paris).

Secondly, CFTC Commissioners are largely able to speak their mind, do not need to present a united front, and are clearly identified from the outset by party affiliation. This allows them to influence legislation more directly even prior to the rule-making process. Thirdly, as enshrined in the Maroni Doctrine, which strongly limits the discretion of European agencies, if ESMA wants to make substantial changes to its technical standards, it needs to seek approval from its board of members and eventually the parliament and Commission.[29] The CFTC merely needs to agree internally among its commissioners and then issue no-action letters or directives.

Finally, the consultation process for commodity derivatives was somewhat different, though both agencies instituted various consultative groups. However, the CFTC could generally hold consultations and request input specifically on commodities regulations while in the case of ESMA this could only be solicited as part of either the entire EMIR or

---

[29] A confounding factor in this regard is also the fact that appointees come from different countries with different economic legal systems and regulatory cultures. This, as shown in Chapter 6, can become relevant in a supranational supervisory context like ESMA.

Table 11.2 *Agency Role in Implementation of Commodity Derivatives Regulation*

	CFTC	ESMA
Ability to influence legislative process	More formalized	Primarily informal
Political neutrality of leadership	Lower – political appointees	High – pure technocrats
Modifying and adapting rules	Relatively simple	Onerous and complex
Consultation processes on commodity derivatives	Less structured and more ad-hoc	Relatively structured with some informal consultation mechanisms

MiFID package. Section 11.3 will address how this played out for two specific issues: the development of the position limits regime, and the exemptions from the swap dealer/investment firm designations.

11.3 Conceptualizing the Politics of Commodity Derivatives Regulatory Reforms

11.3.1 *The Political Economy of Commodity Derivatives Regulation*

The increased "financialization" of commodity markets was part of a broader trend of securitization and capital market integration, in which the largely deregulated OTC commodity derivatives market played a particularly prominent role in the spectacular growth in bank balance sheets.[30] The instability of this system became vividly clear during the 2008 Global Financial Crisis. Derivative markets, Haldane and May argue, increased "the dimensionality and complexity of the network at a cost in terms of stability, with no welfare gain."[31] Bank balance sheets,

---

[30] See L. A. Stout, "Derivatives and the Legal Origin of the 2008 Credit Crisis," *Cornell Law Faculty Publications*, 720 (2011); D. Awrey, "FSA, Integrated Regulation, and the Curious Case of OTC Derivatives," *University of Pennsylvania Journal of Business Law*, 13(1) (2010) 1–58.

[31] Andrew G. Haldane and Robert M. May, "Systemic Risk in Banking Ecosystems," *Nature*, 469 (2011), 351–355 at 352.

in other words, had grown on an edifice of claims positions within the financial system itself, which was greatly facilitated by the proliferation of new financial instruments of questionable social value. Within the academic literature on the regulatory response to the financial crisis and development of new financial regulatory frameworks, the role of OTC derivatives reform has been a significant focus.

Despite their central importance in global finance, derivative markets had been one of the less studied areas of regulation in the social science literature prior to the crisis.[32] In part this was due to the fact that following regulatory reforms in the 1990s and 2000s, there was not a great deal of activity to analyze, given the very light-touch regulatory approaches taken both at national levels and through transnational bodies (such as the Basel Committee, as well as through IOSCO).[33] This changed significantly following the crisis, with a proliferation of scholarship aiming to understand regulatory outcomes, both in terms of pre-crisis under-regulation (and, arguably, regulatory capture) and post-crisis re-regulation.[34] Helleiner and Pagliari argue that the crisis dramatically revealed the enormous systemic and global consequences of international financial and macroprudential regulation and recent scholarship has focused on the limitations of current forms of financial regulation, and particularly the technical and financial risks inherent in existing regulatory institutions monitoring increasingly complex regimes.[35] This has led to the delegation of extensive authority to non-governmental bodies, whose incentives were frequently not aligned with those of the regulatory agencies or with what can be broadly defined as the "public interest" of financial stability.[36]

---

[32] Nonetheless, there are some notable exceptions here, including S. Strange, *Casino Capitalism* (Oxford: Basil Blackwell, 1986); E. Helleiner, *States and the Reemergence of Global Finance: From Bretton Woods to Global Finance* (Ithaca, NY: Cornell University Press, 1994).

[33] In the lead-up to the financial crisis there were a number of more substantial contributions on the international political economy of finance and financial standards; for an overview, see E. Helleiner and S. Pagliari, "The End of an Era in International Financial Regulation? A Postcrisis Research Agenda," *International Organization*, 65(1) (2011), 169–200.

[34] D. A. Singer, *Regulating Capital: Setting Standards for the International Financial System* (Ithaca NY: Cornell University Press, 2010); T. Büthe and W. Mattli, *The New Global Rulers: The Privatization Of Regulation In The World Economy* (Princeton NJ: Princeton University Press, 2011).

[35] See Helleiner and Pagliari, "End of an Era."

[36] A more recent contribution to this literature by Peter Knaack focuses in particular on the reasons behind the institutional arrangements to address the re-regulation of OTC derivatives: a minilateral approach restricting the number of participants to a few highly

Following the relative neglect of commodity derivatives in international political economy (IPE) scholarship, this has been taken up in recent years both in the literature looking at financial and food systems governance. In the case of the former, Helleiner argues that recent OTC derivatives market regulations were the product of three interconnected developments: i) ideational shifts among trans-governmental networks (particularly the G-20); ii) domestic political pressures within the United States and EU; and iii) the interest of officials in these jurisdictions in preventing interstate regulatory arbitrage and thus coordinating regulatory changes, which "demonstrates the case for integrative explanations of international financial regulatory change that focus on developments in transnational, interstate and domestic political contexts."[37]

Related work focuses in greater depth on the causes of this heightened public concern, emphasizing that in the case of the United States, the engagement by large agricultural interests in favor of stronger regulation effectively countered the active lobbying of the finance industry, which favored the status quo.[38] These actors "were able to boost their influence by allying with other domestic actors concerned about volatile energy prices and those concerned with consumer, social, and development issues."[39] This was, broadly speaking, indicative of a paradigm shift in the nature of the international financial standards regime toward "cooperative decentralization" characterized by "the uneven implementation across jurisdictions as well as the territorialization of new central nodes being cultivated by the standards."[40] This dynamic is particularly strong for commodity derivatives due to their post-crisis politicization, the increased diffusion of interstate power, and heightened political risk aversion.

---

involved stakeholders and a reliance on government networks did not lead to a more effective system of cross-border regulatory cooperation, resulting in a large gap between commitment and reality. He argues this was primarily due to a wariness by authorities of the distributional consequences of cross-border harmonization, obstacles created by legislators, and a pre-existent weak and fragmented domestic regulatory system in both the EU and the United States; P. Knaack, "Innovation and Deadlock in Global Financial Governance: Transatlantic Coordination Failure in OTC Derivatives Regulation," *Review of International Political Economy*, 22(6) (2015), 1217–1248.

[37] Helleiner, "Towards Cooperative Decentralization," 132.

[38] E. Helleiner, "Out from the Shadows: Governing Over-the-counter Derivatives after the 2007–8 Financial Crisis," in Best and Gheciu (eds.), *The Return of the Public in Global Governance* (Cambridge: Cambridge University Press, 2014).

[39] Clapp and Helleiner, "Troubled Futures?" 202.

[40] Helleiner, "Towards Cooperative Decentralization," 132.

On the outcomes of commodity derivatives regulation, there have thus far been two main debates. Firstly, on the causes of the reforms, there have been various analyses focusing on the issue of political salience and particularly on the role of civil society pressure, as well as the declining clout of the financial sector in stopping these measures. Others have pointed to the importance of corporate "end user" groups – agribusiness, airlines, and energy utility companies, among others – in agreeing to these new measures. Johannes Petry for example focuses in particular on the role of civil society groups.[41] Gibbon sees the outcome as a result of the diminishing clout of the financial sector.[42] Baines takes a similar stance, seeing the outcome as the result of effective lobbying by corporate derivative "end user" groups such as large agribusiness conglomerates and trading firms.[43]

Secondly, there has been a debate over how effective these measures would be in achieving the desired outcomes. For example, Clapp and Helleiner see it as an important step forward to rein in excess speculation.[44] However, others argue that new measures constitute regulatory overreach due to misunderstanding of how commodity markets operate[45] or as largely toothless reforms, likewise because regulators don't grasp the complexity of modern commodity markets.[46] Nonetheless, there is a widespread consensus that this question will only be answerable during the regulatory implementation – and eventually – enforcement stage. This means there is a likelihood, as Peter Gibbon argues, that "the main market participants have lost through the front door of regulation, only to regain advantage through the side doors of exemptions and arbitraging the rules of private exchanges."[47]

A central premise to the analysis in this chapter is that focusing on the processes itself may yield a more fruitful analysis than just looking at outcomes. This also follows Moschella and Tsingou's argument for the

---

[41] Petry, "Regulatory Capture."

[42] Gibbon, "Commodity Derivatives."

[43] J. Baines, "Accumulating through Food Crisis? Farmers, Commodity Traders and the Distributional Politics of Financialization," *Review of International Political Economy*, 24 (3) (2017), 1–41.

[44] Clapp and Helleiner, "Troubled Futures."

[45] Irwin and Sanders, "Index Funds."

[46] Chadwick, "Regulating Excessive Speculation."

[47] Gibbon, "Commodity Derivatives," 24. In a more recent contribution finalized in February 2017, Eric Helleiner takes a similar view, arguing that despite the large constituency for tighter regulation, outcomes have been characterized by "unexpected delays and inconsistencies." Helleiner, "Positioning for Stronger Limits," 220.

need to focus on the outcomes of regulation and the process of regulatory change.[48] The political economy of financial regulation remains a black box and the agency itself remains an even more opaque box within this. This justifies a focus on the politics of implementation, and more specifically the internal dynamics and capacity of the key regulatory agencies, as well as their interactions with legislators and interest groups. Nonetheless, there is only a limited literature focusing on the regulatory agency itself as an internally complex and often divided actor that has to decide which issues to prioritize and which battles to pick based on an internal plurality of views and opinions, that moreover change throughout economic and political cycles.

11.3.2   Theoretical Framework

It is hypothesized that the relatively far-reaching legislative success in reining in certain risky practices in the derivatives industry would be followed by efforts to undercut these, a dynamic described as the "regulatory sine curve" characterized by "equivocal implementation of the new legislation, tepid enforcement, and eventual legislative erosion" due to a change in the relative power balance in favor of vested interests favoring lax regulation.[49] Coffee's theory has two premises: firstly "regulatory intensity is never constant, but rather increases after a market crash, and then wanes as (and to the extent that) society and the market return to normalcy" and secondly "the public's passion for reform is short-lived and the support it gives to political entrepreneurs who seek to oppose powerful interest groups on behalf of the public also wanes after a brief window of opportunity."

The implementation of commodity derivatives regulation provides a relevant test of this. As such, this chapter addresses how the regulatory implementation dynamics in these processes differ from the respective legislative processes. One could hypothesize that in this more technical, complex and arguably less politicized environment, the returns to lobbying are higher and one might see more active or different forms of political engagement. Young argues that industry strategies in the

---

[48] Moscella and Tsingou, "Regulating Finance after the Crisis."

[49] Coffe, Jr., "Political Economy of Dodd-Frank," 1029. This contrasts with the view articulated most prominently by Roberta Romano that financial crises tend to result in hasty, ill-conceived legislation to channel public anger. See R. Romano, "The Sarbanes-Oxley Act and the Making of Quack Corporate Governance," *Yale L.J.* 114 (2004), 1521–1612.

financial sector differ substantially during the legislative and implementation phases.[50]

With reference to the above, this chapter sees two independent variables as central to determining outcomes during the rule-making process: the breadth and intensity of opposition from interest groups, and the internal level of agreement within the agency itself (Figure 11.2). In cases of both limited opposition and internal agreement within the agency, technical rules will largely follow the intent of the legislation. At the opposite extreme, if there is strong external opposition and internal disagreement within the agency, rules will be modified as much as possible within the legal constraints. Finally, if there is only internal or external opposition, the emergence of a few quite substantial revisions through new exemptions, carve-outs or changes to thresholds is most likely.

While there are a lot of similarities between the two regulatory regimes, some important differences remain – starting with the fact that regulations relevant to commodity derivatives are encompassed in six different EU directives, while rules on commodity derivatives are mostly contained in Title VII of Dodd-Frank (see Table 11.3). Some of the core differences of interest relate particularly to the development of the position limits regime by each agency as well as the legal definition of what in the United States is called a "swap dealer" and in the EU has the

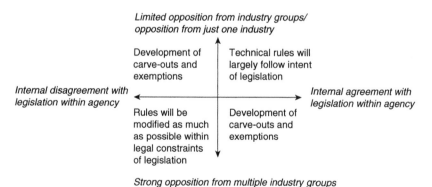

Figure 11.2 Theoretical Framework

[50] K. Young, "Financial Industry Groups' Adaptation to the Post-crisis Regulatory Environment: Changing Approaches to the Policy Cycle," *Regulation & Governance*, 7 (4) (2013), 460–480. See also Chapter 5 in this volume.

Table 11.3 *Select Comparison of EU and US Legislative Outcomes for Commodity Derivatives*

Issue area	EU (EMIR, MiFID II /MiFIR Level 1, MAR/ CSMAD, REMIT, AIFMD)	US (Dodd-Frank Wall Street Reform and Consumer Protection Act, Title VII)
Prior legislation	No EU legislation – national laws or regulations specific to commodity exchanges.	Commodities Exchange Act (1936) and CFMA (2000).
Clearing obligation	Still being developed but generally applies to all OTC contracts among financial parties and non-financial parties beyond clearing thresholds.	All standardized swaps must be cleared through CCPs, including for end users engaging in speculative swap trading for all counterparties.
Exemptions from clearing	Bona-fide hedging by NFCs; non-hedging contracts by non-financial parties' intra-group transactions; pension funds (3 years).	End-users hedging commercial risks; affiliated entities transacting with each other; some intra-group transactions.
Swap dealer definition/ MiFID investment firm	Entities dealing more than $3bn per year ($8bn until 2018).	Investment firm designation applies for all financial counterparties in OTC derivatives with some exceptions.
Position limits	Introduced in MiFID 2 to be set by NCAs based on ESMA methodology. Exemptions for non-financial entities bona fide hedging position. Very broad.	Applied to 28 commodities (strengthened from pre-crisis) and to be set by CFTC or all exchanges and set at 25% of deliverable supply – exemptions for bona fide hedging from commercial risk.

Table 11.3 (*cont.*)

Issue area	EU (EMIR, MiFID II /MiFIR Level 1, MAR/ CSMAD, REMIT, AIFMD)	US (Dodd-Frank Wall Street Reform and Consumer Protection Act, Title VII)
Position limit objectives	Prevent market abuse; support orderly pricing and settlement conditions and price convergence between spot and derivatives prices.	Prevent excessive speculation; deter/ prevent market manipulation; ensure sufficient liquidity for hedgers; ensure undisrupted price discovery process.
Proprietary trading	In progress. No direct equivalent to push-out rule but regulated through capital requirements.	Banks prohibited from proprietary trading in comm. derivatives; swap activities pushed out; trading in physical commodities allowed but eventually banned.

designation of "investment firm," and more specifically how this would apply to non-financial firms that have large-scale swap dealing operations. These two differences provide the empirical focus of the remainder of this chapter.

Methodologically, I am focusing on two aspects central to the re-regulation of commodity markets through both an across-case and within-case comparison. This is based on twenty-two interviews with industry and civil society representatives and current and former regulators in both jurisdictions, as well as a review of consultation documents. There are some limitations to this framework, including that as of late 2017, these processes are still ongoing, and – more importantly – these agencies remain largely opaque, black boxes for a reason: Interviews were incapable of shedding light on the backstage dynamics of implementation in Paris and Washington, which remain elusive. Also, as demonstrated in section 11.2.2, these two agencies do not represent a completely like-with-like comparison: they have different governance structures, degrees of autonomy, and relationships to legislative bodies. Finally, one should not necessarily treat these processes as exogenous to each other; they have not taken place simultaneously and regulatory outcomes on one side of the Atlantic inevitably influence those on the other. These issues are significant, but as argued in the remainder of this chapter, less so than one might assume.

11.4   The Implementation of Post-Crisis Commodity Derivatives Regulations

11.4.1   The Battle Over Position Limits

Speculative position limits are defined in the 1936 Commodities Exchange Act as the maximum number of contracts that can be entered into by a non-hedger in a given time period,[51] and their rationale is to proactively prevent speculators from gaining power to exert undue influence on markets in order to ensure efficiency and authenticity of price movements. Exchanges generally set position limits in an ad hoc manner and based on underlying fundamentals specific to the commodity.[52] Position limits can be set both at the individual level (for one trader) and in aggregate (across one class of traders). Position limits do not, however, apply to market actors who use commodity derivatives to hedge against commodity price risks (or other risks related to commodity trading) if this is not more than what a producer can deliver or what an intermediate or end-user can consume.

Position limits were a central part of efforts to regulate the derivatives market and were integral to regulatory efforts at the international level, as well as in the two primary trading jurisdictions where over 90 percent of all derivatives are traded – the EU and the United States. The Dodd-Frank Act applied position limits to twenty-eight derivatives for commodities ranging from oil to frozen concentrated orange juice (both OTC and exchange-traded), including both individual and aggregate limits for classes of traders.[53] Limits were extended to all exchange-traded commodity contracts and aggregation of individual positions would occur across all exchanges and trading venues (including swap venues and non-US exchanges). Spot month position limits were set at 25 percent of estimated deliverable supplies.[54]

---

[51] Ch. 545, 49 Stat. 1491, enacted June 15, 1936.

[52] Gibbon, "Commodity Derivatives."

[53] See Pub.L. 111–203, H.R. 4173 (2010).

[54] In drawing up its rules on position limits, the CFTC has made proposals that have fallen short of the strictest interpretation of Dodd-Frank, for example in defining "deliverable

EU rules have traditionally not relied on position limits, but following international pressure and the rules in Dodd-Frank, have now included such regulations. EU rules in EMIR and MiFID II do not explicitly include both individual and aggregate limits, with concern by some that the absence of the latter would not curb speculation. The EU legislation in MiFID II on position limits requires market participants to declare their positions at least daily. They further defer to national authorities to limit the size of net positions traders can hold (with some exemptions for oil and coal trading), resulting in risks that this may lead to competition among member states to weaken rules and open the door for regulatory arbitrage.[55]

While position limits are just one of several regulatory tools to restrict market abuse and excessive speculation, and to prevent the risk of cornering certain commodities or manipulating prices, they have become the most prominent and contentious. There are at least three primary critiques in the literature and in ongoing policy debates about the outcomes of position limits. One argues that they are economically inefficient and self-defeating. Another takes almost the opposite view and focuses on the inadequacy of the actual policy outcomes currently set out in EU and US regulations to achieve their desired end. A third focuses on the hedging exemption and argues that this has been misapplied and is outdated, given the reality of how modern commodity markets function.[56]

---

supply," and relied on "netting" in calculating traders' position, rather than aggregation, i. e. using net long or short positions rather than the sum of fall long and short positions. See Gibbon, "Commodity Derivatives."

[55] Specifically, position limits will have to be objectively justifiable and to take into account the liquidity of a specific market. However, this allows for limits to be set in variance to ESMA criteria in "exceptional cases." See Gibbon, "Commodity Derivatives."

[56] More specifically, the first critique focuses on the liquidity-reducing and market-distorting effect of position limits, and is largely rooted in variants of the efficient market hypothesis and/or a general distrust against regulatory overreach. For example, Easterbrook and Fischel and Ross argue that exchanges have sufficient incentives to take precaution themselves. See F. H. Easterbrook, "Monopoly, Manipulation, and the Regulation of Futures Markets," *Journal of Business*, 59(2) (1986) S103–S127; D. R. Fischel and D. J. Ross, "Should the Law Prohibit 'Manipulation' in Financial Markets?," *Harvard Law Review*, 105(2) (1991), 503–553. This has been challenged by Pirrong, who has argued that the effects of manipulation on infra-marginal traders are likely to be ignored, and more significantly, that price informativeness and competition between exchanges may be limited in practice with collective action problems precluding interventions. See C. Pirrong, "The Self-regulation of Commodity Exchanges: The Case of Market Manipulation," *The Journal of Law and Economics*, 38(1) (1995), 141–206. Other studies argue that position limits reduce liquidity, increase execution costs and impact price volatility, moving business to OTC markets (this is also the argument made by the

Some of the key differences in the implementation process are captured in Table 11.4. For one, in terms of the main issues at stake, in the United States, use of position limits as a tool to curb speculation and address market manipulation was openly questioned, while this was a largely settled matter in the EU. In Europe, the key issues were more nuanced and related to the number of contracts for which position limits would have to be set and where they should be set. In terms of the engagement by interest groups, in the United States there was intense lobbying against the regime by the financial industry and large agribusiness and energy conglomerates. It was moreover successfully challenged at the level of the US district court by the International Swaps and Derivatives Association (ISDA), forcing a comprehensive revision by the CFTC. In turn, the CFTC brought forth new regulations that would exempt large traders and carve out a few new exemptions for different divisions of the same company to bundle commodities positions under the new rule.[57] In the EU, there was opposition by individual member states and national authorities (especially the UK), as well as exchanges, but no concerted effort to challenge a position limit regime as such.

---

opponents of the CFTC rules in the recent lawsuit). See R. ap Gwilym and M. S. Ebrahim, "Can Position Limits Restrain 'rogue' Trading?," *Journal of Banking & Finance,* 7(3) (2013), 824–836. The second critique focuses on the inadequacy of current position limit regulations in effectively limiting excess speculation, i.e., that they do not do enough. This view, espoused by Gibbon, argues that current limits should be set lower and need to be broader (i.e. set uniformly and covering all markets, aggregating across classes of actors and excluding hedging exceptions). See Gibbon, "Commodity Derivatives." A final critique relates to the hedging exemption from position limits and to the increasingly blurred boundaries between physical and financial commodity trading (and actors engaging in these). Position limits currently distinguish between "speculators" (defined by the CFTC as "a trader who does not hedge" and a hedger – end users or intermediate users employing futures to protect themselves against adverse price developments. The border between these two classes of market actors – which the current CFTC classifications of traders aims to differentiate between – may be inadequate given current realities and regulatory agencies, most notably the CFTC – is now attempting to decide how to best address this gap. See G. Mayer, "US Commodities Regulator Wrestles Hedgers and Speculators," *Financial Times,* June 20, 2014. As a recent report by the FCA argues, "[t]rading companies will not be entirely unaffected due to the cross-border impact of, for example, Dodd Frank and EMIR, as well as the regulatory changes affecting the commodity derivatives markets in which the trading firms operate. But the regulatory reform measures will not fall evenly on [all] types of market participants, which is likely to accelerate the current trends in changes to market structure." See FCA, "Commodity Markets Update," 7.

[57] G. Chon and G. Meyer, "CFTC in Fresh Bid to Impose Position Limits," *Financial Times,* November 5, 2013.

Table 11.4 Regulatory Issues Pertaining to Position Limits in the EU and United States

Jurisdiction	Main issues	Interest group opposition	Internal dynamics within agency	Outcome (as of early 2017)
US	Validity of position limits as means to curb excess speculation and address market manipulation.	Intense lobbying against regime by financial industry and large agribusiness/energy firms.	Heavily contested, including among some Commissioners and among agency economists.	Substantial carve-outs for corporate end-users (definition as hedgers).
		Successful challenge at US district court forces CFTC revision.		Substantial delegation to exchanges.
		Senate tied reauthorization to hedging exemptions for agribusiness.		
EU	Number of contracts for which position limits will have to be set (potentially up to 30,000 vs. 28 in US).	Individual member states and national authorities, exchanges and civil society organizations.	Effort to accommodate interests by reducing number of contracts and facilitating implementation.	Reduction in number of contracts that NCAs must set limits for.
	Where to set limits in relation to total deliverable supply.	No effort to challenge position limit regime as such.	Concern about administrative burden involved in process.	Large scope for discretion (limits set at 25% ±15%).

Furthermore, this was a priority for campaigning groups and civil society organizations.

In terms of the intra-agency dynamics, the issue was heavily contested within the CFTC, including among some commissioners and among agency economists. A former high-level CFTC official (interviewed in May 2015) claimed: "We found that there really wasn't a very good argument to be made that speculation caused the problem. So, Chairman Gensler came in, ... [and said] that didn't matter to him at all. He was convinced that speculation did matter ... no amount of arguing is going to convince him otherwise. At ESMA, the main concerns revolved around the administrative burden of setting and monitoring limits for a potentially enormous number of contracts.

These procedural differences at the regulatory level resulted in different outcomes: in the United States, substantial carve-outs for corporate end-users were decided and decision-making around the setting and enforcement of limits was delegated to exchanges resulting effectively in self-regulation. At ESMA, there was primarily a focus on reducing the number of contracts that national authorities are required to set limits for, while providing a substantial discretionary scope: limits would be set at 25 percent, ±15 percent of deliverable supply, depending on the liquidity of markets for specific commodities. One ESMA official working on MiFID II (interviewed in May 2016) claimed: "for ESMA what's important is that this is feasible. The EU scope [of the EU position limits regime is vast and] presents a major drain on our resources. We need to find solutions to make this manageable. ... Our approach is focusing on those contracts that are important and really matter. But if we have thousands of opinions you have to be cautious."

11.4.2   Setting Exemption Thresholds and Defining Hedging and Speculation

A central – and previously underestimated – layer of complexity in regulating the commodity derivatives market arises from the increasingly blurred lines between physical and financial commodity markets and the actors that engage in these. Most notable in this regard has been the growth of commodity trading houses (CTHs), which have grown substantially in size in the past decades.[58] The aforementioned FCA report argues

---

[58] According to a 2011 Reuters investigation, the top five commodity firms grossed almost as much in revenues in the previous year (2010) as the top five financial companies and

that while "[t]here have always been ebbs and flows in the prominence of differing segments of market participants … currently, the trend is toward a decline in the activity of the banks and a rise in the role played by commodity trading companies."[59] This has been central to recent studies on CTHs.[60] The limited regulatory oversight (in part due to their private ownership structure and the lax oversight of Switzerland and Singapore, where many CTHs are headquartered), contrasts markedly to the recent regulatory activity and increased oversight for the financial sector.[61] Trading houses at this stage now operate their own trading desks and are headquartered in countries that provide fiscal advantages or synergies with asset holding, most notably Switzerland.

They are likely to only grow in significance as trading houses both become increasingly involved in financial commodity markets and begin to integrate the physical trading operations of banks, which are exiting the sector following lower profit margins and increasing regulatory pressures. CTHs are gradually acquiring commodity trading personnel from banks and are relatively unconstrained by recent regulations. However, trading houses are beginning to act increasingly like large investors and banks in financial commodity markets, although far less constrained in their behavior – even under the new regulatory regimes – as they have argued that they engage in hedging, rather than specula-tion.[62] A central issue pertinent to these firms therefore relates to whether they are in fact hedging against risks and not purely betting on the market, and thus, whether the hedging exemption is justified – a distinc-tion that is often more one of semantics. Trading houses, which have complex derivatives operations, have lobbied extensively to ensure they do not lose exemptions that would cap their positions.[63] These firms have argued that their derivatives activity is a bona fide hedge against risks in physical markets and that they should not be subject to position limits

---

more than the leading telecoms firms. See J. Schneyer, "Commodity Traders: The Trillion Dollar Club," *Reuters*, October 28, 2011.

[59] FCA, "Commodity Markets Update," 6.

[60] See S. Murphy, D. Burch and J. "Clapp, Cereal Secrets: The World's Largest Grain Traders and Global Agriculture," *Oxfam Research Reports* (2012); C. Pirrong, "Risk Management by Commodity Trading Firms: The Case of Trafigura," *Journal of Applied Corporate Finance*, 27(1) (2015), 19–26.

[61] N. Hume and X. Rice, "Trading Houses in Line for Increased Regulator Scrutiny," *Financial Times*, February 26, 2014.

[62] See Mayer, "Commodity Regulator."

[63] P. Gibbon, "Trading Houses during and since the Great Commodity Boom: Financialization, Productivization or … ?" (2014) 12 DIIS Working Paper.

due to their end-user status or be required to clear their transactions. This emphasizes the complexity of how hedging is defined in CFTC rules.

Thus, the departure of banks from physical commodities may not address systemic risk concerns, but rather could "mean the dominant market participants will be low-profile companies far less sensitive to public criticism."[64] This is also central to the FCA, which sees these firms as "known unknowns" that are attracting increased attention as they are able to leverage less stringent capital requirements and operate without enforced restrictions and disclosure requirements that afflict banks.[65] It is particularly the absence of this uncertainty that concerns regulators – currently there is only very limited information on their activities – whether in aggregate form or on a confidence basis to regulators. Thus, a Centre for European Policy Studies report, for example, argues that "coordination at international level among public authorities might be needed to share and reconcile information about physical holdings of these companies."[66] However, progress on disclosure remains slow, with the Swiss government indicating that in light of mounting criticism, it would be willing to force CTHs to clarify disclosure requirements of payments to foreign governments if this was required by other jurisdictions.[67]

In examining the main regulatory issues pertaining to the hedging exemption it is noticeable that outcomes also differed significantly in the EU and the United States (Table 11.5). In the former, exemptions would be provided under MiFID II for investment firms dealing on their own account or to customers as ancillary activity (to be defined further by ESMA). In the United States, the (broadly equivalent) swap dealer designation would apply to any firm dealing more than $8 billion per year of swaps ($3 billion after 2018). In the EU, this ruling faced intense opposition by utilities, energy and agribusiness firms, with particularly the latter threatening regulatory arbitrage and moving their headquarters out of Europe and to Asia.[68]

---

[64] Trading houses have lobbied extensively to ensure they are not restricted in their activities despite recent CFTC interest in their activities.

[65] FCA, "Commodity Markets Update," p. 8.

[66] D. Valiante, *Price Formation in Commodities Markets. Financialisation and Beyond* (Brussels: CEPS, 2013), 16.

[67] A. Hofman, "Swiss Won't Force Commodity Traders to Join Transparency Drive," *Bloomberg*, October 23, 2015.

[68] According to the CFO of a large oil trading firm (interviewed in May 2015), "if as European traders we are submitted to tough regulation but you have traders outside of Europe that manage to circumvent this regulation … then there won't be any level playing field anymore so in that case, the temptation could be significant to get out of Europe."

Table 11.5 *Key regulatory issues pertaining to hedging exemptions in the EU and US*

Jurisdiction	Main issues	Interest group opposition	Internal dynamics within agency	Outcome (as of early 2017)
US	Swap dealer designation – anyone dealing more than $8 bn per year of swaps ($3 bn after 2018). Entails increased oversight, recordkeeping and disclosure requirements.	Some opposition from large agribusiness and energy firms, but most affected firms have registered as swap dealers. Limited congressional interference.	Limited controversy. Hedging definition has long tradition and is largely accepted.	Large firms (BP, Shell, Cargill) almost immediately registered as swap dealers. CFTC has sought to accommodate smaller firms.
EU	Exemption as investment firm under MiFID II for firms dealing on own account or to customers as ancillary activity (to be defined further by ESMA).	Intense lobbying by utilities, energy and agribusiness firms – threats of moving headquarters to Asia. Rejection of draft technical standards by ECON and the Commission.	Development of new accounting rules to accommodate industry and European Parliament concerns.	Provisions repeatedly sent back and subject to continued revision.

This in part contributed to a rejection of ESMA's draft technical standards by the ECON committee and the Commission. In the United States, there was some opposition from large agribusiness and energy firms, but most affected firms had registered as swap dealers. There was moreover very limited congressional interference. Within the respective agencies, there was also very little controversy: the hedging definition had a long tradition and was largely accepted among stakeholders. In the case of ESMA, this required the development of new accounting rules to accommodate industry and European Parliament concerns,[69] while in the United States large firms exceeding the threshold (such as BP, Shell, or Cargill) did not have significant problems complying with the new regulations and almost immediately registered as swap dealers. In turn, the CFTC has sought to accommodate smaller firms – including by only slowly lowering the swap dealer threshold from $8 billion initially to $3 billion in 2018.

11.5   Conclusion: the Role of Agency within Regulatory Agencies

This chapter has traced the post-crisis processes of regulatory reform of EU and US commodity derivative markets, focusing on the "long tail" of regulatory implementation and technical rule-making by ESMA and the CFTC. It has aimed to address both why this relatively minor area of financial market regulation has attracted so much attention and consumed so much of regulators' time, and secondly, why in two central areas of regulation, different outcomes have emerged in the EU and the United States. The chapter focuses on two aspects of the regulatory framework – the development of position limits regimes and the setting of hedging exemptions – and argues that two variables have been central to determining outcomes during the technical rule-making process: i) the breadth and intensity of opposition from interest groups, and ii) the internal level of agreement within the agency itself.

Based on the analysis above, and returning to the framework developed in section 11.3, these cases provide support for each of the four potential regulatory outcomes (Figure 11.3). In the United States, rules on position limits emerged despite strongly divergent views on the

---

[69] According to one ESMA official (interviewed in May 2016), "A lot of lobbying is going on by very powerful organisations. ... On ancillary activities everyone is saying we need to find exact data to make these calculations. We are trying to construct something out of existing data from trade repositories. ... But in the end, we wish we had more influence on Level 1."

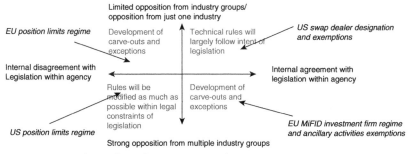

Figure 11.3 Analysis of Regulatory Outcomes by Late 2017

legislation within the respective agency. Thus, the rules governing this area of regulation were modified as much as possible within the legal constraints provided by Dodd-Frank. However, in the EU there was comparatively little external opposition to the imposition of a position limits regime as such. In turn, the objective of regulators was to develop carve-outs and exemptions that would simplify the regime and make it less onerous on businesses, while still ensuring that monitoring was not delegated to exchanges.

In the case of setting the definitions for hedging via the swap dealer and investment firm designation, on the other hand, the outcomes were reversed: in the United States, there was little disagreement with the legislation within the CFTC and limited opposition from industry groups, as few non-financial firms met the swap dealer definition, and those that did, did not see the additional compliance costs as too onerous. This resulted in technical rules that were broadly in line with the legislation. On the other hand, in the case of the EU's investment firm regime, within ESMA the need for these rules was broadly understood. However, given the strong opposition from multiple industry groups, extensive efforts were made to develop carve-outs and exemptions for large industries.

In this context, the chapter has aimed to make several contributions. It has applied simplified framework that aims to incorporate internal dynamics of regulatory agencies into an institutional interest group-based hybrid explanation of divergent regulatory outcomes. It moreover has aimed to complicate existing narratives about post-crisis commodity derivatives regulation: who benefits most from outcomes varies by jurisdiction and issue area. Furthermore, outcomes are highly dynamic and subject to substantial changes throughout the rule-making process and beyond. Finally, it has attempted to demonstrate, based on the example of ESMA and the CFTC, that financial regulatory agencies are not monolithic entities and over time undergo substantial shifts in key personnel and institutional outlook.

In addressing the first research question – why these rules have taken so long to develop – it is useful to return to the governance of these agencies. They are accountable to different institutions and have both engaged in extensive consultation processes. Given the complexity of some of these issues, many of the most technical details were often neglected during the legislative process and left for regulators to determine. In this case, the internal capacity of the agencies becomes a significant constraining factor. Finally, it is important to consider the evolution of commodity markets during the time period under investigation. This was marked by a retreat of investment banks and the emergence of more "physical" actors, such as commodity trading houses. This has in turn influenced the evolution of core interest groups aiming to influence regulators. And finally, it is important to bear in mind that this remains a moving target: almost a decade after the Pittsburgh G-20 summit, final texts have not been decided and consultations, lobbying, and agency efforts to gain approval for final rules from legislative oversight bodies continues.

12

The Political Economy of Cross-Border Banking Regulation in Emerging Europe, 2004–2010

IVAYLO IAYDJIEV[1]

Who governs cross-border banking? This question has received extensive attention, but a relative blind spot remains when it comes to the specific challenges of countries with financial systems dominated by foreign banks in Eastern Europe, Latin America, and sub-Saharan Africa. Host regulators find themselves with a de facto lack of control over their financial systems, while being at the same time largely shut out from key international decision-making fora.

The main contribution of this chapter is to further develop the notion of Pistor's "host's dilemma" by focusing on the role of international institutions in addressing the specific challenges that host states face.

The empirical focus is on emerging Europe, where in the 2004–2007 period cooperation in the governance of cross-border banking was rare, with host countries bearing the costs of adjustment. Yet, once the external shock of the global financial crisis hit the region, there was extensive cooperation between all actors in the crisis response, facilitated by the informal Vienna Initiative.

This demonstrates that international institutions could be an effective solution to the host's dilemma – at the cost of accepting reduced sovereignty. Host states should therefore focus on ensuring adequate representation in the governance of relevant international bodies, and the institutions themselves need to be responsive to such demands.

[1] The author would like to thank the participants in the Political Economy of Financial Regulation conference held at CUHK Faculty of Law, Hong Kong (June 2–4, 2016), and in particular Emilios Avgouleas, for their useful comments and suggestions, and gratefully acknowledges financial support for travel expenses received from the organizers. The author also thanks Ngaire Woods and an anonymous reviewer for comments on an earlier draft presented to the Global Economic Governance Programme, University of Oxford.

12.1 Introduction

In the 1990s and the early 2000s the world saw a dramatic expansion of financial integration, driven by ever-increasing international capital flows. An important part of this trend was a series of bank-sector openings to foreign investment in emerging Europe, Latin America, and sub-Saharan Africa. From being virtually non-existent, foreign banks came to dominate the banking systems of most countries in these regions. Today, foreign banks own more than 50 percent of all banking assets in fifty-two countries, and in seventeen countries that level exceeds 90 percent.[2] Economists widely welcomed these developments, as the efficiency benefits foreign banks brought were seen to largely exceed potential costs in terms of financial stability or access.[3] However, the Global Financial Crisis of 2008–2009 demonstrated that global banks, poorly supervised by their home authorities, could also be a significant source of financial contagion.

Given the Janus-faced nature of banking integration, how can host countries on the receiving end of cross-border flows harness its benefits while minimizing the risks? Economic theory suggests that banking integration carries the promise of catching-up and convergence with advanced countries. This occurs most visibly through the transfer of capital from countries with already high savings, to capital-poor host countries; thus, the population in the home countries gets a higher return on its investments, while entrepreneurs in the host country get improved access to capital. In addition, it also brings collateral benefits such as improvements in technology and governance, and serves as a sign of approval for local banking systems.[4]

However, while relinquishing de facto control over their financial systems in the pursuit of financial integration, host states have had to also accept a regulatory agenda set overwhelmingly by countries, which are home to cross-border banking groups. This situation in which a host country has effectively relinquished de facto control over its financial systems, while relying on international institutions from which they are excluded to ensure

---

[2] S. Claessens and N. van Horen, *The Impact of the Global Financial Crisis on Banking Globalization* (Washington DC: IMF, 2014).

[3] R. Cull and M. S. Martinez Peria, *Foreign Bank Participation in Developing Countries: What Do We Know about the Drivers and Consequences of This Phenomenon?* (Washington DC: World Bank, 2010).

[4] D. Gros, *Who Needs Foreign Banks?* (Brussels: CESifo Working Paper No. 998, 2003); A. Kose, E. Prasad, K. Rogoff and S.-J. Wei, *Financial Globalization: A Reappraisal* (Washington, D.C.: IMF, 2009).

cooperation, can be described, following Pistor, as "host's dilemma."[5] The goal of this chapter is to investigate the extent to which international institutions can offer a way out of this dilemma for countries with systems dominated by foreign banks.[6] This necessarily entails a further loss of sovereignty for host jurisdictions. However, effective governance and representation can mitigate such costs and provide a solution.

The governance regime for cross-border banking has been developed in forums such as the Basel Committee on Banking Supervision (BCBS), from which host countries are largely excluded (see Figure 12.1). In the years before the crisis only three BCBS countries had levels of foreign ownership of local bank assets higher than 10 percent (Belgium, Germany, and the United States), and none were higher than 20 percent – in sharp contrast with levels of 70–80 percent not uncommon for host countries.[7] The situation has not changed much since the crisis, despite the much-advertised increase in BCBS membership – only one out of the twenty-seven members is predominantly a host country (Mexico).[8] Host countries, which have often given up control domestically, have thus been asked to rely on cooperative solutions by fora in which they have little voice.

This dilemma is particularly acute in emerging Europe,[9] where at the time of writing foreign banks clearly dominate credit allocation in all but one country (see table 12.1).[10] Yet, in their negotiations with the EU, countries in the region relinquished the use of their prudential carve-outs under the GATS in order to adopt in full the EU *acquis communautaire* required for membership. They thus adopted rules which were largely shaped before their accession to the EU in 2004[11] and which "hardened"

---

[5] K. Pistor, *Host's Dilemma: Rethinking EU Banking Regulation in Light of the Global Crisis* (New York: European Corporate Governance Institute, Columbia University Law School, 2010).

[6] This scope means both hosts with relatively low levels of foreign bank ownership and home regulators are excluded from the following discussion, since they are either less dependent on the decisions of foreign banks, or have a different set of tools at their disposal to address eventual problems.

[7] Claessens and van Horen, "The Impact of the Global Financial Crisis."

[8] The other countries with foreign ownership of bank assets exceeding even the low bar of 25 percent are either offshore centers (Luxembourg, Hong Kong) or saw a one-off spike due to events during the financial crisis (Belgium).

[9] For the purpose of this chapter, emerging Europe denotes the ten countries that joined the EU in 2004 and 2007. While a priori applicable to non-EU member countries, this analysis does not explicitly address their situation as they have recourse for tools such as capital controls that are prohibited under the EU legal framework. Croatia for example made use of similar tools in the run-up to its accession, to mitigate the credit cycle.

[10] Claessens and van Horen, "The Impact of the Global Financial Crisis."

[11] The only exceptions are Bulgaria and Romania, which joined the EU in 2007.

Table 12.1 *Foreign Bank Assets in Emerging Europe, % of Total Banking Assets, 2004–2010*

Country	2004	2005	2006	2007	2008	2009	2010
Bulgaria	72	76	77	79	82	82	79
Czech Republic	84	83	84	85	84	83	83
Estonia	95	100	99	99	99	99	99
Hungary	65	67	65	64	67	64	63
Latvia	51	57	63	65	66	67	66
Lithuania	91	92	92	92	93	92	90
Poland	72	76	77	76	78	75	73
Romania	54	58	89	89	89	85	85
Slovak Republic	95	91	90	89	90	85	86
Slovenia	21	25	24	24	26	25	24

Source: World Bank Global Financial Development database; Claessens and van Horen, "The Impact of the Global Financial Crisis."

the soft law prescriptions of the BCBS, in which none of the countries from the region are represented.[12] Emerging Europe, therefore, represents an interesting case to examine in more details the implications of the host's dilemma for receiving states between joining the EU in 2004 and the global financial crisis of 2008. During this period host regulators struggled to restrain a credit boom, which led to increasing vulnerabilities. Equally intriguing, however, is how the dilemma was overcome in 2008–2009 through successful crisis management led by the international financial institutions and comprising multiple stakeholders, including home regulators, host authorities, and the private sector.

This question builds on and extends existing international and comparative political economy research on the politics of foreign banking, which has so far paid somewhat limited attention to specific circumstances and challenges of host countries. A first set of studies analyzed the reasons for bank-sector openings in various regions and the respective influence of structural changes, financial crises, and international institutions.[13] While

---

[12] L. Quaglia, *Governing Financial Services in the European Union: Banking, Securities and Post-Trading* (Abingdon: Routledge, 2010).

[13] L. W. Pauly, *Opening Financial Markets: Banking Politics on the Pacific Rim* (Cornell University Press, 1988); R. A. Epstein, *In Pursuit of Liberalism: International Institutions in Postcommunist Europe* (Baltimore MD: Johns Hopkins University Press, 2008);

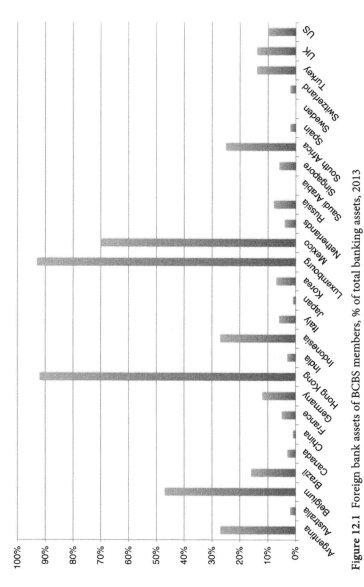

Figure 12.1 Foreign bank assets of BCBS members, % of total banking assets, 2013
Source: Claessens and van Horen, "The Impact of the Global Financial Crisis' and BCBS.

those studies focused on explaining the rise of foreign banking in particular contexts, the goal of this chapter is to analyze the politics of cross-border banking after the liberalization of bank-sector investment. A second and growing line of enquiry has examined who makes the rules in international standard-setting bodies, thus focusing on great power regulatory politics.[14] As it seeks to explain interactions among regulators with significant power and high institutional access, it often presents the exact opposite of the "host's dilemma." Another set of literature seeks to explain the politics of institutional change in global financial governance, again focusing by definition on countries with access to international fora.[15] Finally, some study developing countries with limited institutional access and their resistance to regulatory harmonization, but they tend to examine countries with low levels of foreign bank ownership.[16]

This chapter aims to develop analytically the notion of the "host's dilemma" of countries where foreign banks dominated the financial system, to demonstrate empirically its existence and relevance, and to explore the conditions under which host countries can have their interests meaningfully represented in international institutions. It first differentiates the "host's dilemma" in opposition to the dominant view of the "regulator's dilemma" in the literature on international political economy,[17] traces its different functional demands and considers the problems that arise because of asymmetrical interdependence. It then

---

L. Martinez-Diaz, *Globalizing in Hard Times: The Politics of Banking-sector Opening in the Emerging World* (Ithaca NY: Cornell University Press, 2009).

[14] D. Drezner, *All Politics Is Global: Explaining International Regulatory Regimes* (Princeton NJ: Princeton University Press, 2007); T. Büthe, and W. Mattli, *The New Global Rulers: The Privatization of Regulation in the World Economy* (Princeton NJ: Princeton University Press, 2011); E. Posner, "Making Rules for Global Finance: Transatlantic Regulatory Cooperation at the Turn of the Millennium," *International Organization*, 63 (2009), 665–699; D. A. Singer, *Regulating Capital: Setting Standards for the International Financial System* (Ithaca NY: Cornell University Press, 2007).

[15] M. Moschella and E. Tsingou (eds.), *Great Expectations, Slow Transformations: Incremental Change in Post-Crisis Regulation* (Colchester: ECPR Press, 2013); E. Helleiner, *The Status Quo Crisis: Global Financial Governance after the 2008 Financial Meltdown* (Oxford: Oxford University Press, 2014).

[16] A. Walter, *Governing Finance: East Asia's Adoption of International Standards* (Ithaca NY: Cornell University Press, 2008); L. Mosley, "Regulating Globally, Implementing locally: The Financial Codes and Standards Effort," *Review of International Political Economy*, 17 (2010), 724–761; H.-K. Chey, *International Harmonization of Financial Regulation? The Politics of Global Diffusion of the Basel Capital Accord* (Abingdon: Routledge, 2014).

[17] E. B. Kapstein, "Resolving the Regulator's Dilemma: International Coordination of Banking Regulations," *International Organization*, 43 (1989), 323–347.

proceeds to apply this framework empirically to cross-border banking by exploiting the within-case variance in the case of emerging Europe between 2004 and 2010, in particular the differing response to the credit boom (2004–2007) and to crisis management (2008–2010). Throughout, the focus is on the response of host states and international institutions during the boom and then during the bust phase of the credit cycle. The conclusion offers some implications for host countries based on this analysis.

12.2 Host's Dilemma and the Need for International Cooperation

12.2.1 Whose Dilemma? Regulator's Dilemma vs. Host's Dilemma

Host supervisors are on the receiving end of large international banking flows, which in the run-up to the crisis were the largest component of the capital inflows to emerging European countries.[18] Such flows are particularly problematic in comparison to FDI flows, which are much more stable because of a longer commitment, or equity flows, for which holders take automatic hits when the value of the liabilities declines. In contrast, banking flows represent debt which must be repaid in full and on time regardless of changes in the financial situation of the debtor. The resulting public or private debt can quickly become a significant vulnerability if capital flows experience a "sudden stop."[19]

Moreover, bank-intermediated credit flows are particularly procyclical and driven by the balance sheet management of global banks. When risks appear low during the boom phase, this allows an expansion of the balance sheet, often through wholesale funding and the accumulation of non-core liabilities.[20] Such externally fueled credit growth thus contributes to the emergence of bubbles in the host state. Conversely, when risk perception rises during the bust phase, such funding quickly becomes too expensive, leading banks to pull out the "easy money" and leaving significant debt problems and overhang in the host country. In short, there is a significant synchronization of cross-border bank

[18] The structure of capital flows differed importantly among countries. For example, in Bulgaria an overwhelming part of capital flows came in the form of FDI.

[19] G. A. Calvo, "Capital Flows and Capital-market Crises: The Simple Economics of Sudden stops," *Journal of Applied Economics*, 1 (1998), 35–54.

[20] M. Brunnermeier, et al., *Banks and Cross-Border Capital Flows: Policy Challenges and Regulatory Responses* (Washington DC: Brookings, 2012), 8–11.

flows that depends on global factors and risk perception rather than local financial "fundamentals."[21] This volatile nature and influence of global conditions gives national regulators significant incentives to keep a close eye on cross-border banking.

Scholarship has explored the implications of such global interdependence for regulatory cooperation for several decades.[22] According to the original regulator's dilemma, "with the globalization of capital markets, public officials have been forced to make tradeoffs between domestic regulation on the one hand and international competitiveness on the other."[23] However, this analysis is based on an assumption common in much of the existing scholarship that countries have banks which compete externally against other banks from other countries, and that they might benefit from lower costs due to lighter regulation at home. This particular dilemma is premised, often implicitly, on the notion of "banking nationalism," or the idea that countries do indeed seek to promote abroad the interests of "their" banks.[24]

Given a generally high level of foreign ownership and the low internationalization of domestic banks, host regulators face a rather different dilemma than home regulators preoccupied by a possible tradeoff between international competitiveness and domestic regulation. Their worries often directly reflect the procyclical features of such flows, as during the boom phase they are concerned about excessive credit growth leading to bubbles, especially in real estate. During the bust phase, the main concern is that liquidity could just as easily reverse direction and flow out of local affiliates and toward parent banks, provoking a systemic crisis and leaving the host state to foot the bill.

Analytically, therefore, the "host's dilemma" differs from that of home supervisors in two key aspects. First, they usually have no own banks to promote abroad; hence they are not subject to the competitiveness

---

[21] V. Bruno and H. S. Shin, "Cross-Border Banking and Global Liquidity," *Review of Economic Studies*, 82 (2011), 535–564; K. J. Forbes and F. E. Warnock, "Capital Flow Waves: Surges, Stops, Flight, and Retrenchment," *Journal of International Economics*, 88 (2012), 235–251; H. Rey, *Dilemma Not Trilemma: The Global Financial Cycle and Monetary Policy Independence* (National Bureau of Economic Research, 2015).

[22] Kapstein, "Resolving the regulator's dilemma"; Drezner, *All Politics Is Global*; Singer, *Regulating Capital*; T. Oatley and R. Nabors, "Redistributive Cooperation: Market Failure, Wealth Transfers, and the Basle Accord," *International Organization*, 52 (1998), 35–54.

[23] Kapstein, "Resolving the Regulator's Dilemma," 324.

[24] N. Veron, *Banking Nationalism and the European Crisis* (Brussels: Bruegel, 2013); R. Epstein and M. Rhodes, "International in Life, National in Death? Banking Nationalism on the Road to Banking Union," KNF Working Paper No. 61 (2014).

constraint. Instead, they need to address another risk – that of foreign banks "cutting and running" in a crisis.[25] The performance of national banks in their home jurisdiction, both in terms of financing the real economy and in terms of tax revenues, depends on their success abroad, but ultimately they would find it hard and costly to leave and relocate elsewhere. Yet, that is precisely the threat that host countries face, with potentially devastating consequences as demonstrated by the Argentinian and Asian financial crises.

The second key issue where host regulators differ is in their access to international standard-setting bodies and other financial institutions with responsibilities for maintaining global and national financial stability. Unlike many of their largest home counterparts, who negotiate directly key standards between themselves, host supervisors are largely rule-takers. Therefore, they generally face a different choice than the dilemma whether to negotiate or to compete: namely, whether to adopt rules, which might not suit their economic circumstances, or to risk incurring the costs of a national approach in a largely international capital market.

12.2.2 Demand for Cooperation: Information, Enforcement, Burden-Sharing

Given the different challenges host regulators face, the functional demands for cooperation they are likely to encounter differ from those of home regulators. In the standard home regulator's dilemma, international cooperation is a way to prevent a regulatory race to the bottom induced by global competition that might undercut domestic stability at home;[26] hence the stated objective is often to create a "level playing field" or to "close loopholes." The demand for cooperation for host regulators is also connected to domestic financial stability, but given large foreign-bank ownership, this goal is understood in a different way. In particular, host regulators require cooperation to address specific problems with the supervision, regulation and resolution of cross-border banks, which shapes the dynamics of host–home interaction.

The first issue host regulators face is related to acquiring the necessary information to make judgments on the potential risk exposure of their

---

[25] N. Roubini and B. Setser, *Bailouts or Bail-ins?: Responding to Financial Crises in Emerging Economies* (Washington DC: Institute for International Economics, 2004).

[26] Singer, *Regulating Capital.*

economies. Whereas home supervisors often have an overview of the situation of the parent bank group as a whole, their counterparts in the host country can largely only "see" the situation in the local part of the group. Thus, host regulators are reliant on whatever information the home country has gathered for its own microprudential purposes. This informational asymmetry can lead to potentially serious incentive conflicts in information-sharing between home and host supervisors. In normal times, home supervisors do not derive a significant benefit from engaging with counterparts in non-systemic (for the bank group) jurisdictions. More worryingly, they have a strong interest in limiting any information about deteriorating performance of the bank group as a whole as that is likely to provoke calls for intervention from host authorities. The latter, recognizing that negative information is likely to be restricted, have therefore an incentive themselves to quickly move to ring-fencing and other forceful measures at the slightest hint of trouble.[27] Thus, in the absence of suitable governance arrangements information-sharing arrangements are likely to fall apart precisely when they are most needed.

A second issue often faced by host supervisors is that of potential regulatory arbitrage by systemic banks in their own jurisdiction, which undermines their ability to enforce regulations. Host countries that try to implement measures to reduce credit growth or other financial risks are creating incentives for banks to look for ways of minimizing the regulatory "burden." In cross-border banking, they can generally take two approaches: banks can move lending to other less regulated domains, such as leasing companies, and continue their activities while evading the legal requirements of banking; or they can switch to direct cross-border lending from the foreign bank abroad to the customer in the host country as local affiliates simply pass their loan books to their parent banks. Such challenges are not unique to host country regulators as home country regulators similarly worry about credit supply shifting to "shadow banks" in response to regulatory changes.[28] However, the cross-border aspect of banking introduces specific challenges, as host countries are dependent

---

[27] K. D'Hulster, "Cross-border Banking Supervision: Incentive Conflicts in Supervisory Information Sharing between Home and Host Supervisors," *Journal of Banking Regulation*, 13 (2012), 300–319.

[28] J. F. Houston, C. Lin and Y. Ma, "Regulatory Arbitrage and International Bank Flows," *Journal of Finance*, 67 (2012), 1845–1895; D. Reinhardt and R. Sowerbutts, "Regulatory Arbitrage in action: Evidence from Banking Flows and Macroprudential Policy," Bank of England Staff Working Paper No. 546 (2015).

on cooperation and reciprocity from the home regulator. This might not be forthcoming, as the home regulator might regard the foreign jurisdiction chiefly as a source of profit for "its" banks.

These supervisory and regulatory challenges stem, to a certain extent, from the well-known resolution challenges national authorities face in the absence of supranational resolution tools.[29] Given the lack of a global resolution framework for failing banks, regulators accountable to their national constituency are unlikely to take into account possible externalities and will instead seek to minimize the fiscal costs for their own country and citizens.[30] Thus, in a multi-country setting, ex-post negotiations after a crisis can lead to the underprovision of support as national authorities seek to limit the exposure of national taxpayers by dividing and "carving out" the existing capital. What is needed, therefore, is an ex-ante agreement on burden sharing which will enable the orderly resolution of cross-border banks.[31] In its absence, once a crisis strikes, the protection of domestic stakeholders precedes that of international creditors.

For host states, these resolution dynamics present an even more acute problem of burden-sharing than for home states. If a banking group experiences significant problems, it could be forced to withdraw capital or liquidity, or ultimately even to sell otherwise healthy and systemic subsidiaries in the host state. This can sometimes happen even without the host supervisor participating in the discussions. The burden of responding to the consequent banking problems falls on the host country and its regulators even though they might not bear a large share of the blame. In turn, this creates a divergence between who takes the decisions with systemic implications and who is responsible for the financial consequences of these actions.[32]

To sum up, host regulators depend on cross-border cooperation to underpin cross-border banking by mitigating information asymmetries, by limiting regulatory arbitrage, and by providing burden-sharing agreements. These challenges are magnified by other practical challenges, such as generally more limited resources making host states particularly

[29] E. Avgouleas, *Governance of Global Financial Markets: The Law, the Economics, the Politics* (Cambridge: Cambridge University Press, 2012), 394–424.

[30] D. Schoenmaker, *Governance of International Banking: The Financial Trilemma* (Oxford: Oxford University Press, 2013).

[31] C. Goodhart and D. Schoenmaker, "Fiscal Burden Sharing in Cross-border Banking Crises," *International Journal of Central Banking*, 5 (2009), 141–165.

[32] Pistor, "Host's Dilemma."

reliant on analysis conducted by home authorities, international institutions, or global banks themselves. If cooperation successfully responds to these demands, then host states can reap the benefits of banking integration. However, if such cooperation fails, they are then left with the financial consequences.

12.2.3 Supply of Cooperation: Asymmetric Interdependence and International Institutions

How could these demands for cooperation by host regulators be realized? Given mutual interdependence, in theory both regulators would have incentives to cooperate. Thus, cooperation can be the outcome of self-enforced bargaining outcome and does not necessarily rely on formal institutional mechanisms.[33] As long as both regulatory authorities have significant "skin in the game," this would induce them to work together to reach a solution through Coasian bargaining, provided transaction costs are low enough. However, if the two sides are in a situation of asymmetric interdependence, that creates a bargaining situation which empowers the less dependent side and suggests the final outcome is likely to be closer to its initial preferences.[34] In other words, this introduces an element of power in the relationship, shifting the outcome to the benefit of one of the sides. In these cases, soft law and informal institutions would be unlikely to significantly affect the unfavorable bargaining situation of the more dependent state.

In the case of cross-border banking, the key measure of interdependence is the extent to which a certain foreign affiliate is systemic to the home[35] and to the host country. Following Herring, if the affiliate is systemic to both financial systems, then regulators are likely to reach a cooperative solution through Coasian bargaining.[36] Alternatively, if the costs of the problems in cross-border banks are insignificant to both jurisdictions, it will likely not be a cause for major concern. However, the situation can quickly turn into a "nightmare scenario" if there is an

---

[33] R. M. Axelrod, *The Evolution of Cooperation* (New York: Basic Books, 1984); K. A. Oye, *Cooperation under Anarchy* (Princeton NJ: Princeton University Press, 1986).

[34] R. O. Keohane and J. S. Nye, *Power and interdependence* (Harlow: Longman, 1989).

[35] More precisely, to be systemic for the home country, the affiliate needs to first be systemic to its parent group, which in turn should be systemic to the home state.

[36] R. Herring, *Conflicts between Home & Host Country Prudential Supervisors* (Wharton School, University of Pennsylvania: Financial Institutions Center, 2007).

asymmetry of exposure to the consequences of a bank failure.[37] From the home regulator's point of view, this involves a systemic bank in its jurisdiction with a significant exposure in a host's country, which is however *not* systemic to the host itself. These countries are empirically rare and home authorities dispose of significant means accorded by global and European law to address such a situation. However, whenever a bank which is systemic to the host is either not systemic for the home market or its activities in the host countries represent an insignificant part of its global operations, it is the host authorities that face a "nightmare scenario." Yet, this is precisely the situation of many countries in emerging Europe, but also in Latin America and sub-Saharan Africa.

The dilemma for host regulators is that the institutional structures that are supposed to mitigate the power asymmetry resulting from their exposure to foreign ownership, such as the BCBS, are likely to be created by and confined to home country regulators. There are two ways out of this dilemma. First, states might seek to align their interdependence with that of home countries. It is unlikely they could achieve a more symmetrical exposure to each other's banking system given the large differences in the size of financial markets (which are themselves the source of the gains from banking integration that host states are looking to harvest in the first place). Therefore, to achieve this, host states could seek to reduce foreign ownership within their banking system to a situation in which it is no longer systemic. This means a conscious choice in favor of national approaches, eschewing the benefits of banking integration. The second way out of the host's dilemma would be to make sure that formal institutional arrangements respond to their demands for cooperation, which is most unambiguously achieved through their inclusion in decision-making forums and by granting them real voice.

The choice between these two approaches to addressing the host's dilemma hinges on the role of international institutions. If such institutions are responsive to host countries' demands for cooperation, this would make it possible for countries on the receiving end of large debt flows to reap the benefits of such integration while minimizing potential risks. In turn, that should foster a more sustainable form of banking integration. On the other hand, without such a "supply" of cooperation, ensuring financial stability in host jurisdictions is likely to prove difficult and the risks might outweigh the benefits of integration. Given that the

---

[37] Herring, *Conflicts between Home and Host*, 14–19.

optimal policy choice by decision-makers in host jurisdictions is likely to be conditional on the role of international institutions, it is necessary to understand the conditions under which host countries can rely on such institutions to meaningfully represent their interests.

12.3   The Host's Dilemma during the Boom in Emerging Europe (2004–2008)

The host's dilemma was a serious problem in emerging Europe in 2004–2008, when cross-border banking led to significant vulnerabilities. Host countries, however, were constrained by a European legal framework that gave them few tools to address such problems. Meanwhile, despite some internal discussions, major international institutions largely failed to address the emerging issues. This section presents an initial application of the analytical framework presented above. It begins by outlining the difficulties posed by banking integration for host regulators before then presenting how the governance framework strengthened home supervisors. It then discusses in more details the benign neglect of such issues by international institutions and considers interest-based, ideational, and institutional explanations for this outcome.

12.3.1   Cross-Border Banking and Increasing Vulnerabilities

Starting with the collapse of command economies in 1989, countries in emerging Europe embarked on a path toward their transformation into market economies with corresponding modern banking sectors. Under the pressure to find new capital to finance their development, they dismantled state-owned banking systems in the hope of improving efficiency and reducing political interference, and brought in foreign capital.[38] After a decade and a half of transition, the accession of eight countries from emerging Europe to the EU in 2004, and then Bulgaria and Romania in 2007, raised hopes that integration would enable local economies to partly catch up with Western Europe. The expectation was that given better growth prospects, capital would flow from the west, where returns to savings were low, to capital-poor countries in the east, helping them to satisfy their large demand for investment. This would improve the economic potential, the legal framework, and, ultimately, the political institutions of the recipient states.

---

[38] Epstein, *In Pursuit of Liberalism.*

For a while it appeared that this "convergence machine" was working beautifully; it even exceeded expectations. During the honeymoon period between EU accession and the financial crisis of 2008–2009, countries in the region were growing at annual rates of 5–6 percent, with some in the Baltics even exceeding 10 percent. Income levels began to catch up with the most prosperous half of the continent. Capital inflows played a key role in this process since the late 1990s, attracted by low wages, low capital–labor ratios, and fairly skilled populations. Many Western European manufacturers, led by German automakers, sought to integrate countries from the region into their global production and value chains as intra-European trade boomed.

However, around 2004 the pattern of growth began to shift away from tradable exports and moderate capital inflows, toward increasing levels of domestic demand and consumption. Annual demand rates regularly exceeded GDP growth and reached double-digits in some countries, such as the Baltics, Bulgaria and Romania.[39] The rise in consumption was financed by ever-increasing capital inflows. Thus, the region experienced a threefold increase in net capital inflows between 2004 and 2008, rising from around $100 billion to more than $300 billion, or around 10 percent of GDP. This was not only high by historical standards, but also in comparison to other emerging markets – indeed, in terms of net capital inflows in the four years preceding the crisis, "the unweighted average in the EU-9 (107 percent of 2003 GDP) was almost three times as large as in pre-crisis Indonesia, the Philippines, and Thailand (38 percent of 1992 GDP).[40]

What provided the fuel for this process was accelerating credit growth driven by banking inflows. Given very low levels of financial development, this was initially welcomed. However, while the absolute level remained moderate, the speed of credit growth began to cause worries among economists and regulators in the region.[41] In particular, credit was largely directed toward the non-tradable sector, and thus supporting consumption or real estate investment. Housing prices and equity markets rose rapidly, with real estate prices increasing by between 250 percent and 300 percent in just five years between 2003 and 2008 in the Baltic

---

[39] Bakker, B. and C. Klingen (eds.), *How Emerging Europe Came through the 2008/09 Crisis: An Account by the Staff of the IMF's European Department* (Washington DC: IMF, 2012), 3.

[40] Bakker and Klingen, "How Emerging Europe Came through the 2008/09 Crisis," 7.

[41] C. Enoch and I. Ötker (eds.), *Rapid credit growth in Central and Eastern Europe : Endless Boom or Early Warning?* (London: Palgrave, 2007).

countries and Bulgaria.[42] This drove ever-widening current account deficits, largely correlated with the level of credit growth, which in turn had to be financed through external capital inflows. As some IMF economists highlighted at the time, in previous crises even lower current account deficits than the ones observed in emerging Europe in 2004–2008 have caused significant problems, as they made countries vulnerable to a reversal of capital flows.[43]

The crucial component driving this surge of capital flows was bank loans from Western Europe (see figure 12.2). Facing low margins in overbanked Western European countries, and looking for a source of profits, Western banks eagerly embraced a "second home market" strategy focused on Eastern Europe.[44] Thus, they responded to significant global "push" factors, such as the low interest rate environment in advanced economies and high risk appetite. Such flows were also stimulated by "pull' factors, such as transition reforms and the dismantling of barriers to capital movements in the run-up to EU accession. These factors combined to lead banks to expand aggressively in emerging Europe, with their exposure rising by 20 percent of local GDP in Romania and Hungary, and over 40 percent in the Baltics and Bulgaria.[45]

The expansion of cross-border bank flows had profound effects on host economies. By one official estimate, 80 percent of Western bank exposure translated into additional credit growth, thus raising annual domestic demand growth in the region by 2 percent.[46] Their aggressive competition for market share in this newly emerging corner of Europe with its bright growth prospects shaped their approach to lending which relied on intra-capital markets. Thus, they funded the new loans with capital raised cheaply on (calm) international capital markets using the name of the Western parent bank, rather than through local deposits. This was crucial as it allowed credit growth to continue even as deposit growth in emerging Europe countries slowed.[47] In short, in the words of

---

[42] Bakker and Klingen, "How Emerging Europe Came through the 2008/09 Crisis," 7.

[43] P. Sorsa, et al., "Vulnerabilities in Emerging Southeastern Europe – How much cause for concern?," IMF Working Paper (2007).

[44] R.A. Epstein, "When Do Foreign Banks 'cut and run'? Evidence from West European Bailouts and East European Markets," Review of International Political Economy, 21 (2014), 847–877.

[45] Bakker and Klingen, "How Emerging Europe Came through the 2008/09 Crisis," 14.

[46] International Monetary Fund, "Regional Economic Outlook Europe: Navigating Stormy Waters," IMF World Economic and Financial Surveys (2011), 94.

[47] R. Cull and M. S. Martinez Peria, "Bank Ownership and Lending Patterns during the 2008–2009 Financial Crisis: Evidence from Latin America and Eastern Europe," World

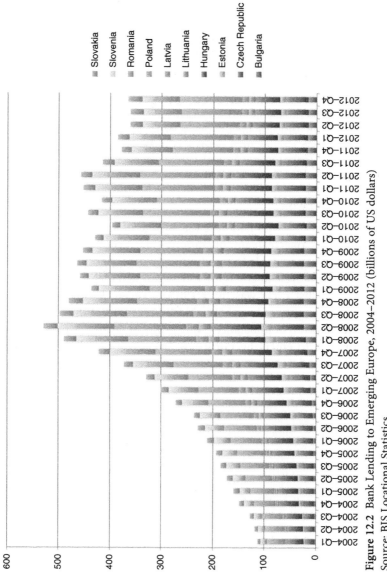

Figure 12.2 Bank Lending to Emerging Europe, 2004–2012 (billions of US dollars)

Source: BIS Locational Statistics.

the IMF, "the magnitude of the credit boom ... was closely linked to the size of the influx of capital from western banks."[48]

Host states in emerging Europe struggled to address increasing vulnerabilities in the run-up to the crisis. Various conventional measures related to loan classifications, reserve requirements, fiscal stance, and monetary policy, wherever possible, made little difference in reducing credit growth.[49] Some countries, such as Bulgaria and Romania, sought to introduce de facto credit ceilings through high reserve requirements and/or capital weights on foreign liabilities, to little avail as financial intermediation quickly circumvented them through direct cross-border loans or loans by leasing companies.[50] It is worth citing the IMF (ex-post) analysis of financial sector policy during the pre-crisis period:

> A related problem was insufficient collaboration between home and host supervisors. In particular, the activities of foreign banks in the region did not get enough scrutiny from supervisors in Western European home countries ... In the context of consolidated supervision, those banks were subject to home country oversight, leaving host supervisory agencies under the impression that the institutions were monitored also at the home country level.[51]

Home supervisors, who had little knowledge of local conditions, had little incentive to "overregulate" operations in host countries, which were typically the most profitable stream for their banks. Another IMF assessment of the credit cycle in emerging Europe argued that to a large extent the boom-and-bust cycle was the result of "bad luck" and that "even perfect policies might not have been able to prevent all of the rapid credit growth and build-up of imbalances" due to global factors.[52] This was not a story confined to emerging Europe, or even host jurisdictions, as the example of Iceland demonstrates, but the governance framework at that

Bank Policy Research Working Paper, 2012); E. Feyen, R. Letelier, I. Love, S. Maimbo and R. Rocha, *The Impact of Funding Models and Foreign Bank Ownership on Bank Credit Growth: Is Central and Eastern Europe Different?* (Washington DC: World Bank, 2014).

[48] Bakker and Klingen, "How Emerging Europe Came through the 2008/09 Crisis," 10.

[49] P. Hilbers, I. Otker-Robe and C. Pazarbasioglu, "Analysis of and Policy Responses to Rapid Credit Growth," in C. Enoch and I. Otker-Robe (eds.), *Rapid Credit Growth in Central and Eastern Europe: Endless Boom or Early Warning?* (London: Palgrave, 2007), 84–136.

[50] A. Bennett, et al., *Economic and Policy Foundations for Growth in South East Europe: Remaking the Balkan Economy* (London: Palgrave Macmillan, 2015); C. Lim, et al., "Macroprudential policy: What Instruments and How to Use Them – Lessons from Country Experiences," IMF Working Paper (October 2011).

[51] Bakker and Klingen, "How Emerging Europe Came through the 2008/09 Crisis," 22.

[52] B. Bakker, and A.-M. Gulde, "The Credit Boom in the EU New Member States: Bad Luck or Bad Policies?," IMF Working Paper (May 2010), 26.

point put host states within the EU into a particularly challenging situation.

12.3.2   The European Governance Framework for Cross-Border Banking: A Home Bias

Given the buildup of vulnerabilities stemming from cross-border banking, how was financial integration regulated? The pre-crisis global framework gave the home (also known as consolidated) regulator the lead without considering potential conflicts of interest.[53] The standards on home–host division of responsibilities were developed at the BCBS, which was set up in 1974 as an informal forum for discussions among G-10 members in response to the globalization of financial activities.[54] The resulting Basel Core Principles (BCP), successively updated in 1975, 1983, 1997 and 2006, were concerned primarily with addressing problems arising from the international activities of large domestic banks in home markets as demonstrated by the collapse of the German Herstatt bank in 1974, the problems of US and European banks in the Latin American debt crisis, and the collapse of BCCI in 1991. The drafters of these accords saw the quality of home country regulation as higher; hence the general direction was to eliminate supervisory gaps by increasing the power of the consolidated supervisor to oversee the activities of "its" banks outside its jurisdictional borders. Therefore, the BCP are mainly aimed at mitigating problems related to inadequate regulation in emerging markets, which is reflected in the way they empower home supervisors at the expense of host ones.[55]

At the European level this global logic and division of responsibilities was if anything further strengthened and hardened in legal terms. Financial integration in the EU was initially driven by the development of the Single Market in the mid-1980s and was stimulated by competition from US and Japanese banks and the active role of the European Commission.[56] It is in this period that the rules regarding the home country principle of the BCP were initially introduced into EU

---

[53] Pistor, "Host's Dilemma."

[54] C. Goodhart, *The Basel Committeeon Banking Supervision : A History of the Early Years, 1974–1997* (Cambridge: Cambridge University Press, 2011).

[55] A. Persaud, "The Locus of Financial Regulation: Home versus Host," *International Affairs*, 86 (2010), 637–646.

[56] G. R. D. Underhill, *The New World Order in International Finance* (New York: St. Martin's Press, 1997).

legislation. The introduction of the EMU stimulated another round of efforts in driving financial integration, centered on the legislative proposals of the five-year Financial Services Action Plan (FSAP) of 1999 aimed at securities markets. To implement the FSAP, the ECOFIN Council appointed a Committee of Wise Men, led by former BIS general manager Alexandre Lamfalussy, in 2000. Once the Committee submitted its proposals in 2001, they were extended by the ECOFIN to the banking and insurance sectors.[57]

The result was a three-level, committee-based system of supervision and cooperation between national authorities. The top level represented the Community method, where framework legislation is proposed by the Commission and is co-decided by the ECOFIN Council and the European Parliament. The second-level committees, chaired by the EC, dealt with technical and implementing measures. In the case of banking, the relevant committee is the European Banking Committee composed of national civil servants from the economic and finance ministries. Although qualified majority voting was a possibility, consensus among participants was the norm. The main focus of its work was on the "technical" transposition of Basel II in EU legislation. The relevant Level 3 committee was the London-based Committee of European Banking Supervisors (CEBS), composed of national banking authorities. Its main role was to advise on implementing measures and legislation proposals (levels 2 and 1) and to issue standards and guidelines for consistent implementation and convergence. As with the EBC, consensus was often sought.[58]

This EU-level "Lamfalussy framework" aimed to stimulate convergence between various national-level regulations in the EU in order to foster a single market in financial services to accompany the launch of the monetary union and to parallel the single market in goods. In particular, the framework sought to provide integrated governance across the banking, securities and insurance sectors, and a more efficient and responsive method for agreeing financial services legislation. However, in pursuing this harmonization objective, policy-makers proceeded by strengthening a global template that gave room for policy choice to home countries,

---

[57] S. Lütz, "Convergence within National Diversity: the Regulatory State in Finance," *Journal of Public Policy*, 24 (2004), 169–198; N. Jabko, *Playing the Market: A Political Strategy for Uniting Europe, 1985–2005* (Ithaca NY: Cornell University Press, 2006); D. Mügge, "Competition Politics in European Finance," *Journal of Common Market Studies*, 44 (2006), 991–1022.

[58] Quaglia, *Governing Financial Services in the European Union*, 37–38.

while reducing host countries to often passive implementers of decisions taken elsewhere, as outlined below. This leads to two sets of problems for host states: first, they are adopting rules that might be ill-suited to their economic circumstances and, second, they participate in a governance architecture that gives them only limited voice.

First, the *acquis communautaire* includes a number of requirements that strengthen home supervisors and remove certain tools from the hands of host regulators. Most importantly, countries joining the EU renounce capital controls as a policy tool for all but the most critical cases (such as Cyprus in 2013). This is a direct implication of the freedom of capital, enshrined as one of the core four freedoms of the EU, into the TFEU. Related to this is "passporting," or the right of an entity that is properly regulated by its home regulator in the EU to carry out financial services or open branches in other member states subject only to notification (and not approval) by host authorities. This is enshrined in community law under the Directive of Credit Institutions, revised in 2006, which only allows for certain limited liquidity regulations of branches by host states.[59] Furthermore, the Capital Requirements Directive (CRD), adopted in 2006, made Basel II legally binding (unlike the soft law recommendations of the BCBS) for all countries in the EU. In addition, the CRD obliges all domestic banks to comply with Basel II requirements, including banks in new member states, despite well-known worries about the effects of these rules on poorer countries.[60] Moreover, the directive stresses the role of home country authorities as lead supervisors. For example, they are in charge of coordinating the approval of applications to use more sophisticated capital calculation rules and, in the case of absence of agreement within six months, can make a decision not to impose extra burdens on companies dealing with multiple supervisors.[61] The prevalence of such home-oriented rules is hardly surprising as the FSAP and the Lamfalussy process took place between 1999 and 2004, just before the first eight emerging European states joined the EU. Thus, as Quaglia puts it, "the new member states either had not yet joined or had only recently joined when the vast majority of financial services rules were negotiated and agreed upon during the first five years of the twenty-first century."[62]

---

[59] Pistor, "Host's Dilemma," 29–34.
[60] S. Claessens, G. R. D. Underhill and X. Zhang, "The Political Economy of Basle II: The Costs for Poor Countries," *World Economy*, 31 (2008), 313–344.
[61] Quaglia, *Governing Financial Services in the European Union*, 57.
[62] Ibid., 8.

Second, in addition to adopting regulations designed by and for home regulators, host regulators were further constrained by their limited voice in the governance architecture. CEBS was supposed to be the forum where home and host regulators coordinate, cooperate, and exchange information.[63] Yet, this consultative body lacked enforcement power, and consensus was sought in taking decisions. Given this and a membership comprising fifty-one regulators from twenty-seven countries, it is hard to see how it could have served as mediator between home and host supervisors. Furthermore, the two main tools on which CEBS relied to promote and sustain regulatory cooperation also strongly favored home-regulators and provided little leverage to host countries to defend their interests. The first one was a college of supervisors, which should facilitate the supervision of systemically important cross-border financial institutions by encouraging the exchange of information and cooperation between different national regulators. However, before the crisis such colleges were relatively rare, largely limited to considerations of capital requirements, and with restricted participation by host authorities as consolidated home supervisors took the lead. Crucially, they operated by consensus decision-making and without a mediation mechanism to resolve potential conflicts other than bargaining among the parties involved.[64] The second instrument to address cross-border banking challenges was a memorandum of understanding between regulators (MoUs). The EU put in place a multilateral MoU on high-level principles among central banks and supervisors in 2003, increasing it in scope to include finance ministers in 2005.[65] However, as the cases of Fortis and the Icelandic banks operating in the UK illustrated, such principles were quickly swept aside once the crisis struck. The IMF assessment is particularly damning: "As MoUs were nonbinding and supervisory colleges were not empowered to make decisions, many MoU commitments – such as timely sharing of information – were quickly abandoned as domestic financial stability concerns became paramount. Supervisory colleges could not restrain unilateral action."[66]

[63] L. Quaglia, "Financial Sector Committee Governance in the European Union," *Journal of European Integration*, 30 (2008), 563–578.

[64] D. Alford, "Supervisory Colleges: The Global Financial Crisis and Improving International Supervisory Coordination," *Emory International Law Review*, 24 (2010).

[65] L. Quaglia, "Is European Union Governance Ready to Deal with the Next Financial Crisis?," in H. K. Anheier (ed.), *Governance Challenges and Innovations: Financial and Fiscal Governance* (Oxford: Oxford University Press, 2013), 63–88, 69–70.

[66] International Monetary Fund, "Cross-border Bank Resolution – Recent Developments," Board Paper (June 2014), 6.

Overall, the regulatory framework at the EU level reflected a desire to foster financial integration by harmonizing regulatory rules on the basis of strengthening the principle of home supervision. This has the clear benefit of reducing transaction costs and ensuring harmonization, but comes at the expense of host countries. Thus, host regulators found themselves operating with a legal framework that they did not participate in developing and within a governance structure that granted them only limited voice in case of conflicts. In short, host regulators had to operate within a context shaped by the "home regulator's dilemma" as "the existing governance structure gives [host regulators] neither powers nor responsibilities to participate in the allegedly coordinative governance structure."[67]

12.3.3   International Institutions and the Host's Dilemma

Given large-scale cross-border banking flows and a EU governance framework that failed to address the needs of host regulators, what was the response of international institutions to the credit boom? The European Commission (EC) is the institution that is tasked to act in the general European interest in mind within the EU policy-making process. Yet, "EU officials generally either did not recognize that EU membership was amplifying the boom, or they attributed the beneficial trends they observed in CEE to a one-way trajectory towards convergence with the EU-15. Most saw nothing to worry about."[68] Meanwhile, the IMF should have been uniquely placed to warn about overheating in emerging Europe due to its specialization in balance of payments problems, its long practical experience with such issues, and the presence of multiple departments, which should help mitigate the pro-European mindset of the EC. However, both the EC and the IMF failed to articulate a clear public position warning of the rising vulnerabilities in emerging Europe. This reflects their relative lack of bargaining power vis-à-vis member states, the lack of ideational consensus among staff, and their institutional and bureaucratic constraints.

First, developments in financial markets over the 2004–2007 period put both institutions in a weak position in discussions with European countries. The literature on economic diplomacy has long recognized the

---

[67] Pistor, "Host's Dilemma," 38.
[68] W. Jacoby, "The EU Factor in Fat Times and in Lean: Did the EU Amplify the Boom and Soften the Bust?," 52 *Journal of Common Market Studies*, 52 (2014), 52–70.

crucial if somewhat endogenous role that markets play in shaping negotiations among governments, particularly in shaping outside options of
financing.[69] Thus, as long as countries retain access to capital markets at
reasonable rates, international institutions are reduced to their surveillance function and deprived of their main instrument for leverage.

Between 2004 and 2008 global liquidity conditions were generally
benign, but they were even more favorable for countries in emerging
Europe than elsewhere, for three reasons. First, EU membership also
promoted policy liberalization reforms, leading many countries to lift
restrictions over the capital account.[70] Second, expectations of euro
adoption prompted many customers to consider loans, especially mortgages, in foreign currency. These FX loans were mostly in euros in
countries with currency boards (Baltics and Bulgaria), where they were
often seen as a one-way bet, or in Swiss francs in countries with floating
currencies where the interest rate differentials were significant (Romania,
Poland). Third, the introduction of the euro in Western Europe spurred
banks to consider cross-border models, which changed their perception
on emerging Europe and prompted capital outflows exceeding market
conditions.[71] In short, studies of capital inflows and cross-border banking in emerging Europe also find an effect above and beyond global
liquidity conditions.[72] Thus, "the prospect of EU membership helped
encourage risky behavior by lending implicit credibility to CEE emerging
markets that previously appeared to be in unstable investment
climates."[73]

Particularly benign financial conditions also undercut the influence of
international institutions by making it hard to warn against rising vulnerabilities. Attempts to point to the possible buildup of problems due to
current account deficits were easily dismissed by national policy-makers,
who pointed out that financial markets were providing financing at
declining risk premia.[74] This significantly undermined the credibility of

---

[69] J. S. Odell, *Negotiating the World Economy* (Ithaca NY: Cornell University Press, 2000);
N. Bayne and S. Woolcock (eds.), *The New Economic Diplomacy: Decision-making and Negotiation in International Economic Relations* (Abingdon: Ashgate, 2011).

[70] D. R. Cameron, "Creating Market Economies after Communism: The Impact of the European Union," *Post-Soviet Affairs*, 25 (2009), 1–38.

[71] J. Jones, "Cross-Border Banking in the Expanded European Union," *Eastern European Economics*, 51 (2013), 54–74.

[72] E. Berglof, et al., "Understanding the Crisis in Emerging Europe," *European Bank for Reconstruction and Development* (November 2009).

[73] Jacoby, "The EU Factor in Fat Times and in Lean," 59.

[74] Bakker and Gulde, "The Credit Boom in the EU New Member States."

warnings by institutions, which felt that they would be considered as "doomsayers" by their national interlocutors.[75] Furthermore, the benign financial conditions weakened incentives to address the buildup of problems. Rising capital inflows and credit booms led to a temporary surge in public revenues, which reduced worries about public debt. Thus, the mispricing of risk was key in making the boom larger than it would have been if risk premia had risen, which would have moderated both inflows and public expenditure.[76] In this way financial developments made it hard for both institutions to convince reluctant policy-makers of the need for reform, while simultaneously providing a way for them to rationalize inaction.

The second factor that accounts for the limited role of international institutions during this period is the lack of ideational consensus among staff regarding the risks posed by such vulnerabilities. At the EC, financial sector developments were generally perceived as the intended and positive outcomes of policy actions. Discussions within the Commission began in 2004 when some officials began to notice a mispricing of risk. However, there was confusion regarding whether that was genuine mispricing or whether it reflected a change in the financial system. The EC at the time was persuaded by academic consensus that the financial system has developed sophisticated mechanisms, which allow risk to be allocated more efficiently across the system. In this interpretation, rising asset prices and underpricing of risk simply reflected a system, which is getting better at managing risk.[77] By 2006 the EC was sufficiently worried, but felt constrained from going public by fear of causing the very crisis it was trying to avoid in the first place. This lack of consensus left policy-makers equally confused; in the words of Lorenzo Bini Smaghi, then a member of the ECB Executive Board: "Should policy-makers get comfort from the fact that the imbalances in central, eastern and southeastern Europe are in line with standard economic theory? Or should we be worried that these imbalances can be very disruptive for convergence if they prove to be unsustainable, as corrections can be painful and costly?"[78]

Unlike the EC, the IMF experienced a more vigorous internal debate over emerging Europe, but ultimately staff also remained internally

---

[75] Interview with senior EC official, Brussels, February 2016.
[76] Bakker and Klingen, "How Emerging Europe Came through the 2008/09 Crisis," 28.
[77] Interview with senior EC official, Brussels, February 2016.
[78] L. Bini Smaghi, "Real convergence in Central, Eastern, and South-Eastern Europe," ECB Conference on central, eastern, and south-eastern Europe, 2007, www.ecb.europa.eu/press/key/date/2007/html/sp071001_2.en.html.

divided on the issue. One view came from the then Policy, Development and Review department, which was tasked with conducting vulnerability exercises for emerging market countries. In 2004 it noticed a relative complacency in the European Department regarding the high levels of current account deficits in emerging Europe, in sharp contrast to the worries among for example the Western Hemisphere Department. The result was a presentation given internally to a number of departments drawing systematic comparisons with the Asian financial crisis and highlighting that emerging Europe faced larger vulnerabilities.[79]

One significant problem, however, was that it was hard to see where a crisis trigger might come from, apart from the withdrawal of non-residency deposits; there was no consideration of a possible contagion from Western European banks.[80] In response, other economists at the IMF, especially at the European Department, argued that such developments reflected rather the successful transformation of the countries and an equilibrium phenomenon related to the process of catch-up and convergence; their point was summarized in the title of a working paper, which clearly stated that "Europe is different."[81] They also contended that the parallel with the Asian crisis was inaccurate, as emerging Europe has much better transparency and governance arrangements, which differed sharply from the "crony capitalism" that characterized earlier crises. Thus, they argued, emerging Europe should not be judged according to emerging market standards. An additional point raised by some was that ultimately banks knew better how to manage risks on their balance sheets.[82]

Finally, international institutions were also somewhat hamstrung in terms of their institutional capacity to carry out comprehensive surveillance and analysis of vulnerabilities in host countries. In the case of the EC, it was expected that a comprehensive framework to underpin European-wide cross-border banking would emerge after the launch of the EMU, including the ability to pool resources.[83] Instead, there were just seven people working on financial stability issues for the whole of the

---

[79] B. Bakker and I. Vladkova Hollar, "Asia 1996 and Eastern Europe 2006 – Deja Vu all Over Again?" unpublished paper (IMF, 2006).

[80] Interview with senior IMF official, Warsaw, February 2016.

[81] A. Abiad, D. Leigh and A. Mody, "International Finance and Income Convergence: Europe Is Different," IMF Working Paper (March 2007).

[82] Interview with senior IMF official, Warsaw, February 2016.

[83] S. Berrigan, "The Global and Euro Area Crises: Will Next Time Be Different?," Oxford University Podcasts (May 2013).

EU at the EC, comprising just a single unit (the lowest institutional building bloc at the EC). In that sense, financial surveillance for all EU countries – not just emerging Europe – was based on reliance on market discipline. The unit was generally engaged in high-level surveillance with very few field missions and was largely focused on public debt dynamics. The logic was that the IMF, OECD, and central banks were already involved in financial stability, so there was no need for large-scale EC effort. Even within this very limited institutional capacity, analysis was focused on developments in the euro area, largely neglecting the experience of new, non-euro, member states.[84]

The IMF was also facing some institutional challenges, although they seemed to be a result of conjuncture rather than design. Overall, its European surveillance suffered from the same macro-level approach as the EC (despite emerging Europe having benefited from better staffing through a dedicated division within the European Department). Compounding this, as a result of a downsizing drive the European Department was without a permanent director or a deputy director for a considerable amount of time just before the global financial crisis.[85] In addition, some Article IV consultations about emerging Europe were never discussed by the IMF Board. Thus, the 2007 consultation on Latvia, which included warnings about its exchange rate, was never sent to the Board, while the 2008 discussion was sent to the Board, but never discussed. This left the IMF facing the crisis in Latvia without ever discussing its exchange rate, which was the key policy issue during the IMF/EU program.[86]

Overall, between 2004 and 2008 emerging Europe experienced a buildup of financial vulnerabilities stemming from the large-scale increase in capital flows, in particular bank inflows by Western European banks. Yet, the framework for regulating cross-border activities was shaped by the "home regulator's dilemma" and hence provided host authorities with only limited legal tools or voice in governance arrangements. In the face of this "host's dilemma," international institutions largely remained silent and passive due to limited bargaining power, internal ideational divisions, and some issues with institutional

---

[84] Interview with senior EC official, Brussels, February 2016.

[85] P. Blustein, "Over Their Heads: The IMF and the Prelude to the Euro-zone Crisis," CIGI Paper No. 60 (April 2015), 8.

[86] G. R. Kincaid, "The Troika – past and future? A view from Washington," Political Economy of Financial Markets Speaker Series, Oxford, European Studies Centre (October 2015).

capacity. Therefore, it is not surprising that when the global financial crisis hit emerging Europe, there were significant worries that the region would experience a crisis of a magnitude comparable with previous emerging market crises.

12.4 The Great Escape: Crisis Management in Emerging Europe (2008–2009)

What were the effects of the global financial crisis on emerging Europe, and how were they managed? In addressing the question, this section looks in-depth at the crisis response and provides a general assessment. It first focuses on the channel of transmission of the crisis and demonstrates how host states were constrained and overwhelmed by the scale of problems originating from outside their financial systems. It then proceeds to outline the response by international institutions, and in particular the role of the IMF/EU financing packages and the EBRD. Finally, it assesses the outcomes from crisis management by drawing a comparison to previous crises.

12.4.1   The Financial Crisis and Bank Flows in Emerging Europe

By leaving the countries exposed to the movements of international capital flows, the host's dilemma led to the buildup of significant vulnerabilities in emerging European financial systems. Current account deficits in 2008, fueled by cross-border banking flows, were at very high levels, reaching a staggering 25 percent of GDP in Bulgaria and 22 percent of GDP in Latvia. Private debt was at historically unprecedented levels at above 100 percent of GDP in Bulgaria (where it increased eight-fold in just five years), Latvia, Estonia and Slovenia, and at around 65–70 percent elsewhere, vastly outstripping GDP growth. Meanwhile, public debt was reduced to very low levels across the region, with the notable exception of Hungary (67 percent of GDP in 2007) and Poland (45 percent of GDP in 2007).

Some problems were becoming visible in the region in late 2007 and early 2008, but it was the collapse of Lehman Brothers that led to a sharp reversal of capital flows and a full-blown regional financial crisis. For a short while, the region appeared little exposed to the "toxic" products in the subprime mortgage sector in the United States. However, as CDS spreads shot up, interbank lending dried up, and cross-border banking slowed to virtually zero, it soon became clear that emerging Europe stood on the brink of a classic emerging market crisis triggered by the sudden stop of capital.[87] With no new private financing, large current account deficits and private debt were impossible to sustain, leading to a sharp adjustment. This was particularly painful in the Baltics, but also significant in all countries except Poland.

The crucial transmission mechanism for the crisis was cross-border lending flows. During the pre-crisis period, emerging Europe had experienced significantly higher net capital inflows compared to other emerging markets at around 5 percent of regional GDP, accelerating to 10 percent of GDP in 2007.[88] Once the crisis hit, Western European banks, facing capital and liquidity pressures at home, reversed their strategy of funding local lending through internal capital markets and instructed affiliates to fund lending only through local deposits. This resulted in a sharp slowdown in bank lending across all countries in emerging Europe. Given the large role of bank lending for the region, its collapse was reflected almost one-to-one in the decline of overall capital inflows, although FDI and remittances flows remained relatively stable. In turn, this put local currencies under pressure, falling in countries in floating regimes or requiring significant use of reserves in countries with fixed exchange rates. It also led to the bursting of real estate bubbles in many countries, a slowdown in investment, and a debt overhang that caused double-digit drops in GDP in some countries (Table 12.2).

The crisis experience confirms both the relevance and the consequences of the host's dilemma. Prior to the crisis, research showed that foreign banking can enhance efficiency and competition in the host country, but also be stabilizing for lending during local downturns.[89] The concerns of host authorities about possible contagion effects from cross-border banking during a crisis, and hence the basis for their demand for cooperation, were however now validated.[90] It was indeed multinational bank subsidiaries that cut lending more than domestic banks, suggesting that the risks of "cut and run" are real for host financial

---

[87] Calvo, "Capital Flows and Capital-market Crises."

[88] Berglof et al., "Understanding the Crisis in Emerging Europe," 3–4.

[89] R. de Haas and I. van Lelyveld, "Internal Capital Markets and Lending by Multinational Bank subsidiaries," European Bank for Reconstruction and Development (2008); Cull and Martinez Peria, "Foreign Bank Participation in Developing Countries."

[90] Z. Kudrna and D. Gabor, "The return of Political Risk: Foreign-owned Banks in Emerging Europe," *Europe-Asia Studies*, 65 (2013), 548–566.

Table 12.2 *The Impact of the Global Financial Crisis in Emerging Europe*

Country	Change in GDP growth (%) (1)	Change in current account (% of GDP) (2)	Change in cross-border bank lending (%) (3)
Bulgaria	−5.0%	13.8%	−25.1%
Czech Republic	−4.8%	−0.5%	−9.1%
Estonia	−14.7%	11.2%	−13.6%
Hungary	−6.6%	6.3%	−16.1%
Latvia	−14.2%	20.4%	−16.3%
Lithuania	−14.8%	15.0%	−21.4%
Poland	2.6%	2.6%	−8.9%
Romania	−7.1%	7.0%	−14.5%
Slovakia	−5.3%	3.0%	−16.4%
Slovenia	−7.8%	4.8%	−20.6%

Source: (1) IMF World Economic Outlook database, annual GDP growth rate for 2009; (2) IMF World Economic Outlook, difference between current account position in 2009 and 2008; (3) BIS locational statistics, change from 2007Q3-2008Q3 to 2008Q3-2009Q3; IMF World Economic Outlook database.

systems.[91] Moreover, the crisis reflected problems of parent banking groups in funding themselves in the wholesale markets, spurred by problems in third countries, rather than any particular problems in host countries.[92] In turn, this left their financial system exposed to changes in strategy by large multinational banks.[93]

The host's dilemma is also evident in the cross-country impact of the crisis. It is the countries that managed to mitigate the cross-border banking-led credit boom that experienced the lowest bust. Before the crisis their policy choices were singled out as standing in the way of financial development and economic growth in comparison to other less-worried peers. The countries with the largest vulnerabilities fueled by cross-border banking suffered the most severe crisis: "pre-crisis current account gaps and pre-crisis net external positions help explain an important part of

[91] R. de Haas and I. van Lelyveld, "Multinational Banks and the Global Financial Crisis: Weathering the Perfect Storm?," *Journal of Money, Credit and Banking*, 46 (2014), 333–364.

[92] A. Popov and G. F. Udell, "Cross-border Banking, Credit Access, and the Financial Crisis," *Journal of International Economics*, 87 (2012), 147–161.

[93] Brunnermeier et al., "Banks and Cross-Border Capital Flows."

subsequent cross-country differences in demand growth."[94] More importantly, even beyond the costs of output volatility among countries with larger booms and busts, GDP growth for 2003–2010 as a whole was *higher* for the countries with the *lower* credit growth.[95] Hence, it would appear that there is no tradeoff between higher growth and more vulnerability in terms of credit growth – indeed, it is the countries with low vulnerability that had the highest growth.

12.4.2   Resolving the Host's Dilemma through International Institutions

Considering the scale of the financial shock in the fourth quarter of 2008, host authorities were quick to react. Yet, this only served to highlight their limited capacity to address extensive vulnerabilities at the national level. The first measure was to relax reserve requirements to stimulate lending while also increasing deposit insurance coverage in a coordinated manner. Regulators advocated a no-dividend policy and the conversion of profits into capital, while also relaxing loan classification and provisioning requirements in Bulgaria, Romania, and Estonia. Some countries, such as Hungary, Romania and Latvia, were pushed into recapitalization measures. Those which had enough policy space reduced interest rates (Czech Republic, Poland) or enacted some limited fiscal stimulus (Bulgaria, Poland). Yet, by October 2008 a sell-off in government securities and the plunge of the florint pushed Hungary to seek external support from the IMF, followed soon by Latvia in December 2008, due to worries about its banking sector, and Romania in early 2009 following problems with the maturity structure of its public debt. Worries were also mounting about the sustainability of currency pegs in the rest of the Baltics and Bulgaria, and there were concerns about the extent of currency depreciation in other countries, especially Poland. It was clear that the scale of the shock outstripped the ability of small open economies to cushion a sudden stop to years of excess.

Worries centered on the possible withdrawal of cross-border banking from the region. Given the large market share of foreign banks and the importance of cross-border banking, a mass withdrawal would cause banking crises in numerous countries. Such worries intensified as home

---

[94]   G. M. Milesi-Ferretti and P. R. Lane, "Global Imbalances and External Adjustment after the Crisis," International Monetary Fund Working Paper 14/151 (2014), 18.
[95]   Bakker and Gulde, "The Credit Boom in the EU New Member States," 25.

authorities stepped in with various commitments to save their parent banks, often on condition that the money is used only for domestic lending. For example, Austria, home of a number of banks with large subsidiaries in emerging Europe, restricted its bailout facilities to institutions regulated under its banking legislation, that is, banks in Austria and their branches, but *not* their subsidiaries abroad.[96] Meanwhile, French banks receiving state support promised to increase domestic credit by 3–4 percent annually, while the Dutch ING announced a further $32 billion worth of loans to Dutch borrowers in exchange for government support.[97] As a response, host regulators looked to renege on obligations to insure deposits or provide liquidity to foreign subsidiaries. In particular, they largely sought to restrict the reallocation of funds from subsidiaries with excess capital or liquidity to their parents through the non-distribution of dividends or the capitalization of profits, a mild form of ring-fencing[98].

Support from international institutions came from three main sources. First, the EU revived a largely forgotten balance-of-payments facility to support non-euro countries, quadrupling its resources to 50 billion euros by mid-2009. It disbursed a total of 14.6 billion euros to Hungary, Latvia, and Romania, or around 30 percent of the overall financing package. The EU also made use of its structural and cohesion funds, which were frontloaded and their flexibility relaxed, and stepped up the lending activities of the EIB and the EBRD.[99] The second source was support from the IMF, which after a period of downsizing saw its resources tripled by the G-20 in response to the crisis. It quickly put these to work, with a total of 27.2 billion euros lent to just three EU countries by 2009. Finally, the Vienna Initiative provided a coordination platform to prevent a run to the exit by foreign banking groups in the region. This was underpinned by a 24.5 billion euros joint action plan for bank lending by the EBRD, EIB, and the World Bank. The role of the IMF, the EU,

[96] J. Pisani-Ferry and A. Sapir, "Banking Crisis Management in the EU: An Early Assessment," *Economic Policy*, 25 (2010) 62, 341–373; K. Pistor, "Governing Interdependent Financial Systems: Lessons from the Vienna Initiative," *Journal of Globalization and Development*, 2 (2012), 11.

[97] "Globalisation under Strain: Homeward Bound," *The Economist* (February 5, 2009).

[98] E. Cerutti, et al., "Bankers without Borders? Implications of Ring-Fencing for European Cross-Border Banks," International Monetary Fund Working Paper 10/247 (2010).

[99] Jacoby, "The EU Factor in Fat Times and in Lean"; Z. Darvas, "The EU's Role in Supporting Crisis-hit Countries in Central and Eastern Europe," Bruegel.org (December 31, 2009).

and the Vienna Initiative in emerging Europe has been discussed extensively in other studies.[100]

In the context of this chapter, however, the focus is on how these institutions helped to address the three interlinked challenges of the host's dilemma outlined in section 12.2. The first problem highlighted above is acquiring timely and accurate information on the state of the parent banking group, which was addressed by the Vienna Initiative. As part of it, the EBRD, alongside other institutions such as the BIS, provided extensive information about the network of mutual exposure, which also raised awareness of the problem faced by emerging European countries. The issue of uncoordinated bank withdrawal was recognized from the outset and the EBRD was active in drawing it to the attention of policy-makers in both home and host countries. Of more operational importance, the Vienna Initiative provided a forum, which gathered foreign banks, home and host regulators, and international institutions. This made possible a set of commitments which softened the obstacles to information sharing by alleviating at least partly the worries of both home and host regulators. Thus, home regulators committed to not constrain how parent banks use bailout money, while their host counterparts committed to not ring-fence assets.[101] These commitments were complemented by public agreements by banks to maintain their exposure to the region and the financial health of their subsidiaries.

Such "soft" promises might not by themselves necessarily alleviate the concerns of host concerns unless there are some enforcement mechanisms in place, which directs attention to the second aspect of the host's

---

[100] Darvas, "The EU's Role in Supporting Crisis-hit Countries"; A. Aslund, "The Last Shall Be the First: the East European Financial Crisis, 2008–10," *Peterson Institute for International Economics* (2010); Pistor, "Governing Interdependent Financial Systems"; Bakker and Klingen, "How Emerging Europe Came through the 2008/09 Crisis"; J. Pisani-Ferry, A. Sapir and G. Wolff, "EU-IMF Assistance to Euro-area Countries – an Early assessment," Bruegel.org (2013); Epstein, "When do foreign banks 'cut and run'?," Independent Evaluation Office, IMF Response to the Financial and Economic Crisis (2014); Jacoby, "The EU Factor in Fat Times and in Lean"; S. Lütz and M. Kranke, "The European Rescue of the Washington Consensus? EU and IMF Lending to Central and Eastern European Countries," *Review of International Political Economy*, 21 (2014), 310–338; D. Gabor, "The IMF's Rethink of Global Banks: Critical in Theory, Orthodox in Practice," *Governance* 28 (2015), 199–218; R. D. de Haas, et al., "Taming the Herd? Foreign Banks, the Vienna Initiative and Crisis Transmission," *Journal of Financial Intermediation*, 24 (2015), 325–355; Blustein, "Over Their Heads"; D. Hodson, "The IMF as a de facto Institution of the EU: A Multiple Supervisor Approach," *Review of International Political Economy*, 22 (2015), 570–598.

[101] Pistor, "Governing Interdependent Financial Systems."

dilemma. To be sure, banks themselves had significant incentives not to disengage from the region, not least of which were reputational concerns and the desire to maintain a relationship with countries which were the source of significant profits.[102] It would also have been operationally difficult to pull out, given the large brick-and-mortar lending operation.[103] Nevertheless, there was a very real prisoner's dilemma: no single bank would prefer to leave, but should there be a run to the exit, it would be rational for each bank to try to be the first one out so that it could preserve the value of its investment. In order to prevent this, the international financial institutions used a mixture of moral suasion and financial incentives to ensure enforcement of these non-legally binding commitments. On the "stick" side, as early as Hungary the IMF sought commitment letters from banks as a precondition to supporting the countries in which they were doing business, with the practice becoming formalized within the context of the Vienna Initiative, later.[104] On the "carrot" side, the EBRD, EIB and World Bank prepared a financing package aimed at the private sector, ultimately providing 33 billion euros of debt funding, equity, trade finance, support for SMEs, small infrastructure projects, multilateral guarantees, syndicated loans, and other financing support.[105]

Perhaps the most visible way international institutions addressed the host dilemma was through providing significant help to ensure burden-sharing once the crisis hit. As with any balance of payments crisis, this was a function of the level of capital outflows, and the mix between external financing and domestic adjustments that compensates it. Given the potentially significant financing gap estimated by the World Bank, the EBRD, and the IMF of around \$250–300 billion overall,[106] the Vienna Initiative also played an important role in limiting banking outflows.[107] Countries also significantly cut their expenditures, and when possible, provided limited fiscal stimulus. However, they also received large packages to support their adjustments, limiting somewhat the fallout from the financial turmoil imported from abroad (see table 12.3). Total IMF/EU support

---

[102] Interview with senior World Bank official, Washington, September 2015.

[103] Interview with senior IMF official, Warsaw, February 2016.

[104] Interviews with senior IMF official, Washington, September 2015 and with senior IMF official, Warsaw, February 2016.

[105] EBRD, EIB and World Bank, "Final Report on the Joint IFI Action Plan," European Bank for Reconstruction and Development (2011).

[106] S. Wagstyl, "IMF Urges Eastern EU to Adopt Euro," *Financial Times* (April 5, 2009); S. Wagstyl, "Variable Vulnerability," *Financial Times* (25 February 2009).

[107] de Haas et al., "Taming the herd?"

Table 12.3 *Financial Assistance to EU Member States, 2008–2009 (billions of euros)*

	IMF	EC	Others*	Total	% of 2008 GDP
Hungary	12.5 (62.5%)	6.5 (32.5%)	1.0 (5%)	20.0	19%
Latvia	1.7 (22.6%)	3.1 (41.3%)	2.7 (36%)	7.5	32%
Romania	13.0 (65%)	5.0 (25%)	2.0 (10%)	20.0	15%
Total	27.2 (57.2%)	14.6 (30.7%)	5.7 (12%)	47.5	18%

*Others involve World Bank (all countries), bilateral assistance from all four Scandinavian countries and Estonia (for Latvia), assistance from the EBRD, Czech Republic, and Poland (for Latvia), and the EBRD and EIB (for Romania). Source: IMF program documents, EC MoUs, and Darvas, "The EU's role in supporting crisis-hit countries."

for Hungary, Latvia, and Romania reached $62.2 billion between 2008 and 2010, alongside a precautionary $20.5 billion credit line agreed with Poland. Total packages amounted to 32 percent of GDP for Latvia, 19 percent of GDP for Hungary, and 15 percent of GDP for Romania.[108] IMF funding exceeded 1000 percent of each country's quota, and programs were three to five times as large as previous SBAs approved for Thailand, Indonesia and Korea in terms of GDP. The Executive Board processed applications very quickly, with the Hungarian and Latvian programs taking as little as four weeks from initial request to approval. Funding was significantly frontloaded, committed upfront, and disbursed fast in order to respond to a rapidly worsening financial situation. Finally, conditionality was more streamlined and limited, with a gradual fiscal adjustment path, and budgetary support, reflecting an attempt to account for the social costs of the programs.[109]

12.4.3   Outcomes of Crisis Management

How can one assess the impact of international institutions in emerging Europe in 2008–2009? One approach, taken by analysts at the time, is to draw parallels with the outcomes of previous similar emerging market

---

[108] Darvas, "The EU's role in supporting crisis-hit countries."
[109] S. Takagi, et al., "A review of crisis management programs supported by IMF Stand-By Arrangements, 2008–11," Independent Evaluation Office of the International Monetary Fund, Background Paper 14/12 (2014).

crises. Indeed, many pointed out the similarities with the Asian financial crisis of 1997: "The vulnerabilities in many CEE countries – high foreign-currency borrowing, hefty levels of external debt, massive current-account deficits – suggest the classic makings of a capital account crisis à la Asia in the late 1990s"; meanwhile "Central and Eastern European policymakers are in a virtual straitjacket, having fairly limited tools to cope with the crisis."[110] Other high-profile voices ran articles such as "Eastern crisis that can wreck the Eurozone,"[111] "The bill that could break up Europe,"[112] or "Eastern Europe 2008=Southeast Asia 1997."[113] If anything, emerging Europe looked substantially more vulnerable than East Asia had been on the eve of the crisis. Its current account deficits often reached double digits, whereas already much smaller deficits have proven problematic before when financing conditions reversed, particularly in Latin America. Equally worrying, the levels of foreign currency loans among total loans significantly exceeded the levels seen in Thailand, Indonesia and Turkey in all but one of the countries in the region, while reserve coverage was also thinner than in previous crises.[114]

However, despite such large vulnerabilities, when measured by speed of recovery, by the risk of currency collapse, or by the presence of systemic banking crises, emerging Europe confounded the pessimistic predictions. Thus, what observers found most surprising was that "the crisis is missing some of the defining attributes of emerging market crises in the past."[115] First, the region experienced a sharp fall but an equally quick rebound back to growth, with recovery well under way by late 2009, just one year after the collapse of Lehman Brothers. That is not to say that emerging Europe did not suffer from a painful downturn – indeed, it was the region hardest hit by the global financial crisis. The output collapse was significant, and, given high growth rates pre-crisis, the declines from peak to trough were even larger.[116] However, the current account balance sharply improved in the space of several months, including by between

---

[110] N. Roubini, "Will The Economic Crisis Split East and West in Europe?," *Forbes* (26 February 2009).

[111] W. Munchau, "Eastern Crisis that Could Wreck the Eurozone," *Financial Times* (22 February 2009).

[112] "The Bill that Could Break Up Europe," *The Economist* (February 26, 2009).

[113] P. Krugman, "Eastern Europe 2008 = Southeast Asia 1997," *New York Times* (October 31, 2008).

[114] Bakker and Klingen, "How Emerging Europe Came through the 2008/09 Crisis," 76.

[115] Berglof et al., "Understanding the Crisis in Emerging Europe," 2.

[116] Darvas, "The EU's Role in Supporting Crisis-hit Countries."

12 percent and 18 percent in the case of Bulgaria and the Baltics. Therefore, by 2010 countries in the region, with the exception of Latvia and Romania, had returned to growth, even if their economic output remained considerably below pre-crisis levels.

Second, the region avoided currency crises on the scale of those in Indonesia, Thailand, Turkey, and Argentina, whose currencies crashed spectacularly after exchange pegs had collapsed. The exchange rate was the most contentious issue in countries with currency boards (Bulgaria and the Baltics). Entry into the EU alongside easy global monetary conditions stimulated a large inflow of capital to such countries, while EU rules prohibited capital controls; in turn this led to higher inflation, which was used as an argument about not letting them join the euro.[117] As a consequence, these countries were caught in the impossible trinity, leading to significantly overvalued exchange rates. Hence, it is easy to see why many prominent commentators, including Paul Krugman, Nouriel Roubini, and Kenneth Rogoff argued that Latvia should devalue early on by drawing parallels with Argentina in 2000–01.[118] Furthermore, the IMF was criticized by many outside observers for agreeing to a program that did not include a devaluation of the lat.[119] Yet, the Latvian currency peg held through the crisis, although this necessitated draconian "internal devaluation." Estonia, Lithuania, and Bulgaria also managed to protect their pegs through fiscal consolidation and without recourse to international funds. Meanwhile, after steep falls, the currencies of the floaters such as Poland, the Czech Republic, Hungary, and Romania quickly recovered, thus avoiding the risk of prolonged currency mismatches in the banking system.

The third surprising outcome was the lack of a systemic banking crisis in the region. Such system-wide contagion is often the most painful aspect of emerging market crises, costing between 10 and 57 percent of GDP in public support.[120] To be sure, Latvia's Parex did require restructuring, but no other bank failed (although Hungary's OTP did come

---

[117] Aslund, "The Last Shall Be the First," 59.

[118] P. Krugman, "Latvia Is the New Argentina (slightly wonkish)," *New York Times* (December 23, 2008); N. Magnusson, "Rogoff Says Latvia Should Devalue Its Currency, Direkt Reports," *Bloomberg* (June 29, 2009); N. Roubini, "Latvia's Currency Crisis Is a Rerun of Argentina's," *Financial Times* (June 10, 2009).

[119] E. Hugh, "Why the IMF's decision to agree a Latvian bailout programme without devaluation is a mistake" (December 22, 2008); Roubini, "Latvia's Currency Crisis Is a Rerun of Argentina's."

[120] L. Laeven and F. Valencia, "Resolution of Banking Crises: The Good, the Bad, and the Ugly," International Monetary Fund Working Paper (June 2010).

close). However, while there were some fears about the domestic banks in some countries, and worries about foreign currency mortgages in others, the key issue at the time was whether foreign banks which dominated the region would "cut and run" as they had in previous crises.[121] Given the large foreign bank presence in emerging Europe, such a "run on the region" would not only have undermined the efforts of the IMF and the EU, but it would have also precipitated a significant banking crisis, further complicating crisis resolution efforts. In the event, no foreign bank withdrew from the region. Although they largely curtailed lending to zero, leading to an abrupt change in credit conditions compared to when credit was growing at double digits per annum, they did not repatriate large amounts of capital or liquidity from their subsidiaries. Indeed, in comparison to other regions, emerging Europe suffered the largest output collapse during the global financial crisis, but cross-border banking claims fell the least.[122] Overall, net exposure of Western banks fell by 1.3 percent of GDP between 2008Q3 and 2010Q2 – considerably less than the average of 9 percent of GDP net declines witnessed within the same timeframe in previous crises.[123]

12.5   Conclusion

Overall, this chapter has sought to demonstrate that countries on the recipient end of large cross-border banking flows face a host's dilemma, which differs significantly from the well-studied regulator's dilemma between international competitiveness and domestic stability. Instead, such host countries with largely foreign-owned domestic banking systems are caught between their special needs for supervision, regulation, and resolution, and international institutions designed to meet such needs from which they are largely excluded. It then demonstrated that countries in emerging Europe largely found themselves facing the host's dilemma between 2004 and 2007, leading to a significant credit boom and increasing vulnerabilities due to accelerating cross-border banking inflows and a largely unresponsive governance framework. However, once the crisis hit the region between 2008 and 2010, international institutions responded and successfully mitigated a potentially significant collapse. This provides empirical evidence for both the relevance and the

---

[121] Roubini and Setser, *Bailouts or Bail-ins?*; Epstein, "When Do Foreign Banks 'Cut and Run'?"

[122] Berglof et al., "Understanding the Crisis in Emerging Europe."

[123] Bakker and Klingen, "How Emerging Europe Came through the 2008/09 Crisis," 86.

costs of the dilemma for host states and demonstrates the need to consider the specific challenges that host states face, a topic which still receives limited attention in the literature on international political economy of financial regulation.

There is clearly scope for both theoretical and empirical further research on the host's dilemma. On the theoretical side, a key takeaway refers to the need of cross-border institutional mechanisms to underpin financial stability in host countries as absent this they find themselves exposed to the ebbs-and-flows of cross-border banking flows.[124] One area for fruitful inquiries is identifying the crucial components of international institutions that could make them responsive to non-members or marginal members. Another issue for scholars is to study the relationship between independence, ideational consensus and capacity, and tease out more precisely which way the causality is running. Finally, there is scope to explore how institutions interact –both between themselves and with private-sector actors, and under what conditions such interaction can allow them to respond to the needs of host states. There are various approaches to examine how and whether the costs to host states in terms of sovereignty can be mitigated, even if they cannot be eliminated.[125]

On the empirical side, further inquiry is needed into the factors, which explain the switch in international institutions from the boom to the bust period, exploring in particular the impact and consequences of crisis conditions. Additionally, it would be clearly beneficial to confirm the generalizability of the host's dilemma in other regions with significant foreign-bank ownership and presence, such as sub-Saharan Africa or Latin America. Furthermore, while this chapter has restricted itself to countries with large-scale foreign bank ownership, it is evident similar boom-and-bust dynamics played out in countries where the banking system was not foreign-owned, but nonetheless relied extensively on cross-border banking flows. This was notably the case of Spain, Ireland, and to a lesser extent the rest of the countries caught in the euro area crisis. This suggests that perhaps the dilemmas facing host countries are more widely applicable to countries on the receiving ends of large-scale capital flows. Examining this claim would require going beyond the scope and task of this chapter.

---

[124] E. Avgouleas and D. Arner, "The Eurozone Debt Crisis and the European Banking Union: 'Hard Choices', 'Intolerable Dilemmas', and the Question of Sovereignty," *International Lawyer*, 50 (2017), 29–67.

[125] Avgouleas and Arner, "The Eurozone Debt Crisis and the European Banking Union."

The implications arising from the analysis presented here for host states are considerable, but somewhat mixed. On the one hand, the host's dilemma is not as inescapable as it would appear at first sight, and that international institutions can indeed help mitigate many of its problems. Therefore, it is possible to manage the challenges of banking integration in ways, which allow countries on the receiving end to harness the ensuing benefits. Yet, on the other hand, this comes at a cost of reduced sovereignty as host states have very limited control on the variables shaping the behavior of supranational bodies.[126] As host's states are often marginal, if at all, members with sometimes opposing interests to powerful home states, this presents significant political obstacles to sustainable and equitable banking integration. In short, the experience of emerging Europe shows that international institutions can help to resolve the dilemma, but that it is also far from guaranteed that they will do so.

Nonetheless, from the perspective of host states, the conclusions are twofold. If they are to reap the benefits of banking integration, they need to ensure a degree of influence in international institutions through adequate representation in their governance, or, at the very least, that the institutions tasked with financial stability have the independence, expertise, and resources to address their problems. This draws explicit attention to the institutional and governance underpinnings required for sustainable banking integration, and holds lessons for both the ongoing development of the European Banking Union, and for future projects of banking integration in South-East Asia and elsewhere. However, this analysis also suggests that in the absence of appropriate institutional safeguards and resources, host states should be ready to forgo the alluring benefits of foreign banks. In particular, they need to be wary from the impact of foreign banks on credit growth and be ready to implement measures, which might be seen by others as preventing the full freedom of movement of banking flows. While the quandary is hard to resolve and the stakes are high, indecision and a refusal to address the challenge head-on appears to be the worst of both worlds.

---

[126] Avgouleas and Arner, "The Eurozone Debt Crisis and the European Banking Union."

The Preferential Treatment of Government Debt in Financial Law: The Case of Europe

AD VAN RIET[*]

13.1 Introduction

Responding to the Global Financial Crisis of 2008, the leaders of the Group of Twenty (G-20) major economies, including the European Union (EU), committed to restoring the health and stability of the global financial system.[1] Following the G-20 initiatives, the competent authorities in the EU set out to correct financial market failures, tighten financial regulation, enhance financial supervision and improve the resilience of financial institutions in Europe.

This chapter shows that the reform of European finance went further than just removing financial market distortions, correcting deficient regulations and strengthening supervisory institutions: it also significantly widened the scope of the existing preferential regulatory treatment of sovereign debt that makes it easier for governments to obtain market funding at favorable interest rates and to manage the crisis legacy of high public debt.

First, the authorities have tightened EU prudential legislation for banks as well as for collective investment funds, money market funds, institutional investors and central counterparties. As a result, the existing preferential treatment of claims on the government in European banking law has gained in weight and has been extended to other financial services. This regulatory provision encourages the financial industry to disregard the risks from high government exposure and contributes to captive sovereign credit markets. Second, EU financial market legislation has been tightened in several respects, notably constraining the operations of credit rating agencies and the ability to engage in short-selling

---

* Comments from Emilios Avgouleas, Sylvester Eijffinger and Lex Hoogduin are gratefully acknowledged.
1 Group of Twenty (G-20), "Declaration of the Summit on Financial Markets and the World Economy" (Washington DC, November 15, 2008).

and credit default swaps. Several aspects of these legal changes reduce market pressure and benefit governments in times of funding stress. Third, the majority of euro area countries are considering how best to impose a harmonized financial transactions tax. Governments could well decide to exempt market trading in sovereign bonds, thereby favoring public debt management in addition to receiving extra tax revenues.

Taking a political economy perspective, European policy-makers may have felt compelled to follow relevant parallel regulatory developments in other advanced economies, notably the United States. Beyond this political desire for maintaining a "level playing field," the extension of market access support for governments in EU financial law may be related to three (complementary) explanations: a reappearance of financial repression to reduce the burden of high public debt; a return to the traditional close relationship between the government and the financial sector so as to align mutual interests in fiscal and financial stability; and the wish to increase explicit and implicit taxes on finance and recoup public revenues lost during the financial crisis. The broadening base of this "regulatory tax on finance" has largely escaped attention.[2]

Enabling national governments to protect themselves from market pressure may be understandable, given the heavy fiscal legacy of the crisis, the systemic role of government bonds as safe and liquid assets, and the view that the financial sector should in future make a larger contribution to the European tax bill. This may offer EU countries some compensation for the fact that their ability to exercise political dominance over the domestic financial industry and capital markets in general is being constrained by two recent developments: first, the centralization of banking supervision and resolution under the European Banking Union, and second, the planned harmonization of capital market law as part of the Capital Markets Union.[3]

However, extensive government privileges in public debt financing create moral hazard on the part of sovereigns and undermine incentives for fiscal adjustment and economic reforms. They put a heavy burden on the successful implementation of the reinforced EU economic governance framework that seeks to ensure sound macroeconomic and fiscal policies. Moreover, the regulatory bias toward large sovereign exposures

---

[2] For a detailed analysis, see A. van Riet, *Financial Repression and High Public Debt in Europe*, CentER Dissertation Series, 551 (Tilburg, Netherlands: Tilburg University, Center for Economic Research, February, 2018).

[3] See N. Véron, "Banking Union or Financial Repression? Europe Has Yet to Choose," VoxEU – CEPR's Policy Portal (April 26, 2012); and N. Véron, "Defining Europe's Capital Markets Union," Policy Contribution, 12 (Brussels: Bruegel, November 2014).

in financial institutions may become an economic and prudential concern, given the possible crowding out of private sector funding and the risks for financial stability in times of fiscal stress.[4] Discussions at the European and international level on whether, how and at what pace to phase out these fiscal favors in prudential banking legislation have not led to any agreement. The evidence in this chapter shows that an encompassing approach covering the whole financial system would be warranted, taking account of the risk of regulatory arbitrage.

The remainder of this chapter is structured as follows. Section 13.2 discusses the regulatory foundation of government bonds as safe and liquid assets and proposes three political economy arguments that may explain why European policy-makers wanted to stay with this prudential fiction. Sections 13.3, 13.4 and 13.5 document the main cases where the crisis-driven overhaul of European financial governance over the period 2008–2017 has extended the existing preferential treatment of sovereign debt in banking, investment and market law, respectively (see Table 13.1 for the ten main legislative measures selected for this chapter; see Table 13.4 for a detailed overview).[5] Section 13.6 concludes.

13.2   The Regulatory Foundation of Government Bonds as Safe and Liquid Assets

Over the course of the 1970s to 1990s, financial markets in advanced economies were widely liberalized. This evolving trend had at least two consequences for governments: first, they had to introduce prudential regulation and supervision of the financial sector to protect savers and investors and preserve systemic stability; second, they had to pursue credible stability-oriented economic policies in order to convince market participants of their creditworthiness, as a pre-condition for attracting savings at affordable, market-determined (real) interest rates.

---

[4] See also C. Castro and J. Mencía, "Sovereign Risk and Financial Stability," Banco de España, *Financial Stability Journal*, 26 (May, 2014), 75–107; and European Systemic Risk Board (ESRB), *Report on the Regulatory Treatment of Sovereign Exposures* (Frankfurt am Main: ESRB, March 2015).

[5] This review focuses on regulatory privileges for EU sovereigns (central governments), while acknowledging that in many cases similar advantages apply to the central bank, regional and local governments, public-sector entities, multilateral institutions and third-country governments. Moreover, many EU financial laws are of relevance for the whole European Economic Area.

Table 13.1 *Selection of European Financial Reforms 2008–2017*

Main reforms of EU financial legislation	Announced	Applies	Status
1. EU banking regulation/ directive (CRR/CRD IV)	July 2011	Jan 2014	In force, phased in
EBA capital exercise	Oct 2011	Oct 2011– Dec 2014	Ad hoc measure
2. EU banking structure regulation (proposal)	Jan 2014		Withdrawn
3. EU investment funds directive (UCITS IV)	July 2008	July 2011	In force
4. EU regulation on money market funds (MMF)	Sept 2013	July 2018, Jan 2019	In force
5. EU insurance and reinsurance directive (Solvency II)	Mar 2008	Jan 2016	In force
6. EU directive for occupational pension funds (IORP II)	July 2010	Jan 2017	In force
7. EU market infrastructure regulation (EMIR)	Sept 2010	Aug 2012	In force
8. EU regulation on credit rating agencies	July 2011	June 2013	In force
9. EU regulation on short-selling and CDS contracts	Sept 2010	Nov 2012	In force
10. Common financial transactions tax (FTT) (proposal)	Feb 2013	?	Under discussion

Source: Compilation based on (proposed) changes in EU financial law 2008–2017. Cut-off date: 31 December, 2017.

Gelpern and Gerding observe in this light that the law plays an important role in making investors believe that specific assets are safe.[6] Beyond the core powers of a nation state to access the country's resources, national policy-makers use their powers of legislation, regulation and contract design to coordinate market participants toward selecting the sovereign benchmark asset promoted by law and to make them act as if it was a safe haven, even if

[6] A. Gelpern and E. F. Gerding, "Rethinking the Law in 'Safe Assets'," in R. P. Buckley, E. Avgouleas and D. W. Arner (eds.), *Reconceptualising Global Finance and Its Regulation* (New York: Cambridge University Press, 2016), 159–189.

the reality is different. Governments greatly facilitated meeting their new challenge of financing public debt in open capital markets by making sure that the prudential requirements for financial intermediaries, notably banks and institutional investors, would not impose any restrictions on holdings of domestic government debt. Accordingly, they labeled government bonds as "safe" for regulatory purposes, and so promoted a liquid market for public debt instruments. Also supported by favorable credit ratings and the absence of defaults, market participants thus generally perceived the sovereign bonds of advanced economies as safe and liquid assets, and over time these functioned as a cornerstone for the development of the financial system.[7]

After the onset of the Global Financial Crisis in September 2008, the G-20 set out to strengthen financial markets and remedy the shortcoming of regulatory regimes so as to avoid future crises. Following the lead of the G-20, the European Commission embarked on a comprehensive financial reform program with the overall objective to create a more resilient and growth-supportive EU financial system and to secure financial stability.[8] However, this comprehensive policy response also significantly broadened the scope of the existing preferential regulatory treatment of sovereign bonds at the European level.

Looking beyond the wish to coordinate financial reforms at the global level, this remarkable development may reflect at least three (complementary) political economy considerations: first, it may be interpreted as a revival of financial repression, i.e. a comprehensive regime of government interventions in the financial system with the intention to gain fiscal benefits;[9] second, it could be seen as a return to the traditional close relationship between the government and the financial industry, whereby a strong role of the state in finance is again necessary to preserve the benchmark role of government bonds as safe and liquid

---

[7] See International Monetary Fund (IMF), "Safe Assets: Financial System Cornerstone?," *Global Financial Stability Report: The Quest for Lasting Stability* (Washington DC: IMF, April 2012), chap. 3; and A. van Riet, "Addressing the Safety Trilemma: A Safe Sovereign Asset for the Eurozone," ESRB Working Paper, 35 (Frankfurt am Main: European Systemic Risk Board, February, 2017).

[8] European Commission, "Communication on regulating financial services for sustainable growth," COM(2010) 301 (Brussels: June 2, 2010); and European Commission, "Communication on a reformed financial sector for Europe," COM(2014) 279 (Brussels: 15 May, 2014).

[9] See C. M. Reinhart, "The Return of Financial Repression," Banque de France, *Financial Stability Review*, 16 (April, 2012), 37–48; and A. van Riet, *Financial Repression and High Public Debt in Europe*, (Tilburg University, February, 2018).

assets as precondition for a stable financial system;[10] and third, it can be regarded as a way to counter regulatory capture by the financial industry, increase the taxation of finance and recoup public revenues lost during the financial crisis.[11]

13.3   The Preferential Treatment of Government Debt in EU Banking Law

13.3.1   EU Prudential Banking Legislation

A privileged market access for governments based on prudential considerations can be found already in the Basel Accord of 1988. This agreement among the G-10 major economies determined the supervisory regulations governing the capital adequacy of international banks based on the weighted relative riskiness of broad categories of assets, focusing on credit risk. One of the contentious issues was how to treat bank claims on foreign governments relative to those on the domestic government which were deemed to be safe.[12]

As documented by Goodhart, Europe insisted on applying the basic principle of the EU Treaty that all Member States should be treated equally and hence be given the same high credit standing, a point of view which translated in a zero credit risk for bank claims on all EU sovereigns.[13] To allow for an equal assessment of sovereign instruments among the "club" of G-10 members and other advanced economies, the Basel Committee on Banking Supervision then decided to extend the preferential treatment of sovereign exposures by default to those vis-à-vis all OECD countries.[14]

---

[10] See E. Monnet, S. Pagliari and S. Vallée, "Europe between Financial Repression and Regulatory Capture," Working Paper, 8 (Brussels: Bruegel, July 2014).

[11] See IMF, "A fair and substantial contribution by the financial sector," Final Report to the G-20 (Washington DC: IMF, June 2010); S. M. Chaudry, A. Mullineux and N. Agarwal, "Balancing the Regulation and Taxation of Banking," *International Review of Financial Analysis*, 42 (December 2015), 38–52; and M. Devereux, N. Johannesen and J. Vella, "Can Taxes Tame the Banks? Evidence from the European Bank Levies," Research Paper, 5 (Oxford: Saïd Business School, April 2015).

[12] The idea was that a sovereign can always meet its nominal payment obligations by issuing more of its own currency. This argument raised questions for those countries where the central bank was independent and later for the governments of the euro area, since monetization of their debt by the European Central Bank was excluded by the EU Treaty.

[13] C. A. E. Goodhart, *The Basel Committee on Banking Supervision: A History of the Early Years 1974–1997* (New York: Cambridge University Press, 2011).

[14] More precisely: all full OECD members or countries which had concluded special lending arrangements with the IMF associated with the Funds' General Arrangements to Borrow (the club was subsequently extended to include those countries having signed the New

Goodhart notes that true economic risk played no role in this decision, but it was the only way to reach a political agreement on the subject.

The revised Basel Accord (known as Basel II) of 2004 introduced a significantly more risk-sensitive framework, based on two credit rating approaches: a standardized one and another based on banks' internal risk models. OECD membership was thus no longer a sufficient condition for sovereign claims to attract a zero-risk weight. However, national authorities were given the choice to give bank claims on the sovereign a preferential zero-risk treatment if certain conditions were met.

At the European level, the Basel Accords I and II found their way in successive versions of the Capital Requirements Directive (CRD), which were transposed into national law of the Member States for supervisory application to credit institutions and investment firms. These EU directives essentially considered government securities as safe assets by definition, irrespective of credit, market and concentration risks.

Following the global financial crisis, tighter Basel III standards were approved by the G-20 in November 2010 and published by the Basel Committee on Banking Supervision one month later. The EU Capital Requirements Regulation (CRR) and update IV of the Capital Requirements Directive (CRD IV) transposed these new international standards into EU law; they entered into force in July 2013, taking effect gradually from January 2014 onwards, with full implementation to be achieved within five years.[15] Their overall aim is to enhance the quantity and quality of bank capital, limit large capital exposures, ensure liquidity, promote stable funding and constrain leverage. This revamped EU prudential banking legislation contains several important cases of a preferential treatment of bank claims on the government, some of which will be limited over time while some others are additional compared to those in the earlier CRDs.

Arrangements to Borrow). Later it was added that any country which reschedules its official external debt is precluded from this group for a period of five years.

[15] See Regulation (EU) No. 575/2013 of the European Parliament and of the Council of 26 June 2013 on prudential requirements for credit institutions and investment firms and amending Regulation (EU) No. 648/2012 [2013] OJ L176/1–337; and Directive 2013/36/EU of the European Parliament and of the Council of 26 June 2013 on access to the activity of credit institutions and the prudential supervision of credit institutions and investment firms, amending Directive 2002/87/EC and repealing Directives 2006/48/EC and 2006/49/EC [2013] OJ L176/338–436.

13.3.1.1   Capital Adequacy

According to the Basel II and III agreements, banks must hold a minimum amount of capital against the credit risk of all their exposures in the banking book, including their sovereign exposures. Two methodologies for calculating the credit risk weights may be adopted: the standardized approach, which relies on external credit ratings; and the internal-rating based approach, which relies on (large) banks' own risk assessment models. Under the standardized approach of the Basel II/III framework, national authorities have the discretion to allow banks to apply reduced credit risk weights on their sovereign exposures in the banking book.[16]

The new EU Capital Requirements Regulation (CRR) grants, as before, a zero-risk weight to exposures vis-à-vis the central government of any Member State if these are denominated and funded in the domestic currency. For banks in the eurozone, this preferential treatment covers by default their claims on all member countries of the European Economic and Monetary Union (EMU) if these are denominated and funded in the euro, since this is their relevant domestic currency. Until 2017, the standardized approach, as applied in the EU, also continued to extend the zero-risk weight to all EU sovereign exposures denominated and funded in any other EU currency than that of the issuing Member State; in subsequent years, this transitional provision is phased out. From 2020 onwards in these cases the assessment of external credit rating agencies will have to be followed (see Tables 13.2 and 13.3).

For euro area banks, this forthcoming more realistic risk weighting of sovereign claims in non-domestic EU currencies is of only modest relevance; as mentioned above, banks based in the eurozone can automatically value all their euro-denominated and funded exposures vis-à-vis EMU governments as zero-risk claims. This implies that, for example, the government bonds issued by eurozone countries hit by the sovereign debt crisis will continue to be treated as risk-free for all euro area banks.[17]

---

[16] Note that sovereign claims held in the trading book also receive a reduced risk weight for specific market risks, notably for credit spread risk.

[17] Among others, this feature is viewed critically by D. Nouy, "Is Sovereign Risk Properly Addressed by Financial Regulation?," Banque de France, *Financial Stability Review*, 16 (April 2012), 95–106; D. Gros, "Banking Union with a Sovereign Virus: The Self-serving Regulatory Treatment of Sovereign Debt," *Intereconomics*, 48(2) (March/April 2013), 93–97; and J. Weidmann, "Stop Encouraging Banks to Buy Government Debt," *Financial Times* (1 October, 2013).

Table 13.2 *Credit Risk Weights for Exposures to Central Governments* (Standardized approach; ratings from nominated external credit assessment institutions)

Credit quality step	1	2	3	4	5	6	unrated
External credit rating (example S&P)	AAA, AA	A	BBB	BB	B	CCC and below	unrated
Credit risk weight	0%	20%	50%	100%	100%	150%	100%

Source: Final draft implementing technical standard jointly prepared by EBA, EIOPA and ESMA (November 2015); mapping between the long-term issuer credit assessments of Standard & Poor's, the credit quality steps and the credit risk weights under the standardized approach of the EU Capital Requirements Regulation, in accordance with Articles 114, 136(1) and 136(3) of Regulation (EU) No. 575/2013.

Table 13.3 *Regulatory Capital Treatment of Bank Claims on the Government*[a] (EU prudential banking legislation – CRR/CRD IV; in percent of standard credit rating)

Claims issued and funded in:	Domestic currency	Other EU currency			
Year of application:	*permanent*	*2014–17*	*2018*	*2019*	*2020*
Claims issued by:					
Domestic government of a euro area country	0%	0%	20%	50%	100%
Government of any other euro area country	0%	0%	20%	50%	100%
Government of any other non-euro area EU country	0%	0%	20%	50%	100%
Government of any non-EU country[b]	0%				

Notes

[a] Claims on EU governments include claims on central government and the central bank and may include claims on regional and local governments and in exceptional cases those on public sector entities.

[b] 0% on condition that the regulatory authorities have at least equivalent prudential legislation in place and give claims on their sovereign issued and funded in domestic currency a risk weight of zero; otherwise standard credit rating.

The Basel II/III framework allows banks using internal risk models to permanently adopt the standardized approach for assessing credit risk for non-significant business units and asset classes that are immaterial in terms of size and perceived risk profile. Going beyond this Basel II/III "carve out," the EU regulation (CRR) permits such banks to apply the standardized approach to a wide range of sovereign exposures (covering the whole public sector of the Member States) – even those of material size and perceived risk – as long as they would be assigned a standardized zero-risk weight. The European Banking Authority (EBA) is required to issue guidelines at the latest in 2018 that limit over time the use of the standardized approach by banks that normally use internal ratings.

Overall, the zero-risk assessment applicable to all sovereign exposures in EU prudential banking regulation continues to be misaligned with the more differentiated views of markets and credit rating agencies regarding Member States' fiscal fundamentals and their probability of default. This amounts to a preferential regulatory treatment of bank claims on the public sector relative to exposures vis-à-vis the private sector, which benefits in particular the more vulnerable euro area governments. Since the EU bank capital requirements have been tightened with the implementation of Basel III, in terms of the capital definition, the capital criteria and five extra capital buffers for specific situations, the weight of this preferential treatment has increased even further. All else equal, this should be expected to further raise the banking sector's structural demand for sovereign assets labeled as safe.

According to the IMF, the zero-risk weighting of domestic sovereign exposures contributed to an upward bias in the end-2007 capital adequacy ratios of banks (in terms of regulatory capital to risk-weighted assets) of 0.5 to 2.0 percentage points across European countries. This regulatory capital bias has grown since the financial crisis, because fiscal fundamentals have deteriorated and many banks have increased their sovereign exposures.[18] Moreover, it has tightened the nexus between banks and their own government, which turned vicious during the euro area sovereign debt crisis.[19]

Hannoun suggests that the regulatory authorities should move toward a more realistic assessment of sovereign risk and stricter capital requirements where necessary.[20] Consistent with this advice, the EBA issued

[18] IMF, "Safe Assets: Financial System Cornerstone?" (April 2012).
[19] See P. Angelini, G. Grande and F. Panetta, "The Negative Feedback Loop between Banks and Sovereigns," Occasional Paper, 213 (Rome: Banca d'Italia, January 2014).
[20] H. Hannoun, "Sovereign risk in bank regulation and supervision: where do we stand?," speech delivered at the Financial Stability Institute, Abu Dhabi (26 October, 2011).

in December 2011 a recommendation to the national competent authorities which sought to increase the transparency about unrealized losses hidden in the government bond portfolios of systemic banks. Large European banks were asked to create by mid-2012 an exceptional and temporary capital buffer against their fair valued sovereign exposures toward the countries belonging to the European Economic Area and to raise in this connection their core tier 1 capital ratio to 9 percent. The EBA's capital exercise may be interpreted as de facto introducing realistic risk weights on the sovereign exposures of the participating large banks.[21] This prudential intervention sought to reassure markets about the banking sector's ability to absorb unexpected losses and remain solvent. Most large banks were able to fulfill the EBA's temporary capital requirements by mid-2012.[22] As a transition to the full implementation of the Basel III capital standards in EU law, in July 2013 the EBA adopted a new recommendation to preserve the enhanced level of bank capital. Also taking account of the market environment, the additional capital buffer against sovereign risk thus remained in force, until the EBA recommendation was repealed in December 2014.

13.3.1.2   Liquidity Coverage Ratio

The misalignment between regulatory and market-based sovereign credit risk in the EU's capital adequacy rules has been extended to the new EU liquidity and funding standards that follow the Basel III framework as published in December 2010. Starting with liquidity, the CRR requires credit institutions and investment firms to hold enough unencumbered high-quality liquid transferable assets to cover their net cash outflows over a thirty-day period of liquidity stress. Observance of this liquidity coverage ratio should increase the short-term resilience of banks against shocks that drain their liquidity. For certain types of liquid assets, the market value used in the calculation of the liquidity coverage ratio is to be reduced by a specific haircut. A further differentiation is made between assets of extremely high liquidity and credit quality (so-called level 1 assets) and assets of high liquidity and credit quality (level 2 assets, which are subdivided in level 2A and 2B). Given the importance attached to

---

[21] See J. Korte and S. Steffen, "Zero Risk Contagion – Banks' Sovereign Exposure and Sovereign Risk Spillovers," Working Paper (Frankfurt am Main and Berlin: Frankfurt and European School of Management and Technology, April 7, 2015).

[22] European Banking Authority (EBA), "Final report on the implementation of Capital Plans following the EBA's 2011 Recommendation on the creation of temporary capital buffers to restore market confidence" (London: EBA, October 2012).

a strong liquidity position, EU banking legislation set October 2015 as the starting date and asked for a full implementation of the liquidity requirement as from 2018 – one year earlier than agreed in the Basel Committee on Banking Supervision.

A European Commission delegated act specifies the details of the liquidity coverage ratio.[23] A liquid asset is defined as "a freely transferable asset that can be converted quickly into cash in private markets within a short timeframe and without significant loss in value." All claims on or guaranteed by the central government of a Member State have level 1 status and count in full (without haircut) toward meeting the liquidity coverage ratio irrespective of the actual market situation. Furthermore, the rules state that liquid asset holdings must always be appropriately diversified per asset class. As another preferential treatment, sovereign-based assets with level 1 status enjoy an exemption from this diversification requirement. Credit institutions are allowed to hold them in their liquidity buffers without limit. Hence, also these liquidity provisions are likely to raise the banking sector's demand for central government bonds, since these are regarded as liquid by definition.[24]

13.3.1.3   Net Stable Funding Ratio

Another new element of Basel III introduced in EU banking legislation is the requirement for credit institutions (and systemic investment firms) to maintain a stable funding profile in relation to the composition and maturity of their assets and off-balance sheet activities. The objective is to reduce the longer-term funding risk of banks, i.e. the likelihood that disruptions in regular funding sources could endanger their liquidity position, which in turn could undermine their solvency and cause broader systemic stress.

The Basel Committee on Banking Supervision defines the net stable funding ratio – which should always be equal to at least 100 percent – as the available amount of stable funding relative to the required amount of stable funding over a one-year period. Both amounts are calibrated reflecting the stability of a bank's liabilities and the liquidity of its assets. An important assumption is that unencumbered high-quality and liquid assets that can be securitized or traded can easily be used as collateral to secure additional funding, or sold in the market and, therefore, do not

---

[23] See Commission Delegated Regulation (EU) 2015/61 of 10 October 2014 to supplement Regulation (EU) No. 575/2013 of the European Parliament and the Council with regard to liquidity coverage requirement for Credit Institutions [2015] OJ L11/1–36.

[24] See also IMF, "Safe Assets: Financial System Cornerstone?" (April 2012).

need to be fully financed with stable funding. Claims on or guaranteed by sovereigns are regarded as extremely high-quality and liquid assets (level 1), in line with the liquidity coverage ratio (see above), and therefore receive a preferential treatment. The Basel Committee agreed that only 5 percent of their value needs to be covered by stable funding, irrespective of the actual credit quality and market liquidity of these assets.

The European Commission's legal proposal[25] – which at the time of writing this chapter was still under discussion – reduces this stable funding factor to 0 percent for central government bonds with level 1 status in the EU liquidity coverage ratio, so as to avoid negative impacts on the liquidity of national sovereign bond markets in the specific European context. If accepted, this favorable treatment would make it even more attractive for banks to buy and hold sovereign bonds, as these assets make it easier for them to meet the net stable funding ratio than when they invest in private securities.

13.3.1.4   Large Exposures Regime

The large exposures regime in EU banking legislation focuses on avoiding concentration risk arising from large asset holdings, i.e. the risk that losses vis-à-vis a given counterparty or in particular instruments could become so large as to threaten a bank's solvency. To ensure adequate diversification across counterparties and assets, EU credit institutions and investment firms must generally keep their large exposures below the maximum of 25 percent of eligible capital. Governments enjoy a preferential treatment. As claims on the government or claims carrying their guarantee are perceived to be risk-free and liquid, as before, credit institutions do not face a maximum on their sovereign exposures. At least the new EU banking rules do ask banks to put in place effective internal controls that address concentration risks, including those arising from large sovereign exposures.

13.3.1.5   Leverage Ratio

An important new regulatory tool put forward in the Basel III framework is the 3 percent minimum leverage ratio (in terms of tier 1 capital relative

---

[25] European Commission, "Proposal for a Regulation of the European Parliament and of the Council amending Regulation (EU) No. 575/2013 as regards the leverage ratio, the net stable funding ratio, requirements for own funds and eligible liabilities, counterparty credit risk, market risk, exposures to central counterparties, exposures to collective investment undertakings, large exposures, reporting and disclosure requirements and amending Regulation (EU) No. 648/2012," COM(2016) 850 (Brussels: November 23, 2016).

to gross total asset exposure including off-balance sheet positions), which restricts the build-up of excessive leverage in the banking sector and supplements the risk-based capital requirements with a non-risk-based backstop measure. EU banking legislation also introduced the minimum leverage ratio as a new prudential tool in Europe. After a period of mandatory reporting and public disclosure, the European Commission proposes to follow the Basel III leverage ratio requirement of 3 percent and to make it binding two years after the specific regulation enters into force.[26]

A leverage ratio that simply relates a bank's core capital to its non-risk-weighted assets has the potential to counter the many uncertainties surrounding a risk-based system of capital requirements and, therefore, also the preferential treatment of claims on the government compared to those on corporations. A bank's sovereign exposures will be fully included in the assets entering the calculation of the leverage ratio, although in the EU context some specialized credit institutions can make particular adjustments. Some credit institutions may have to adjust their portfolios in order to comply with the 3 percent minimum leverage ratio, in which case changes in public and private sector exposures will generally count the same and do not give rise to a funding privilege for governments.

13.3.1.6   Reducing the Preferential Treatment of Sovereign Exposures

Looking ahead, several experts have advised European authorities to reduce or eliminate the preferential treatment of sovereign exposures in EU prudential banking legislation, as part of an international agreement.[27] The main objectives of this amendment would be to better align the regulatory treatment of credit risk and interest rate risk, remove regulatory distortions among asset classes, discourage large bank exposures to their own sovereign and improve the incentives for sound fiscal policies. Given the special role of sovereign debt as safe and liquid asset in the financial system and the pervasive impact of the existing preferential

---

[26] See again European Commission, COM(2016) 850 (November 23, 2016).

[27] See among others European Systemic Risk Board, "Report on the regulatory treatment of sovereign exposures" (March 2015); Deutsche Bundesbank, "Reducing the privileged regulatory treatment of sovereign exposures," *Annual Report 2014* (Frankfurt am Main: March 2015), 23–40; and Bank for International Settlements (BIS), "Towards a financial stability-oriented fiscal policy," *86th Annual Report 2015/16* (Basel: BIS, June 2016), chap. V.

regulatory treatment of government bonds on both sovereign debtors and their creditors any limitation should be carefully calibrated and allow for a reasonable transition regime – although financial markets would likely frontload expected regulatory changes.[28] For example, one could phase in requirements that banks apply realistic risk weights to their holdings of government debt, use more cautious liquidity assumptions, hold more stable funding, and/or put a limit on the size of their domestic government bond portfolios or on their overall exposure to European governments. However, the Basel Committee on Banking Supervision could not reach a consensus on specific regulatory amendments.[29]

13.3.2   EU Banking Structure Regulation

The favorable regulatory treatment of sovereign debt can also be found in the European Commission's proposal for an EU banking structure regulation that addresses concerns about large banks being "too big to fail, too big to save and too complex to resolve," especially at the national level.[30] Given the threat that systemic banks pose to the stability of the financial system and the implicit subsidy they enjoy from a potential bailout by the public sector in times of banking stress it is considered important to improve the resilience of important credit institutions and, if necessary, to break them up.

The proposed regulation therefore contains two key elements. First, it would prohibit major EU banks from carrying out proprietary trading in financial instruments and commodities, i.e. taking speculative positions for making a profit for their own account. Second, if there is a risk of circumvention of this prohibition, it would give the national competent authority the power (or even the obligation) to require from major EU banks that they separate all high-risk investment activities that are not related to their traditional retail financing of the economy and place them in a distinct trading entity.

---

[28] See for example M. Lanotte, G. Manzelli, A. M. Rinaldi, M. Taboga and P. Tommasino, "Easier Said than Done? Reforming the Prudential Treatment of Banks' Sovereign Exposures," Occasional Paper, 326 (Rome: Banca d'Italia, April 2016).

[29] Basel Committee on Banking Supervision, "The Regulatory Treatment of Sovereign Exposures," Discussion Paper (Basel: Bank for International Settlements, December 2017).

[30] European Commission, "Proposal for a Regulation of the European Parliament and of the Council on structural measures improving the resilience of EU credit institutions," COM (2014) 43 (Brussels: January 29, 2014).

A notable feature of the European Commission's proposal is that it exempts the buying and selling of financial instruments issued by Member States from the ban on proprietary trading and from a possible separation of risky trading activities. This exemption is explicitly made consistent with the zero-risk treatment of bonds issued by central and regional governments (as well as by the EU and other public entities) under the EU banking legislation (as discussed in section 13.3.1), in order to avoid disturbing sovereign debt markets. Again, investments in government bonds are assumed not to pose any credit risk to major banks, and accordingly they are unrestricted in taking significant speculative trading positions in sovereign financial instruments, even in those which in the end might harm their balance sheet. While the envisaged structural reform of the EU banking sector would reduce the implicit public-sector subsidy to large banks, it would extend the privileged treatment of government debt.

The EU Council determined in June 2015 its position on the draft EU banking structure regulation as a starting point for negotiations with the European Parliament. This position suggests including a clause in the regulation that would mandate a review of the exemption given to trading in government bonds so as to take account of possible new views on the treatment of sovereign risk at the European and international level. Views in the European Parliament were split. Since political support rapidly faded and a common agreement appeared no longer feasible, the European Commission decided in October 2017 to withdraw its proposal.

13.4 The Preferential Treatment of Government Debt in EU Investment Law

13.4.1 EU Investment Funds Directive

As regards other financial institutions than credit institutions and investment firms, the EU legal provisions relating to undertakings for collective investment in transferable securities (UCITS) must be considered. The EU Investment Funds Directive – the first version of which (UCITS I) dates from December 1985 – provides an umbrella for asset managers to develop their activities across Europe subject to prudential requirements. As noted by Kopf, the UCITS Directive restricts the investment policies of collective investment funds, but offers ample scope for national regulators to exempt government debt from standard exposure limits that apply to private sector instruments.[31]

Ever since UCITS I, national authorities have been able to authorize collective investment funds to place up to a maximum of 35 percent of their net assets (in terms of transferable securities or money market instruments) in instruments issued or guaranteed by a single Member State, its local authorities, a third country, or a public international body to which one or more of the Member States belong. By way of derogation, they can be allowed to invest up to 100 percent of their assets in different transferable instruments issued or guaranteed by one of these public sector bodies. The conditions are that the securities cover at least six different issues of a single issuer, those from any single-issue account for not more than 30 percent of total assets, and unit-holders must have equivalent protection. Moreover, the authorization must be expressly mentioned in the fund rules and prominently communicated to the public. This legal provision compares with a standard counterparty exposure limit of 5 percent for this type of assets when they are issued by the same private sector entity (or by entities belonging to the same group). This ceiling may be raised to 10 percent on the condition that the total value of all such assets exposed to the same private sector entity stays within 40 percent of the value of all the investment fund's assets.

Considering the applicable concentration limits, collective investment funds may acquire no more than 10 percent of either all the debt securities or all the money market instruments issued by a single body. Again, national regulators may waive this restriction in case a Member State, a local authority, a third country or a public international body to which one or more of the Member States belong is the issuer or guarantor. Allowing for very large collective investments in assets related to a single public sector body goes beyond prudent concentration limits and the authorization of very large sovereign exposures mentioned above goes against the principle of risk diversification. These government funding privileges can nevertheless also be found in the latest form of the EU Investment Funds Directive (UCITS IV), which entered into force in December 2009 and took effect from July 2011.[32]

---

[31] C. Kopf, "Restoring financial stability in the euro area," CEPS Policy Brief, 237 (Brussels: Centre for Economic Policy Studies, March 15, 2011).

[32] See Directive 2009/65/EC of the European Parliament and of the Council of 13 July 2009 on the coordination of laws, regulations and administrative provisions relating to undertakings for collective investment in transferable securities (UCITS) [2009] OJ L302/ 32–95.

13.4.2   EU Regulation on Money Market Funds

Money market funds are part of the asset management sector and provide short-term finance to financial institutions, non-financial corporations and governments. Traditionally, they offer to their investors either a variable net asset valuation per unit or share (VNAV funds) that is calculated marked-to-market and therefore linked to money market interest rates; or they aim to maintain a constant net asset valuation per unit or share (CNAV funds) that is based on amortized cost calculations and seeks to preserve the face value of the investment. Money market funds are prone to investor runs, as became evident in the United States during the global financial crisis. The risk of a run is highest for CNAV funds in times of volatile markets if investors were to believe that they could fail to live up to the expectation of redemption at par (known as "breaking the buck"). Liquidity shortages at redemption raise concerns about financial stability and the supply of short-term credit to the economy.

The EU regulation on money market funds, which entered into force in July 2017 and applies from July 2018 for new money market funds and from January 2019 for existing ones, seeks to address such concerns.[33] The main objective of the regulation is to introduce common standards across the Member States that increase the ability of money market funds to withstand redemption pressures in stressed market conditions and thereby protect investors, safeguard financial stability and preserve the integrity of the EU internal market. The common rules ensure that money market funds only invest in eligible liquid assets and that these are of high credit quality, well-diversified and subject to concentration limits. In addition, the regulation seeks to address the risk of regulatory arbitrage, leading certain banking activities to migrate toward the comparatively less regulated shadow banking system, including money market funds.

Most of the CNAV funds in Europe invest in both public and non-public debt instruments and are domiciled in Ireland and Luxembourg, while the VNAV funds are mostly found in France. The EU regulation on money market funds determines that, in order to mitigate systemic risk, CNAV funds are no longer allowed to invest in private debt but only in public debt – without restricting this requirement to EU public debt.

---

[33] See Regulation (EU) 2017/1131 of the European Parliament and of the Council of 14 June 2017 on money market funds [2017] OJ L169/8–45. Note that the vast majority of money market funds in Europe operate under the UCITS Directive (see section 13.4.1).

In addition, it introduces a new Low Volatility Net Asset Value (LVNAV) fund as a close alternative to a public debt CNAV fund. The Commission is mandated to review within five years the prudential and economic adequacy of the regulation, covering inter alia the role that money market funds play in purchasing debt issued or guaranteed by the Member States, taking into account international and European regulatory developments. In addition, the European Commission must report on the feasibility of establishing a quota whereby at least 80 percent of the assets of public debt CNAV funds are to be invested in EU public debt instruments, having regard to the availability of short-term EU public debt instruments and whether LVNAV funds might be an appropriate alternative to non-EU public debt CNAV funds which would allow taking them out of the CNAV funds altogether. A preferential treatment of EU versus non-EU public debt – so it is argued in a recital – is justified from a prudential supervisory point of view, because the issuance of EU short-term public debt instruments is governed by EU law.

The EU regulation on money market funds includes several additional provisions that create privileges for EU public debt financing. First, the requirement that money market funds can only invest in eligible money market instruments for which both the issuer and the quality have received a "favorable assessment" does not apply to those instruments issued or guaranteed by a central authority or central bank of a Member State, or by specific European institutions. This provision is beneficial to central governments that do not enjoy a high credit standing.

Second, money market funds are explicitly allowed as part of a reverse repurchase agreement to receive non-eligible liquid transferable securities or money market instruments, provided these are issued or guaranteed by a central authority or central bank of a Member State or of a third country, or by specific European institutions, and these have received a favorable credit quality assessment. A lenient interpretation of what constitutes a favorable assessment in this regard might still lead central governments that do not really have a high credit standing to qualify for this derogation.

Third, the provisions on the investment policies of money market funds contain derogations for public sector debt that are similar to the UCITS Directive (see section 13.4.1), both with regard to the diversification requirement to contain the exposure of money market funds to counterparty risk and the concentration limit to prevent a money market fund becoming excessively important for a single issuing body. Hence, the EU regulation creates considerable leeway for national competent authorities when assessing the mutual exposure between money market funds and public sector entities issuing money market instruments.

There are nevertheless a few common factors relating to the management of fund-specific risks that mitigate the preferential treatment of public sector versus private sector funding. First, all money market funds are subject to specific portfolio obligations concerning the minimum share of total assets that must mature daily and weekly (although in the latter case, as another exception, a public debt CNAV fund and an LVNAV fund can within limits also include highly liquid assets from public sector bodies with a residual maturity of up to 190 days). Second, each money market fund must undertake a sound stress testing of its capability to withstand the adverse impact of severe economic and financial conditions on the liquidity level or credit quality of its assets and on the possibility that this might trigger large redemptions. Third, both a public-debt CNAV fund and an LVNAV fund must publish every day the difference between the constant net value of its assets per unit or share calculated on the basis of the amortized cost method and the valuation derived from a market-to-market or market-to-model calculation. Finally, the management of both a public debt CNAV fund and an LVNAV fund must have prudent and rigorous liquidity management procedures in place. When the liquidity of their money market funds is quickly deteriorating, adequate countermeasures to deal with large redemptions must be considered or have to be initiated. Accordingly, a deteriorating credit quality of a sovereign and a falling market price of its short-term debt instruments will likely hit the liquidity position of money market funds that are heavily invested in its public debt, and trigger an appropriate response to contain the risk of redemption pressures.

13.4.3   EU Prudential Legislation for Insurance Undertakings

European institutional investors tend to have long-dated liabilities on their balance sheets which they seek to cover with long-term assets. Low-risk government bonds with long maturities are therefore an attractive instrument for these "buy and hold" investors. This is one reason why the successive EU Directives for Insurance Undertakings contain a preferential treatment of sovereign exposures, in particular by allowing national regulators to exempt claims on the government in domestic currency from standard exposure limits that apply to claims on the private sector (in a way similar to the UCITS Directive; see section 13.4.1).

The EU Directive for Insurance Undertakings, known as Solvency I, became law in end-2002. While it did not set capital requirements, it gave Member States the freedom to introduce their own risk-based frameworks in national legislation. The main sovereign privilege remained that investments in central, regional and local government debt could be exempted from asset diversification requirements. This exemption could be interpreted as a regulatory encouragement to hold government debt, although insurers were not (or not anymore) constrained by law to invest in domestic government bonds, since such a restriction would amount to financial repression.[34]

Under the new EU Insurance and Reinsurance Directive, named Solvency II, insurance companies are required as of 2016 to value both their assets and liabilities consistent with market prices and to hold adequate capital against an array of risks related to their investments, the so-called Solvency Capital Requirement (SCR).[35] The SCR may be calibrated using the standard formula as specified in the legislation, or an internal model approved by the national supervisory authority. Under the standard formula, Solvency II requires insurers to hold adequate capital to cover for interest rate risk and currency risk associated with their sovereign bond holdings. By contrast, claims on or guaranteed by EU central governments issued in their own currency enjoy a capital exemption with regard to the market risk related sub-modules for concentration risk (stemming either from lack of diversification in the assets portfolio, or from large exposure to default risk by a single issuer of securities or a group of related issuers) as well as for spread risk (i.e., the sensitivity to changes in level or volatility of credit spreads over the risk-free interest rate term structure).

Solvency II further includes a similar transitional approach as the new EU banking legislation (see Table 13.3): until 2017, a capital exemption also applied for concentration risk and spread risk related to those EU sovereign exposures that are denominated and funded in any other EU currency than that of the issuing country, while subsequently this preferential treatment is phased out. As from 2020 in these cases the standard model's computation based on credit quality must be applied. Given the fact that euro area countries share the same currency, insurance companies in the eurozone can by default apply a zero capital charge

---

[34] See again D. Nouy, "Is Sovereign Risk Properly Addressed by Financial Regulation?"

[35] See Directive 2009/138/EC of the European Parliament and of the Council of November 25, 2009 on the taking-up and pursuit of the business of Insurance and Reinsurance (Solvency II) [2009] OJ L335/1–155.

for concentration risk and spread risk related to all EMU sovereign exposures denominated and funded in the euro.

Many larger insurance groups instead apply their internal models to compute the SCR and therefore have to make more accurate assumptions regarding the market-related sovereign risks in their portfolio and ensure an appropriate amount of capital to cover for them. Comparing the biased assumptions under the standard formula with more realistic partial internal model calculations of sovereign credit risks, Gatzert and Martin conclude that the degree of underestimation of the SCR depends on the credit quality of the government bonds and is especially severe for lower-rated sovereigns.[36]

Höring conducts a review of the literature on the impact of Solvency II on the investment portfolios of insurance companies. He finds many studies expecting a reallocation to less capital-intensive assets and a greater appetite for EU sovereign bonds issued in domestic currency, in particular lower-rated government debt.[37] At the same time, Solvency II also enhances governance and risk management and explicitly asks insurance companies to invest all their assets in accordance with the "prudent person" principle so as to ensure the security, quality and liquidity of their portfolios. This also applies to investments in European government bonds. In addition, they are obliged to conduct an adequate own risk and solvency assessment, even in those cases where the standard formula for the calculation of credit risk allows them to consider EU government bonds as risk-free. Since all assets covered by this assessment are to be valued at market prices, insurers have to take account of the credit and market risks related to all their counterparties, also those for governments.[38]

13.4.4   EU Prudential Legislation for Occupational Pension Funds

A European prudential legislative framework for occupational pension funds was established in 2003 with the EU Directive on the Activities and Supervision of Institutions for Occupational Retirement Provision (IORP). Member States were given discretion on the precise investment rules that they

---

[36] N. Gatzert and M. Martin, "Quantifying Credit and Market Risk under Solvency II: Standard Approach versus Internal Model," *Insurance: Mathematics and Economics*, 51 (3) (2012), 649–666.

[37] D. Höring, "Will Solvency II Market Risk Requirements Bite? The Impact of Solvency II on Insurers' Asset Allocation," *The Geneva Papers on Risk and Insurance – Issues and Practice*, 38(2) (2013), 250–273.

[38] See again European Systemic Risk Board, *Report on the Regulatory Treatment of Sovereign Exposures*.

wanted to impose at the national level: they could be made more stringent, but could also entail a preferential treatment of government debt. Similarly to Solvency I (see section 13.4.3), national regulators could decide to exempt investments in government bonds from diversification requirements, thereby offering occupational pension funds the opportunity – if not an incentive – to create a substantial exposure to sovereign risk. However, Member States could generally not require them to invest in domestic government bonds, whereas this had been quite common in the past.

After the introduction of Solvency II, to ensure a level playing field with insurance undertakings offering pension products, the European Commission suggested in 2010 that also occupational pension funds should hold a sufficient capital buffer.[39] Originally, it planned to extend the preferential treatment of government exposures in Solvency II to the new solvency requirement for occupational pension funds, to be introduced in a recast of the IORP Directive (IORP II). Following critical comments from stakeholders, however, it decided in May 2013 to defer the introduction of a harmonized solvency rule for occupational pension funds. The IORP II Directive that entered into force in January 2017 instead focuses inter alia on improving risk management and enhancing information for pension scheme members.

As shown in the empirical literature, imposing a minimum solvency requirement could lead occupational pension funds to rebalance their portfolios in favor of low-risk assets, including government bonds. Already the announcement of the possible introduction of a new solvency rule caused some de-risking of pension fund portfolios toward fixed-income instruments.[40]

13.5   The Preferential Treatment of Government Debt in EU Market Law

13.5.1   EU Market Infrastructure Regulation

Following a G-20 agreement, EU legislation has also been implemented to increase the transparency of over-the-counter (OTC) derivative contracts such as credit default swaps, reduce the uncertainty about the risks

---

[39] European Commission, "Green paper towards adequate, sustainable and safe European pension systems," COM(2010) 365 (Brussels: July 7, 2010).

[40] See the study by A. Amzallag, D. Kapp and C. Kok, "The impact of regulating occupational pensions in Europe on investment and financial stability," ECB Occasional Paper Series, 154 (Frankfurt am Main: European Central Bank, July 2014).

involved in derivative transactions, protect against market abuse, and thereby allay the related financial stability concerns. The European Market Infrastructure Regulation (EMIR) of August 2012 requires 1) the reporting of all derivative contracts to trade repositories, making them accessible to supervisory authorities; 2) the clearing of all standardized OTC derivative contracts through a central counterparty and liquid, high-quality collateral assets to be posted by the parties to both centrally and non-centrally cleared derivative contracts; and 3) the implementation of stringent organizational, business conduct and prudential rules for the central counterparties.[41]

EU public bodies and central banks charged with intervening in the management of public debt are excluded from the scope of this market regulation in order to avoid limiting their power to perform their tasks of common interest. For reasons of international coherence and consistency, the same exemption is being extended to public bodies and central banks outside the EU to the extent that these enjoy a similar treatment in their national legislation. EMIR in this respect avoids any interference in the operation of independent central banks using government securities for the conduct of monetary policy in derivative markets. Placing similar activities of public debt management offices in sovereign securities markets on one line with those of central banks is surprising, because it appears to assume that the two public bodies still are (or should be) closely intertwined.

EMIR has contributed to more clearing taking place via central counterparties. A central counterparty can only accept highly liquid collateral with minimal credit and market risk to cover the initial and ongoing exposure to its clearing members. The legal provisions and regulatory technical standards specify the exact types of highly liquid collateral, i.e. cash, financial instruments, bank guarantees and gold.[42] For financial instruments to qualify, they should normally be debt instruments issued or explicitly guaranteed by a government, a central bank or a supranational institution.

EMIR also defines a framework for determining valuation haircuts and collateral concentration limits to restrict the exposure. Central counterparties are required to establish prudent valuation practices and develop

---

[41] See Regulation (EU) No 648/2012 of the European Parliament and of the Council of 4 July 2012 on OTC derivatives, central counterparties and trade repositories [2012] OJ L201/1–59.

[42] See European Central Bank, *Collateral Eligibility Requirements: A Comparative Study Across Specific Frameworks* (Frankfurt am Main: July 2013).

haircuts that are regularly tested and that take into account stressed market conditions. Some of them impose minimum credit rating standards for the acceptance of collateral assets. The concentration limits differ across the various arrangements. For example, they may set a maximum for a certain rating per category of collateral in the basket, or set a limit on the share of certain issuers (such as regional governments) of the assets in the collateral basket.

The empirical literature suggests that EMIR will raise the net demand for high-quality, liquid collateral assets, including sovereign bonds. This may contribute to easing government funding constraints, especially when the additional demand for this type of assets due to EMIR and other EU legislation (as discussed in this chapter) is structural and would exceed the growth in supply.[43]

As regards the prudential rules applicable to central counterparties, the European Commission has issued regulatory technical standards to ensure that they are at all times safe and sound and hold sufficient capital against a range of risks (except those risks stemming from clearing activities that are largely covered by specific financial resources). Since these risks are similar to those of credit institutions and investment firms, the capital standards in EU prudential banking legislation serve as the relevant benchmark. For credit risk, the standardized approach must be applied, indicating that the preferential treatment of sovereign exposures in the banking sector (as discussed in section 13.3.1) is extended to central counterparties.

13.5.2   EU Regulation on Credit Rating Agencies

Since the Global Financial Crisis, credit rating agencies have come under severe criticism from policy-makers for having underestimated the credit risks associated with structured financial products. They have also received critical comments for downgrading distressed euro area countries, even after these had just committed to serious policy adjustments that improved their fundamental outlook. Eijffinger concludes in this

---

[43] See A. Levels and J. Capel, "Is Collateral Becoming Scarce? Evidence for the Euro Area," *Journal of Financial Market Infrastructures*, 1(1) (2012), 29–53; and A. Houben and J. W. Slingenberg, "Collateral Scarcity and Asset Encumbrance: Implications for the European Financial System," Banque de France, *Financial Stability Review*, 17 (April 2013), 197–206.

respect that the credit rating agencies generally lagged behind markets in their judgment.[44]

Following the financial crisis, three EU regulations affecting the operations of credit rating agencies in Europe have been adopted. Those registered in the EU were first placed under stricter authorization requirements and new rules of conduct applicable in full from December 2010. A subsequent amendment of the regulation brought them under exclusive supervision by the European Securities and Markets Authority (ESMA) as from July 2011. Further EU legislation in force since June 2013 seeks to reinforce the independence of credit rating agencies, enhance the transparency and quality of credit ratings, reduce the risk of over-reliance on external credit ratings, limit the high degree of concentration in the rating market, and control the risks associated with the business model of rating agencies. In addition, it introduces a right of redress for investors in and issuers of financial instruments.[45]

This new EU legislation also made credit rating agencies subject to specific requirements for sovereign ratings. They have to publish annually at the end of December a calendar for the next 12 months setting two or three dates for issuing unsolicited sovereign ratings and rating outlooks, from which they can only deviate for legal reasons. Sovereign ratings must be accompanied by detailed research reports explaining the assumptions, perceived risks and other key elements on which they are based. While specific national policies may constitute one of these elements, rating agencies are to refrain from giving policy recommendations to a country. Governments are also given more time (a full working day, instead of just twelve hours) to react to a change in their credit rating before this is made public, so that they can better verify the underlying data, which must have been taken from generally accessible sources. When a rating agency breaches the obligations, it may be held liable for damages caused intentionally or with gross negligence.[46]

---

[44] S. C. W. Eijffinger, "Rating Agencies: Role and Influence of Their Sovereign Credit Risk Assessment in the Eurozone," *Journal of Common Market Studies*, 50(6) (2012), 912–921.

[45] See Regulation (EU) No 462/2013 of the European Parliament and of the Council of 21 May 2013 amending Regulation (EC) No 1060/2009 on credit rating agencies [2013] OJ L146/1–33.

[46] For a legal and economic analysis see J. de Haan and F. Amtenbrink, "Taming the Beast? New European Regulation for Credit Rating Agencies," *Zeitschrift für Staats- und Europawissenschaften/Journal of Comparative and European Policy*, 10(4) (2012), 433–458.

European Commission staff also examined the policy option of granting ESMA the power to restrict or ban temporarily the issuance of
sovereign debt ratings.[47] This could become relevant, in particular,
when exceptional events could trigger contagion and excessive market
volatility or when complete information on timing, amount and conditions of EU/IMF financial support to stabilize the economy of a troubled
member country, was still missing. The staff study also considered the
option of a permanent prohibition of sovereign credit ratings. For clearly
defined exceptional circumstances a temporary suspension was regarded
as an acceptable precautionary measure of last resort, although its effectiveness was probably limited. By contrast, a permanent prohibition was
in conflict with the fundamental freedom to conduct a business and the
principle of proportionality. None of these repressive policy options were
in the end seriously considered, as "shooting the messenger" for the bad
news on a country's credit standing was no solution to the underlying
fiscal problem.

While there are legitimate concerns with how credit rating agencies
operate, the impression is that policy-makers wanted to "punish" them
for unduly downgrading euro area sovereigns. During 2012–2014 the
credit rating agencies were in any case more conservative in their credit
risk assessment of crisis-affected euro area countries than before the
sovereign debt crisis.[48] This greater caution may also be due to the stricter
EU legislation, the supervision by ESMA, or a deliberate strategy of credit
rating agencies to regain their reputation.

13.5.3   EU Regulation on Short-Selling and Credit Default Swaps

Speculators are another typical target of the authorities in times of market
stress. As the financial crisis and sovereign debt crisis intensified,
several euro area countries introduced emergency measures to counter
excessive speculation by announcing a temporary restriction or ban on
short-selling in certain market segments. Short-selling is the practice of
investors to sell borrowed securities (including sovereign bonds) with the
intention to cover their positions later by repurchasing them at a lower
price. This attracts concern from regulators, as short-selling is seen as

---

[47] European Commission, "Impact assessment accompanying the Proposal for a Regulation
amending Regulation (EC) No 1060/2009 on credit rating agencies," Commission Staff
Working Paper, SEC(2011) 1354 (Brussels: November 15, 2011).

[48] See T. de Vries and J. de Haan, "Credit ratings and bond spreads of the GIIPS," *Applied
Economics Letters*, 23(2) (2016), 107–111.

artificially driving prices to lower levels and spurring market volatility during a crisis. Also attempts by investors to protect themselves against losses on sovereign debt by purchasing credit default swaps (CDS) are sometimes associated with higher government bond yields. Particular concerns arose regarding naked (i.e., uncovered) short-selling and naked buying of sovereign CDS, because these activities are seen as contributing to negative price spirals and disorderly markets.[49]

A new EU regulation harmonized with effect from November 2012 the rules for short-selling and certain aspects of credit default swaps and conferred powers of coordination and intervention on the European Securities and Markets Authority (ESMA).[50] The common regulatory framework gave national competent authorities the possibility to prevent short sales during periods of market stress, introduced a reporting requirement for net short positions above specific thresholds for European shares and sovereign bonds, restricted uncovered short-selling of shares and debt instruments and prohibited uncovered sovereign credit default swap positions in view of their speculative nature. A safeguard clause allows the national competent authorities to suspend the regulation temporarily if the restrictions on sovereign credit default swaps were found to lead to a significant decline in the liquidity of the sovereign debt market. With regard to hedging, market-making activities in general and operations of primary dealers in sovereign debt are exempted from the new requirements.

Arguably, uncovered positions pose a danger of settlement failure and market disruption and should be restricted or banned. However, short-selling also supports market efficiency in terms of liquidity, risk allocation and price formation. As argued by the public debt managers of OECD countries, the ability to manage risk through short-selling operations supports a better functioning of both primary and secondary markets for sovereign instruments.[51] A restriction of uncovered short-selling of government bonds could lead investors to demand a higher risk premium and increase borrowing costs.

---

[49] On 8 June, 2010, the French President and the German Chancellor sent a joint letter to the President of the European Commission, asking the Commission to come forward with a legal proposal to ban naked short-selling and naked sovereign CDS purchases.

[50] See Regulation (EU) No 236/2012 of the European Parliament and of the Council of 14 March 2012 on short selling and certain aspects of credit default swaps [2012] OJ L086/1–24.

[51] See H. J. Blommestein, "A Public Debt Management Perspective on Proposals for Restrictions on Short-Selling of Sovereign Debt," *OECD Journal: Financial Market Trends*, 2010/2 (March 2011), 179–185.

Also, the new legal requirement that only investors who actually hold EU government bonds (or meaningfully correlated private sector instruments) are allowed to buy protection against sovereign default could reduce market volumes. Trades in sovereign credit default swaps have become dependent on investors that are willing to buy the underlying government bonds and wish to hedge against the risk of losses. The more speculative traders have to turn to unrestricted proxy markets (for example, using futures contracts on sovereign debt, or CDS contracts on financial firms that are correlated with a country's credit risk), if they want to place their bets on European sovereigns. This could have the unintended effect of causing dislocations in these other markets and undermining financial stability. A reduced liquidity in the market for sovereign debt protection, moreover, raises the costs of hedging and could drive up the costs of sovereign debt issuance.

Overall, this EU regulation may be seen as constraining or even preventing market participants from expressing a negative view on the creditworthiness of sovereigns and as another example of "messenger shot, message not."[52] Already in the run-up to the date of its introduction, the unwinding of net short positions in sovereign debt reportedly contributed to a decline in government bond yields. The longer-term impact of the short-selling restrictions may, however, be a higher cost of government funding. The IMF observed that the phasing out of all uncovered positions in European sovereign credit default swaps coincided with a material decline in spreads and reduced market liquidity, although other factors may also have played a role.[53] A first review by the ESMA noticed a slight decrease in Member States' sovereign CDS spreads after the introduction of the prohibition on uncovered sovereign CDS transactions.[54] The liquidity of EU sovereign CDS markets was in general not adversely affected, although CDS markets for specific Eastern European countries experienced a significant deterioration. The CDS indices on groups of EU sovereigns (the purchase of which now requires

---

[52] See the article entitled "Sovereign Credit-default Swaps: Messenger Shot, Message Not," *The Economist* (27 October, 2012), 64.

[53] International Monetary Fund (IMF), "A New Look at the Role of Sovereign Credit Default Swaps," *Global Financial Stability Report: Old Risks, New Challenges* (Washington DC: IMF, April 2013), chap. 2.

[54] European Securities and Markets Authority (ESMA), "Short-selling in the EU: Initial Evidence after Entry into Force of the Regulation," *Trends, Risks and Vulnerabilities*, 2 (September 20, 2013), 35–42.

investors to hold the underlying bonds of all countries represented in the index) saw a significant decline in liquidity.

13.5.4   European Financial Transactions Tax

Following a request from the European Parliament, the European Commission put forward a proposal in 2011 for an EU-wide financial transactions tax (FTT). The main objectives were to counter excessive market activity, contribute to avoiding future financial crises and ensure that financial institutions (as compared to other sectors) make a fair and substantial contribution to covering the fiscal costs of the crisis. The initiative was also meant to avoid the single market for financial services becoming fragmented by uncoordinated national indirect taxation of financial transactions. A suggestion to add the revenues to the EU budget received a cool reception in national capitals.

As many Member States were opposed to such a uniform tax, the European Commission proposed instead to introduce in January 2014 a common financial transactions tax in the eleven euro area countries (Belgium, Germany, Estonia, Greece, Spain, France, Italy, Austria, Portugal, Slovenia and Slovakia) that had expressed their willingness to go ahead with it under the so-called enhanced cooperation procedure.[55] The harmonized tax regime would be applied at each stage of a financial transaction and through each financial intermediary, covering secondary-market transactions in shares, bonds and derivatives, while excluding primary market activity. Transactions undertaken for the purpose of monetary policy, public debt management and some international public policies would be exempted, as well as foreign exchange trading in the spot market (to preserve the free movement of capital) and day-to-day financial transactions of households and firms. Further provisions aimed to avoid tax evasion, distortions and transfers to other jurisdictions.[56]

Some of the participating euro area countries have indicated a wish to exclude trade in government debt securities from the scope of the financial transactions tax. This would, however, create an arbitrary cost advantage for secondary market purchases of public sector debt compared to alternative financial instruments. As a transitory alternative

[55] European Commission, "Proposal for a Council Directive implementing enhanced cooperation in the area of financial transaction tax," COM(2013) 71 (Brussels: 14 February, 2013).

[56] See T. Hemmelgarn, N. Gaëtan, T. Bogdan and P. Vermote, "Financial Transaction Taxes in the European Union," *National Tax Journal*, 69(1) (March 2016), 217–240.

option, the European Parliament suggested limiting the tax rate on government bond transactions to half the standard rate, for a few years.[57] Additionally, it proposed applying that reduced tax rate until the same end-date to all financial trades by pension funds. Other policy-makers suggested exempting pension funds altogether from the financial transactions tax in order to avoid pensioners being hit by the higher costs of trading.[58] For a level playing field, such an exemption would have to be extended to life insurance companies. As pension funds and insurers typically invest a large part of their reserves in government paper and are regular traders in public sector bonds, this would be a convenient way for the participating countries to ensure a more liquid government bond market with lower trading costs than for other financial instruments. Advocates of an encompassing approach countered that a financial trans-actions tax could nudge asset managers further toward "productive" longer-term investment strategies and that pensioners would also benefit from the broader effect of more stable financial markets.[59]

Acknowledging the need for further technical work, the participating euro area countries committed in May 2014 to implementing the harmonized financial transactions tax in a progressive manner. As a first step, they planned to start with the taxation of shares and some derivatives on 1 January, 2016, allowing each further step toward full implementation to take due account of the economic impact. A negative impact on the real economy and on pension schemes was to be minimized. As both public-sector and private-sector debt securities would not be part of the tax base, the extent of the implied sovereign privilege would be more limited than in the initial proposal. Regarding derivatives, it was agreed that the tax rate should be low but based on the widest possible tax base, without impacting the cost of sovereign borrowing. This suggests that derivative contracts for sovereign bonds might be (temporarily) exempted from the tax. Estonia decided to step out from the planned introduction, because with the envisaged small tax base it expected the costs to be higher than the benefits. After several delays, in December 2017, politicians were still unable to agree on the final mod-alities of the common financial transactions tax.

---

[57] European Parliament, "Financial Transaction Tax: Wide Scope and Attention to Pension Funds and SMEs," Press Release (Brussels: 3 July, 2013).

[58] See A. Botsch, "Financial Transaction Taxes in the EU," *ETUI Policy Brief*, 8 (Brussels: European Trade Union Institute, 2012).

[59] See J. Gray, S. Griffith-Jones and J. Sandberg, "No Exemption: The Financial Transaction Tax and Pension Funds," Network for Sustainable Financial Markets (December 2012).

13.6 Conclusions

Since the Global Financial Crisis of 2008 European authorities have set out to strengthen financial governance in order to create a more stable and resilient financial system. As discussed in this chapter, the new and updated EU legislation addressed to a wide array of financial markets and institutions also significantly broadened the scope of the existing preferential regulatory treatment of sovereign bonds at the European level. This benefits public debt management in many ways.

The fiscal advantages occur (or could occur), in particular, through the fact that EU prudential legislation for banks, collective investment funds, money market funds, institutional investors and central counterparties in many cases disregards the risks from high sovereign exposures. Furthermore, new EU restrictions placed on short-selling of government bonds, buying sovereign default protection and issuing sovereign credit ratings reduce market pressure. In addition, the proposed common financial transactions tax not only promises a new source of public revenues, but might also exempt trading in government bonds.

Taking a political economy perspective, the growing scope of these government funding privileges in EU financial law may be interpreted in three (complementary) ways: as a reappearance of financial repression to reduce the burden of high public debt; as a return to the traditional close relationship between the government and the financial sector so as to align mutual interests in fiscal and financial stability; or as a way to increase explicit and implicit taxes on finance and recoup public revenues lost during the financial crisis.

The many European regulatory incentives for investors to buy and hold government debt carry the risk of crowding out private-sector funding and will raise financial stability concerns every time one or more governments face distress. Moreover, a privileged access to capital markets reduces market discipline and may lead to moral hazard on the part of sovereigns.

As the discussion in this chapter demonstrates, the preferential treatment of sovereign exposures and governments' market access is found in a growing body of EU financial law. Any regulatory attempt to reduce it would therefore have to take account of the financial structure to avoid regulatory arbitrage and necessitate a carefully crafted common approach at the global level that allows for a (long) period of transition to avoid market disruption.

Table 13.4 *Preferential Treatment of Government Debt in European Financial Law*

EU prudential legislation	Preferential treatment
1. EU Banking Regulation/Directive (CRR/CRD IV)	
a) Capital adequacy requirements	EU sovereigns in domestic currency risk free, but phased out for non-domestic EU currencies
EBA capital exercise	Temporary capital buffer against sovereign risk
b) Liquidity coverage ratio/ diversification rule	EU sovereigns highest liquidity and credit quality
c) Net stable funding ratio	EU sovereigns highest liquidity and credit quality
d) Large exposures regime	Exempts EU sovereign bonds, but sovereign concentration risks a bank issue
e) Leverage ratio	Focus on total non-risk weighted assets
2. EU Banking Structure Regulation (proposal withdrawn)	
a) Ban on proprietary trading	Exempts EU government securities
b) Separation of high-risk investment activities	Exempts EU government securities
3. EU Investment Funds Directive (UCITS IV)	
a) Portfolio diversification rules	Allows much higher limits for public sector exposures
b) Portfolio concentration limits	Allows waiver for public sector bodies
4. EU Regulation on Money Market Funds (MMF)	
a) Public sector CNAV money market funds	Excludes private debt, possible future EU public debt quota
b) Favorable assessment of issuer and quality of assets	Exempts EU public debt instruments
c) Portfolio diversification rules	Allows much higher limits for public sector exposures
d) Portfolio concentration limits	Exempts public sector bodies
e) Resilience against redemption pressures	Mandatory risk assessment/ management for all assets

Table 13.4 (*cont.*)

EU prudential legislation	Preferential treatment
5. EU Directive for Insurance Undertakings (Solvency II)	
a) Asset diversification requirement	Allows to exempt government securities
b) Capital requirements for specific market risks	Exemptions for concentration risk and spread risk related to EU sovereigns in domestic currency, but phased out for non-domestic EU currencies
c) Own risk and solvency assessment (ORSA)	All assets valued at market prices, prudent person principle
6. EU Directive for Occupational Pension Funds (IORP II)	
a) Asset diversification requirement	Allows to exempt sovereign bonds
b) Capital requirements (deferred)	As Solvency II (excl. ORSA)
7. EU Market Infrastructure Regulation (EMIR)	
a) Mandatory central clearing of OTC derivatives	Exemption for official public debt management
b) Only high-quality and liquid collateral	Favors high-quality sovereign bonds
c) Capital requirements for central counterparties	As CRR/CRD IV
8. EU Regulation on Credit Rating Agencies	Restrictions on sovereign credit ratings and rating outlooks
9. EU Regulation on Short-Selling and CDS Contracts	Restricts uncovered short-selling and bans uncovered sovereign CDS positions
10. Common Financial Transactions Tax (FTT) (proposal)	
a) Common financial transactions tax under enhanced cooperation	Curbs trading in all financial instruments except primary issuance and public debt management
b) 1st step: shares and some derivatives	Exemption of public and private debt

PART IV

Financial Regulation and State Capitalism:
A Political Economic Perspective

Rethinking State Control over the PRC Financial System

The Black Box of Proactive Intervention

GUO LI AND XIA DAILE

14.1 Introduction

Capital is one of the most important economic resources. No explanation of the booming Chinese economy can ignore the contribution of the Chinese financial system. A financial system helps to allocate funds efficiently. This resource allocation function is either performed by a financial market or financial institutions. The financial market helps to allocate resources efficiently through a price mechanism. When the price of securities fully reflects all available information, the market allocates funds to securities issuers more efficiently.[1] In this system, the liquidity of the market and the informed traders' pricing accuracy is key.[2]

The financial institutions can also allocate resources, because they can solve the information asymmetry problem that cannot be eliminated by the financial market. For example, Leland and Pyle suggested that financial intermediaries have special knowledge so that they can gather information not available to the public and properly price the information. Usually, intermediaries would invest wealth in the asset to show the credibility of the information they gathered.[3] Diamond argued that intermediaries over-come asymmetric information problems by acting as "delegated

---

[1] B. G. Malkiel and E. F. Fama, "Efficient capital markets: A Review of Theory and Empirical Work," *The Journal of Finance*, 25 (1970), 383.

[2] Z. Goshen and G. Parchomovsky, "The Essential Role of Securities Regulation," *Duke Law Journal* 55 (2006), 711.

[3] H. E. Leland and D. H. Pyle, "Informational Asymmetries, Financial Structure, and Financial Intermediation," *The Journal of Finance*, 32 (1977), 371.

monitors."[4] In this mechanism, the ability to gather information, the knowledge of prices and monitoring techniques of the financial intermediaries are especially important. Traditionally, the market mechanism also works for financial intermediaries.[5] The intermediaries with more advanced techniques to select promising investment projects and effectively control the following risks will beat the competition, and thus are able to attract investors. Meanwhile, "profitable projects" are more likely to be funded.

Unfortunately, the Chinese financial system does not work in the preceding way. The Chinese government frequently intervenes in the process of funding resource allocation, largely replacing the price mechanism in the financial markets and distorting financial institutions' business judgments. These interventions are often read as a manifestation of state capitalism; the Chinese economy is enormously diversified. The state is unable to control the whole economy by dominating a small amount of industries. Thus, controlling the financial system becomes particularly important. The government needs to control the financial system to guide the flow of money and credit within the national economy.[6] If the state capitalism hypothesis is fully correct, the strong state control of the financial system is only rent-seeking.

The only conclusion we could then draw from the Chinese financial system is in line with the claims of some scholars: this system is not efficient at all.[7] It would follow from this conclusion that the flourishing of the Chinese economy could largely be attributed to underground financing[8] or to the fact that the goal of the government has not yet significantly conflicted with economic growth.[9]

---

[4] D. W. Diamond, "Financial Intermediation and Delegated Monitoring," *The Review of Economic Studies*, 51 (1984) 393.

[5] We are also aware of the many ways that market forces are deflected and eliminated in "free market" economies. Each economy stands in the market spectrum between Utopian communism and Utopian libertarianism, but the extremes have never existed. See I. Bremmer, *The End of the Free Market. Who Wins the War between States and Corporations?* (New York: Portfolio, 2010), 43–44.

[6] See ibid., 134–135.

[7] See P. C. Chang, C. Jia and Z. Wang, "Bank Fund Reallocation and Economic Growth: Evidence from China," *Journal of Banking & Finance*, 34 (2010), 2753–2766. This paper finds no correlation between bank fund reallocation and regional economic growth or between bank loans and regional economic growth. Instead, the authors find a positive association between bank deposits and growth.

[8] F. Allen and J. Qian, "China's Financial System and the Law," *Cornell International Law Journal*, 47 (2014), 499; J. Aziz and C. Duenwald, "Growth-financial intermediation nexus in China" (2002), IMF, http://lnweb90.worldbank.org/CAW/Cawdoclib.nsf/0/4F843CF9E134EA8185256C8A00599FDA/$file/WP02194.pdf.

[9] See Bremmer, *The End of the Free Market.*

Our analysis takes a more positive perspective: we assume the government also cares about the efficiency of the financial system, and these interventions are more than mere rent-seeking. We also admit that although these interventions may have solved some urgent problems for the economy, change remains necessary. The rest of this chapter is organized as follows.

Section 14.2 provides a review of the Chinese government's strong control over the financial system. Section 14.3 explains the efficiency concerns regarding state control. Many financial institutions rely on the government's implicit safety net to survive, because they have cultivated little public trust on their own. Such a safety net however is costly to maintain and often gives rise to moral hazard. The government has strong incentives to contain moral hazard and reduce the bailout cost through ex-ante intervention. Section 14.4 focuses on the drawbacks of the current "heavy control and heavy insurance" regulatory strategy, including the formidable costs of unlimited implicit insurance and its perverse impacts on the financial system.

14.2   The State-Centered Nature of the Chinese Financial System

The most distinctive characteristic of the Chinese financial system is its state-centered nature. China went through a centralized economic period (1949–1978), when there was virtually no market, and the economy was operated by central planning. The central bank, the People's Bank of China (PBOC) was the only financial institution and was responsible for almost all financial activities. All money went into PBOC, and PBOC distributed funds to state-owned enterprises throughout China in accordance with the central plan. During this period, modern financial activities in China were very rare.

Within the last two decades, the Chinese financial system has evolved from a wholly state-owned system into a hybridized system,[10] but the state-centered nature of the Chinese financial system largely remains. Path dependence might play a role. Even with the growth of financial market and other financial institutions, China's financial system is still dominated by several large state-owned banks.[11] Nowadays, the Chinese government can influence the financial system by the following means.

---

[10] See K. Pistor, L. Guo and C. Zhou, "The Hybridization of Chinese Financial System," in Benjamin L Liebman and Curtis J. Milhaupt (eds.), *Regulating the Visible Hand? The Institutional Implications of Chinese State Capitalism* (Oxford: Oxford University Press, 2015).

[11] Allen and Qian, "China's Financial System and the Law."

14.2.1 Ex-Ante Authorizations and Limitations

Financial systems are rule-bound and need more regulation than regular industries all over the world,[12] but China has taken this a step further. Financial activities are strictly restricted by ex-ante authorizations and limitations. In China, nearly all activities concerning borrowing and lending are regarded as financial activities. Lending between enterprises has been generally prohibited until recently; this business is only allowed with ex-ante authorization.[13]

As financial activities are controlled by ex-ante authorization, Chinese financial institutions and services are not inventions of the market, but rather created and designed by the government. Normally, a new form of financial institution or activity can appear in the market only after issue of the specific laws, regulations or other legal authorizations designed to govern it, and the relative regulatory authority issues licenses. These specific laws or regulations provide the establishing requirements and procedure for each kind of financial institution or activity, and usually require them to pass examinations administered by the relevant authorities. Those authorities possess a high degree of discretion. Fulfilling all the requirements designated in the regulations will not, however, guarantee a license for the applicant.

Aside from the ex-ante authorizations, the scope of business and the model of these financial institutions are also prescribed by the regulations. Commercial banks remain today the most important and influential financial institutions, as they are the only kind of financial institutions that are entitled to raising money from the public. By the end of 2015, the total assets of the Chinese banking sector amounted to RMB199.35 trillion.[14] An institutional separation similar to that required by the Glass-Steagall Act generally forbids Chinese commercial banks from taking part in securities business, trust business and real estate business.[15] The most important banking businesses are lending and

[12] K. Pistor, "A Legal Theory of Finance," *Journal of Comparative Economics*, 41 (2013), 315.

[13] Art. 61 of DaikuanTongze (贷款通则) [General Provisions on Lending] stipulates: "Lending and borrowing activities, overt or otherwise, shall not be handled between and among enterprises in violation of government regulations." DaikuanTongze (贷款通则)[General Provisions on Lending] is promulgated by the People's Bank of China, June 28, 1996, effective August 1, 1996).

[14] China Banking Regulatory Commission, "China Banking Regulatory Commission Annual Report 2015" (Beijing: China Banking Regulatory Commission, 2016).

[15] Art. 43 of the Law of the People's Republic of China on Commercial Banks (ZhonghuaRenminGongheguoShangyeYinhang F,a 中华人民共和国商业银行法, which was promulgated and took effect in 1995, and was revised in 2003; hereinafter

deposit-taking. Since establishing commercial banks in the 1980s, banks' discretion on interest rate has been subject to interest rate floors and ceilings set by the central bank.[16] Only recently are the interest rate floors and ceilings being removed.[17] Even today, the prudential requirements for Chinese banks are higher than global practice: banks must stick to the strict loan-to-deposit ratios that do not allow banks to lend funds over 75 percent of their deposits; the reserve requirement imposed by the central bank is also high compared with that of other countries.[18]

Although the banking business in other countries has evolved from the originate-to-hold model to the originate-to-distribute model,[19] the key technique of credit securitization is still at a pilot period in China.[20] As credit securitization requires approval of the China Banking Regulatory Commission (CBRC) on a lengthy, case-by-case basis, the development largely depends on the attitude of the government. The pilot had paused for about four years after the 2008 financial crisis and restarted at the end of 2012. At the end of 2015, the government ended case-by-case approval and instead required issuers to register their securitization products. It was only then that securitization business in China began to boom.

Other financial institutions enjoy even less freedom. The business type and model of most financial institutions are provided clearly in the relevant regulations, and the activity actually undertaken is generally not allowed to exceed it. Microloan companies can only grant microloans

---

"Commercial Bank Law") provided that "Commercial banks are not allowed to make trust investment, trade in shares or make investment in fixed assets of non-self-use within the People's Republic of China."

[16] Art. 31 of Commercial Bank Law provided: "A commercial bank should decide its own interest rates and announce them in accordance with the upper and lower limits for deposit interest set by the People's Bank of China."

[17] Until the end of 2015, the People's Bank of China (PBOC for short; China's central bank) removed all ceilings and floors of interest rates except for demand deposit and short-term deposit under one year. See People's Bank of China, "Annual Report 2015," People's Bank of China (2016), 24.

[18] E. Avgouleas and D. Xu, "Overhauling China's Financial Stability Regulation: Policy Riddles and Regulatory Dilemmas," *Asian Journal of Law and Society*, 4(1) (2017) 9.

[19] For more details of this trend, please see V. M. Bord and J. A. C. Santos, "The Rise of the Originate-to-Distribute Model and the Role of Banks in Financial Intermediation," *Federal Reserve Bank of New York Economic Policy Review*, 18 (2012), 21.

[20] See Notice of the People's Bank of China, the China Banking Regulatory Commission and the Ministry of Finance on Relevant Matters Concerning Further Expanding the Pilot Securitization of Credit Assets (Guanyu Jinyibu Kuoda Xindai Zichan Zhengquanhua Shidian Youguan Shixiang De Tongzhi 关于进一步扩大信贷资产证券化试点有关事项的通知) Yin Fa [2012] No. 127.

largely by using their own capital;[21] pawn shops are allowed to offer collateralized loans only;[22] financial guarantee companies' business is restricted to providing insurance for financing activities.[23]

There were two safe harbors: the first one is lending amongst natural persons, and the other is wealth management activities.[24] Financial regulation did not reach personal lending because it is hard to draw a clear line between lending business and the lending and borrowing in everyday life. Moreover, the scope of the lending business among natural persons is not large enough to cause large-scale instability. So the government left such lending unregulated as long as usury is not concerned.

The wealth management activities free harbor can be read as a government's compromise to market pressures. The government also worries about the profitability of financial institutions when it does not conflict with higher political goals. This concern becomes more severe when financial institutions in China face more and more market assessments. Wealth management products seemed like a good choice because wealth management products would not appear in the balance sheet of the issuing financial institutions and thus would not add up liabilities on financial institutions, at least in theory. The government chose to provide leniency in this field partly because global best practices are lacking, and partly because the financial institutions issuing wealth management products are under heavy regulations. The government is still able to set regulations after these financial institutions begin the wealth management business.

These safe harbors have become narrower as the government finds market players increasingly made use of them to game regulations. Peer-to-peer (P2P) lending market places have boomed in China since 2006 because they were set up freely under the regulatory exemption of

---

[21] See Guiding Opinions of the China Banking Regulatory Commission and the People's Bank of China on the Pilot Operation of Small Loan Companies (Guanyu Xiaoe Daikuan Gongsi Shidian De Zhidao Yijian 关于小额贷款公司试点的指导意见), Yin Jian Fa [2008] No. 23.

[22] See Measures for the Administration of Pawning (Diandang Guanli Banfa典当管理办法), Ministry of Commerce and Ministry of Public Security(Order No.8 [2005]).

[23] See Interim Measures for the Administration of Financing Guarantee Companies (Rongzixing Danbao Gongsi Guanli Zanxing Banfa 融资性担保公司管理暂行办法), Order of the China Banking Regulatory Commission, the National Development and Reform Commission, the Ministry of Industry and Information Technology, the Ministry of Finance, the Ministry of Commerce, the People's Bank of China and the State Administration for Industry and Commerce (No. 3 [2010])

[24] Wealth management business includes wealth management products issued by the banks and other financial institutions or trust products issued by trust companies.

lending between natural persons. However, most Chinese P2P lending market places are much more than information intermediaries. They actually conduct credit intermediation like banks, which would be illegal fundraising.[25] As more and more unregulated P2P marketplace scandals erupt, the government has also begun to impose ex-ante authorization regulation on this industry and planned to fix the loophole in the natural person lending free harbor. The legislative affairs office of the State Council issued a draft of a regulation on non-deposit-taking lending institutions, which eliminates the difference between lending by natural persons and by enterprises and sets up a uniform licensing mechanism. Only occasional acts of lending or non-profit lending can be exempted.

Wealth management businesses are also used by financial institutions to game the heavy financial regulations. After several rounds of interplay with the regulators, wealth management businesses also evolved into shadow banking businesses. In this "catch me if you can" game, regulators continuously tried to fix the loopholes in regulation. As a result, the restrictions on investment behaviors of wealth management products have gradually become much tighter.

14.2.2   Ownership Control in the Financial System

State ownership is another distinctive feature of the Chinese financial industry. State ownership dominates the banking sector, the most significant financial sector by far in China. Nearly all major nationwide banks are state-controlled. One exception is China Minsheng Bank. China Minsheng Bank received a banking license in 1996. It is the eighth largest bank in China. By the end of 2016, its total assets reached 5.9 trillion RMB.[26] But China Minsheng Bank is not a typical private bank.

[25] Illegal fundraising is severely punished in China. Currently, "illegal fundraising" is identified as follows: (1) absorbing funds without approval from the relevant government department in accordance with the law; (2) making use of public means of solicitation such as the media, promotion conferences, leaflets and text messages on mobile phones; (3) engaging in undertakings to repay the principal and interest or to pay a return in the form of currency, property in kind, or equity within a certain time limit; or (4) absorbing funds from the general public, i.e., non-specific targets in society. Any disguised act to achieve the above goals is also the target of legal enforcement. See Interpretations of the Supreme People's Court on the Specific Application of Laws in the Trial of Criminal Cases of Illegal Fundraising (Zuigao Renmin Fayuan Guanyu Shenli FeifaJizi Xingshi Anjian Juti Yingyong Falv Ruogan Wenti De Jieshi最高人民法院关于审理非法集资刑事案件具体应用法律若干问题的解释), Fa Shi [2010] No. 18.

[26] China Minsheng Bank, "China Minsheng Bank Annual Report 2016" (Beijing: China Minsheng Bank, 2017).

It has had a close relationship with the Communist Party and the government from its birth. China Minsheng Bank was launched under the aegis of the All-China Federation of Industry & Commerce (ACFIC), which is a long-time alliance of the Communist Party of China (CPC), and a key unit of the Chinese People's Political Consultative Conference. All fifty-nine of Minsheng Bank's sponsors are members of ACFIC. Minsheng Bank's connection with the CPC and the government never faded after its founding. The senior managers of Minsheng Bank are either assigned by the CPC or get approval from the party before they take office.[27] Minsheng Bank's former president Xiaofeng Mao used to work in the Communist Youth League in Hunan Province and then Beijing before he joined Minsheng Bank. Mao received a prominent position at that time and eventually became the president of Minsheng Bank after six years. Mao used to be the youngest leader in the Chinese financial sector, but was suddenly removed on January 25, 2015 by the Central Discipline Inspection Commission (CDIC), the party's graft-buster.[28]

The government has recently shown signs of relaxing ownership control in the banking industry. In July 2013, the State Council office issued guidelines encouraging private capital to enter into the financial sector, establish private banks, financial leasing companies and financial companies.[29] In 2014, the government launched a pilot project to permit five new entirely privately owned banks.[30] The businesses of these five banks are so far restricted, either to a certain region or to a certain business. For example, Wenzhou Minshang Bank's customers must be micro-size enterprises in Wenzhou City.[31] Tencent-backed Webank is an online-only bank[32] and focuses on personal business and micro-enterprise

---

[27] J. Anderlini, "China Opens Door to Private Banks," *Financial Times* (March 11, 2014), www.ft.com/intl/cms/s/0/7096239e-a8e0-11e3-bf0c-00144feab7de.html#axzz3UlYiqzul.

[28] H. Wu, "Minsheng Bank President Resigns amid Corruption Investigation," *Caixin*, February 2, 2015, http://english.caixin.com/2015–02-02/100780797.html.

[29] See State Council guidance on financial support for economic structure adjustment and transformation and upgrading (Guowuyuan Bangongting Guanyu Jinrong Zhichi Jingji Jiegou Tiaozheng He Zhuanxing Shengji De ZhidaoYijian 国务院办公厅关于金融支持经济结构调整和转型升级的指导意见), Guo Ban Fa [2013] No. 67.

[30] Anderlini, "China Opens Door to Private Banks."

[31] See Reply of China Banking Regulatory Commission Zhejiang Office on Opening Wenzhou Minshang Yinhang (Zhongguo Yinjianhui Zhejiang Jianguanju Guanyu Wenzhou Minshang Yinhang Gufen Youxian Gongsi Kaiye De Pifu 中国银监会浙江监管局关于温州民商银行股份有限公司开业的批复), Zhe Yinjian Fu [2015], No. 142.

[32] G. Wildau, "Tencent launches China's first online-only bank," January 5, 2015, www.ft.com/intl/cms/s/0/ccc5a6dc-9488-11e4-82c7-00144feabdc0.html#axzz3V4SOi8LH.

lending. Tianjin Jincheng Bank, meanwhile, is only open to legal persons in Tianjin City.[33]

More importantly, although all the promoters of these five private banks are private companies, they are carefully selected. The private promoters include Alibaba, Tencent, Wanxiang, JuneYao, Meters/bonwe, Fosun International, Chint Electrics Co. The boundary between these elite private companies and state-owned enterprises (SOEs) is blurred because their connection to the state power is arguably as close as SOEs.[34]

14.2.3   The State's Influence on Business Operation

To be sure, in industries that are so tightly constrained, the ownership control is not as important as in industries that enjoy higher degree of freedom. The regulatory power creates rents,[35] especially in industries that government enjoys wide discretion (like financial industry). Entrepreneurs must please the regulatory authorities to capture these rents.[36] Even assuming the financial institutions and their controllers have no ownership connection with the government, they would comply with the will of the government. For example, each time when Alibaba launches a new financial product, it must first inform the PBOC. The informal acknowledgment guarantees that the products will avoid most discretionary intervention afterwards. But in some extreme circumstances, for example, if the impact of the product becomes too significant, the regulatory attitude may change. Thus, in reality, the restrictive ex-ante authorization and limitation also gives the government power to influence the business decisions of financial institutions, even when it does not have ownership.

The power of the regulatory authorities is reflected not only by the sea of regulation documents. Their more mysterious weapon is window guidance. Window guidance is a kind of informal one-to-one soft regulation, which might be a face-to-face talk or just a phone call, but the

---

[33] F. Shang, "Three Private Banks Are Allowed to Be Established," China Banking Regulatory Commission, July 25, 2014, www.cbrc.gov.cn/chinese/home/docView/29F3A2B79D234AC0965715757F2F3252.html.

[34] C. J. Milhaupt and W. Zheng, "Beyond Ownership: State Capitalism and the Chinese Firm," *Georgetown Law Journal*, 103 (2015), 665.

[35] See C. A. Reich, "The New Property," *Yale Law Journal*, 73 (1964), 733.

[36] A. O. Krueger, "The Political Economy of the Rent-Seeking Society," *American Economic Review*, 64 (1974), 291.

conversation may cover all aspects of the operation, regardless of whether the laws have delegated the powers for regulatory authorities to step into the field. In theory, window guidance is not mandatory. Nevertheless, due to institutions' disclosure obligation to regulatory authorities and regulatory authorities' influence on their future business, it is nearly impossible for financial institutions to say no to such window guidance.

14.3 The Efficiency Concern in Proactive Intervention

The Chinese government has long used its influence in the financial sector to enforce industrial policies. The most apparent example can be found in the real estate industry. The real estate market in China has grown rapidly since 1998, when the State Council issued a document ending the welfare-oriented public housing supply system.[37] But the skyrocketing housing prices also suffocated long-term development and divided society by widening the wealth gap. Therefore, reining in the unreasonably high prices of real estate became the most urgent mission of central government. Among all the methods adopted by the government, credit policy is one that cannot be ignored. Both bank loans and trust loans to the real estate industry are restrained (if not forbidden) either via formal regulatory documents or via informal window guidance.[38] A mortgage loan to a second home purchaser requires higher interest rates and higher down payments.[39]

---

[37] See Notice of the State Council on Furthering the Reform Regarding Housing Issues and Speeding up Housing Construction (Guowuyuan Guanyu Jinyibu Shenhua Chenzhenghua Zhufang Zhidu Gaige Jiakuai Zhufang Jianshe De Tongzhi 国务院关于进一步深化城镇化住房制度改革加快住房建设的通知), Guo Fa [1998] No. 23.

[38] Since 2009, the State Council has released a series of documents, trying to control house prices. Correspondingly, the CBRC urged, and sometimes mandated, commercial banks to reduce loans to real estate developers, especially for commercial residential buildings. In 2010, it proposed drawing up a "white list" of real estate developers; only enterprises on the list would be eligible for bank loans. The proposal was implemented soon and was enforced more strictly in the following years. At the 2013 National Bank Regulatory Conference, the CBRC requested banks to enforce the controlling policy on real estate loans and enhance management of the white list. At the 2014 Conference, the management of the white list was again emphasized. See China Banking Regulatory Commission, 2013 and China Banking Regulatory Commission 2014.

[39] See Notice of the People's Bank of China and China Banking Regulatory Commission on Strengthening the Administration of Commercial Real Estate Credit Loan (Zhongguo Renmin Yinhang Zhongguo Yinhangye Jiandu Guanl iWeiyuanhui Guanyu Jiaqiang Shangyexing Fangdichan Xindai Guanli De Tongzhi 中国人民银行中国银行业监督管理委员会关于加强商业性房地产信贷管理的通知), Yinfa [2007], No. 359.

The Chinese financial system's favorable treatment of SOEs is also obvious.[40] Bank loans to SOEs are a form of subsidized funding because the interest rate ceiling set by the government is far below the market rate. The flow of bank loans empowers the state even further in the following two ways: first, SOEs acquire competitive advantage through their easy access to cheap money, and secondly, bank loans become a tool of the state to control the private owned enterprises (POEs). POEs must keep a close relationship with the government, or they have little chance to get bank loans.

But political goals are not the only concerns the government took into account when it intervened in financing activities. The government also cares about the efficiency of the financial system. The state may also control the financial system to enhance the efficiency of the system when the market mechanism does not work correctly.

14.3.1   The Mystery of Chinese Financial Institutions: How Do They Attract Customers?

Investors give money to financial institutions when the ex-ante information asymmetry problem is serious and screening borrowers is costly.[41] Thus, financial institutions must usually show their comparative advantages in selecting and monitoring borrowers in repeated practice in order to attract customers.

However, Chinese financial institutions have not won a good reputation from their previous performance. In China, financial institutions are relatively young. The government stopped interest-free budgetary grants to SOEs and began to establish commercial banks and other financial institutions in the late 1970s. Financial institutions still served as a financial agent of the government at the beginning. It was a few years later that financial institutions started to have discretion in making business decisions.

In their short history of performing financial functions, these financial institutions have not shown professionalism. Non-performing loans (NPL) have been a serious burden for both financial institutions and the government[42]. According to the International Monetary Fund's (IMF)

---

[40] S. J. Wei and T. Wang, "The Siamese Twins: Do State-Owned Banks Favor State-Owned Enterprises in China?," *China Economic Review*, 8 (1997), 19.

[41] C. Wang and S. D. Williamson. "Debt Contracts and Financial Intermediation with Costly Screening," *Canadian Journal of Economics*, 31 (1998) 573.

[42] E. Avgouleas and D. Xu, "Overhauling China's Financial Stability Regulation: Policy Riddles and Regulatory Dilemmas," *Asian Journal of Law and Society*, 4(1)(2017), 11–12.

April 2016 Global Financial Stability Report, more than 15.5 percent of a total USD 1.3 trillion PRC corporate debt may be at risk of default.[43] Even referring to the official figure, which claims NPLs only account for 1.75 percent of total bank lending, the amount is still as large as RMB 1.4 trillion (Reuters, 2016).

The NPL problem cannot be exclusively attributed to the poor professional techniques and skills of the financial institutions. A strong SOE lending preference under the pressure of the government is another crucial driver.[44] The information asymmetry problem itself is also more serious in China than in the developed economies. There are at least two institutional drawbacks that increased the costs of financial institutions. The first is the lack of a social credit information system; the second is weak anti-fraud enforcement. The first drawback prevents Chinese financial institutions from obtaining basic information to make proper judgments about previously unknown counter-parties; the second drawback makes information identification costs extremely high. One thing is certain: Chinese financial institutions have barely proven their professionalism in financial activities.

This raises the question: why do investors still trust Chinese financial institutions and let these financial institutions manage their money?

14.3.2 Government as the Source of Trust in the Financial Sector

As discussed above, financial institutions attract customers by building a track record of professionalism that reflects the trust between the market players, which leads to prosperity in developed countries.[45] This kind of trust is largely absent in Chinese society.[46] But there is an alternative: the public's confidence in the government is strong.[47] Such confidence also appears in financial sector. Although the public does not believe in financial institutions' ability to make profits, they do believe that the government fully guarantees stability. This notion is strengthened by the practice.

---

[43] International Monetary Fund, "Global Financial Stability Report," International Monetary Fund, October 2016 (available at https://www.imf.org/en/Publications/GFSR/Issues/2016/12/31/Fostering-Stability-in-a-Low-Growth-Low-Rate-Era.)

[44] Avgouleas and Xu, "Overhauling China's Financial Stability Regulation," 9–10.

[45] See F. Fukuyama, *Trust: The Social Virtues and The Creation of Prosperity* (New York: Free Press, 1995).

[46] Fukuyama classified China as a society with low levels of trust. Ibid., chap. 9.

[47] Z. Wu, "Trust and Rule of Law in the Capital Market," *Securities Law Review*, 8 (2013), 23.

All financial institutions comply with an unwritten rule, namely "no default, no surprise." Financial institutions would like to bear the loss of investment even when the product contract attributed these kinds of risk to investors. In other words, the product issuers will almost always pay back the principals and fulfill expected yields, so the risk-allocation term in the written contract is not important, nor is the profitability of the project.[48]

Under the "no default, no surprise" rule, it is the financial institutions who bear the investment risks. However, many assets underlying the products are impossible to generate sufficient cash flow to meet repayment obligations.[49] Sometimes issuers roll over the program to pay the earlier creditors with new money coming into the pool. Xiao Gang, the former Chairman of Bank of China, found the mechanism of wealth management products was to some extent a Ponzi scheme.[50] When the losses do happen, financial institutions simply write them off. The bad debts accumulate in the financial institutions and gradually weaken the balance sheet, inevitably resulting in insolvency for some institutions. However, they seldom go bankrupt.

The only financial institution bankruptcy to date is the case of Guangdong International Trust and Investment Corporation (GITIC 广东国际信托投资公司). GITIC functioned as the main fund-raising arm of the Guangdong government. It borrowed billions of dollars – mostly in foreign currency and without approval from Beijing – to pay for a reckless expansion into real estate, hospitals, securities trading, and even silk weaving. But most of the businesses failed, and the company sank under $4.3 bn. of debt. On October 6, 1998, the central government abruptly shut down GITIC and entrusted the People's Bank of China to start liquidating it, which was completely unexpected.[51] On January 16,

---

[48] The "no default, no surprise" rule has become a common practice in the industry. It has been regarded as a severe source threatening the stability of China's financial system and drew attention at a high level of the central government. 12th National People's Congress Finance and Economy Committee specially listed orderly breaking "No Default, No Surprise" rule as one of the suggestions to the draft of 2017 Plan on National Economic and Social Development. See Examination Report of 12th National People's Congress Finance and Economy Committee on the Execution of 2016 Plan on National Economic and Social Development and the Draft of 2017 Plan on National Economic and Social Development.

[49] X. Gang, "Regulating Shadow Banking," *China Daily* (October 12, 2012).

[50] Ibid.

[51] M. Landler, "Bankruptcy the Chinese Way; Foreign Bankers Are Shown to the End of the Line," *The New York Times* (January 22, 1999), www.nytimes.com/1999/01/22/business/

1999, Guangdong High Court declared the bankruptcy of GITIC. It was the first time that financial institution creditors were not fully repaid.[52] In most cases, PBOC will designate a financial institution (usually a commercial bank) to take over all the unwinding business of the institution in trouble, along with all the liabilities and rights. Creditors would be repaid in full by the institution designated to take over.

Bail-outs are not only reserved for firms on the brink of bankruptcy. For some important financial institutions, the government helps them to write-off bad debts when the balance sheets need to look cleaner. The central government launched two large-scale write-offs for the four biggest commercial banks (the Big Four) in China: Industrial and Commercial Bank of China, China Construction Bank, Agricultural Bank of China and Bank of China. The first was in 1999, when the State Council approved the establishment of four financial asset management companies (AMCs) to buy out up to CNY 1,400 bn. of non-performing loans of the Big Four.[53] Some scholars believed the Big Four were technically insolvent before the spin-off.[54] After the restructure, the officially recognized ratio of non-performing loans to total outstanding loans remained as high as 25 percent.[55] The second capital restructuring occurred before the Big Four went public.[56] Bank of China and Construction Bank received a $45 bn. bailout to cut their bad-loan ratio and render them more attractive to investors and to compete with overseas competitors.

The government even expanded the implicit safety net to the capital market. If a big shock hits the capital market, the China Securities

---

international-business-bankruptcy-chinese-way-foreign-bankers-are-shown-end-line
.html?pagewanted=1.

[52] T. K. Chang, "The East Is in the Red," *International Financial Law Review*, 18 (1999), 43.

[53] Y. Ye, "The Way of Dealing with Non-performing Loans and Its Effects on Macro-statistics in China," International Monetary Fund, May 16, 2003, www.imf.org/external/np/sta/npl/eng/2003/051603a.pdf.

[54] For example, see N. R. Lardy, 'China and the Asia Financial Contagion," Foreign Affairs, July/Aug 1998, www.foreignaffairs.com/articles/54212/nicholas-r-lardy/china-and-the-asian-contagion).

[55] J. Lou, "China's Bank Non-Performing Loan Problem: Seriousness and Causes," *The International Lawyer*, 34 (2000), 1147, 1148.

[56] China Construction Bank went public on the Hong Kong Stock Exchange in October 2005 and then on the Shanghai Stock Exchange in September 2007; Bank of China went public on the Hong Kong Stock Exchange in June 2006, and then on the Shanghai Stock Exchange in July 2006; in October 2006, Industrial and Commercial Bank of China went public on the Hong Kong Stock Exchange and Shanghai Stock Exchange simultaneously; and Agricultural Bank of China went public on July 2010 on the Hong Kong Stock Exchange and Shanghai Stock Exchange at almost the same time.

Regulatory Commission (CSRC) along with PBOC would implement a series of measures to prevent the market from dropping too sharply.[57] Besides suspending the trading of particular shares, closing the market or other methods to limit transactions, the regulatory authorities may also command the large shareholders (usually SOEs) to buy some big chunk of shares.

From this perspective, in China, the public's trust that supports the financial system is not exactly in financial institutions themselves, but derives from the public's confidence in the government.

14.3.3   The Role of Ex-Ante Intervention in the Story

14.3.3.1   Mitigating Moral Hazard

As shown above, the government acts as the source of trust that supports the financial system, and it does not limit bailouts to financial institutions suffering liquidity crises. On the contrary, insolvent financial institutions are usually the target.

Financial institutions do not fear failure since they will not bear the costs. They lose incentives to act prudently. Meanwhile, market forces also encourage financial institutions to take risks: as the investors know they do not assume the risk associated with their choice of financial institution, they do not take the financial condition of the institutions into consideration.[58] Instead, they hand their money to institutions that choose more risky strategies and usually yield higher returns.

In these circumstances, both self-regulation and market forces fail to constrain financial institutions. The government becomes the only force that can prevent financial institutions from taking on more risks than optimal. The heavy ex-ante regulations decrease the possibility of financial institution failure, and thus reduce the probability of bailout cost and

---

[57] For example, in July 2015, the Chinese capital market dropped dramatically. To stop the fall, the China Securities Regulatory Commission (CSRC) soon issued a notice encouraging the big shareholders, directors, supervisors and senior officers of listed companies to stabilize the stock price of their companies by increasing their shareholdings and by other means when the stock price of the company had declined significantly. CSRC even exempted the legal responsibility of these behaviors if they breached any provisions of the securities law and regulations. See Notice of the China Securities Regulatory Commission on Issues concerning the Increase of Shareholding in a Listed Company by Its Principal Shareholders, Directors, Supervisors, and Senior Executives, No. 51 [2015] of the China Securities Regulatory Commission, July 8, 2015.

[58] S. H. Talley and I. Mas, "Deposit Insurance in Developing Countries," World Bank Policy Research Working Paper, WPS 548, November 1990.

enhance the efficiency of the market in the long-term. When market competition can no longer select the more efficient financial institutions, ex-ante administrative examination and authorization also play the role of selector. Extra limitations on the financial institutions, such as high debt-loan ratio or high reserve ratio, are imposed as higher prudential requirements.

The Chinese financial system's favorable treatment of SOEs can also be explained. Generally speaking, SOEs have access to all kinds of resources. Regardless of their operating efficiency, SOEs always have enough cash flow to pay back loans. Even when SOEs are unprofitable, loans to SOEs enjoy implicit state guarantees.[59] For example, the government decided to issue bonds to pay back the loans borrowed by some local government financial vehicles (LGFVs).[60] LGFVs had this chance because they are state-owned companies that raise funds for local governments, a kind of SOE that has very close connections with the government. These privileges made SOEs popular borrowers compared with POEs.

14.3.3.2   Precondition of Implicit Safety Net

Strong ex-ante control is also the key precondition to implement an implicit safety net.[61] As mentioned above, in most bailout cases, the government needs to persuade another financial institution to merge with the troubled institution and take over the bad debts. The Chinese government's bargaining power results from its heavy controls over the financial industry.

The first is the value of financial license/charter. When the value of a financial charter is high, other financial institutions, especially ones that have not been granted the specific charter, may wish to merge with the troubled institution, to gain the charter. The higher the entry barrier to the financial market, the higher the value of the charter will be. Thus the current austere ex-ante authorizations actually increase the value of financial charters and strengthen the government's power of negotiation in the bailout context.

---

[59] Avgouleas and Xu, "Overhauling China's Financial Stability Regulation," 9.
[60] A. Back, "China Bailout Falls on Banks' Shoulders," *The Wall Street Journal*, March 10, 2015, www.wsj.com/articles/china-bailout-falls-on-banks-shoulders-heard-on-the-street-1425979781.
[61] See C. J. Milhaupt, "Japan's Experience with Deposit Insurance and Failing Banks: Implications for Financial Regulatory Design?" *Washington University Law Quarterly*, 77 (1999), 399, 427.

The second source of the government's bargaining power is the ability to bestow favorable treatment. For example, in 1996, PBOC decided to close Zhongyin Trust Investment Company and designated Guangdong Development Bank (a state-owned financial institution) to take over the business of Zhongyin Trust. Guangdong Development Bank paid as much as CNY 4 trillion to clear the debts of Zhongyin Trust. In return, the central government allowed Guangdong Development Bank to expand its business from Guangzhou province to the entire country. This kind of ability is based on the government's broad discretionary power.

Regulatory deterrent force may also facilitate the government's negotiation with potential acquirers. In the circumstances where the government exercises broad policymaking autonomy, it is also able to legitimately limit the further development of a financial institution by disapproving a new business, turning down expensing plans, or not giving pilot permissions, among other actions. Some financial institutions would be in a weak position in such negotiations.

State ownership also makes the negotiation process smoother. The government may use its shareholder rights to propose and approve a merger proposal, especially when the same particular department is executing the shareholder rights of both the troubled institution and the potential acquirer.

14.4   The Problem of the Current "Heavy Insurance, Heavy Intervention" Strategy

Aside from the political purpose, the government's rescue strategy might also result from efficiency concerns: the government offers implicit insurance to the whole financial system so that financial institutions are able to attract customers. Meanwhile, although maintaining control in the financial industry sets up numerous limitations to the industry, such controls are also the only force able to reduce the possibility of institution failure in the current situation, and the precondition that assures the operation of the current implicit safety net. Nonetheless, these efficiency concerns are short-term. The current strategy would impose huge adverse impacts on the financial system and even the whole economy in the long-term.

14.4.1   Huge Bailout Costs

The most direct drawback of the rescue strategy is that the government needs to bear huge bailout costs. As proved by worldwide practices, a safety net that consists of deposit insurance and the lender of last resort is necessary to prevent systemic risks and promote financial system stability. But the Chinese bailout mechanism that offers implicit insurance to the whole financial system is too expensive. As most bailouts in China have involved asset instead of liquidity problems, rescues are not a method to reduce risks but to redistribute risks (because of the moral hazard problem, bailouts may increase the risk for the whole system), which means the bailout authority is unable to achieve a positive return from the bailout business. Even worse, the total loss would be huge.

An important difference between institutional deposit insurance and an implicit safety net is the source of funding. As no funding is contributed by market players for the safety net, the government needs to use the fiscal budget or central bank resources to absorb these losses from rescues.[62] Although strict regulations may help to reduce costs to some extent, the burden on the government is still heavy. Sometimes, bailout happens in the form of the government injecting money directly into the financial institution in trouble or the designated acquirer.[63] In more cases, the government would designate another financial institution to take over all the debts and liabilities of the troubled institution.[64] In the latter cases, there may not be straightforward fiscal expenditures, but the government will have to give the acquirers some preferential treatments in exchange for its cooperation. Moreover, the acquirer is usually a state-owned bank, which means when the acquirer is ruined by the burden it inherited,[65] the collapse can be counted as a loss of the government.

---

[62] Talley and Mas, "Deposit Insurance in Developing Countries," 22.

[63] In 2005, the State Council approved the plan to inject CNY 6 bn. to rescue and restructure Yinhe Securities Company when it was in the brink of bankruptcy.

[64] For example, in the case of Guangdong Development Bank Takeover Zhongyin Trust Investment Company mentioned in section 14.3, Guangdong Development Bank took over all the debts and liabilities of Zhongyin Trust Investment Company.

[65] In the case of Guangdong Development Bank Takeover Zhongyin Trust Investment Company, mentioned in section 14.3, eight years after Guangdong Development Bank took over all the debts and liabilities of Zhongyin Trust Investment Company, Guangdong Development Bank also encountered financial troubles because of the political burdens it took on. The government finally had to restructure Guangdong Development Bank. See "The Restructuring of Guangdong Development Bank Is Full of Twists and Turns," *Caijing* (August 22, 2005).

14.4.2   Financial Repression

Government's frequent intervention plays an important role in the financial system,[66] but it also inevitably creates a big drawback: financial repression.

Financial repression means that state power prevents the financial system from functioning at full capacity, and drives money supply below its effective level.[67] The financial repression strategy was believed to facilitate economic growth in some developing countries, including China. As the artificial interest rates under Chinese financial repression policies made considerable price differences between loans and deposits, it also guaranteed the profitability of commercial banks in China in the last two decades. However, in the current stage, its use in China stifled financial institutions' growth. To assure commercial banks a central position in the financial system, current regulations give non-bank institutions little space to thrive.[68] In theory, financial guarantee companies take banks or other lenders' credit risk. However, the interests of lending belong to the lenders, and the financial guarantee companies can only charge lenders a service fee that is far from able to cover the risks the guarantee companies have assumed. Non-deposit-taking lending institutions like micro-loan companies and pawn shops are able to charge higher interest rates than commercial banks, but their customers are also riskier.[69] In addition, the limits on fund resources and leverage also erode their ability to make profits.

Although commercial banks are in a superior position compared with other financial institutions, the government's intervention in their operation also set up obstacles for them in market competition. In the deposit-taking business, as the interest rate has long been artificially depressed, bank deposits have steadily lost their attraction. The government now seldom directly intervenes in banks' particular decisions, but the constraints on commercial banks are still heavy and impose a high cost on banks' lending businesses. The deposit reserve ratio in China is now as

---

[66] See Chapter 16 of this volume.

[67] See E. S. Shaw, *Financial Deepening in Economic Development* (Oxford: Oxford University Press, 1973); see also R. I. McKinnon, *Money and Capital in Economic Development* (New York: Brookings Institution Press, 1973).

[68] See Chapter 15 of this volume.

[69] Most of banks' customers are state-owned enterprises. The efficiency of these enterprises might not be high, but they are able to access many resources and the implicit guarantee of the government. Thus lending to them is safe. See Avgouleas and Xu, "Overhauling China's Financial Stability Regulation," 9.

high as 16.5 percent and even reached as high as 21 percent in 2011. In operation, banks also need to comply with the strict loan-to-deposit ratios that do not allow banks to lend funds over 75 percent of their deposits; the loan volumes control which limits the total loan volume granted by commercial banks each year; and other regulations like credit policies.

Customers, no matter whether investors or borrowers, are also not satisfied with the current financial system. As both financial institutions and financial markets are strictly restricted by ex-ante authorization, the investment channel is very limited. Especially for those who want to invest in short-term low-risk investments, the unappealing bank deposit is the only legal choice. In the long period of depressed interest rates, the deposit interest rate was not only much lower than the market rate, but also lower than the inflation rate.[70] Although the Chinese government began to liberalize interest rate regulation in 2013, the deposit products are still not attractive vis-à-vis wealth management products.

On the borrowers' side, the distribution of funding resources is not fair. Some borrowers face serious financial exclusions.[71] As interest rates are artificially repressed, the funds that banks can gather are limited. Plus, the cheap interest rate of loans granted makes them precious resources that every borrower wants. Under this circumstance, banks are unable to satisfy all financing needs in the market, so the government is able to guide the flow of the loans through credit policies. Between 1991 and 2009, cheap funding to all non-state and non-listed companies accounted for only around 20 percent of the total; the rest went to SOEs and listed companies. Meanwhile, the respective contributions to GDP of these sectors was the reverse. In 2011, the total output of the all non-state and non-listed companies was almost $11,444 bn., as opposed to the approximate $4,812 bn. total output produced by the state and listed sectors.[72]

14.4.3   Distorted Behaviors and the Extra Costs

Market players found a way to circumvent the restrictive Chinese financial regulatory system. Commercial banks, trust companies, securities

---

[70] See Chapter 15 for further discussions on the depressed interest rate in China.

[71] See S. Collard, E. Kempson and C. Whyley, *Tackling Financial Exclusion: An Area-based Approach* (Bristol: The Policy Press, 2011), Introduction. See also L. Lin, "Managing the Risks of Equity Crowdfunding: Lessons from China," *Journal of Corporate Law Studies*, 17 (2017) 327, 328.

[72] Allen and Qian, "China's Financial System and the Law," 517.

companies and informal financial institutions, together with borrowers who have difficulties accessing bank loans, created Chinese shadow banks.[73]

According to the official document, some shadow banks are products of formal financial institutions, like wealth management products issued by banks, securities companies, insurance companies and fund management companies, or trust products issued by trust companies. The rest consists of informal financing in China, including P2P lending marketplaces, micro-loan companies, pawn shops, financial guarantee companies, and private equity funds.[74]

Different from the typical shadow banking system that triggered the 2008 financial crisis overseas, Chinese shadow banks were not the result of disintermediation.[75] There's almost no involvement of securities or direct financing. Chinese shadow banks simply created a gray or black market that served to replace commercial banks to be the new financial intermediary between the ultimate borrowers and investors.

Some shadow banks, offering wealth management and trust products, are not legal persons themselves, instead, they are a part of duly licensed financial institutions. Some shadow banks may cooperate to conduct full intermediation. For example, P2P market places may ask financial guarantee companies or other third parties to provide guarantee to the loans in the market places. Banks would use their own wealth management products to gather funds, but usually ask other financial institutions for bridge loans. No matter whether the credit intermediation process is done under one roof, the shadow banks work as intermediaries. When borrowers are unable to payback their loans, shadow banks would stand out and make up for the losses of ultimate investors.

As Chinese shadow banks only replace banks' place in the financial chain, their business model is just as same as that of traditional banks. Which means Chinese shadow banks did not bring about the benefits of disintermediation. Their risks of conducting credit intermediation are no

---

[73] Regulation arbitrage has been regarded as a strong force that stimulate the growth of Chinese shadow Banks; see Chapter 15.

[74] According to world bank, the key difference between formal financing and informal financing is whether they are regulated by financial regulatory authorities. See World Bank, "Informal Financial Markets and Financial Intermediation in Four African Countries," World Bank, January 1997, http://documents.worldbank.org/curated/en/800841467990343381/pdf/570510BRI0Find10Box353745B01PUBLIC1.pdf.

[75] Disintermediation is an important character of shadow banks. See S. L. Schwarcz, "Regulating Shadow Banking," *Review of Banking & Financial Law*, 31 (2011), 619, 626–627.

less than traditional banks. Chinese shadow banks contributed to the efficiency of the financial system by extending credits to those enterprises with no access to bank loans. This kind of efficiency was however not an outcome of developments in financial technology, but the regulatory advantage under the financial depression background. Chinese shadow banks exist only because traditional banks are forbidden or limited from performing some functions. Compared with the financing service of traditional banking, shadow banks actually impose extra costs on financial institutions, borrowers, and the whole system.

Financial institutions face risks of breaching laws and regulations. Credit intermediation activities of Chinese shadow banks are largely illegal.[76] In China, only commercial banks are entitled to gather money from the public. While conducting credit intermediation, Chinese shadow banks inevitably need public funds, otherwise the leverage is not high enough to make a profit. Except for wealth management funds issued by commercial banks, other shadow banks commit "illegal fund raising" when they reach out to the public. As to banks' wealth management products, they are regarded as an off-balance sheet activity, but the banks stick to the unwritten rule "no default, no surprise." As a result, it is still the banks who are bearing the investment risks. Although there are no specific rules which prohibit financial institutions from doing so, it certainly runs against the spirit of relative regulations.

The above costs would ultimately be transferred to the borrowers. The interest rates of loans from shadow banks are much higher than those of traditional banks. Certainly, the artificially repressed bank interest rates should be considered as the main reason, but shadow banks would also translate the possible penalties for their violation into their operation costs, and proportionately increase their charges.

The Chinese shadow banking system may also threaten the stability of the whole financial system. Commercial banks are deeply involved in the shadow banking system. In their wealth management activities, just as in traditional loan business, commercial banks themselves work as credit risk bearer. The losses of the wealth management products may cause banks liquidity or solvency problems, and may even trigger bank runs. In other shadow banking activities, traditional banks may play the role of important investors because they are still the most important financial institutions and possess the most social assets. The collapse of shadow

---

[76] Chapter 15 goes into detail of how Chinese shadow banks are largely illegal activities.

bank financial chain would likely trigger financial contagion in the traditional banking system.

Moreover, in contrast to the traditional banking system, the bailout costs of the Chinese shadow banking system would be higher. The shadow banking system looms in a gray area with less supervision, especially of their illegal credit intermediation activities. The regulatory authorities are less able to detect risks preventatively. Usually, the government discovers the business chain and the risks associated with it only when the chain has broken down and the loss is already widespread.[77]

14.5   Conclusion

The Chinese financial system is operated in a different way from those in Western countries, and in China the heavy intervention of the government plays a pivotal role. Without the support of the government, financial institutions are unable to gain trust from the public to run their business. Yet the current strategy is not a sustainable one.

The first challenge is the heavy fiscal burden of an implicit safety net. The Japanese government also tried to be responsible to the whole financial system from the 1970s through 1990s, but failed in the after-bubble era due to the expensive bailout costs.[78] The Chinese government has also felt the pressure. The government keeps claiming that they will break the "no default, no surprise" norm in the near future. In October 2014, the government launched the explicit deposit insurance scheme after decades of discussion, effective since May 1, 2015. It remains unknown whether this formal explicit deposit insurance might be a paper tiger, as proved to be the case in Japan during 1970s–1990s.

The government also needs to reckon with the adverse impacts of its heavy intervention. The current regulation has disappointed both the financial institutions and their customers. Market players created the Chinese shadow banking system to defend against financial repression

---

[77] For example, the underground financial system of Wenzhou city drew the attention of the government only after the 2012 "runaway" debt crisis, in which at least 80 percent of business people were reported to have disappeared, committed suicide or declared bankruptcy. For more information of this case, please see W. Shen, "Shadow Banking System in China – Origin, Uniqueness and Governmental Responses," *Journal of International Banking Law and Regulation*, 1 (2013), 20, 22–24.

[78] C. J. Milhaupt, "Japan's Experience with Deposit Insurance and Failing Banks: Implications for Financial Regulatory Design," *Monetary and Economic Studies*, 17 (1999), 21.

policies. But the government has not really understood why all of this happened. Since 2013, the government has implemented a series of regulations aiming to push financial institutions back to their regulatory blueprint. The hope is that these heavy regulations will be able to control the risks of Chinese shadow banks; however, they might lead to another round of financial repression. In this sense, the "return to the blueprint" strategy may push the market players even further from the government's control.

15

The Political Economy of China's Shadow Banking

SHEN WEI

China's shadow banking system attracted little attention before the latest Global Financial Crisis starting in 2007, but turned out to be one of the main causes[1] for "the worst financial crisis since Depression."[2] It was plausibly claimed that the Global Financial Crisis started as a liquidity run on the repo market, categorized as one of the most important sectors in the shadow banking system.[3] Accordingly, there are two schools of thought explaining the cause of the Global Financial Crisis. According to the global savings glut theory, it was high-savings that fueled flows of money from emerging market economies and pushed long-term interest rates down to rock-bottom levels, leading to asset bubbles in the United States and other countries.[4] By contrast, the global credit glut theory diagnosed the illness in the opposite way: it was the scale of global shadow banking that caused the trouble.[5]

Globally, the scale of shadow banking assets exceeds GDP. Non-bank financial intermediation grew to reach $71 trillion, which accounted for 117 percent of GDP.[6] The largest shadow banking system exists in advanced economies, while emerging economies have seen the growth of

---

[1] J. Hu and M. Moroz, "Shadow Banks and the Financial Crisis of 2007–2008," (2010), http://ssrn.com/abstract=1574970.

[2] International Monetary Fund, "World Economic Outlook: Financial Stress, Downturns, and Recoveries," (2008), www.imf.org/external/pubs/ft/weo/2008/02/pdf/text.pdf.

[3] G. Gorton and Andrew Metrick, "Securitized Banking and the Run on the Repo," Yale ICF Working Paper No. 09–14 (2009), http://papers.ssrn.com/sol3/papers.cfm?abstract_id=1440752.

[4] G. Gorton, *Slapped by the Invisible Hand: The Panic of 2007* (Oxford: Oxford University Press, 2007); Hsu and Moroz, "Shadow Banks."

[5] Financial crisis can be divided into three categories. The 2008 crisis came with the collapse of previously rock-solid institutions such as Lehman Brothers. The 1997 crisis was unfolded when global investors lost faith in countries and pulled their money out of Asian countries. The 2007's Northern Rock crisis in the UK was more about a public run on one or more financial institutions. For a detailed account of a variety of financial crises, see generally, C. M. Reinhart and K. S. Rogoff, This Time Is Different: Eight Centuries of Financial Folly (Princeton University Press, 2009).

[6] Financial Stability Board, "Global Shadow Banking Monitoring Report 2013," (2013), 2.

shadow banking outpace that of the traditional banking system.[7] The broadest measure of shadow banking assets tracked by the Financial Stability Board (FSB) surpassed \$75 trillion in 2014 in twenty countries plus the euro area. That represented 120 percent of G20's GDP – approaching the high of 123.4 percent recorded in 2007.[8] In the US, the shadow banking assets, starting from 1993, exceeded the value of assets in the traditional banking sector, and exceeded GPD by over three times.[9] Shadow banking assets in emerging economies increased from 30 percent to 70 percent of GDP from 2002 to 2012.[10] In 2014, shadow banking comprised 24.5 percent of financial assets in emerging economies, the highest share since 2007. By contrast, traditional banks' share of the sector slipped to 45.6 percent from a high of more than 49 percent in 2008.

It is fair to state that the shadow banking sector is growing in size and significance, not only in the world but also in China. China now has the world's third-biggest shadow banking sector after the US and the UK. Some Chinese institutions estimate that the shadow banking sector's size may be in the range of CNY 20 to 30 trillion.[11] The FSB projected that China's shadow banking assets have experienced a growth rate of 42 percent.[12] It was estimated by Goldman Sachs that 24 percent of total credit to corporates and consumers were extended through shadow banking in China, accounting for 45 percent of GDP in 2012.[13] The staggering value of shadow banking assets, the unprecedented speed of its growth, and the complexity and novelty of its products have made this sector a rather urgent task for regulation and monitoring. The IMF has warned that China's shadow banking sector requires particular monitoring[14] as shadow banking social financing had risen to 35 percent of GDP.[15]

---

[7] International Monetary Fund, "Risk Taking, Liquidity, and Shadow Banking – Curbing Excess While Promoting Growth," Global Financial Stability Report (October 2014), 65.

[8] S. Fleming, "Shadow Banking Nears Pre-Crisis Peak," *Financial Times* (October 31, 2014).

[9] Z. Pozsar et al., "Shadow Banking," Federal Reserve Bank of New York Staff Report No. 458 (2010), p.65, available at http://ssrn.com/abstract=1645337.

[10] International Monetary Fund, "Risk Taking, Liquidity, and Shadow Banking: Curbing Excess While Promoting Growth," *Global Financial Stability Report* 73 (October 2014).

[11] Y. Zhao, "A Comparison of Shadow Banking Credit Risk Aggregation from the Perspective of Global Financial Crises in the Past," *Finance and Economics Science*, 11 (2013) (in Chinese).

[12] Financial Stability Board, "Global Shadow Banking Monitoring Report 2013," (2013), 12.

[13] Goldman Sachs, "China: Banks," *Equity Research* (2013), 4.

[14] International Monetary Fund, "Financial Stress and Deleveraging Macrofinancial Implications and Policy," *Global Financial Stability Report* (2008), 90.

[15] International Monetary Fund, "Risk Taking, Liquidity, and Shadow Banking – Curbing Excess While Promoting Growth," *Global Financial Stability Report* (2014), 77.

The political economy of regulation usually focuses on the way in which regulators are appointed and appraised, and the mechanisms of accountability to democratically elected politicians. The conventional topics in this school also include the tensions between electoral cycles, volatility of public interest in financial regulation, and technocratic expertise in agencies.[16] These topics may be less relevant to China, given its regime's authoritative nature. However, the political economy of regulation is still relevant to China's financial market and financial regulation, as the politics and ideology matter in the Chinese context when the mounting shadow banking sector needs to be understood and contained in a more sensible manner.

The key thesis of this article is that the government has inefficiently overregulated finance, and market forces have efficiently provided liquidity and return to those neglected by the government through the medium of shadow banking. A sensible response to an increasingly sizable shadow banking sector is a free-market approach allowing the financial market more effectively and efficiently to allocate financial resources in the lending market. A political economy approach pierces the veil of such questions as why the government has chosen to enter the financial market heavily as well as to take a more tolerant and passive approach to the regulation of shadow banking sector given its hands-on approach on the financial market. The state ownership alone may not be a strong reason to explain why the government favors state-owned banks and borrowers. Nevertheless, when we connect the continuing state ownership (i.e., majority ownership of large SOEs)[17] with the political foundation and legitimacy of the ruling party or state capitalism, the political economy paradigm well justifies the government's more favorable economic, fiscal and industrial policies toward the state-owned sector as the state-owned enterprises and state-owned banks are the economic pillar of China's party-state.[18] State ownership also explains regulatory capture in

---

[16] J. Armour et al. (eds.), *Principles of Financial Regulation* (Oxford: Oxford University Press, 2015), chap. 27.

[17] The CCP's 14th Central Committee issued the CCP Central Committee's Resolution on Several Issues Regarding the Establishment of a Socialist Market Economic System which explicitly stated that small SOEs could be leased, restructured as joint-stock companies, or sold to collectives or individuals. According to the CCP Central Committee's Resolution on Several Major Issues Pertaining to the Reform and Development of SOEs, issued in September 1999, the state-owned economic sector is the main component of the Chinese economy, and the chief goal of the SOE reform is to turn large SOEs into competitive firms through various strategies such as the one to grab the big and let go of the small.

[18] M. X. Pei, *China's Crony Capitalism- The Dynamics of Regime Decay* (Cambridge MA: Harvard University Press, 2016), 264.

China's banking sector.[19] While China is still in a transition period moving from the planned economy to a socialist market economy and is in a process of developing a long-time desired vibrant capital market, shadow banking indeed becomes a legal institution,[20] through which the government is trying to achieve adaptive efficiency.

15.1 Shadow Banking in Global and Chinese Contexts: Definition and Main Characteristics

It is technically hard to define shadow banking in a concise and precise manner. The term "shadow banking system" was first used by American economist Paul McCulley in 2007,[21] who referred to it as "the whole alphabet soup of levered up non-bank investment conduits, vehicles and structures," "unregulated shadow banks [which] fund themselves with uninsured commercial paper [and] which may or may not be backstopped by liquidity lines from real banks" and which stand in contrast to "regulated real banks, who fund themselves with insured deposits, backstopped by access to the Fed's discount window.[22] According to a report issued by the Financial Stability Board (FSB) in November 2011, shadow banking is defined as "credit intermediation involving entities and activities outside the regular banking system."[23] There are other ways of mapping the broad shadow banking system by applying both an "entity-based" approach and an "activity-based" approach. The advantage of this "mapping" approach is to allow a focus on examining liquidity and maturity transformation, leverage, interconnectedness between the shadow banking and regular banking sectors.[24]

Defining shadow banking in China is a challenging task. Participants in China's shadow banking sector include a wide range of nonbank

---

[19] W. P. He, *Banking Regulation in China: The Role of Public and Private Sectors* (Basingstoke: Palgrave Macmillan, 2014), 40.

[20] M. Ricks, "'Money and (Shadow) Banking: A Thought Experiment," *Review of Banking and Financial Law*, 31 (2011), 731, 748.

[21] P. A. McCulley, "Teton Reflection," *PIMCO Global Central Bank Focus* (2007), www.pimco.com/Documents/GCB.

[22] Ibid.

[23] It is widely recognized that the concept of credit intermediation involves maturity, credit, and liquidity transformation which can significantly reduce the cost of credit relative to direct lending. For details, see Z. Pozsar, T. Adrian, A. Ashcraft and H. Boesky, "Shadow Banking," (2010), http://ssrn.com/abstract=1645337.

[24] L. Grillet-Aubert, J.-B. Haquin, C. Jackson, N. Killeen and C. Weistroffer, "Assessing Shadow Banking – Non- bank Financial Intermediation in Europe," *European Systemic Risk Board Report* No. 10 (2016), 2.

market players such as trust companies, brokerage firms, microfinance firms and financial guarantee companies. Underground lending and some off-balance-sheet activities are also included. The rationale of their inclusion into the scope of shadow banking is that these firms or activities involve regulatory arbitrage and systemic risk, which are two key concerns linked by the FSB to the shadow banking sector.[25]

In 2013 the People's Bank of China (PBOC), China's central bank, made the first attempt to define shadow banking, as follows: credit intermediation involving entities and activities outside the regular banking system, with the functions of liquidity and credit intermediation, which could potentially cause systemic risks or regulatory arbitrage.[26]

The State Council, China's cabinet, in 2013 issued the Circular of the General Office of the State Council on Relevant Issues of Strengthening the Regulation of Shadow banking (Circular No. 107), which indicated its preliminary but technical attempt to tackle the shadow banking sector. Circular No. 107, as the first legal or administrative document, set out an overarching regulatory framework for monitoring shadow banking in China. The Circular defines shadow banking as "credit intermediation entities and activities outside the traditional banking system."

Circular No. 107 takes a functional approach, classifying shadow banking into three categories, covering both traditional and shadow banks. The first category is credit intermediation entities that do not have financial licenses and that are completely unregulated, such as the so-called internet financing companies and third-party wealth management entities. These shadow banks are not licensed or regulated financial businesses. The second category includes credit intermediation entities that do not have financial licenses and that are subject to an inadequate level of regulation, such as financing guarantee companies and petty loan companies. The third category includes those licensed financial institutions that have activities which are not adequately regulated such as money market funds, asset securitization and some types of wealth management products.

These three categories are divided according to their degree of institutionalization or intimacy with the traditional banking sector. The closer one category is to the traditional banking sector, the more likely

---

[25] Financial Stability Board, "Shadow Banking: Scoping the Issues – A Background Note of the Financial Stability Board," 3.

[26] This is not an official definition but was made by an official, Sheng Songcheng, of PBOC in a media conference on January 15, 2014, http://finance.people.com.cn/money/n/2014/0115/c42877-24126410.html.

it may fall into the existing regulatory space and entail documented banking rules and procedures. This definition is still quite broad, encompassing some forms of lending activities that have not been widely recognized as shadow banking activities. Including local government financing vehicles and underground lending into shadow banking shows the regulators' anxiety about the accumulation of systemic risk and potential financial instability. Compared with other forms of shadow banking activities, underground (or informal) lending has the weakest tie with the formal banking sector, and is the least regulated sub-sector in shadow banking albeit some funding connections between underground lending and formal lending through letters of credit, short-term loans, discounted bills, and group or residential mortgages.[27]

Circular No. 107's way of defining shadow banking or grouping shadow banking forms in China also reflects the level of benefits a particular shadow banking activity can contribute to the real economy. In this sense, these three categories can be placed in a spectrum ranging from credit disintermediation to credit intermediation. At one extreme of the spectrum are the non-bank lenders, which can be categorized as the typical form of credit disintermediation without the involvement of traditional banks. The other extreme of the spectrum is represented by credit intermediation involving traditional banks, but through off-balance-sheet financing techniques. In the middle is something combining both credit intermediation and credit re-intermediation with a changing role of either a bank or a non-bank institution. This has been described as a credit enhancement layer of shadow banking,[28] due to the fact that non-bank lenders channel additional funding to the borrowers which have no access to formal bank loans.

In essence, this triple-tiered framework involves a differentiated level and nature of risks. The credit intermediation process involves banks or other traditional financial institutions. Therefore, systemic risk remains the key concern for this category of shadow banking. Banks' participation also determines that the regulatory instruments relied on by the regulators to address systemic risk in this section will be those regulatory tools widely used in banking regulation. Credit disintermediation does not

---

[27] Bank of America Merrill Lynch, "Shadow Banking: Risky Business," *Investment Strategy* (2012).

[28] A. Sheng, C. Edelmann, C. Sheng and J. Hu, "Bringing Light Upon the Shadow: A Review of the Chinese Shadow Banking Sector," Hong Kong Oliver Wyman and Fung Global Institute Report (2015), www.oliverwyman.com/content/dam/oliver-wyman/global/en/2015/feb/Bringing-Light-Upon-The-Shadow.pdf.

involve traditional banks or financial institutions. Those lenders will encounter credit failure and credit risk. The lack of connection among lenders may not lead to system-wide failure or collapse. In other words, systemic risk may not be the key concern for this category of shadow banking activities. Instead of bank-type regulatory instruments, resolutions or contract-based enforcement mechanisms may be more important for the purpose of containing credit risks and protecting creditors. The quasi-intermediated and institutionalized shadow banking sector presents some challenges to regulators partly because the relevant institutions are not heavily regulated like typical banks and partly because they positively contribute to the private sector and small businesses. Regulators must strike a sensible balance between heavy regulation (in order to avoid systemic risks) and effective regulation (to ensure some benefits can still be channeled to the real economy). The regulatory devices used are licensing plus exclusion (or inclusion) rules. For instance, financing guarantee companies are only allowed to carry out the licensed financing guarantee business. The banks are clearly excluded from the financing guarantee business for the issuance of bonds and negotiable instruments.[29]

Circular No. 107 also outlines a regulatory framework, summarized in Table 15.1, corresponding to the sectoral regulatory model for regulating the financial market. It adopted a regulatory-based structure by dividing the regulatory space into three sections. Each regulatory authority has its own jurisdiction over a specific section. For instance, while the Circular only briefly mentions that private equity funds are strictly prohibited from carrying on debt financing businesses,[30] this is not the end of the story. The China Securities Regulatory Commission (CSRC), China's securities authority, is still relied on to supervise and regulate private investment funds, including the qualifications of the fund manager, the process of offering fund units, information disclosure requirements and the scope of financial products private equity funds can invest in. The market entry approval allows each regulator to regulate a group of shadow banks once they are incorporated.[31] Therefore, this three-tiered definition actually serves clear regulatory purposes with the aim of effectively containing risk and regulating shadow banks or shadow banking activities. Monitoring shadow banking presents a challenge to the existing sectoral regulatory

---

[29] Circular No. 107, Art. 3(6).
[30] Circular No. 107, Art. 3(8).
[31] PRC Securities Investment Fund Law.

Table 15.1 *Triple-tiered Definition of Shadow Banking and Key Parameters*

Tier	1	2	3
Layer	Unlicensed and unregulated financial operators	Entities operating without a finance license and inadequate supervision by credit agencies	Inadequate supervised activities of licensed financial institutions
Coverage (major subsectors)	Underground lending, internet finance, P2P lending	Pawnshops, credit guarantee companies, microfinance companies	Money market funds, wealth management products, asset securitization
Intermediation	Disintermediation	Not typically involved in traditional credit intermediation; re-intermediation	Intermediation
Relationship with the bank	Distance from banks	Microfinance firms, which are regulated like banks	Banks or bank-type of financial institutions
Institutionalization	Least institutionalized	Quasi-institutionalized	Institutionalized
Economic benefits	Providing additional sources for funding	Existing funding channels	Formal funding channels
Potential risk	Credit risk, liquidity risk and market risk; Less likely to see system-wide risk	Credit risk, liquidity risk, and market risk; Possible systemic risk if the scale of lending through these shadow banks becomes large	Systemic risk
Licensing requirement for shadow banks	Unlicensed	Licensed	Licensed
Regulation	Private lending, based on contract and court enforcement for credit protection	Microfinance rules, subject to market entry rules and business scope rules	Subject to sector-based financial regulation including banking law and securities law, in particular, the financial safety net: prudential regulation, deposit insurance scheme and lender of last resort

model. The newly established State Council's Financial Stability and Development Commission, an overarching regulatory and coordinative framework, may help address the potential regulatory arbitrage. The China Banking Regulatory Commission (CBRC), China's banking regulator, stated in its 2011 annual report that "[a]ccording to the definition by FSB, the supervision by the CBRC over non-bank financial institutions does not fall into the scope of shadow banking." This statement was technically correct, in the sense that the CBRC has no jurisdiction over non-banks except trust companies. Circular No. 107 remedied this mismatch between shadow banking and the current financial regulatory framework. Consequently, shadow banking in China is also subject to a sectoral regulatory framework depending on the nature of shadow banks. For example, brokerage firms and insurance companies are regulated by the CSRC and CIRC respectively. Banks and trust companies are still regulated by the CBRC. While this regulatory framework maintains consistency with the one for the formal financial market, it may leave some shadow banking activities or institutions unregulated. A large number of local government financing vehicles may have to be regulated differently.

Circular No. 107 applied a balanced approach to shadow banking reflecting the government's permissive stance. It recognizes both benefits and risks of shadow banking due to the demand and supply imbalance in the lending market and the shadow banking's potential function to fill in the gap. The risk side is not only about the systemic risk attached to the shadow banking sector but also a dangerous market-driven competitor against a government-dominated banking sector. It is stated that the advent of shadow banking is the necessary product of financial development and financial innovation, and that as a beneficial supplement to the traditional banking system, it plays a positive role in serving the real economy and widening investment channels for businesses. On the other hand, it is also clearly recognized that shadow banking is vulnerable to systemic risks due to its complexity, uncertainty and propensity to augment contagion. For instance, Circular No. 107 is to limit off-balance sheet lending by banks and place non-bank institutions under closer scrutiny. The general tolerance showed in Circular No. 107 is to maximize the benefits shadow banking can bring to the financial sector and real economy.

Meanwhile, Circular No. 107 attempts to work out a structure to minimize the risk that shadow banking activities may cause financial instability. It is clear that the Circular's approach is to delegate regulatory responsibilities to multiple regulators based on the existing lines of financial sectors. The adherence to the traditional division of financial sectors is a clear-cut approach, matching the regulatory architecture for the traditional financial market. This regulatory arrangement may work by relying on the existing sectoral regulatory structure. Other benefits include continuity, efficiency, and coherency saving additional regulatory or switching costs for the change of existing regulatory model.

However, the defect of this regulatory or institutional build-up is clear in that the shadow banking sector often is cross-sectoral and a sectoral division may create regulatory arbitrage, overlap, inconsistency, and even omission. Shadow banking involves innovative products and services which are hard to fit neatly into the typical sector or category. For instance, private investment funds[32] and financing guarantee business[33] are regulated separately from other shadow banks which can be easily placed in existing financial sectors and regulatory spaces. Strengthening interagency cooperation is probably not sufficient to deal with the structural fluidity or organic fragmentation in shadowing banking. This may explain why Circular No. 107 does not specify regulators for some shadow banking activities. The mismatch between the shadow banking market and the shadow banking regulatory structure is likely to affect the efficacy of regulation. In this sense, the less integrated regulatory framework outlined in Circular No. 107 is sub-optimal. As far as some cross-institution financial products are concerned, the Circular stresses contracts and contractual enforcement between the risk-bearing and the channel-providing entity, and the industry regulator's jurisdiction over the risk-bearing entity.[34]

It is worth noting that, although Circular No. 107's regulatory framework is not optimal, it is consistent with the regulatory approach adopted by the FSB and the European Union. The FSB in October 2011 made recommendations for regulation in relation to various aspects of shadow banking along with several key shadow banking sectors: banks' interactions with shadow banking entities, money market funds, shadow banking entities, securitization and securities lending and repos.[35] This sector-based framework can also be seen in the EU's Green Paper Shadow Banking 2012.[36]

---

[32] Circular No. 107, Art. 3(6).
[33] Circular No. 107, Art. 3(8).
[34] Circular No. 107, Art. 3(4).
[35] Financial Stability Board, "Shadow Banking: Strengthening Oversight and Regulation – Recommendations of the Financial Stability Board," (October 27, 2011), www.financialst abilityboard.org/wp-content/uploads/r_111027a.pdf?page_moved=1.
[36] European Commission, "Green Paper Shadow Banking," (March 19, 2012), http://ec .europa.eu/finance/bank/docs/shadow/green-paper_en.pdf.

Circular No. 107 tackles various perspectives of shadow banking. It addresses market failure by requiring banks to establish proper mechanisms for internal control, risk management and risk segregation. Banks are required to comply with the proportionality principle, that is, the business scale must be commensurate with risk bearing capacity. At the firm level, senior management control must be put in place to correct agency failure.

Although the Circular represents a sound regulatory approach and constructive guidance to improving the regulation and monitoring of shadow banking, it is merely a policy document setting out broader legal, economic and policy consideration, and has limited utility, clarity and specification of details. The sectoral approach means that Circular No. 7 works only if separate financial regulators lay out their implementing rules later on. More importantly, the effectiveness of shadow banking regulation not only depends on the implementation by various financial regulators, but also the re-balancing of China's economic structure as a whole. Regulators and policymakers must keep a close look at the market so as to keep up with the market developments.

15.2   The Effects of a Distorted Supply and Demand Equilibrium

A political economy analysis will help us to identify the legal, economic and technological shocks that shaped the long-standing regulatory equilibrium in the banking and financial markets.

In terms of China's shadow banking sector, shadow banking emerges, survives and grows in conditions of supply–demand (dis)equilibrium. When regular banks fail to function as a credit intermediary responsible for credit, maturity and liquidity transformation, and become unable to meet the financing demands of businesses, shadow banks quickly kick in and fill the vacuum left by regular banks.

China's shadow financing market is a symptom of China's financial system – a result of China's rapid growth of underground financing and unregulated off-balance-sheet lending by China's state banks as well as a soaring credit growth. In addition to the further reform of the lending system, a deeper problem of popular shadow lending is related to China's economic distortions – the advantageous or dominant position occupied by a large number of state-owned enterprises (SOEs) and listed companies.[37] China's growth is largely powered by high investment in the state

---

[37]   SOEs' dominant position in the market can be evidenced by the revenues at two of China's largest SOEs, Sinopec and China Mobile, which multiplied nearly eight times over the last

sector, which made interest rates artificially low. Chinese banks have rationed their credit by doling out captive saving deposits to, at lending rates scarcely above the inflation rate,[38] large SOEs, which are more often conceived as good borrowers posing little default risks. The state sector is heavily dependent on privileged access to cheap loans from state banks. On the contrary, small and medium-sized enterprises accounting for over 60 percent of economic activity only get 30 percent of the financing and are the first victims in bad time's economy.[39]

The predominant position helps SOEs or listed companies obtain money from the formal banking sector at lower interest rates while less favored borrowers may have to rely on the informal lending market to finance at much higher rates. Even in the formal lending market, banks often impose more rigid terms on private borrowers which are required to guarantee corporate loans with personal assets or to use disproportionate land and equipment as collateral. In some extreme cases, borrowers may have to redeposit half of the loan with the same bank at a lower interest rate.[40] In addition, the borrowers will incur significant transaction costs involved in preparing paperwork and completing the approval process. Given these, borrowers are likely to end up in paying a much higher interest rate than the heavily regulated interest rate for loans, usually 7 or 8 percent. This lending practice further squeezed out private enterprises[41] and strengthened SOEs' dormant market status. The

decade, twice the rate of economic growth. "China's Leadership – Appearance and Reality," *Financial Times* (November 16, 2012) (online). State firms still lead, but private firms increase their grip on the market through better promotion and innovation. It is reported by Millward Brown, a global research agency, that the brand value of top privately held companies in China grows faster than that of SOEs. In its 2012 BrandZ List of the fifty most valuable mainland brands, non-SOEs' share of brand value rose to 27 percent. The list is based on the views of more than 35,000 mainland consumers, financial data and market information. C. Sun, "Private Mainland Brands Accelerate Growth, Report Finds," *South China Morning Post* (December 5, 2012) (online).

[38] It is estimated that the real return on 12-month time deposits in the past seven years averaged minus 0.5 percent, which has changed the depositors' mindset not to save as much as they did. T. Holland, "Reformers Aiming to Achieve Bank Liberalization by Stealth," *South China Morning Post* (April 3, 2012), B8.

[39] H. Sender, "Monetary Tightening by China to Be Felt across Globe," *Financial Times* (January 7, 2011), 20.

[40] "Cutback on Lending Puts Chinese Businesses in a Bind," *International Herald Tribune* (November 9, 2011), 14.

[41] Most private enterprises are struggling except those in the sectors where state giants are absent. For example, Tencent, an internet company, multiplied its revenues more than 580 times. "China's Leadership – Appearance and Reality," *Financial Times* (November 16, 2012).

intimacy between the state-owned banks and state sector is path-dependent. The dominance of SOEs constitutes a strong political lobby group, which, together with their entrenched interests, has made any reform difficult.

Financial regulation is always mixed with increased financial innovation, which in turn evolves with and affects the risk allocation function of the financial system.[42] Chinese regulators have been tolerant for the financial sector to experiment with new products or off-balance sheet activities, allowing the system gently to displace state allocation of capital through decreed interest rates, loan quotas, loan-to-deposit ratios and specific credit restrictions. However, regulators disapprove of banks and financial institutions taking advantage of financial innovation to bypass administrative and regulatory measures governing capital adequacy and loan-to-deposit ratios.

As discussed above, China's shadow banking refers to lending that is free from the regulation applicable to bank loans, and includes banks' off-balance-sheet vehicles such as commercial bills, entrusted loans, underground lending as well as wealth management products (WMPs).[43] The WMP market is the major sector in which banks are deeply involved in the shadow banking sector. Trusts and securities brokerages emerged as new conduits for shadow lending.[44] Incentivized by tightly controlled credit limits in China, part of China's domestic bank loans and savings moved from banks into opaque, off-balance sheet, risk-laden vehicles or underground financial networks.

The economic model of supply and demand well explains the rationale of WMPs, or shadow banking as a whole in a larger context. The supply and demand of deposits depend on the rate of interest. The equilibrium interest rate is that rate which makes the quantity supplied equal to the quantity demanded. In a market economy, the interest rate will reach this equilibrium rate. In other words, demand and supply determine price in equilibrium and leads to an efficient allocation of financial resources in the market. If the rate of interest is arbitrarily set below the equilibrium rate, the amount that the depositors are willing to supply is less than the

---

[42] D. B. Crane et al., *The Global Financial System: A Functional Perspective* (Cambridge MA: Harvard Business School Press, 1995), 153.

[43] The account of shadow banking in the US and worldwide, see generally S. Schwarcz, "Regulating Shadow Banking," *Boston University Review of Banking and Financial Law* (2011–2012), 619–642.

[44] S. Rabinovitch, "Surge in Chinese Credit Raises Fears," *Financial Times* (February 8, 2013).

amount that the banks wish to obtain. This inevitably results in a shortage of deposits in the market. This shortage is the source of shadow banking system: some banks are willing to pay a higher interest rate to attract more deposits whilst some borrowers are willing to pay an even higher interest rate. The origin of this shortage, however, is the government's control (or market manipulation) over the interest rate. Seen from this vein, WMPs (or even the shadow banking system) solve the shortage problem and improve economic efficiency, which has been distorted by administrative interference.

The cause of WMPs (or shadow banking as a whole) springs in part from the distorted interest rates system in China. The PBOC previously had set both a floor for lending rates and a ceiling for deposit rates, which guaranteed a sizeable net interest margin for state-owned banks but mispriced credit. A floor for lending interest rates provides an artificial subsidy to banks so that they can borrow less expensively and then invest in higher-yielding safe assets such as government bonds and the property market. By offering interest rates that exceed the benchmark deposit rate[45] and providing more WMPs, banks can secure more funds, which however may accumulate risks in the financial system. The lender in a shadow banking system, built on a lattice of interlocking credit, usually borrows money from banks and other private lenders with the aim of arbitraging interest rates. A mandatory ceiling on deposit interest rates deprives savers of the market return on their money. Inflation in China, which in most cases exceeded official interest rates, left savers suffering losses. Chinese banks, therefore, earn almost all of their income from government-set interest rate margins, leaving depositors with little profit and choice except pouring money into the shadow banking sector.

Chinese savers have piled into WMPs in recent years and made them the fastest-growing investment vehicles in the country. The popularity of these products is largely strengthened by the fact that (i) a mandatory ceiling on deposit rates (interest rates) deprives savers of the market return on their money, and (ii) inflation in China surged past official interest rates. For example, in February 2013, the deposit rate was only 3 percent, while the consumer price index increased by 3.2 percent,[46]

---

[45] Low rates do not necessarily increase the supply of credit. Risk aversion and higher returns on capital would encourage banks to eschew loans so that they can put more money in government securities or property market. This is also the case in the United States where banks are holding more cash and government securities than the outstanding volume of commercial and industrial loans.

[46] G. C. Chow, "Stop Tinkering," *South China Morning Post* (July 26, 2013), A19.

providing depositors with a negative return for their deposits. This effectively is a system of "financial repression" that caps the deposit interest rates on offer, which are much lower than the higher returns promised by WMPs. A moribund stock market during the 2008 financial crisis left investors with few meaningful investment opportunities to turn profits. Consequently, investors were forced to seek higher returns by investing in more profitable products rather than effectively lose money in bank deposits.[47] A huge pool of hard-earned savings either runs the risk of investing in dubious products or is parked in savings accounts paying extremely low interest.

High yields are closely related to the lending rates in the P2P sector. Annualized lending rates are roughly maintained at the rate of 15 percent in the small-loan sector, more than twice the benchmark bank loan rates. Large Chinese internet companies are following suit and offering higher returns than Alibaba's Yu'E Bao, a money fund. The P2P sector and internet-based money funds could inflict a serious blow to the banking sector, as the interest rate is one of the crucial instruments the Chinese government uses to manage the economy. The winners are Chinese savers, who now earn up to 7 percent annually on cash deposits compared to 3.3 percent paid by commercial banks. However, after the PBOC loosened its grip on the interbank market as its effort to push down the currency, yields have fallen as more cash floods into the market. The decline shows the mounting complexity of the regulators' efforts to control China's financial system, making it harder for money funds to lock in competitive yields.

A thriving underground lending market has bloomed due to depositors' zeal to put their money for higher returns or better use. As much as 90 percent of underground lending is used for speculative trades in financial markets.[48] Interest rates on loans provided by China's underground lending institutions are often 10 percent per month or even higher.[49] Some offered an annual interest rate as high as 100 percent, 180 percent[50] or even 200 percent.[51] Chinese banks were offering lending

[47] While savers are fed up with the miserable returns on their deposits and are demanding alternatives, capital is less captive. In April 2012, deposits expanded by only 11.4 percent, the slowest rate since at least 1998. "The Air Is Thinning," *The Economist* (May 19, 2012).

[48] "Chinese Lenders: Black Market Banking," *The Economist*, www.economist.com/node/9622318.

[49] M. F. Martin, "China's Banking System: Issues for Congress," *Congressional Research Service Report* (February 20, 2012), 6.

[50] G. Y. Ma, "What Do We Have for Wenzhou's Rescue," *China-US Focus* (November 16, 2011).

[51] "China's Economy: Bamboo Capitalism," *The Economist* (March 10, 2011).

rates between 7 percent and 8 percent for commercial loans. China's one-year deposit rate stands at 3.5 percent, under the PBOC's 2011 inflation target of 4 percent and below actual inflation which recently has exceeded 6 percent. Higher interest rates attached to underground loans may be justified by high administration costs to secure repayment and higher rates of default. Informal lenders are not under downward pressure from formal banks to lower their interest rates as the demand side is guaranteed by the financing needs of SMEs.

15.3   Regulatory Arbitrage and Regulatory Capture: A Regulatory Perspective

Behavioral public choice suggests a cautious approach to policy-making and a skepticism of government involvement in economic activities. Based on this school of thought, government action may be motivated by market failures or by paternalism. The call for greater government intervention is often directed at firm biases.[52] While legislation is often adopted in response to a perceived emergency, regulation also involves hidden costs.[53] In the context of US securities regulation, excessive regulation will reduce investment gains by one-half of one percent per year.[54] The pursuit of investment return drives market players to invest into less-regulated financial sectors, which may lead to deeper market failures. Regulatory arbitrage explains the existence of a mounting shadow banking sector and a failing banking sector even though the banking regulation has been gradually tightened up. In the regulatory framework, cognitive regulatory capture occurs when bureaucrats "internali[ze], as if by osmosis, the objectives, interests, and perception of reality of the vested interest they are meant to regulate and supervise in the public interest instead."[55] The US Federal Reserve's policy response to the 2008 financial crisis, as it was said, has been detrimental to the broader economy. It was argued that the Federal Reserve's inferior policies were

---

[52] J. C. Cooper and W. Kovacic, "Behavioral Economics: Implications for Regulatory Behavior," *Journal of Regulatory Economics*, 41 (2012), 41, 43.

[53] D. Hirshleifer, "Psychological Bias as a Driver of Financial Regulation," *European Financial Management* (2008) 856, 859.

[54] S. J. Choi and A. C. Pritchard, "Behavioral Economics and the SEC," *Stanford Law Review*, 56 (2003), 1, 39.

[55] W. H. Buiter, "Lessons from the North Atlantic Financial Crisis," unpublished manuscript, on file with the Federal Reserve Bank of New York (May 28, 2008), http://new yorkfed.org/research/conference/2008/rnum/buiter.pdf.

based on financial institutions' special pleadings and were a result of cognitive regulatory capture.[56]

The underground credit market is estimated by the PBOC and private sector analysts at CNY 2 to 4 trillion ($325 to $650 bn.),[57] or as much as 7 percent of total lending.[58] In some areas, informal lending exceeds that of official banks.[59] It has been estimated that such informal lending amounts to about $630 bn. (or even $2.6 trillion)[60] a year, or the equivalent of about 10 percent of China's GDP,[61] while the formal lending market offers 135 percent of GDP as of 2012. Comparatively, the underground lending market in China is smaller than in India (26 percent of GDP) and Thailand (47 percent of GDP).[62] Some sources notice that the size of undergrounding lending in China accounted for 33 percent of the entire shadow banking sector in 2011.[63] Unlike other major sources of funding for shadow banks, an assessment of what underground lenders get up to are intelligent guesses at best as informal lenders are the least transparent of the market players in China's shadow banking system.[64]

China's Ministry of Finance and the State Administration of Foreign Exchange have been cracking down on underground banks since 2002. The Chinese authorities have shut down over 500 underground banks,

[56] Ibid., 36.

[57] BBC, "China to Control Shadow Banking and Private Lending," (19 October 2011).

[58] H. M. Zhao & G. Q. Koh, "China's Runaway Bosses Spotlight Underground Loan Market," (September 29, 2011), www.reuters.com/article/2011/09/29/china-economy-runaway-bosses-idUSL3E7KS1B120110929. In March 2010, PBOC estimated that the underground lending market was worth CNY 2.4 trillion, or 5.6 percent of China's total lending.

[59] J. McDonald, "China's Unofficial Lending Falters, Savers Protest," www.businessweek .com/ap/financialnews/D9T11K7O0.htm.

[60] S. Sen, "Finance in China after WTO," Economic and Political Weekly, 40 (2005), 565–571.

[61] D. Barboza, "In cooling China, Loan Sharks Come Knocking," New York Times, October 13, 2011 (citing UBS's estimation), www.nytimes.com/2011/10/14/business/global/as-chinas-economy-cools-loan-sharks-come-knocking.html?_r=0.

[62] Milken Institute, "Underground Lending: Submerging Emerging Asia?' (April 2014), p. 7.

[63] J. H. Mao and J. Luo, "An Analysis of China's Underground Lending," Capital Markets (in Chinese), 11 (2011).

[64] Almost half of families in China have been involved in private lending, according to a survey of more than 28,000 families published last month by the Survey and Research Center for China Household Finance at the Chengdu-based Southwestern University of Finance and Economics. The figures show that about 49 percent of families in China's western regions had participated in private lending, around 46 percent in central China and 38 percent in eastern China. Nearly 320,000 households in western regions offered high interest loans totaling CNY 100 bn. in 2013. Y. Chen, "Wenzhou to Legalize Private Loans," Global Times, February 18, 2014, www.globaltimes.cn/content/843104.shtml.

with over 100 cases involving more than CNY 20 bn. in illegal funds.[65] Leaders including the ex-Premier Wen Jiabao and other top economic officials repeatedly promised more credit for small companies.[66] The government allowed the underground lending market to grow over the past decade, apparently seeing it as necessary to support entrepreneurs.

Zhejiang province alone has about 1.19 million non-state companies contributing 65 percent of its total GDP,[67] and abounds with underground banks for cash-strapped small businesses. About 80 percent of the SMEs in Zhejiang are using underground banking loans to fund their businesses, even though the black market interest rates in the province have surged as high as 10 percent monthly. About CNY 600 bn. flows through the province's underground banking system a year.[68] In 2011, Wenzhou's underground lending market was approximately CNY 110 bn., which was 20 percent of the whole city's banking loans.[69]

Underground lending markets often trap households and entrepreneurs in a cycle of debt, with high interest rates and predatory lending practices, leading to social problems and criminal activity. More than 7,300 companies in Zhejiang were forced to close between January and April 2011 due to the central government's monetary tightening measures.[70] The number of civil cases involving underground lending disputes rose dramatically after 2008, increasing to 747,809 cases in 2012 from 488,301 cases in 2008. The caseload of underground lending

---

[65] "China Shuts Down 500 Underground Banks in 8 Years: Ministry," Xinhua, November 22, 2010.

[66] J. McDonald, "China's Unofficial Lending Falters, Savers Protest," *Business Week* (February 20, 2012), www.businessweek.com/ap/financialnews/D9T11K7O0.htm.

[67] "Zhejiang: Private economy accounts for 65 percent of GDP in the province," Xinhua, September 28, 2017, http://news.xinhuanet.com/2017–09/29/c_1121747335.htm; "Statistics Communique on the National Economic and Social Development of Zhejiang Province in 2016," Xinhua, http://tjj.zj.gov.cn/tjgb/gmjjshfzgb/201702/t20170224_192062.html (in Chinese).

[68] Empirical research shows that the largest amount of bank financing funded to private firms is in the coastal (23.3 percent) and southwest (26 percent) regions, which were said to have an investment climate that facilitates access to formal sources of external finance. M. Ayyagari, A. Demirguc-Kunt and V. Maksimovic, "Formal versus Informal Finance: Evidence from China," *Review of Financial Studies*, 23 (2010), 3048–3097.This may suggest that Wenzhou probably is not the worst place to see a large amount of informal lending, compared to other surveyed areas in China.

[69] G. L. Wu, "An Investigation into the Current Underground Lending Market," *Zhejiang Finance* (in Chinese), 8 (2011).

[70] "China Squeeze Drives Boom in 'Black' Banks," *Asia Times*, www.atimes.com/atimes/China_Business/MH26Cb02.html.

disputes was around 10.22 percent first instance civil cases in 2012, or 48 percent of disputes arising out of loan agreements.[71]

The Chinese government's regulatory responses to the underground lending sector are largely premised upon a misperception about the nature of risks associated with informal financial intermediation in China. The emergence of systemic risks usually justifies regulation and regulatory responses. The apparent consequences of the return of political action may be the return of government as pro-active agent and the return of political risk.[72]

The risk of default is real. Lending to SMEs carries a higher perceived risk of payment delays, if not defaults. Lending savings to firms is more lucrative than putting their money in banks that give negative returns. Interest rates can be as high as multiple times of banks' lending rates, which trap households and entrepreneurs in a cycle of debt and predatory lending practices. Borrowers cannot afford such sky-high rates, significantly increasing default risk at the end of the debt cycle.

Speculative private lending is outside of the banking system and such loans are generally embedded in an excessively lengthy credit chain even though they are not necessarily used to fund speculative businesses. Despite government messages that no large-scale collapses among small firms or extreme credit shortages among SMEs exist, private lending can increase credit risk and systemic risk. Credit woes faced by one small firm can affect its peers through "debt triangles." This is the case when a firm that is short of cash delays payments to its suppliers, causing suppliers to suffer cash flow problems which in turn can affect others higher up the supply chain. To this specific firm, the risk is a credit risk but involves operational risk management. In other words, management of business processes[73] can influence the probability of a failing event occurring[74] even though credit risk is exogenous while operational risk is

---

[71] J. Tong, "An Analysis of Underground Lending Case Data in Recent Five Years in Court Nationwide," *Legal Daily* (in Chinese) (February 19, 2014), 9.

[72] J. Nugee, "Current Issues in Financial Regulation, and the Return of the Political Economy," *Journal of International Business and Law*, 11 (2012), 333, 335.

[73] Basel II lists seven event types and one of them is called clients, products, business practices. Basel III however focuses on other risks and additional capital requirements without touching upon operational risk. A. A. Jobst, "The Treatment of Operational Risk under the New Basel Framework: Critical Issues," *Journal of Banking Regulation*, 8 (2007), 316.

[74] M. Power, "The Invention of Operational Risk," *Review of International Political Economy*, 12 (2015), 577.

endogenous.[75] In a larger picture, the risk is that a major default of an underground loan could trigger a domino effect threatening the wider financial system. Then, credit risk of a firm, apart from its risk-rewarding consideration, can easily turn to systemic affecting much of the financial system. Among the anecdotal evidence of the growth in loan sharking, media reports said Inner Mongolia saw an "explosion" in the number of court disputes over underground loans in 2013, to as many as 43,000,[76] which indicates a connection among lenders and borrowers in the underground lending market.

Banks are not entirely insulated. Savers' reluctance to put their money in banks has sparked a "war for deposits." Banks are seen to be channeling capital into the underground lending market.[77] The collapse of the underground banks thus threatens to spread to the formal banking system. Underground banks are seen as a major conduit for the illegal flow of overseas capital in China because the two money markets show differentials in exchange rates of renminbi and foreign currencies.

As far as the government is concerned, social stability remains a leading concern. Financial stability is an essential component of this overarching social goal. Rising defaults threaten to aggravate social tensions, leading to social problems and criminal activity. The social instability risk lies in the government's potential inability to effectively intervene in the underground lending market if the default risk unacceptably increases because there is no centralized pool for the funding, as in a bank bailout or bail-in.[78] The other related risk is the central bank's inability to implement effective monetary policy if a large scale of lending takes place outside of the formal banking system. Consequently, it will become more difficult for the government and financial regulators to maneuver the levers of the economy such as fiscal stimulus and dampening. The risk will become a real one should there be a fiscal or economic crisis.

---

[75] For a comparison of operational risk and credit risk, R. Doff, "Why Operational Risk Modelling Creates Inverse Incentives," *Journal of Financial Regulation*, 1 (2015), 284, 286–287.

[76] J. Woo, "China's Loan Sharks Circle in Murky Shadow Bank Waters," *Chicago Tribune*, January 30, 2014, http://articles.chicagotribune.com/2014–01-30/business/sns-rt-us-china-loans-underground-20140130_1_shadow-bank-underground-banking-under ground-loans.

[77] B. Zhang, F. Zheng and J. T. Zhao, "Cash Crash for Wenzhou's Private Loan Network," *Caixin*, October 11, 2011.

[78] The bail-in process is superior to bailouts in the case of idiosyncratic failure, but can still entail risks. E. Avgouleas and C. Goodhart, "Critical Reflections on Bank Bail-ins," *Journal of Financial Regulation*, 1 (2015), 3–29.

The absence of a balanced financial sector itself presents a risk to economic growth. The market does not play a decisive factor in forming interest rates and other lending terms. Interest rate ceilings or floors and other restrictions in the financial market inhibit the banks from pricing loans to reflect the trade-off between profit and risk, which leads to allocative inefficiency. The fact that the scale of shadow banking assets is close to the value of assets in regular banks itself presents a risk for the financial market, and shows the severity of this distortion. The strategy to mitigating this risk is to balance the distorted financial sector through market-oriented approaches.

The problems of interest group lobbying, in particular by financial sector firms, is one of the key political economy issues in financial regulation. Regulatory reform can be caused by the change in the relative strength of competing interests. We live in a world of value-pluralism and there is no single public interest.[79] When it comes to regulation or legislation, the outcome is likely to be a natural result of competing lobbying efforts by various constituencies. The best example may be the lobbying efforts made by banks to call for harsher regulation over P2Ps. Banks are lobbying regulators to tighten rules governing online products they see as unfair, given their own 20 percent capital reserve requirements and other regulatory restrictions, which increase transaction costs. The Chinese Banking Association, a government-backed industry group, is lobbying regulators to cap the yields on online money market funds and reserve requirements as banks have felt a threat from online financial products.[80] If adopted, online money market products would be subject to the same regulatory cap that governs conventional term deposits. This again is a valid example showing that the rival interest groups may make use of various policymaking processes to influence financial services modernization legislation. Regulation is largely acquired by industry and is operated primarily for its incumbents' benefits. In this sense, a range of mechanisms including increasing competition in the market, lowering the state-owned banks' market share, and strengthening the financial regulators' independence can be considered as regulatory devices serving to ameliorate the interest group lobbying problems.

Bureaucrats can be viewed as a distinct interest group, concerned about expanding the scope of their jurisdiction, size and influence over

---

[79] E. Butler, *Public Choice – A Primer* (London: The Institute of Economic Affairs, 2012) 15.
[80] "Chinese Banks Call for Cap on Online Interest Rates," *South China Morning Post* (February 28, 2014) (online).

the sector they regulate. The key argument of the leviathan approach is to say that the objective of the government is to maximize or increase its size and expenditures.[81] This well explains the increasing size of the local government financing vehicles (LGFVs). A possible local government debt crisis in China, at the same time, has received continuing attention in the Chinese and global press. Local governments' huge and opaque debt, totaling $3.8 trillion by the end of 2014,[82] has been seen as one of the significant risks threatening China's overall economy. Unfortunately, the phenomenon has yet to be understood adequately both in terms of its magnitude and its origins.[83]

The fiscal demands of the government trigger a close relationship between politics and the banking and financial sectors. LGFVs arise as a way for local governments to maximize their revenues in order to fill in the expenditure gaps. This practice created a constituency of LGFVs that are organized and involved in the financing businesses in order to protect local governments' vested interest to maintain financial soundness and economic growth. Local governments come to rely on deficit financing through the issuance of sovereign debt. Reforms of the government bond markets can then be understood as an alternative financing mechanism which delays the crisis resulting from the LGFVs. The changes to the Budget Law can also be seen in this light.[84]

---

[81] See generally A. P. Martinich and B. Mattiste (eds.), *Leviathan*, revised edn. (Peterborough, ON: Broadview Press, 2010).

[82] A. Mukherjee, "Debt Relief for China's Local Governments," *International New York Times*, September 15, 2015, p. 20 (citing the Chinese government's official statistics).

[83] There has been some literature on this topic. The angle is the prism of inadequate public service provisions in poor rural areas owing to fiscal stress. See generally, C. Wong (ed.), *Financing Local Government in the People's Republic of China* (Oxford: Oxford University Press, 1997); World Bank, *China: National Development and Sub-national Finance – A Review of Provincial Expenditure* (Beijing: Poverty Reduction and Economic Management Unit, East Asia and Pacific Region, 2002).

[84] PRC Budget Law was first promulgated twenty years ago, and the amendments were initiated ten years ago. The newly amended Budget Law is now double the size of the old one, with changes in eighty-two areas, many of which are worth highlighting. The most important achievement of the amended Budget Law is its compliance with the framework set out by the CCP's Third Plenum's reform blueprint. The Budget Law has strengthened oversight by the legislatures at all levels, in line with the Third Plenum's call for a law-based and transparent budgeting system. The shift is reflective of the ruling party's changing attitude toward the budgeting, which is no longer a private matter to the government. The Budget Law, amended by the National People's Congress in August 2014, now ends the direct borrowing ban and allows local governments to issue bonds directly for "public-welfare capital expenditure," providing a legal basis for the formalization and expansion of the pilot scheme.

15.4   Dichotomy between SOEs and SMEs:
A Political Ideology Perspective

Banking regulation is only one arena where political factors can play a role. The structure of regulatory and government institutions also plays an important part. From a Minsky perspective, understanding the financial market should include cyclical and structural perspectives, which will then facilitate the design of a policy strategy for further reform.[85] On the other hand, as it has been pointed out, the relationship between politicians and regulation is often unhelpful: electorates are interested in financial regulation in times of crisis. As a result, politicians have incentives to be interventionist in bad times while being lax in good times.[86] However, in the Chinese context, the government may be keen to be interventionist due to the state-owned shareholding connection between the government and banking sector. Apart from its shareholder's role, financial soundness is the fundamental principle to keep state-owned banks and financial institutions intact.

The underground lending market connects China's army of savers with mostly small borrowers unable to access formal lenders and who can end up paying exorbitant annual interest rates. As informal financing institutions are not viewed as formal banks, the informal lending market has not been targeted by national or international financial regulatory reform efforts. This however does not suggest that the risk is minimal and there is no systemic risk. As a matter of fact, the risk of informal lending is mounting in China while the government intensifies its efforts to discipline risky lenders and calm exuberant credit growth with the purpose of pushing away borrowers from informal lenders. Due to the lack of regulatory oversight and uncertainty of the macroeconomic environment, the underground lending market could be the most vulnerable sector in China's shadow banking sector and is thus viewed as the largest risk to China's financial stability.

Underground lending can be divided into gray and black forms of financing. The gray market, encompassing a large number of microfinance firms,[87] trust and investment companies, pawnshops and credit

---

[85] H. P. Minsky, *Stabilizing an Unstable Economy*, 2nd edn. (New York: McGraw-Hill Education, 2008) xiii.

[86] J. Amour et al. (eds.), *Principles of Financial Regulation* (Oxford: Oxford University Press, 2016) chap. 1.

[87] L. Wang, "Microfinance Play Seeks Macro Boost," *The Standard* (January 5, 2015), www .thestandard.com.hk/news_detail.asp?art_id=152860&con_type=3.

guarantee companies, may be economically beneficial to some innovative activities and cash-constrained market players. Such firms play a gap-filling role in providing financial services that are unavailable from the bank-centered financial system.[88] This gap-filling function justifies the existence of shadow banking, which can be viewed as a market response to financial exclusion. The black market, on the other hand, has detrimental effects only. However, in the activity occurring, there is no clear line between gray and black markets. For instance, some of China's credit guarantee agencies have moved beyond their intended business scope and effectively become banks, taking deposits and providing loans. Some investment brokers and private fund managers also used their capital to provide illegal commercial and personal loans. Pawnshops can be offering some banking services to individuals and firms.[89]

Banks are not necessarily free of risk from either gray or black financing markets, as banks are involved in the credit chain (or financial (re-) intermediation chain), upstream or downstream. Some foreign investors seeking entry into China's financial market are also attracted to credit guarantee agencies, thereby turning themselves to financial intermediaries. When a business faces debt service challenges in a reciprocal loan guarantee network, bank loans guarantee or guaranteed by that business may be at risk. Certainly, the black lending market may be more distant than the gray one from the banking system and may pose limited systemic risk to the banking system.

After the financial crisis, the Chinese government once tried to tighten monetary policies to clamp down on a credit boom, combat inflation and cool its economy, which overheated after CNY 4 trillion was pumped in as stimulus to counteract the financial crisis in 2008. In the economic downturn, the credit tightening has been hurting China's 7.5 million or so non-state small and medium-sized companies (SMEs). State-owned banks cut the small amount of private sector lending they were doing while continuing support to state-owned sector. Many cash-strapped firms have been unable to borrow from banks amid a credit clampdown by the government while struggling with slumping global demand, and some of them have had to turn to China's underground lending market – which pools money from individuals and firms.

---

[88] W. Vlcek, "From Road Town to Shanghai: Situating the Caribbean in Global Capital Flows to China," *British Journal of Politics and International Relations*, 16 (2014), 539–540; World Bank, "Enterprise Survey China," (2012).

[89] M. F. Martin, "China's Banking System: Issues for Congress" (February 20, 2012) 6.

SMEs and farmers are generally poorly served by the larger state-owned banks and frequently have no option but to turn to these informal lending firms. SOEs however are easier to secure funding from the state-owned banks. Large SOEs are able to obtain over 75 percent of loans from state-owned commercial banks[90] at a 7.2 percent interest rate, compared with the one-year benchmark interest rate of 6.56 percent. Through third-party companies such as financing firms, they can then lend the money on at higher rates, ranging from 36 percent to 60 percent, to SMEs.[91] SMEs have been severely marginalized by the state banking system. In 2011, only 19 percent of bank lending went to small businesses, while total loans fell 6 percent from 2010 to RMB 7.5 trillion ($1.2 trillion).[92] In 2013, 23.2 percent of bank loans, of which 4.7 percent were short-term working capital loans, were extended to SMEs.[93] The World Bank's survey confirmed that, during the period from 2011 to 2013, only 25 percent of SMEs obtained bank credits, and 90 percent used internal financing.[94] The general estimation was that 10 percent of SMEs have access to formal bank loans, while they account for 65 percent of the workforce and 60 percent of China's GDP.[95]

SMEs have thus been forced to resort to non-banking sources of credit due to structural constraints on their borrowing from state-owned banks. Underground lending firms provide as much as a third of the loans to SMEs and 55 percent of the loans to farmers.[96] Against this backdrop, informal lending has been surging while the state has been trying to reduce legitimate lending to cool the economy. Its popularity reflects widespread desperation for an alternative financing source to China's banking sector, which pays low deposit rates that fail to keep up with inflation and channel savings.

---

[90] C. Leung, "It's Far From Enough to Only Adjust Stock Structure of SOEs," http://money.163.com/14/0811/15/A3CI99HS00254TFQ.html.

[91] O. Chung, "China Squeeze Drives Boom in 'Black' Banks," *Asia Times* (August 26, 2011), www.atimes.com/atimes/China_Business/MH26Cb02.html.

[92] J. McDonald, "China's Unofficial Lending Falters, Savers Protest," www.businessweek.com/ap/financialnews/D9T11K7O0.htm.

[93] China Banking Regulatory Commission, "CBRC Vice Chairman Yan Qingmin Attended Small- And Micro-Sized Financial Service Sub-forum of Boao Forum for Asia," www.cbrc.gov.cn/Chinese/home/docView/C1B3D38F6C61440B024B7FABEAD15A57.html.

[94] World Bank, "Enterprise Surveys: China" (2012).

[95] Milken Institute, "Underground Lending: Submerging Emerging Asia?" (April 2014), 13.

[96] "Chinese Lenders: Black Market Banking," *The Economist*, www.economist.com/node/9622318.

Entrepreneurs and private firms face barriers in accessing credit, which is an enduring structural feature in both advanced and emerging economies.[97] Research concludes that SMEs are financially more constrained than large companies in both developed and developing countries.[98] Serving small enterprises can be a high-risk, high-cost business for banks as such borrowers have neither stable revenue streams nor repayment capabilities. Small, short-term and unsecured loans do not economically justify the extension of credit from formal banks to SMEs. Borrowers usually do not have sufficient collateral assets and credit information, increasing not only the default risk of lending to them but also the transaction costs for banks. Small enterprises, unable to meet the lending criteria set out by banks, may prefer informal lending as the loan approval process is much more straightforward. The difficulty in financing for SMEs is more severe in China. SMEs' access to financing is more limited than large companies in China[99] as well as than their counterparts in other Asian countries. The World Bank's survey shows that on average, Chinese SMEs receive 12 percent of their working capital from bank loans, compared to 21 percent in Malaysia, 24 percent in Indonesia, 26 percent in Korea, and 28 percent in Philippines.[100]

In the Chinese context, this structural bias against SME financing not only has an economic logic but also reveals political priority. It has been pointed out that politicians often use the financial system to provide low-cost financing to targeted industries or groups, either through explicit state-owned banks or implicit guidance.[101] Compared to SMEs, SOEs and larger firms usually have stronger connections with the government,

---

[97] Organization for Economic Co-operation and Development, "Financing SMEs and Entrepreneurs 2014," 35.

[98] A. N. Berger and G. F. Udell, "The Economics of Small Business Finance: The Roles of Private Equity and Debt Markets in the Financial Growth Cycle," *Journal of Banking and Finance*, 22 (1998), 613; T. Beck and A. Demirguc-Kunt, "Small and Medium-Size Enterprises: Access to Finance as A Growth Constraint," *Journal of Banking and Finance*, 30 (2006), 2931.

[99] J. Y. F. Lin and Y. J. Li, "Promoting the Growth of Medium and Small-sized Enterprises through the Development of Medium and Small-sized Financial Institutions," *Economic Research Journal*, 1 (2001), 11; H. S. Xu, "Financing Gap and Minimization of Transaction Cost: Why SMEs Have Problems in Financing and How to Improve the Policy," *Journal of Financial Research*, 11 (2001).

[100] D. Dollar, et al., "Improving the Investment Climate in China, Investment Climate Assessment," http://info.worldbank.org/etools/docs/library/113671/madagascar/english/china_climate.pdf.

[101] R. S. Kroszner, "On the Political Economy of Banking and Financial Regulatory Reform in Emerging Markets," (1998) CRSP Working Paper No. 472, https://ssrn.com/abstract=143555.

which provides an implicit guarantee or subsidy to the bank credit. The result of limited access to the formal lending market is an increasing reliance on underground lending markets by SMEs. Financial exclusion worsens the equilibrium between demand and supply of financial resources. Commercial bank branches and ATMs per 100,000 adults are two key measures of financial outreach,[102] evidencing a lack of access to formal finance. In China, there are only eight commercial bank branches per 100,000 adults, fewer than nineteen worldwide and thirty-five in G-7 countries, and thirty-eight ATMs per 100,000 adults, fewer than forty-three worldwide and 135 in G-7.[103] China has a small micro-finance penetration rate compared with other Asian countries, evidenced by the number of active borrowers from microfinance institution. In 2011, China only recorded 0.57 million active borrowers, far less than 26.49 million borrowers in India or the 20.88 million in Bangladesh, and only slightly more than the 0.46 million borrowers in Indonesia.[104]

Parts of the financial sector are regulated and used as a means to provide subsidized credit or services to targeted groups (including the government itself) and to protect particular groups from such activities as competition, hostile takeovers, and expropriation.

Most underground lending businesses are not truly illegal or prohibited. In jurisdictions where there is an interest rate cap, underground lending offering a higher interest rate above the cap is then prohibited. A closed financial market imposing restrictions on market entry also disallows underground lending, which operates outside of the formal banking sector without regulatory approval and regulatory oversight. These happen to be the restrictions in China. An excessive size of underground lending market may impede a country's economic development due to its distorting impact on the financial market and banking regulation. Lack of access to credit is identified as one of the major constraints for entrepreneurial activities in developing economies,[105] and an obstacle to economic growth and development. Empirical work confirms a correlation

---

[102] In Chinese context, bank branches and ATMs are being phased down as electronic alternatives take over. Simply put, China is simply more modern, and bank branches and ATMs may be less important to China when it comes to financial outreach.

[103] International Monetary Fund, "Financial Access Survey (2014)."

[104] N. Zhang and P. Wong, "Sustainable Microfinance in Asia: Landscape, Challenges, and Strategies," (January 2014), 11.

[105] T. Beck and A. Demirguc-Kunt, "Small and Medium-Size Enterprises: Access to Finance as a Growth Constraint," *Journal of Banking and Finance* (2006), 2931–2943.

between the lack of credit access and poverty.[106] Formal financing, as empirical research confirmed, plays a larger role in enhancing productivity and economic growth.[107] Higher interest rates, heightened costs of borrowing, and coercive measures for debt collections lead to larger household debt and massive social disruption. Therefore, social risks and impacts become the main concerns over the informal lending market.

Economics may not be the only tool for the understanding of China's shadow banking. Rather, ideology may be a strong theoretical foundation for the explanation. Identifying the driving force behind changes in ideology over time has been difficult. The "too big to fail" principle may be reflective of an ideology protecting state-owned banks and state-owned sectors. Ideology can also explain the policy shift toward deregulation, reregulation and privatization. The government's role may determine the extent of government intervention. Given the large number of state-owned banks and SOEs, the financial regulatory structure and policy responses are likely to be more favorable toward SOEs and state-owned banks when the government crafts its banking regulation and fiscal or monetary policies. The private interest theory of regulation can also be relied upon to justify a variety of regulatory interventions which are difficult to be rationalized on public interest grounds. Due to the strong political and economic connection between the government and state-owned sector (including both state-owned banks and SOEs as borrowers), the government is keen to ensure the economic soundness of state-owned banks and the stability of financial resources available to SOEs.

15.5   Financial Repression vs. Financial Liberalization: A Public Choice Perspective

The entire architecture of financial regulation may need to be revisited and redesigned given the dynamic and complex nature of shadow banking.[108] In terms of China's shadow banking sector, it is worth enhancing both demand and supply sides of shadow banking. Shadow banking

---

[106] P. Honohan, "Cross-Country Variation in Household Access to Financial Services," *Journal of Banking and Finance*, 32 (2008), 2493–2500.

[107] Ayyagari, Demirguc-Kunt and Maksimovic, "Formal versus Informal Finance," 3048–3097.

[108] S. L. Schwarcz, "Regulating Financial Change: A Functional Approach," *Minnesota Law Review* 100 (2016) 1441–1494.

emerges, survives and grows in supply-demand (dis)equilibrium. When regular banks fail efficiently to supply credit, maturity and liquidity transformation, and become unable to meet the financing demands of businesses, shadow banks act to fill the vacuum. The public choice school argues the role of the government in correcting market failure which is perceived as arising from externalities while the market itself is a process of competition but the market competition is never perfect. Public choice economists seek to make the same assumption about human behavior in the political sphere as the way how the markets are analyzed. Market failures would not give rise to the problems that concern us if the self-interest had not operated within the market. It is the self-interest that drives banks not to respond to government guarantees by increasing the risks they take.[109] While technological innovation and regulatory arbitrage lend convincing force to the explanation of the popularity of shadow banking in China's financial market, financial repression is a theoretical framework laying down a solid foundation for more effective regulatory design and policy responses. The orthodox thinking is that policy decisions are made logically and rationally by enlightened and impartial officials who are keen to pursue public interest with the purpose of enlarging social welfare or the well-being of the community as a whole. Nevertheless, public choice shattered this assumption, that is, the process of making public decisions falls far short of the welfare economists' assumed ideal. In other words, public-decision makers are self-interested and regulation is likely to serve special interests rather than the general public.

Financial regulation is always mixed with increased financial innovation, which in turn evolves with and affects the risk allocation function of the financial system.[110] Chinese regulators have been tolerant of financial sector experimentation with new products or off-balance sheet entities, allowing the system gently to displace state allocation of capital through decreed interest rates, loan quotas, loan-to-deposit ratios and specific credit restrictions. However, regulators disapprove of banks and financial institutions taking advantage of financial innovation and bypassing administrative and regulatory measures governing capital adequacy and loan-to-deposit ratios.

---

[109] G. M. Lucas, Jr. and S. Tasic, "Behavioral Public Choice and the Law," *West Virginia Law Review*, 118 (2015), 200–255.

[110] D. B. Crane et al., *The Global Financial System: A Functional Perspective* (Cambridge MA: Harvard Business School Press, 1995), 153.

In order to secure the least expensive source of funding to sustain long-term economic growth, China has been applying more favorable monetary policies and regulatory devices, mainly in the form of interest rates and exchange rates, to state-owned banks. The consequence of such a financial repression model is two-fold. First, state-owned banks are able to secure the least expensive source of deposit, and ensure a sizable profit margin.[111] Related to this is the commercial banks' lending behavior in favor of state-owned sectors and discriminating against non-state players in the market. Second, the private sector, including start-up firms and privately owned enterprises has the difficulty in financing their business and expansion and creating the demand side of shadow banking. Viewed thus, regulating shadow banking at a technical level is insufficient to contain the growth of shadow banking. Rather, the government and regulators have to adopt a more holistic solution or scheme to deal with both the supply and demand sides of financing. It has been proposed that the holistic solution should include better demographic, industry and urban planning.[112] What can be achieved through this holistic solution appears to ensure that all of the parts of the financial market (whatsoever they may be labeled) that perform economically equivalent functions are, to the fullest extent possible, subject to functionally equivalent forms of prudential regulation. In this author's view, this holistic solution (howsoever it may be conceived) is merely to address the narrow scope of regulatory net, but yet tackle the fundamental flaw in market-disequilibrium. Seen from this angle, as far as China's shadow banking is concerned, a "visible" device is to rely on the "invisible hand" by injecting more competition into the financial market and removing restrictions on market entry, interest rate and exchange rate so that the market can shape the equilibrium of demand and supply sides[113] in an efficient and cost-effective manner.

In order to diminish the motivation for arbitrage, the proposal has been made to reform the existing financial regulatory regime. China's current

---

[111] The real sources of the high profitability of Chinese banks revealed by some empirical research not only include the managed interest system, but also unsustainable low staff costs. It appears that the high net interest margin alone did not guarantee the "windfall" profits for Chinese commercial banks. H. Löchel and H. X. Li, "Understanding the High Profitability of Chinese Banks," Frankfurt School of Finance & Management Working Paper Series No. 177 (2011), www.frankfurt-school.de.

[112] L. Guo and D. Xia, "In Search of a Place in the Sun: The Shadow Banking System with Chinese Characteristics," *European Business Organization Law Review*, 15 (2014), 387, 417.

[113] P. C. Carstensen, "Antitrust Law and the Paradigm of Industrial Organization," *UC Davis Law Review*, 16 (1983), 487.

sectoral (or sector-based) regulatory regime facilitates regulatory arbitrage between the discrete segments of the financial regulatory framework (designed originally to respond to a fragmented financial sector). While this sectoral regulatory regime guarantees a higher level of responsiveness, specialty and relevance, regulatory arbitrage and regulatory loopholes are natural byproducts of such a regulatory architecture. As discussed above, some major shadow banking subsectors span a number of regulatory arenas while others may fall outside the entire regulatory space of the financial market. Circular No. 107, presents a clear example showing the limitation of the sectoral regulatory model, the effectiveness of which relies on the implementing rules each financial regulator may have in the future. The latest reform taken by the Chinese government to tackle regulatory arbitrage in the financial sector is to set up a Financial Stability and Development Commission under the State Council to oversee and coordinate three regulatory bodies in banking, securities and insurance sectors. However, the regulatory effect of this Commission is unclear at this point.

15.6   Conclusion

The political economy approach deployed in this article attempts to provide an account of how and why a sizable and complicated shadow banking system has evolved and taken shape in China, and what forces have led to its status quo. This approach explains the heavy involvement of the government in the banking and financial system and the subsequent impact. The political connection (in the form of and due to state ownership) between the banking sector and the government has not diminished after the so-called corporatization or commercialization (if not privatization) reform through which major state-owned banks have been listed in domestic or foreign stock exchanges.[114] This political connection drives the government and regulators to continue to apply more favorable policies toward state-owned banks. The favorable policies inevitably discriminate against non-state-owned borrowers who in some sense compensate and subsidize state-owned banks and state-owned borrowers. Figure 15.1 indicates a low percentage of loans foreign-invested enterprises, privately owned enterprises and individuals have obtained from banks in the period between 1999 and 2009. This low percentage is a natural result of favorable and unfavorable policies applied by the government and regulators toward

---

[114] W. P. He, *Banking Regulation in China: The Role of Public and Private Sectors* (New York: Palgrave Macmillan US, 2014), 149.

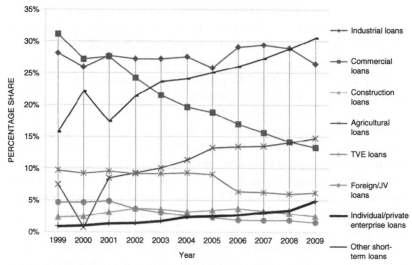

Figure 15.1 Distribution of Short-Term Bank Loans, 1999–2009

different borrower, and a significant driver of a sizable shadow banking sector. A strong political connection between banks and the government as well as the state ownership of the state-owned banks certainly create a moral hazard issue, meaning that banks may take riskier decisions even with macro- and micro-prudential regulation in place.

Regulatory arbitrage and the imbalancing of supply and demand sides in the lending market, among others, are the key determinants shaping the current shadow banking sector. The banking and financial system is particularly vulnerable to politicization. To a certain extent, this political economy perspective complements the traditional normative analysis undertaken by lawyers or economists studying "optimal" regulation. Among others, this chapter examines the influence of public and private interest, ideology, the institutional shape of government and the financial industry, and the impact of interest groups and public expectations on the evolution of shadow banking in China, underlining why the banking and financial system appear particularly vulnerable to politicization. The chapter highlights the impact of Chinese political institutions on the shape of the financial market. It seeks to identify the particular manner in which legal, economic and technological shocks are interrupting the long-standing regulatory equilibrium in Chinese banking markets and regulation, and how this evolutionary path relates to major trends in financial reform. It is the political economy factors that drive the recent trend toward financial regulatory reform and policy responses.

Public choice theory suggests the ineffectiveness of relying on the government or regulation to fix the defects of the banking sector, which is the main cause of shadow banking. In other words, regulation may not be an effective way of containing the growing shadow banking sector in the Chinese context given the repressed nature of the banking sector. Regulation, as a matter of fact, may lead to more harm than good.[115] If regulation is not a solution to the shadow banking sector, what will be the right one? This article argues for the use of market-oriented reform policy as an effective way of changing the demand-supply disequilibrium in the financial market, which is not only the main cause of a booming shadow banking sector but also the natural result of a dominant state-owned sector (including both the state-owned banks and SOE borrowers). The possible solution is for the government to overhaul its financial repression model to a financial liberalization model so that the market can play a larger role in fixing the demand-supply disequilibrium. Due to its doubt over the value of regulation, much of which is driven by psychological bias, the behavioral approach of public policy also supports the case for laissez-faire.[116]

A balanced policy framework has been proposed by the FSB to achieve two objectives: ensuring financial stability and promoting financial and economic development. National regulators must appreciate the importance of shadow banking in filling a credit void, broadening access to finance and deepening the financial market. More importantly, shadow banking is valuable to promote financial inclusion, which hints toward the "democratization" of finance. The state of financial services industry is highly institutionalized insofar as it comprises of highly organized and politically focused economic actors.[117] Corresponding to this institutionalization of finance is a regulatory framework with greater hierarchy and vested interest. Shadow banking is a viable agent of the "democratization" of finance[118] as it disrupts the dominance of traditional institutional actors

---

[115] See generally D. C. Mueller, *Public Choice* II (Cambridge: Cambridge University Press, 2003); D. C. Mueller, *Perspectives on Public Choice* (Cambridge: Cambridge University Press, 1997); P. J. Hill, "Public Choice: A Review," *Faith & Economics* 34 (1999), 1–10.

[116] D. Hirshleifer, "Psychological Bias as a Driver of Financial Regulation," *Eur Fin Management*, 14 (2008), 856.

[117] S. Soederberg, "The New International Financial Architecture (NIFA): An Emerging Multi-level Structure of Neo-Liberal Discipline," in A. Baker, D. Hudson and R. Woodward (eds.), *Governing Financial Globalization: International Political Economy and Multi-Level Governance* (Abingdon: Routledge, 2005), 189.

[118] R. J. Shiller, "The Democratization of Banking," www.theglobalist.com/the-democratiza tion-of-banking-nobel/.

such as banks in financial industry and economic development.[119] Seen through this lens, shadow banking optimizes the distribution of financial resources thereby improving economic efficiency and increasing social welfare. This is particularly relevant to China, which is a heavily repressed financial market. Shadow banking is a result of financial repression and can be relied on to improve the financial market.

Regulators should avoid over-regulation of shadow banking. This shows the importance and relevance of local peculiarities and circumstances, i.e., the stage of financial development and the level of financial innovation, which need to be taken into account to warrant policy relevance and efficacy. The regulators and policymakers instead need to prioritize risk prevention and continuously stress that financial innovation should serve the needs of the real economy. Implementing these large-scale economic and financial reforms take years. In the ongoing financial services modernization debate, the market plays a key role in liberalizing the financial market. Apart from the mounting concern over the sizable shadow banking sector (indeed a potential debt-fueled crisis), it is in China's own best interest to improve the breadth and sophistication of financial markets and implement its "mass entrepreneurship and innovation"[120] scheme or the idea of "inclusive economy,"[121] which will help avoid economy's hard landing, and more importantly, drive Chinese economic and societal growth in the future.

---

[119] W. Dobson and A. K. Kashyap, "The Contradiction in China's Gradualist Banking Reforms," *Brookings Papers on Economic Activity* 103–162 (2006) 2, www.frbsf.org/economic-research/publications/working-papers/wp2014-07.pdf (claiming that the fact that 90 percent of financial assets flows through the banking system is a truly striking feature of China's financial system).

[120] "China Eyes Mass Innovation, Entrepreneurship as New Engine," *Xinhua News* (January 28, 2015), www.globaltimes.cn/content/904599.shtml and "China Boots Mass Entrepreneurship and Innovation," *Xinhua News* (June 16, 2015), http://english.gov.cn/policies/latest_releases/2015/06/16/content_281475128473681.htm (reporting that the government is determined to innovate its institutional mechanisms to facilitate mass entrepreneurship and innovation).

[121] Inclusive growth is imperative not only for achieving the equity objective but also for sustaining the growth momentum. The major policy to achieve inclusive growth is to encourage easier and affordable access to financial services. China, together with other developing countries, has been including inclusive growth into the policy package. See generally, S. M. Hali, "APEC 2015 Lays the Foundations for Inclusive Economies" (November 23, 2015), www.china.org.cn/opinion/2015-11/23/content_37133786.htm; F. Peng, "China to Foster 'Inclusive Development' with Britain: Premier Li," http://news.xinhuanet.com/english/bilingual/2014-06/18/c_133417232.htm; U. Thorat, "Inclusive Growth – The Role of Banks in Emerging Economies," *RBI Monthly Bulletin* (2008), 411–424.

The A-share Bailout and the Role of China's Securities Watchdog in Regulating a Policy-driven Market

JIN SHENG[*]

16.1   Introduction: The 2015–2016 Stock Market Crash and A-Share Bailout

16.1.1   The Three Rounds of the 2015–2016 Stock Market Crash

China's stock market experienced three crashes from June 12, 2015 to January 2016. The first crash occurred from June 15 to July 8, 2015, when the Shanghai composite index lost 32 percent and the Shenzhen market dropped 41 percent.[1] On June 12, the A-share market reached a peak of 5178.19. Thereafter, the market tumbled began. Within one month, the market value of A-shares dropped by one-third. On July 8, 2015, the suspension of trading in the stocks of more than 1,400 Chinese listed companies was approved. On July 9, 97 percent of stocks were frozen.[2] It was noted that the CSRC's failure to regulate clearances of over-the-counter (OTC) stock financing triggered the market downturn.[3] In the first round, the stock market fell into a liquidity crisis.

---

[*] The paper on which this chapter is based was funded by the National University of Singapore Centre for Banking and Finance Law. The author sincerely thanks Professor David Donald for his valuable insights on revising the paper. The author is particularly grateful for the excellent editing and insightful suggestions of Professor Priscilla Roberts, Co-Director of the Asia Pacific Business Research Center of the City University of Macau.

[1] C. Riley, "China stocks hammered as market crash continues," CNN (July 8, 2015).

[2] P. Spence, "China's stock market crash: five numbers you need to know," *The Telegraph* (July 31, 2015).

[3] X. Wu, J. Li, and Z. Wang, "Improve Institutional Arrangements and Boost Market Confidence: Build Long-term Healthy Capital Markets with Steadily Development," *Tsinghua Financial Review* (December 2015), 14–23.

The second big crash occurred on August 18–26, 2015, when the Shanghai composite index dropped from 4,006 points to 2,850 points (a loss of 29 percent).[4] On the August 24, or "Black Monday," the Shanghai main share index plummeted 8.49 percent. On international stock markets, the Dow Jones Industrial Average dropped over 1,000 points (from 16,700 to 15,400) in the first ten minutes after opening.[5] On the following day (August 25), the market suffered similar losses of 7.6 percent. By August 25, 2015, the Shanghai Composite Index had crashed 42 percent from its peak of June 12.[6] At this stage, the market slide caused investors to panic; while deleveraging margin trading and swaps trading prompted a further round of market turbulence. In the second round, a "liquidity spiral" emerged, meaning that margin calls reinforced and accelerated the decline in liquidity.[7]

The third round of the crash was the "January 2016 meltdown." On December 4, 2015, the CSRC announced the introduction of the mechanism of circuit breakers, also known as trading curbs, which had been designed as a financial regulatory instrument in the United States, France, Japan and Singapore, to prevent stock market slumps.[8] It transpired that the introduction of trading curbs did not work well in the Chinese context, as the emergency shutdown caused investors to panic; even worse, the shutdown blocked purchasing bids. In particular, the A-share market already had a "daily price limit" for individual stocks.[9] Generally, the daily limit of price volatility was ±10 percent; while the daily limit for stocks under special treatment (ST and *ST shares[10]) was ±5 percent. The dual systems of "daily price limit" and the index fuse mechanism overlapped and might counteract each other. Recognizing that the negative effects were greater than the positive ones, the Chinese securities regulator (CSRC) decided to suspend the circuit-breaker mechanism. In the evening of January 7, 2016,

---

[4] Ibid.

[5] M. Egan, "After Historic 1,000-point Plunge, Dow Dives 588 Points at Close," CNN (August 25, 2015).

[6] C. Riley, "China Needs to Open up about Its Economy," CNN (August 25, 2015).

[7] M. K. Brunnermeier and L. H. Pedersen, "Market Liquidity and Funding Liquidity," The Review of Financial Studies, 22 (2009), 2201–2238.

[8] Wikipedia, "Trading Curb."

[9] Price limit = previous closing price × (1 ± price up/down limit percentage)

[10] "ST Company" means special treatment company. A listed company which does not meet the listing requirements but which the regulatory authority may not allowed to be delisted from the stock market, is termed an "ST company."

the Shanghai Stock Exchange,[11] the Shenzhen Stock Exchange[12] and the CFFEX issued notices to suspend the implementation of the index-based circuit-breaker mechanism from January 8, upon approval from the CSRC.

From January 4 to January 15, 2016, the Shanghai Composite Index fell 18 percent.[13] On January 26, 2016, the Shanghai Composite Index declined 6.4 percent in the last few trading hours and the Shenzhen Composite was down 7.1 percent.[14] In the third round, the introduction of the fuse mechanism is regarded as the cause of the flash crash. Additionally, the depreciation of the Chinese currency after August 11, 2015 and the reduction of holdings by large shareholders also contributed to the market turmoil.[15] The market plunges on the two trading days of January 4 and 7 indicated that the introduction of the "index fuse" mechanism represented a regulatory failure by the CSRC.

16.1.2   Bailout or Not? And How?

In late June and early July 2015, Chinese economists debated whether the 2015–16 stock market crash might trigger contagious effects or a financial crisis. Qingping Nie, Chairman of the Board of China Securities Finance Corporation Ltd, believed that a bailout was the only choice to deal with the stock market turmoil, since the abnormal volatility had created a liquidity crisis, a leveraged crisis, and a speculative crisis. He voted for various bailout policies, such as restrictions on arbitrage and speculations between the stock exchange and the futures exchange market, a CSRC deleverage policy, and government intervention.[16]

Other voices questioned the need for the bailout and associated measures. Anbound, a Beijing-based think tank, evaluated the potential influence of the bailout and concluded that excessive government intervention would have negative effects.[17] Shuguang Li believed that any

---

[11] Notice of the Shanghai Stock Exchange on Suspending the Implementation of the Index-Based Circuit Breaker Mechanism (promulgated by the Shanghai Stock Exchange, January 7, 2016, effective January 8, 2016).

[12] Ibid.

[13] J. Mullen, "Chinese Stocks Enter Bear Market," CNN (January 15, 2016).

[14] S. Yan, "China Stocks Plunge 6% as Rout Continues," CNN (January 26, 2016).

[15] J. Anderlini, "China Defends New Currency Regime," *Financial Times* (August 13, 2015).

[16] Q. Nie, "Cause, Nature and Countermeasures of the Stock Market's Abnormal Volatility," *WallStreetCN* (June 13, 2017).

[17] Anbound, "The Stock Market Crash Has More Influence beyond the Market," *Financial Times* (Chinese edition) (July 9, 2015).

government intervention must have a legal basis, since the intervention would change the existing market rules and the result of the bailout was uncertain. In particular, moral hazard, market risks, and legal risks were consequences that might ensue from excessive intervention by the government. He suggested enacting financial emergency law or amending the securities law and including the bailout in the legislation. Li also questioned certain bailout measures. For example, there was no legal basis for China's Central Bank to announce that it would provide unlimited liquidity for the China Securities Finance Corporation; joint purchases of stocks by the twenty-one securities firms might violate the stipulations on market manipulation of Article 77 of the PRC Securities Law.[18]

Another issue was whether the stock market turmoil would trigger a systemic crisis. At the beginning of July 2015, some Chinese economists assessed the causes and effects of the market turbulence. Gao Xu and Wei Zhong,[19] members of the China Finance 40 Forum, believed that the market downturn would not lead to a systemic crisis at that time. Gao Xu further analyzed the potential financial sector losses of securities, trusts and banks, as well as the contagious effects of the stock market turmoil on the financial system and real economy. He tended to conclude that the stock market turbulence would not cause a financial or economic crisis.[20]

In addition, Anthony Neoh, the former Chairman of the Securities and Future Commission of Hong Kong and former Chief Consultant of CSRC, believed that the bailout decision was reached in haste, and that defects in China's stock markets and loopholes in the PRC Securities Law were also responsible for the market turmoil.[21]

Nevertheless, in early July 2015 the government quickly decided on overall intervention and a national bailout. To some extent, for top-level Chinese decision-makers, the bailout decision reflected not just economic considerations but also political considerations, namely, the maintenance of stability.

---

[18] S. Li, "Thinking on the 'Stock Market Crash' and the 'Bailout' from the Legal Perspective," seminar on "Stock Market Activities and Market Rules" *China Law Review*, 3 (2017), 201–6.

[19] W. Zhong, "Bailout? Why? and How?" *China Finance 40 Forum* (7 July 2015).

[20] G. Xu, "Will the Stock Market Turbulence Trigger China's Economic Crisis? The Report Claims that the Probability Is Low," 8 July 2015, http://m.jiemian.com/article/322263.html.

[21] G. Ma, "Anthony Neoh Made Comments on Three Lessons of the 2015 Stock Market Crash: The Bailout Was a Hasty Decision," *Caijing* (May 29, 2016).

16.1.3   The National Bailout Team

On July 4, twenty-one major securities firms set up a joint bailout team known as the national bailout team. The Chinese Central Bank promised to provide unlimited liquidity to back the team's operations. On July 5, the CSRC suspended all IPOs. At the end of August 2015, immediately after the second market crash, CSRC instructed securities companies to examine margin trading and clear up accounts with margin calls.[22]

The government intervention in the first round failed to resolve the liquidity crunch, as the national team tried to stabilize the prices of blue chip stocks (e.g., the banking sector) and mega-capitalized stocks such as Sinopec and the China National Petroleum Corporation (CNPC), for the purpose of propping up the stock index. It transpired that the bailout was quite costly. As a result of this massive state bailout, at the end of November 2015, China's "national team" owned 742 different stocks, which accounted for at least 6 percent of the mainland stock market.[23]

In particular, several issues related to the national bailout team's actions gave cause for concern, including moral hazard, price manipulation, and when to cease the bailout. In practice, worries about the retreat of the national bailout team hit market confidence in August 2015, and the stock markets tumbled again. A series of later investigations revealed that insiders in some bailout securities firms, such as CITIC Securities, Haitong Securities, and Guosen Securities, had taken advantage of their access to insider information to place trades and make huge profits at public expense.

16.2   The Securities Regulator and a Policy-driven Market

16.2.1   Establishment of the Regulatory System of China's Securities Industry

China's stock markets were established in 1991 for the purpose of raising capital for state-owned enterprises (SOEs).[24] In the early stages, as the

---

[22] Wikipedia, "National Bailout Team."

[23] G. Wildau, "China's 'National Team' Owns 6% of Stock Market," *Financial Times* (November 26, 2015).

[24] China's earliest stock trading first appeared in the 1860s in Shanghai. The People's Republic of China (PRC)'s Shanghai Stock Exchange was founded on November 26, 1990 and started operations on December 19, 1990. See the website of Shanghai Stock Exchange, "Brief Introduction." The Shenzhen Stock Exchange was founded on December 1, 1990 and started formal operations on July 3, 1991. See the Shenzhen Stock Exchange, "SZSE Overview," www.szse.cn.

sole regulator of the financial sector, the People's Bank of China (PBOC) was responsible for surveillance over securities issuance and trading. In December 1993, the State Council decided to reform the financial structure and implement the policy of classified management for banking, securities, insurance and trust industries.[25] In 1995, commercial banks were forbidden to trade in securities within the People's Republic of China.[26] Meanwhile, three surveillance models for the securities industry were discussed: a subordinate administration under the Central Bank, a subordinate administration under the Ministry of Finance as in Japan, or a securities administrative authority independent of the Central Bank and the Treasury, as with the US Securities and Exchange Commission (SEC). The US model was partially adopted, although, unlike the SEC, the newly established China Securities Regulatory Commission (CSRC) was not an independent securities supervisory body answerable to Congress.[27] Instead, CSRC is a public institute at ministry level directly under the State Council, which shall, according to the powers authorized to it by the state, exercise administrative functions, and in addition supervise and manage the national securities and futures markets.[28]

As an organization endowed with administrative functions directly under the State Council, the CSRC possesses legislative powers.[29] Like other competent ministries and commissions, the CSRC is authorized to issue orders, instructions and regulations within its jurisdiction in accordance with the law and decisions of the State Council, under the Organic Law of the State Council[30] and the PRC Constitution.[31] Some legal scholars challenged the independence of the CSRC and argued that it

---

[25] Art. 6, Decision of the State Council on Reform of the Financial System (promulgated by the State Council, December 25, 1993).

[26] Art. 43, Law of the People's Republic of China on Commercial Banks (promulgated by the National People's Congress Standing Committee, May 10, 1995, amended in 2003)

[27] Q, Nie and X. Cai, *The Long on China: History of Capital Markets and Strategy of Financial Openness* (China Machine Press, 2012), 38–40

[28] Circular of the General Office of the State Council on Issuing the Regulation on the Main Functions, Interior Institutions and Staffing of the China Securities Regulatory Commission (promulgated by the State Council, [Guo Ban Fa (1998) No. 131], September 28, 1998).

[29] Art. 71, Law on Legislation of the People's Republic of China (promulgated by National People's Congress, March 15, 2000).

[30] Art. 10, Organic Law of the State Council of the People's Republic of China (promulgated by the National People's Congress Standing Committee, December 10, 1982).

[31] Art 90, Constitution of the People's Republic of China (promulgated by the National People's Congress, December 4, 1982, amended in 1993, 1999 and 2004).

had exceeded its authorized legislative powers.[32] Additionally, the quality and application of the CSRC's legislation has been questioned. According to Gang Xiao, the former Chairman (March 2013 to February 2016) of CSRC, by mid-2013 there existed over 1,200 rules and regulations concerning capital markets, as well as more than 200 accountability terms concerning administrative or economic liabilities. However, two-thirds of the accountability terms have never been applied.[33] Since 2013, the CSRC has moved to integrate its large number of regulations and to classify them into eight categories: (i) "Financing and M&A" Subsystem; (ii) "Market Trading" Subsystem; (iii) "Product Business" Subsystem; (iv) "Market and Institutional Investors" Subsystem; (v) "Market Openness" Subsystem; (vi) "Prudent Supervision" Subsystem; (vii) "Investor Protection" Subsystem; and (viii) "Regulatory Enforcement" Subsystem.[34] This integration of CSRC rules should strengthen its legal authority over capital markets.

Although the CSRC has been granted wide supervisory power, it still faces difficulties in investigating, collecting evidence and law enforcement. The CSRC's enforcement capacity and efficiency have also been questioned. For example, prior to 2007, the CSRC only sanctioned twelve cases of insider trading.[35] Between 2008 and 2013, the CSRC investigated 785 insider-trading cases, ninety-five of which resulted in criminal proceedings.[36] However, the real number of genuine self-dealing cases is likely to have been higher. From 2008 to 2013, about 110 cases annually were placed on file for investigation by the CSRC, but on average no more than sixty of them led to any imposition of administrative punishment. Overall, more than half the cases filed each year were eventually left unsettled.[37]

---

[32] X. Ke, "A Study on the Legislative Power of China's Securities Supervisory Authority," *The Theory and Practice of Finance and Economics*, 32 (January 2011) 123–127.

[33] G. Xiao, "Regulation Enforcement: Cornerstone of the Healthy Development of Capital Markets," *Qiu Shi* (August 1, 2013), 29–31.

[34] G. Xiao, "A Strong Legal System Brings Forth the Market's Rising: To Complete Legal Norm Subsystems from Eight Aspects," *Caixin* (December 9, 2013).

[35] These insider-trading cases from 1993 to 2002 include the cases of *Gao Fashan* (000537), *Yu Mengwen* (000629), *Wang Chun* (6006011), *Agriculture Bank Xiangfan Trust* (6006012), *Dai Lihui* (000583), *Qingqi Group* (000566), *Liaoning Province Jindi Construction Group* (600758), *Nanfang Securities* (600878), *Zhangjiajie Company* (000430), *Minyuan Hainan Company* (000508) and *Wingqi Group* (600698). Source: CSRC www.csrc.gov.cn/pub/newsite/jcj/dxal/.

[36] CIB Fund, "Insider Trading Has Been the Big Problem of the Capital Markets" (May 22, 2015) www.cib-fund.com.cn.

[37] G. Xiao, "Regulation Enforcement."

In the reformed CSRC, a reconciliation system has been introduced into its administrative regulations. This mechanism leaves room for the regulator and wrongdoers to reach a compromise instead of always relying on the application of administrative punishment or sanctions. In terms of cost-benefit analysis, this system is suitable for resolving minor violations and reduces the CSRC's exposure to administrative lawsuits. It also provides a means to avoid administrative sanctions. This legal reform is an attempt to improve regulatory interactions and increase the flexibility of current executive sanctions. The CSRC's law enforcement powers have been enhanced. The CSRC can freeze suspect bank accounts and may also take measures to restrict the purchase and sale of securities.[38] These restrictions can last no longer than fifteen trading days but can with approval be extended for up to a further fifteen trading days.[39] These new measures are intended to make enforcement more efficient.

16.2.2   The Era of Zhuanggu: From an Information Market to a Policy-driven Market

Stock markets in mainland China are separated into A-share and B-share markets. A-shares are issued to domestic investors; B-shares, which account for a very small proportion of China's stock market, were formerly issued to foreign investors, and then opened to domestic investors after 2001. Prior to 2005, A-shares were divided into non-tradable stocks held by the state and legal persons[40] and under employee ownership plans, as well as transferable stocks held by institutional investors and retail investors. The CSRC implemented share structure reform, which significantly boosted A-shares' tradability from 32.78 percent of total market value in August 2005 to 78.66 percent in 2014, as shown in Figure 16.1.[41]

Stock price manipulation was common in the early stage of China's stock markets. From 1998 to 2004, during the era of "zhuanggu," most Chinese

---

[38] Art. 4, Measures of China Securities Regulatory Commission for Restricting the Purchase and Sale of Securities (promulgated by CSRC, May 18, 2007).

[39] Ibid., Art. 5.

[40] "Legal person shares" are shares held by corporations or institutions and social groups who qualify as legal persons. Legal person shares are not transferable but enjoy priority in dividends in proportion to the amount of assets invested in these companies. State and state-owned enterprises owned approximately 70 percent of A-shares prior to the share structure reform.

[41] Calculation of the liquidity ratio and Figure 16.1 are based upon CSRC's monthly reports on China's stock markets (2003–2016).

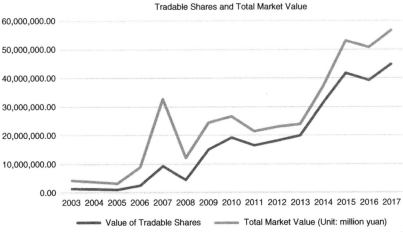

Figure 16.1 2003–2017 Tradable A-shares and Total Market Value (A-shares & B-shares)[42]

private equities, as "underground private equities," were involved in stock manipulations.[43] Zhuanggu refers to seizing profits by manipulating the price of a certain stock in which an institution or investor controls a considerable amount of its transferable shares (e.g., 30 percent). As non-tradable shares accounted for 66 to 70 percent of the market at that time, it was easy to manipulate the stock price with a small amount of capital. In such cases, stock prices usually are not decided by business performance and investment value, but by manipulation based on the zhuanggu's operational and capital capacity.

Thanks to low penalties and weak enforcement of the laws against securities fraud, violations of insider trading and market manipulation used to generate "high profits but low costs," with manipulators taking advantage of slack surveillance and legislative loopholes to commit fraud. The PRC Securities Law lists the circumstances of manipulation, stipulating three types: consecutive trading manipulation,[44] agreement transaction manipulation,[45] and self-trading manipulation.[46] However, these

---

[42] Source: CSRC statistical data.

[43] W. Han and S. Wu, "The Era of Zhuanggu Closes to End in 2003," *New Finance Economics*, 5 (2004), 40–42. Examples of zhuanggu include D'Long, Mingtian, Jinxin, Taiyue and Yong Jin. The collapse of D'Long in 2004 indicates the end of the era of zhuanggu.

[44] Art. 77(1), PRC Securities Law (promulgated by the National People's Congress Standing Committee, December 29, 1999, amended in 2004, 2005, 2013, 2014 and 2017).

[45] Ibid., Art. 77(2).

[46] Ibid., Art. 77(3).

were obscurely defined and lacked enforceability. The CSRC did not issue implementing rules until 2007, when two sets of Guidelines were drafted – Guidelines for Identification of Insider Trading in Securities Market (for Trial Implementation) and Guidelines for Stock Market Manipulation (for Trial Implementation). The latter Guidelines stipulate five other types of manipulation: demagogic manipulation of transactions; pre-emptive transaction manipulation; false declaration manipulation; specific price-fixing; and specific period trading manipulation.

The development of an A-share market relied heavily on external expansion, such as IPOs, secondary offerings, and follow-up offerings, rather than the appreciation of existing stocks. Disappointing earnings of companies and low dividend (or even non-dividend) yields could barely attract long-term investments.[47] The lagging legislation on securities violations and its slack enforcement enhanced widespread speculation. It transpired that individual investors in the markets frequently fell victim to securities fraud. Inadequate legal enforcement and an ineffective disciplinary system led directly to low recognition of fraud costs, which in turn further boosted pervasive fraud. To date, neither China's regulators nor courts have gained adequate experience in dealing with cases concerning market manipulation. Weak legal enforcement leaves public investors in an absolutely disadvantageous situation.

16.2.3   A Policy-driven and Highly Leveraged Bull Market in 2014 to mid-2015

China's stock market is regarded as "a policy-driven market." Government policies have greatly affected the fluctuations of bear markets and bull markets. From November 2014 to June 2015, the PBOC repeatedly cut interest rates and the RMB deposit reserve requirement ratio (RRR) for financial institutions in order to promote the stock market boom. For example, the PBOC cut interest rates on November 14 and 21, December 28, 2014, February 28, May 10, and June 27, 2015; and the PBOC cut RRR on February 4, April 19, and June 27, 2015.[48]

Financial leverage greatly promoted the "bull market." Leverage, as a popular financing tool, was widely used by both institutional investors and retail investors. From October 2014 to June 2015, new capital invested

---

[47] S. Gao, "China Stock Market in a Global Perspective," Dow Jones Indexes Research Report (September 2002).

[48] PBOC, "China Monetary Policy Reports – Quarter Four, 2014, Quarter One and Quarter Two, 2015."

in the stock markets increased to CNY 5 to 6 trillion at its peak, including CNY 3–4 trillion of OTC equity financing (except margin trading).[49] As of June 17, 2015, the balance of margin financing and securities lending reached CNY 2.26 trillion,[50] which occupied nearly 5 percent of tradable stocks. One should note that the ratio between short selling and long selling was extremely out of balance. Funds for short selling only accounted for less than 1 percent.[51] Since the threshold for accredited investors of margin trading[52] is CNY 500,000, this could not satisfy the needs of retail investors with only small amounts of money. Other equity financing tools such as umbrella trusts, structured trusts, peer-to-peer lending, and private stock matches endowments attracted large numbers of retail investors. Table 16.1 compares margin trading with OTC equity financing.

Additionally, China's public media fueled retail investors' pessimism by issuing editorials and articles on the prosperous bull market in April 2015, when the Shanghai composite doubled in nine months.[53] At the beginning of April 2015, the Xinhua News Agency, the government's official press agency, issued three articles on the red hot stock market and confirmed the need and rationale for a new bull market round – "a reform bull market."[54] On April 22, 2015, *People's Daily*, the Party's official newspaper, claimed that 4,000 points was only the start of the bull market, and denied that bubbles existed on the A-share market.[55]

16.2.4 The Stock Market Crash: From a Policy-driven Market to a "Political Market"

Facilitated by the stimulus effects of various policies, the Shanghai Composite Index peaked at 5,178.19 on June 12, 2015. The A-share

---

[49] Wu, Li and Wang, "Improve Institutional Arrangements and Boost Market Confidence," 15.

[50] T. Mitchell, G. Wildau and J. Noble, "Equities: A Bull Market with Chinese Characteristics," *Financial Times* (July 10, 2015).

[51] Wu, Li and Wang, "Improve Institutional Arrangements and Boost Market Confidence," 18

[52] Margin trading was introduced in August 2006 as a pilot program. In October 2011, margin trading and short selling officially became the business of securities companies, subject to the approval of the CSRC. On April 17, 2015, securities investment funds were allowed to engage in margin trading and short selling transactions.

[53] J. Xu, "Study on the Risks and Supervision of China's OTC Stock Financing," *Journal of Finance and Economics*, 2 (2017), 75–79 at 77.

[54] Ibid.

[55] J. Cai, "Who Let Out the Bull in the China Stock?," *South China Morning Post* (July 17, 2015).

Table 16.1 *Margin Trading vs. OTC Stock Financing*

	Margin Trading	OTC Stock Financing
Accredited Investor	(i) 18 months after opening a securities account; (ii) Threshold is CNY 500,000 for margin financing and securities lending.	Threshold for umbrella trust: CNY 3 million; structured trust and stock return swaps: CNY 10 million. But in reality, sub-accounts via HOMS or P2P lowered threshold for retail investors
Liquidation & Margin Closeout	(i) Open line is 175%; (ii) Must provide 100% loan guarantee	(i) Sub-accounts lowered requirements for loan guarantee; (ii) Open line can be 105% in P2P
Restrictions on Stock Selection	Limited to about one-third A-share stocks	Any except ST stocks ("ST" means special treatment)
Period of Stock Financing	Capped at six months	No such requirement
Leverage Ratio	No more than 1 time	From 1 to 10 times
Interest Rate	8–9% (lower costs)[56]	Trusts: 8.8–10.5%; P2P: 13–18%[57]

market rose in twelve months and created \$6.5 trillion of value.[58] Thereafter, however, the stock market was transformed from a "mad bull"[59] into a bear market. From June 12 to July 2, 2015, the stock market dropped 28 percent on book value.[60] The stock market crash in June and July 2015 wiped out \$5 trillion of market value, although the subsequent rescue propped up the stock index by 20 percent in mid-

---

[56] J. Cheng, "Third Editorial of Xinhua News Agency on the Bull Market: The Policy Bonus Promoted the Reform Bull Market," *People's Daily* (April 8, 2015).

[57] R. Wang, "4000 Points Is Just a Start of A-Shares' Bull Market; There Are No Bubbles," *People's Daily* (April 21, 2015).

[58] A. Sweanson, "Meet the World's Biggest Stock Market Bubble Since the Dot-com Boom," *Washington Post* (June 24, 2015).

[59] Chinese use "flash bear" to describe when the stock market suddenly becomes a bear market, from being a bull market.

[60] M. Pei, "China's Big, and Misguided Stock Market Gamble," *Fortune* (July 6, 2015).

Table 16.2 *2008–2009 Market Turmoil vs. 2015–2016 Stock Market Crash*

	Oct. 2007–2008 Market Turbulence	2015–2016 Stock Market Crash
Changes of Shanghai Composite Index (SCI)	SCI dropped from 6,124 points on October 16, 2007 (A Shares' peak point) to 1,664 points at the end of 2008.	First round: SCI dropped nearly 1/3 from 5,178 points; Second round: SCI dropped 29%; Third round: two flash crashes on January 4 and 7, 2016
Duration of Stocks Tumble	More than one year (from late October 2007 to 2008)	From mid-June 2015 to January 2016, three rounds crashes
Market Decline	The cumulative decline was over 70% (65% decline in 2008)	By mid-December 2015, the A-share market had lost value of an accumulated CNY 22.3 trillion in six months. Average loss of retail investors was CNY 43,700.[61]
Short Selling Mechanisms	Short selling was not allowed	Stock index futures (CSI 300, SCI 500, SSE50); Securities lending and short selling; Offshore A-share derivatives
Leveraged Funds	Very few	Maximum leveraged funds reached CNY 5–6 trillion[62] (margin trading + OTC stock financing CNY 3 – 4 trillion); Leverage ratio: 1–10 times
Bailout or not	Followed market principles; No extra government intervention	The government organized ten departments and major brokers in order to prop up the market

December.[63] Table 16.2 compares the 2015–2016 stock market crash with the one in late 2007–2008.

---

[61] L. Wei, "Beijing Probes Architects of Stock-Market Rescue: Senior Regulators Are Caught up in Investigation," *Wall Street Journal* (December 17, 2015).

[62] L. Wu, "A-share Market Has Lost Value of CNY 22 Trillion in the Second Half Year of 2015," *Economic Information Daily* (December 14, 2015).

[63] Wu, Li and Wang, "Improve Institutional Arrangements and Boost Market Confidence," 33–34.

In order to avoid the financial systemic risk or contagion effect, on June 27, ten government agencies, including the securities regulator, CSRC, jointly engaged in the bailout and tried to halt the stock market crash. The ten government agencies were the People's Bank of China (PBOC), the CSRC, the China Banking Regulatory Commission (CBRC), the China Insurance Regulatory Commission (CIRC), the Ministry of Finance, the State-owned Assets Supervision and Administration Commission (SASAC), the National Development and Reform Commission (NDRC), the Ministry of Human Resources and Social Security, the National Social Security Fund Council and the Ministry of Public Security. On July 8, the PBOC announced that, in order to avoid systemic risk, it would provide ample liquidity through lending, issuing financial bonds, mortgage financing and refinancing for the China Securities Finance Corporation Limited.[64] On July 9, Qingfeng Meng, a vice minister in the Public Security Ministry, and his team started to investigate insider trading, manipulation of the securities and futures market, and "malicious short-selling."[65]

Meanwhile, the China Securities Finance Corporation Limited (CSF) became the bailout platform. On July 4, twenty-one major brokers, subsequently known as the "National Bailout Team," agreed to contribute 15 percent of their net assets as bailout funds.[66] The twenty-one securities companies transferred CNY 128 bn. to the CSF. The CSF, as China's only financial institute providing financing services (margin funds and securities loans) to qualified securities firms for their margin transactions, was incorporated in October 2011, with CSRC approval.[67] The CSF launched the stabilization fund on July 5.[68] In the following

---

[64] PBOC, "The Announcement on Supporting the Stable Development of the Stock Market," July 8, 2015, www.pboc.gov.cn.

[65] K.H. Kim, "Chinese Police Visits Regulator, to Probe 'Malicious' Short-selling," Reuters (July 9, 2015).

[66] The securities companies were CITIC Securities (600030), Haitong Securities Co. Ltd., China Galaxy Securities Co., Ltd., GF Securities Co., Ltd., Shenwan Hongyuan Group Co., Ltd. (000562), China Merchants Securities Co., Ltd. (600999), Guotai Junan Securities Co., Ltd., Guosen Securities Co., Ltd. (002736), China Securities Co., Ltd. (CSC), Huatai Securities Co., Ltd. (601688), Oriental Securities Co., Ltd., Essence Securities Co., Ltd., Everbright Securities Co., Ltd., Founder Securities Co., Ltd., Dongxing Securities Co., Ltd., Changjiang Securities Co., Ltd., Industrial Securities Co., Ltd., Soochow Securities Co., Ltd., Southwest Securities Co., Ltd., Sinolink Securities Co., Ltd. and Qilu Securities Co., Ltd. Of these twenty-one domestic securities companies, CITIC Securities was the largest one in China's securities industry. See Wikipedia, "The National Bailout Team."

[67] China Securities Finance Corporation Limited, "Introduction," www.csf.com.cn.

[68] Ibid.

week, the CSF focused on propping up blue chip stocks, while the sense of panic grew within the SME Board and the Growth Enterprise Board (GEB).

On July 5, the CSRC suspended all IPOs. On July 12, securities account holders were prohibited from conducting securities trading in violation of regulations by placing sub-accounts, subsidiary accounts, or virtual accounts under securities accounts.[69] In addition, the CSRC took a series of bailout measures to avoid another market crash. According to the CSRC's spokesman, at the end of August 2015, the CSRC directed securities companies to examine their own margin trading and clear up accounts with margin calls. As of September 11, 2015, 3,255 accounts carrying out margin trading were cleared up, which amounted to 60.85 percent of margin trading funds; the remaining 2,094 accounts still had a market value of CNY 187.627 billion.[70] RoyalFlush, Hundsun Technologies Inc. and Huatai Securities came under investigation and faced huge penalties.[71]

If we compare China's stock market crash in 2015 with the stock market crash in late 2007–2008, when the Shanghai Composite Index declined over 70 percent,[72] on the earlier occasion, the government did not undertake any large-scale bailout. However, due to the economic slowdown and worries over financial system risk, in mid-2015 the Chinese government moved aggressively to control the crisis. The 2015 national bailout action indicates that decision-makers in the CSRC and other government agencies have clearly abandoned market principles when dealing with an immediate crisis. The question is: will they abandon the pursuit of market-oriented economic reform?

16.3   Regulatory Hand vs. Invisible Hand

Chinese regulators deemphasized administrative enforcement related to investor protection in favor of a "policy-driven market." The following section examines this shift, including the treatment of asymmetric

---

[69] Art. 2, Opinions on the Cleanup and Rectification of Illegal Securities Business Activities (promulgated by CSRC (No. 19 [2015]), July 12, 2015).

[70] Y. Ma, L. Ye and L. Dong, "A Hundred Days on the National Bailout: Crackdown of Short-selling and Exploring Experience by Trial and Error," *Beijing Business*, September 17, 2015.

[71] Y. Tang, "The 'Culprit' of Stock Market Crash Will Be Fined CNY 1 Billion: Hundsun Technologies Inc. Is Fined CNY 530 Million," *Pengpai News* (February 22, 2016).

[72] Z. Liu, D. Han, and S. Wang, "Bursting Bubbles in China's Stock Market," (December 8, 2016).

information and rent seeking, using game theory to model the interaction between the regulator and regulated bodies.

16.3.1   The Government's "Never Idled Hand" vs. The Invisible Hand

The stock market may overreact or underreact to information. Overreaction involves sharp changes in market prices, clearly exceeding the anticipated level, after a certain event. Underreaction means that stock prices change less than was expected by the regulator following a certain event.[73] However, many Chinese economists believe that the relationship between stock prices and information may be distorted by the government's "Never Idled Hand."[74] In other words, the government's excessive or undue interference may cause the failure of the price mechanism.

From March 13 to June 12, 2015, when the stock market was red hot, the Shanghai Composite Index rose 54 percent; the SZSE SME Composite rose 75 percent; and the Growth Enterprise Index (GEI) rose 93 percent. Meanwhile, the average P/E ratio of listed companies (except banks, CNPC and Sinopec) was 51, and the average P/E ratio of listed companies on the Growth Enterprise Board reached 142, a serious deviation from A-shares' actual values.[75] This indicated that many A-shares were over-valued.

Government supervision is necessary for the healthy operation of the stock market. Moderate government intervention may manage abrupt events, regulate the impacts of price swings on the national economy, and maintain market stability. However, like individual investors, the government is also a "limited rational person."[76] Government intervention can result in high costs and weaken the resource allocation function of the market. The Shanghai and Shenzhen stock exchanges were established in the early 1990s, when China started its transition from a planned economy. Government intervention in markets has been a Chinese characteristic, even when no market failure has occurred.

---

[73] Y. Song, "Stock-Market Failure and the Selection of Government Behavior," unpublished PhD thesis, Jilin University (2006).

[74] Y. Lu, *Never Idled Hand: Evolution of China's Stock Market System* (Beijing: CITIC Publishing House, 2008).

[75] Wu, Li and Wang, "Improve Institutional Arrangements and Boost Market Confidence," 15.

[76] The theory of public choice regards government behavior as being only of "limited rationality," since government intervention is implemented after the occurrence of market behavior.

Reuters lists about twenty instances of direct Chinese government inter-ventions in the stock market from 1992 to 2010, ranging from the CSRC's suspension or resumption of IPOs, government purchases of stock in major state-owned banks, and utilizing editorials in Party newspapers to affect the stock index, to using monetary easing or tax cuts to support the market.[77]

Aside from administrative intervention, the government has been deeply involved in the market's operations, as China's stock market was founded to raise capital for state-owned enterprises. The dual role of government as both supervisor of securities market and the representa-tive of state-owned assets also results in conflicts of interest. To date, state-owned listed companies have enjoyed priorities in public offerings, refinancing and takeovers. To some extent, the government is both a coach and a player on the stock market.

16.3.2   Capital Market Efficiency and Asymmetric Information

The efficient-market hypothesis (EMH)[78] gives an interpretation of the relationship between stock price and market information, which explains information efficiency and resource allocation within a stock market. In a mature securities market, these two factors are highly connected. According to the EMH, stock markets are categorized as weak-form efficient, semi-strong form efficient and strong form efficient markets. In a weak-form market, stock prices rapidly reflect all information found in past prices and volume.[79] Li (2007) believes that the Shenzhen stock market reached weak-form efficiency after 2001.[80] Lim et al. (2013) find that China's stock markets were still weak-form efficient.[81] These studies demonstrate that the information efficiency and resource allocation of

---

[77] Reuters Staff, "Timeline: China's Intervention in the Stock Market," Reuters (July 7, 2010).

[78] The efficient market hypothesis (EMH) has implications for investors and firms: (a) If information is fully and rapidly reflected in security prices, investors should be unable to make excess profits by relying on published information. (b) Similarly, sellers and issuers of securities in the market should expect to receive their fair value. See S. A. Ross, R. W. Westerfield and J. Jaffe, *Corporate Finance* (Boston MA: McGraw Hill/Irwin, 2008).

[79] P. Liu, "Positive Study on the Weak-form Efficiency of China's Stock Markets," *World Economic Information*, 8 (2006), 13–15.

[80] Q. Li, "Positive Study on the Weak-form Efficiency of Shenzhen Stock Market" *Securities Study*, 9 (2007), 142–144.

[81] T. C. Lim, W. Huang, J. Lim and D. Zhao, "Has Stock Market Efficiency Improved? Evidence from China," *Journal of Finance & Economics*, 1(1) (2013), 1–9.

stock markets were low-efficient during the early stages and further reforms would enhance their connectivity.

Compared with advanced stock markets where institutional investors play a dominant role, more than 80 percent of investors in the A-share market are retail investors. A-share accounts have continued to increase in the last few years. There were 168,283,300 accounts in 2016, 135,863,200 accounts in 2015, and 95,807,300 accounts in 2014.[82]

Unlike institutional investors who enjoy advantages in market information and investment strategy, retail investors contribute approximately 85 percent of the turnover of the A-share market.[83] However, it is said that overall 90 percent of retail investors received no actual returns from 1992 to 2011.[84] In practice, the top five winners in China's stock markets are: (i) SOEs and their management (because the objective of establishing the A-share market is to provide capital for SOEs); (ii) the government (through imposing stamp duty for shares); (iii) securities brokers (from commissions); (iv) original shareholders of listed companies (through acquiring shares with a book value of CNY 1 or less and then selling out at a much higher market value); and (e) professionals in the securities sector (such as fund managers, securities analysts and traders, etc.).[85]

16.3.3 Government Intervention: Market Failure vs. Government Failure

Government intervention may produce externalities. From the perspective of "Capture Theory," interest groups take advantage of the supervisory body to grab benefits. From 2003 to 2009, at least seven CSRC officials, including Xiaoshi Wang, Xiaolong Lu, Zhiwei Zhong, Ming Liu, Yi Wang, Shiqing Xiao and Po Lei, were prosecuted for bribery and corruption. It is said that behind each corrupt officer, there is an interest group. In late 2015, a few senior CSRC officials such as former Vice Chairman Gang Yao, former Assistant Chairman Yujun Zhang, and Zhiling Li were caught in the anti-corruption crackdown. This illustrates

---

[82] *Shanghai Stock Exchange Statistics Yearbook 2017*, p. 6.

[83] Y. Xun, "A-share Market Examination: Structure of Market Players, Trading Characteristics, and Chip Allocation Decide the High Volatility of A-shares," *Caijing* (May 18, 2016).

[84] D. Fan, "90 percent Chinese Investors Lose Money: Retail Investors Suffered Losses of CNY 86,600 in Average," *Henan Business Daily* (February 27, 2015).

[85] Ibid.

another externality of government intervention – rent-seeking. Rent-seeking in the examination and approvals of IPOs, secondary seasoned offerings, and other monitoring administrative activities may lead supervision into a vicious circle. For instance, some listed companies passed examination for stock issuance through bribery. In the bribery case of *Xiaoshi Wang*,[86] Wang, a former CSRC official, who was in charge of the assignment of IPO examination committees, sold name lists of IPO examination committee members to prospective listed companies. He charged CNY 200,000–300,000 for each name list, which included the names, addresses and phone numbers of seven committee members, and extracted nearly CNY 10 million in a few years.[87]

Another bribery case involving Yi Wang, former Vice Chairman of the CSRC (1995–1999) and Vice President of the China Development Bank (1999–2008), indicates rent-seeking and moral hazard arising from loopholes in the IPO approval system, too. Wang was investigated for corruption in June 2008. It was widely reported that Wang was involved in the IPO of Pacific Securities Co., Ltd. (SH, 601099),[88] Sinolink Securities Co., Ltd. (SH, 600109) and GF Securities (SZ, 000776). Wang was also accused of bribery in approving bank loans. He was sentenced to death, with a two-year reprieve and deprived of political rights for life, with all his personal assets confiscated, for accepting bribes of over CNY 11 million.[89]

16.3.4 A Perspective of Game Theory: CSRC and Market Manipulators

To some extent, the policy-driven market operates between the government and investors according to repetitive game theory.[90] From the

---

[86] *No. 1 Branch of the Beijing Municipal People's Procuratorate v. Xiaoshi Wang* (Beijing No. 1 Intermediate People's Court, Criminal Case No. (2005) 3580 (first trial), December 9, 2005) (Higher People's Court of Beijing, Criminal Case No. (2006) 65 (final trial), April 17, 2006).

[87] H. Xie, "The Rent-seeking Link of IPO Examination Exposed; Xiaoshi Wang Got Nearly CNY 10 Million," *Sanlian Lifeweek Magazine* (November 26, 2004).

[88] "The Abnormal IPO of Pacific Securities Co., Ltd. Is Related to Wang Yi," *The Beijing News*, March 30, 2010. See also H. Zhang and Z. Shi, "The Trial of Wang Yi Is Suspicious for Not Concerning Securities Big Cases," *Economic Information Daily* (April 1, 2010).

[89] *No. 1 Branch of the Beijing Municipal People's Procuratorate v. Yi Wang* (Beijing No. 1 Intermediate People's Court, Criminal Case No. (2010) 355 (first trial), April 15, 2010 (Higher People's Court of Beijing, Criminal Case No. (2010) 303 (review of death sentence), May 25, 2010).

[90] G. Qiao, "The Game Theory Analysis on China's 'Policy-driven' Stock Market," *Economic Science*, 2 (2004), 65–73.

perspective of game theory, the supervisory behavior can be tested by the following model:

		Player 2: CSRC	
		Supervise	Not Supervise
Player 1:	Manipulate	-Cm-F, Gs-Cs ⟶	Gm, 0
Traders	Not Manipulate	0, -Cs ⟵	0, 0

Figure 16.2 Game Theory

C_S: Costs of CSRC to supervise the stock market;
C_M: Costs of the manipulator to undertake his market manipulation;
G_S: Gains made by CSRC from its supervisory operation;
G_M: Gains or extra profits made by the manipulator from his manipulation;
F: Fines levied by CSRC to punish market manipulation or false statements.

This is a mixed strategy game involving the supervisory body and the manipulator of the securities market. The supervisor has two strategies: "supervise" and "not supervise." The supervised also employs two strategies: "manipulate" and "not manipulate." There are four kinds of payoffs for the CSRC and the traders in this game. Assume that player 1 chooses the strategy of "manipulation," the best strategy for player 2 is to choose "supervision" to perform the monitoring function as the supervisory body. Nevertheless, when player 2 chooses "supervision," then the best strategy for player 1 is to choose "no manipulation." When player 1 chooses the strategy of "no manipulation," then player 2 should choose "no supervision" based upon the consideration of costs and benefits. Once player 2 chooses the strategy of "no supervision," player 1 appears to choose the strategy of "manipulation." This process of dynamic games can be repeated, unless player 2 regulates and enforces the law effectively.

Moreover, whether or not player 1 chooses to manipulate and player 2 chooses to supervise can be measured by probability. If the government strengthens the punishment for securities violations, then the probability of manipulation by player 2 decreases. A situation of equilibrium emerges. However, decreased manipulation may result in the reduction of supervision; when player 1 reduces supervision, the probability of manipulation by player 2 increases.

16.3.4.1 Parameters in this Model

In this model, suppose the probability of the CSRC's "Supervision" and the probability of the traders' "Manipulation" are as follows:

p: CSRC: probability p for "Supervising";

$1-p$: CSRC: probability $1-p$ for "Not Supervising";

q: Traders: probability q for "Manipulating";

$1-q$: Traders: probability $1-q$ for "Not Manipulating."

There are situations concerning p and q in the game:

(i) With the probability of pq, a trader gets caught. It is obvious that the smaller the p, the lower the probability that he will get caught. Since q is less than 1, the probability of a trader being caught is less than p. For instance, if the probability of CSRC supervision is 5 percent, then the probability that a trader will be caught must be less than 5 percent.

(ii) With the probability of $(1-p)$ q, a trader manipulates without being caught. The smaller the p is, the greater the probability that he/she will manipulate without being caught by the regulator.

(iii) With the probability of $1-q$, a manipulator does not manipulate and his/her payoffs are "0."

When probability p is too low, many traders are "encouraged" to take the risk of committing securities fraud. For instance, the CSRC implemented ten administrative sanctions concerning false statements in 1997, which means the punishment rate was only 1.34 percent for the year.[91] In many cases, such as *Zhong Ke Chuang Ye* (2000) and *D'long* (2004), the regulator failed to monitor the securities fraud; even if the wrongdoers were caught, the costs of punishment only accounted for a small proportion of the benefits arising from market manipulation. Thus wrongdoers believed that the costs of punishment were much lower than the benefits arising from market manipulation.

Additionally, actual fines for securities fraud are typically low. By April 2003, the CSRC had only implemented sixteen administrative sanctions penalizing market-price manipulations.[92] The criminal fine for

---

[91] Source: CSRC, www.csrc.gov.cn.
[92] Ibid.

securities fraud is also low.[93] Traders may illegally transfer their assets before the enforcement of administrative or criminal fines, ensuring that some judgments or administrative penalties cannot be fully implemented. If we examine the small proportion of violators punished by the regulator, we discover that administrative fines or market entry inhibition were much lower than their gains from the stock market. As a result, traders may consider improbable the danger of the imposition of supervisory punishments and accept the risk so as to make illegal profits through market-price manipulation or insider trading.

16.3.4.2   Regulator's Strategies

For the CSRC, when E1 = E2, the government will choose to "Supervise" or "Supervise" not randomly. Suppose

$$E1 = (G_S\text{-}C_S) \text{ X } p + (\text{-}C_S) \text{ X } (1\text{-}p)$$

$E2 = 0 \text{ X } p + 0 \text{ X } (1\text{-}p)$Then assume E1 = E2, then when the game reaches its equilibrium, the optimal probability for CSRC to "Supervise" is: $p = C_S/G_S$.

Suppose $p > C_S$ / G_S, which means E1 > E2, CSRC will choose to "Supervise." The CSRC is also concerned over its monitoring costs. Taking the example of costs of issuance examination, the CSRC Accounting Department is responsible for the examination of information disclosure of listed companies. In 2007, 1,547 public companies were listed on the Shanghai Stock Exchange and Shenzhen Stock Exchange. This department had fewer than thirty staff members.[94] The supervisory workload was heavy.

Assume $p < C_S$ / G_S, which means E1 < E2, CSRC will choose not to "Supervise" since its costs are greater than its gains.

Note: The probability of CSRC supervision is decided by the ratio between "C_S" and "F." That is, if CSRC increases its administrative costs on punishing securities fraud, the probability p can rise.

---

[93] See Arts. 180, 181 and 182 of PRC Criminal Law (1997). The PRC Criminal Law (1997) sets punishments for insider trading, false statements, and market-price manipulation: (i) The violators shall be sentenced to no more than five years in prison or criminal detention, provided the circumstances are serious; (ii) He or she shall be fined, additionally or exclusively, a sum not less than 100 percent and not more than 500 percent as great as his or her illegal profits.

[94] CSRC, www.csrc.gov.cn.

16.3.4.3   Manipulator's Strategies

For traders, when E3 = E4, traders will choose randomly either to "Manipulate" or not. Suppose:

$$E3 = (-F-C_M) \times q + (G_M) \times (1-q)$$

$$E4 = 0 \times q + 0 \times (1-q)$$

Then assume E3 = E4, the game reaches its equilibrium, and the optimal probability for the manipulator to "Manipulate" is $q = G_M/(F+G_M+C_M)$.

Suppose $q > G_M/(F+G_M+C_M)$, which means E3 > E4, traders will choose to "Manipulate" since they will obtain extra profits from their manipulation. From the 1990s to early 2000s punishment was not serious, and many traders tended to make huge profits from market-price manipulation or insider trading.

Suppose $q < G_M / (F+G_M+C_M)$, which means E3 < E4, the optimal strategy for traders is "Not Manipulate" as the costs are greater than the gains from manipulation.

Note: The probability of manipulation is decided by "F" and "C_M" rather than "G_M." That is, if the CSRC increases punishment (administrative fines), market manipulation can clearly be reduced. At the same time, if a trader considers that the probability of supervision is very low, he tends to choose to "Manipulate"; however, if CSRC supervision is strict, even if manipulation produces huge extra profits, traders may not take the risk of incurring punishment from the regulatory authority.

16.3.4.4   Costs and Benefits of the Regulator and Regulatory Capture

As more than 80 percent of investors are retail investors who generate approximately 85 percent of the turnover in a market with asymmetric information, the success of manipulation depends on manipulators' skills in inducing "herding." Prior to the 2015 stock market crash, the costs of manipulation and the probability of being caught were low, whereas the benefits accruing from it were quite lucrative. Therefore, insider trading and market manipulation were pervasive.

Subsequently, regulatory capture became a serious problem. In late 2015, significant numbers of CSRC officials were detained due to suspected bribery or corruption. Most of them were in charge of IPO approvals. For example, Gang Yao, the former director of the Department of Public Offerings Supervision and former CSRC Vice Chairman, was detained in November 2015 for abusing power for personal gain and his acceptance of extensive property holdings. From 2004 to April 2017, Yao controlled the CSRC's IPO approvals. Liang Li, the former Deputy Director of the Department of GEM Public Offerings Supervision and the former Director of the China Securities Investor Protection Fund Corporation Ltd, was arrested on December 1, 2014. On August 25, 2015, Shufan Liu, the former Division Chief of the 3rd Division of the Department of Public Offerings Supervision and former secretary of Gang Yao, was detained for suspected insider trading and forging official documents and seals. Before their downfall, these officials had been very powerful influences in IPO approval, and they finally involved themselves in rent-seeking.[95] The name list of CSRC officials who committed crimes related to IPO approvals also included Xiaoshi Wang, the former Deputy Director of the Department of Public Offerings Supervision, and Zhiling Li, the former Division Chief of Department of Public Offerings Supervision.

16.3.5   Finding Insiders during the Bailout

In August 2015, the CSRC began to investigate insider dealing within the national bailout team. On August 25, it was reported that some financial institutions had focused on how to make money from the national stability funds, thereby damaging national financial security.[96] From that moment, any trading jeopardizing the government's bailout was regarded as threatening national financial stability. On the same day, four securities companies – Haitong, GF, Huatai and Founder – announced that they were under investigation by the CSRC over "suspected illegal activities of not examining and acknowledging the identities of their clients according to regulations."[97] On September 15, three top executives of CITIC Securities were detained by the PSB for insider trading and disclosure of inside information. On October 23, it was reported that the regulatory authority was investigating the management of Guosen Securities for short-selling.[98] On November 26, both CITIC Securities and Guosen Securities announced that the CSRC had decided to officially investigate the company due to "suspected violation of [the] Regulation on the Supervision and Administration of Securities Companies."[99]

---

[95] C. Ye, "The Downfall of Gang Yao," *Financial Times* (Chinese edition) (November 16, 2015).

[96] S. Dong, "Destroying the Confidence of China's Stock Market Will Endanger the Overall Reform," *Securities Daily* (August 25, 2015).

[97] Wikipedia, "The National Bailout Team."

[98] Ibid.

[99] Y. Wang, "Six out of 21 Securities Companies in the National Bailout Team Have Been Investigated," *Legal Evening News* (November 27, 2015).

Further investigations by the CSRC and PSB uncovered additional "inside jobs" in some securities companies. As of November 26, 2015, six of the twenty-one securities companies that constituted the national bailout team – CITIC, Guosen, Haitong, Huatai, Founder and GF Securities – were under investigation by CSRC for short selling A-shares.[100] Two top CSRC executives in particular, Yujun Zhang and Gang Yao, were suspected of "leaking the government's moves" to rescue the stock market in order to reap profits. It was reported that Gang Yao leaked classified bailout information to executives at brokerages such as CITIC Securities and Guotai Junan Securities Co.[101] In November 2015, the graft watchdog probed Guotai Junan Securities and Haitong Securities.

Rent-seeking became business-political collusion during the A-share market bailout. It was widely reported by Sina, Sohu, and other public media that a few major securities firms on the national bailout team and private equity firms colluded with two senior CSRC officials, such as Gang Yao and Yujun Zhang, in short selling and insider trading. Yujun Zhang, assistant CSRC Chairman and the "commander" of the national bailout team, was investigated by the Central Commission for Discipline Inspection (CCDI) for "disturbing the order of capital markets" and corruption.[102] More than ten executives, including the CEO of CITIC Securities, the largest brokerage in mainland China, were investigated for breaching rules on short selling and margin contracts.[103] In 2017, the CSRC announced that CITIC Securities, Haitong Securities and Guosen Securities, former national bailout teammates and China's large investment banks, would be punished for facilitating short selling of Citadel Securities, a US-based high-frequency trader, in late 2015. CITIC, Haitong and Guosen were fined CNY 308 million ($45 million), CNY 105 million, and CNY 3 million respectively.[104] In November 2016, Qingdao Municipal People's Procuratorate sued Xiang Xu, the "Big man of Private placement" and CEO of Shanghai Zexi Investment, for market manipulation. Xu and his co-conspirators made huge illicit gains during the stock market crash. Xu was sentenced to a fixed-term imprisonment of five and half years and fined CNY 11 billion (the harshest

---

[100] T. Xu, "Six Securities Companies out of the 'National Bailout Team' Have Been Investigated," *Legal Evening News* (November 26, 2015).

[101] L. Wei, "Beijing Probes Architects of Stock-Market Rescue."

[102] Reuters Staff, "Ex-China's Securities Regulator Assistant Chairman to Be Prosecuted: Graft Watchdog," Reuters (July 21, 2017).

[103] Bloomberg, "Facing a probe over China Stock Market Rout, Brokerage CITIC 'Unable to Contact Executives'," *The Strait Times* (December 7, 2015).

[104] G. Wildau, "China's Biggest Investment Banks Fined for Role in Short Selling," *Financial Times* (May 26, 2017).

fine, historically). On March 20, 2017, the China Securities Investment Fund Association disqualified Xiang Xu from membership as a private fund manager.[105]

16.4 CSRC's Role of Overregulation and Underregulation

16.4.1 CSRC's Overregulation of the Primary Market and the Protracted Transition from the IPO Approval System to the Registration System

16.4.1.1 The IPO Approval System and the Pre-marketization Process

The evolution of China's IPO approval system has experienced four stages: "Quotation Management" (1993–1995), "Index Management" (1996–2000), "Channel System" (2001–2004), and "Sponsor System" (after 2004).[106] The CSRC's examination of new stock issuance reveals administrative interference over the stock market. Since the Shanghai and Shenzhen stock exchanges were founded in the early 1990s, when China embarked on its economic transition from a planned economy, CSRC's regulatory policies at its early stage had features of a planned economy. For example, quotation management and index management were command economy methods whereby SOEs could become listed. Subsequent reforms added some market factors, but the IPO approval system, which accommodated "business-political exchanges" and the bureaucracy, was not market-oriented. Under quota control or another reformed procedure, administrative examination and approval, issuing new shares became a rare resource. The supply and demand of new shares were thus out-of-balance. Huge amounts of capital invested in IPO shares, high earnings from new shares, and an over-speculative secondary market were byproducts of this system.

Aside from the examination and approval of new share issuance, the CSRC used to manage IPO pricing by exercising regulatory control over the IPO price or P/E ratio. The IPO price system has experienced three stages: fixed IPO price (1991–1998), inquiry pricing (1999–2004), and book building (2005-present).[107] Over the 1990s, the CSRC adopted

---

[105] X. Zhao, "China Securities Investment Fund Industry Association Punished Zexi and XU Xiang and Warns Fund Manager in Four Aspects," *Securities Daily* (June 8, 2017).

[106] CSRC Research Center, "Evolution of China's Equity Issuance Approval System," July 3, 2013, www.csrc.gov.cn.

[107] CSRC Research Center, *"Development of China's IPO Pricing and Placement,"* July 3, 2013

a fixed IPO pricing mechanism.[108] IPO pricing was inclined to settle at a certain average price rather than a market-oriented pricing. Tian and Zhang (2014) find that IPO underpricing averaged 181.6 percent in the past two decades, although it decreased from 491 percent in 1993 to 42 percent in 2010.[109] Tian's (2011) empirical study demonstrates that the extreme IPO underpricing was caused by the A-share market's institutional arrangements that favored inefficient SOEs.[110] As a result, IPO underpricing caused the price spread between the primary market and the secondary market, prompting particularly big jumps in stock prices after an IPO absorbed liquidity on the secondary market. The stock market crash of late 2007, for example, was triggered by the IPO of PetroChina (CNPC). In the 2017 Bo'ao sub-forum on China's capital markets, most economists suggested the desirability of speeding up the reform of the market-oriented IPO registration system.[111]

16.4.1.2 Regulatory Control over the IPO Approval Pace and the Exit Mechanism

Supply of new stocks has been controlled by China's securities watchdog. The CSRC frequently utilizes suspensions and resumptions of IPOs to affect the supply of public offerings, demonstrating strong intervention by the regulator. From 1994 to November 2015, on nine occasions the CSRC froze new stock offerings.[112] The longest IPO suspension lasted from November 16, 2012 to January 7, 2014.

The absence for a long time of any exit mechanism also affected the A-share pricing system. The CSRC issued no delisting rules until the "Opinions on Reforming, Improving and Strictly Implementing the Delisting System for Listed Companies" became effective, in November 2014. The CSRC's Opinions listed twenty-seven circumstances that justified active or compulsory delisting. The Shanghai and Shenzhen Stock Exchanges then issued correspondingly detailed and amended delisting rules.

---

[108] Ibid.

[109] L. Tian and W. Zhang, "Extreme IPO Underpricing: Can the Market-oriented Incremental Reform Work in China," *Nankai Business Review*, 5(2) (2014), 225–255.

[110] L. Tian, "Regulatory *Underpricing*: Determinants of Chinese Extreme IPO Returns," *Journal of Empirical Finance*, 18(1) (2011), 78–90.

[111] Bo'ao Sub-forum for Asia Annual Conference 2017, "Correct an Error: Let Capital Markets Return to Their Nature," 23–26 March 2017.

[112] X. Yu, "China Ushers in New IPO Registration System But It's Likely to Come with "Chinese Characteristics," *South China Morning Post*, December 9, 2015.

16.4.1.3   Transition to a Registration System

Since 2009, the CSRC has reformed its IPO approval system, but only limited progress has been made and the pace was slow. In November 2013, the CSRC issued its "Opinions on Further Promoting the IPO System Reform," intended to improve the transparency of the IPO review process. The CSRC submitted a draft plan for stock issuance reform to the State Council in November 2014 and has been planning since 2015 to introduce the registration-based IPO system. On December 27, 2015, the National People's Congress Standing Committee passed a decision authorizing the State Council to adjust the relevant applicable provisions of the PRC Securities Law when implementing the reform of stock issuance registration system in two years' time. In July 2017, the CSRC announced it would speed up the establishment of a registration-based IPO system.[113]

However, those who have high expectations of the marketization reform of the IPO system may be disappointed. It is said that the CSRC will remain a system with Chinese characteristics rather than a US-style system. Nor will the CSRC give up its control over stock prices and listing pace, as when, for example, the CSRC requests an unofficial P/E ratio capped at twenty-three times.[114] Also, it is noted that the registration-based IPO system was not included in the latest amendment of the PRC securities law, which indicates that implementing the registration-based IPO reform will take some time.

16.4.2   The CSRC's Underregulation of the Secondary Market

16.4.2.1   Large Shareholders' Tunneling

One of the main factors triggering the 2015 stock market turmoil was that large shareholders sold out their own stocks in May 2015, when the A-share market was red-hot. In the first half-year of 2015, the directors and management sold off around 70 billion shares, whose market value amounted to approximately CNY 900 bn.[115]

Tunneling profits and benefits and misappropriation of assets from listed companies by large shareholders have been pervasive. Large shareholders take advantage of various opportunities such as related party transactions, corporate restructuring, secondary offerings, diluting

---

[113] X. Yu, "Regulator to Fast-track Reform of Registration-based IPO System," *China Daily* (July 25, 2017).

[114] X. Yu, "China Ushers in New IPO Registration System."

[115] Wu, Li and Wang, "Improve Institutional Arrangements and Boost Market Confidence," 20

equity, management buyouts, earnings management and acquisitions to grab control benefits.[116] From 1992 to 2011, retail investors contributed around CNY 6 trillion, including capital of nearly CNY 5 trillion raised for listed companies on the Shanghai and Shenzhen Stock Exchanges, stamp duty for shares of CNY 600 billion, and commissions for securities firms of CNY 400 billion. However, as of the end of 2010, dividends paid by all Chinese listed companies totaled CNY 500 billion during the first twenty years of China's stock markets.[117] In other words, the few large shareholders were winners, while 90 percent of retail shareholders received zero or negative returns.[118]

16.4.2.2 Weak Enforcement over False Statements, Insider Trading and Market Manipulation

Prior to the 2015–2016 stock market crisis, the CSRC's enforcement of securities laws violations had been weak. Insider trading and market manipulation have been serious problems over the past two decades, while the CSRC's law enforcement remained weak. Without a well-functioning legal system, manipulation is quite profitable because the regulator's inefficiency in law enforcement further lowers the costs of securities violations. After the stock market crash, the CSRC has enhanced its investigative and enforcement measures targeting market manipulators. In particular, big data have been applied to collect evidence and conduct investigations.[119]

16.4.2.3 Regulatory Arbitrage and Cross-market, Cross-sector Trading

It has been noted that in 2014, one year before the stock market crash, financial leverage and policy tools were widely used to boost a bull market. According to a research report published by the Tsinghua University National Institute of Financial Research (NIFR), several factors contributed to the first round of the stock market crash.

- When the stock market was red hot, large shareholders sold off stocks, sales amounting to CNY 130.7 billion in May 2015 and CNY 103.4 billion in June 2015.

---

[116] J. Sheng, *China's Listed Companies: Conflicts, Governance and Regulation* (Alphen aan der Reijn: Wolters Kluwer, 2015), 136–149.
[117] D. Fan, "90 percent Chinese Investors Lose Money,"
[118] Ibid.
[119] Y. Yue, "CSRC Uses 'Big Data' to Conduct Investigations," *Caixin* (November 20, 2015).

- A large amount of capital was frozen due to subscriptions of initial public offerings, including CNY 11 trillion frozen for the IPOs of the China National Nuclear Corporation (CNNC) and Guotai Jun'an Securities, as well as CNY 4 trillion frozen for newly approved IPOs.
- The People's Bank of China (PBOC), the Central Bank, decided not to inject funds again via the medium-term lending facility (MFL).
- The supply of bank capital was reduced due to mid-year settlements, payments to fiscal deposits and required reserves.

These factors resulted in low market liquidity. Meanwhile, trading volumes between the stock exchange and the futures exchange were out of balance in the futures exchange. From January to August 2015, the total trading volume of stock index futures reached CNY 37 trillion, while the trading volume of stock spot was much lower.[120] The CSRC's sudden announcement that it would clean up the stock matches endowments triggered the stock market meltdown.[121]

Due to mismatched trading rules between the stock exchanges and the futures exchange, it was possible for short-sellers such as Citadel and Yishidun (Eastern Dragon) to take advantage of regulatory arbitrage and make huge profits. Table 16.3 compares the differences between the two.

Following the first market turbulence, the CSRC tried to crack down on speculation via cross-market and cross-exchange trading. Under the current framework of separate supervision over mixed operations in China's financial industry, the CSRC had to overcome regulatory arbitrage between sectors. After the 2015 stock market crash, the CSRC turned to applying big data to detect abnormal trading, which improved its supervisory efficiency.

16.5 Conclusion: More "State Interference," or a Market-Oriented Transition?

The 2015–2016 stock market crash was a product of both market failure and regulatory failure. The subsequent bailout policy reflected both regulators' economic objective of avoiding financial systemic risks and the political consideration of stability maintenance. Following the market turbulence, the CSRC substantially strengthened its enforcement policies over various securities trading violations. In 2017, the CSRC initiated 478 investigations, which led to the filing of 312 cases by the CSRC. Of these 312 filed cases, 203

---

[120] P. Liu, "NIE Qingping: I Have Three Suggestions on Quantitative Trading," *Tencent Finance* (November 19, 2016).

[121] Wu, Li and Wang, "Improve Institutional Arrangements and Boost Market Confidence," 15.

Table 16.3 *Comparison of Trading Rules of Stock Spot and Futures*

	Stock Spot	Futures
Settlement Cycle	T+1	T+0
Buy and Sell	Must buy first and sell later	Short selling available
Trading Exchange	Shanghai Stock Exchange; Shenzhen Stock Exchange	China Financial Futures Exchange
Transaction Costs	Normally high	Much lower – about 10% of stock transactions
Leverage Level	Full amount; Margin financing; Securities lending	High leverage – 3–10% margin deposit
Delivery	Practical delivery	Mostly hedging rather than practical delivery

cases of false statements (sixty-four cases), insider trading (101 cases) and market manipulation (thirty-eight cases) accounted for 65 percent.[122] In the same year, the CSRC completed 335 filed cases, 303 of which were transferred to related government bodies, either the administrative penalty apparatus for trial or the public security organs for further investigation. However, securities-related violations still represent a serious problem.[123]

Meanwhile, this stock market crash forced people to rethink the role of China's securities watchdog. As the regulatory authority of China's securities industry, the CSRC is not an independent agency. Under the current supervisory system, the administrative regulator has overly expansive powers, while courts and self-regulatory organizations only play a passive role in the protection of securities investors. State interference is becoming more active and frequent. This presents an uncertain future for the CSRC's IPO system reform, since judicial efficiency and the rule of law are more essential to investor protection than administrative punishment.[124] Further, it is found that using the planned economy approach to control IPO pricing and pace has resulted in an imbalance in the supply and demand of new stocks on the primary market; while inadequate surveillance of trading on the secondary market leaves loopholes for market manipulation, insider dealing and false statements.

---

[122] CSRC, "Briefing on CSRC's Handled Cases in the Year of 2017," January 19, 2018.
[123] Ibid.
[124] R. La Porta, F. Lopez-de-Silanes, A. Shleifer, and R. W. Vishny, "Law and Finance," *The Journal of Political Economics*, 106 (1998), 1113–1155.

INDEX